Managing Conflict in the Former Soviet Union:
Russian and American Perspectives

CSIA Studies in International Security

Michael E. Brown, Sean M. Lynn-Jones, & Steven E. Miller, series editors
Karen Motley, executive editor
Center for Science and International Affairs (CSIA)
John F. Kennedy School of Government, Harvard University

Published by The MIT Press:

Allison, Graham T., Owen R. Coté, Jr., Richard A. Falkenrath, and Steven E. Miller, *Avoiding Nuclear Anarchy: Containing the Threat of Loose Russian Nuclear Weapons and Fissile Material* (1996)

Allison, Graham T., & Kalypso Nicolaïdis, eds., *The Greek Paradox: Promise vs. Performance* (1996)

Blackwill, Robert D., and Michael Stürmer, eds., *Allies Divided: Transatlantic Policies for the Greater Middle East* (1997)

Brown, Michael E., ed., *The International Dimensions of Internal Conflict* (1996)

Elman, Miriam Fendius, ed., *Paths to Peace: Is Democracy the Answer?* (1997)

Falkenrath, Richard A., *Shaping Europe's Military Order: The Origins and Consequences of the CFE Treaty* (1994)

Feldman, Shai, *Nuclear Weapons and Arms Control in the Middle East* (1996)

Forsberg, Randall, ed., *The Arms Production Dilemma: Contraction and Restraint in the World Combat Aircraft Industry,* (1994)

Shields, John M., and William C. Potter, eds., *Dismantling the Cold War: U.S. and NIS Perspectives on the Nunn-Lugar Cooperative Threat Reduction Program* (1997)

Published by Brassey's, Inc.:

Blackwill, Robert D., and Sergei A. Karaganov, eds., *Damage Limitation or Crisis? Russia and the Outside World* (1994)

Johnson, Teresa Pelton, and Steven E. Miller, eds., *Russian Security After the Cold War: Seven Views from Moscow* (1994)

Mussington, David, *Arms Unbound: The Globalization of Defense Production* (1994)

Published by CSIA:

Allison, Graham, Ashton B. Carter, Steven E. Miller, and Philip Zelikow, eds., *Cooperative Denuclearization: From Pledges to Deeds* (1993)

Campbell, Kurt M., Ashton B. Carter, Steven E. Miller, and Charles A. Zraket, *Soviet Nuclear Fission: Control of the Nuclear Arsenal in a Disintegrating Soviet Union* (1991)

Managing Conflict in the Former Soviet Union: Russian and American Perspectives

Editors
Alexei Arbatov, Abram Chayes,
Antonia Handler Chayes, and
Lara Olson

CSIA Studies in International Security

The MIT Press
Cambridge, Massachusetts
London England

Library of Congress Cataloging-in-Publication Data

Managing conflict in the former Soviet Union: Russian and American perspectives / Alexei Arbatov . . . [et al.], eds.
        p.   cm.—(CSIA studies in international security)
        Includes bibliographical references and index.
        ISBN 0-262-51093-6 (pbk.: alk. paper)
1. Russia (Federation)—Ethnic relations—Government policy. 2. United States—Ethnic relations—Government policy. I. Arbatov, Aleksei Georgievich.
        II. Series.

DK510.33.M36   1997   97-11343
327.47—dc21   CIP

10 9 8 7 6 5 4 3 2 1
Printed in the United States of America

Contents

Acknowledgments   vii

Maps   ix

Part I   Introduction   xvii

Chapter 1   Transition and Conflict: Russian and American Perspectives on the Former Soviet Union
Abram Chayes and Antonia Handler Chayes   1

Chapter 2   A Framework for Assessing Post-Soviet Conflicts
Alexei Arbatov   19

Part II   Cases of Conflict   25

Chapter 3   North Ossetia and Ingushetia: The First Clash
Olga Osipova   27

Chapter 4   Commentary on North Ossetia and Ingushetia
David Mendeloff   77

Chapter 5   The Crimean Republic: Rivalries for Control
Edward Ozhiganov   83

Chapter 6   Commentary on the Crimean Republic
Michael Lysobey and Tonya Putnam   137

Chapter 7   The Republic of Moldova: Transdniester and the 14th Army
Edward Ozhiganov   145

Chapter 8   Commentary on Moldova   211
               Brian D. Taylor

Chapter 9   Latvia: Discrimination, International   219
               Organizations, and Stabilization
               Alexander Yusupovsky

Chapter 10   Commentary on Latvia   267
               Brian J. Boeck

Chapter 11   Kazakhstan: How Long Can Ethnic   273
               Harmony Last?
               Vladimir Barsamov

Chapter 12   Commentary on Kazakhstan   333
               Henry Hale

Chapter 13   The Republic of Georgia: Conflict in Abkhazia   341
               and South Ossetia
               Edward Ozhiganov

Chapter 14   Commentary on Georgia   401
               Arthur G. Matirosyan

Part III   What Will the Future Hold?   409

Chapter 15   Russian Security Interests and Dilemmas: 411
               An Agenda for the Future
               Alexei Arbatov

Chapter 16   Horror Mirror: Russian Perceptions of the   459
               Yugoslav Conflict
               Nadia Alexandrova-Arbatova

Chapter 17   The Development of U.S. Policy   493
               Toward the Former Soviet Union
               Abram Chayes, Lara Olson, and George Raach

Contributors   537

Index   541

About the Belfer Center for Science and International Affairs   557

Acknowledgments

This volume was made possible through the generous support of the Carnegie Corporation of New York. Jennifer Leonard provided all-around invaluable editorial and research assistance over the life of the project. Tonya Putnam also provided not only unique translation services, but became a trenchant editor, as well.

Maps

Russia   x

The Baltic States   xi

Chechnya   xii

Georgia   xiii

Moldova   xiv

Ukraine   xv

All of these maps come from U.S. government sources.

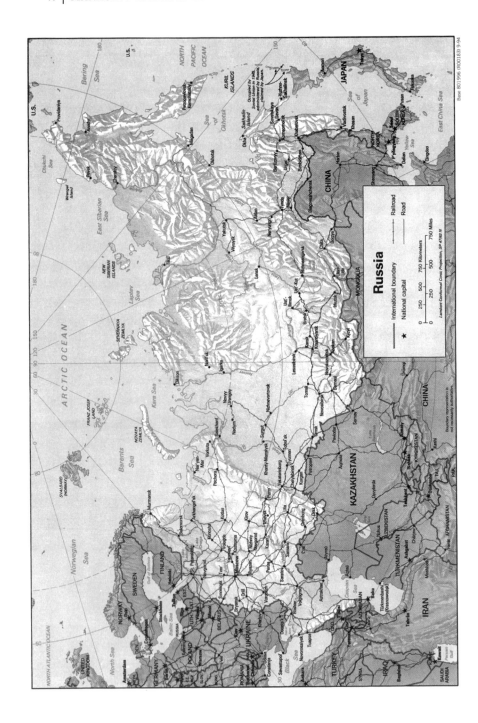

The Baltic States

Legend:
- International boundary
- ★ National capital
- Railroad
- Road

Estonia, Latvia, and Lithuania have
no internal administrative divisions.

0   50   100 Kilometers
0   50   100 Miles

FINLAND

Kouvola
Vyborg
Lake Ladoga
Sosnovo
Turku
Kotka
Primorsk
Porvoo
Helsinki
St. Petersburg (Leningrad)
Hanko
Porkkala   Gulf of Finland
Gatchina
Paldiski
Tallinn
Kohtla-Järve
Narva
SWEDEN
Tapa   Rakvere
Slantsy
Hiiumaa   Haapsalu
Gdov
Luga   Batetskiy
ESTONIA
Lake Peipus
Ozero Il'man
Saaremaa
Viljandi
Tartu
Pärnu
Lake Pskov
Kuressaare
Gulf of Riga
Valga   Võru
Kolka
Valmiera
Pskov   Ono
Gotland (SWEDEN)
Ventspils
Alūksne
Ostrov
Mērsrags
Cēsis
Gulbene
Pytalovo
Sushchëvo
Stende
SOVIET
Baltic Sea
Riga
LATVIA
UNION
Tukums   Jūrmala   Ogre
Liepāja
Saldus   Jelgava
Rēzekne
Novosokol'niki   Velikiye Luki
Jēkabpils
Pustoshka
Mažeikiai
Nevel'
Šiauliai
Daugavpils
Kretinga   Rietavas
Panevėžys
Klaipēda
Novopolotsk   Polotsk
Šilutė
LITHUANIA
Utena
Vitebsk
Zelenogradsk
Tauragė   Kėdainiai   Ukmergė
Švenčionėliai
Postavy
Babichi
Kaliningrad
Neman
Jonava
Gdynia
SOVIET UNION
Kaunas
Vilnius
Orsha
Gdańsk
Pregolya   Chernyakhovsk
Alytus
Molodechno
Borisov
Mogilev
Elbląg
Suwałki
Druskininkai
Tczew
POLAND
Ełk
Minsk
Olsztyn
Grodno
Lida
Neman

Final boundaries of Estonia, Latvia, and Lithuania with the USSR are expected to be confirmed by agreement. Other boundary representation is not necessarily authoritative.

801946 (R00112) 10-91

Chechnya

Georgia

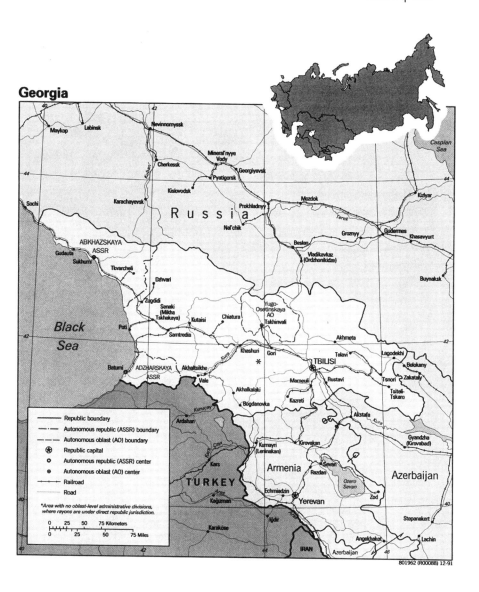

Republic boundary
Autonomous republic (ASSR) boundary
Autonomous oblast (AO) boundary
⊛ Republic capital
⊙ Autonomous republic (ASSR) center
◉ Autonomous oblast (AO) center
⊢⊢⊢ Railroad
.... Road

*Area with no oblast-level administrative divisions,
where rayons are under direct republic jurisdiction.*

0   25   50   75 Kilometers
0   25   50   75 Miles

801962 (R00088) 12-91

Base 802163 (R01013) 7-93

Ukraine

― International boundary
★ National capital
┅ Railroad
― Road

0 100 200 Kilometers
0 100 200 Miles

Lambert Conformal Conic Projection, SP 47N/62N

Boundary representation is
not necessarily authoritative.

Base 802139 (R00339) 4-93

Part I
Introduction

Chapter 1

Transition and Conflict: Russian and American Perspectives on the Former Soviet Union

Abram Chayes and
Antonia Handler Chayes

When in 1994 Russian troops stormed Grozny, the capital of the breakaway province of Chechnya, most Americans even in policy-making circles had never heard of the place. Chechnya, a primarily Muslim territory in the remote vastness of the Caucasus between the Black and Caspian seas, had proclaimed its independence from the Russian Federation. Although Western diplomats were at first inclined to acquiesce to Russian President Boris Yeltsin's attempts to preserve the territorial integrity of the federation, they were unprepared for the brutality of the tactics of the Russian armed forces or the ferocity of the defense under the command of Dzhokhar Dudaev, then president of the self-proclaimed Chechen state. After several years of inconclusive fighting, with massive civilian and military casualties, President Yeltsin acknowledged that his reelection depended on his ability to restore peace in the area. After Yeltsin won the election in late 1996, even the cease-fire negotiated by Alexander Lebed, who was subsequently fired, remained perilously fragile.

Chechnya was only the latest in a long series of ethnic conflicts that flared up within the Russian Federation and in the new states on its borders as the Soviet Union dissolved. Though many of these conflicts are centuries old, they had been kept in check under both the tsarist and Soviet empires. In the trauma and confusion of the Soviet collapse, ethnic identities became the framework around which struggles for political and economic power were organized, and in numerous regions increasingly nationalistic local ethnic groups confronted stranded Russian populations who were now minorities in "foreign" lands. Not far from Chechnya, Armenians and Azeris are locked in combat over Nagorno-Karabakh that began while Mikhail

Gorbachev was still in power. In Moldova, Georgia, and Tajikistan, open warfare broke out. It continues today in Tajikistan, although in the others there is a shaky truce. In the Baltic states and Ukraine, the confrontations did not slide over the brink into systematic warfare, but they poisoned relations between the new countries and Moscow in the early years of independence and continue to be a source of unease and friction. Within the Russian Federation itself, there was fighting in 1993 in North Ossetia, neighbor to Chechnya and to the rebel South Ossetia in Georgia. Indeed, Moscow's inordinately harsh response to the Chechen rebellion reflected its fear that the entire Russian position in the strategic North Caucasus might disintegrate if Dudaev succeeded in maintaining Chechen independence.

The way Russia deals with ethnic tensions, both inside and outside the federation, decisively affects Russia's effort to transform itself into a democracy and a market economy in good standing in the international community. Since the success of this transition is a primary goal of U.S. policy, these conflicts, though they occur in unfamiliar and distant locations, are of crucial importance to the United States in at least three different ways.

First, instability stemming from ethnic conflicts threatens Russia's own security. Centrifugal forces within the Russian Federation divert energies, attention, and resources away from the primary business of constructing a democratic society and a viable market-based economy. As for the neighboring states of the "near abroad," Moscow cannot be indifferent to the fate of the large populations of ethnic Russians residing there. Moreover, ethnic conflict creates fertile fields for the involvement of other powers, including Iran, Turkey, and China, and major economic interests are implicated as well.

Second, the character of the Russian response to these problems will necessarily affect its own political evolution and the way Russia is perceived abroad. The attempted military solution in Chechnya has, according to some, already affected the democratic character of Russia's institutions; the United States and other nations, which were initially willing to give Yeltsin a good deal of slack on the issue, have been appalled by the resulting slaughter. Russian efforts to deal with the problems in the near abroad can take many forms, ranging from neo-imperialist revivalism (which some Western observers purport to see already) to cooperative efforts with friendly states and international organizations. The choices Russia makes along this spectrum will inevitably color its relations with the United States and the West.

Third, tensions in the border regions, and especially the status of the

Russian populations there, feed into Russian internal politics, tending by and large to strengthen the hand of the most nationalistic and reactionary elements.

Despite the importance of the instability along the Russian perimeter, U.S. policy has in general failed to engage seriously or systematically the problems that have been raised. This book, however, is not, for the most part, an attempt to prescribe policy responses for the United States to this intricate complex of ill-understood problems. Rather, its purpose is to provide one necessary component to the development of a wise and sustainable U.S. policy. It seeks to give U.S. readers a sense of how these issues look to well-informed and relatively nonpartisan observers in Russia itself. For it is our conviction that U.S. policy toward these conflicts must be fashioned with full and sympathetic understanding of these viewpoints, even if they reflect an inherent bias.

The Approach Used in This Book

The heart of this book consists of six case studies of post–Cold War conflict and potential conflict in the former Soviet territory and in Russia itself. In addition to the Baltics (primarily Latvia) and Crimea, the other subjects of intensive study are Kazakhstan, Moldova, Georgia, and the North Caucasus. The selection does not represent all cases in which either Russia or the United States has a particular interest; they were chosen to represent a wide geographic range, and to exemplify conflicts at different stages where policy intervention has been or might be effective. Each of the studies provides as rich a historical background as space permits.

The case studies do not aim for complete scholarly objectivity. As Alexei Arbatov says in his foreword to the case studies, it is worth the risk of some imbalance and even bias to get a perspective that is not ordinarily available in the West. What is presented in each study is a careful and well-documented analysis from a moderate Russian perspective. The authors are affiliated neither with the Yeltsin administration nor with the nationalist opposition. Individually, they have extensive scholarly backgrounds and firsthand knowledge of the areas about which they write. Collectively, they make up a substantial part of the Policy Analysis Section of the Council of the Russian Federation, the upper house of the Russian Parliament. This section functions as an advisory body to the Council on a wide range of issues. Thus the perspectives reflected in the case studies are not without real policy implications.

In order to provide a contrasting point of view, each Russian account is followed by a commentary written by a young American scholar, drawing upon Western literature and academic work. These American commentators worked with the Russian authors during an intensive workshop and met with them thereafter in late 1994 and some through mid-1995, discussing the issues and background of the conflicts treated in this volume. Even though there are new events in each of these areas, the editors believe that the Russian perspective is well captured in the case studies. It is a perspective that U.S. foreign policymakers and analysts should understand.

The Lessons of the Case Studies

Emerging from the case studies are a number of recurring themes of central importance for Russian policymakers, Western nations, and international organizations in formulating policies for preventing and resolving internal conflict and promoting stability and democracy in the newly independent states. The most important of these themes are: 1) the significance of President Yeltsin's support of nationalism in the republics as a weapon in his struggle against Mikhail Gorbachev; 2) the situation of Russian minority populations in the new states; 3) the importance of laws governing citizenship and language both in generating and managing ethnic conflict; 4) the pressures created by continued deployment of Russian troops in the territories of the new states; and 5) the limited impact of international organizations, at least from the Russian perspective.

YELTSIN'S SUPPORT OF NATIONALISM

A striking feature of the internal conflicts considered in this book is the extent to which Boris Yeltsin's promotion of nationalism in the new states later came back to plague both his foreign policies and his domestic political position. The case studies reveal a characteristic pattern marking political developments in the republics of the Soviet Union from 1989 through the end of 1991. Unionist groups, consisting primarily of the old communist leadership and bureaucracy and supporting the preservation of the Soviet Union, maneuvered against opposition nationalist parties committed to autonomy or independence. The logic of the power struggle between Yeltsin and Gorbachev led Yeltsin to support these nationalist parties as an element of his drive for leadership of the Russian Federation. Indeed,

Yeltsin himself was the head of the nationalist faction in Russia. He and his advisers apparently gave little thought to the consequences of this strategy for future relations between the federation and any new states that might emerge.

After the breakup of the Soviet Union, Yeltsin had to reap what he had sown, not only in the near abroad, but also in the parallel separatist movements within Russia itself, such as those in North Ossetia and Chechnya. All the studies discuss, in greater or lesser detail, the impact of the initial support of national independence by the "radical democrats" around Yeltsin. But as time passed and nationalist sentiments revived in Russia itself, the parliament exploited the situation of Russians in the near abroad as a weapon in its opposition to Yeltsin. The Russian administration was under increasing pressure to wiggle out of its earlier positions.

Thus Yeltsin, as president of the Russian Federation, recognized the Baltic states before Gorbachev, but soon after independence the governments of these republics introduced policies that discriminated against their ethnic Russian minorities and agitated for the immediate withdrawal of Russian troops. In Moldova, Russia became increasingly critical of the use of force by the nationalist government of President Mircea Snegur against the dissident ethnic Russians in Transdniester. In Georgia, Yeltsin supported the early efforts for Georgian independence because, according to Edward Ozhiganov, he saw Zviad Gamsakhurdia as an ally in the struggle against Gorbachev. Later, however, in order to shore up the Russian position in the North Caucasus and to meet domestic criticism, Yeltsin lined up at least temporarily with the Abkhazians against the new Georgian government under Edward Shevardnadze and with the South Ossetians against the Ingush. In both Moldova and Georgia, Russian troops wound up in uneasy and ill-defined peacekeeping missions to separate government and separatist forces.

RUSSIAN MINORITY POPULATIONS IN THE NEW REPUBLICS

The breakup of the Soviet Union transformed the substantial Russian populations in the republics into minorities in foreign lands, creating a new layer of ethnic issues on top of what in many of the republics was a potentially explosive ethnic mix resulting from centuries of large-scale population movements. Moreover, as a consequence of historic policies and subsequent political and economic transitions, the Russians outside the Russian Federation are concentrated in urban industrial locations, and comprise a disproportionate part of the population that possesses the skills needed for a modern industrial economy. They are seen as colonizers and interlopers, interfering with a nationalist agenda. This resentment has translated into discrimination against Russian ethnic minorities during the transitions to independence, although the form, level, and intensity differ among the cases.

Whatever the details of the particular situation, the demographic composition of the former Soviet republics was determined by a number of factors that were roughly similar in all cases.

TSARIST COLONIZATION. As imperial Russia extended itself eastward, the tsars encouraged the migration of their subjects to settle the new lands, sending Cossack bands to defend the empire's frontiers.

THE NATIONALITIES POLICIES OF THE SOVIET UNION. The Soviets purported to give the union republics autonomy under indigenous local leadership through the device of *korenizatsia* or indigenization, which placed indigenous people in official positions, often with major roles in the Communist Party and *nomenklatura*. In all important cases, however, a Moscow-appointed official, usually Russian, was second in command. These policies created the myth of ethnic-based national unity and autonomy that was ready to assert itself once the ties with Moscow were shattered.

SOVIET ECONOMIC POLICIES. Massive development and industrialization projects prompted tens of thousands of Russians to relocate to remote areas, especially in the Caucasus and Central Asia. Partly in consequence, Russian military policy called for large numbers of Russian officers and their families to be stationed along the Soviet periphery.

STALINIST DEPORTATIONS AND COERCED POPULATION MOVEMENTS. During World War II, thousands of persons of minority ethnic identity were forced into exile, especially from Crimea, the Caucasus, and Kazakhstan.

Tension with the residual Russian populations is a salient political element in many former Soviet republics. In Kazakhstan, for example, the present more or less equal division between ethnic Russians and ethnic Kazakhs (each comprising about 40 percent of the population) derived from centuries of colonization, beginning with Russian Cossack settlements in the early eighteenth century and continuing through the nationalities and industrialization policies of the Soviet period. The resulting ethnic mix (complicated by a scattering of Germans, Ukrainians, Tatars, Uzbeks, and others) is superimposed on an ancient clan structure dating back to the thirteenth century, the social and political impact of which persists to the present. In Crimea, there were massive population shifts in the mid-1930s, when the collectivization of agriculture resulted in mass deportations and death, and the Russian portion of the population increased to 43 percent. The creation of shipbuilding, machine-building, chemical, and tourist industries cemented the substantial presence of Russians. In Latvia, as Alexander Yusupovsky points out in Chapter 9, although Russians had been in residence for centuries, the Russian population in 1939 was only 10 percent, compared with 75 percent Latvian. However, by 1989, the Latvian population had declined to 52 percent, while Russians increased to 34 percent. The forcible incorporation of the Baltic nations into the Soviet Union in 1940 and mass deportations of alleged Latvian collaborators provided a justification for Latvians, once independence was consolidated in 1991, to enact laws that denied citizenship in the new nation to resident Russians, leaving many of these ethnic Russians as stateless persons. In many cases, these population changes reflect the Soviet industrialization policy that began in the 1950s, resulting in the ethnic distinction between urban and rural areas. The irony is that where the large Russian population retains the principal industrial skills necessary to a strong economy in the transition to independence, discriminatory policies of the newly independent states punish the states themselves.

CITIZENSHIP AND LANGUAGE LAWS

The status of the Russian language in the newly independent states looms large in almost all the cases studied. Insistence on the primacy of the local language, even though most of the local ethnic populations speak Russian and the ethnic Russians use their mother tongue, is a subtle method of exclusion that often exacerbates ethnic tensions between titular majorities and the Russian minorities as much as overt discrimination. The case studies of Latvia and Kazakhstan bring this out most clearly, although the same issue has arisen in the other Baltic republics. Similarly, the legislation that made Moldovan the official state language of Moldova, though not an initial cause of the conflict in Transdniester, was certainly a contributing factor, and led to a series of strikes in 1989 that nearly paralyzed the Moldovan economy.

The Latvian case is perhaps the sharpest example of overt and legal discrimination. In Yusupovsky's account, the focus of the tension is citizenship policy, which is harsh in the letter of the law, and even more so in its implementation. Because the new nationalists regarded the years after the Soviet takeover in 1940 as a foreign occupation, the

Latvian government refused to treat Russians who took up residence during that period as citizens in the new state, and the new citizenship laws raised severe barriers to naturalization of Russians. In 1994, 85 percent of the resident noncitizens were ethnic Russians. To Russians who have lived in Latvia for their entire lives and even for generations, this represented a deprivation of rights that they believed they had and should have. Moreover, the impact on civil and political rights does not end with the denial of the vote. Noncitizens may be excluded from government jobs, universities, and professions and have only limited rights to own property or form corporations. The pervasiveness of the discriminatory treatment and frictions over the withdrawal of Russian troops brought ethnic tensions to the boiling point in Latvia. But by the same token, they provided a lever for international intervention to find a solution before the situation deteriorated into unresolvable violent conflict.

THE CONTINUING PRESENCE OF THE RUSSIAN MILITARY
The end of the Soviet Union left Soviet military formations in place throughout the former empire. Although the successor states, convened as the Commonwealth of Independent States (CIS), divided the former Soviet military assets among themselves, and Russia was to withdraw its share into its own territory unless otherwise agreed, these arrangements were not implemented automatically or swiftly. Through much of the immediate transition period, the Russian military units remained in their old bases in the republics, providing further flash points for hostility against both resident Russians and the Russian government, and in some cases intervening in local conflicts. In Latvia, Crimea, Moldova, and Georgia, the Russian military presence was a major irritant.

The problem of the division of the personnel, ships, and shore installations of the Black Sea Fleet between Ukraine and Russia has been especially complex. In the first place, it has plagued bilateral relations between Ukraine and Russia. Second, it has fueled tensions within Ukraine between the Ukrainian and Russian communities. While Ukraine had nuclear weapons, the United States saw the ongoing failure to resolve the issue of the Black Sea Fleet as presenting continuing risks to the outside world. Third, since the fleet was traditionally based in Crimea, the issue became central to the movement of ethnic Russians on the peninsula: they maintain that Nikita Khrushchev's "gift" of Crimea to Ukraine in 1954 was invalid, and support its reintegration with Russia. The question of whether the ships and facilities of the Black Sea Fleet should be manned and maintained primarily by Crimeans or by others was as much an economic as a political or ethnic issue; however, nationalistic rhetoric from Russians, whether in Crimea, Ukraine, or Moscow, revolved to a considerable extent around the status of the fleet.

Edward Ozhiganov's account of the 14th Army in Moldova is quite different from those found in the Western press, as Brian Taylor points out. Ozhiganov argues that in many republics during the chaos following the breakup of the Soviet Union, weapons stores were simply seized by those who had the means to do so. The situation in Transdniester was far more complicated. It has been charged that the 14th Army, which was historically deployed there, did not relinquish its weapons and did not play either a conflict-prevention role or one limited to self-defense. Rather, it participated in the hostilities on the side of the Transdniester separatists. Ozhiganov argues that the Transdniester soldiers, who made up the bulk of the 14th Army, were acting defensively and on their own as individuals whose homes were under attack. Nevertheless, President Snegur protested to President Yeltsin, and the activities of the 14th Army were an issue of enduring friction between Moldova and Russia. Ozhiganov argues that the 14th Army became a problem for the Moldovan government. He contends that the replacement of General Yuri Netkachov by General Lebed later in the conflict was intended by Moscow to bring the situation under control and to prevent both men and matériel from going over to the Transdniester separatists. Whether or not his is an accurate perspective on the situation, it certainly highlights vividly how complex and explosive the continuing presence of the Russian military has been in situations of internal conflict and threatened secession.

The Georgian case study also gives a more favorable view of Russian activities in Abkhazia than is generally accepted by Western analysts. Nevertheless, it shows pretty clearly how messy and confusing the military situation was in the conflict that raged there in the aftermath of the dissolution of the Soviet Union. At the outset, vast stores of sophisticated weapons from the Soviet Army became available to all sides in the Georgian conflict, by illegal sale, seizure, or in the normal course of devolution of weapons under the agreement among the CIS states. Even after Edward Shevardnadze took power and requested that the remaining stores be destroyed, much Soviet Army equipment was left in the Transcaucasus Military District, where it was seized by combatants. Even more serious was the actual use of force against the Georgians by Russian military forces in Abkhazia. Whether or not this was self-defense, as Ozhiganov suggests, or partisan actions, as claimed by others, there is no doubt that Russian military involvement aggravated the conflicts in Georgia, and delayed, if not diminished, the credibility of subsequent peacekeeping efforts after the cease-fire.

THE WORK OF INTERNATIONAL ORGANIZATIONS

On the whole, the authors of the case studies do not offer a very sanguine view of the past actions or future prospects of international organizations in the area. They see little value in the many study missions and "get acquainted" visits, and have little patience with the mediative and facilitative activities of the organizations. They look instead for concrete proposals for practical solutions. In the absence of a strong effort by the organizations to define and impose such solutions, the Russian commentators see the various parties trying to use the organizations to their own advantage in a complicated game of internal political maneuvering in which the established government, as the member and chief interlocutor of the organizations, seems to come out ahead.

Both the United States and Russia have officially committed themselves to work to prevent and manage internal conflicts through international and regional organizations such as the United Nations and the Organization for Security and Cooperation in Europe (OSCE). Although these organizations remain weak and lack adequate resources, and are themselves in transition to new roles of conflict management, there were some manifestations of international organization activity in each of the conflicts discussed in this volume, while frequent actions at headquarters and in the field were directed at conflict prevention or resolution.

The involvement of international and regional organizations covers a broad range of subject matters, including human and political rights, democratization, and journalistic freedom. OSCE observers issued a critical report on the March 1994 parliamentary elections in Kazakhstan, and the Council of Europe has kept up pressure for new parliamentary elections after the dissolution of parliament a year later and the concentration of power in the hands of President Nursultan Nazerbaev. In the Baltics, the activity of international organizations focused on citizenship laws and other forms of discrimination against resident Russians. The OSCE High Commissioner on National Minorities has been particularly active in Latvia and Estonia, and

Yusupovsky acknowledges that the efforts of regional organizations and nongovernmental organizations (NGOs) such as Helsinki Watch have had some success in softening the harsher features of these laws. Ozhiganov chronicles a long series of OSCE actions in Georgia, including observer missions and roundtable discussions between South Ossetians and Georgians. Although the various cease-fires did not hold and tensions have continued, he gives credit to the intensity of effort and even accomplishments of the OSCE in helping to restore stability and renew movement toward resolution. However, he regards the extensive UN involvement in the negotiations at various stages of the Abkhazia conflict as of little practical significance. Moreover, he raises questions about proliferation of uncoordinated missions both within the UN and between the UN and OSCE.

The studies do not provide a full account of the activities of international organizations. Rather they are of interest because they reflect informed Russian perceptions of what the international organizations did and how effective their efforts were. In the Abkhazia case, Ozhiganov complains that the visiting international delegations were monopolized by the Georgian government and received little exposure to the Abkhaz point of view. Despite the OSCE's success in ameliorating the Baltic citizenship laws, Yusupovsky is critical because it did not accept the argument that Latvia's and Estonia's refusal to recognize resident Russians as citizens of the new state was a violation of OSCE organizational norms.

In all, the picture as seen by these Russian analysts is neither flattering to the organizations nor reassuring to those who consider them major actors. Unlike in Western Europe and, to a lesser extent, in the United States, where international organizations, whatever their effectiveness, occupy a significant part of the foreign policy space, on the basis of these studies the conclusion would have to be that in Russia, these organizations are quite marginal. Nevertheless, although the authors take a skeptical view of their accomplishments, acceptance of the OSCE and the UN remains high. There seems to be a reservoir of good will, and a willingness to cooperate with the organizations in their efforts to prevent or mitigate conflict.

Yugoslavia—Similarities and Differences in Impact and Perception

As a counterpoint to the case studies of ethnic conflict in the former Soviet territory, Nadia Arbatova traces the perceptions and reactions in Moscow to the crisis in the former Yugoslavia. Yugoslavia is often cited as an example of nationalism and ethnic separatism parallel to those in the former Soviet Union. There is no doubt that, as Yugoslavia began to disintegrate, there was fear in both Washington and Moscow that the infection would spread to the former Soviet Union. As in the other case studies, however, a Russian perspective emerges that differs markedly from that of the United States. The differences are manifested in two dimensions. First, although Arbatova acknowledges the excesses of the Bosnian Serbs, she contends that U.S. media and politicians have misconceived the equities underlying the starting positions of the parties to the conflict and have not evaluated their subsequent conduct evenhandedly. She presents a fully articulated statement of the Russian "pro-Serb" position. Second, she contends that the significance of the Russian interests in the region and the importance of Moscow's contribution to the efforts to obtain peace have been undervalued, even ignored, by the United States. There remains a sense of unfairness that Russia has not been treated with due respect and deference. An important reason for including this chapter is to illuminate the gap that must be bridged and the very different perceptions that must be reconciled before the major powers can act in concert to prevent conflict.

Arbatova's account of Russian attitudes is shadowed, however, by the metaphor of her chapter's title: Yugoslavia as a "horror mirror" of what is in store for Russia if it cannot manage the ethnic tensions within and around it. Is the former Yugoslavia a unique case for which all parties were unprepared? Will it serve as a precedent for ethnic and separatist conflict, or as a vaccination against it? Will the horrors of ethnic cleansing, broken agreements, hostage-taking, and wholesale murders establish what is acceptable by the international community in other conflicts? Or will the violence and cruelty of the prolonged war in the former Yugoslavia remain as a stark example of futility, never to be repeated by the current generation? These questions haunt Arbatova's analysis as they do, implicitly, the other case studies in the book.

Implications for Russian and U.S. Policy

RUSSIA: CLEAR INTERESTS, UNCERTAIN POLICIES

Alexei Arbatov brings to his overview of Russian policy toward the new states his long experience as an analyst of U.S.-Soviet arms control relationships and, beginning in 1993, as a member of the Duma and as deputy chairman of its Defense Committee since December

1995. As his starting point he outlines what he sees as Russia's legitimate interests in the near abroad. Not only are there historic ties and sympathies; in many areas, economic cooperation remains vital to the further development of both Russia and the newly independent states. Rampant nationalism in the near abroad is a matter of concern for Russia on many grounds, just as Russian nationalism and expansionism is for these states. In particular, Russia has a legitimate interest in the welfare of the Russian population remaining in the newly independent states, whatever the origins of their presence—whether from Cossack settlements under the tsars or Stalinist policies of forced removal. Minimal international standards of fairness to ethnic Russian minorities have not always been met. Their grievances, complaints, and protests are amplified in the increasingly strident internal political discourse in Russia. Arbatov shows how, under pressure from both internal politics and external events, Moscow has come to adopt a more independent line, and cooperation with the West now requires harder negotiation and efforts to reconcile different perspectives. He concludes that Russia's policy in the near abroad will be a major factor not only in its external relations but in its domestic politics. Thus he sees the conditions of Russians in the near abroad as Russia's paramount foreign policy problem.

Arbatov rejects the view of some Western analysts that the series of Russian military and political interventions from Tajikistan to Moldova adds up to a policy of neo-imperialism and renewed hostility toward the West. Instead, like the other Russian authors of this book, he sees them largely as ad hoc, opportunistic reactions, dominated by internal political currents and maneuvers, against a background of chaotic decision-making procedures, loss of control at the center (especially of the Russian military), and Yeltsin's eroding political position. But Arbatov recognizes that over time, such a series of responses could feed a new Cold War mentality in both East and West. However, he argues that such an evolution is not at all inevitable, and preventing it should be a major objective of foreign policy on both sides.

One alternative would be a return to a system of spheres of influence where, by tacit agreement, Russia has a free hand to deal with conflicts in the territory of the former Soviet Union, while the United States is accorded similar freedom of action in the Western hemisphere and other regions of major U.S. interest. Arbatov calls this the "Monrovsky Doctrine," and writes that it finds support not only among extreme nationalists but also among more moderate advocates of democratic reform, who face the domestic backlash against Russian foreign policy defeats and failures and what is seen as overreaching by the West. However, Arbatov thinks such a division of responsibilities would surely fail; over time it would not be accepted and could not be maintained in the present circumstances of international life. Russian resources in both the military and economic spheres would be inadequate to impose Moscow's will in the region, and the effort to do so would strengthen extremist forces within Russia, destabilize the new states, and ultimately earn the hostility of the West. Such a policy would create the very conditions it is designed to avoid.

Arbatov's basic position is that "the first priority of Russia's foreign policy should be to support the emergence of independent, stable, peaceful, and neutral new states in place of the former Soviet colonies." This means that Russia should take great care not to get involved in internal conflicts in these states. What is required instead is a flexible, steady, and mature course of action, tailored to the specific circumstances of each state, within an overall framework of normal interstate relations. Arbatov's chapter develops in general terms what would be involved in such a policy, country by country; for convenience in exposition, he divides them into four groups.

The first group consists of Ukraine and Belarus, which Arbatov considers "by far the most important subject of Moscow's policy in the near abroad." For Ukraine, he sees increasing economic integration under the umbrella of a strict Russian respect for Ukraine's political independence and integrity. In Belarus, the likely outcome is some kind of political reintegration, though not one forced by Russia. The obstacle here is that Belarus has not undergone democratic political reform or economic transition to anything even approaching the extent to which Russia has.

The second group comprises Georgia, Armenia, Kazakhstan, and Kyrgyzstan. These states have little prospect for economic or political reintegration with Russia. Nevertheless, they need security guarantees and a Russian military presence to protect their outer borders against foreign threats, which are also threats to Russia's security interests. Such arrangements could perhaps be made within the framework of the CIS. Kazakhstan, which Arbatov says "is second only to Ukraine" in its importance to Russia, presents one of the trickiest problems, because the Kazakh leadership itself seems to support some kind of federative reintegration. Arbatov thinks this would be a mismatch, and the effort to achieve it would be dangerous. Instead he proposes normalization of economic cooperation including

Russian investment, financial aid, and technological assistance, combined with military cooperation.

The third group consists of the Baltics and Moldova. Arbatov's prescription for Russia is to maintain normal diplomatic and trade relations with them as with any other foreign country. There is little prospect or reason for closer economic or political integration. The implication is that these states should be treated like Poland or Hungary, disregarding the period during which they were under Soviet or Russian rule. This outcome would depend to a considerable degree on developments within NATO. Russia could not be expected to maintain such a complacent attitude if these countries were to join or even align themselves with a military alliance that Moscow viewed as potentially hostile.

The last group includes Azerbaijan and the Central Asian states of Tajikistan, Uzbekistan, and Turkmenistan, which Arbatov sees as "formerly communist semi-feudal regimes . . . trying to secure Russian military support to fight local opposition movements." Russia should strictly avoid such entanglements. In fact, according to Arbatov, Central Asia is the least important region for Russia in the entire former Soviet territory. He foresees a gradual withdrawal of Russian interest and concern, especially if democratic reform continues in Russia, and Central Asia gravitates politically and economically toward South Asia.

Russian meddling is not the only or even the main cause of ethnic and internal conflict in the former Soviet Union (FSU), and so Russian disengagement will not end it. If there is no alternative method of resolving or at least containing these sources of instability on the Russian periphery, Russia will inevitably be drawn in and the policy directions Arbatov outlines will be undermined. The situation will slide toward Russian hegemony, with all the negative consequences for both internal and external Russian politics. The only alternative, Arbatov recognizes, is for Russia to engage the organized international community, primarily the United Nations or the OSCE, in the effort to manage ethnic conflicts on its borders. Neither the United States nor Russia has been very effective in using these institutions in the pursuit of a common and cooperative security system. As noted above, the case studies show that Russia and Russian policymakers do not have a very well-developed understanding of the functions and *modus operandi* of such organizations. And the United States has more often seemed to be trying to bend them to its own will, rather than seeking a common will. In any event, they suffer from serious structural and organizational weaknesses.

Arbatov recognizes all this. He assumes that the OSCE will be, at least in the first instance, the organization of choice for conflict situations in East Central Europe (ECE) and the former Soviet Union. He sketches some of the reforms he thinks are needed in decision processes and other aspects of the organization. His basic appeal, however, is for a common effort by both Russia and the United States to use the OSCE in a responsible and impartial manner, which will mean defining objectives and policies that are truly policies of the international community rather than the objectives of one side or the other dressed up in multilateral costume, and the willingness on the part of both countries to accept results from time to time that are less than their preferred outcomes. These are perhaps utopian prescriptions, and Arbatov is fully cognizant of how slender the chance is that they will prevail. However, he believes that this is the only way to avoid another long half-century of global confrontation.

THE UNITED STATES: REVERSING NEGLECT OF THE NEAR ABROAD

Working out a new relationship with Russia has been perhaps the major U.S. foreign policy priority since the end of the Cold War, but the ethnic problems of the new states and their impact on Russian domestic and foreign policies have been curiously neglected elements in this process. U.S. policy evolution—if it can be called that—is chronicled in the chapter by Abram Chayes, Lara Olson, and George Raach. For most of the post-Soviet period, U.S.-Russian relations have been conducted within a broadly cooperative framework. Both nations, looking outward, have sought to use their influence in a cooperative manner to reduce conflict, and particularly to reduce the threat of weapons of mass destruction throughout the world. The new relationship appeared to respond quite well when tested in 1991 in the Gulf War: Iraq's cross-border aggression violated clear-cut international norms; there was no direct threat to either Russia or the United States; and the firm U.S. commitment to act created favorable conditions for cooperation.

Reflecting the long Cold War practice, U.S. policies under both Republicans and Democrats have been Moscow-centered and personalized in their focus on the leader in the Kremlin. Initially, both the Reagan and Bush administrations gave strong support to Secretary General Mikhail Gorbachev's efforts to open up the Soviet Union and begin a transition to democracy. The objective was a stable, democratic Soviet Union. There was little anticipation and even less planning for the breakup of the Soviet Union. The instability that such an upheaval would inevitably entail was not fully appreciated. Support for a democratic Soviet Union under Gorbachev persisted until the very last moment, but ultimately had to give way in light of the reality of the drive for independence of the republics of the Soviet Union. Even after recognition of the fifteen newly independent states of the former Soviet Union, the U.S. focus remained on Russia and the new man in the Kremlin, Boris Yeltsin. This has made it difficult for the United States to forge comprehensive policies that support Russian democratization and at the same time steer an independent course toward other newly emerging states, apart from the Ukraine and the Baltics, where special considerations are at work.

As for Ukraine, the central issue for the United States was nuclear disarmament, and denuclearization efforts in many ways are the most successful of the Clinton administration policies toward the FSU. The Trilateral Agreement of January 1994, in which the United States provided needed security assurances, helped to resolve some immediate tensions between Ukraine and Russia, and to ensure that Ukraine would not develop independent nuclear capability. The defeat of Ukrainian President Leonid Kravchuk by Leonid Kuchma seems to have resulted in a good-faith effort at full implementation of the Trilateral Agreement, dissipating the uncertainties caused by the maneuvering of the Kravchuk administration. As an adjunct of U.S. denuclearization efforts, U.S. officials worked to ameliorate friction between Russia and Ukraine over Crimea and the disposition of the Black Sea Fleet.

U.S. policy toward the Baltics has strong historic roots reflecting the strength of the Latvian and Lithuanian communities in U.S. politics. High-visibility pressure on Moscow for troop withdrawal was accompanied by lower-key efforts to induce the independent governments of Estonia and Latvia to give more equitable treatment to Russian inhabitants and to enact more generous citizenship laws. The culmination was President Bill Clinton's trip to Riga in July 1994, the first time an American president had ever visited the Baltic states. The avoidance of violent conflict in the Baltics and some easing of restrictive policies were a cumulative result of many factors, most notably the effort and persistence by the Council of Europe and the High Commissioner on National Minorities of the OSCE. Yet U.S. policy did have its impact on all the involved states.

Apart from these two special cases, a differentiated U.S. policy focus on the many conflicts that have cropped up elsewhere in the former Soviet Union has been slower to develop. Other conflicts have not engaged the United States to the same degree. There has been ongoing dialogue with the Russian government, but little knowledge or support among the American people for any active engagement. Moreover, both Russia and the United States have been slow to offer encouragement, and slower still to provide tangible support to the international institutions that might work to help prevent, resolve, or even mitigate conflict in the former Soviet territory.

Conclusion

The enormity and the complexity of transition from Soviet rule emerges powerfully from the case studies in this volume. This complexity and the legacies of the abuses of the totalitarian past should no longer be underestimated. In this context, the amount of ethnic violence that has actually occurred could be considered astonishingly low. As Keitha Fine has commented in an essay on East Central Europe:

No single approach to making a transition from authoritarian practices and mentalities, active or passive, can alone repair long-lived economic-structural, political-social or individual dysfunctionality. The weakness and corruption of national elites, the continuing presence of the old bureaucratic class, the absence of universal agreement about either the terms of or the transition itself, unpreparedness for emerging problems once central planning and social control disappear, the early fragmentation of oppositions, and inexperience with and misunderstanding of the sphere of so-called civil society was almost universal in the ECE.[1]

On its borders and within Russia itself, the transition continues to be plagued by smoldering ethnic tensions. Although the focus of U.S. policy has been on reform of Russia's political and economic institutions, the success of any effort to build a network of prosperous democracies under the rule of law will depend in large part on how Moscow and Washington deal with the legacy of ancient and more recent misrule.

---

1. Keitha Sapsin Fine, "Fragile Stability and Change: Understanding Conflict During the Transitions in East Central Europe," in Abram Chayes and Antonia Handler Chayes, eds., *Preventing Conflict in the Post-Communist World* (Washington, D.C.: Brookings, 1996), p. 543.

Chapter 2

A Framework for Assessing Post-Soviet Conflicts

Alexei Arbatov

The following section of this book contains case studies of some of the principal post-Soviet conflicts that have already erupted or may do so in the near future. For all the economic, political, cultural, and ethnic peculiarities of these conflicts, as well as their varying geopolitical locations and environments, they share some fundamental features. These commonalities make them a legitimate subject for systematic analysis and generalizations that provide the groundwork for recommendations on the policies required of Russia and the West with regard to conflict management and peacekeeping in the vast transcontinental post-communist space: Central, Eastern, and Southern Europe; Central Asia; and Siberia.

Basically, the problems and conflicts in the post-Soviet space are typical of historical post-colonial relationships. Nonetheless, several crucial differences must be taken into account in applying standard post-colonial conflict management to the former Soviet space: 1) the empire was conceived to obtain security, not resources and wealth; 2) dissolution was by choice—not defeat; and 3) Russians are disappointed by and resentful of the Western response to the end of the empire. These peculiarities are not always adequately understood in the West, but they strongly affect the attitude of Russians in the newly independent post-Soviet states, including Russia itself. These factors will become clearer to the interested Western audience after reading the case studies in this volume, which to varying degrees reflect perceptions and concepts predominant among the new Russian political elite. Thus, the editors decided to preserve as many of these particular features as possible in the chapters that follow, even if they did not always fully agree with the interpretations of events and the arguments of the authors of the case studies.

Risking some imbalance and even bias in the analysis of particular post-Soviet conflicts seems warranted in order to shed light on the views of this new Russian political elite. The Soviet, Russian Federation, and ethnic Russian perspectives on the problem reflected here usually escape the Western public, which is mostly exposed to the views and complaints of the national-liberation political elites of the newly independent states bordering Russia, or at best to the self-recriminations of pro-Western liberal Russian intellectuals. In the wake of the collapse of the huge and oppressive Soviet empire, these views may be historically justified and natural, but they are also quite biased and therefore inadequate as a basis for Western policymaking.

An Empire for Security, Not Wealth

The tsarist and then the Soviet communist empires were different from classic Western empires of the eighteenth, nineteenth, and first half of the twentieth centuries. Unlike the Western metropolises that prospered and flourished by exploiting colonies overseas, the Russian/Soviet empire was much more similar to Eastern empires that conquered colonies by expanding their continental perimeters. Even more important, Moscow did not seek economic enrichment so much as the aggrandizement of its military power, thus fortifying its security at the expense of the security of others and enhancing its geopolitical status in the world. Ordinary Russians did not profit much from colonialism, and in many cases were made to pay more to support the empire economically and militarily, often at the cost of their rights and freedoms. For geographic, ethnic, and psychological reasons, Russians moved to the colonies in much greater numbers and accepted greater immigration from the colonies than the French, British, or Germans did. Because of Russia's relative social and political backwardness and the more advanced state of development of some of the colonized nations (such as the Poles, Finns, and Balts), intermixing of Russians with other nations was incomparably broader on all social levels and across all regions.

Moreover, in both Russia and its colonies (which were not perceived as such, but rather as provinces of a single integrated state), ethnic Russians as a rule lived worse than the people of the colonized nations. Apart from subsidizing them economically, the Russian/Soviet empire repaid the loyalty of its colonies by giving local elites significant domestic autonomy and privileges, by accepting non-Russians into the Moscow and St. Petersburg aristocracy and into top governmental posts, and by tolerating the gain by large non-Russian communities of advantageous economic and social positions in Russia. Thus, the overwhelming majority of Russians do not feel any guilt for past colonial oppression, and many are offended by a lack of gratitude on the part of former colonized nations.

Dissolution by Choice, Not Defeat

The Soviet empire, in contrast to most others, collapsed not as a result of defeat in a world war with stronger, more advanced opponents (Spain, Turkey, Austria-Hungary, Japan, Germany), or after exhaustion in continuous colonial wars (Spain, Netherlands, Portugal, France, Britain), but rather as a result of a free choice by the mother country—Russia. By the early 1990s, Moscow's relations with other major powers were better than ever, and the outside world was interested in keeping the Soviet Union integrated (except for the Baltic states). Only portents of potential colonial wars were evident in the bloody clashes in Dushanbe, Fergana, Tbilisi, Baku, Vilnius, and Riga in 1989–91. Russian democratic forces, led by Boris Yeltsin, supported national liberation movements in other republics against Soviet attempts at colonial suppression. The escalation of violence was interrupted by the failure of the Moscow coup in August 1991, and preempted by Yeltsin and the new Russian elite's liberation of Russia and the other republics from the Soviet imperial superstructure in December 1991.

That is why Russians in Russia and in other former Soviet republics, who overwhelmingly encouraged the dissolution of the empire, feel entitled to at least a modicum of appreciation and respect from the public and elites of other post-Soviet states. They received their independence and statehood at almost no cost, as a gift from Russia, and were spared the horrible losses of fighting for their freedom themselves. (A glimpse of what could have been in store for them if there had been no Russian consent can be seen in the Chechen debacle.) Instead, Russians see violation of the rights of ethnic Russians in many post-Soviet republics, and the separation of their compatriots by the new borders. There are never-ending tensions between the Russian Federation and its neighbors over territorial, economic, defense, and other issues. All this makes many Russians feel betrayed and deceived by developments since 1991. These ethnic

Russians in the near abroad are now immigrating to Russia en masse and starting to doubt that supporting democrats and discarding the empire was the right choice in 1991.

Resentment at the West's Response to the End of the Empire

There is a strong sense among Russians of disappointment with and recrimination toward the United States and other Western powers. The Soviet Union was never defeated in the Cold War. The Soviet Union was originally created and organized for waging both hot and cold wars, and that was its natural environment. With modest corrections, improvements, and savings, the Soviet Union could have continued the Cold War for decades. The Soviet Union disintegrated not because of the military-political pressure of its external opponents, but under the powerful impact of internal social developments and the sincere, albeit utopian, desire of Mikhail Gorbachev and Edward Shevardnadze to end the arms race, establish genuine peace in the world, and renovate the communist system ("socialism with a human face") so that it could coexist and cooperate with the West. Instead, in such an unnatural domestic and external environment the Soviet empire suddenly collapsed. Russia was the driving force behind the democratic offensive inside the Soviet Union, ending the Cold War and liberating other nations from communist oppression.

The Russian Federation emerged out of the wreckage of the Soviet empire as a new state. Everything was different: the people in power, the territory, the population, the economic and political systems. Communist ideology had been replaced by the ideals of democracy. Were it not for Russia as the center of Soviet power under Gorbachev and as the most democratic Soviet republic under Yeltsin, the Cold War would not have ended and the communist empire would not have fallen. Russia, as one of the principal victors in the bloodless defeat of Soviet communism, felt it deserved better treatment by other major powers.

But it soon became clear that this was not a common perception in the West. As the natural successor to the Soviet Union in many physical respects, Russia was also seen as the inheritor of the responsibility for numerous Soviet (and even tsarist) crimes and offenses, including those perpetrated in Central Europe and other former Soviet republics. In fact Russia was treated like a defeated power, deserving of economic help and political sympathy perhaps, but by no means entitled to an equal and respected place in relations with other victors in the Cold War. In some influential Western political circles, Russia was even denied any legitimate foreign geopolitical or strategic interests beyond its borders, reasonable sufficiency in the military balance, or any independent role in the "far abroad" (e.g., in the Yugoslavian crisis).

True, this treatment was largely self-inflicted on account of the naiveté, lack of dignity, incompetence, and euphoria of Russia's top leaders during 1991–93. It was also the result of Russia's enormous perceived economic dependence on Western aid and credits, although in fact this assistance and Russian economic reform, associated with the requirements of the International Monetary Fund and World Bank, failed both economically and politically. The West was not wise enough to help Russia out of such a humiliating position, to assuage its national pride, and to make concessions to it while it was so weak. On the contrary, Western leaders used the situation to the utmost to gain maximum unilateral concessions from Moscow in foreign trade and in geopolitical and military terms, as well as to virtually dictate Russia's domestic economic reforms and influence its internal political affairs and even cadres policy.[1] Some weak and hesitant attempts by Russian officials to deviate from the course prescribed by the West and to raise points about Russia's own interests were cut short by U.S. and European "big brothers."[2] And the West did much less than Russia had expected to take care of Russian security needs and support Russian economic, humanitarian, and other interests in the "near abroad." In most cases, the West either abstained or took the side of other post-Soviet states in their controversies with Moscow. Even when the West pressured other republics to respect the rights of ethnic Russians and other minorities, this Western policy was perceived in Russia as too little, too late. (On this point, see especially Chapter 9, "Latvia: Discrimination, International Organizations, and Stabilization.")

The West's treatment of Russia is what might have been expected if it were dealing with a defeated and disbanded empire, but not a

---

1. "Cadres policy" is a Soviet term for political appointments to key positions on all societal levels.

2. One typical episode occurred in 1993, when Russian Foreign Minister Andrei Kozyrev tried to explain to U.S. Secretary of State Warren Christopher that it would be hard for Yeltsin to renege on the missile engines deal with India for domestic reasons. What he got in response was: "Andrei, you've got to do better than that." A. Pushkov, "The West Doesn't Care Where Kozyrev Will Write his Memoirs," *Moskovskie novosti*, No. 31 (April 30, 1995), p. 12.

young and enthusiastic state that had torn the Soviet empire apart and was longing to join the community of civilized nations as soon as possible. The Western stance on Russian relations with other post-Soviet states—suspicion of Russian neo-imperialism and reluctance to assume a greater burden in cooperating with Russia to resolve post-Soviet problems—had a negative impact on both Russia's attitude to the near abroad and its perceptions of the Western role and goals there. These tendencies are also reflected in the following case studies.

These factors helped to produce a backlash in Russian domestic politics and in Moscow's relations with the near abroad as well as with the major Western powers. The first inklings of this backlash appeared as early as the middle of 1992, but the real turning point came in December 1994 with the beginning of the savage suppression by Russian armed forces of the secessionist Chechen republic. The case studies shed some light on that disaster, which is discussed more fully in Chapter 15, "Russian Security Interests and Dilemmas: An Agenda for the Future."

Part II
Cases of Conflict

Chapter 3

North Ossetia and Ingushetia: The First Clash

Olga Osipova

It is ironic that one of Russia's most serious problems in the North Caucasus today arises out of conflict of two peoples—the Ossetians and the Ingush—traditionally regarded as perhaps the most pro-Russian of all the North Caucasian ethnic groups.

—Paul B. Henze

The terrible violent clashes that erupted in late 1992 between the two small republics of North Ossetia and Ingushetia in the North Caucasus were the first armed conflicts to occur within the Russian Federation itself following the breakup of the Soviet Union in 1991. On November 1 and 2, 1992, what had been sporadic violence in the region turned into bitter fighting with the use of heavy weaponry in the Prigorodny ("outlying") district of the left bank of the North Ossetian capital, Vladikavkaz. Armed paramilitary groups of Ingush and the armed forces of the North Ossetian Autonomous Republic revived an old territorial dispute over control of this district. The worst armed clashes lasted only three days, but according to official sources, around 600 people were killed, and as many more were wounded. Around 3,500 homes were destroyed, and approximately 50,000 Ingush became refugees.[1]

---

1. "A Political Assessment by the Security Council of the Russian Federation of the Circumstances Surrounding the Armed Conflict on the Territories of the North Ossetian SSR and the Ingushetian Republic in October, November 1992." *Nezavisimaia gazeta*, March 23, 1994. Official statistical figures are from the ABD.1.S., version 6.50, computerized data bank of the State Committee for Statistics of the Russian Federation, Statistics on the Republic of North Ossetia (NO ASSR).

Despite imposing a state of emergency in the North Caucasus in December 1992, Russian authorities still have failed to disarm the population, and the issues that led to this tragic conflict remain unresolved. The devastated Prigorodny district is virtually uninhabitable and remains extremely dangerous. Armed bands roam the area and the situation resembles a low-intensity guerrilla war, with frequent acts of sabotage, terrorism, and hostage-taking. A large number of refugees from the Prigorodny district have been forced to live in very poor conditions in other parts of Ingushetia, making conditions in this tiny, already impoverished republic much worse.[2] On December 8, 1994, the Council of the Federation (the upper chamber of the Russian Parliament) refused to renew the state of emergency in the region, and instead formed a commission to "look for peaceful solutions to the crisis."[3] But this refusal to extend the state of emergency reflects only an assertion of power against the status quo policies of the Yeltsin government, and does not indicate that significant changes have occurred in the situation on the ground. Unfortunately, in the face of increasingly harsh policies on all sides, none of the Russian, Ingush, or Ossetian political leaders seems capable of moving beyond rhetoric and achieving concrete steps toward compromise.

The conflict over the Prigorodny district has deep roots in the troubled history between the Ingush, the Ossetians, and the Russians, who have always played a critical role in the politics of the North Caucasus. The most important factor underlying the conflict was the repeated recarving of boundaries during the Soviet period based on the old dictum, "divide and rule." Under the Russian Empire and the Soviet Union, Russia's internal administrative divisions underwent numerous forced changes. The Ingush were initially rewarded for their allegiance to the Bolsheviks during the Civil War, but in the 1930s Ingushetia lost its status as an independent republic, and during World War II, the Ingush were accused of disloyalty to the Soviet state and,

---

2.   There are no official statistics on the number of refugees from Prigorodny, and the situation in the region has become even more confused since the beginning of the Chechen crisis. Based on numerous visits to the area and contacts with officials there, the author estimates that, as of summer 1995, there were upwards of 100,000 refugees in Ingushetia.

3.   In the Russian parliamentary system, the imposition and suspension of a state of emergency inside the Russian Federation is exclusively within the control of the Council of the Federation. Perhaps ironically, December 8, 1994, is also the generally accepted date of the start of the Chechen war, since it was on this day that federal troops amassed on the Chechen border first began crossing over into Chechen territory.

together with other North Caucasian peoples, were forcibly deported to Central Asia. Most of their lands, including the Prigorodny district, were given to the neighboring republic of North Ossetia.

The Ingush were rehabilitated during the Khrushchev years, and many of them returned to their traditional territory in the Chechen-Ingushetian Autonomous Republic, which was formed in 1934. However, the Ingush were not authorized to return to the Prigorodny district of Vladikavkaz, though over the years many returned illegally despite bureaucratic barriers established by the North Ossetian authorities. In 1989, the Ingush decided to separate from Chechnya and declared their independence. In this volatile context, the Russian Supreme Soviet passed a law on full territorial rehabilitation for the Ingush, which declared the right of the Ingush to their original territories, including the Prigorodny district. Although this law gave the Ingush a basis for legitimizing their long-standing territorial claims, it did not establish a procedure for the actual transfer of territory. Nor did the law stipulate what would happen to the existing North Ossetian population of these regions. As a result of this legislation and the Russian Parliament's subsequent recognition of the Republic of Ingushetia, the latent dispute over Prigorodny became ripe for open conflict.

A second cluster of factors explaining the level of social tension that mobilized people to violence arose from the general economic and social crisis in the region. The independent Ingushetia that emerged after the break with Chechnya was a tiny and overwhelmingly rural republic with a very low standard of living. There were no services or hospitals, sanitary conditions were poor, and many places lacked running water. The region's main industrial facilities were all located in Chechnya and North Ossetia; Vladikavkaz and Grozny were the only major urban centers capable of providing services, medical care, and non-agricultural employment. Although economic depression was pervasive throughout the region, the North Ossetians were generally much better off than the Ingush, who had absolutely no industry and few economic prospects. This disparity caused deep resentment among the Ingush, since the Prigorodny district had been their only center of industry. The gradual departure of the non-native population (i.e., Russians) from the increasingly tense Prigorodny district contributed to the acceleration of economic decline and removed a neutral moderating presence. These conditions led to high levels of social frustration, which were easily manipulated by ambitious political leaders. The rapid decline of the economy also increased the importance to the Ingush of regaining the valuable Prigorodny district as one of the few potentially viable economic areas of an independent Ingushetia.

The third important factor was the general instability of the Russian Federation's authority in all of the regions and border territories and many of the other post-Soviet states, culminating in the war in Chechnya. This larger political context and the absence of clear and effective political structures led both the Ingush and the Ossetians to assume that they could achieve their goals by force. More difficult to define is Russia's role in the conflict. Moscow was too distracted by its own political struggles to take decisive measures to resolve the conflict. However, at least some parties within the Russian government and military were clearly conducting a pro-Ossetian policy. The general chaos of the situation, combined with the fact that the self-proclaimed independent republic of Ingushetia had no formal government institutions or status to enable it to press its claims at an official level, increased the calls within the Russian government to resolve the situation through the use of force. In mid-1995, Ingushetia's biggest problem appeared to be facilitating the return of the tens of thousands of Ingush refugees from Chechnya, Dagestan, North Ossetia, and other areas of the North Caucasus. Negotiations among Russian, Ossetian, and Ingush representatives on the issue of refugee return, which began in 1993, have achieved few results.

The inadequacy of Russian endeavors to predict and manage crises in this volatile region has been acutely demonstrated by the tragic war in Chechnya, which added a new dimension to the crisis in Ingushetia. The Chechen conflict left Grozny more devastated than Stalingrad was in 1941 following Hitler's attack, and in need of at least 15 trillion rubles for reconstruction. In addition to the danger that the war in Chechnya might spread into Ingush territory, this overburdened region has been the destination of over 60,000 Chechen refugees. Ingushetia has no resources to care for the refugees. It receives 80 percent of its budget from the central Russian treasury, and the Russian Federal Migration Service can only provide 20,500 rubles—approximately U.S. $4.00—plus one small piece of soap per refugee.

A possible flare-up of the Ossetian-Ingushetian conflict, combined with the civil war in Chechnya, threatens the peace and stability of the whole North Caucasus and adjacent regions of the Russian Federation. The leaders of the republics and national movements of the North Caucasus and Transcaucasia understand that the present situation is fraught with danger and are making efforts to ease tensions. However, in the absence of a solution to the root territorial and refugee problems, a new explosion of violence is a constant threat.

A grasp of the historical, social, and political background of the dispute between the groups in the North Caucasus is critical to understanding the intractability of the issues at the heart of the present conflict. Since the evolution of this conflict is very complex and not widely understood, the bulk of this chapter will be devoted to sketching relevant aspects of the larger historical background. Particular emphasis is placed on the complexity of Russia's role in the region's past, and its responsibilities today.

The Historical Origins of the Ossetian-Ingushetian Conflict

The Caucasus Mountains form the natural frontier between Russia on the one side and Azerbaijan and Georgia on the other. Over the last two hundred years, the Caucasus region has been the site of both open and covert struggles between Turkey, Iran, and Russia.

The Ossetians and Ingush, two peoples differing greatly in national culture, customs, religion, and standards of living, share a complex history in a small area in the valley between the upper reaches of the Terek and Sunzha rivers in the North Caucasus. The incorporation of parts of Georgia and Armenia into the Russian Empire at the end of the eighteenth and beginning of the nineteenth centuries spurred Russia to conquer the North Caucasus. The fifty-five-year war waged by Russia in that ethnically variegated region faced bitter resistance from the "mountain peoples" under the leadership of the Imam Shamil and led to the forcible exile (*makhadzhir*) of many of the North Caucasian peoples to Turkey.[4]

The legacies of the war combined with the ruinous nationalities policies of the Soviet Union constitute the basis for many of the contemporary ethnic conflicts in the wider region, which includes parts of the Russian Federation, Georgia, Armenia, and Azerbaijan. The North Caucasus is now a region of the Russian Federation comprising six national republics and three administrative-territorial entities, many of which are multinational. In Dagestan, for instance, there are more than forty ethnic groups belonging to four different language families

---

4.   The term *makhadzhir* is the Russian transliteration of the oft-used Turkish term *muhacir*.

(Terskoe, Dagestani, Iranian, and Caucasian). The sheer number of languages and peoples thrown together in a relatively small territory, coupled with frequent, dramatic changes of administrative boundaries during the Soviet period, has given rise to a plethora of mutually incompatible territorial claims by these national groups against each other. Clan, tribal, and (loosely) ethnic divisions form the main cleavages between the mountain peoples. And between the Caucasus mountain peoples and Russia, there is also a division along religious lines in the confrontation of Islam and Christianity.

The Ossetians belong to the Iranian language group. In the early Middle Ages, the ancestors of the Ossetians, the Alans, created a large feudal state, Alania, in the steppes and foothills of the North Caucasus. The Alans converted to Orthodox Christianity and maintained close ties with Byzantium, Kievan-Rus', and the states of the Caucasus until the Tatar-Mongolian invasions in the thirteenth century. Driven southward by the Golden Horde, some of the Alans settled on the territory of present-day North Ossetia, while the rest crossed the Caucasus Mountains into what is now South Ossetia in the Republic of Georgia. Although some Ossetians later converted to Islam, they have remained a Christian people in the minds of Russians. During the Russo-Turkish War of 1768–74, detachments of Ossetians fought in the Georgian army on the side of the Russians against the Turks. Russia's annexation of the territory of present-day North Ossetia was recognized in the 1774 peace treaty with Turkey (the Treaty of Kiuchuk-Kainardzhi). At the time of Russia's conquest of the North Caucasus, the Ossetians were subjects of Kabarda; since the Russians freed them from this condition of dependence, they were seen as liberators.[5]

In order to propagate Orthodox Christianity in the Caucasus, the Ossetians instituted a spiritual commission in the eighteenth century and eventually founded seminaries in Vladikavkaz and Ardona for training Ossetian missionaries. At the beginning of the nineteenth century, part of the Ossetian nation moved from the mountains to the Mozdok district and the plains of Vladikavkaz, where they took up agriculture. Russia always distinguished the Ossetians from the other mountain peoples of the North Caucasus, considering them

---

5.   Kabarda is a generic term in Russian historiography denoting Abaza-Adygean ethnic groups (this includes most of the ethnic groups from the western North Caucasus). The ethnonym was derived from the most populous group, the Kabardinians.

co-religionists, and with Ossetian help Russia conducted its own policies in the region.

The Ingush and Chechens belong to the Hakho-Dagestani language group and are members of the same ethnic group, the Vainakhians. They are the original inhabitants of the Northern Caucasus. In 1810, the Ingush voluntarily became Russian subjects and did not fight with the mountain peoples against Russia in the Caucasian war, thereby incurring the resentment of the Chechens. At that time, the tsarist government encouraged the Ingush to descend from the mountains and settle on the plain and engage in farming. Nevertheless, over the course of the nineteenth century the ethnic affiliation of the Ingush with the Chechens and their conversion to Islam combined to alienate the Ingush from the Russians. In Russian society, Chechens and Ingush were seen as wild peoples and bandits; the Ossetians, by contrast, were viewed as allies of Russia in the region.

The Chechens were the most active adversaries of Russia during the Caucasian war, and as a result, they experienced repeated repressions and deportations. In the twentieth century, they fought with the White Russians during the Civil War, while the Ingush favored the Bolsheviks. Chechen resistance persisted after the Soviets came to power, with Chechen bands continuing to operate in the mountains until the People's Commissariat of Internal Affairs (NKVD) ferreted them out and eventually destroyed them.

A sense of historic grievance toward the Russian state remains alive among the North Caucasian peoples.[6] It is rooted in the Russian Empire's harsh policies in the North Caucasus, Russia's complete subjugation of the region in 1864 in the aftermath of the Caucasian Wars, and the unequal pattern of treatment of Ingush, Chechens, and Ossetians by the Russian authorities. There is a kind of unity among the Caucasian peoples in their indictments against Russia, which finds expression today in the revived Confederation of Mountain Peoples, first formed in 1917 in reaction to the Russian Empire's policy of divide and rule.[7] However, while the members of the Confederation are united against Russia, they are divided among

---

6. Kh. M. Ibragimbeily, "The North Caucasus: Genocide, Deportation and States of Emergency," *Nezavisimaia gazeta*, July 12, 1994.

7. The Confederation of Mountain Peoples continued to exist in some form throughout the Soviet period, although, politically at least, it was driven deep underground.

themselves. Thus Confederation members have intervened in some conflicts, such as Abkhazia, but have ignored others.

ETHNIC FOUNDATIONS OF THE SOVIET STATE

The Russian Empire was organized according to purely administrative units known as provinces (*gubernia*). The idea of political legitimacy based on national characteristics simply did not exist prior to the Soviet period. The revolutionary terrorist organization Narodnaia Volia (People's Will, 1879–81) was the first in tsarist Russia to proclaim the principle of national self-determination as a political slogan.[8] Because of Narodnaia Volia and other, later organizations, the image of Russia as a "prison house of nations" and an amalgamation of plundered provinces was fixed in the consciousness of the anti-tsarist Russian intelligentsia. As a result, the intelligentsia established and strengthened national revolutionary organizations, which struggled for the creation of national states. The Social Revolutionaries and the Bolsheviks took up the principle of national self-determination, viewing it as a weapon in the fight against the Russian autocracy. It became a key slogan used by Bolshevik agitators in the outlying areas of the Empire.

The rise of separatism on the national periphery played an important role in both the 1905 and 1917 revolutions. The ideological core of the Bolshevik program was the principle of proletarian internationalism under the slogan "Proletarians of All Countries Unite!" However, in the years leading up to the revolution, the Bolsheviks tactically adopted the principle of national self-determination for the many peoples of Russia in order to help foment revolution. Once they gained power, the Bolsheviks found themselves in an awkward position. On the one hand, they were obliged to fulfill their promises and concede autonomy to the nations they had helped to awaken in the periphery, yet on the other, they also had to check real national self-determination in order to build a new unitary communist state. The Bolsheviks adopted a policy that became known as autonomization, and in the first years of Soviet power, they created a series of internal administrative boundaries nominally based upon ethnic identity.

As a result of many subsequent delimitations, a complex system of national entities and administrative hierarchies emerged in the Soviet Union. The top level was occupied by the fifteen union-level

---

8. Based in St. Petersburg, Narodnaia Volia was an organization of intellectuals of various ethnic backgrounds, not just Russians.

republics, which did have some real autonomy and which themselves contained several strata of autonomous areas and regions. Below the level of the union republics, known as Soviet Socialist Republics (SSRs), the national element in the other administrative units was largely formal. In actuality, the Soviet government suppressed the natural right of minority peoples to an autonomous national life. In the end, these ethnically based territorial divisions turned out to be timebombs inside the Soviet state.

The Russian Soviet Federated Socialist Republic (RSFSR) as the only union republic constituted as a federation. Today, although the various subunits of the Russian Federation enjoy equal rights, the national-state entities (republics), the national-territorial entities (autonomous districts), and the administrative-territorial entities (krais and oblasts) find themselves in very unequal relationships with the federal administrative bodies. This asymmetry within the Russian Federation in turn stimulates these units to seek to raise their own status.

In retrospect, it is clear that the tactic of promulgating paper autonomies on the basis of national groupings laid the foundation for many of today's conflicts. The explosive potential of this arrangement did not go completely unnoticed in Russian legal circles. For example, the émigré Russian theoretician on the state and law N.N. Alekseyev wrote in 1927: "The well-known slogan 'national self-determination' has been shown by experience to bring with it least of all rest and peace. On the contrary, it separates and contains in itself the seeds of disintegration and enmity. Inspired by this slogan, peoples, as if delirious, destroy the true basis of their economic existence, put themselves in an obviously unprofitable position and ignore their real interests."[9] However, at the time nationalities policies were being formulated and implemented, legal scholars and practitioners trained in the pre-revolutionary school were not in a position to influence the process. In a multinational state like the Soviet Union, it might have been wiser to incorporate all nations into one economic and political process. The introduction of the national principle by the Bolsheviks, even though it was only nominal, contributed to the development of nationalist communist party structures, which subsequently demanded the right to full national self-determination.

---

9. N.N. Alekseyev, "Soviet Federalism," *Yevraziiskii vremennik*, No. 5 (1927).

THE OSSETIAN-INGUSH SITUATION BEFORE 1917

Territorial claims by both Ossetians and Ingush on the city of Vladikavkaz and the adjoining Prigorodny district are at the heart of today's Ossetian-Ingushetian conflict. Vladikavkaz was founded by the Russian government in 1784 as a military fortress on the river Terek, and it has always been looked upon as the *de facto* capital of the North Caucasus. Russia paid special attention to this city, largely because of its military significance, and it became the center of Russian influence in the North Caucasus. A key Georgian military road to Transcaucasia ran through Vladikavkaz, which promoted the city's industrial and cultural development.

Both the Ossetians and the Ingush have always contested the ownership of the land on which Vladikavkaz was built. The Ingush allege that the original fortress was constructed on the location of the village (*aul*) of Angusht, from which the Russian name for the Ingush is derived. The Ossetians claim it was the site of an Ossetian village called Dzaudzhikan. As long as the town was an administrative unit of the Russian Empire, none of these claims could be acted upon and the groups shared Vladikavkaz between them. Moreover, the Ingush and Ossetians constituted only part of the population in the region, and in fact until 1919, the disputed land was mainly settled by Terek-Cossacks of the Terek province of the Russian Empire.[10]

Many representatives of the Caucasian peoples played an active role in the revolutionary events of 1905–07 and 1917, motivated in part by the desire to resolve some of the region's nationality problems. Many groups sided with the Bolsheviks in the hope of creating their own national governments. As noted above, in the years leading up to the revolution, a key slogan of the Bolshevik Party—and it was a legitimate political party at that time—called for autonomy and self-determination for non-Russian peoples.[11] After the first Russian revolution in 1905–07, the tsarist government, perhaps as an attempt to undermine the appeal of the Bolsheviks, tried to forge a compromise with national groups in the North Caucasus. The Ingush were granted some autonomy in a new "Nazran" (Ingushetian) national district with Vladikavkaz as its administrative center, in what had previously been the Terek province.

---

10. The Cossacks were the military class of the Russian Empire who served on the frontiers and played an active role in the colonization policies of the Empire.

11. Although the Bolshevik-Menshevik split did not become formal until 1903, the first marked differences between the two competing strands of National Socialists were apparent as early as 1893.

SOVIET NATIONALITIES POLICY IN THE REGION

During the Russian Civil War (1918–21), the sides that the various peoples of the North Caucasus took determined their future in the new Soviet state. The Terek Cossacks, along with other Cossack groups, fought with the White Army. Following the Red Army victory, the new Soviet authorities conducted a massive deportation of Cossacks to Siberia in reprisal. As a direct result of the deportations, the traditional lands of the Terek Cossacks were vacated.[12]

In return for Ingush support of the Bolsheviks, at an August 1918 Congress of the Ingush people, the prominent Bolshevik Sergo Ordzhonikidze promised them the land of the Terek Cossacks. In the years leading up to the 1917 revolution, the Ingush had been a critical base of Bolshevik power on the Terek River, and they took an active part in the Civil War on behalf of the Bolsheviks.[13] The Ingush began to settle in the former Cossack farms and villages—the very same villages that were the focus of large-scale fighting in 1992, and that remain under dispute today. The Ingush assert that they were simply reclaiming former Ingush villages from which they had been driven during the Caucasian war in the previous century.[14]

Following the Civil War, Soviet authorities began the process of creating new administrative entities in the North Caucasus. On the territory of the Terek province, they proclaimed the Mountain Autonomous Soviet Socialist Republic (ASSR), which included districts inhabited by Ossetians, Ingush, Chechens, Balkardians, and Karachais (from the Turkic language group) and Cherkessians (from the Abkhazo-Adygean language group). The capital of this new republic, Vladikavkaz, was given a separate administrative status directly subordinate to the highest bodies of the Mountain ASSR.

In 1921–22, the Soviet government began to carve out autonomous territorial entities for Kabardinians, Balkardians, Karachais, and Chechens from the Mountain ASSR. For the first time in history, these peoples had the opportunity to take part in building their own state. The Mountain ASSR, comprising only Ossetia, Ingushetia, and the Sunzha district, lasted until 1924.

---

12. This activity was part of the Soviet government's policy to eliminate the Cossack estate. In 1919, the Central Committee of the Russian Communist Party adopted a directive on "de-Cossackification" toward this end.

13. In all, 20,000 Ingush lost their lives in the Civil War out of a total population of 90,000.

14. A. Petrovich, "The Cossacks and the North Caucasus," *Nezavisimaia gazeta*, June 4, 1994.

In 1924, the Ingush were presented with the Ingushetian Autonomous Region (oblast). Vladikavkaz was made a dual city and fulfilled administrative, industrial, and cultural functions for both the Ingushetian Autonomous Region and the Ossetian Autonomous Region. The Terek River, which demarcated the border between the Ossetian and Ingushetian Autonomous Regions, literally divided Vladikavkaz in two. The administrative center of the Ossetian Autonomous Region was located on the left bank of the river, while that of the Ingushetian Autonomous Region—which included the Prigorodny district—was on the right bank. This division was largely formal since the two populations were highly intermingled, sharing one university, one theater, and a number of major administrative buildings. Later, the Ingush Regional Committee of the Communist Party of the Soviet Union (CPSU) petitioned to have Vladikavkaz renamed Ordzhonikidze after Sergo Ordzhonikidze, who had been their special patron.

In the 1930s, a new series of major adjustments to the administrative divisions in the North Caucasus occurred. On January 15, 1934, the right to self-determination that the Soviet government had granted to the North Caucasian peoples in the 1920s was revoked, and the Chechen Autonomous Region and Ingushetian Autonomous Region were united to form the Chechen-Ingushetian Autonomous Region. In 1936, this region was transformed into the Chechen-Ingushetian Autonomous Republic, with Grozny as its capital. As part of the shift to create the Chechen-Ingushetian ASSR, North Ossetia was granted a portion of Ingushetian territory, including the Ingushetian part of the city of Ordzhonikidze, and the valuable industrial enterprises and official institutions there. The loss of their capital, with its role as cultural, industrial, and administrative center, was a major blow to the Ingush.

It is still not entirely clear why the Politburo made this decision. It was part of a larger shake-up of the whole region. Other oblasts had their autonomy revoked and were combined into strangely amalgamated republics. Sometimes completely unrelated peoples were put into a single republic, or a single people was divided among different republics. Most likely, these changes reflected the classic imperial strategy of divide and rule and were undertaken to ensure that the North Caucasian peoples could not unite against the Soviet center.

Changes in the borders in the North Caucasus were also connected to political struggles and intrigues among various communist national elites in Moscow. In the 1930s, Joseph Stalin purged many of his closest colleagues, influential older Bolshevik leaders who could pose a threat to his authority. Among the victims were Sergei Kirov and Sergo Ordzhonikidze, both from the "Sons of the Caucasus" group of Soviet leaders, which included Stalin himself. Kirov was assassinated in 1934 and Ordzhonikidze died soon after, allegedly by suicide. Stalin may have perceived the need to eliminate any loyalty to these leaders among certain North Caucasian groups. There have been some rumors as well that Stalin may himself have been an ethnic Ossetian, rather than a Georgian as is generally supposed. Whatever the motivations behind the border changes, they essentially amounted to a huge reward for North Ossetia, which gained full control over the city of Ordzhonikidze.

The changes were devastating for the economic well-being and status of the Ingush and left them deeply embittered. Grozny, the new capital of the Chechen-Ingushetian Autonomous Region, was a former Russian fortress (Groznaia), which served the cultural needs (schools, newspapers, theaters, and broadcasting stations in the national languages) of both Russians and Chechens in the region. However, Grozny was far from Ingushetian territory. In practical terms, the transfer of the administration of Ingush affairs to Grozny imposed great hardships on the Ingush. They had to travel three hours for services that only an urban center could provide, including medical clinics, higher education, and administrative offices, while Ordzhonikidze was within twenty minutes of most of the Ingush population. Furthermore, the Ingushetian portion of Ordzhonikidze had been the most economically valuable part of the Ingushetian territory, and one of the few sources of industry and employment opportunities for the Ingush. As a result, many Ingush had to move to Grozny for work and services.

WORLD WAR II AND THE DEPORTATION OF THE INGUSH

The beginning of 1944 marked the start of a tragic period of repression and forcible deportation of Ingush, Chechens, and other Caucasian peoples. Decree No. 1118-342 cc of the Council of People's Commissars of the Soviet Union of October 14, 1943, ordered the deportation of 100,000 Ingush. On January 31, 1944, the State Committee for Defense of the Soviet Union issued a decree ordering the deportation of Chechens and Ingush. The deportation, which began on February 23, 1944, was brutally carried out by NKVD troops, who offered no explanation to the victims and allowed them no time for preparation. The deportees were loaded into trains and sent to desolate areas on the harsh steppes of Kazakhstan. The conditions were so horrendous that around 25 percent of the deportees perished on the journey.[15] There was no official announcement of the deportations, which were carried out secretly. Across the Soviet Union and especially in the Caucasus, rumors were spread that the deportees had betrayed the Soviet Union and had taken part in preparing for the Nazi advance in the Caucasus.[16]

On March 7, 1944, immediately after the deportations, the Presidium of the Supreme Soviet of the Soviet Union abolished the Chechen-Ingushetian ASSR and ordered an administrative reorganization of the territory, which increased the area of the North Ossetian ASSR by 50 percent.[17] A decree issued a few days earlier, on March 1, 1944, had transferred the town of Mozdok, which was inhabited mostly by Russians, from the Stavropol region of the RSFSR to North Ossetia. In addition, most districts that had previously been inhabited by Ingush were joined to the North Ossetian ASSR, with the exception of the southernmost part of the Prigorodny district, which was transferred to the Georgian Soviet Socialist Republic. Nearly the whole Sunzha district, which had been heavily populated by Ingush, was attached to the Grozny region, which was newly created on the remaining lands of the old Chechen-Ingushetian ASSR. A part of the Kursky district of Kabardino-Balkaria that had been inhabited by Ingushetians was also given to North Ossetia. By order of the Presidium of the Supreme Soviet of the Soviet Union, the districts and villages that had been transferred to the North Ossetian ASSR were given new Ossetian names. The vacated Ingush lands were

---

15. Report of the Commission for the Restoration of the Ingushetian Autonomy of the Soviet of Nationalities of the RSFSR (material provided by the Russian Central State Archive, USSR, Moscow, 1990).

16. For more on the deportations, see A. Pristavkin, "The Golden Storm Cloud Spends the Night," (Nochevala Tuchka Zolotaia) in *Banner*, No. 3–4 (1987).

17. The Ossetian people were the titular nationality in both the North Ossetian ASSR, which was part of the RSFSR, and in the South Ossetian Autonomous Region, which belonged to Georgia. The question of how this autonomous region became part of Georgia is fairly complex, since the vast majority of Ossetians lived in districts of Georgia that were not included in the territory of South Ossetia. The South Ossetian Autonomous Region was set up in 1922, following the victory of the 11th Red Army under the command of Sergo Ordzhonikidze, against the Menshevik Government of independent Georgia. In 1990, an ethnic conflict erupted between Georgians and Ossetians in which North Ossetia took part. This conflict also influenced the development of Ossetian-Ingushetian relations, and is examined in more detail in Chapter 13, "The Republic of Georgia: Conflict in Abkhazia and South Ossetia."

resettled by ethnic Russians (mainly in the Sunzha district) and ethnic Ossetians (mainly in the Prigorodny district). The authorities often carried out these resettlements by force. Whole villages were forcibly transported to the deserted Ingush and Chechen villages to salvage the farms, livestock, and crops left behind by the deportees.

It is difficult to do more than guess at the motives behind the deportations of the Ingush and other Caucasian peoples. Most likely it was the Soviet Union's countermove to Germany's attempt to play the "Turkish card."[18] The deportations affected the Turkic-speaking peoples and the Vainakhians. The Chechens' history as the most anti-Russian of the North Caucasian peoples likely made them a particular target for such measures. Some of the Turkic-speaking peoples of Dagestan were also exiled, and evidence suggests that plans to organize similar mass deportations in Dagestan had progressed to the point that railway cars stood ready.[19]

THE POST-STALIN ERA AND THE REHABILITATION OF THE INGUSH

In his famous speech at the Twentieth Congress of the CPSU in February 1956, newly appointed Secretary General Nikita Khrushchev accepted the task of correcting the policies of Stalinism, including those affecting the "repressed peoples" of the Caucasus and other regions. On July 16, 1956, the Supreme Soviet lifted all restrictions associated with the so-called "special settlements," including those affecting the deported Ingush. Six months later, on January 9, 1957, the Supreme Soviet restored the Chechen-Ingushetian ASSR and gave the deported peoples the right to return to their lands. However, the Prigorodny district and part of the former

---

18. The threat that Turkey might enter the war as a German ally was always considered quite real by the Soviet leadership. Germany sought to draw Turkey into the war on the side of the Axis powers by promising to grant independence to the mountain peoples of the Caucasus. The deterioration of Germany's situation on the Eastern front had, by 1944, compelled Germany to double its efforts to bring Turkey into the war. Though the Caucasus Mountains presented an enormous natural obstacle to a Turkish invasion, it was calculated that disloyalty among the population in the northern foothills of the Caucasus could open a wide passage for Turkish forces to advance on the South European steppe of the Soviet Union when the bulk of Soviet forces were concentrated on the German front. Thus, it is necessary to think of the deportation of North Caucasian peoples in 1944 in the context of the perceived danger of the situation.

19. From private conversations with Sibir Magomedov, head of the Faculty of History and Cultural Theory at Dagestan State University, and the Chairman of the Shamil Foundation. See also Daniyalov, "Memoirs," *Vatan*, No. 2 (1990). Daniyalov was the First Secretary of the Dagestan Regional Party Committee during the war.

Psedakh district, situated in the southern part of the present Mozdok district, remained part of North Ossetia. As a result, the Ingush territory was reduced by one-sixth of its former size. By 1956—twenty-two years after the Prigorodny district was transferred to North Ossetia—the plains and industrially developed lands of this district where the Ingush had previously lived had become home to more than 26,000 Ossetians from the harsh, mountainous South Ossetian regions of Georgia, 15,000 Ossetians from other districts of North Ossetia, and 14,000 people from Russia proper.[20]

Because this part of the original Ingushetian territory was left out of the new Chechen-Ingushetian Republic, the rate of Ingush return was considerably slower than that of other deported peoples of the North Caucasus. A large part of the Ingush stayed in Central Asia, and by 1959, only 50 percent had returned to their homeland; by 1970, the figure had increased to 85 percent.[21] The North Ossetian authorities did everything in their power to block the return of Ingush to the Prigorodny district, appealing for support even to the highest bodies of the Soviet Union. Because the Soviet decree that reestablished the Chechen-Ingushetian Republic did not mandate the restoration of Ingush property confiscated during the deportation, the government of North Ossetia issued an order restricting the issuance of residence permits and the sale or renting of houses to Ingush trying to return to their old lands. These restrictions became grounds for territorial claims by the Ingush against the North Ossetian ASSR. After 1957, the Ingush were again allowed to work in the Prigorodny district, but the top positions were almost always filled by Ossetians; this was a key socioeconomic factor in the development of tensions.

The Ingush did not let matters rest. In 1973, Ingush nationalist groups held demonstrations in Grozny and Ordzhonikidze to demand the return of the disputed districts. Barricades were set up and tanks were sent in to break up the demonstrations. Ingush groups came to Moscow in 1981 to demand that the Central Committee of the CPSU resolve the problem. Some of the demonstrators were harshly suppressed, but no action was taken to resolve

---

20. *Two Years after the War: The Problem of Forced Settlers in the Zone of the Ossetino-Ingushetian Conflict* (Moscow: Center for the Defense of Human Rights Memorial, 1994).

21. Ibragimbeily, "The North Caucasus: Genocide, Deportation and States of Emergency."

the issue in favor of the Ingush. At the initiative of the North Ossetians, a decree of the Soviet Council of Ministers of March 5, 1982, gave the North Ossetian authorities the right to grant residence permits in the Prigorodny district; residence permits are necessary to obtain work, to gain access to education and health care, and to receive a pension.[22] This step was considered unusual, since the region in question was largely rural and residence permits are generally used primarily to control the population of highly urbanized areas such as Moscow and Leningrad. However, even the residence permit requirement could not halt the spontaneous return of Ingush to the district. By 1990, more than 60,000 Ingush were living in North Ossetia, more than half of them without residence permits.[23]

A tragic result of this ongoing dispute is that a stubborn reciprocal "enemy image" became entrenched in generations of Ingush and Ossetians. This image has itself become a factor driving the dispute. Until the beginning of perestroika, Soviet nationality policy was based on the overarching goal of creating a new, distinctly Soviet society that attempted to blur the ethnic and religious differences of groups residing within Soviet borders. The effect of this policy was to essentially ignore, and therefore freeze, the Ossetian-Ingush dispute. The Soviet authorities never seriously discussed the issue and the conflict was generally interpreted as the work of troublemakers, bandits, and dissidents. For Moscow, admitting the existence of nationalist problems meant acknowledging the failure of the "internationalist" enterprise. Consequently, there was no attempt to provide a public assessment of the events of 1944 even from a purely legal perspective. Nor did the state officially offer any apologies to the Ingush or other peoples for the deportations.

The Evolution of the Conflict, 1988–92

Soon after perestroika was initiated by Soviet Secretary General Mikhail Gorbachev, it became clear that the Soviet state could not

---

22. Decree 183 of the Council of Ministers of the USSR, "On The Restriction of Residence Permits For Citizens in the Prigorodny District of the North Ossetian ASSR," March 5, 1982.

23. Until 1944, the population of the Prigorodny district numbered 34,000, including 31,000 Ingush. In 1990, of the 40,000 registered residents, only 17,500 were Ingush, although the number of Ingush actually living there was much greater. See *Two Years after the War: The Problem of Forced Settlers in the Zone of the Ossetino-Ingushetian Conflict*.

avoid addressing the volatile nationality problems that had accumulated during the years of Brezhnev-era stagnation. The democratization of public life and the newly granted freedom of speech in the
mass media stirred up latent issues with increasing frequency.

In 1988, a powerful social-political movement called Niiskho
(Justice) that was based on national traditions and supported by the
clergy and the Council of Elders—the heads of the clans (*teips*)—galvanized social activism among the Ingush. The clan and tribal structure of Vainakh society was preserved during the Soviet period, and in
this structure the Council of Elders embodied supreme authority and
formulated basic policies and priorities for the entire Vainakh nation.
Niiskho called the first Congress of the Ingush people and made an
appeal to the Central Committee of the CPSU and the Soviet government to partition the Chechen-Ingushetian Republic and restore the
Ingushetian Republic to its 1924–34 boundaries, which would include
the Malgobek, Nazran, Sunzha, and Prigorodny districts.

In 1989, a second Ingush Congress also took up this appeal. In
November 1989, the newly elected Supreme Soviet of the Soviet
Union adopted a declaration "recognizing the illegal and criminal
repressive actions taken against forcibly deported peoples and concerning the safeguarding of their rights." All corresponding discriminatory legislation against these peoples was rescinded. For the first
time the Soviet government—in this case the Supreme Soviet, which
was already adopting different policies than the CPSU and the central authorities—admitted its guilt and offered apologies to the peoples that had suffered at its hands. The declaration provided a legal
basis for the Ingush deputies to prepare legislation for the restoration
of Ingushetia within the 1924–34 borders. The corresponding documents were studied in commissions of the Council of Nationalities of
the Supreme Soviet, and Ingush claims to the Prigorodny district
were pronounced well founded. The Council of Nationalities
acknowledged that the infamous 1982 decree of the Council of
Ministers restricting the issuance of residence permits in the
Prigorodny district had violated the rights of the Ingush and should
be repealed.[24]

The Russian Supreme Soviet became involved early on, and the
question of the Ingush situation came under the jurisdiction of the

---

24. "Report of the Commission of the Council of Nationalities of the Supreme
Soviet of the USSR on the Appeal of the Ingush Population," *Bulletin of the
Supreme Soviet of the USSR*, No. 5 (March 26, 1990).

Russian Parliament. However, the legislative branch of the government of the Russian Federation lacked expertise on issues concerning relations between nationalities, and a number of the laws it passed reflected immediate political considerations without any clear anticipation of their consequences. For example, the law "On the Rehabilitation of Repressed Peoples," passed on April 26, 1991, by the Russian Supreme Soviet, recognized the right of those peoples repressed during the Stalin years to the restoration of their national-state formations and to compensation for damage inflicted by the state. Article 6 of this law states:

The territorial rehabilitation of the repressed peoples anticipates the implementation, in accordance with their expressed will, of juridical and organizational measures to restore the national-territorial boundaries existing before their unconstitutional and forcible change.[25]

However, the law was passed with no attempt to define exactly how it could be implemented. Government commissions were set up to implement the law but did not follow through with any concrete initiatives. There were no steps to open talks between the deported peoples and the current residents of the lands in question. Thus the territorial dispute was not seriously addressed. In retrospect, the enactment of this law, with its vague and ill-defined terms, contributed to the development of further tensions.

In the period before his election as the first president of the Russian Federation, Boris Yeltsin made promises to the Ingush and other groups in order to win their loyalty. As chairman of the Russian Supreme Soviet, he voiced his support for full rehabilitation of the Ingush. In the spring of 1991, at a meeting in Nazran attended by thousands, Yeltsin announced:

So far, national discord that would lead to bloodshed has not erupted on the territory of the Russian Federation. You and I should do everything in our power to make sure that this will not happen. The people are always right and the fact that the day before yesterday the Supreme Soviet has rehabilitated all the repressed peoples of Russia means that the repressed Ingush people have also been rehabilitated. The Ingush people have demonstrated throughout their history that they are not aggressive, that they are kind and industrious, that they are not conquerors—no, they simply demand justice. And whether

---

25. The Law of the RSFSR, "On the Rehabilitation of Repressed Peoples," *Bulletin of the Congress of Peoples' Deputies and the Supreme Soviet of the RSFSR*, No. 18 (1991).

you decide on an Ingush autonomous region or an Ingush republic, whatever you ask of the Supreme Soviet of Russia, we shall approve.[26]

This declaration must be understood in the context of the struggle under way at that time between Yeltsin and Gorbachev, and Yeltsin's attempts to undermine the leadership of the Soviet Union and win independence for Russia. That these promises to the Ingushetians reflected only the political utility of the moment is evidenced by the fact that Yeltsin promised exactly the same thing to the Ossetians, as if these two claims were not mutually exclusive.

After this law was passed, a meeting of Ingush rural council representatives decided to halt the activities of all Ingush social associations. They wanted to preclude the possibility that resolutions and statements by the leaders of Ingush associations would provoke conflicts with Ossetians.[27] The Ingush reaffirmed their complete refusal to resort to force in a draft treaty between the public and social organizations of Ingushetia and North Ossetia. However, the North Ossetian social groups that signed the treaty did not represent the North Ossetian government. The Ingush tried to reach a consensus in the hope of avoiding violence, but because they had no state structure, they were easily marginalized. In the absence of state institutions, the only form of political activity and mobilization available to the Ingush were independent social organizations, including Niiskho. It was very difficult for these organizations to be heard in Moscow or to command the attention of the national government. The North Ossetians, by contrast, had government structures that enabled them to represent their case officially to the Russian government and to pursue their aims politically.

Nevertheless, inspired by strong support from the Soviet and Russian authorities, the Ingush and their leaders set a firm course for separation from Chechnya and considered themselves on the brink of having their claims satisfied.

THE IMPACT OF THE CONFLICT BETWEEN SOUTH OSSETIA AND GEORGIA
By early 1990, the Georgian-South Ossetian conflict had erupted and the capital of South Ossetia, Tskhinvali, was completely cut off. The renewal of violence prompted approximately 100,000 South

---

26. S. Byelozertsev and L. Duvanova, *The Mechanics of Death* (Moscow: Simbvestinfo, 1993).

27. Ibid.

Ossetians to flee to North Ossetia where most of them found shelter in Vladikavkaz[28] or with relatives in the Prigorodny district.[29] Vladikavkaz also became a haven for waves of refugees from other ethnic conflicts in the Caucasus, including Armenia-Azerbaijan and Abkhazia-Georgia. Social tensions in the Prigorodny district reached crisis levels. The apparent progress toward a solution to the Ingushetian question in the Supreme Soviets of the Soviet Union and Russia in no way contributed to the relaxation of these tensions.

North Ossetia was the first republic to be confronted with the realities of war as the Soviet Union began to unravel in the late 1980s and early 1990s.[30] Conflict erupted between South Ossetian and Georgian forces at a time when the Supreme Soviet of North Ossetia, headed by Askharbek Galazov, still exercised considerable authority in the region. In order to defend its position with regard to the Ingush, in 1990, the North Ossetian Supreme Soviet declared the North Ossetian ASSR an independent republic. Stated somewhat differently, North Ossetia attempted to secure the Prigorodny district for itself by asserting the precedence of republic acts over federal laws.

Furthermore, in September 1990, a decree of the North Ossetian Supreme Soviet, "On the Temporary Restriction of Unrestrained Population Growth on the Territory of the North Ossetian Autonomous Soviet Socialist Republic," established a moratorium on the issuance of residence permits in the district. Moreover, the North Ossetian Supreme Soviet took the initiative in coordinating military and other aid to South Ossetia and in providing for the many refugees. The North Ossetian Supreme Soviet repeatedly turned to federal authorities with requests to legalize the unification of North and South Ossetia and to incorporate a united Ossetia into the Russian Federation. All this placed the North Ossetian Supreme Soviet at the center of national consolidation, playing the same role as national movements and political parties in other North Caucasian republics.

---

28. Ordzhonikidze had again become Vladikavkaz in 1980.

29. *South Ossetia: Blood and Ashes* (Moscow: 1991).

30. According to the 1989 census, the population of the North Ossetian ASSR numbered 632,400, including 334,900 ethnic Ossetians (Digors, Irons, and Kudars); 189,200 ethnic Russians; 32,800 ethnic Ingush; 13,600 Armenians; 12,300 Georgians; 10,000 Ukrainians; 9,500 Kumyks; and 3,100 Germans. According to data supplied by the State Committee for Statistics of the Russian Federation, the population of North Ossetia in 1993 numbered 650,400. Its territory covers an area of 8,000 square kilometers, bordering on Kabardino-Balkaria, Ingushetia, Chechnya, the Stavropol region of Russia, and Georgia.

The participation of North Ossetia in the conflict in South Ossetia had consequences that could not help but affect North Ossetia's ongoing conflict with Ingushetia. These circumstances drew the Russian leadership into an intricate political game. Through involvement in the Ingush-Ossetian conflict, Russia could influence the state of affairs in Georgia. This in turn led to the development of a special trust between the leaders of North Ossetia and Russia.

THE CHECHEN DECLARATION OF INDEPENDENCE

On November 27, 1991, the Republic of Chechnya proclaimed its independence from the Russian Federation. The difficulties this step caused in Russian-Chechen relations had serious consequences for political developments in Ingushetia. The Ingush had to make a political choice between maintaining close relations with Russia or with Chechnya. The Ingush had de facto already made this choice. By participating in the Russian referendum in the spring of 1991 (which the Chechens had boycotted) and by voting over 95 percent for Yeltsin as president in the summer of 1991, the Ingush apparently decided to remain loyal to Russia in the hope of gaining Moscow's leverage in resolving the territorial dispute with Ossetia. Opting to split from Chechnya and form an independent republic, Ingushetia found itself in a dangerous geopolitical situation. Squeezed between three key centers for the export of raw materials and resources (Mozdok, Vladikavkaz, and Grozny), Ingushetia's entire industrial capability consists of an oil-and-gas processing plant and a brick factory in the town of Malgobek, a gas processing plant in the settlement of Voskresenskoe, a knitwear factory in Nazran, a chemical factory in Karabulak, and a few small factories for processing agricultural products. Immediately after the election in which the Ingush voted overwhelmingly for Yeltsin as president, Ingush were purged from leadership positions in industrial enterprises and organizations in Chechnya. Literally within days, ethnic Ingush elites found themselves excluded from all important affairs in Grozny and were essentially forced out of the republic. Furthermore, Ingush agitation in Chechnya was creating problems in the delicate balance of Chechen relations with the Russian government.[31]

---

31. This was the moment when criminal structures (arms trade, narcotics) were set up to move illegal goods through Chechnya, and arms were delivered to Dzhokhar Dudaev by certain factions in the Russian government. With these illicit ties growing between Moscow and Grozny, there was no need for the Ingush, and there was a concerted policy to force them out.

Within a year after the Chechen declaration of independence, the political situation in Chechnya was chaotic. All kinds of illegal trade flourished—including trade in weapons—and large amounts of arms flowed to both sides in the Ingush-Ossetian conflict. Political groups in power and among the opposition fought over control of the oil industry, Chechnya's principal source of wealth. Since the late 1930s, the Chechen-Ingushetian ASSR had been a crucial refinement center for Russian oil. Sixteen to twenty million tons were processed there annually, although not more than five million tons were extracted in the republic itself. Furthermore, Chechnya had a virtual monopoly on the production of industrial aviation lubricants—92 percent of the national total—making Russian aviation fully dependent on Chechnya.[32] Chechens believed that oil could provide Chechnya with real economic and political independence and allow it to break off all relations with Moscow.[33]

In the period of Chechnya's self-proclaimed independence, however, the Chechen oil industry suffered greatly. The deterioration of equipment, the sharp drop in capital investment, the general political crisis, and the outflow of the Russian population, which had been principally engaged in this business, all contributed to the virtual destruction of the oil industry. Political and financial lobbies became active in Moscow and sought to influence decisions regarding Chechnya. According to some experts, groups representing the interests of very powerful sectors of the Russian economy, primarily oil and metal industries, currently occupy a dominant position. These interests have sought to reestablish control over the oil business in Chechnya and the large amounts of money involved in this trade.[34]

THE CONFLICT BECOMES A WAR

The first armed clashes between Ossetians and Ingush broke out in April 1991 in the village of Kurtat in the Prigorodny district. The North Ossetian Supreme Soviet proclaimed a state of emergency in the district and instituted a curfew, document checks, confiscation of illegal weapons, and the demolition of dwellings built (illegally) by

---

32. Statistical data from the ABD.1.S. version 6.50, of the computerized data bank of the State Committee for Statistics of the Russian Federation.

33. On Chechnya, see "Democracy, Chechnya, and Narcotics," *Zavtra* (newspaper of the Research Center "Felix"), No. 12–14 (1995); also, "What Does the Kremlin Reap after the Storm in the Mountains?" *Pravda*, April 2, 1995.

34. Edward Ozhiganov, "The North Caucasus Triangle," *Megapolis Express*, No. 21 (1993), p. 23.

Ingush who did not have residence permits. By the end of 1991, both sides began to arm themselves. This was not difficult, given the disintegration of the Soviet Union and its armed forces, the other wars in Transcaucasia (especially in South Ossetia), and the unrestricted trade in weapons in Chechnya following its declaration of independence. The organization of irregular armed groups in Ossetia and Ingushetia was not unusual in the context of the chaos generated by the breakup of Union structures. After the disintegration of the Soviet army, in fact, many Russian analysts note that independent armed formations began to appear throughout the former Soviet Union. Even when attempts were made to give these units legal status, they were inevitably penetrated by criminal elements.[35]

The weapons for the arms buildup in North Ossetia came primarily from Russian Ministry of the Interior stocks earmarked for peacekeeping battalions in South Ossetia. Large supplies of weapons and ammunition were "stolen" and turned up in North Ossetia. In the fall of 1991, the North Ossetian Supreme Soviet tried to give this armed buildup a legal foundation by issuing a decree giving the republic the right to create its own defensive forces, essentially a type of National Guard. However, according to the RSFSR Constitution and the Federal Treaty, the arms buildup in North Ossetia was patently illegal, since a member of the Russian Federation does not have the right to maintain its own armed forces.[36] In October 1992, a new security law was passed uniting the republic's security services, the Department of the Interior, the people's volunteer corps, and the republican guard into a single armed service. Though the Russian Supreme Soviet considered these moves unconstitutional and in violation of the contravening federal treaty, North Ossetia ignored Moscow's protests, and no further reaction was forthcoming from Moscow.

Ingushetia, having no state or executive institutions to create such armed formations, armed itself haphazardly and created volunteer armed detachments for the defense of Ingush settlements in the Prigorodny district. The Ingush Council of Elders tried to halt the slide toward violence but in the end could not.

---

35. Kh. Tsgoyev, "The People's Volunteer Corps, an Interview on this Theme," Otchizna (Vladikavkaz), No. 1 (March 1992). See also *Gazette of the Interim Administration*, No. 40 (August 26, 1994).

36. See "On the Formation of a Republican Guard"; in addition, Article 92 was added to the North Ossetian Constitution, giving it the right to form republic defense forces.

A significant change occurred in the North Caucasus in June 1992 when Russia passed a law creating an Ingushetian Republic within the Russian Federation.[37] However, as with the earlier law on territorial rehabilitation, the consequences of such recognition were not well thought out. The Ingushetian Republic was to consist of three rural districts with no defined borders, and no state institutions or administrative bodies of any kind. In an attempt to address the growing tensions in the republic, the Russian Supreme Soviet charged a State Commission to submit recommendations by December 31, 1993, delimiting the borders of the new republic, taking into account the interests of all parties concerned. It also decided to appoint an interim representative of the Supreme Soviet to the republic.

The Republic of Ingushetia was a tiny area with virtually no industry, poor communications, and few public facilities, and it was entirely dependent on subsidies from the federal budget. Considering these problems, it is clear that the decision to grant autonomy to the republic was foolhardy. While it could be argued that there was some ethnic legitimacy to this decision after the breakup of the Chechen-Ingushetian Republic, no possibility existed for this region to become economically and politically self-sufficient. In recognizing Ingushetia, the Russian Supreme Soviet in fact aggravated the conflict. North Ossetians felt threatened by this development, and the Ingush were no doubt encouraged to think they might augment their new republic with the Prigorodny district. It is difficult to understand Russia's decision, particularly considering the challenges of transition politics. In 1991 and 1992, Russia was in the process of drafting a new constitution of its own, and creating new national entities did not make this task any easier.

The difficulties in resolving the question of territorial rehabilitation for the Ingush soon became clear, and on July 3, 1992, the Russian Supreme Soviet announced a moratorium on the raising of territorial problems until 1995,[38] and criminal penalties were established for

---

37. The Ingushetian Republic founded on June 4, 1992, has no defined frontiers so far. It comprises, for the time being, the Nazran, Malgobek, and Sunzha districts. No official census has been conducted in the republic. According to the electoral register for the republic's presidential elections, the population numbers 192,800, including 20,000 Russians. Seventy-five percent of the population lives in rural areas. Its territory covers an area of 4,200 square kilometers (the area of the three districts). The republic borders on North Ossetia, Chechnya, and Georgia. Under the treaty of August 23, 1993, with the republic of Chechnya, the territorial borders between the two republics are not delimited.

38. This moratorium has since been extended until the summer of 1997.

any unauthorized changes in territorial boundaries. Thus the promised delimitation of the borders of Ingushetia was postponed, leaving the new republic without any established borders, and its people increasingly frustrated by the inability of the federal organs to resolve its case.

It cannot be stressed enough that at this critical moment in the advent of Ingushetian statehood, no state institutions existed. Sole decision-making authority rested with President Yeltsin's representative in the republic, Issa Kostoyev, a former official in the Russian Prosecutor General's office. Kostoyev, a renowned criminal investigator, was not an expert on state law. The rural councils and tribal leadership played a symbolic role early on and to some degree filled in the gaps left by the absence of government structures. The only other groups with any real authority in Ingushetia at the time of the republic's creation were various religious organizations.

Ingush-Ossetian relations had seriously deteriorated by autumn 1992. Cases of sectarian murder on ethnic grounds grew more frequent. In the first nine months of 1992, approximately three hundred serious crimes were committed in Vladikavkaz and the Prigorodny district, thirty-one of which were murders or disappearances.[39] Ingush villages were patrolled by North Ossetian forces, and acts of intimidation against the Ingush population were committed frequently and with impunity. In October, an Ossetian armored car crushed a young Ingush girl, provoking a strong reaction from the Ingush, who began to patrol their own villages with self-defense forces. In the meantime, the North Ossetian authorities and the mass media continued to whip up anti-Ingush hysteria.[40]

In late October, the violent situation in the densely populated villages of the Prigorodny district was debated in the North Ossetian Parliament. At this session, First Deputy Chairman Yuri Biragov reported:

the situation in the last four days has seriously deteriorated, [and] a number of armed clashes have taken place which have led to loss of life. In the villages of Kambileyevka, Chernorechenskoye, Terk, and Kartsa and the settlement of Yuzhnoye, extremist Ingush elements have set up road blocks, positioned armed picketers and formed armed bands. The leaders of these formations declare that the Prigorodny district is Ingushetian territory and that the laws of that republic should prevail there. All territorial questions should be

---

39. "A Political Assessment by the Security Council of the Russian Federation."
40. Byelozertsev and Duvanova, *The Mechanics of Death.*

decided in accordance with the will of the people, the laws and constitutions of Russia and North Ossetia, and the provisions of the
Federal Treaty.[41]

This statement was endorsed by much of the North Ossetian leadership and no doubt reflects the dominant opinion in the North
Ossetian Parliament that the Ingush had instigated aggression
against their Prigorodny district.

That same day, Kostoyev and the Ingush deputies in the Russian
Parliament presented a petition requesting that the state of emergency being enforced by North Ossetia be placed under Russian
jurisdiction. They also requested that Yeltsin establish presidential
rule, an investigation of ethnically motivated crimes, the appointment of an interim head of administration for Ingushetia, and the
delimitation of territorial borders under Yeltsin's control. Since the
appeal came only from Yeltsin's special representative, there was no
obligation to take it seriously, and Yeltsin rejected it. Yet again, the
Ingush suffered from having no representatives to the official organs
of power in Moscow.

A few days later, on October 29, 1992, Russian troops stationed in
North Ossetia were put on a state of alert. The previous evening, a
meeting of the president's Security Council in Moscow had decided
to set up a joint command of Russian and North Ossetian forces
under the official rubric of restoring the Constitutional order in the
region. Since the self-built armed forces of North Ossetia were in fact
illegal, the decision to establish a joint command was very unusual
and conferred upon the North Ossetian forces a *de facto* legitimacy.
On October 30, an armed group of about 150 Ingushetians seized a
traffic police post near the North Ossetian village of Chermen. Two
soldiers from Russia's interior forces were wounded, an armored
vehicle captured, and a police station set on fire. Later, in the same
area, an armed band of Ingushetians besieged a Russian Interior
Ministry unit and captured a number of armored cars, sixty-two
automatic rifles with ammunition, five machine guns, and four mortars. Seventy-eight soldiers were taken hostage and transported to
Nazran. The North Ossetian Parliament pronounced the incident a
case of armed Ingush aggression. The Russian Parliament forwarded
no countervailing assessment.[42]

---

41. Itar-Tass, reported by special correspondent Valery Shanayev, Vladikavkaz,
October 27, 1992.

42. Itar-Tass, the Public Relations Center of the Russian Ministry of the Interior,
November 1, 1992.

On October 31, a high-level delegation from Moscow, comprising Georgi Khizha, Deputy Chairman of the Russian government; Sergei Shaigy, Chairman of the State Committee for Emergency Situations; and Vasili Savvin, Commander of Russian Internal Ministry Forces, arrived in Vladikavkaz. The Ossetians reported to them that the recent Ingush military action had been part of an overall plan to seize the Prigorodny district. Khizha, after consulting the Council of Ministers of North Ossetia, stated that

the main threat to the North Caucasian region comes from Chechnya. Grozny is continually inflaming the situation. This problem is constantly at the center of attention of the Russian government. As far as the conflict between Ossetians and Ingush is concerned, the first thing to do is to set up administrative bodies in Ingushetia and establish constitutional order there. The Russian troops will remain in the region until the territory of Ingushetia is free from illegal armed formations.[43]

Khizha was referring specifically to Ingush groups created in the Prigorodny district to protect Ingush settlements from outrages by North Ossetia, and the special police units created by the North Ossetian Parliament to administer the state of emergency. In agreement with the government and the Ministry of Defense, Khizha issued written instructions about the distribution of weapons, ammunition, and armored vehicles to the North Ossetian volunteer force and the North Ossetian Ministry of the Interior. Khizha's actions, along with those of Russia as a whole, were naturally considered by the Ingush as blatantly pro-Ossetian.[44] Russian policy toward this skirmish was suggestive of Moscow's general view of the conflict, as well as its preoccupation with Chechnya and maintaining the allegiance of the Ossetians.

On November 1 and 2, the worst fighting of the Ingushetian-Ossetian conflict—involving heavy weapons and armored vehicles—broke out in the Prigorodny district in the villages of Kartsa, Kurtat, Dachnoye, Komgaron, Kambeleyevskoye, and Redant. Detachments of the North Ossetian Republican Guard, the people's volunteer force, and troops of the North Ossetian Ministry of the Interior succeeded in driving the Ingush out of these villages. The South Ossetian government sent a volunteer unit to fight with the North Ossetian forces, which distinguished itself by its particular cruelty

---

43. Itar-Tass, special correspondents Leonid Timofeyev and Valery Shanayev, Vladikavkaz, November 1, 1992.

44. Itar-Tass, special correspondent Sharip Asuyev, Grozny, November 2, 1992.

toward the Ingush civilian population;[45] in three days of fighting accompanied by terrible violence and barbaric atrocities, approximately six hundred people were killed and many were forced to flee.

During the three or four days of the worst fighting, the Ingush were left undefended, although high-ranking generals of the Russian Army were in Vladikavkaz. The troops of the Russian Ministry of the Interior (MVD) took no action, thereby tacitly encouraging both sides to intensify military operations. A garrison of the Russian Army—the same forces that had entered into the joint Russian–North Ossetian Command—was stationed in the North Ossetian district.[46] At that point, Russia initiated a major military operation in the Prigorodny district, mobilizing the Don division, the Pskov division, special purpose units, the Vladikavkaz garrison, the Ossetian Guard, the special militia (OMON) of the North Ossetian Interior Ministry, an Ossetian volunteer force, and two Cossack regiments.[47] There were numerous Ingush civilian casualties from the fighting and the punitive actions subsequently carried out by North and South Ossetian armed detachments.[48] Of the 60,000 ethnic Ingush who had been living in the Prigorodny district, 50,000 had to flee their homes. In addition, around 3,500 houses were destroyed and camps were established where hostages were kept.[49] Many Ingush went to Nazran or Grozny and were given shelter, just as many Chechen refugees have escaped to Ingushetia. Those Ingush left behind were isolated in their own villages, ostensibly protected by Russian troops against North Ossetians crossing into these regions. Ingush villagers could not leave to obtain goods and services as there was no guarantee of their safety or that they would be allowed to return. The fighting died down to sporadic outbursts of gunfire and the situation has remained unchanged since 1992. Although Russian troops remain, it is not safe for an Ingush to be in Vladikavkaz.[50]

---

45. Byelozertsev and Duvanova, The Mechanics of Death.

46. No action was taken, however, until November 5, after additional Russian Army troops from outside the region were brought in to stop the conflict.

47. Byelozertsev and Duvanova, *The Mechanics of Death.*

48. According to official information from the investigative arm of the Russian public prosecutor's office, at least 583 people were killed—including 407 Ingush, 105 Ossetians, and 17 Russian soldiers—and 168 Ingush and 418 Ossetians were wounded.

49. "A Political Assessment by the Security Council of the Russian Federation."

50. Russian policy appears to be linked to influences within the joint force. That different Russian forces acted differently indicates the persistence of a general

There is much speculation that the joint Russian–North Ossetian command was created with an eye toward Chechnya, and that the events in the Prigorodny district were, in fact, intended as a warning to Chechnya. The arming of North Ossetia and the establishment of a joint command comprising illegally formed armed detachments and the Russian Army was absolutely unconstitutional and confirms that the Russian Army was not a neutral force in the conflict. There is no consistency to the government's policy in the region; although the armed formations of North Ossetia were identical to the illegal bands being hunted down in Chechnya, they were legitimized by the Russian Army. Furthermore, as in most post-Soviet states, there are no competing political forces to counter unlawful and arbitrary elite politics, and no conception of citizens' right to influence or check the government. The role of the Russian Army in these events is best summed up by a group of independent experts:

As a result of the absence of even a single Ingush administrative or state structure, there was no concerted preparation for the conflict as was the case on the Ossetian side. Ingush activities had a spontaneous character. In North Ossetia, by contrast, there was a planned buildup of armed detachments, both constitutionally sanctioned and illegal. The Russian leadership proceeded from a mistaken conception of its interests in the North Caucasus, and the Russian Army Command wanted to use the situation to resolve the painful problem with Chechnya by force once and for all. The introduction of censorship all across Russia put obstacles in the way of the search for a peaceful solution. The participation of armed bands from South Ossetia in military operations was unconstitutional as was the joint action of Russian troops with the illegal formations of North Ossetia.[51]

Implicitly, the objective behind the attack of the Russian troops was to provoke a conflict with rebellious Chechnya, inasmuch as the attack brought the Russian troops right up to the Chechen frontier in the Sunzha district. Sunzha was inhabited only by Ingush and Chechens: there were no Ossetians in this district. Furthermore, there had been no armed conflict or fighting of any kind there following the Ingush split from Chechnya, and no border delineation between

---

pattern within the Soviet, and now the Russian, armed forces with regard to inter-ethnic conflict: units of the armed forces tend to actively or tacitly adopt the position of the local actors with whom they lived and interacted before the conflict. Evidently, it is psychologically very difficult to take an objective position in such situations.

51. Berezovsky, Kulikov, Moskovchenko, and Novikov, *Conclusions about the Role of the Russian Army in the Ossetino-Ingushetian Conflict* (Moscow: 1993).

Chechnya and Ingushetia. Chechnya found itself in a strategic pincer that gripped it from three sides: Dagestan, the Stavropol region of Russia, and now Ingushetia.[52] Chechens thus viewed the introduction of Russian troops into Sunzha as an act of aggression. Suddenly, a real danger of confrontation had arisen between Russian and Chechen troops.

Nevertheless, and contrary to expectations, Chechnya did not join in the armed conflict on the side of Ingushetia. The president of Chechnya, Dzhokhar Dudaev, said the decision to proclaim a state of emergency in North Ossetia and Ingushetia was

a dangerous maneuver, while the Decree on the State of Emergency once more demonstrates the falsity of the Russian leadership's policies and the colonial nature of the Federal Treaty. The introduction of the state of emergency will convince the peoples of the Caucasus that the only guarantee for their security is the union of their peoples, founded on complete independence from whomever it may be.[53]

Dudaev called on the Ossetians and Ingush to resolve their conflict at the negotiating table and assured them that Chechnya was ready to act as a mediator. With respect to the Russians, the Chechen Republic demanded the withdrawal of Russian troops from its territory—meaning the Sunzha district—and accused the Russian government of aggravating the conflict.

The Search for a Peaceful Solution

The joint efforts of the Russian Army and the internal troops brought an end to the most violent phase of the Ingushetian-Ossetian conflict. Russian federal authorities have had to deal with the aftermath of the violence, including its psychological effects on the population, and to facilitate the return of the refugees and the exchange of hostages. From the beginning of the conflict, many hostages were seized by both sides. A commission was formed to implement a hostage exchange, and in the first two or three months of its existence, a large number of hostages were traded. Then the exchange stopped. Hostages continue to be taken, a factor that has contributed to the ongoing violence.

---

52. According to data provided by the Russian State Committee for Statistics, the population of the Chechen Republic numbered 1,097,200 in 1993. The republic covers a territory of 15,100 sq. km.

53. Itar-Tass, special correspondent Sharip Asuyev, Grozny, November 2, 1992.

The first priority for all sides was to help life in the Prigorodny district return to normal. Normalization has not been easy to achieve, especially considering the specific history and mentality of the mountain peoples, their customs and traditions, and their traditional lack of respect for state structures. Yet precisely at the moment when intensive, coordinated efforts by the Russian federal authorities were most needed, Russia was itself experiencing a deep political crisis. In spite of all kinds of consultations, meetings, decrees, and instructions, no serious action was taken or proposals put forth by the Russian authorities that would bring about a peaceful resolution of this conflict. As a result, the situation in the Prigorodny district has not changed fundamentally since early 1993.

RUSSIAN ADMINISTRATIVE MEASURES

With the first outbreak of fighting on November 2, 1992, President Yeltsin proclaimed a state of emergency in two districts of North Ossetia and Ingushetia to stop the fighting from spreading. The State Committee on Nationality Policies characterized these armed clashes as the first serious armed conflict on the territory of the Russian Federation, one that threatened to destabilize the whole Caucasus region.[54] The Russian government set up a special interim administration for these districts (like that established by the Soviet government in Nagorno-Karabakh) and headquartered it in Vladikavkaz.[55] Georgi Khizha was appointed head of this interim administration. By order of the Russian president, all district and rural councils and executive committees ceased to function. The presidential representative became the only authority in North Ossetia and Ingushetia, and he was subordinate to the head of the interim administration. During the period that the state of emergency remained in effect, all meetings, demonstrations, strikes, and other mass events were prohibited, censorship was introduced, and weapons and ammunition were temporarily confiscated from civilians, enterprises, and organizations.

Immediately after the large-scale fighting of November 1992, Khizha was replaced as head of the interim administration by Sergei Shakhrai. A number of other appointees to the position followed in

---

54. Statement of the Government Commission of the Russian Federation for Nationality Policies, Itar-Tass, November 2, 1992.

55. Many disagreed with the decision to put the headquarters of the interim administration in Vladikavkaz and argued that it should have been located in the area of the conflict itself, such as in the village of Chermen.

rapid succession—Alexander Kotenkov, Yuri Shatalin, Victor Polyanichko, and Vladimir Lozovoi. Such rapid turnover in the leadership in the space of only a few years led to confusion in the implementation of measures already under way, as well as difficulties in the development of new ones.

The Russian mass media usually referred to the Russian Army and Interior troops deployed in the area of conflict as "peacemaking forces," although legally—not to mention their actual role—they never had this status. These forces control the military situation in the area under the state of emergency. Russian Interior troop units and the North Ossetian militia are concentrated at roadblocks and control posts to patrol the main roads and arteries. The situation as of mid-1995 was still quite unstable and could be characterized as a low-scale partisan war. There were ongoing sporadic bursts of shooting by all sides, armed bands were still at large, hostage-taking continued, and it was impossible to travel in the area without the protection of a motorized armored vehicle. In addition, North Ossetians intermittently attempted to attack the remaining Ingush villages under protection of Russian troops.

The official Russian policy on the conflict was expressed by Sergei Shakhrai, who maintained that a small circle of people are interested in escalating the tensions in the area:[56] 1) dishonest politicians who, by continuing and extending the conflict, are trying to achieve their own self-seeking ends; 2) groups linked to the Mafia who seek to make money out of the misfortune and suffering of their fellow countrymen; and 3) extreme nationalist elements trying to undermine order from within and thus bring Russia to the brink of destruction.[57] Shakhrai did not implicate any specific groups; several teams of investigators have been appointed to inquire into the causes and main instigators of the dispute, but have yet to reach any conclusions.

At the end of 1992, Major General Alexander Kotenkov became head of the interim administration. He tried to concentrate the administration's efforts on disarming the population in an effort to eliminate so-called "bandit formations." However, because of the continued violence in the district and people's fear of being left defenseless, his goal proved impossible to accomplish. Colonel

---

56. Itar-Tass, special correspondents Leonid Timofeyev and Valery Shanayev, November 28, 1992.

57. Ibid.

General Yuri Shatalin, appointed head of the interim administration in March 1993, linked the continued instability of the Prigorodny district to the intractability of the situation with arms and hostages. Shatalin stated that

the peacemaking forces of Russia will remain in the area of the state of emergency as long as is necessary for the complete stabilization of the situation in the region. About 150,000 firearms are in the possession of the local population and illegal armed formations have so far not been disbanded. The principal destabilizing factor is the fact that the two sides have not exchanged any hostages for several months.[58]

In the summer of 1993, a restructuring of military districts of the Russian internal troops occurred. The North Caucasus, the first of the new districts, was manned by Interior Ministry troops stationed in the North Caucasus and the Lower Volga region under the command of Yuri Kosolapov. On August 1, 1993, a new head of the interim administration, Russian Deputy Prime Minister Victor Polyanichko, was murdered in the Prigorodny district just before he was to oversee the repatriation of Ingush to their homes there. In spite of Interior Ministry investigations and assurances by Vladimir Kolesnikov, chief of the Criminal Investigation Department, that the investigation into Polyanichko's death was being conducted with "great urgency and thoroughness," the perpetrators have so far not been found. Certain investigative journalists have since published reports in the Russian press alleging that the official authorities in Vladikavkaz were directly involved in Polyanichko's murder. The head of the North Ossetian government, Sergei Khetagurov, was forced to issue an official denial of an accusation that he was implicated in the murder of Polyanichko.[59]

The next head of the interim administration in Ingushetia, Russian Deputy Prime Minister Vladimir Lozovoi, tried to learn of North Ossetia's and Ingushetia's positions with regard to specific localities where returning refugees and deportees might be resettled. In mid-1993, the interim government formed a Mixed Commission for the Resolution to the Problem of Refugees and Resettlers on the Territory of Ingushetia and North Ossetia in Vladikavkaz to decide how to implement the return of refugees. The Commission was made up of representatives from government structures in North Ossetia and

---

58. Itar-Tass, special correspondent Vadim Byrkin, Vladikavkaz, March 22, 1992.
59. Krutakov, "The Fifth Version of the Murder of Victor Polyanichko," *Komsomolskaia Pravda*, September 24, 1993.

Moscow, and an attempt was made to incorporate representatives of the different ethnic groups involved. The Ingush demanded that all refugees be allowed to return, while the North Ossetians demanded the right to approve all requests for resettlement. In the end, the Commission supported the North Ossetian position, and decided the case of each family separately. This meant that only those families that all sides could agree upon were allowed to return, which effectively barred the return of families that took part in the violent events of November 1992. The Commission began by verifying and registering documents confirming the former residences of Ingush who wanted to return to live on the territory of North Ossetia. The Ossetian side argued that the consent of Ossetian fellow-villagers to the return of Ingush families would be a guarantee of future reconciliation, and this became an essential condition in the consideration of individual cases. However, the return of refugees proceeded so slowly that the Ingush side demanded Lozovoi's replacement, and accused the interim administration of delaying the return of refugees.

POLITICAL DEVELOPMENTS IN INGUSHETIA AND NORTH OSSETIA

An Extraordinary Commission, headed by the Russian People's Deputy, Bembulat Bogatyryev, was established in Nazran to deal with the aftermath of the November 1992 conflict. The Ingush side, headed by General Ruslan Aushev, a veteran of the war in Afghanistan and head of administration of the Ingushetian Republic, held talks with the Ossetians on the exchange of hostages and POWs. The Ossetian side handed over 1,360 Ingush hostages and the Ingush side returned 580 Ossetian hostages; 291 Ingush and 27 Ossetians had disappeared without a trace. Seven thousand five hundred refugees were registered in North Ossetia and more than 50,000 in Ingushetia.[60] In December 1992, Aushev resigned from the Commission, stating that

since the first days of the proclamation of the state of emergency in the North Ossetian SSR and the Ingushetian Republic, the Interim Administration has been unable to resolve the question of the return of hostages and has taken no steps toward the return of the deported inhabitants of Ingushetian nationality to the Prigorodny district. The security of the civilian population has not been assured and the illegal armed formations of North and South Ossetia have not been disarmed. On the contrary, without even preliminary permission, they

---

60. "A Political Assessment by the Security Council of the Russian Federation." The official statistics in this article with regard to refugees were gathered under the auspices of the Russian Prosecutor General.

have been legalized. Nothing was done to find a political solution to the conflict nor was there a juridical and political assessment of the intervention of the South Ossetian leadership and its armed formations. No federal rule was introduced in the Prigorodny district, although the Ingushetian side had repeatedly requested it, nor were Russian troops withdrawn from Ingushetian territory. In the eyes of a considerable part of the Ingush population, the Russian army has discredited itself. One of the main reasons for this is the inappropriate behavior of the troops themselves: lack of discipline, disrespect for local customs, and confusion about their proper functions in conditions of a state of emergency.[61]

Aushev counseled that the formation of a battalion of internal troops, partly made up of Ingush and operationally subordinate to the president of the Ingushetian Republic, would have been the best solution. The Russian side defended its role in the conflict, arguing that without the involvement of Russian internal troops, the destruction in the region would have been far greater than that which actually occurred.

In March 1993, Aushev was elected the first president of Ingushetia after receiving 99.9 percent of the votes.[62] Ingushetia at last had its own plenipotentiary representative and its first state and administrative bodies began to take form. In July Aushev and Chechen President Dudaev signed a treaty in Grozny by which each side agreed not to proceed with unilateral territorial delimitation of borders between the Republics of Chechnya and Ingushetia. They also agreed not to permit the participation or mediation of any third party in negotiations on border questions, which was a change in the Ingush position that had been maintained since their 1989 break with Chechnya. After the war with the North Ossetians, both groups felt that the division of Chechnya-Ingushetia was a great tragedy caused by outside intervention, and that it had only made it easier for Russia to manipulate them. The war in Chechnya has confirmed these suspicions, and both sides believe that the separation should be revoked once the situation stabilizes.

Soon after the Aushev-Dudaev agreement, an extraordinary session of the Congress of the Ingush people was held in Nazran, with four hundred delegates in attendance. Among the guests were delegations

---

61. Itar-Tass, special correspondent Mikhail Shevtsov, December 21, 1992.

62. At a press conference with Magomet Sakolov, Chairman of the Central Electoral Commission, on March 2, 1993, it was reported that 153,590 people were entered on the electoral register. Of that number, 142,318 people voted and 142,223 of those who voted preferred Aushev.

from Chechnya, Kabardino-Balkaria, Dagestan, Kalmykia, Karachayevo-Cherkessia, and the Stavropol region. Before the opening of the Congress, President Aushev stated that nothing had been solved in the previous nine months and everything remained the same as on the first day of the conflict, but the participants went on to discuss questions connected with the settlement of the Ossetian-Ingush conflict and land reform, and reviewed a draft constitution for Ingushetia. In August 1994, an Ingushetian government conference also devoted to the refugee problem was held in Nazran, but the problem remained unresolved.

In January 1994, North Ossetia elected Askharbek Galazov president. The results of the election have been questioned, largely because Ingush refugees forced to flee to other areas were deprived of their constitutional right to vote or be elected in North Ossetia.[63] On March 24, 1994, the North Ossetian Supreme Soviet rescinded the controversial security law passed in autumn 1992 that had united all the forces of North Ossetia. In autumn 1994, a proposal was put forward in the North Ossetian Parliament to create a new republic of Alania that would unite the North and South Ossetians. Although such a proposal had failed in the past, the prospect alone was disturbing to the Ingush; the forces of a united Ossetia would pose a much greater threat to Ingush interests, particularly once the South Ossetians were no longer fighting the Georgians.

According to data supplied by the Russian Migration Service as of 1993, more than 46,000 refugees from Georgia, South Ossetia, Abkhazia, Tajikistan, Chechnya, Ingushetia, Armenia, and Azerbaijan have found a haven on the territory of North Ossetia. The flow of refugees to the republic continues to grow, but the Russian authorities simply do not have the funds that would be required to deal with the refugee problem. North Ossetia has held up many peace initiatives for fear of lifting the moratorium on the revision of borders passed by the Supreme Soviet in July 1992. If this moratorium is lifted, then Article 6 of the 1991 law passed by the Russian Supreme Soviet mandating territorial rehabilitation for the Ingush

---

63. The effect of displaced populations on electoral outcomes is a ubiquitous problem throughout the North Caucasus. When individuals are forced to flee an area, they nevertheless remain officially registered there, regardless of where they settle. Thus, in virtually all electoral districts in the region, both territorial and national, either a significant portion of the official population—in particular large proportions of minority groups—is now elsewhere, or a meaningful number of those actually residing in the district are not entitled to vote.

would automatically come into effect. Thus North Ossetia has a vested interest in maintaining a state of emergency.

THE RUSSIAN PARLIAMENT AND FEDERAL AUTHORITIES

Soon after the outbreak of the worst fighting in November 1992, the upper chamber of the Russian Supreme Soviet, the Soviet (or Council) of Nationalities, headed by Ramazan Abdulatipov, assumed the task of facilitating a dialogue between the Ingush and the Ossetians. With the aid of the State Committee on Nationality Affairs, Abdulatipov organized a consultative assembly in Kislovodsk comprised of legislative and executive leaders of the members of the Russian Federation in the North Caucasian region. The leaders of sixty national and public movements were invited, and the first meeting was held in January 1993, only two months after the terrible violence in the Prigorodny district. A declaration on the "Principles of Relations between Nationalities in the North Caucasus" was adopted, and representatives of civic organizations in North Ossetia and Ingushetia signed a joint document, "Measures for the Resolution of the Ossetian-Ingushetian Conflict," which placed priority on the return of refugees. This statement was of great symbolic importance at the time, since it also declared that there could be no resolution of the conflict through military means.

At this and subsequent meetings, urgent measures were formulated to resolve the conflict, and especially the refugee problem. Provisions were made for the repatriation of refugees from the Ossetian-Ingushetian and Ossetian-Georgian conflicts, and for the settlement in new localities of those refugees who were unable to return to their permanent place of residence. The refugee problem was particularly acute because of the inhuman conditions in which people had to live, especially in Nazran. If this problem was not solved, the social tensions could erupt into more violence.

In March 1993, a fifth round of negotiations between the Ossetian and Ingushetian delegations began with representatives from Dagestan and the Stavropol region acting as mediators, and the presence of Ingushetian President Aushev lent special significance to the event. These negotiations concluded with the signing of the "Agreement on the Measures for a Comprehensive Solution to the Problems of Refugees and Forcibly Deported Persons on the Territories of the Ingushetian Republic and the North Ossetian SSR," which stipulated concrete measures for political management of the conflict. At the same time, an appeal to the press was circulated that called for help in spreading the idea of national reconciliation, and the strengthening of civil accord and good-neighborliness.[64]

However, the forced dissolution of the Russian Supreme Soviet in October 1993 following the standoff at the Russian Parliament building in Moscow interrupted the negotiation process; it was renewed only after the election of a new parliament on December 12, 1993. In accordance with the Russian Constitution, also adopted in December 1993, questions of conflict between members of the federation come under the jurisdiction of the upper house of Parliament—the Council of the Federation—of which both Askharbek Galazov, president of North Ossetia, and Ruslan Aushev, president of Ingushetia, are members.

The Council of the Federation has held several closed sessions and hearings devoted to the Ossetian-Ingushetian dispute, and deputies from the Council of the Federation have repeatedly visited the Prigorodny district as observers. In June 1994, on the initiative of the Council of the Federation and the Ministry for Nationality Affairs, both sides agreed to a timetable for the return of refugees to four villages in the Prigorodny district.[65] However, this timetable was continually frustrated and the resettlement proceeded quite slowly. Often local inhabitants barred the return of Ingushetians, preventing them from entering their houses and threatening to beat them up if they did so. The Ossetians used provocative tactics, including protests and blockades, and they placed women and children at the front of these demonstrations in order to inhibit attack.[66]

Another meeting between Aushev and Galazov was organized in Nalchik in August 1994 within the framework of the First International Congress of Mountain Peoples, in which leaders of all the republics of the North Caucasus and Transcaucasia, as well as the leaders of national movements, participated. The goals of the Congress were to consolidate forces for the maintenance of peace and to preserve the culture and environment of the mountain peoples of

64. *Etnopolis*, February 1993, pp. 44–70.

65. The timetable for the return of refugees was set up as a supplement to the decree "On the Order of Return and Settlement of Refugees and Forced Settlers in the Places of their Former Habitation in the Populated Areas of Chermen, Dongaron, Dachnoye and Kurtat of The Prigorodny District of The Republic of North Ossetia," signed by the presidents of both republics on June 26, 1994, in the town of Beslan. The timetable itself was approved by North Ossetia somewhat later.

66. I. Rotar, "Not Everyone Awaits the Ingushetians in North Ossetia," *Nezavisimaia Gazeta*, September 10, 1994.

the Caucasus. The Congress adopted an appeal to the mountain peoples to halt all armed conflicts and to find peaceful solutions to ethnic disputes.

As a result of these efforts, a certain measure of understanding was reached between the leaders of Ossetia and Ingushetia; however, the return of refugees and their resettlement continue to proceed with great difficulty. Only near the end of 1994 did the rate of return of refugees to the Prigorodny district increase.[67] In accordance with the agreed timetable, 638 families were to have been resettled in their former places of residence by January 1, 1995. This goal was not met.[68]

Prompted by events in Chechnya, in mid-July 1995, Aushev and Galazov began meeting one-on-one in Vladikavkaz to search for a solution to the Ingush-Ossetian conflict. The two leaders purposely shunned established federal channels for the resolution of internal conflicts, considering them to have contributed both to the deterioration of conditions in Chechnya and the stagnation of their own situation. Both leaders have affirmed their commitment to continuing efforts to implement the decrees of the president of the Russian Federation and the recommendations of its government as well as all agreements intended to remedy the damage from the Ingush-Ossetian conflict.[69] The talks were scheduled to continue in the fall of 1995 in Nazran.

The work of the investigative group of the Russian prosecutor general's office on the motivations of the main parties involved in the November 1992 clashes was conducted under extremely difficult conditions and met with much resistance—frequently accompanied by threats—from both the local authorities and the populace.[70] Both sides have expressed national solidarity by covering up the facts.

---

67. According to information supplied by the interim administration on the resettlement of refugees in Vladikavkaz, from August 1 to November 1, 1994, 113 families were resettled in their former places of residence, 75 in the first half of November alone. *Bulletin of the Interim Administration*, No. 1 (1995).

68. Federal authorities have not been able to manage resettlement at a micro level, and, as a result, the process has begun to unwind. In June 1995, for example, an entire Ingush family that had been granted official permission to return to the Prigorodny district was killed, likely by local bands opposed to Ingush resettlement.

69. Aleksander Aleshkin, "The Long Road Home: The Return of Refugees is the Main Topic of Talks in Vladikavkaz," *Rossiiskaia gazeta*, July 12, 1995, p. 2.

70. The prosecutor general of the Russian Federation is responsible for investigating and supervising the implementation of legislation. All activities of public prosecutors are nominally coordinated by and subordinated to the office of the prosecutor general.

This resistance affected the results of investigations: in the two years following the violence, only thirteen criminal prosecutions against a total of fifteen defendants reached the trial stage. The identities of the actual organizers of the large-scale armed clashes were never established, nor was a judicial assessment of the conflict ever provided.

It took the federal authorities an entire year to work out specific measures to settle the conflict. In December 1993, President Yeltsin chaired a meeting in Nalchik of the heads of republics and regions of the North Caucasus that adopted a detailed settlement program. All ministries and departments concerned were given detailed instructions, and an official statement was issued. Later that month, Yeltsin signed a decree ordering the repatriation of refugees and deportees to North Ossetia and Ingushetia. Unfortunately, in the year following, not one of the forty instructions to the Russian ministries was fully carried out, and in many cases implementation was not even attempted. In May 1994, Yeltsin issued a decree that again charged the government with the task of quickly solving the problem of the return of refugees to the Prigorodny district. In the summer that followed, the government continued its attempts to normalize the situation.

On June 19, 1994, the Russian government issued a decree, "On a Free Economic Zone on the Territory of Ingushetia," as an experiment to attract investments and capital. The "special economic zone of Ingushetia," was set up, accompanied by a federal government loan to the Ingushetian Council of Ministers. This special status meant that tax rates in Ingushetia were much lower than in the surrounding regions as an incentive for businesses to start operations there. Taxes collected went directly to the government of Ingushetia. This quickly helped to start many building projects by Russian and foreign firms, and strongly improved Ingushetia's economic prospects.[71] By January 1995, 152 new enterprises were registered in Ingushetia, bringing about $200 million into the republic.[72] However, as experience has shown, the creation of such zones during times of crisis contributes to the enrichment of a small elite. In the author's opinion, based on conversations with aides to Ingushetian President Aushev, as well as with experts from the North Caucasian Personnel Center, Ingushetia was not an exception to this rule. Businessmen from the

71. See the interview with Ruslan Aushev, "'Baki Dom' Unites the Nation in the New Capital of Magas," *Golos*, No. 31 (August 1, 1995), p. 3.

72. Yelena Ilina, "What's Growing in the Zone?" *Komsomolskaia Pravda*, No. 64 (April 4, 1995).

neighboring Stavropol and Krasnodar regions have created problems by registering enterprises in Ingushetia that were not located on Ingushetian territory. The flow of taxes out of domestic budgets into the Ingushetian budget as a result of such arrangements has prompted officials from Stavropol and Krasnodar to press for the elimination of the special economic zone. In his fight to prolong the term of the zone, Aushev cited the extraordinary burden Ingushetia bears in providing for refugees.

In September 1994, the Russian government acknowledged the unsatisfactory efforts of the ministries and departments of the Russian Federation in implementing the presidential decrees on the resettlement of refugees, and it modified its instructions to the ministries of Finance, Nationality Affairs, and Emergency Situations. At the end of 1994, a large delegation from the Moscow municipal government headed by Mayor Yuri Luzhkov visited Ingushetia. An agreement was signed on the investment of Moscow funds in building houses and communications infrastructure in Nazran. These intentions may have been serious since the fruition of this project could be a trump card for Luzhkov if he were to decide to run for president of Russia.[73]

On December 8, 1994, the routine extension of the state of emergency in Ingushetia was not supported by the Council of the Federation, and the state of emergency was formally lifted. However, nothing changed in Ingushetia with the exception of the name of the interim government, which officially became the "Government Commission on the Liquidation of the Consequences of the Ingushetian-Ossetian Conflict."

EFFORTS OF PUBLIC ORGANIZATIONS AND "PEOPLE'S DIPLOMACY"

The peacemaking efforts of public organizations, which primarily provide charity and humanitarian aid, have not had much success in helping to resolve conflicts. Independent "Track II" peacemaking activities have helped to regularize the situation, and public and religious organizations have helped to bring people together. Ultimately, however, the role of disparate and uncoordinated humanitarian interventions is not great.

In February 1993, a "mobile reconciliation group" comprised of veterans of the war in Afghanistan participated in a conference in Nalchik that brought together Northern Caucasian and

---

73. In the spring of 1995, Moscow signed a similar agreement with the Kirovskaia oblast in northern Russia.

Transcaucasian Afghan war veterans following similar meetings in numerous towns and villages. An observer committee of Ingush and North Ossetians was set up at the conference assisting the authorities and law-and-order agencies with enforcing the state of emergency.[74] In March 1993, the same reconciliation group spent a week in the Prigorodny district to distribute 100 million rubles' worth of clothing, food products, medicines, and medical equipment to inhabitants of both republics.[75]

With the assistance of the head of the interim administration, Vladimir Lozovoi, meetings were organized in Vladikavkaz with women, young people, representatives of the intelligentsia, and elders from both North Ossetia and Ingushetia to help renew the dialogue between the two sides. However, in spite of the interim administration's activities in the sphere of people's diplomacy, both the Ingush and the Ossetians viewed the results with skepticism.

A public political association called the Senezh Forum, which is based in Moscow and comprises well-known Russian experts on ethnic questions, organized meetings of Northern Caucasian leaders of government and public organizations in Pyatigorsk. The meetings were of a consultative nature, and their role was only to prepare documents to be presented during the Kislovodsk negotiations. The forum might have eventually contributed to the resolution of the conflict, but the meetings were held under the auspices of the Council of Nationalities of the Supreme Soviet of the Russian Federation and were terminated along with that entity in October 1993. The creation of a similar follow-on project to facilitate regional cooperation between the North Ossetians and the Ingush, including meetings between officials from lower levels of government and the leaders of local administrations, could be very important and productive.

THE ROLE OF INTERNATIONAL ORGANIZATIONS

The conflict between North Ossetia and Ingushetia is contained within the internationally recognized borders of the Russian Federation, and according to traditional international standards, the participation of international peacemaking organizations in this conflict without the agreement of the Russian federal authorities would be unacceptable. Although both the Ingush and the Ossetians have appealed to world public opinion, Russia has tried to resolve the

---

74. Itar-Tass, special correspondent Vladimir Gondusov, February 27, 1993.
75. Ibid.

problem itself. Nevertheless, a number of representatives of international foundations and organizations have visited the zone of conflict since 1992, and each side has naturally made efforts to find support in the outside world through these organizations.

In January 1993, a delegation of the Conference on Security and Cooperation in Europe (CSCE) headed by Khalil Akinzhi, Minister at the Turkish Embassy in Moscow, arrived in Vladikavkaz on a fact-finding mission. The delegation met with Sergei Khetagurov, head of the North Ossetian government, and also visited refugee camps in the Prigorodny district. Although a certain amount of humanitarian aid was promised, the visit was strictly of a fact-finding nature, and it was clear that no substantial follow-up was intended.

In January 1994, the Republic of Ingushetia was accepted as a member of the International Organization of Non-represented Peoples (ONP). In February 1994, at a special meeting of the Managing Committee of the ONP in the Hague, Mustapha Bekov, the plenipotentiary representative of the Republic to the ONP, submitted a report on the situation in Ingushetia. In summer 1994, the Andrei Sakharov Foundation organized a special conference in Stockholm at which attempts were made to work out recommendations for a settlement of the Ingushetian-Ossetian conflict.

In November 1994, a delegation of the European Bureau of the United Nations High Commissioner for Refugees arrived in Vladikavkaz. At the invitation of the Russian government, the delegation, which included UN human rights experts, visited the Caucasus to acquaint itself with the refugee situation. The members of the delegation showed great interest in the political aspects of the problems in Southern Russia; however, their main purpose, as stated during a meeting with journalists, was to organize humanitarian aid in cooperation with all interested parties. Although the recommendations of peacemaking organizations have all stressed the need for a speedy return of refugees and the disarmament of illegal formations in the region, constructive measures to achieve this have yet to be proposed by these groups.

In the author's opinion, the lack of any concerted action to address problems in Ingushetia constitutes the greatest difficulty. International organizations in general, and the Council of Europe in particular, should directly pressure the Yeltsin government as they have done with regard to events in Chechnya. They should also work indirectly to mobilize constituencies in Western countries to pressure their national leaders to achieve some progress on a resolution of basic issues and perhaps for some funding for this effort as well. However, the fact remains that this is an internal Russian problem, and Russia must solve it. A solution requires focused politicking in Russia, and the participation of an objective, neutral party that can ensure fair distribution of government resources—in contrast to the current situation in which the North Ossetians end up with a disproportionately greater share.

The Chechen Crisis

The outbreak of the war in Chechnya had a direct impact on the situation in Ingushetia. A wave of Chechen refugees flowed into Ingushetia, worsening the humanitarian and refugee problems there. In addition, the Ingush are very fearful of the Chechens' clear attempts to draw Ingushetia into the conflict. The Ingush see a great deal of potential for Russian military action against Ingushetia and Dagestan—the Caucasus republics that supported Chechnya and whose nationals are ethnic kin of the Chechens. The situation remains very volatile. Ingush Vice President Boris Agapov identifies three different forces with an interest in extending the war to Ingushetia. The first is a group of upper-level Russian authorities who see the Ingush as potential separatists and wish to "demonstrate the strength of the federal center" in order to deter other potential separatists inside Russia. The second group includes some Chechen leaders and a portion of the Chechen people who would like to see the Ingush enter into the fight against Russia. The third includes certain political circles in North Ossetia who would like to use the situation in Chechnya to settle the prolonged Ossetian-Ingushetian conflict in favor of Vladikavkaz.[76]

More worrisome, however, is that Russian politicians and military leaders have evinced a desire to identify Ingushetia with Chechnya and to solve the problem with Ingushetia in the same way that the problem with Chechnya is being "solved." In particular, Vladimir Shumeiko, speaker of the Council of the Federation, has labeled Ingushetia an "artificial formation." At a press conference in the president's office on February 1, 1995, Sergei Shakhrai referred to a report of the Federal Counterintelligence Service and the Ministry of the Interior that claimed to have proof that Chechen President Dudaev

---

76. Boris Agapov and Vladimir Kiselev, "Three Signs of Disaster," *Obshchaia Gazeta*, No. 5 (February 2–8, 1995).

was orchestrating Chechen resistance efforts from a location in Ingushetia. The report also asserted that arms depots and training camps for Chechen fighters had been set up on Ingushetian territory.[77]

Meanwhile, while Russian politicians talked, the military took action. In Chechnya, Russian federal forces had by February 1, 1995, carried out a number of bombing raids and artillery bombardments of Ingushetian territory, killing twenty-six Ingush and injuring thirty.[78] Boris Agapov has pointed out that in the text of Yeltsin's well-known presidential decree on the disarmament of illegal formations, "not only Chechnya is mentioned, but also North Ossetia and Ingushetia. Thus, after Chechnya, the formal justification for continuing military operations on the territory of Ingushetia allegedly exists. Our people feel that something terrible is approaching."[79]

Conclusion

Because of Russia's current economic and political crisis, the obligations assumed by the Russian federal authorities to solve the problem of refugees and deported peoples in the North Caucasus are not being met. Both sides understand the consequences if the refugee problem is not resolved, but their approach to a solution differs: the Ingush believe that the settlement should be immediate and unconditional, while the Ossetians demand that the settlement be gradual and carried out under a joint coordinating commission.

The measures undertaken by federal authorities have not achieved any tangible results. Illegal armed formations continue to operate and build up their military capabilities, and the military balance in the region has changed as a result. The civilian population on both sides is in possession of large quantities of arms, while, at the same time, the public mood, whipped up by nationalist hysteria, is becoming more radical and aggressive. The government and the interim administration on the territory of the republics cannot ensure that Yeltsin's presidential decrees or the Security Council's orders will be implemented, which has led to a considerable lack of trust in federal authorities among the populace of both republics. The funds allocated for settling the conflict and ameliorating its consequences are being spent on

---

77. Vladimir Shumeiko, *Kommersant Daily*, February 4, 1995.

78. Boris Agapov and Yelena Tregubova, "Moscow Provokes the Ingushetians to Extreme Forms of Protest," *Segodnia*, February 2, 1995.

79. Agapov and Kiselev, "Three Signs of Disaster."

other purposes. The use of armed violence has created deep hostility and suspicion between the two sides. At the government level in North Ossetia, the idea that it is simply impossible for Ossetians and Ingush to live together is not uncommon, and the Ingush continue to advance their claims on the Prigorodny district. The Ingushetian side proposed introducing a "special administration" in the Prigorodny district that would be subordinate to the federal government; the Ossetian side views this as flagrant intervention in the internal affairs of North Ossetia.

The catastrophic results of the conflict have led the Ingush to view the Russian central authorities not as independent arbiters, but as outside forces trying to take advantage of the situation. National elites on both sides consider the real intentions of Russian authorities to be unclear, fluctuating, and dependent upon the twists and turns in the struggle for power in Moscow. Nevertheless, Ingushetia has confirmed its status as a member of the Russian Federation and is likely, in view of the civil war and complete chaos reigning in Chechnya, to distance itself more and more from that republic and look instead for support from Moscow. Ingush president Ruslan Aushev is essentially a pragmatist and understands that the best way to help his people in the short term is to dissociate Ingushetia as much as possible from Chechnya and Dudaev. Ingushetia has taken in 120,000 Chechen refugees and will likely continue to provide assistance to the Chechen people. At the same time, it will attempt to maintain a strong allegiance to Moscow and to preserve the economic zone that is helping Ingushetia build a real economic base. In spite of the general weariness caused by the conflict and the desire for some return to normalcy on both the Ingushetian and Ossetian sides, there is a high probability of more violent outbursts.[80]

The conditions that led to the tragic and bloody outcome in Northern Ossetia, Ingushetia, and now Chechnya are traceable to a number of fundamental problems prevalent in contemporary Russia. One key cause of the intensity of these conflicts is the proliferation of weapons and military equipment throughout former Soviet territory. After the 1991 breakup of the Soviet Union, the country's enormous military inheritance was divided among the newly formed national armies of the newly independent states. While Russian government

---

80. Ruslan Aushev has been quoted as saying, "Yes, we are brother nations but each brother has the right to live in his own house." Interview with Ruslan Aushev on the radio station Novaia Volna, February 6, 1995.

institutions, along with Western leaders, attempted to ensure strict control over the Soviet Union's nuclear legacy, far less control was achieved over the flow of conventional weapons. The division of these non-nuclear military spoils was undertaken amid great confusion and with little official supervision. Weapons rapidly began to flow to areas of instability, including the Caucasus region. In the Caucasus, arms and munitions were freely bought and sold, resulting in the indiscriminate arming of the population.

Political instability and the weakness of Russian federal authorities have also played a large role in the outbreak of violence in the Prigorodny district, and will continue for some time to be a feature of the Russian political landscape. Still in their formative stage and absorbed by internal political problems, the federal structures took no action before the conflict had reached a highly volatile stage. When conflict did break out, Russia's federal structures were unable to react fast enough to contain the armed clashes and at the same time maintain strict neutrality in the conflict. It is becoming widely recognized that operations of this kind should be carried out by peacekeeping forces with special training in the historic, ethnic, and religious particularities of the peoples involved in the conflict. Russia has never had such forces and does not have them now. Consequently, the federal government is limited to dispatching ordinary army subunits and detachments of internal troops. The forces that were sent to the North Caucasus did not take a neutral position and instead supported the Ossetians. Further evidence of the weakness of Russian government structures is the fact that it took a whole year to work out a document specifying measures to resolve the conflict. Although this document was finally ready by the end of 1993, so far not one of its measures has been implemented by the federal authorities. The failure can be traced to a lack of will combined with the general level of incompetence in government structures. Russian political leaders are preoccupied with other affairs, such as the struggle between Yeltsin and the Parliament, the economic crisis, and elections. In the face of so many crises, resolving a territorial dispute between Ingushetia and North Ossetia has taken a rather low priority.

Constant internal struggles within the Russian government itself are also to blame for the lack of serious attention to this conflict. No attention is given to unifying or rationalizing policy, and decisions end up being made largely on an ad hoc basis. Moreover, there is simply no tradition of negotiation in most of the post-Soviet governments and the dominant inclination is to use force to resolve disputes. Reliance on the use of force characterizes Russian politics in general, as has been abundantly illustrated by the handling of affairs in Chechnya. As under the Soviet regime, local conflicts, like that in the Prigorodny district, often become pawns in political games being played out far away in Moscow. At present no mechanisms exist in Russia to compete with or counteract this type of elite-driven politics.

The legacy of the Soviet period is a veritable powder keg of grievances between ethnic groups within Russia, and it is apparent that Russia's lack of a coherent nationality policy has created a dangerous vacuum. Unlike Soviet federalism, which existed in name only, the federal structure of the Russian state is real, and the actions of the autonomous regions within the Russian Federation as they seek to improve their political and economic status threaten Russian federalism because they foster the same centrifugal forces that unraveled the Soviet Union. The lesson that Russia should draw from the Ossetian-Ingushetian conflict is that it must develop a nationality policy worthy of a multinational state that ensures peaceful coexistence and cooperation among its many ethnic groups and enables these groups to satisfy their national cultural needs. Without such a policy, it is clear that the nationality-based conflicts, in the North Caucasus and elsewhere in Russia, will only increase.

Chapter 4

Commentary on North Ossetia and Ingushetia

David Mendeloff

The study of the Ingush-Ossetian conflict in Russia's Northern Caucasus offers valuable insight into the management of interethnic and territorial conflicts throughout the former Soviet Union. Since 1992, the Russian government has actively intervened to help settle the conflict. Since any solution to ethnic violence in the former Soviet Union, especially within Russia itself, requires some form of Russian involvement, Moscow's role in the Ingush-Ossetian conflict merits serious attention and evaluation. To the degree that the chapter by Olga Osipova takes on this task, it is highly informative, if not provocative.

This brief commentary addresses a central question raised by Osipova's well-informed study. What explains the failure of recent efforts to manage the Ingush-Ossetian conflict? More specifically, what are Moscow's primary interests in the conflict? Russian apathy—or worse, cynical manipulation of these events—is a major stumbling block to managing and settling this conflict. Thus the question of Moscow's motivation is vital to comprehending the lessons for ethnic conflict management and resolution both in Russia and on its periphery.

The Failure of Conflict Management: Russian Machinations and Manipulation

While the violence in North Ossetia has lessened somewhat since the introduction of Russian troops in late 1992, a permanent cessation of violence and a comprehensive solution to the conflict have yet to be achieved. Despite Ingush demands and Russian and North Ossetian promises, the resettlement of Ingush refugees—driven from their homes in the wake of fighting in North Ossetia's Prigorodny district in 1992—has occurred at a glacial pace. The resettlement is indeed the biggest obstacle to an immediate lessening of the violence. And while resettlement is only a first step to a comprehensive settlement of the conflict, it is a vital one. At a minimum, a solution to the refugee problem would show good faith on the part of the Russian and North Ossetian authorities to settle the more fundamental issue of territorial control.

So why has the refugee issue continued to fester? According to Osipova's study, the failure of efforts to stem the violence in the North Caucasus rests largely with the Russian political leadership. While other factors that have contributed to the conflict are astutely considered—notably the political machinations, blunders, and insensitivities of the Soviet-era government—it is the actions, and inactions, of the Yeltsin regime that have prevented its cessation. As evidence, Osipova notes Moscow's failure to enforce its own decrees on the refugee issue and other official measures to lessen the violence.

This is perhaps the most provocative aspect of Osipova's analysis. Yet what explains this? Is it an intentional unwillingness on Moscow's part to enforce its decrees, or an inability to do so, or perhaps both? Osipova's analysis tends toward the former, arguing that the Russians did not intervene to achieve a political solution to the conflict. Instead, they had an ulterior motive—namely Chechnya. Moscow, she argues, intervened militarily in North Ossetia as a show of Russian resolve—to serve as a deterrent to the insolence of neighboring Chechnya, and as a warning to other secession-minded republics.

Others go further than Osipova in describing Russia's cynical interest in the Ingush-Ossetian conflict. Some Ingush leaders, as well as Chechen President Dzhokhar Dudaev, have accused Russia of deliberately instigating the violence that broke out in 1992, exploiting the territorial conflict, and fanning the flames of ethno-nationalist violence not only to intimidate Chechnya, but to crush any potential Ingush independence drive. These critics accuse the Russians of arming and training the North Ossetians, and of regularly disbanding armed Ingush formations, while ignoring illegally armed Ossetian ones. Further evidence was offered after the Russian intervention in Chechnya in December 1994: the decree banning armed formations applied not only to Chechnya but to North Ossetia and Ingushetia as well. Both Ingush President Ruslan Aushev and Vice President Boris Agapov expressed fear that Moscow would likely use the opportunity presented by the Chechen intervention to crush what they believed to be an increasingly secessionist-minded and pro-Chechen Ingushetia.[1]

An Alternative Explanation: The Structural Impediments to Conflict Management and Resolution

However, imputing the failure of peacemaking to Russian machinations alone gives Russia a great deal more credit than perhaps it deserves. It assumes significant coordination, foresight, planning, and careful calculation on the part of the Russian leadership, currently rife with division, mistrust, and conflict. A more plausible interpretation seems to be that Russian policy is essentially inconsistent, ill thought-out, and perhaps even contradictory. Russia may indeed have multiple and overlapping interests in the conflict: first, to stop the Ingush-Ossetian violence because of the danger of instability—and the resultant decline of Russian influence—in the Caucasus; second, to challenge Chechen belligerence, and prevent other rebellious regions of the federation from following in its footsteps; and third, to contain any nascent Ingush rebelliousness. Upon the outbreak of violence in 1992, Russia focused on claims that Chechnya had armed Ingush militants, confirming Moscow's belief that the region was prone to rebellion, as well as hardening the Russian position against Chechnya. Indeed, Boris Yeltsin justified the state of emergency in November 1992 not as a means of stopping interethnic territorial conflict, but as a necessary response to "militant nationalists [who] have unleashed a direct armed attack on the constitutional order of Russia, its security and territorial integrity."[2]

Furthermore, focusing solely on Russian interests and behavior ignores the serious structural impediments to a solution, which Osipova's own analysis clearly reveals. Whether or not Russia had wanted to achieve a political solution to the conflict, doing so would have been—and remains—extremely difficult given economic and political constraints. Moscow pledged to fund and coordinate the resettlement of the refugees, which includes temporarily housing Ingush

---

1. See Suzanne Goldenberg, *Pride of Small Nations: The Caucasus and Post-Soviet Disorder* (London: Zed Books, 1994), p. 202. The comments by Agapov appear in *Obshchaia gazeta*, No. 5/81 (February 2–8, 1995), p. 1, in *Foreign Broadcast Information Service Daily Report: Central Eurasia* (hereafter *FBIS*), February 23, 1995, pp. 47–48. Also see Agapov's comments in Robert Orttung, "Ingush Denounces Shakhrai," *OMRI Daily Digest*, No. 24 (February 2, 1995).

2. Quoted in Serge Schmemann, "Russian Troops Arrive as Caucasus Flares Up," *New York Times*, November 11, 1993, p. A6.

returnees, rebuilding housing and infrastructure, and providing jobs and other basic necessities. Financially this is no small task, even in the best of economic times. Further, North Ossetia, which is also responsible for carrying out the resettlement, has faced significant challenges. The republic has had to absorb and accommodate a flood of refugees into the city of Vladikavkaz from conflicts in Abkhazia, Armenia, and Azerbaijan. At the same time, authorities there have been required to build housing for some 20,000 Russian servicemen.[3] These factors have not only caused further financial strain, requiring even more funds and building materials, but have greatly increased the organizational and bureaucratic demands on the North Ossetian government. It is little wonder that the refugee problem continues unresolved.

Yet such material impediments could conceivably be overcome through the involvement of international organizations. The provision of financial assistance, building materials and supplies, civilian volunteer workers, and peacekeepers could remedy much of these problems, speeding up the resettlement, and alleviating much Ingush suffering. However, as Osipova's chapter reveals, international organizations have played a marginal, if not irrelevant, role in the conflict, largely because of Russian resistance. Again, this says much about Moscow's interests in the conflict. If the Russians desire only a military solution— to quash nascent Ingush separatism—then lack of Russian interest in international involvement makes sense. If they sincerely desire stability in the region, then why not take advantage of the international assistance, however meager, that has already been offered?

Again, though, Russian interests are likely more complex and even contradictory. Clearly Russia has vital strategic and economic interests in the Caucasus.[4] It wants stability (i.e., the absence of conflict), productive economic activity, and acquiescence to Russian control of the region. It is these interests that have made Russia leery of foreign involvement, even if it may help prevent further violence. More important, Moscow may have chosen to avoid international participation

---

3. Goldenberg, *Pride of Small Nations*, p. 202. See also the comments by Ilia Kostoev, chairman of the Federation Council Committee on Constitutional Legislation, on *Vremya*, February 7, 1995, in *FBIS*, February 8, 1995, p. 26; and the interview with Galazov, ITAR-TASS, February 12, 1995, in *FBIS*, February 13, 1995, p. 39. For the text of the Russian government's edict on the state of emergency, see ITAR-TASS World Service, January 31, 1995, in *FBIS*, February 1, 1995, pp. 25–27.

4. For a good discussion of Russian interests in this region, see Umirserik Kasenov, "Chego khochet Rossiia v zakavkaz'e i tsentral'noi azii (What Russia Wants in Central Asia)," *Nezavisimaia gazeta*, January 24, 1995, p. 3.

because such intervention may not have broad popular support out-side of the Caucasus. Given the Russian public's increasing hostility to Western involvement in Russian affairs, such a position may, in this case, make perfect political sense. Therefore, this must not necessarily be seen as hard evidence of deliberate Russian unwillingness to solve the refugee problem. In short, one finds numerous factors—economic and political constraints, even simple incompetence—other than sim-ple malign intent on the part of Ossetians and Russians, which have prevented a solution to the refugee problem.

Implications for the Future

This brief essay has argued that the failure of efforts to manage and resolve the Ingush-Ossetian conflict, especially the refugee problem, cannot be attributed solely to Russian machinations and manipulation. Russian interests in the conflict are largely inconsistent, contradictory, perhaps even self-defeating. More important, serious economic and political constraints, as well as the added burden of non-Ingush refugees and Russian servicemen in North Ossetia, have all exacerbat-ed and prevented a speedy cessation of the violence.

So what then are the implications for this and future conflicts in Russia and the former Soviet Union? Even if Moscow purposefully intends to resolve the Ingush-Ossetian conflict (that is, once the "Chechen question" is solved), a successful outcome would still not be guaranteed. Although the state of emergency in the region has not been allowed to lapse, Moscow's plenipotentiaries and the Russian armed forces have decided to remain and continue, at least in word, to help realize an end to the conflict.[5] Yet such efforts are likely to fail if they do not include some foreign assistance to help remove the struc-tural impediments to lessening the violence. As long as an internation-al role remains politically unpalatable inside Russia, the structural problems are bound to continue, resettlement of refugees will occur slowly, and the Ingush will grow increasingly more impatient.

Furthermore, following the events in Chechnya, a continued Russian presence may be even less useful than it was from 1992 to

---

5. On the refusal of the Russian Federation Council to ratify the state of emer-gency, see Robert Orttung and Liz Fuller, "Federation Council Fails to Ratify State of Emergency," *OMRI Daily Digest*, No. 26 (February 6, 1995); Robert Orttung, "Federation Council Rejects State of Emergency," *OMRI Daily Digest*, No. 28 (February 8, 1995); and Interfax, February 10, 1995, in *FBIS*, February 13, 1995, pp. 38–39.

1994. As many commentators have noted, the Chechen invasion may have been a self-defeating and self-punishing policy, undermining Moscow's legitimacy in the region. Indeed, in light of the intervention, the Ingush have grown increasingly bitter toward Moscow. Ironically, Russian fears of potential Ingush separatism, clearly exaggerated in 1992, are now much closer to reality. The Ingush openly distanced themselves from the secessionist Chechnya in 1991, remaining firmly within the Russian Federation, largely in the hope that the territorial question with North Ossetia could best be resolved in that way. While Ingushetia's leaders still declare that they have no intention of seceding from Russia, the Ingush population has grown increasingly weary of the violence associated with the Chechen conflict, the burden of some 98,000 war refugees, and especially of repeated Russian accusations of Ingush disloyalty.[6]

Other ethnic groups in the North Caucasus may also become embittered by Russian behavior in Chechnya, proliferating interethnic violence and further complicating a resolution of the Ingush-Ossetian conflict. The intervention, for example, has already led to nascent unrest in the ethnically heterogeneous republic of Dagestan, which has absorbed several thousand refugees from the Chechen conflict. As one observer put it, "This republic has finally woken up."[7] Dagestan could very well become the next tragedy for the Caucasus and Moscow. Sadly, in that case, the Ingush-Ossetian conflict would likely continue unresolved.

---

6.   On the growing unrest of the Ingush population, see the comments by Agapov, ITAR-TASS World Service, February 1, 1995, in FBIS, February 1,1995, p. 24. On the continued loyalty of the Ingush leadership, witness the comment by Arkadii Popov, of the Russian President's Analytical Center, who has noted that Aushev "enjoy[s] support from the majority of republican population and remain[s] loyal to the Russian state," and is "the sole stabilizing factor in such an extremely volatile region as Ingushetia." Quoted in Interfax, January 31, 1995, in FBIS, February 1, 1995, p. 24. Accusations of Ingush disloyalty were made explicitly by Deputy Prime Minister Sergei Shakhrai on "Vesti," February 1, 1995, in FBIS, February 1, 1995, pp. 23–24, and Orttung, "Ingush Denounces Shakhrai." The refugee figures represent Ingush government estimates, as cited in Interfax, February 15, 1995, in FBIS, February 15, 1995, pp. 31–32.

7.   Vadim Shorokhov, "Chechenskoe protivostoianie i vokrug nego: Groznii na politicheskoi stsene (The Chechen Counterinsurrection and its Environs: Grozny on the Political Scene)," Nezavisimaia gazeta, January 20, 1995, p. 3. Shorokhov also argues that separatism in the Caucasus, as well as throughout the Russian Federation, will become a self-fulfilling prophecy given Moscow's use of force against Chechnya. On this, also see Ronald Grigor Suny, "Moscow's Dangerous Game," New York Times, December 22, 1994, p. A19. For a brief overview of the ethnic makeup and precarious unity of Dagestan, see Goldenberg, Pride of Small Nations, pp. 203–207.

Chapter 5

The Crimean Republic: Rivalries for Control

Edward Ozhiganov

Throughout Crimea's complicated history, the peninsula's strategic location on the Black Sea has made it a desirable military outpost and warm-water port, leading to territorial claims by a great variety of political forces. Since the demise of the Soviet Union, the unstable situation in Crimea has threatened to turn the Black Sea region of Russia and Ukraine into a hotbed of tension similar to Transdniester or Abkhazia. The scale of the Crimean conflict allows it to be classified as a "serious dispute" in which "at least one of the parties has implicitly or explicitly threatened to use force and some small-scale violence has occurred."[1]

The conflict over Crimea has its roots in the region's demographic and geopolitical history. The Crimean peninsula, which covers 27,000 square kilometers, has an extremely complex demographic structure. Although dominated by ethnic Russians and Ukrainians, over 100 other ethnic groups inhabit Crimea.[2] In 1979, before the policies of Soviet President Mikhail Gorbachev permitted the large-scale return of Crimean Tatars who were deported by Stalin during World War II, the population of Crimea was approximately 2.5 million. Immediately after the war, there had been a large influx of Russians and other nationalities, and following Crimea's incorporation into

---

1. "Wars, Low-Intensity Conflicts and Serious Disputes," Interdisciplinary Research Program on Root Causes of Human Rights Violations (PIOOM), Leiden University, The Netherlands, Working Paper I (Summer 1993), p. 1.

2. The 1979 census records the following ethnic composition in the Crimean oblast: 1,460,980 Russians (68.4 percent of the peninsula's population); 547,336 Ukrainians (25.6 percent); 43,214 Belarusans (2 percent); 22,597 Jews (1 percent); 15,078 Crimean Tatars (0.7 percent); 6,092 Poles (0.3 percent); and 40,619 people of other ethnic groups (1.9 percent).

Ukraine in 1954, large numbers of Ukrainians also moved to the peninsula. The Crimean Tatars represented only a small portion of the Crimean population until the 1980s, when their numbers increased at least tenfold.

Since the collapse of the Soviet Union, Crimea has been the object of two overlapping rivalries for control: first between the Crimean Republic authorities and the Crimean Tatars, who demand recognition of their historic and territorial rights to the peninsula; and second between pro-Russian leaders of the Crimean Republic, who want either independence or reunification of the peninsula with Russia, and the Ukrainian authorities, who oppose Crimean separatism and insist that Crimea remain an integral part of Ukraine. These movements revolve around the same basic political question: who has sovereignty over the Crimean peninsula—its original Tatar inhabitants; the government of the Ukrainian Republic, which has, in one form or another, presided over the region since 1954; or the predominantly Russian population that currently inhabits the peninsula?

The internal divisions within both the Crimean authorities and the Crimean Tatar nationalist movement have so far prevented this conflict from erupting into open clashes. Thus the bitter struggle waged by the President of the Crimean Republic, Yuri Meshkov, against the Crimean Parliament resulted in the resignation of the pro-Moscow government and the substantial weakening of the Crimean president's powers. At the same time, Crimean Tatar nationalists are split into several rival factions, ranging from moderates seeking compromise with the Ukrainian authorities and the Crimean Republic to extreme nationalists pushing for uncompromising, exclusionist solutions.

These conflicts are further aggravated by a number of external issues that affect the question of Crimean sovereignty. Disagreement over the legitimacy of Crimea's transfer in 1954 from Russia to Ukraine is exacerbated by the dispute between Ukraine and Russia over the fate of the Black Sea Fleet and its main naval base in Sebastopol and by the constantly worsening economic crisis in Ukraine. Whether the Crimean Republic's authorities can prevent the situation from exploding depends to a large degree on how the relationship between Ukraine and Russia evolves. Future policies with respect to Ukraine's debt for Russian energy deliveries, nuclear weapons (which appears to be settled), and the status of the Black Sea Fleet could ameliorate or worsen the relationship between the two states. The accession to power of pro-Russian political parties in Crimea set a precedent for all Russian-speaking regions in eastern

Ukraine, which are suffering from the disruption of economic ties with Russia. At the same time, the instability of the Yeltsin regime in Russia has often led to sudden changes in its policy toward the "near abroad" as well as in its nationalities policy. In 1992–93, Russia changed its stance on the Crimean problem a number of times as a result of internal power struggles among the elites and advisers surrounding President Boris Yeltsin. In the author's opinion, the election of Leonid Kuchma to the Ukrainian presidency in July 1994 has not changed the balance of forces on the Crimean issue.

Another unpredictable and dangerous factor that affects the Crimean situation is the potential for other countries in the region to exploit for their own purposes the Ukrainian political elite's resistance to Russia. For example, Turkish President Suleiman Demirel advised Kiev to permit all Turks of Crimean Tatar origin—more than half a million people—to return to the Crimean peninsula, in exchange for which Turkey would provide Ukraine with economic assistance and political support in the world arena.[3] Another worrisome trend is that radical forces among both Ukrainian and Crimean Tatar nationalist movements are trying to exploit the split between Ukraine and Russia to promote their own interests, thereby increasing tensions between these two countries, which could lead to serious instability in the region as a whole.

Historical and Sociopolitical Background

Throughout its history, Crimea has been inhabited by many tribes and peoples—Goths and Taures, Polovtsians and Turks. Numerous states and empires have ruled the peninsula: Scythia (700–200 B.C.), Greek city-states (around 500 B.C.), the Bosphorus kingdom (also in the fifth century B.C.), the Roman Empire (100 B.C.–100 A.D.), Byzantium (the fourth and fifth centuries), the Khazar Khanate (eighth and ninth centuries), the Old Russian Tmutarakan princedom (10th–12th centuries), the Mongolian Golden Horde (13th–15th centuries), and the Crimean Khanate (15th–18th centuries). The advantageous location of the peninsula made it a crossroads of ancient naval civilizations—Greece, Rome, Byzantium, Genoa—and the steppes around the Black Sea were populated by various nomadic peoples—Huns, Scythians, Khazars, Nogais, and others. The interaction and mixing of different

---

3.   General Dogon Gyuresh, "Russia Has Become a Serious Threat to Turkey," *Nezavisimaia gazeta*, July 16, 1994, p. 1.

civilizations and ethnic influences had created a vibrant economic culture on the Crimean peninsula long before the appearance of Turkic nomads.

The beginning of the gradual "turkicization" of the population is connected with the Khazar Khanate. Beginning in the ninth century, the Turkic-speaking Pecheneg tribes began to move into the region, later followed by Polovtsians. Turkish tribes from Asia Minor invaded Crimea and resettled there just before the Mongols conquered the peninsula in the thirteenth century. In 1243, Crimea became an administrative region (ulus) of the Golden Horde, and when the Horde split in 1443, the Crimean Khanate was established as an independent state. The Crimean Khanate subdued the entire peninsula and areas to the north of the Black Sea. In 1475, Ottoman Turks invaded and, after three years of fighting, the Crimean khans agreed to allow Crimea to become an Ottoman vassal state. As a result, the multiethnic population of Crimea was almost completely "turkicized," with the exception of small groups of Greeks, Armenians, Karaites, and indigenous Crimeans.

Over time, the Crimean Tatars divided into two primary groups on the basis of specific tribal characteristics, including descent lines, dialects, and cultural variations. The Northern Crimeans call themselves the Nogais and inhabit the steppe areas. The Nogais belong to the northwestern (Kipchak) branch of Turkic languages and were the strongest of the nomadic peoples who came to the peninsula from the areas around the Black Sea in the thirteenth century. Southern Crimeans, the Tati, live mostly along the southern coast. The Tati belong to the southwestern (Oguzian) branch of Turkic languages and are therefore more closely related to the Osmanli (Ottoman) Turks who came to the southern coast of the peninsula in the fifteenth century. An intermediate geographical and cultural position between the two main groups was occupied by Tatars inhabiting the mountainous regions and the foothills of the Crimean peninsula around Bakhchisarai and Old Crimea. The dialect of this group provided the basis for the Crimean Tatar literary language.

After the collapse of the Golden Horde, the Crimean Khanate claimed the Horde's Russian principalities, and beginning in 1502, it embarked on an exhausting struggle with Russia that did not abate for almost three centuries.[4] From 1475 to 1774, the Crimean Khanate

4. Vasili Osipovich Kliuchevsky, *The Course of Russian History*, Vol. 2, trans. Natalie Duddington (Armonk, N.Y.: M.E. Sharp, 1994), p. 96.

held the status of a dependent vassal of the Ottomans and acted as an instrument of Turkey's foreign policy toward Russia. In that period the Crimean Khanate took part in six different Russian-Turkish wars on Turkey's side and was a permanent source of armed aggression against Russia, Ukraine, and Poland.[5]

These struggles concluded with the signing of the Iasi peace treaty ending the Russian-Turkish War of 1782–91, under which the whole Crimean peninsula and areas to the north of the Black Sea were recognized as Russian territory. The commander in chief of the Russian Army during this war was General Field Marshal Grigory Potemkin, who was rewarded with the title of Prince of the Tavric, from Tavria, the old Russian name for Crimea. Potemkin founded such Crimean cities as Kherson, Simferopol, and Sebastopol and was also the founder of the Russian Black Sea Fleet.

Under the Russian Empire, the Cossacks played a critical role in settling the Crimean peninsula. They were pioneers in these new Russian lands, defending the borders of the empire against incursions and developing agriculture in the region according to a long Cossack tradition of common lands. Crimea and the steppe areas around the Black Sea were opened up for settlement and became part of the national economy of Russia, fueling the economic growth of the region.

THE NINETEENTH CENTURY

The Ottoman Empire, supported by Napoleonic France, tried to win Crimea back during the Russian-Turkish War of 1806–12, but again suffered defeat. Just before the Crimean War of 1853–56, the British allied with the Ottoman Turks in their attempts to regain Crimea, in hopes of weakening the pressure of the Russian Empire on India, the most prized British colony. During the Crimean War, the Russian authorities feared that the Crimean Tatars would collaborate with the Ottoman Turks, and to prevent this they deported a large part of the population to remote provinces of Russia. As news of the deportations spread, over 140,000 Crimean Tatars fled Crimea and settled in the Near East, primarily in Turkey. Traditional Crimean Tatar mistrust of the Russian authorities and the Russian policy of colonizing the Crimean peninsula combined to precipitate several waves of Tatar emigration in the latter half of the nineteenth century.

---

5. G.A. Sanin, *The Relationship of Russia and Ukraine with the Crimean Khanate in the Mid-Seventeenth Century* (Moscow: Nauka, 1987), pp. 240–242.

According to the 1897 census, the population of the Crimean peninsula numbered 532,200 people, including 186,200 Crimean Tatars.
The majority of these Tatars lived in the mountainous regions of the
peninsula—only approximately 20 percent were urban dwellers.

The first ethnic nationalist organizations of Crimean Tatars were
established in 1908–12 on the basis of the Crimean Students Alliance.
These organizations, including the underground political organization Vatan ("motherland" in Tatar), fought for Crimean independence,
were linked closely to Pan-Turkic movements in Turkey, and took a
pro-Turkish and pro-German stance. In World War I, Russia fought
against Turkey and the Crimean Tatar ethnic nationalist organizations, including the very influential Milly Firka (National Party) with
its Pan-Turkic ideology. In the anarchy that followed the collapse of
the Russian monarchy in February 1917, an All-Crimean Muslim
Congress in Simferopol elected an Executive Committee headed by
Tatar ethnic nationalist leaders who attempted to take control of
Crimea. In December 1917, the Crimean Tatar Parliament (*Kurultai*)
passed the Crimean Tatar Law and formed an executive body known
as the Directorate, headed by the *Mufti* (leader) Chelibeev.

The Tatar Directorate's attempts to assume control over Crimea
were strongly resisted by political groups representing the interests of
the Russian and Ukrainian bourgeoisie on the one hand, and the
Bolshevik Sebastopol Revolutionary Military Committee on the other.
Armed conflicts broke out in January 1918, when the Bolsheviks over-
threw the Directorate, whose leaders fled to Turkey. The Bolsheviks
created the Soviet Socialist Republic of Tavrida on the territory of
Crimea, but the republic lasted only a month before it was crushed by
the German Army, which occupied the peninsula in April 1918.

Armed formations of Crimean Tatar nationalists helped to estab-
lish German rule over Crimea, and a puppet government for the
region was set up with a Russified Lithuanian Tatar, General
Suleiman Sulkevich, who had commanded the First Muslim Corps in
the tsarist Russian Army, as its head. Milly Firka and the Crimean
Kurultai proposed to the German Emperor Wilhelm II that the
Crimean Khanate should be reestablished as a joint protectorate of
Germany and Turkey, a proposal that was strongly supported by the
Turkish rulers. However, Hetman Skoropadsky, head of the German
puppet government in Ukraine, strongly opposed the creation of an
independent Crimea and prevented adoption of the plan. The
Crimean Tatars had no choice at this point but to accept the creation
of the Ukrainian-Crimean Federation with Kiev as its center.

With Turkey's surrender in October 1918 and the defeat of Germany in November 1918, the plans of Crimean Tatar ethnic nationalists were irretrievably frustrated. The peninsula was occupied by a British-French expeditionary corps, and pro-Germans were removed from the regional government. In April 1919, the regional government was overthrown by the Bolsheviks, and a Crimean Soviet Socialist Republic (SSR) was established, but it was eliminated following the June 1919 invasion by the tsarist White armies under the command of Generals Denikin and Wrangel. At this point, most of the Tatar ethnic nationalist leaders emigrated to Turkey since the Whites regarded them as traitors and enemies of "Great Russia" because of their pro-Turkish orientation. However, during the Russian civil war, Wrangel's troops were defeated and forced to flee the Crimean peninsula.

THE SOVIET PERIOD

In 1920–22, the Soviet Council of People's Commissars repeatedly addressed the issue of a state and administrative system for Crimea. On October 18, 1921, the Crimean Autonomous Soviet Socialist Republic (ASSR) was formed within the framework of the Russian Soviet Federated Socialist Republic (RSFSR). The decree "On the Formation of the Crimean ASSR" did not include special rights of autonomy for the Crimean Tatar people, though it did provide a basis for territorial autonomy. The only provision in this decree relating specifically to the Crimean Tatars was that the Crimean Tatar language was to be one of the official languages of the republic, although Tatars were not defined as the titular nation.

The subsequent industrialization programs and the forced collectivization of agriculture carried out across Russia in the 1930s significantly changed the social structure of the population of the Crimean peninsula. According to the official data for 1936, 43.5 percent of the Crimean population were Russians, 23.1 percent were Tatars, 10 percent were Ukrainians, 7.4 percent were Jews, 5.7 percent were Germans, and the remaining 10.3 percent were represented by other nationalities. The largest population influx occurred between 1930 and 1940 as a result of new shipbuilding, machine-building, and chemical industries in the region, as well as specialized agricultural industries, such as wineries, and the development of the region as a tourist resort for the entire Soviet Union.

The pre–World War I Tatar nationalist organization Milly Firka, which had been forced to go underground after the Bolshevik takeover, tried to work within the system through the Communist Party and administrative institutions of the Crimean ASSR. Veli Ibragimov, a former member of the left wing of Milly Firka, became the chairman of the Crimean ASSR Central Executive Committee. During this pre-war period of the 1920s and 30s, the Soviet government was implementing its policy of *korenizatsia* (indigenization) in the national autonomous republics, promoting literacy and elevating a local elite into local administrative and party positions. Ibragimov pursued similar "national communist" policies in Crimea, which included plans for the resettlement in Crimea of 20,000 descendants of Crimean Tatars from Romania and the transfer of more than 3,000 Crimean Tatar families from areas of high Tatar population on the southern coast of the peninsula to the northern steppes where the numbers of Tatars were smaller. The intent was to change the demographic situation in favor of the Tatars. In 1926–28, a struggle arose within the Communist Party in Crimea over the question of official languages and the conversion of the written language of the Soviet Turkic peoples from Arabic script to Latin script. The uproar caused by this policy coincided with the end of the New Economic Policy (NEP) period in the Soviet Union and a growing harshness in Soviet policies. Ibragimov was convicted of having contact with illegal nationalist formations like Milly Firka and pursuing an openly pro-Tatar policy. He was shot in 1928.

The Soviet collectivization of agriculture was conducted between 1931 and 1934. In Crimea, as elsewhere in the Soviet Union, collectivization resulted in mass deportations and repression of wealthy peasant kulak families. Crimean Tatars were often successful agriculturalists, compared to other ethnic groups who tended to be more involved in industry and commerce, and as a result many Tatar families were labeled kulaks. Large numbers of Tatars were deported to Central Asia, and many died either en route or under the terrible conditions that awaited them. The terrible famine that struck Ukraine affected all groups on the Crimean peninsula. Some sources say that between 1921 and 1941, no fewer than 160,000 Crimean Tatars perished—almost a half of their total number in Crimea.

During World War II, the Crimean peninsula was an arena of fierce fighting and partisan warfare with heavy casualties. The Crimean Tatars were themselves divided about which side to support in the war, with a minority that included the leaders of nationalist Crimean Tatar emigrant groups in Turkey opting to side with Germany. Those who helped Germany were counting on German support for their goal of a Crimean Tatar state on the Crimean peninsula.[6] Hitler's long-term plan for the region was to make it into the *Gottenland* resort area for German aristocracy, but more immediately he wanted to exploit the Crimean Tatar nationalists for military and strategic purposes. Consequently, following the German invasion of Crimea in November 1941, Nazi occupation authorities permitted the establishment of local Crimean Tatar committees. In 1942, the Central Muslim Committee was formed under the guidance of Ahmed Ozenbahsli, a key Crimean Tatar nationalist leader who had been exiled in Turkey and been brought back by the Germans. Also in 1942, six Crimean Tatar battalions numbering 20,000 troops were formed in the rural regions of Crimea under the auspices of the German SS and joined forces with police "self-defense contingents." These battalions were made up mostly of local Tatars and some who had returned from Turkey, and acting under the command of German officers, they carried out harsh reprisals against civilians. However, it should be emphasized that they by no means represented all Crimean Tatars. The majority supported the Soviet war effort and fought in the Soviet army against the Germans.

After the defeat of the German troops in the region, the remaining Tatar armed formations were taken to Romania and Hungary in April 1944, where they joined the ranks of the SS division of the Eastern Turkic Military Alliance. A mere three weeks before Germany's capitulation, the Germans established the Crimean Tatar National Committee headed by Edige Kirimal, a Milly Firka leader, and recognized the "independent" Crimean Tatar state.

In 1944, the State Defense Committee of the Soviet Union adopted a resolution ordering the deportation of Crimean Tatars and persons of other nationalities from Crimea on the charge of collaboration with German occupation authorities. It is very difficult to determine exactly how many Tatars were deported because different researchers provide

---

6. An analysis of the Crimean Tatar nationalist organizations' activities in Crimea during the German occupation of the peninsula which was conducted by German historians using German archives, shows that these organizations collaborated closely with and depended on the German authorities. See, e.g., M. Luther, *Die Krim unter deutscher Bezatzung im zweiten Weltkrieg* (Berlin: 1956). Turkish and Crimean Tatar historians, however, are inclined to deny this and put the main emphasis on the contradictions between the German leadership and the Crimean Tatar organizations. This is the viewpoint of Edige Kirimal, who had been the leader of the Crimean Tatar nationalists' representation in Berlin during the years of the German occupation of the peninsula. See Edige Kirimal, *Der nationale Kampf Krimturken* (Emsdetten: 1952).

very different figures. Official statistics put the total number of deported Tatars and other groups at 190,000.[7] The London-based International Alert, using different sources, writes that in May 1944, "some 188,000 Crimean Tatars were forcibly deported from their homeland."[8] In the period before the deportation, the Crimean Tatars made up 19 percent of the peninsula's population. The whole nation suffered repression, although most Crimean Tatars had remained loyal to the Soviet state during the war and suffered from German occupation no less than other ethnic groups. The deportees that survived the journey ended up in Central Asia, mostly in Uzbekistan. Everything they owned was confiscated by the government, and later used by the Russians and other Slavs who came to Crimea.

On June 30, 1945, soon after the end of the war, the Crimean ASSR was demoted to oblast status, thus canceling the limited autonomy Crimea had previously exercised and turning the region into a regular administrative unit of the RSFSR. On February 19, 1954, the status of the region again changed drastically when the entire peninsula was transferred from the RSFSR to the Ukrainian SSR at the initiative of Nikita Khrushchev.[9] Khrushchev explained his actions, on the basis of communist internationalism, as a "gift" to the Ukrainian SSR in honor of the 300th anniversary of Ukraine's reunification with Russia. The decree, "On the Transfer of the Crimean Oblast from the Russian Federation to the Ukrainian SSR," issued by the Presidium of the Supreme Soviet of the Soviet Union, stated that the transfer had been prompted by "the common character of economy, territorial proximity and close economic and cultural links between the Crimean oblast and the Ukrainian SSR." The decree cited a "joint

---

7. "Moving the Crimean Tatars," TASS, May 16, 1987. In June 1944, the "NKVD also deported some 20,000 Greeks, 20,000 Armenians, and 17,000 Bulgarians from the Crimea (45,000 Germans had already been deported in 1941)." Other Moscow-based researchers, referring to Crimean Tatar sources, claim that 238,500 Crimean Tatars alone were deported from Crimea in 1944, and they point out that "official Soviet statistics never indicate how many Crimean Tatar people were victims of this action, as many people died en route, never reaching their destinations. The only source regarding these losses that modern researchers can use are the figures provided by the Crimean Tatar movement." M. Guboglo and S. Chervonnaia, *Krimskotatarskoe natsionalnoe dvizhenie* (the Crimean-Tatar Nationalist Movement) Vol. 1 (U.K.: Russian Academy of Sciences, Institute of Ethnology and Anthropology, Moscow: 1992), pp. 81–82.

8. Andrew Wilson, "The Crimean Tatars: A Situational Report on the Crimean Tatars for International Alert," (Cambridge, U.K.: International Alert, 1993), p. 37.

9. The decision on the transfer was not taken in accord with the appropriate legal procedures, which later served as grounds for denying its validity.

request" by the Presidiums of the Ukrainian and Russian Supreme Soviets to justify the transfer, although it was in direct violation of constitutional norms existing at the time and of the formal rules for changing administrative borders.[10] In fact, Khrushchev, who previously had been the leader of the Ukrainian communist organization, made this decision in the context of the vicious internal struggle within the Communist Party of the Soviet Union (CPSU) for succession after Stalin's death. The real motivation for this decision has not yet been fully established, but in this author's view, a strong case can be made that the transfer of Crimea strengthened support for Khrushchev as the General Secretary of the CPSU among Ukrainian Communist Party leaders, who were at that time very influential.[11]

Most of the Crimean Tatars deported forcibly from the peninsula were resettled in Central Asia, primarily in rural areas of Uzbekistan. In accordance with the decree issued by the Presidium of the Supreme Soviet of the Soviet Union on April 28, 1956, Crimean Tatars were taken off the list of so-called "special settlements" and were freed from administrative supervision by the Ministry of Internal Affairs. However, Crimean Tatars were still forbidden to return to Crimea. Following the decree, a movement arose among Crimean Tatars that supported a return to their historic homelands. In September 1967, the Presidium of the Supreme Soviet of the Soviet Union issued a new decree restoring the full rights of Crimean Tatars under the Soviet Constitution and issued an additional resolution that made it formally possible for Crimean Tatars to settle in any region of the country "in accordance with labor and passport legislation currently in force."[12] The Soviet laws regulating the passport regime at that time gave local administrations the power to grant residence permits (*propiskas*), which were required for residence in any city. This allowed local Crimean authorities to legally prevent a massive influx of Crimean Tatars by refusing to grant *propiskas* to returning families. After 1968, approximately 3,000 Crimean Tatars were

---

10. *Vedomosti Verkhovnogo Soveta SSSR* (The Gazette of the Soviet Union Supreme Soviet), No. 4 (1954), p. 64. According to the legal norms that were written into the Soviet Union Constitution of 1936, Article 18 provided that the territory of a Union Republic could be changed without its agreement. Similar provisions existed in Article 16 of the Constitution of the RSFSR and Article 19 of the Constitution of the Ukrainian SSR. *Constitutions of Union Soviet Socialist Republics* (Moscow: Juridical Literature, 1951), pp. 8, 9, 36, 68.

11. Khrushchev's well-known willfulness and recklessness were key elements of his political life, and led ultimately to his ouster in 1964.

12. *Vedomosti Verkhovnogo Soveta SSSR*, No. 36 (1967), p. 532.

allowed to move to Crimea on the basis of what was known as "organized admission," but various roadblocks were put in their way, and the program was stopped altogether in 1978. These and other obstacles to return stirred up discontent among the Crimean Tatars. By this time over 10,000 Crimean Tatars were already living in Crimea, one-third of them illegally, without official residence permits and without legal work.[13] Near the end of 1978, the local authorities started to force some Tatar families out of Crimea for violating the passport regime, heightening social tensions throughout the region.

The Crimean Tatar national movement has never achieved a unified position on how to treat the national interests of other peoples and ethnic groups inhabiting the Crimean peninsula.[14] In the pre-perestroika period (1956–87), the movement was united by the single objective of resisting the Soviet system, and only a few minor issues stood in the way of full agreement among its founding leaders. But later a sharp cleavage developed between the two central groups in the Crimean Tatar movement. The Organization of the Crimean Tatar National Movement (OCNM), headed by Mustafa Dzhemilev, operated on the principle of the "cultural integrity" of the Crimean Tatar people and their "exclusive rights" to the Crimean territory, which were assumed to take priority over the rights of other ethnic groups. The second group, the Crimean Tatar National Movement (CTNM), headed by Yuri Osmanov, endorsed the principle of solidarity with other ethnic groups on the peninsula, assuming that the Crimean

---

13. The passport regime was very strict in Crimea because of its status as a health resort for the entire Soviet Union.

14. There is some disagreement about how to categorize the stages of development of the Crimean Tatar nationalist movement. In the most comprehensive historical work on the subject, Edward Allworth's *Tatars of the Crimea: Their Struggle for Survival: Original Studies from North America, Unofficial and Official Documents from Tsarist & Soviet Sources* (Durham, N.C.: Duke University Press, 1988), the development of the Crimean Tatar movement is divided into three main stages: 1) the period of Ismail Gasprinski and his circle (from the early twentieth century to the 1930s); 2) the Soviet period of the "founding fathers" of the Crimean Tatar movement (1930s–60s); and 3) the period of Mustafa Dzhemilev, who personified the new type of nationalist movement. Michael Guboglo and Svetlana Chervonnaia observe in their study that "the theorists and those involved in practical activities, the leaders and ideologists of the Crimean Tatar movement, divide its developmental history into three main periods: 1) 1956–64, the movement in the making; 2) 1964–69, the peak of its activities; 3) from 1970 on—the crisis of the movement." However, Guboglo and Chervonnaia argue that "we can talk about five, not three main stages. The two stages we can add to the above-mentioned ones are the periods before 1956 and after 1985." Guboglo and Chervonnaia, *Krimskotatarskoe natsionalnoe dvizhenie*, p. 98.

Tatars should have some special status in Crimea, but no special rights over other ethnic groups.[15]

Starting in April 1987, the CTNM began to conduct mass actions in Moscow with the intent of putting pressure on the Soviet central authorities and focusing the attention of the government and the Western public on its situation. During June and July 1987, about 1,000 Crimean Tatars picketed government buildings and went on hunger strikes in Moscow. At the same time mass demonstrations were organized in Uzbekistan and other places where large numbers of Crimean Tatars lived. In July 1987, the Council of Ministers of the Soviet Union established a state commission headed by Andrei Gromyko to study and make recommendations on the problem of the Crimean Tatars' return to Crimea. The local Crimean authorities set up ad hoc committees to look at the issue of residence permits and jobs for the Crimean Tatars. At the same time, preventive measures were taken to remove Crimean Tatars from Moscow, and diplomatic steps were also taken to put an end to the support of some Western embassies for these groups, on the grounds that this constituted intervention in the internal affairs of the Soviet Union.[16] Some Crimean Tatars had appealed to the U.S. Embassy for assistance, which refused Gromyko's request to stop these contacts. The Ministry of Foreign Affairs made an oral demarche to the U.S. Embassy which asserted that "some American diplomats were attempting to inspire nationalist demonstrations and to encourage some Crimean Tatars in Moscow to undertake antisocial actions."[17]

In the midst of these events, the Gorbachev government spelled out its position in a TASS statement on August 23, 1987, which said that although many Crimean Tatars had collaborated with the Nazis and committed atrocities, the punishment of the entire people, including Tatars who fought against the Germans, was not right and had been corrected with the rehabilitation of the Tatars in 1967. However, the statement continued, the population of the Crimean peninsula had changed greatly since the prewar period. In fact, it had doubled since then, and the Tatars had to see the question of restitution and historical justice in a "realistic way," taking into account the

---

15. Gumboglo and Chervonnaia give a more detailed analysis of the ideological contradictions within the Crimean Tatar movement. See *Krimskotatarskoe natsionalnoe dvizhenie*, pp. 171–262.

16. "In the Interest of Public Order," TASS, July 30, 1987.

17. TASS, July 30, 1987.

interests of all the peoples in Crimea. It also stated that the attempt to stir up conflict and to make appeals to outside (i.e., Western) opinion was not constructive, and it characterized the political aspirations of the CTNM as extremist.[18] A confidential resolution (No. 1476) passed by the Presidium of the Supreme Soviet of the Soviet Union on December 24, 1987, listed towns and villages in the Crimean oblast where a ban was imposed on giving any citizens rights of permanent residence, and where the local executive authorities could lay down the rules of the passport regime. These measures were cast in general terms, but were targeted at preventing the return of Crimean Tatars and posed a legal obstacle to their repatriation from other regions of the Soviet Union. By the late 1980s, although the total Crimean population had remained roughly constant at the level recorded in the 1979 census—2.5 million people—the nationality breakdown showed an increasing number of Crimean Tatars, balanced by the out-migration of other groups. According to the 1989 census, 67 percent of Crimea's population were ethnic Russians, 25 percent Ukrainians, and only 1.5 percent Crimean Tatars. The remaining 6.5 percent of the population included more than 110 nationalities, including Belarusans (2 percent) and Jews (.7 percent). The social and ethnic structure of the peninsula remains complicated.[19] According to the 1989 census, over 270,000 Crimean Tatars were living on the territory of the Soviet Union, of whom only 38,400 officially resided on the Crimean peninsula. In the mid-1990s, an estimated 350,000 Crimean Tatars reside on the territory of the former Soviet Union.[20]

A government commission on the Crimean Tatar problem was established in Moscow on July 12, 1989, to address the question of how to help Crimean Tatars return home. It achieved little. During 1990 and in the first half of 1991, Crimean Tatar organizations attempted to consolidate their presence on the peninsula by legal

---

18. TASS, August 23, 1987.

19. *National Composition of the Population of the Soviet Union According to Data from the 1989 Census* (Moscow: Report of the Soviet Union State Statistics Committee, 1991), p. 82.

20. "The Crimea: Will the Return Take Place? An Interview with a Member of the Soviet Union Supreme Soviet Commission on the Crimean Tatar Problem," *Sobesednik*, No. 40 (September 1989), p. 13. Some sources say that there are many more Crimean Tatars living on the territory of the Soviet Union. There is no official data for Crimean Tatars living in Crimea in the mid-1990s. According to figures supplied by Mustafa Dzhemilev, Chairman of the Majlis, in 1995, 250,000 people could have returned to Crimea. "Third Power of the Crimea," *Morning of Russia*, No. 46–47 (1994), p. 10.

means such as applying for *propiskas*, but they encountered opposition from the local administration. Meanwhile, at the end of 1990, a referendum held in Crimea supported the conversion of the Crimean oblast into an autonomous socialist republic within the Ukrainian SSR. This endorsement, which represented a return to the status Crimea had previously held as part of the RSFSR, was made during a period when all internal entities were striving to improve their legal status once the breakup of the Soviet Union seemed likely. This newly proclaimed autonomy was not much help to the Crimean Tatars, however; rather, it lent support to the Russian population's efforts to regain some autonomy from Ukraine. There was no mention of reinstituting Crimean Tatar as one of the official languages.

On August 6, 1991, the Soviet Council of Ministers adopted a resolution, "On the Organized Return of Crimean Tatars to the Crimean ASSR and Guarantees of Their Resettlement," and a draft of the government return program was prepared. According to a report presented by the State Commission of the Soviet Union, 350,000 Soviet citizens claimed to be Crimean Tatars. By mid-1991, about 135,000 Crimean Tatars had resettled in the Crimean Autonomous Republic, most of them having returned during the preceding two years. By September 1993, 260,000 Crimean Tatars had returned, and the forecast was that by 1995 a total of 350,000 would have resettled on the peninsula.[21] The Soviet government approved a resettlement plan that allotted Tatars strips of land on which to build cottages, but the resources allocated were insufficient. The unregulated return of the Crimean Tatars to the peninsula created acute economic problems with respect to the supply of food and manufactured goods, housing, health care, and education, all of which were still provided by the state. At this point, Crimean Tatars began to seize land and buildings in formerly Tatar towns, which created the threat of clashes with local authorities and local populations whose lands were being illegally occupied. Many of the Soviet Union Council of Ministers' decisions were simply ignored by the local authorities, who lacked resources and resisted the implemention of such programs.[22]

Other peoples who had been deported from Crimea in the 1940s also sought the legal right to return, including Germans, Bulgarians,

---

21. Wilson, "The Crimean Tatars," p. 37.
22. The documentary side of the Crimean Tatar people's homecoming is described in detail in *Belaia Kniga natsionalnogo dvizhenia Krimskikh Tatar* (The White Book of the Crimean Tatar National Movement) (Simferopol: 1991).

Greeks, Armenians, Crimeans, and Karaims. The Supreme Soviet of the Crimean Republic adopted a resolution containing some practical measures for the organized return of these groups and the restoration of their rights on the same terms as the Crimean Tatars.

In June 1991, the first *Kurultai* was convened.[23] Elections had been held in every region of the Soviet Union inhabited by Crimean Tatars. The 280 elected delegates raised the issues of the return of the Tatars to their homeland and the restoration of their statehood. The *Kurultai* elected a national parliament, the Majlis. The establishment of a parallel power structure in Crimea made the other ethnic groups apprehensive. The *Kurultai* issued a Declaration on the National Sovereignty of the Crimean-Tatar People which stated that "Crimea is the national territory of the Crimean Tatars, who have an exclusive right to self-determination in this region."[24] Accordingly, the *Kurultai* announced that the land and natural resources (including health resorts) on the peninsula constituted the national property of the Crimean Tatars and could not be used without their consent. The other inhabitants of Crimea were referred to as "invaders" and "colonialists."[25] The Majlis was authorized to create local councils of national self-government and corresponding committees. To finance such political activities, a national fund for Crimea was created.[26] On July 29, 1991, a month after the *Kurultai* met, the Supreme Soviet of the Crimean Republic announced that the decisions of the *Kurultai* were illegal and violated the constitutions of the Soviet Union and Ukraine. It singled out in particular the decrees proclaiming that Crimea was a Crimean Tatar national territory with all attributes of a state; asserting that Crimean Tatars have exclusive property rights to the land and natural resources of the peninsula; and creating parallel power structures and administrative institutions.

The situation in Crimea was aggravated by the disintegration of the entire political system of the Soviet Union following the unsuccessful coup attempt in Moscow in August 1991. On August 24, Ukraine adopted an act proclaiming Ukraine's independence, and on August

---

23. "On the Eve of the Crimean Tatar Congress," Ukrinform-TASS, June 24, 1991.

24. "The Declaration of the Crimean Tatar People's National Sovereignty," in Guboglo and Chervonnaia, *Krimskotatarskoe natsionalnoe dvizhenie*, Vol. 2, p. 110.

25. "The Crimean Tatar Congress," Ukrinform-TASS, June 26, 1991.

26. The Charter of the Crimea Fund says that it is "designed to put the decisions of the Crimean Tatar *Kurultai* and its representative body, the Majlis, into practice.

29, the Presidium of the Ukrainian Supreme Soviet announced that Ukraine had become an independent democratic state. The Ukrainian Supreme Soviet also pledged that the independence of Ukraine would never result in the infringement of any nationality's rights and that Ukraine, as an independent democratic state adhering to the generally recognized rules and principles of international law, would secure equal political, economic, and social rights for every citizen as well as full freedom for all national languages and cultural development.[27] At that time 52 million people were living in Ukraine, including Russians, Jews, Belarusans, Moldavians, Poles, Bulgarians, Hungarians, Crimean Tatars, Romanians, Greeks, and Gagauz.

In response to this action, a special session of the Supreme Soviet of the Crimean Republic on September 5, 1991, issued a "Declaration of Crimean State Sovereignty." Although this document confirmed that Crimea remained an integral part of Ukraine, its authors emphasized the supremacy, independence, integrity, and indivisibility of the Crimean Republic. Moreover, it declared that the people of Crimea had the exclusive right to possess, use, and dispose of the land, mineral wealth, airspace, water, and natural resources within the republic's territory and in its continental shelf. The declaration contained a firm guarantee that all inhabitants of Crimea, irrespective of their nationality, political views, and religion, would have equal rights.[28]

At this point then, there were three active claimants to legitimate power over Crimea: the Ukrainian authorities, the Crimean Republic authorities, and the Crimean Tatar groups. The first legislation passed by the self-proclaimed Crimean Republic was adopted on September 5, 1991, and declared that both state-owned property and CPSU property located on the peninsula's territory belonged to the Crimean Republic. This development stimulated greater activity among those who wanted the 1954 Act of Transfer of Crimea from the Russian Federation to Ukraine declared illegal. Revoking this transfer

---

For that purpose the Crimea Fund finds and uses the material means for the realization of social-political, economic, and cultural programs related to the Crimean Tatar people's homecoming and the restoration of their rights." See Guboglo and Chervonnaia, *Krimskotatarskoe natsionalnoe dvizhenie*, Vol. 2, p. 140.

27. "Appeal to the People," Ukrinform-TASS, August 29, 1991.

28. "The Decision of the Special Session of the Supreme Soviet of Crimea," Ukrinform-TASS, September 5, 1991.

became the main goal of the 20th of January Movement, which convened its Constituent Conference in Simferopol on October 7, 1991.[29]
This movement openly advocated the preservation of the Soviet
Union, with Crimea itelf an SSR rather than part of the Ukrainian
SSR. Actually there were two closely related positions held by the
Slavic population of Crimea: some wanted Crimean independence
and stronger links with Russia, whereas others wanted reunification
with Russia. The goals of the pro-independence and the pro-unionist
factions were not far apart. However, one must bear in mind that official Russian policy supported the territorial integrity of Ukraine. The
20th of January Movement demanded an all-Crimean referendum on
the issue of Crimea's secession from the independent Ukrainian state.
The Presidium of the Crimean Supreme Soviet also issued a statement that the 1954 Transfer Act had been taken with absolutely no
consideration for the will of the people. With these actions, a new
group claiming legitimacy was added to the political game in
Crimea, the Russian element.

At the same time, still another political force, the Cossacks, was
active in Crimea. The Cossacks also advocated the reunification of
Crimea with Russia, since their basic creed was to support "Great
Russia." In January 1992, a Constituent Assembly, a so-called
Cossack krug, of the Azov-Black Sea Cossack Union was convened in
Simferopol in which the Don, Zaporozhian, Uralian, and Terian
Cossacks were represented. The delegates adopted the "Regulations
and Code of Cossack Honor," and a well-known Crimean entrepre-
neur, Sergei Potamanov, was elected as their *ataman* (leader). It is
notable that Yuri Meshkov, the leader of the Crimean Republican
movement and the future president of the Crimean republic, was
elected the ataman of the Crimean section of the Don Cossacks.
Although this section did not become an influential political force in
Crimea, it played a clear role in the movement for the reunification of
Crimea with Russia.[30]

---

29. The movement was named after the referendum of January 20, 1991, when
most of the peninsula's inhabitants voted to restore the Crimean Autonomous
Republic as a subject of the Soviet Union.

30. This section was reorganized into the Crimean Cossack Circle, which first
met on November 27, 1994, in Simferopol. If a conflict situation were to arise in
Crimea, the Cossack Circle intended to take a neutral position. This organization
considered its immediate task to secure the passage of a law in Crimea on the
rehabilitation and the status of the Cossacks.

The Conflict after the Collapse of the Soviet Union

THE FIRST YEARS OF INDEPENDENCE

On May 5, 1992, the Supreme Soviet of the Crimean Republic passed the Act of the Crimean Republic's Independence, which proclaimed the establishment of a sovereign state covering the entire Crimean peninsula, subject to a popular referendum.[31] The Crimean Constitution, adopted the following day, declared that the Republic of Crimea was an integral part of Ukraine and that relations between them were to be maintained on the basis of appropriate treaties and agreements. These provisions meant that the Crimean Republic was demanding the de facto federalization of Ukraine, which, not surprisingly, Ukraine refused to accept.[32] Nor did these developments suit the Crimean Tatar Majlis, headed by Mustafa Dzhemilev. Dzhemilev considered the separatist policy pursued by the Crimean administration to be one of the obstacles to the return of the Crimean Tatars to the peninsula, and he therefore declared that he would never accept the results of any referendum that ignored the issue of the Crimean Tatars' exclusive right to self-determination.[33] Dzhemilev insisted on the creation of a "national-territorial formation," i.e., an autonomous region, on the peninsula that would be an integral part of Ukraine. He also sought to gain general recognition of the Majlis as the only representative body of the Crimean Tatar people.[34]

The OCNM set an ambitious agenda for itself. Its objectives included: 1) the completion of the return of the Crimean Tatars to their national homeland under the auspices of the Ukrainian state authorities on the basis of the appropriate state programs and international treaties; 2) the settlement of the returning Tatars in the regions of the peninsula they had traditionally inhabited, so as to assure that they again constituted a majority in those regions (i.e., a "compact" settlement so that they could re-create the Crimean Tatar

---

31.   The Act was to enter into force after its approval by the all-Crimean referendum scheduled for August 2, 1992, which would pose the following two questions: "Are you in favor of an independent Crimea in alliance with other states?" and "Do you approve the Act of the Crimean Republic's Independence?"

32.   "The Act of Crimean State Sovereignty is Adopted," Ukrinform-TASS, May 5, 1992.

33.   The Majlis warned that the Tatar movement would find an effective means to protect this right.

34.   "Crimean Tatars Mark a Day of National Trauma in the Crimea," Ukrinform-TASS, May 18, 1992.

communities that were destroyed); 3) the restoration of national statehood for the Crimean Tatar people that would be no less than that of the Crimean Autonomous Republic of 1921–44; and 4) material compensation for the losses incurred by the Crimean Tatars since 1944, as well as for their contribution to the economy of the Soviet republics to which they had been deported. According to this approach, the restoration of statehood for the Crimean people meant that the Crimean Constitution should offer firm guarantees that the core of the Crimean Tatar nation would be given a wide scope for national development, that their national territory would be regarded as indivisible, that their rights within this territory would be properly secured, and that Crimean Tatars would be represented in every structure of the legislative, executive, and judicial branches of power in Crimea as well as in Ukraine. In line with these demands, the OCNM demanded the right to amend the Ukrainian and the Crimean Constitutions and to be allotted 36 percent of the seats in the unicameral Crimean Parliament.

This position received some support from the Ukrainian central authorities, who were constantly trying to play the "Tatar card" in their struggle against the pro-Russian Crimean separatists. The most important concern of the authorities in Kiev was the preservation of Crimea as part of the Ukrainian state. The return of the Crimean Tatars to the peninsula and their autonomous formation of economic and political structures were secondary questions. After the declaration of Ukrainian independence, the new government began to understand that factions in Crimea held incompatible political goals: pro-Russian Crimean separatism and Crimean Tatar self-determination. The situation of parallel authority, which arose in the second half of 1991 as a result of the formation of the Majlis, created an opportunity for the Ukrainian authorities to use Crimean Tatar political structures to restrain pro-Russian separatism. Kiev did not formally recognize the legal authority of the Majlis, but strengthened its contacts in the wake of the pro-Russian separatist movement in Crimea.[35] At the same time Kiev completely opposed any attempts to federalize the Ukrainian state, and prospects for the creation of a Crimean Tatar national state, in Crimea, even within Ukraine, were slim. The law on national minorities debated at the beginning of 1992

---

35. This was particularly true, for example, in May 1992, at the time of the Declaration of the Independence of Crimea, and in April 1994, during the rising constitutional crisis in Crimea.

in the Ukrainian Parliament did not provide a special status or special rights for the Crimean Tatars in Crimea to the degree that the
Majlis and OCNM were demanding. Moreover, political moves by
the Kravchuk government were designed to defeat serious separatist
efforts.[36]

Kiev exploited the conflict emerging between the legislative and
executive branches of the local Crimean authorities and between
groups headed by the chairman of the Crimean Supreme Soviet,
Nicholas Bagrov, and the head of the Crimean government, Vitaly
Kurashik. The main struggle was over which body would play the
dominant role in the privatization of former state property. In
exchange for support from Kiev, Bagrov secured the passage of a
decision by the Supreme Soviet of Crimea to postpone the referendum and the date on which the Crimean Constitution would go into
effect. In return, Ukrainian President Leonid Kravchuk removed
Kurashik from his post and agreed to the introduction of the institution of a presidency in Crimea. The understanding was that Bagrov,
who was loyal to Kiev, should become the president of Crimea. This
step prompted the pro-independence and pro-Russian forces—the
Republican Movement of Crimea, the movement of the Crimean electorate for an independent Crimea, and the 20th of January
Movement—to demand legal proceedings against Bagrov and other
leaders of the Crimean Supreme Soviet, on charges of breaking the
referendum law. At the same time, the Russian Parliament weighed
in on behalf of the separatists by passing a resolution on the uncon-
stitutionality of the transfer of Crimea from Russia to Ukraine.

In May 1992, the Russian Supreme Soviet conducted several special sessions on Crimea, and made an appeal to the Ukrainian parliament to "refrain from any actions directed toward the suppression of
the free expression of the Crimean population, which has in accordance with international norms the full right to determine its own
destiny."[37] The Ukrainian authorities considered this action "an
attempt to apply political pressure, and an act of political blackmail

---

36. The Organization of the Crimean Tatar National Movement was the most
influential of the three Tatar political groupings (the moderate CTNM and the
reestablished radical nationalist Milly Firka are the others). The OCNM is the
equivalent of an organized political party, has 600–800 members, and overlaps
substantially with the leadership of the Majlis. Wilson, "The Crimean Tatars," p.
29. See also *RFE/RL Research Report*, Vol. 2, No. 45 (November 12, 1993), pp. 6–8.

37. "Statement of the Supreme Soviet of Russia to the Supreme Soviet of
Ukraine," TASS, May 23, 1992.

toward Ukraine." The Ukrainian Supreme Soviet announced that it "rejected the attempt of the Russian Parliament to carry out a policy of great-power chauvinism toward Ukraine" and also rejected "its groundless demands to settle the question of Crimea through inter-governmental negotiations between Russia and Ukraine."[38] Thus, by the middle of 1992, conditions were ripe for open clashes between the Crimean Tatars (operating through the Majlis) and Ukrainian nationalists on the one hand, and the pro-Russian separatists in the Crimean Supreme Soviet on the other. Ukraine and Russia had their own agendas in this dispute, and offered varying degrees of support to the respective sides in the conflict depending on their domestic political situation at the moment.

A "test of strength" between the Crimean Tatars and the Crimean Republic began on October 2, 1992, when a serious clash erupted on a state agricultural enterprise where groups of recently arrived Crimean Tatars had set up an encampment. The local authorities issued an order to tear down the illegal Tatar constructions and to clear the entire piece of land. Casualties from the clash that followed included 24 militiamen, 6 locals, and 26 Crimean Tatars.[39] On October 5, 1992, the Tatar protesters attempted to block the traffic on the roads to Simferopol while more than 1,000 people picketed the Supreme Soviet and the office of the public prosecutor of the Republic. The Presidium of the Majlis warned that it would take measures to pro-tect Crimean Tatar settlements, and Tatar political organizations were alerted. The Majlis had formed its own paramilitary groups, under the guise of construction gangs. On October 6, several thousand peo-ple armed with homemade weapons attempted to seize the Crimean Supreme Soviet building, which was guarded by the local militia. Massive disorder followed, during which 114 officials and 31 Tatars were injured and the Supreme Soviet building sustained damage estimated at two million rubles. The Majlis ordered a full mobiliza-tion of its followers and the creation of "self-defense groups." The Crimean Supreme Soviet adopted a resolution on October 8, 1992, declaring the actions initiated by the Majlis, its local sections, and the OCNM to be illegal and authorizing Republic law enforcement agen-cies to stop them.[40]

---

38. "The Supreme Soviet of Ukraine Passes a Resolution Related to the Decision of the Supreme Soviet of Russia on the Question of Crimea," Ukrinform-TASS, June 3, 1992.

39. "The Clash in Crimea," Ukrinform-TASS, October 2, 1992.

40. "The Special Session of the Crimean Parliament," TASS, October 8, 1992.

After this clash, the Crimean Tatar political organizations were not interested in searching for a workable political compromise. They had staked out an extreme nationalist position, relying on the support of the Ukrainian central authorities and the Ukrainian radical nationalist parties, which they considered the lesser of two political evils and the most plausible means of combating the pro-Russian majority. But the economic and political crisis in Ukraine itself turned out to be so grave that Ukraine failed to provide strong support for the Tatars. The Crimean Republic authorities, still oriented toward Russia, were suspicious of the pro-Ukrainian inclinations of the Crimean Tatar leaders, and consequently made every effort to prevent the Tatars from gaining stronger influence in the governing structures of the Crimean Republic.

KRAVCHUK AND MESHKOV

The Crimean struggle was taking place in the context of a troubled Ukrainian political and economic scene. Ukraine is divided into 24 administrative districts, with a total population of 51,940,000 people, 73 percent of whom are Ukrainians, 22 percent Russians, 1 percent Jews, and the remaining 4 percent comprised of mixed nationalities. Since the breakup of the Soviet Union, the economic situation in Ukraine has declined disastrously. The Ukrainian national currency essentially collapsed after its value depreciated from 6,000 *karbovanyets* to the dollar in mid-August 1993, to 19,000 by early September. The monthly inflation rate rose to 50 percent in real terms, and by the fall of 1993, hyperinflation had begun. Most of Ukraine's vital energy supplies are imported. Therefore, when Russia increased its gas and oil prices to world market levels, the impact on Ukraine's economy was profound. Ukraine failed to prepare itself for these drastic changes and to adapt once they occurred. Ukraine's oil-processing enterprises, which had previously refined Russian petroleum and exported finished products back to Russia, began to close because of acute resource shortages. In general, production fell in Ukraine at a much higher rate than in Russia. Between the first quarter of 1991 and the first quarter of 1992, Ukraine's gross domestic product declined by 20 percent; in the first quarter of 1993, by an additional 10 percent; and by the first quarter of 1994, it was still declining at an annual rate of 10 percent. In concrete terms, these trends translated into the general impoverishment of the entire population of Ukraine.

After some initial success, Ukrainian nationalist movements began to experience internal difficulties over their divergent views on the aims, tactics, and terms of creating their own institutions of state power and administration. One major problem was the emerging conflict between notions of individual freedom and ethnic loyalty. All ethnic nationalist movements restrict the freedom of individuals in the name of the sacred rights of the nation. Moreover, the adherence of ethnic nationalists to the principles of a national language and a national territory allows little room for the free existence of other national groups. Tension between these two norms developed against a background of a very corrupt privatization process, a drastic decline in living standards, and growing disillusionment with the new politics among the populace. Politically, eastern Ukraine remained pro-Russian, thereby creating a cleavage with Ukrainian nationalists in western Ukraine.[41] The Ukrainian economy became extremely politicized in the struggle over the redistribution of state property, and most workers and engineers in the eastern industrial regions of Ukraine were perceived by Ukrainian nationalists as Russian-speaking "outsiders." The Donetsk coal basin and the Kharkov industrial district, the location of Ukraine's largest productive enterprises—coal mining and machine-building—experienced the deepest economic decline. Attempts in September 1993 by Ukrainian President Leonid Kravchuk and Russian President Boris Yeltsin to resolve outstanding differences between Ukraine and Russia caused the next Russophobic outburst in western Ukraine. Ultranationalists, including Ukrainian People's Deputies at all levels, began to blame the Russian-speaking population of Ukraine for the violent clashes and the continued conflict in Crimea.[42] The Ukrainian

---

41. Other Ukrainian political forces include the following: centrist forces are represented by electoral blocs created by former parliamentary and governmental leaders headed by Vladimir Grinev and Leonid Kuchma on the one hand, and by the Lvov "New Wave" Association headed by Yukhnovsky on the other. The leftist bloc that exerts the strongest influence in the eastern industrial Russian-speaking regions includes Socialists, Agrarians, and Communists who are primarily Russian speakers who want closer links with Russia. The ultranationalist parties and organizations that exert the strongest influence in western Ukraine include the Social-Nationalist Party, headed by Yuri Krivoruchko; the Ukrainian Self-Defense National Forces, headed by Oleg Vitovich; the Ukrainian National Assembly; and the Ukrainian Conservative Republican Party, headed by Ivan Khmara. The nationalist parties and organizations that are influential in central Ukraine as well are Rukh, the main opposition party, headed by Vyacheslav Chornovil; and the Congress of National Democratic Forces and the Ukrainian Republican Party, which form the so-called National Democratic Bloc, headed by Vyacheslav Chornovil and Levko Lukjanenko.

42. "The Western Ukraine: Nationalists Are Fomenting an Anti-Russian Mood and Breaking Glass in Russian Schools," ITAR-TASS, September 15, 1993. On

Officers Alliance, a Lvov-based nationalist organization, joined forces with the Special Committee on Saving the National and State Honor—an organization known for its radical views—to call for the resignation of the Ukrainian Supreme Soviet and President Kravchuk. This Special Committee opposed signing an economic treaty with Russia and, in the event of its ratification, advocated a continuous struggle against Russian hegemony by any means, including constitutional actions and armed resistance.[43]

In Crimea, Ukrainian nationalists did not play a very important role in local politics because of their small numbers and weak base of support. Nonetheless, the Crimean Tatar question occupied Ukrainian nationalists as much as their opposition to pro-Russian separatism. As a result, various Ukrainian nationalist organizations, including the Congress of National Democratic Forces of Ukraine and the neofascist Ukrainian National Assembly, supported strong links with the Majlis and OCNM, viewing them as natural allies in the struggle against Russian influence.

Elections to the Ukrainian Supreme Soviet took place in March–April 1994 and exposed a striking divergence of views on the republic's future. The most significant split was between the eastern and western regions. In the first round of elections, most of the population in the Russian-speaking industrial east voted for Communists and Socialists as well as for industrialists and entrepreneurs. Radical Ukrainian nationalist organizations of all hues suffered an overwhelming defeat in this important region. Only a handful of the hundreds of nationalist candidates in the east managed to survive the first round of elections, and in the final round, nationalists did not win a single seat in eastern Ukraine. Of the 14 deputies elected in the Donetsk and Lugansky oblasts, 11 represented the Communist Party of Ukraine.[44] Out of a total of 450 seats in parliament, Rukh (the

---

September 15, 1993, reprisals against Russians were called for by participants in the so-called Lvov "veche" who proclaimed that groups of vigilantes would be created and headed by Yuri Krivoruchko, one of the leaders of the Ukrainian Social-Nationalist Party. After the meeting, large numbers of "stormtroopers" smashed signboards and shop windows in Lvov, resulting in clashes with the local police.

43. "The Scandal Among the Ukrainian Officers," ITAR-TASS, September 18, 1993.

44. "The New Ukrainian Parliament Will Be Born Only in April," ITAR-TASS, March 31, 1994. Moreover, on March 27, 1994, the Regional Soviets of Donetsk and Lugansk conducted a local consultative referendum in spite of a ban imposed by the Ukrainian central authorities. The citizens were asked whether they agreed

largest nationalist political movement) won 38, and the radical nationalists from the Ukrainian National Assembly (UNA) and Ukrainian
Peoples' Self-Defense (UPSD)—the military terrorist branch of the
UNA—gained only two seats, and all of the deputies were elected by
western constituencies.[45] Thus a significant redistribution of political
forces took place in Ukraine, demonstrating a sharp decline in the
influence of the nationalist *nomenklatura* headed by Leonid Kravchuk
and the rise of centrist and pro-Russian forces in parliament.

The conflict between the Crimean Tatars and the Crimean
Republic's authorities was closely intertwined with these develop-
ments and with issues concerning the internal structure of Ukraine as
well as with the development of Crimean-Russian relations.
Following a special congress in January 1993, the All-Crimean
Electoral Movement elected a new leadership to address the immediate task of consolidating the "patriotic" forces of the republic—i.e.,
those who supported independence and a pro-Russian orientation.
The leaders of the movement demanded that the Crimean Supreme
Soviet lift the 1992 moratorium on the referendum on independence.
An ultimatum was issued insisting that the referendum be held, or
else the All-Crimean Electoral Movement would force the resignation
of the Supreme Soviet and advocate limiting the Ukrainian armed
forces deployed on Crimean territory, the withdrawal of Ukrainian
National Guard units, and a ban on army intervention in any conflict
on the peninsula.

Supporters of the Crimean Republican Movement, which included
the Russian Party and the Crimean Alliance of Russian Officers, had,
since the beginning of 1993, exerted an increasingly strong influence
on the political scene. This movement called for closer relations
between Russia and Crimea, and its members were generally critical

---

that 1) Russian and Ukrainian should both be regarded as national languages; 2)
the Russian language should be made the language of business in the Russian-
speaking Donbass region; and 3) Ukraine should become a full-fledged member
of the Commonwealth of Independent States (CIS) and the CIS interparliamen-
tary assembly. In both industrial regions about 90 percent of those who participated in the plebiscite gave an affirmative answer to all three questions ("The
Donbass Defines Itself in the Elections," ITAR-TASS, March 29, 1994). Of 337
newly elected deputies to the Ukrainian Supreme Soviet (in the remaining 113 districts, the balloting was invalidated and new elections were ordered), 86 were
Communists, 14 were Socialists, and 18 represented the Peasant Party. "Work
Begins in Kiev on the First Session of the Supreme Soviet of Ukraine," ITAR-TASS,
May 11, 1994).

45. Whereas the UNA is a registered political party, the UPSD is not formally
registered as a political organization but is nevertheless very active.

of the Crimean Parliament, accusing it of blocking the constitutionally proclaimed legal status of Crimea. For instance, the Russian Party demanded that the referendum on Crimean independence should be held and insisted that Russian jurisdiction over Sebastopol and the Black Sea Fleet should be maintained. On May 21, 1993, the Crimean Republican Party sent an open letter to the presidents of Russia and Ukraine urging them, in negotiating the draft Union Treaty, to recognize the results of the referendum held in Crimea on January 20, 1991, that endorsed the establishment of the Crimean Republic as an independent entity.

Laws governing the election of the Crimean president and Parliament were enacted in September 1993, which created great discontent among the Crimean Tatars because there was no provision guaranteeing them a fixed quota of twenty seats in parliament. The Crimean Tatars organized a rally near the parliament building while the Supreme Soviet was still in session, demanding that the deputies institute this quota. The Majlis threatened to take "extraordinary" actions against the Crimean authorities, and the Crimean Tatars attempted to block railway traffic in several regions of Crimea. As a result, the Crimean Supreme Soviet adopted amendments that provided special quotas for the representatives of deported peoples. National electoral districts were created for previously deported Armenians, Bulgarians, Greeks, and Germans, in which each group would elect one member of parliament. Multi-member voting districts were created for the Crimean Tatars, which gave the Tatars fourteen seats in the new parliament, and their national parties gained the right to elect nominees representing these districts from party lists.

Nevertheless, leaders of the Crimean Tatar national movement opposed the law on presidential elections and the introduction of a Crimean presidency because they would create more obstacles to the achievement of "national territorial statehood" for the Crimean Tatars. In the meantime, a power struggle had arisen among the Crimean Tatar political organizations over leadership of the movement. In November 1993, Yuri Osmanov, the well-known leader of the CTNM, was murdered. The other CTNM leaders regarded his assassination as an effort by "outside forces" to provoke a civil war among the Crimean Tatars and to help the "national traitors"—i.e., supporters of the presidential and parliamentary institutions—in the forthcoming Crimean parliamentary elections. The election campaign in Crimea was accompanied by a series of apparently uncoordinated attempts upon the lives of Crimean politicians and journalists, illustrating the general political destabilization throughout the peninsula. An attempt was made on the life of Yuri Meshkov, the presidential candidate of the Crimean Republican Party. The Black Sea Press Center chief and presidential nominee Andrei Lazebnikov was assassinated, and there was a terrorist assault on Eksander Memetov, the economic adviser to the chairman of the Crimean Supreme Soviet.

In the January 16, 1994, Crimean presidential elections, six candidates were on the ballot. Two ran as independent candidates: Nicholas Bagrov, Chairman of the Supreme Soviet of the Crimean Republic, and Vladimir Verkoshansky, a Crimean entrepreneur. The others ran on party tickets: Leonid Grach, leader of the Crimean Communist Party; Yuri Meshkov, leader of the Crimean Republican Party and the Crimean Republican Movement; Ivan Ermakov, representative of the Ukrainian president in Sebastopol; and Sergei Shuvainikov, Chairman of the Russian Party. About 77 percent of all adult residents of Crimea went to the polls, and 38.5 percent of them cast their votes for Yuri Meshkov.[46] Meshkov's political program was openly pro-Russian and included the following proposals: 1) that the Black Sea Fleet would remain in Russia's possession; 2) independence for the Crimean Republic that would allow Crimea to maintain many ties with Ukraine but independently manage its economic relations with Russia; 3) a referendum on the status of Crimea; and 4) that residents of Crimea would have the right to dual Russian and Ukrainian citizenship. Meshkov went on to sweep the second round of the elections on January 30, 1994, receiving 72.9 percent of the 1,427,419 votes cast.[47] The leaders of the Majlis and the Crimean Tatar political organizations did not welcome this outcome. Mustafa Dzhemilev announced that Meshkov would not be recognized as the Crimean president unless he agreed to abide by the special quotas for the Crimean Tatar representatives in the Crimean Parliament outlined in the September 1993 election law. This Meshkov refused to do. The western Ukrainian nationalist parties also considered Meshkov's election an extremely negative development since they suspected that

---

46. Ukrinform-TASS, January 17, 1994. Another 17.5 percent voted for Bagrov. Shuvainikov and Grach received somewhat fewer votes. Ermakov polled a little more than 6 percent, and Verkoshanski received about 1 percent. According to the Election Law, two of the six were to participate in a run-off election: Yuri Meshkov and Nicholas Bagrov.

47. "Results of the Presidential Elections in Crimea," ITAR-TASS, January 31, 1994.

the Crimean presidential elections marked the beginning of a de facto federalization of Ukraine. The Ukrainian Supreme Soviet quickly granted President Kravchuk the power to annul any decision taken by the Crimean leader if it ran counter to the Constitution or the laws of Ukraine.

In response to this action, the new Crimean president issued a decree that a public opinion poll should be conducted as a substitute for the referendum on Crimean state sovereignty. The poll, which was conducted on March 24, 1994, posed three questions:

(1) Are you in favor of restoring the Constitution of the Republic of Crimea of May 6, 1992, which determines that Crimean-Ukrainian relations are to be based upon treaties and agreements [rather than laws enacted in Kiev]?[48]

(2) Do you wish to restore the provision of the Crimean Constitution of May 6, 1992, that gives the Crimean people the right to dual citizenship?

(3) Do you wish to give the decrees of the Crimean president on issues not yet governed by republican legislation the status of laws?

Of Crimea's 1,087,000 inhabitants, 1,081,000 participated in this poll: 78.4 percent supported the idea of a negotiated relationship between Crimea and Ukraine; 82.8 percent were in favor of dual citizenship; and 77.9 percent agreed that any decree issued by the Crimean president on problems still not covered by Crimean legislation should acquire the force of law.[49]

The results of the contemporaneous elections for the ninety-six-member Crimean Parliament confirmed the presidential election

---

48. On May 6, 1992, the Crimean Parliament had voted to declare Crimea's independence from Ukraine, subject to a referendum that was scheduled for August of that year. A week later, on May 13, 1992, the Ukrainian Parliament declared the Crimean Parliament's action unconstitutional and insisted that the declaration of independence be annulled by the Crimean Parliament itself by May 20, 1992. On the deadline, the Crimean Parliament annulled its resolution on independence but stopped short of annulling the actual declaration of Crimean independence. In July 1992, the Crimean parliament put off indefinitely the date of the referendum on the Crimean declaration of independence and the adoption of the Crimean Constitution. The issue returned to the political forefront through Meshkov's efforts. See "No Possibility for Statehood," *Foreign Broadcast Information Service* (hereafter FBIS) SOV-92-83, May 6, 1992, p. 46; and "Chronology of Events in Crimea," *RFE/RL Research Report*, Vol. 3, No. 19 (May 13, 1994), p. 28.

49. Interfax, March 28, 1994.

returns and showed that most Crimean citizens—67 percent—supported the program of the Russia bloc[50] which had much in common with Meshkov's policies. Thus Meshkov's political course was legitimized by three separate means: the public opinion poll, the presidential elections, and the parliamentary elections. The Ukrainian and Tatar nationalists had suffered a crushing defeat. They insisted that Meshkov and his administration, together with the newly elected Supreme Soviet, would be unable to maintain peace and stability on the Crimean peninsula and would instead aggravate the political and economic situation.

Immediately following the Crimean elections, Kiev took a number of measures that were precursors to declaring a state of emergency on the peninsula and introducing direct rule by the Ukrainian president. The Ukrainian military presence in Crimea was built up, not only to put pressure on the Crimean authorities, but also to lay the groundwork for possible further actions. As a result, Crimea became the most militarized zone of Europe after Bosnia,[51] further destabilizing the political situation on the peninsula. Kiev also took administrative steps to increase its control over developments in Crimea, such as creating the position of representative of the Ukrainian president to Crimea to oversee the situation and provide information to Kiev.[52] In response, during a televised address, Meshkov accused President Kravchuk of attempting to destabilize Crimea.[53]

Presidential elections in Ukraine were scheduled for June 1994. As the campaign progressed, Kravchuk lost the support of most voters because of Ukraine's economic collapse. In attempting to recoup some of these losses, Kravchuk began to champion Ukrainian independence and sovereignty while branding his opponents as advocates of a return to the old communist order. By contrast, Kravchuk's opponent, Leonid Kuchma, condemned the economic and political course that had been pursued in Ukraine since independence and had isolated the country from other former Soviet republics—especially Russia—and pushed it to the brink of disaster.

---

50. "Some Repeated Elections to be Held" and "Further on Results," in *FBIS SOV-94-060*, March 29, 1994, p. 34.

51. In addition to the Black Sea Fleet and the Ukrainian Navy, 50,000 Ukrainian soldiers and officers of the Ukrainian Army were deployed on the peninsula.

52. One of the losing candidates in the Crimean presidential elections, Ivan Ermakov, became the first representative of the Ukrainian president in Crimea.

53. ITAR-TASS, April 6, 1994.

In early April, high-ranking Ukrainian military officers began to take vigorous measures in Crimea. Without coordinating their actions with the Crimean authorities and without notifying the appropriate bodies, Ukrainian Defense Minister Radetsky, Chief of the Ukrainian Armed Forces Intelligence Agency Major General Vegunnikov, Chief of Staff of the Ukrainian National Guard Major General Mokhov, and others all arrived in Crimea. At the same time, units of the Ukrainian special forces were reported to have been transported to Crimea.[54] The situation was aggravated by the fact that Meshkov was on a working visit to Cyprus and could not come back to Simferopol because the air corridor was unexpectedly blocked by Turkish authorities. The representative of the Crimean president called the Ukrainian president's representative and protested the illegal actions of the Ukrainian officials who had arrived in Crimea. The object of all these activities seemed to be to create a disturbance in Crimea in order to postpone the second round of the 1994 elections, which threatened to remove Kravchuk and his associates from power.[55] The elections went forward as scheduled, with a turnout of 52 percent.[56]

On May 20, 1994, in President Meshkov's absence, the Crimean Parliament adopted a law on the restoration of the Crimean Constitution of May 6, 1992. On the following day, under the provisions of the restored Constitution, the Crimean Parliament suspended a number of decrees of the Ukrainian president, including those dealing with the activities of the Ukrainian Central Security Office and the Central Office of the Ministry of Internal Affairs in Crimea.

President Kravchuk treated the Crimean Parliament's actions as an attempt to violate the territorial integrity of Ukraine contrary to the rules of international law, and as a threat to relations between Ukraine and one of its integral parts. Ukrainian Foreign Minister Anatoly Zlenko sent letters to the UN Secretary General, the president of the UN Security Council, the chairman of the Conference on Security and Cooperation in Europe (CSCE), and other leaders of international organizations, arguing that the government of the Crimean Republic had taken illegal actions aimed at undermining the Ukrainian constitutional system and Ukraine's territorial integrity. He

---

54. "V Sevastpol pribili spetsnazovtsi Ukraini" (Ukrainian Special Forces arrived in Sebastopol), *RIA*, April 5, 1994.

55. The first round had been held in March 1994.

56. "Election Results in Crimea Reported," *FBIS* SOV-94-126, June 30, 1994, p. 39.

characterized those actions as an attempt by separatist forces to jeopardize the internal stability of the region and the overall stability of Europe. Ukraine reserved the right, in the worst-case scenario, to take all measures necessary to preserve its territorial integrity within the framework of international law.[57]

ENTER KUCHMA, EXIT MESHKOV

The two most important political events affecting Ukraine and Crimea in 1994 both helped to decrease the intensity of the conflict between them. First, Leonid Kuchma, a moderate politician, swept Leonid Kravchuk out of office in the Ukrainian presidential elections. When Kuchma assumed power, the Ukrainian leaders who had taken the most belligerent attitude towards Crimea—including Defense Minister Radetsky and Foreign Minister Zlenko—were removed from office.

Second, the Crimean Parliament adopted a law "On the Crimean Government" that deprived President Meshkov of his post as head of state; this second development warrants further elaboration. A conflict between the Crimean president and Parliament over economic issues erupted in September 1994, prompting both sides to seek Kiev's support and thus temporarily removing the threat of Crimean separatism. The conflict had its roots in the struggle over the privatization of state property in Crimea. Before Meshkov came to power, a draft law on privatization had been blocked by parliament because it granted control over the privatization process to Nicholas Bagrov, the former chairman of the Crimean Supreme Soviet. The opposition stemmed from Bagrov's ties to the Party of Economic Revival of Crimea, which was known to defend the interests of the Crimean *nomenklatura* as well as its business and criminal structures. After his election, Meskhkov submitted new legislation giving his government full control over the privatization process. The new plan was prepared by a government team headed by economist Evgeny Saburov and backed by a group of economic experts from Moscow whom

---

57. ITAR-TASS, May 21, 1994. In an interview on the Russian NTV on May 21, 1994, Ukrainian Defense Minister Vitali Radetzsky maintained that Crimea was an integral part of Ukraine and threatened "the violators of the state border and the territorial integrity of Ukraine" with "every measure envisaged by the Ukrainian legislation," including "the most harsh and extreme ones." Nevertheless, the severe economic crisis, the increasing ungovernability of the entire country, the decline in living standards of most Ukrainians, and changes in the population's political inclinations prevented the conflict from turning into outright violence.

Meshkov had invited to serve as ministers in his new cabinet. The attempt at "Moscow-style" privatization did not go well and led to a five-month confrontation between the parliament and Saburov. Ultimately Saburov was forced to resign, which weakened the political standing of President Meshkov. In the ensuing political struggle, both Meshkov and his opponents appealed to the recently elected Ukrainian president, Leonid Kuchma. Immediately after the Ukrainian elections, Meshkov's representative met unofficially with Kuchma, and the two leaders and their advisers discussed a plan to dissolve the Crimean Parliament.[58] The Crimean Supreme Soviet decided to assume responsibility for the economic and political situation in Crimea, and on September 9, 1994, it adopted a resolution relieving the president of his post as head of state. Thereafter the functions of chief executive were to be performed by the prime minister rather than the president.[59]

This political turmoil continued until the end of 1994, with the struggle over privatization at its core.[60] On November 17, 1994, the Ukrainian Supreme Soviet, hoping to take advantage of these events, adopted a resolution canceling all legal acts of the Crimean Republic that contradicted the Ukrainian Constitution and laws. Thirty-nine

---

58. See the review article, "The Time of the Self-Proclaimed State is Ending," *Nezavisimaia gazeta*, No. 62 (April 7, 1995), p. 2.

59. Interfax-Ukraine, September 10, 1994. Sixty-one deputies voted for this proposal. Twelve deputies representing Yuri Meshkov's followers left the hall of the Supreme Soviet directly after the vote, branding the Supreme Soviet's actions as a "constitutional coup." On September 29, 1994, members of parliament debated a bill on the Crimean Republic's government structure and ultimately voted to establish the post of prime minister and to make respective changes in the governmental structure. In essence, these changes were aimed at transferring the functions of the chief executive from the president to the prime minister. Sergei Tsekov, the Chairman of the Supreme Soviet, stated that the appointment of a prime minister in the Crimea was "a vital ingredient in a strong executive authority." "Crimean Deputies Approve the Appointment of a Prime Minister," *POST-FACTUM,* September 29, 1994.

60. However, the socioeconomic conflicts in Crimea over the redistribution of ownership and control of the privatization process continued to worsen. In voting for a new government in September 1994, which would be headed by Anatolii Franchuk, a close relative of the President of Ukraine, the Crimean Parliament hoped to gain full control over economic reform in Crimea. However, conflicts arose as soon as Andrei Senchenko, former first secretary of the Crimean Committee of the Komsomol and a *nomenklatura* protégé who had worked on economic policy under Nicholas Bagrov, was appointed deputy prime minister and given responsibility for the privatization process. By the end of 1994, the situation had reached a standstill, much as had been the case at the end of 1993, when the Crimean *nomenklatura* and the criminal business organizations under its patronage made their first attempts to redistribute ownership to their benefit.

laws were subject to cancellation, including the Declaration of Crimean State Sovereignty of September 4, 1991, the May 5, 1992, Declaration of Independence, and the Resolution on the Crimean Ministry of Internal Affairs. In addition, the Ukrainian Parliament mandated that the cabinet and the national bank should cut off funding to any Crimean institutions that continued to abide by the canceled laws. A number of Ukrainian parliamentary deputies favored taking a tough line on the Crimean problem, and some members of the Presidium of the Ukrainian Supreme Soviet asserted that Ukraine had the right to put an end to Crimean autonomy. There were proposals to eliminate the Crimean presidency, to dissolve the Crimean Parliament, and to return Crimea to its former status as an autonomous oblast.

All these proposals were clearly unacceptable to both the Crimean authorities and the Crimean people. In response to these actions, the Crimean Parliament appealed to the Ukrainian Supreme Soviet not to consider legislation on Crimea until the new Ukrainian Constitution had been adopted. At a closed sitting, the Crimean Parliament considered a number of options, including the radical proposal to dissolve the Supreme Soviet and to rejoin the Russian Federation. Sergei Tsekov, speaker of the Crimean Parliament, stated that the Ukrainian Supreme Soviet's decision could be either suspended or ignored. Tsekov's gravest concern was that the declaration of Crimean state sovereignty of September 4, 1991, had been canceled. He argued that this document had been adopted before both the breakup of the Soviet Union and the Ukrainian referendum on independence, and therefore should serve as the legal basis for Crimean-Ukrainian relations.[61] Debate on the formation of the Presidium of the Crimean Parliament aggravated the crisis. Some deputies insisted that the Presidium should be formed on a fundamentally new basis so as to reflect the actual support for pro-independence and pro-Russian positions. Others believed that a system of equal representation for all factions should be adopted. Finally, deputies from the Republic,

---

61. In the parliament, only the leader of the Crimean Tatar *Kuraltai* faction, Refat Chubarov, was of the opinion that Ukraine should have been more radical—i.e., Kiev should have dissolved the Crimean Supreme Soviet, canceled the presidential regime, and transferred full authority to the Ukrainian president's representative and only allocate power to the Crimean government through him. Apparently this scenario was being considered by the leaders of Ukraine. "Ukrainian Supreme Soviet Reviews the Course of 'Restoring Order' of the Crimean Constitution," *POSTFACTUM*, November 4, 1994.

Russia, and *Kurultai* electoral blocs agreed to set up a conciliation commission to discuss all problems related to the formation of the Presidium and the rotation of parliamentary leadership.

By the end of 1994, none of the parties to the conflict on the Crimean peninsula had achieved either their proclaimed or their implicit goals. But neither had any group been forced to retract its political program. Given the growth of internal differences both within and among various factions, the parties had to temper their respective political demands.

Through early 1995, political conflict between the Crimean Parliament and the executive—now Prime Minister Anatolii Franchuk—continued over the removal of Andrei Senchenko as deputy prime minister in charge of privatization. The Crimean Parliament subsequently passed a resolution dissolving Franchuk's government. Meanwhile, the Ukrainian Supreme Soviet passed a resolution abrogating the Crimean Constitution and a series of Crimean laws, and on April 1, 1995, President Kuchma issued a decree placing the Crimean government under his direct control—Kiev's first major step toward reducing Crimean autonomy. According to this decree, the Crimean government was to be directly subordinate to the Ukrainian Cabinet "until such time as a new Constitution is introduced in the Crimean Autonomous Republic."[62] Kuchma's decision to bring the Crimean government under his control was opposed by many political parties and organizations on the peninsula, especially the Russian Party of Crimea, headed by Sergei Shuvainikov. On April 11–12, 1995, a delegation from the Crimean Supreme Soviet headed by its chairman, Sergei Tsekov, visited Moscow at the invitation of the Russian Duma. There Tsekov called on the Russian Parliament to defend the Russian inhabitants of Crimea and to protect Crimean independence.[63] In response to these actions, the Ukrainian Supreme

---

62. "The Crimean Prime Minister will hereafter be appointed by the President of Ukraine after nomination by the Chairman of the Supreme Soviet of the Crimean Autonomous Republic," while the rest of the government will be appointed by the Ukrainian Cabinet of Ministers after nomination by the Crimean prime minister. "Leonid Kuchma Takes Control of the Crimean Government," ITAR-TASS, April 1, 1995.

63. The Crimean Supreme Soviet decided to hold a referendum in Crimea on June 25, 1995, in which the following questions would be asked: 1) Do you support the Constitution of the Crimean Republic, which was unilaterally abolished by the Ukrainian Supreme Soviet on March 17, 1995? 2) Do you support the Ukrainian law "On the Crimean Autonomous Republic," which was passed on March 17, 1995? and 3) Do you support an economic and political union between

Soviet began discussion of three draft resolutions that would abolish Crimean autonomy, dissolve the Crimean Parliament, and recognize only those Crimean deputies who declared their allegiance to Ukrainian law.

The continuing struggle between the Crimean and Ukrainian authorities for control of the peninsula also affected the Crimean Tatar political organizations. On April 6, 1995, the Ukrainian Supreme Soviet passed a law, "On the Participation of Ukrainian Citizens Deported from Crimea in the Election of Deputies to Local Councils in the Crimean Autonomous Republic," that was designed to ensure that Ukrainian citizens deported from Crimea between 1941 and 1944 and their descendants were represented on Crimean local councils.[64] The law stated that, within the districts of Crimea where previously deported Crimean Tatars, Bulgarians, Armenians, Greeks, and Germans had resettled, provisions would be made for the creation of special electoral districts, in addition to regular electoral districts, so that they could elect their own deputies.[65] The Crimean Tatar Majlis opposed the law, arguing that it would exclude Tatars from voting in regular Crimean elections. The older Crimean law, which had given deported peoples proportional representation in local councils, would be superseded by the new exclusionary law, effectively preventing Tatars from fully participating in Crimea's electoral process. According to the new law, only those Tatars who had returned to Crimea before November 1991 would have the right to vote since those who had returned later (more than 64,000) had not yet been granted Ukrainian citizenship. Ultimately, in order to create ethnic electoral districts, an ethnic group had to present over 300,000 signatures that had been gathered in a particular fashion over a period of less than two weeks.[66]

Belarus, Russia, and Ukraine? According to the Crimean Parliament, the referendum was necessary because of the differing opinions of the Ukrainian and Crimean authorities on the political status of the republic, the ownership of Sebastopol, the status of the Russian and Tatar languages, and the rights of the Crimean peoples to own land and natural resources. "Crimean Autonomy Remains a Central Issue in Ukraine," ITAR-TASS, April 26, 1995.

64. "Parliament Adopts Law on Local Elections in Crimea," *FBIS* SOV-95-067, April 7, 1995, p. 61.

65. In the event that the majority of the inhabitants of an electoral district were former deportees, additional electoral districts would not be created there. "Ukrainian Parliament Passes Law on Crimean Elections," Ukrinform-TASS, April 6, 1995.

66. "Ukraine Denies Many Repatriated Crimeans the Right to Vote in Elections to Local Councils," ITAR-TASS, April 15, 1995.

The Crimean Tatar National Movement demanded that the Ukrainian leadership abolish the April 6 law and take steps to ensure that Crimean Tatars were adequately represented in all Crimean government and administrative structures.[67] As of the beginning of 1995, a new Ukrainian Constitution had not yet been adopted, which prevented Ukraine from becoming a member of the Council of Europe. Indeed, the constitutional draft law "On Power," which was supposed to remain in force until the new Constitution was adopted, was still being debated in Ukraine. In particular, President Kuchma opposed the introduction of the federal-state system in Ukraine. In his opinion, federalism could split the country and therefore Ukraine must remain a unitary state for at least the duration of the transition period.

Thus, in early 1995, Crimean politics looked roughly the same as at the beginning of the conflict. As before, there were two overlapping lines of ethno-political conflict: 1) the Crimean Tatar conflict, in which the Crimean authorities were pitted against Crimean Tatar ethnic nationalists; and 2) the separatism conflict between the pro-Russian Crimean leadership and the Ukrainian leadership. Both the Crimean authorities and the Crimean Tatar nationalist movement continued to be racked by internal rivalries, both open and hidden, which prevented tensions from becoming overly focused. However, the underlying issues remained the same, which meant that conflict could flare up again.

The Role of the Russian Federation

Russian politics encompasses an enormous range of political forces active at various levels of state and society, each of which can be perceived as part of Russia. The tendency, however, is to focus on a handful of characteristics and to attempt to generalize from them in various situations. Because of this mistaken approach, the role that nationalists from Russia play in the politics of Crimea is often exag-

---

67. Vasvi Abduraimov, leader of the CTNM, maintained that the Ukrainian law was passed at the suggestion of Majlis leaders who wished to deprive returning deportees of the vote. He stated that during the election campaign for the Crimean Supreme Soviet, CTNM members had been in the lead in almost all ethnic districts, and that the Majlis got its candidates into parliament only by falsifying the election results. According to Abduraimov, the Majlis feared that during the next campaign it would be unable to stop the CTNM from getting its candidates elected, and thus it turned to the Ukrainian leadership for assistance. "Crimean Tatar National Movement Considers Ukrainian Law on Elections to be Discriminatory," ITAR-TASS, April 19, 1995.

gerated. Relations between Russia and Ukraine concerning Crimea revolve around two issues: the status of Crimea and the Black Sea Fleet. The evolution of these issues has been strongly influenced by the political and economic instability of both countries.[68] The dynamics of the conflict during 1992–94 reveals a connection between the top Russian leadership's willingness to exploit the situation in Crimea and developments in the power struggle between various political forces and factions within President Boris Yeltsin's personal entourage. Russian Vice President Alexander Rutskoi, who advocated the reunification of Crimea with Russia, held an opinion very different from that of Galina Starovoitova, Adviser to the President for National Affairs, who supported the Ukrainian position.[69]

The Black Sea Fleet consisted of 300 combat ships, including 45 large surface ships, 14 submarines, and about 300 sea- and land-based planes and helicopters. The fleet also had a highly developed coastal infrastructure. The disposition of the fleet was not settled by the CIS agreement on the division of the Soviet Union's armed forces. Immediately after the disintegration of the Soviet Union, Ukraine claimed its right to the Black Sea Fleet and all Ukrainian nationalist movements supported this claim. Meanwhile during 1991–93 in Russia, nationalist organizations, styling themselves as true champions of Russia's national interests, repeatedly raised issues related to Crimea and the status of the Black Sea Fleet.

President Yeltsin was the chief initiator of the agreements signed in the Belovezh Forest on December 8, 1991, that led to the dissolution of the Soviet Union and the creation of independent states from the former Soviet republics. His attitude toward problems between Russia and Ukraine derived from his desire to keep his allies in power in the new states, particularly Ukrainian President Kravchuk, who was the former Secretary for Ideology of the Ukrainian Communist Party. While Yeltsin always adopted policies in line with the Belovezh Accords, he was preoccupied with domestic political struggles, and Russian nationalists and their representatives in parliament frequently

---

68. The impact of the economic and political instability within the Russian Federation and the Ukrainian Republic on Russian-Ukrainian relations is analyzed by James A. Duran in "Russia and Ukraine: Political and Economic Update," *Atlantic Council of the United States' Bulletin*, Vol. 5, No. 5 (June 15, 1994).

69. For an analysis of the contradictions among the Russian leaders on the problem of Crimea and the Black Sea Fleet, see Roman Solchanyk, "The Crimean Imbroglio: Kiev and Moscow," *RFE/RL Research Report*, Vol. 1, No. 40 (October 9, 1992).

used the issues of Crimea and the Black Sea Fleet to present themselves as the true defenders of Russian national interests.

During the Gorbachev period, the Russian Supreme Soviet was divided over the issue of Crimea, with "patriotic" groups taking an openly pro-Russian stance, and "radical democrats," who wished to promote the collapse of the empire, arguing that the matter was strictly the concern of Ukraine. Thereafter, however, despite some progress, the Crimean factor continued to play a role in the conflict between supporters of the president and nationalist groups in the Russian Parliament that began in January 1992 and ended in October 1993 with the destruction of the Supreme Soviet by Yeltsin's troops.

In January 1992, immediately after the collapse of the Soviet Union, a group of deputies from the Supreme Soviet of the Russian Federation began to discuss possible statements to be addressed to the Ukrainian Supreme Soviet regarding implementation of the agreement to create the Commonwealth of Independent States. Also under discussion was a possible resolution on the 1954 decisions that transferred the Crimean oblast from the RSFSR to Ukraine. Andrei Kozyrev, Russian Minister of Foreign Affairs, called the transfer "a political decision of the former Politburo," but nevertheless warned the Supreme Soviet against aggravating relations between Russia and Ukraine. A group of Russian deputies visited Crimea and met with representatives of the Black Sea Fleet in Sebastopol. The Russian deputies insisted that the fleet should protect the security not only of Ukraine, but of all the CIS countries as well. Consequently they called upon the Russian Supreme Soviet to defend the interests of the CIS and Russian national interests in the event of any dispute regarding the fleet while still respecting the rights of Ukraine.

In a subsequent resolution on January 23, 1992, the Russian Parliament declared the decisions taken on the Black Sea Fleet by the executive authorities of the Soviet Union and the Russian Federation invalid.[70] However, in light of the Russian-Ukrainian Treaty of November 19, 1990, in which each side pledged not to make territorial claims against the other, the Russian resolution accepted as a practical matter that the Crimean problem would have to be addressed by intergovernmental Russian-Ukrainian negotiations with the participation of Crimean authorities, rather than by legislation of the Supreme Soviet. It also acknowledged that "those serving in the

---

70. Info-TASS, July 3, 1992.

Black Sea Fleet should take the oath laid down in the Agreement on Strategic Forces signed by CIS member nations," and urged the Ukrainian Supreme Soviet to speed up negotiations on all issues relating to the fleet. Moreover, the Russian resolution charged the Committee on International Affairs and Foreign Economic Relations and the Committee on Legislation with the task of investigating and reporting on the constitutionality of the 1954 transfer of the Crimean oblast to the Ukrainian SSR. The Presidium of the Supreme Soviet proposed that the Ukrainian Supreme Soviet conduct its own investigation into the 1954 resolutions.

Over the years since the dissolution of the Soviet Union, there has been a series of crises in relations between Russia and Ukraine, usually provoked by the actions of extreme nationalists on one side or the other. These crises have been extinguished by summit meetings between the Russian and Ukrainian presidents that resulted in a series of agreements and statements designed to strengthen mutual relations and settle the Black Sea Fleet issue.[71] A prime example is the June 1992 Dagomys summit between Yeltsin and Kravchuk precipitated by the May 21, 1992, passage of a Russian parliamentary resolution declaring "the 1954 documents transferring Crimea [to Ukraine] without force of law from the moment they were adopted."[72] Russia and Ukraine signed the Dagomys Accords on future relations between the two countries on June 23, 1992. The Accords emphasized that Russia and Ukraine had no reason to make claims on each other's territory, and that both countries would cooperate in preventing and regulating any conflicts that might threaten their security or otherwise harm their interests. In August 1992, the Yalta Accords provided for the formation of Russian and Ukrainian fleets from the Soviet Black Sea Fleet, and agreed to permit officers and crew members to choose to take the oath of allegiance to either Ukraine or Russia.

The question of possession of Sebastopol, the main base of the fleet, further complicated the picture, since in 1954 only part of Crimea had

---

71. For example, when Yeltsin and Kravchuk met on January 15, 1993, in Moscow, they issued a communiqué stating that Russian-Ukrainian relations were of prime importance for both countries and that "strengthening these ties, based on the Agreement signed by Russia and Ukraine on 19 November 1990 and the Dagomys Accords on future relations between Russia and Ukraine, will not only serve the interests of the peoples of Ukraine and Russia—it will be of major importance to the world as a whole." "Further Reportage of Yeltsin Meeting With Kravchuk," *FBIS* SOV-93-011, January 15, 1993, p. 15.

72. "Chronology of Events in Crimea," *RFE/RL Research Report*, Vol. 3, No. 19 (May 13, 1994), p. 28.

been transferred to Ukraine, and Sebastopol—which was a federal city and not part of the Crimean oblast—was not included in the transfer.[73] On July 9, 1993, the Russian Supreme Soviet adopted a resolution reaffirming "the Russian federal status of Sebastopol within the administrative-territorial urban district as established in December 1991." Thereafter, leaders of Sebastopol's political parties and public organizations appealed to top Russian leaders to recognize and give a legal form to the status of Sebastopol. A public opinion poll conducted in Sebastopol on June 26, 1994, showed that roughly 90 percent of its inhabitants were in favor of making Sebastopol the main naval base of the Russian Black Sea Fleet.[74] Participants in numerous rallies held in Sebastopol demanded that the deputies of the Municipal Soviet petition the Russian Duma for "the immediate practical implementation of the Russian Federation Supreme Soviet's resolution of July 9, 1993, which reaffirmed the Russian federal status of the city of Sebastopol."[75] Accordingly, the deputies of the Sebastopol Municipal Soviet appealed to the presidents of Russia and Ukraine "to implement the will of the people and give a clear definition of the Black Sea Fleet and Sebastopol's status."[76]

The Crimean Supreme Soviet also made an appeal to both presidents about the Black Sea Fleet problem, emphasizing that Crimea wanted the fleet to be indivisible and manned primarily by Crimean conscripts. They asked Yeltsin to pledge to support the Crimean Parliament's resolution, "On Crimean Citizens Performing Their Active Military Service," according to which inhabitants of Crimea called up for active service should serve only on Crimean territory. As was to be expected, the Ukrainian Defense Ministry rejected this demand. The Crimean Parliament again expressed the hope that representatives from Crimea and Sebastopol would be invited to participate in the negotiations on the fleet. On September 3, 1993, Yeltsin and Kravchuk signed a "Protocol Regulating the Matter of the Black Sea

---

73. In 1948, six years before Khrushchev's transfer of Crimea to Ukraine, a decision of the Supreme Soviet of the RSFSR removed the city of Sebastopol from the Crimean oblast of the RSFSR, and included it in a category of cities "under republican authority," which meant that it gained a higher status in the RSFSR and did not fall under the juridical authority of the Crimean oblast. However, in Article 77 of the Ukrainian Constitution of 1978, Sebastopol was unilaterally (without the formal agreement of the authorities of the RSFSR) declared a city "under republican authority" of the Ukrainian SSR.

74. *Krasnaia zvezda*, December 17, 1994, p. 1.

75. Interfax, December 26, 1994.

76. POSTFACTUM, December 26, 1994.

Fleet" at the Massandra Summit, which established that Ukraine would sell its share of the Black Sea Fleet to pay off Ukraine's fuel debt to Russia. The protocol stipulated a one-month deadline for government delegations from Russia and Ukraine to negotiate an agreement, "according to which the whole of the Black Sea Fleet in Crimea, together with its installations there, will be used by Russia and will fly the Russian flag, with the understanding that the Russian side will allow Ukraine to do the same with its half of the Black Sea Fleet, including its installations, which were allotted to Ukraine in previous agreements."

On May 13, 1994, the governments of Russia and Crimea signed an agreement that outlined steps for strengthening economic relations between Russia and Crimea. The agreement recognized Crimea as part of Ukraine, which was significant because the nature of the agreement was such that it could have easily been formulated otherwise. For example, Article 1 of the agreement stipulates that "trade and economic cooperation between parties to the agreement based on the principle of mutual benefit will be realized by direct arrangements between the managing subjects . . . and in observance of legislation acting in the Russian Federation, Ukraine, and Crimea."[77] At the same time, and in the same vein, Ivan Rybkin, chairman of the Russian Duma, outlined the new parliament's much more moderate stance on Crimean affairs to Douglas Hurd, British Minister of Foreign Affairs and Cooperation. Rybkin stated that "whatever occurs in Crimea is an internal Ukrainian matter," and that "the peoples of the peninsula have the right of self-determination, but within the Ukrainian state and within the context of the CSCE."[78]

Since then, the Russian Ministry of Foreign Affairs has frequently affirmed that it considers Crimea to be part of Ukraine. It called on the Ukrainian and Crimean authorities to resolve their differences "through political dialogue, respecting the norms of international law and the democratically expressed desires of the people of the peninsula." The ministry also suggested that "this might be facilitated by a more active use of appropriate CSCE mechanisms."[79] During Russian Vice-Premier Oleg Soskovets's March 1995 visit to Kiev, economic

77. "Agreement between the Government of the Russian Federation and the Government of the Republic of Crimea on Trade and Economic Cooperation," May 23, 1994.

78. "Ivan Rybkin: Crimean Issue Is Too Important to Be Used as a Card in Ukrainian Presidential Campaign," ITAR-TASS, May 23, 1994.

79. "Russian Ministry of Foreign Affairs Issues Statement on Crimean Situation," ITAR-TASS, April 3, 1995.

agreements of particular importance to Ukraine were reached (i.e., regarding debts owed by Ukraine to Russia), yet the Russians did not so much as inquire as to what Ukraine's future policy would be regarding Crimea. President Kuchma expressed his gratitude to the Russian president and Parliament for their sensible approach to the Crimean issue. He emphasized that "the Russian approach was appropriate, and significantly aided in normalizing the situation."[80]

Tensions between Russia and Ukraine decreased somewhat after President Kuchma came to power. He considered it necessary to expedite the signing of all documents governing relations with Russia. In the author's opinion, Kuchma also believed that the main obstacle to an improved relationship with Russia was the Black Sea Fleet, and without a resolution of this and other central problems, the climate of Russian-Ukrainian relations was gradually eroding. Although the general atmosphere around the protracted negotiations regarding the fleet improved, the issue remained unsettled. At a briefing given in Kiev on November 30, 1994, Ukrainian Vice-Premier Evgenii Marchuk, who headed the Governmental Commission for the Preparation of the Ukrainian-Russian Treaty, stated that "Ukraine would not agree [to allow] the Russian Fleet to be based in Sebastopol, Kerch, or Feodosiya." He claimed that Ukraine, which was not a member of any military bloc, could not allow foreign armed forces to be deployed on its territory. Ukraine proposed to solve joint problems on a step-by-step basis, i.e., to reach separate agreements on issues such as hydrographic facilities or the social welfare of Ukrainian servicemen.[81]

Ultimately Russia and Ukraine did manage to reach an agreement on the distribution of the Black Sea Fleet, although it was not initialed in 1994. Ukraine insisted that if Russia retained Sebastopol as its naval base, the very existence of a Ukrainian Navy would be jeopardized. Ukraine was willing to lease particular facilities as necessary for Russia to maintain a limited number of ships. As for other facilities, Ukraine proceeded from the assumption that the entire coastal structure of the Black Sea Fleet was Ukraine's property and would be leased to Russia for basing on a case-by-case basis. Moreover, the leasing period would be limited to the time Russia needed to build appropriate bases on its own territory.

---

80. "Ukrainian President Considers Localization of Crimean Problem to Have Been Timely and Necessary," ITAR-TASS, April 4, 1995.

81. POSTFACTUM, November 30, 1994.

In mid-1995, political conditions in Russia continued to preclude a resolution of the Black Sea Fleet problem. The whole situation was aggravated by shifts in the highest echelons of the Russian military. The status of the main part of the Russian Black Sea Fleet remained undefined and the status of those officers in the fleet who took the oath of allegiance to Russia had yet to be determined legally. However, after a series of Ukrainian and Russian political maneuvers on the issue, Kuchma and Yeltsin signed two documents, an agreement between Russia and Ukraine on the Black Sea Fleet, and a communiqué from the Russian-Ukrainian Summit in Sochi on June 9, 1995. The agreement stated that both the Black Sea Fleet of the Russian Federation and the Naval Forces of Ukraine had been created from the Soviet Black Sea Fleet and were based separately. The Black Sea Fleet Agreement also stipulated that "the main base of the Russian Federation's Black Sea Fleet and its staff is the city of Sebastopol, and it is granted use of facilities and equipment of the [Soviet] Black Sea Fleet in Sebastopol, and other basing facilities, aircraft and coastal forces, operational equipment, and technical and rear service equipment in Crimea."

Questions relating to the property of the Black Sea Fleet would be settled by the governments of Russia and Ukraine in separate agreements based upon the earlier agreement of an equal division of resources. Nevertheless, in terms of the actual division of assets, Russia would receive 81.7 percent of the ships of the Black Sea Fleet, and Ukraine only 18.3 percent—with Russia agreeing to compensate Ukraine for the difference.[82] But the suspicions of the Ukrainian nationalist parties had not diminished. They regarded the Russian Parliament's resolution on Sebastopol's status as the first step toward a takeover of Crimea. Over twenty parties and organizations held a rally of many thousands of people in Kiev under the slogan of "Ukraine in Danger!" Ukrainian President Kuchma and Prime Minister Marchuk were condemned for taking a conciliatory stance toward Russia. The leaders of Rukh maintained that the Russian-Ukrainian agreement on the division of the Black Sea Fleet would involve dividing not only the ships, but also the coastal troops and coastal facilities that had been placed under Ukraine's jurisdiction in accordance with the "Act on Ukrainian Independence." They argued that a dangerous precedent was being set allowing the existence of Russian property and the deployment of Russian armed forces on the

82. ITAR-TASS, June 9, 1995.

territory of Ukraine, which, in turn, could foster the growth of separatist trends in Crimea.

Although the new Russian Parliament generally took a much more moderate stance on Crimea, the issue resurfaced in Russian domestic politics. With instability increasing in Russia throughout 1995 as a result of protracted economic decline, the war in Chechnya, and the approach of parliamentary and presidential elections, criticism of the government's Crimean policy mounted. In early April 1995, policy toward Ukraine and Crimea became the focus of an attempt to get the Russian Duma to pass a vote of no confidence in the government. Konstantin Zatulin, chairman of the Duma's Committee on CIS Affairs and Relations with Russians Abroad, argued that "the government's policy is incomprehensible and secretive, and is beginning to have a negative effect on the prestige and authority of the Russian Federation."[83] Zatulin specifically attacked the March 1995 agreements signed in Kiev by Oleg Soskovets and the Ukrainian authorities. According to Zatulin, "Crimea is witnessing human rights abuses, the imposition of a police state, and continual infringements on the Ukrainian Constitution and Ukrainian law." Sergei Tsekov, chairman of the Supreme Soviet of the Crimean Autonomous Republic, was invited to speak to the Russian Duma, where he stated that "Russia cannot afford to treat the Crimean issue as merely an internal Ukrainian matter since the lack of respect shown for Crimea is above all a lack of respect for Russia."[84] According to Tsekov, Kiev was being aided in its attack on the rights of Crimea by "the total inertia of the Russian Federation on this issue, in particular of its executive authorities, who are attempting to maintain the strategic relationship between Russia and Ukraine, which is itself of questionable benefit." Yeltsin's response was cautious, however. He maintained that "the majority of the people in the Republic of Crimea, which is a part of Ukraine, are Russians. Russia therefore has important interests in the Crimean peninsula. The future of Crimea is important to us, and both the President and the government urge that the differences between Simferopol and Kiev be resolved through dialogue, without the use

---

83. "Konstantin Zatulin May Suggest that State Duma Pass a Vote of No Confidence in the Government," ITAR-TASS, April 3, 1995.

84. "According to Sergei Tsekov, Chairman of the Crimean Parliament, 'Russia Cannot Afford to Treat the Crimean Issue as an Internal Ukrainian Matter'," ITAR-TASS, April 14, 1995.

of force, and with respect for the desires of the Crimean people."[85] He added that a comprehensive treaty between Russia and Ukraine "will be signed once we are convinced that relations between Simferopol and Kiev do not threaten the interests of Crimeans and are in accordance with internationally accepted human rights principles."

The issue of Ukraine's nuclear status and the fate of its nuclear inheritance from the Soviet Union were often considered at the same international summits and meetings at which the future of Crimea and the Black Sea Fleet was discussed, including the Lisbon Summit and the meeting in Kiev between Ukraine, Russia, and the United States, at which the Trilateral Agreement on the denuclearization of Ukraine was hammered out. However, it would be a mistake to attempt to draw a strong causal link between the outcomes of the two issues. The Trilateral Agreement established a formula of compensation and security assurances that was key to convincing Ukraine to commit to becoming a non-nuclear state, and was the focus of great effort and attention on the part of the United States and other Western powers. Insofar as the West promised in the agreement to assure Ukraine's territorial integrity against the use of force by other states, the nuclear issue and the Crimean issue were not completely disconnected. Nevertheless, in terms of the complex politics behind each of the issues, there were no clear signs of a relationship between the two. First of all, it should be recalled that it was Russia's legislature that called into question the validity of the 1954 transfer of Crimea to Ukraine, whereas the agreement on nuclear forces was negotiated by Russia's executive—the stronger of the two branches— which was far more hesitant than the Supreme Soviet to stir up international protest over so tenuous an issue as the status of Ukraine when far more important interests could be damaged by doing so.[86] Second, on the issue of nuclear transfer, where Kiev held most of the cards, it was unlikely that Ukraine's leaders would have signed an

---

85. "Boris Yeltsin Announces that 'Major Political Documents' Will Be Signed by Russia and Ukraine After the Conflict Between Simferopol and Kiev Has Been Settled," ITAR-TASS, April 15, 1995.

86. Ukraine is recognized internationally as including the Crimean peninsula, and for Russia to call that into question would have raised international ire—not least in the United States. At the time of the negotiations over Ukraine's nuclear status, Russian foreign policy was still in the last stages of its period of acquiescence to Western foreign policy preferences, reinforcing the unlikelihood that Yeltsin would make a serious bid to acquire Crimea. Nevertheless, the issue was occasionally used to whip up anti-Ukrainian sentiment among the Russian public when it was convenient to do so.

agreement in which the integrity of Ukraine's 1991 borders was questioned by one of the agreement's primary signatories—i.e., Russia. In other words, the successful conclusion of the Tripartite Agreement was to a large degree based upon the tacit acknowledgment that Crimea was an internal Ukrainian problem.

During 1991–93, Ukraine frequently changed its stance on how to dispose of the nuclear weapons inherited from the Soviet Union. Tensions were heightened between Russia and Ukraine by Moscow's suspicions about Kiev's intentions regarding its nuclear arsenal. Ukrainian leaders made contradictory statements on this issue on a number of occasions. After President Leonid Kuchma came to power, Kiev began to show signs of willingness to sign the Nuclear Non-Proliferation Treaty, and the appropriate law was adopted by the Ukrainian Supreme Soviet on November 16, 1994, by a vote of 301 in favor and eight against. However, the law contained a number of important reservations. The original treaty did not provide for every eventuality. In particular, it had not contemplated the unique situation of the disintegration of the Soviet Union and the creation of several nuclear successor states including Ukraine. According to the Ukrainian law, "infringement of the territorial integrity and the inviolability of [Ukraine's] borders, and the threat of using force or exerting economic pressure by any nuclear state would be regarded by Ukraine as extraordinary circumstances which threaten its vital interests," and thus grounds for withdrawal from the treaty. It was also specified that the law would come into effect only after other nuclear states gave Ukraine firm guarantees of its security.[87] A memorandum on safeguards for Ukrainian security with regard to its joining the Nuclear Non-Proliferation Treaty was signed at a CSCE summit in Budapest on December 5–6, 1994. This long-awaited agreement somewhat improved strained Ukrainian-Russian relations.

The Activities of International Organizations

Because of the particular balance of forces within and around the Crimean peninsula, international govermental and nongovernmental organizations have not played an active role in settling the Crimean conflict. Although Russia and Ukraine declared their intentions to resolve the dispute over Crimea and Sebastopol in accordance with UN and CSCE basic principles, in reality these declarations were

---

87. POSTFACTUM, November 16, 1994.

political tactics rather than serious proposals for a solution to the problem. Nevertheless, international organizations such as the UN and the Organization on Security and Cooperation in Europe (OSCE, the successor to the CSCE) have given greater attention to Ukraine than to other former Soviet republics.

In 1992–93, Ukraine engaged in intensive diplomatic activity focused on the Crimean problem. Foreign Minister Zlenko addressed a number of statements to the UN Secretary General which characterized the Russian Federation's actions concerning the Crimean peninsula as a violation of Ukraine's sovereignty and interference in its internal affairs. In November 1992, following the signing of a host agreement by Ukrainian Foreign Minister Anatoly Zlenko and UN Secretary General Boutros Boutros-Ghali, the United Nations opened an office in Kiev with the dual aim of supporting the development of Ukraine and monitoring the political situation there.[88] Areas of UN concern included disarmament, ethnic and religious conflicts, and Ukraine's relations with its neighbors. UN staff from the Kiev office have undertaken fact-finding missions in Crimea, visiting Sebastopol, Simferopol, and Yalta, as well as in Odessa and the Danube Basin.[89] With technical assistance from the UN Development Program, a joint UN-CSCE team was able to monitor the electoral process leading up to the Ukranian parliamentary elections in March and April 1994 in many areas of the country, including Crimea. The team noted with concern that both international and domestic observers experienced difficulties in obtaining accurate and timely information on the administration and results of the election. On the basis of preliminary observations, the CSCE noticed "irregularities, minor violations and improprieties which, in most cases, were not the result of malicious and dishonest behavior, but rather the likely consequence of cultural habits and a lack of clarity in the electoral law regarding procedures."[90]

88. Specifically, the UN can provide 1) support for legal and constitutional reform, including assistance in the drafting or reform of national constitutions and legal codes, preparations for democratic elections, and aid in training and administration; 2) political monitoring and information—collecting and studying information on political developments, particularly those with a bearing on the peace and security of the region; 3) informational activities, including a monthly UN bulletin on the situation in Ukraine; and 4) monitoring and analysis of political and human rights, and recording violations of these rights.

89. "The United Nations in Ukraine: Who We Are," HREF Internet Base, unual.html.

90. "United Nations and CSCE Monitor First Democratic Parliamentary Elections in Ukraine," Press Release of UN/UNDP Country Office for Ukraine, April 11, 1994.

In early 1994, the CSCE began to play an increasingly active role in the Crimean issue. In February 1994, CSCE High Commissioner on National Minorities Max van der Stoel began to study the situation of national minorities in Ukraine, particularly that of the Crimean Tatars living in Crimea. After visiting Kiev and discussing the issue with President Kravchuk, the Crimean deputies in the Ukrainian Parliament, and a Crimean Tatar delegation from the Majlis headed by Refat Chubarov, van der Stoel concluded that the Ukrainian law on National Minorities not only met international standards but in certain aspects exceeded them. On May 15, 1994, he wrote to Ukrainian Minister of Foreign Affairs Anatoly Zlenko that "I consider it a very positive aspect of the present situation in Ukraine that there are presently no significant ethnic tensions between Ukrainians and Russians. Another positive element is that the Ukrainian legislation concerning minority questions complies fully, in general, with the international obligations Ukraine has entered into."[91] In his opinion, there was every reason to recommend the Ukrainian law as a model for many other European countries.[92]

On May 26, 1994, the CSCE Standing Committee adopted a resolution voicing serious concern over the situation in the Crimean Republic, particularly on the issue of inviolability of borders.[93] After a visit to Ukraine and Crimea, Ambassador van der Stoel stated at a press conference on November 4, 1994, that "Ukraine recognized the autonomy of Crimea as a part of its territory and sought to settle all controversial issues by peaceful means so that the Crimean Constitution and laws might be brought into line with those of Ukraine." He was quoted as saying that "the Head of the Ukrainian state and I share the same view on the issue of the Crimean situation," which implied first and foremost that the Crimean Parliament should bring its constitution into conformity with that of Ukraine.[94] Van der Stoel offered to send CSCE experts to help create the appropriate conditions for settlement[95] and announced that the CSCE planned a mission in Simferopol to monitor developments in Crimea directly. These statements caused a stir among Crimean leaders. Sergei Tsekov, chairman of the Crimean Supreme Soviet, stated that

91. *CSCE Communication*, No. 23 (June 7, 1994).
92. Ukrinform-TASS, February 16, 1994.
93. Ukrinform-TASS, June 6, 1994.
94. ITAR-TASS, November 3, 1994.
95. Ukrinform-TASS, November 4, 1994.

if a CSCE mission were established in Crimea, it should "help to normalize Crimean-Ukrainian relations instead of exerting intense pressure on the Crimean Republic."[96] In January 1995, a Memorandum of
Understanding was signed by the ambassador of the newly established office of the OSCE and the UN office in which both agreed to
share information, consult on subjects of mutual interest, and cooperate on practical matters including logistics, communications, and
ensuring the safety of personnel. Among the UN programs that
showed promise for improving economic and social life in Ukraine
was a five-year, $15 million Crimean Integration and Development
Program aimed at assisting the settlement of returning Tatars and
other peoples in Crimea and contributing to the general development
of the peninsula. The UN office has undertaken a number of missions
to Crimea, including one in December 1994 to gather information on
the demands for humanitarian aid on the peninsula. The UN office
also organized meetings in Kiev with the Ukrainian government and
potential donors to Crimea.[97]

International Alert is the best-known nongovernmental organization active in Crimea. The organization's fundamental goal is "to
endorse all constructive measures aimed at the prevention and
peaceful resolution of conflict in the region,"[98] and its activities have
primarily focused on research related to the economic and political
position of the Crimean Tatars.

The CSCE and the European Parliament have expressed support
for Kiev's attempt to solve the crisis in Crimea by abolishing the
Crimean Constitution and bringing the Crimean government directly under the control of Kiev. Van der Stoel frequently agreed with the
Ukrainian Parliament's resolutions and the Ukrainian President's
decrees on Crimea, and noted that, "the autonomous republic was in
a state of chaos, and Ukrainian laws were not being observed."[99]
Elizabeth Schredter, head of the European Parliament's interparlia-
mentary delegation on relations with Ukraine, Belarus, and Moldova,
met with President Kuchma on April 21, 1995, and subsequently stated that "the authorities are acting in accordance with Ukrainian law,

---

96. Ukrinform-TASS, December 21, 1994.

97. "Monthly Report of the UN/UNDP Country Office for Ukraine," January 31,
1995.

98. See Wilson, "The Crimean Tatars."

99. "Max van der Stoel Arrives in Simferopol," ITAR-TASS, April 6, 1995.

and the European Parliament will provide Ukraine with all the help
it needs in order to maintain its territorial integrity."[100]

An analysis of the activity of international political organizations
throughout 1992–95 shows their clear support for Kiev's actions concerning the Crimean problem. This support was, to all appearances,
guided by broader motives, in particular the strategy of encouraging
any Ukrainian policy directed against the "imperial aspirations" of
Russia. The problem, however, is that as in many post-Soviet conflicts
in which international organizations have been involved, they have
typically supported only one of the parties openly and consistently.
For this reason international organizations cannot be relied upon as
unbiased arbiters in promoting the effective resolution of crisis situations. The OSCE's unilateral support for Kiev's position on the
Crimean problem cannot be challenged objectively—whether this
policy should be criticized or commended is another question. The
role that the OSCE has played in Ukraine has been disappointing; if
the OSCE had taken a more objective stance at the beginning of its
involvement, it could have played a more active role in actually
resolving the conflict—not just in dealing with its effects.

Conclusion

The struggle for ethnic and national self-determination on the
Crimean peninsula has several deeply contradictory dimensions.
From the perspective of Crimean Tatar ethnic nationalists, the
peninsula is their national territory to which they have exclusive
right. According to the Russian-speaking majority inhabiting the
peninsula, Crimea should be an integral part of Russia. Meanwhile,
Ukrainian nationalists are prepared to make any sacrifice to preserve
Ukraine's territorial integrity. Yet despite the strident passions these
convictions evoke, they have not led to violent conflict on the same
scale as in Moldova, for example. Indeed, the conflict over Crimea
suggests that an increase in tensions on the peninsula and an outbreak of violence is not likely. Extremist groups will only be successful if they receive external support.

The future of the Crimean Republic depends directly on relations
between Russia and Ukraine and the internal political stability in
these two states. Russian-Ukrainian relations were strained after

---

100. "European Parliament Supports Ukrainian Approach to Crimean Issue,"
Ukrinform-TASS, April 21, 1995.

August 26, 1991, when Russia declared its right to raise the issue of the revision of its borders with neighboring republics. To justify Russian claims to Crimea and the Black Sea Fleet, some Russian politicians and political organizations began to regard Ukraine as Russia's geopolitical rival. At the same time, the growth of the Ukrainian nationalist movement and the threat of violations of the rights of the Russian population of Ukraine provoked the potential reemergence of conflict.

During the Kravchuk presidency, it was not clear whether the Russian-Ukrainian conflict over control of Crimea would become more serious because of the economic and political instability in both states on the one hand, and the advocacy by some Ukrainian leaders of the use of force to settle the Crimean problem on the other. President Kuchma's accession to power in Kiev and Ukraine's renunciation of nuclear weapons contributed to a significant relaxation in tensions between Russia and Ukraine. According to a number of Russian experts, Russian-Ukrainian relations were likely to continue on roughly the same basis, with the same difficulties and differences of opinion persisting.

But there were other possible scenarios for the future of relations between Russia and Ukraine. If Kuchma and his followers in the Ukrainian Parliament remained in power in Ukraine, and if the "radical democrats"—such as Yegor Gaidar, Boris Fyodorov, and the group of economists who espouse monetarist macroeconomic theory—rose to power in Russia, normal relations could be established between the two states without any elements of a joint political, military, or economic alliance. If Boris Yeltsin were to remain in power, there might be, over time, either the formation of an alliance between Russia and Ukraine or the emergence of friction—particularly if Russia were to attempt to interfere in any conflict in Crimea. A shift to the left in both Russia and Ukraine would provide better grounds for the formation of an alliance. But if nationalists were to come to power in Moscow or Kiev, Ukraine would probably attempt to join an anti-Russian military and political bloc—or even initiate the creation of such a bloc—which would increase the likelihood of a direct conflict developing between Russia and Ukraine.[101] If nationalism were overcome and policy became less vague in both states, Moscow and Kiev might gain breathing space in which to work out a common

---

101. A survey of experts' views on the issue of "Ukrainian-Russian Relations: Possible Scenarios for their Development" was conducted by the department of

approach to the Crimean problem, including the issue of Crimean Tatar self-determination. The conclusion of a comprehensive treaty between Russia and Ukraine could consolidate the territorial integrity and inviolability of both states and expedite a solution to the Black Sea Fleet problem.

---

social-political modelling of the Interfax Information Agency. The experts questioned—political scientists, economists, officials from government agencies, Ukrainian and Russian journalists—tied the relatively high probability of these scenarios to the level of stability of the existing political regimes in the two countries, especially Russia. Interfax, December 19, 1994.

Chapter 6

Commentary on the Crimean Republic

Michael Lysobey and Tonya Putnam

Edward Ozhiganov's account of the conflict over Crimea is a compelling, detail-rich explanation of a case in which violent conflict was avoided in what could have easily become an explosive situation. Ozhiganov's broad base of historical knowledge and his insights as a Russian policy adviser are valuable for Western scholars for whom only a smattering of information and analysis on the Crimean question is available. Nevertheless, Ozhiganov's analysis—particularly regarding Russia's indirect impact on developments in Crimea—comes across as disconnected in places, and stops short of conclusions about the progression of events that seem apparent to an observer with more distance from the situation. This brief commentary will focus on two dimensions of Ozhiganov's analysis that we believe particularly deserve further elaboration and clarification: 1) his hesitancy to recognize Russia's impact on the ebb and flow of tensions in the region; and 2) his treatment of the ethno-political situation, both on the Crimean peninsula and in the larger Ukrainian context.

Although the Crimean question can be approached as primarily an internal Ukrainian affair, a complete picture would have to acknowledge the broader political, military, and diplomatic context in which events were played out. While Ozhiganov does ascribe some significance to Russia's role in the continuing saga, particularly regarding the status of Sebastopol and the Black Sea Fleet, his account makes Russia's involvement appear merely episodic. Ozhiganov rejects the notion that outside actors, including various international organizations operating in the region or even the United States as a key signatory to the January 1994 Trilateral Agreement, have directly affected the outcome of the Crimean crisis.

This, in our estimation, constitutes a serious defect in Ozhiganov's analysis. The opinions and activities of international organizations and international law with regard to Ukraine have been critical to the consolidation of Ukraine's status as an independent state with borders that include the Crimean peninsula.

To describe the politics of the Crimean peninsula as merely a manifestation of an outside party's larger agenda would be, of course, inaccurate. Since 1991, various factions in the Crimean government have attempted to follow a path distinct from both Ukrainian and Russian policies. However, it is similarly inaccurate to depict the development of the crisis in Crimea without giving explicit attention to the role of outside forces in shaping the scope and nature of the conflict. Ozhiganov's consideration of how, both before and after the Soviet collapse, Ukrainian politics fed into the conflict over Crimea is important in explaining the outcome. However, his treatment of Ukraine's sensitivity to developments in Russia not just at the level of official diplomacy, but at many levels in the government and in public opinion throughout the period in which the Ukrainian state was being consolidated, is quite thin. At the same time, political dynamics on the Crimean peninsula determined to a significant degree the approaches open to both Ukraine and Russia in resolving the dispute over Crimea's status. The Crimean secessionist movement created much of the tension seen in 1994, and opened up opportunities for Russia to champion the cause of the separatists. Similarly, Russia's interest in the fate of the peninsula precluded the use of extreme tactics by Kiev to bring the renegades quickly into line, and to some degree forced Ukrainian officials onto the middle path Ozhiganov describes.

Crimean-Ukrainian relations have played an important, independent role in the development of tensions. A more integral analysis of the situation would highlight Russia's part in shaping the general environment of the crisis, even on issues where it had no direct involvement. Western accounts of the situation in Crimea have tended to overlook the significance of the political demands forwarded by Crimean Tatars and to focus instead almost exclusively on the Black Sea Fleet issue. However, Ozhiganov errs in the opposite direction by overstating the impact of the ethnic minority factor, and then failing to develop his account fully in the wider context of Ukrainian politics. While the politics of ethnicity have certainly been critical in drawing the political dividing lines on the Crimean peninsula, the options available to the government in Kiev to quiet the situation throughout were, to an important degree, constrained by the state of Russian-Ukrainian relations. Ukrainian authorities in Kiev could not have undertaken a forceful response to events in Crimea without the risk that Russia would seize such action as an opportunity to intervene on behalf of its co-ethnics. Even considering the recent influx of ethnic Crimean Tatars onto the peninsula, the Tatars and other minorities were never in any danger of displacing the Slavs from their positions of economic and demographic dominance. Although minority politics have at times certainly constituted an important catalyst to events—as was the case when the Tatars attempted to establish parallel power structures—the real struggle has been the Ukrainian-Russian struggle over Crimea.

The Crimean Tatars pose a threat to the stability of the situation on the peninsula because of their consistent focus on ethnic issues, while the Ukrainian government has tried desperately to treat the situation as a matter involving citizens of the Ukrainian state and to deemphasize the ethnic factor. The Tatars' enmity toward the Russians has its roots in the history of deportation and genocide described by Ozhiganov, and Ukrainian authorities fear that these types of tensions might also develop between Russians and Ukrainians. At least in 1992–93, such fears would not have been unfounded, given the separatist rumblings that were heard among the largely ethnically Russian eastern Ukrainians directed against the virulently nationalist western Ukrainians. Ethnic tensions between Slavs on the peninsula have, in fact, remained quite low. Ukrainian nationalists did not find a base for their movement in Crimea, although they attempted for years to establish one. Of far greater relevance to developments in Crimea have been relations between Moscow and Kiev. In contrast to their Ukrainian counterparts, Russian nationalists found a broad base of support, both on the peninsula itself, and within the Black Sea Fleet. Although Yuri Meshkov's campaign for the presidency tapped into ethnic sentimentality, the ethnic angle was not the primary source of tension in Crimea. Rather it was economic considerations, coupled with the friends that groups could make by putting a particular type of ethnic spin on their demands.

In some cases Ozhiganov does not explain the background and impetus for important milestones of the Crimean movement sufficiently for the role of outside forces to be fully appreciated. For example, in his discussion of the restoration of the Crimean constitution in May 1992, Ozhiganov explains neither what Russia's response was, nor the context of this key event. In fact, Russia's role in determining the sequence of events leading to Crimea's declaration of independence from Ukraine turns out to have been quite important. Several weeks before Crimea's declaration of independence, Russian Vice President Alexander Rutskoi, together with presidential adviser Sergei Stankevich and General Boris Gromov, went to Crimea with Yeltsin's full knowledge and made statements claiming Crimea as part of Russia, according to "common sense" if nothing else. On May 21, 1994, the same day that Crimea rescinded its resolution on independence, the Russian Parliament adopted legislation to annul the 1954 transfer of Crimea to the Ukrainian SSR. During this period, powerful groups inside the Russian system, including first and foremost the Russian Parliament, attempted to pressure Crimea to unite with the Russian Federation. The political and other incentives emanating from Russia had a profound effect on Crimean decision-making. Rhetorically, Russia halted all interference in 1994, when the pro-Russian Meshkov began to provide interference for them. However, virtually all the incentives for Russia to meddle in Crimean affairs have remained intact, and when Meshkov was stripped first of his powers, and then the presidency, Russia again stepped up its activities in the region. Beginning in spring 1995, restorationist voices, like that of Konstantin Zatulin, again began to be heard in the Russian Duma, although they have not been echoed at the presidential level.

Russia may have officially renounced its claim to Crimean territory (with the exception of its demand to lease basing rights), but there is reason to suspect that the matter is not quite so simple. The reason is to be found in Ozhiganov's own statement that the Russian government is not a single, monolithic entity, but rather a complex admixture of levels and factions. While Boris Yeltsin and Andrei Kozyrev continued to insist in official statements that the situation in Crimea was an internal affair of the Ukrainian state, this interpretation is unlikely to be universally held among officials in either the presidential administration or the Foreign Ministry, not to mention the succession of Russian parliaments since 1991.

Statements asserting a formal claim to Sebastopol, such as that issued by the Russian Parliament in July 1993 on the basis of the city's Russian federal status at the time of the 1954 transfer, open the door for future challenges to Ukraine's integrity. Ozhiganov characterizes the action of the Russian Parliament in challenging the validity of the 1954 transfer of Crimea as aimed at conducting "intergovernmental Russian-Ukrainian negotiations with the participation of Crimean authorities" and states that Yeltsin has "always adopted policies in line with the Belovezh accords." This conclusion is only significant if one believes that the office of the president has, and will continue to have, the final say on the design and implementation of policy in the states of the Commonwealth of Independent States (CIS). When viewed in this light, official presidential statements hardly appear to be the firm guarantee against Russian exploitation of the situation that Ozhiganov makes them out to be. The parliamentary challenge to Crimea's Ukrainian status was particularly significant because it occurred after a number of important summits, including the June 1992 meeting that produced the Dagomys Accords, at which, as Ozhiganov notes, the dominant theme was the idea that no country was justified in making a claim to another's territory. Yet the Russian Parliament did precisely what Presidents Boris Yeltsin and Leonid Kravchuk had rejected as imprudent policy. Aggressive legal maneuvers such as this clearly illustrate the plurality of official lines within Russian policy and expose the root of Russian-Ukrainian-Crimean tension.

It can be argued that Russian officials have purposefully avoided a full normalization of relations with the Ukrainian state precisely in order to maintain a recognized interest in the Black Sea region. Russia does not now reap any economic benefit from holding on to Sebastopol, nor is it likely to in the near future. It is equally difficult to make an argument justifying Russian possession of the city on military grounds since Novorossiisk could serve perfectly well as the primary base for the Russian Federation's naval forces. The dominant perception in Ukraine is that Russia's interest in Sebastopol can only be viewed as Russian desire to maintain a foothold on the peninsula.

The dispute over the Black Sea Fleet is the largest thorn in the relations between the two states, but others exist as well. Continued Russian pressure for granting dual citizenship, even after Yeltsin himself chalked it up as a non-issue, is interpreted in Ukraine as evidence that certain factions in Russia continue to covet all or part of Ukraine. For example, Russia has continued to send consular groups to the Crimean peninsula ostensibly to "counsel" Crimeans on consular matters, including gaining Russian citizenship.[1] The majority of

---

1. One such group was dispatched on March 21, 1995, three days after the Ukrainian Parliament voted to nullify the Crimean Constitution. Official Russian reports stressed that the consular groups had no authority to issue passports or visas, and that they went to Crimea with the tacit approval of authorities in Kiev. See "Russia Watches Crimean Developments—Sends Consular Group," in *Foreign Broadcast Information Service (FBIS)* SOV-95-055, March 22, 1995, p. 11.

Russians on the Crimean peninsula, especially those in Sebastopol, have backed Russia in these activities. Russia promised all the trappings of a powerful state that would provide Crimeans with a higher standard of living and the civic privileges they had sought unsuccessfully from the Ukrainian state.

Expanding the context still further to the international sphere would tend to support Ozhiganov's conclusions that Russia's direct impact on the situation in Crimea has been negotiable. Ukraine has been formally recognized under international law as a state that includes the Crimean peninsula. Thus constituted, Ukraine has likewise become a full member of a number of international organizations, including international security organizations such as the United Nations and the Organization for Security and Cooperation in Europe (OSCE). Thus, there are a number of potentially powerful mechanisms in place to safeguard the territory of Ukraine against forcible encroachment. Ozhiganov downplays any connection between events such as the conclusion of the Trilateral Accord that secured the removal of Soviet nuclear weapons from Ukrainian territory and the situation in Crimea. It may well be true that the situation in Crimea presented neither a barrier nor a particular incentive to the negotiation of the Trilateral Accord. Nevertheless, the fact of its conclusion and the high degree of importance a non-nuclear Ukraine holds for both Russia and the United States constitute further safeguards against encroachments on Ukrainian interests on the Crimean peninsula. Similarly, Ozhiganov downplays the direct role of international organizations in resolving the situation in Crimea. However, the presence of international organizations in the region and their periodic visits to both Ukraine and Crimea also constrained the options of the actors involved, although no permanent United Nations or OSCE missions to Crimea were organized. This is especially the case given that the activities of international organizations have proven compatible with Russia's interests in other areas of post-Soviet space (for example, in greasing the wheels for the introduction of Russian peacekeeping forces into Georgia and Tajikistan).[2] In this sense the Crimean crisis was played out in the shadow not only of

---

2. The intrusion of the international system into the vagaries of post-Soviet politics has placed serious constraints on Russia's freedom of action, at least in areas where the West, and in particular the United States, has a declared interest. Any prognosis that Russia will continue to conduct its policies and activities with an ear to international public opinion is, of course, predicated on the assumption that the next Russian president will find it in Russia's interest to maintain credibility among Western countries, whether due to pragmatism or genuine political conviction.

Russia, but of international law and world public opinion.

Although Ozhiganov is doubtless far better informed regarding the details of events in Crimea than the vast majority of Western scholars, his analysis of the Russian role in shaping events and sharpening tensions both on the Crimean peninsula and in government corridors in Kiev is largely uncritical. It remains to be seen whether Russia will be able to maintain its edge in Crimea after the war in Chechnya and new efforts to improve Ukraine's economic health. Russia's efforts in the financial and military sectors have secured Crimea's loyalty up to this point, but to rely on continued ethnic loyalty in the absence of incentives would be an enormous mistake for Russia. The Ukrainian state has continued its policy of ethnic nondiscrimination, and if and when the Ukrainian economy begins to strengthen, the Russian Federation may find that the loyalty it has been able to foster can slip away as easily as it was acquired. More important, the resurgence of a Crimean crisis with a heavy measure of Russian involvement would be recognized by all but the most extreme Russian nationalists and restorationists as an international crisis inviting international measures for its resolution. In this sense Russia has a tangible reason for insisting that the Crimean situation is Ukraine's internal affair, while at the same time preventing the stabilization of the situation until a satisfactory agreement regarding Sebastopol and the Black Sea Fleet is reached.

Chapter 7

The Republic of Moldova: Transdniester and the 14th Army

Edward Ozhiganov

The prolonged conflict under way in the Transdniester region of the Republic of Moldova since 1991 has been one of the most violent since the breakup of the Soviet Union. This conflict has raised two ominous questions that directly affect the future stability of the region—separatism and irredentism—and set a very dangerous precedent for developments in the wake of the multinational Soviet state.

Because of its intensity and consequences, the conflict in Moldova can be classified as a full-scale, but localized war.[1] The fighting has involved heavy weapons and resulted in more than 1,000 battle-related deaths. Three main phases can be distinguished in the development of the conflict in Transdniester and will be explored in this chapter: 1) the emergence of the conflict against the background of general social and economic destabilization in Moldova (1989–90);

---

1. According to PIOMM's data bank, no less than thirty-three violent conflicts plague the states of the former Soviet Union; two of these are considered "outright wars," ten "low intensity conflicts," and twenty-one "serious disputes." (PIOMM is a Dutch-based, nonpartisan organization that conducts research on causes of gross violations of human rights.) According to PIOMM's classification, a war is defined as "prolonged combat between the military forces of two or more governments and, at least, one organized armed group, involving the use of weapons and incurring battle-related deaths of at least 1,000 persons." Low intensity conflicts are defined as "political-military confrontations below the level of war, involving counterinsurgency and terrorism as well as certain peace-enforcement activities. Serious disputes occupy a middle position between the upper level of low-intensity conflicts and the lower level of political tension. One of the parties has implicitly or explicitly threatened to use force. Some violent incidents might already have occurred." Ko Colijn, Berto Jongman, Paul Rusman, and Alex Schmid, *Wars, Low-Intensity Conflicts and Serious Disputes: A Global Inventory of 160 Confrontations*, PIOMM Working Paper 1 (Summer 1993), p. 1.

2) intensification and transition to a full-scale local war (1991 to mid-1992); and 3) the relative stabilization of the situation and the search for a settlement (mid-1992 onward). The principal participants in the conflict are the ethno-nationalist regime in the Republic of Moldova and the secessionist Republic of Transdniester on the eastern shore of the Dniester River. The Transdniester area has a primarily ethnic Russian and Ukrainian population and contains the bulk of Moldova's industrial enterprises.

Major fighting erupted in Transdniester in May 1992, resulting in a prolonged armed stalemate accompanied by heavy sporadic fighting until 1994. The conflict has been devastating to Moldova—more than 1,000 people have lost their lives, upwards of 5,000 have been wounded, and more than 100,000 have become refugees. Losses to the republic's economy totaled approximately 12 billion rubles (in 1992 prices). At least 15 billion rubles are needed for the reconstruction of fully and partly destroyed population centers and industrial installations, yet in 1991, Moldova's national income amounted to only 15.4 billion rubles.[2]

The Transdniester conflict has been aggravated by tension in southern Moldovan districts densely inhabited by Gagauz and Bulgarians, who proclaimed the independent Republic of Gagauzia in 1992. In mid-1990, before the breakup of the Soviet Union, these two territories declared themselves independent Union republics of the Soviet Union. Their actions were precipitated by rising Moldovan nationalism in the government structures of the Moldavian Soviet Socialist Republic (SSR) in the late 1980s, and by the perceived threat that Moldova would reunite with Romania.[3] The Gagauz region managed to avoid serious bloodshed and maintained its self-proclaimed independence until an agreement on special autonomous status within Moldova was reached in December 1994, which guaranteed the Gagauz the right to self-determination should Moldova change its own status by uniting with Romania.

The formation of the self-proclaimed Transdniester and Gagauz republics can be explained in part as a reaction to Moldovan nationalism and the intention of part of Moldova's ruling circles to reunite Moldova with Romania. The region's complex population mix, the confused history of its status, and its important geopolitical location

---

2.   Vasile Nedecivc, *The Republic of Moldova* (Kishinev: s.n., 1992), pp. 97–101.

3.   The name Moldavia was officially changed to Moldova following the Moldovan declaration of independence from the Soviet Union in 1991.

explain the involvement of Russia, Ukraine, and Romania, each of which hàs its own strategic interests. The unstable economic and political situation in the Russian Federation has had a negative effect on the behavior of both sides in the conflict, especially since different groups in the Russian Federation have supported different parties in the Moldovan conflicts, thereby exacerbating the situation.

The presence of the 14th Army—initially under the jurisdiction of the Commonwealth of Independent States (CIS), and later under that of Russia—seriously complicated the situation in Transdniester[4] and reflected the struggle among political forces within both the Moldovan Republic and the wider region. The dissolution of the Soviet Union left the 14th Army stranded; while nominally it was in the service of the CIS, in reality it belonged to no country. Only in April 1992, in accordance with a decree issued by Russian President Boris Yeltsin, did the 14th Army come under Russian command. From that moment on, however, the army's legal status on Moldovan territory came into question. Beginning in August 1992, Russia and Moldova participated in ten rounds of talks on the problem, which ended in September 1994 when the two states signed an agreement that mandated that the withdrawal of Russian military forces from Moldova must be completed within three years. Furthermore, the withdrawal of Russian troops would coincide with the political set-tlement of the Transdniester conflict and the definition of a special status within Moldova for the Transdniester region.

The 14th Army clearly played a very particular role in the Transdniester conflict, but not the primary causal role that is usually assigned by Western analysts.[5] Before the collapse of the Soviet Union, the 14th Army was based in the Odessa Military District, which spanned the Soviet republics of Ukraine and Moldavia. After the Soviet Union disintegrated, the 14th Army ended up primarily on Moldovan territory. In accordance with the CIS agreement of December 1991 on the division of Soviet military property among the former Soviet republics, the 14th Army's weapons and supplies were given to the government of the Moldovan Republic. When serious

---

4.   Interfax, August 10, 1994.

5.   The typical Western view on the role of the 14th Army is expressed by Fiona Hill and Pamela Jewett in their report, *Back in the USSR: Russia's Intervention in the Internal Affairs of the Former Soviet Republics and the Implications for United States Policy toward Russia* (Cambridge, Mass.: Harvard University, Kennedy School of Government, Strengthening Democratic Institutions Project, January 1994), p. 61.

fighting broke out between Moldovan government forces and Transdniester forces in the summer of 1992, President Yeltsin removed the 14th Army's commander, Yuri Netkachov, and replaced him with General Alexander Lebed.

Many people, especially outside of Russia, believe that the 14th Army, and Lebed in particular, openly supported Transdniester. Actually, the 14th Army's role was far more complex. In the context of the general disintegration of the Soviet Army, the absence of any real authority, and splits within the officer corps (who were primarily residents of Transdniester), there was a danger that Russia would lose control of the 14th Army and its huge stores of military supplies. Lebed portrayed himself as a "friend" of Transdniester, the residents of which assumed he was on their side. But Moscow's prime reason for sending Lebed in was to prevent the Transdniester militias from taking over the 14th Army's huge military stockpiles. Ironically, Lebed's action in maintaining Russian control over the 14th Army stopped the outright seizure of its remaining stocks of armaments by the Transdniester forces. This chapter sheds light on some of the calculations and determinants of the 14th Army's role—which has been far from one-sided—and illustrates the kinds of dilemmas facing the Russian military since the breakup of Soviet military structures.

Some prospects for a settlement in Transdniester emerged following Moldova's move toward a more moderate brand of nationalism and a decreased likelihood of unification with Romania. Political changes in 1994 in both Russia and Romania, the two outside countries most heavily involved in Transdniester, also affected the situation. The Transdniester region became relatively stable, but no decision on its territorial status was reached. The delay in settling the conflict by negotiating a special status for Transdniester stemmed from the ongoing struggle among Moldovan elites over a federal structure for the Moldovan state, and the unwillingness of the Transdniester authorities to make compromises on the question of special status.

History and Background

Because of Transdniester's long and complex history,[6] ideologues on all sides of the conflict often resort to historical arguments to

---

6. See V. S. Zelenchuk, *The Population of Bessarabia and Transdniester in the Nineteenth Century* (Kishinev: Shtiintsa, 1979); M.V. Sergievskii, *Moldovan Etudes*

substantiate their political and territorial claims.[7] Each side emphasizes the historical stage that best suits it at a given moment. In spite
of the bitterness of these historical quarrels, one fact is not in dispute:
the Transdniester region, situated on the left bank of the Dniester
River, was never part of any Romanian or Moldovan state until 1924,
when Soviet authorities established the Moldavian Autonomous
Republic as part of the Ukrainian Soviet Socialist Republic (SSR).

Since the first independent Moldovan principality was founded in
1359, Moldavia's borders have been defined by the Eastern
Carpathian mountains to the west, the Sylvanian Carpathians and
the Dniester River to the north, the Black Sea and the Seiret and
Danube rivers to the south, and the Dniester and its estuary in the
east. At that time the region was populated by a group closely related
to ethnic Romanians. Another principality of ethnic Romanians—
Walachia (Muntenia)—existed on the territory of contemporary
Romania. Both principalities were subjects of the Ottoman Empire
from the beginning of the sixteenth century until the early nineteenth
century when Russia and Austria ended Turkish domination of the
region. The prolonged confrontation between Turkish, Russian, and
Austrian interests was a key factor in the creation of political entities
in this region. Beginning in the sixteenth century, Russia had strong
diplomatic and military ties with the Moldavian principality, which
it considered a natural ally against the Ottoman Porte and the
Crimean Khanate. Several treaties between Russia and Moldavia
established the Dniester as the principality's eastern border.[8] The ethnic Slavs who settled in the Transdniester region during this period

---

(Moscow: Akademii Nauk SSR, 1936); V. Kubijovych, ed., *Encyclopedia of Ukraine*,
Vol. 1 (Toronto: University of Toronto Press, 1984); and O. Subtelny, *Ukraine: A
History* (Toronto: University of Toronto Press, 1988).

7.   Beginning in March 1992, when the situation in the left-bank districts of the
Dniester grew tense, the Romanian press has harped upon the right of Romania
to Transdniester, although exactly opposite opinions were voiced. Thus, the
weekly *Express Magazine* considers that Transdniester never belonged to Romania
and that the leadership should state: "Romania has no claim to this territory." In
response to this article, the newspaper *Diminiata*, which is close to presidential
circles, tried to substantiate the claim in an article entitled "Romanian Rights in
Transdniester" by giving a historical review beginning with King Buresbeti of the
Dacians (70–44 B.C.) to the "Eastern campaign" of Marshall Antonescu's army
against Russia in World War II. "On the Rights of Romania in Transdniester,"
ITAR-TASS, May 13, 1992.

8.   Two examples of these are the Moscow Treaty of May 7, 1654, and the
Prutskii Treaty of April 13, 1711.

were Little Russian (Ukrainian) Cossacks, and their presence even today has remained a persistently important factor in the conflicts between Russia, the Turks, and the Crimean Tatars.[9]

After two successive wars with Turkey (1768–74 and 1787–91), Russia incorporated the territory of Transdniester into its Empire during the reign of Catherine the Great. The 1774 Treaty of Kuchuk Kainardzhi between Russia and Turkey granted the Danube principalities of Walachia and Moldavia the right, under protection of the Russian ambassador in Constantinople, to appeal to the *chargé d'affaires* at the Ottoman Porte—a right that formed the basis of Turkey's recognition of their autonomy. It is clear that at that time, neither Russia, Turkey, nor any other European power regarded the Transdniester region as a historic part of the Danube principalities. From December 1791 onward, the Transdniester region belonged to the Russian Empire.

In 1775, Austria occupied Bukovina, the northern part of the Moldavian principality. As a result of the Russo-Turkish wars of the eighteenth and early nineteenth centuries, the Gagauz people moved from Bulgaria to southern Bessarabia and settled in the Budzhak Steppe where they have lived in self-contained, densely populated settlements ever since. Scholars remain unsure about the ethnic origins of the Gagauz people. The dominant opinion is that they are of Turkic origin, descendants of nomadic tribes that migrated from Central Asia to the Balkans between the ninth and fourteenth centuries. By the eighteenth century, the Gagauz had emerged as a distinctive ethnic group in northeastern Bulgaria and southern Dobruzha.[10]

After another war with Turkey (1806–12), Russia obtained the northeastern part of Bukovina, which, together with other territories, traditionally bore the name Bessarabia. From 1812 until 1917, Bessarabia existed as an ordinary governmental administrative unit

---

9. During the sixteenth century, Russia had to fight wars on several fronts, and thus was not yet strong enough to prevail in these conflicts. Peter the Great's attempt to gain some ground ended in total failure with the Prutskii Treaty of 1711, which granted Turkey the whole Black Sea and Transdniester region. The victorious but futile war of 1735–39 against Turkey during Empress Anna's reign also ended in diplomatic defeat for Russia.

10. The Gagauz incorporated many ethnic elements, including Greek, Bulgarian, and Seljuk. For more information on the migration of the Gagauz people from Bulgaria, see I. Meshcheriuk, *A Socioeconomic History of the Bulgarian and Gagauz Villages of Southern Bessarabia (1808–58)* (Kishinev: Akademii Nauk Moldausto, 1971).

(*gubernia*) of the Russian Empire. The two Danube principalities, Walachia and Moldavia, united in 1859 as the principality of Romania. Romania became an independent kingdom under the Treaty of San Stefano, which ended the final war between Russia and Turkey (1877–78). With the emergence of Romania, the Moldavian principality, as well as the name Moldavia itself, disappeared from the political map.

Bessarabia fell into chaos during the Russian Civil War, and in March 1918, Romania invaded with 200,000 troops and established its rule there. The union of Bessarabia with the Kingdom of Romania was recognized in 1920 by the European powers in the Treaty of Paris. In 1924, on the territory east of the Dniester bordering directly on Bessarabia (present-day Transdniester), the Soviet Union created the Moldavian Autonomous Socialist Republic (ASR) as part of the Ukrainian SSR. The Bolsheviks probably wanted to attempt to regain Bessarabia and they set up this nominally "Moldovan" republic as a means of agitating for the eventual inclusion of Bessarabia within Moldavia. The population of the Moldavian ASR consisted mainly of Russians, Ukrainians, and Moldovans, along with many refugees from Bessarabia who had fled the harsh policies of the Romanian monarchy.

During the Stalinist political repressions of 1937–38, a large part of the leadership and intelligentsia of Moldavia was eliminated. In a secret protocol—the Molotov-Ribbentrop Pact of August 20, 1939—Germany and the Soviet Union defined respective spheres of influence in Eastern Europe. After addressing two notes to Romania demanding the return of Bessarabia and northern Bukovina (which Russia had lost during World War I), the Soviet Union occupied these territories in June 1940 and made major changes in the administrative borders of the region. The Moldavian ASR was taken away from Ukraine and joined to the Bessarabian territories to form the Moldavian Soviet Socialist Republic. Meanwhile, three districts of northern Bukovina were transferred to the Ukrainian SSR.

With the consolidation of Soviet control in these regions, Stalin initiated mass repressions in which 300,000 people were deported in 1940–41. Deportation occurred primarily for class reasons, but there was an ethnic element as well. Moldovans, who were mainly rural, resisted efforts to collectivize agriculture and were dealt with harshly by the Stalinist regime. During World War II, when Romania was allied with Nazi Germany, the fascist regime of Marshall Ion Antonescu sent 700,000 Romanian troops to fight the Soviets on the southern sector of the Eastern front, and temporarily recaptured the territory of the new Moldavian SSR. However, this Eastern advance turned into a disaster for Romania, which lost 400,000 men in 1941–42 and was completely routed in the battle of Stalingrad. The territories occupied by the German and Romanian armies were liberated by the Soviet Red Army in 1944 and the Moldavian SSR was restored to its 1940 borders, including Bessarabia and northern Bukovina. These frontiers were recognized in a number of agreements among the Allies in the European postwar settlement.[11]

THE SOCIAL AND ETHNIC CONTEXT

In 1989, 80 percent of the secretaries of the Central Committee of the Moldavian Communist Party, 70 percent of the secretaries of the municipal and district party committees, and 74 percent of the chairmen of the Council of People's Deputies were ethnic Moldovans.[12] The dominant influence of ethnic Moldovans in the party and government structures of the Moldavian SSR was a result of the communist

---

11. During the 1947 Paris peace negotiations between the victor states and the former European allies of Nazi Germany, the Soviet-Romanian border was established in accordance with the Soviet-Romanian agreement of June 28, 1940. This border was officially recognized in the peace treaty with Romania. See "Peace Treaty with Romania" in *Anthology of Active Treaties, Agreements, and Conventions Concluded Between the USSR and Foreign Governments*, 13th ed. (Moscow: s.n., 1956), pp. 203–234.

12. Throughout the Soviet period, information on the ethnic composition of the party elites *(nomenklatura)* was carefully guarded as a state secret, and class categories were used in any statistical information which did not distinguish an ethnic basis. For 1989 data, see *Express-Information*, No. 07-13-11, State Committee of Statistics of the Moldavian SSR, February 27, 1990. According to statistical data published in 1992, the national composition of the leading cadres of the republic of Moldova in 1989 was as follows:

	Total	Moldovan	Russian	Ukrainian	Gagauz	Bulgarian
Parliamentary deputies	345	254	45	29	10	7
Presidium of the Parliament	22	18	1	1	1	1
Members of the government	30	24	1	3	1	1
Heads of local administrations	49	38	5	5	1	-

Source: *The Republic of Moldova* (Kishinev: s.n., 1992), pp. 47-51, 97-99.

regime's distinct ethnic policies—specifically the policy of *korenizatsia* (indigenization) of the government apparatus and the use of the titular language in government to encourage this process. The essence of this concept was to ensure that the republican party elites were recruited from the titular population and that Russians did not entirely dominate the power structures of the Union republics. This practice allowed the regime to fill its personnel needs, while also coopting and controlling ethnic elites to prevent them from uniting on a nationalist basis to oppose the center. In order to ensure this central control, people from the central party structures always held several key posts in the republican party structures and organs of repression, including the KGB and its predecessors. These outsiders, however, were not exclusively Russian.[13] In Moldavia, the result of the policy of *korenizatsia* was that political and administrative power was held largely by ethnic Moldovan officials.

A special feature of the creation and development of Moldavia's economic potential was the construction of large industrial facilities in the Transdniester region. The work force and engineering staff of these enterprises were mainly people of non-indigenous, Slavic origin—Russians and Ukrainians were brought to Transdniester by the Soviet government specifically to fill the personnel needs of these industries. These outsiders joined a large Slavic population who had lived in the region for many generations while it was part of the Russian Empire and later the Ukrainian SSR. The ethnic composition of the leadership of Moldavia's industrial sector was quite different from its government structures. Only 46.8 percent of top industrial managers were ethnic Moldovans.[14] The urban intelligentsia and the

---

13. After the death of Stalin, who was the main engineer of the *korenizatsia* policy, Chief of Soviet Intelligence Lavrentii Beria attempted to use this same policy in his struggle for power and secured the party's support for a total *korenizatsia* of republican structures. According to a report by Beria, on June 12, 1953, the Presidium of the Central Committee of the Communist Party of the Soviet Union (CPSU) passed the following decree: "1) All party and state institutions will correct the situation in the ethnic republics and end the distortions of Soviet ethnic policy in favor of the titular groups; 2) A large number of people from local populations will be trained and promoted to management positions, and government employees who do not know native languages will be dismissed and placed at the disposal of the Central Committee of the CPSU; 3) All records and paperwork in ethnic republics will be written in local languages," etc. However, Beria was unable to complete his project of total *korenizatsia* because he was arrested by his rivals in the Politburo on June 26, 1953. See Georgii Bezirgani, "Lavrentii Beria's One Hundred Days," *Delovoi Mir*, April 30, 1993.

14. By the end of 1988, the government television channel, the radio, and the majority of newspapers and magazines in the Moldavian SSR were controlled by

government apparatus were mainly ethnic Moldovans, although they represented only a small portion of ethnic Moldovans, who primarily lived outside the urban centers and were engaged largely in agriculture (with the exception of the Gagauz region). Moldavia's working class, technical and engineering specialists, and leading industrial personnel were, to a significant degree, made up of ethnic Russians and Ukrainians.

As a result of all these developments, the left-bank districts of the Dniester in the Republic of Moldova have a complex ethnic mix. According to the 1989 census, the total population of these districts numbered 601,700, of whom 39.9 percent were Moldovans; 28.3 percent Ukrainians; 25.4 percent Russians; 0.5 percent Gagauz; 1.9 percent Bulgarians; and 4 percent other ethnic groups. The large town of Bender on the right bank of the Dniester, where the most bitter fighting has taken place, had a 1989 population of 138,000, of whom 29.9 percent were ethnic Moldovans; 18.2 percent Ukrainians; 41.9 percent Russians; 1.2 percent Gagauz; 2.8 percent Bulgarians; and 6 percent other ethnic groups.[15] Although only 17 percent of the population of Moldova lives in Transdniester, it is the most developed industrial region of the republic,[16] providing 36 percent of industrial production, 28 percent of consumer goods, and 87.7 percent of energy. Strategically important rail and motor ways cross the region as well as gas pipelines.

The Beginning of the Conflict, 1989–90

The appearance of political tensions in Moldova toward the end of 1989 coincided with the economic depression in the national economy and the failure of Gorbachev's program of perestroika in industry and agriculture.[17] Within the Moldavian Communist Party and government elite in the capital city of Kishinev (Chisinau) two

---

ethnic nationalists whose aim was the Romanianization of Moldova. This situation provided a highly fertile environment for the proliferation of the dominant ethnic ideology, at the core of which was a negative stereotyping of non-Romanian ethnic groups and a celebration of the monoethnic Romanian state.

15. Electronic databases of the CIS Committee for Statistics and the Russian Federation's State Committee for Statistics (Goskomstat).

16. According to the CIS Committee for Statistics, the population of Moldova in 1989 numbered 4,359,000, of whom 64.5 percent were Moldovans; 13.8 percent, Ukrainians; 13 percent, Russians; 3.5 percent, Gagauz; 2.5 percent, Bulgarians; 1.5 percent, Jews; and 1.2 percent, other nationalities.

17. Economic statistics showing the actual progress of the perestroika program were jealously guarded by the central committees of the communist parties of

groups began to form. One, headed by Semyon Grossu, first secretary of the Moldavian Communist Party (MCP), was made up of the communist old guard who followed the internationalist line and supported the preservation of the Soviet Union. The other was headed by the second secretary of the MCP, Pyotr Luchinsky, and had a national communist orientation. The chief goals of the national communist movement, which developed in party organizations in many Soviet republics during the late 1980s, were to reform the party structures; reduce the unpopularity of the Communist Party and the Soviet regime by increasing the autonomy of republics and removing the regime's Russian aspects at the republic level; recruit more members from the titular nationality; increase use of the national language in the party organization; and pay more attention to the ethnic intelligentsia and young people. Personnel decisions were to be made with the clear purpose of ethnicizing republic political and administrative structures at all levels. National communists also demanded more autonomy for local economic organizations and campaigned against industrialization, which had led to a massive influx of non-native specialists and workers into the republics. Although the national communist movement was periodically purged by the party, it was able to successfully take advantage of the party's policy of *korenizatsia*. The movement gained strength during perestroika, and was spurred on by the prospect of republic communist parties independent of the CPSU.

When it became clear that the collapse of communism as a political system was inevitable, the national communists organized ethnic national movements that brought them to power in the republics.[18] The split gradually widened among the political elites, but the national communists kept it hidden to avoid showing their hand, which would have given impetus to the defenders of the status quo.

---

ethnic republics, which were supposed to report on the program to the Central Committee of the CPSU. Thus, economic statistics did not accurately reflect the real economic situation, which could only be evaluated by indirect means. See, for example, Gosudarstvennyi department SSR Moldova po statistike, *The Economy of the Moldavian SSR: Statistical Yearbook 1989* (Kishinev: Kartia Moldoveniaske, 1990).

18. Typically the movement camouflaged its actions, often as campaigns against corruption or infringement of party discipline, which happened to target ethnically "foreign" individuals or groups. An example of this was the ouster in November 1988 of the second secretary of the Central Committee of the Moldavian Communist Party, Vladimir Smirnov, on charges of corruption, which the chief prosecutor of the Soviet Union later admitted to have been completely false.

A common national communist tactic was to use key positions of authority to promote members of the cultural elite to leadership roles. As defenders of the nation and national culture, they could be counted upon to support national communist positions. Indeed, during this period the cultural elites were an inseparable part of the government *nomenklatura*. In Moldavia and elsewhere, organizations such as the Union of Writers and the Union of Journalists, as well as the mass media, were in reality bureaucratic hierarchies intertwined with the top party and state institutions—the Central Committee of the Communist Party of Moldavia, the Ministry of Culture of the Moldavian SSR, and even the KGB.

In Moldavia, the first open split came in 1989 when the Moldovan cultural elite advanced the idea of the priority of the interests of the indigenous nation. A plenum of the republic's artistic unions, together with a constituent congress of the People's Front, demanded limits to the CPSU monopoly on power, the formation of national military units, a strict definition of citizenship on an ethnic Moldovan basis, and the establishment of Moldovan as the official state language. During this period, accounts were published and documentary films were made about the Moldavian famine of 1946–47, the collectivization program under Stalin, and the deportation of part of the population in 1949. They emphasized historical justifications for Romanian ethnic superiority and territorial claims.

From March to August 1989, tension began to develop over the debate on two bills that proposed to make Moldovan the official state language. The first bill, which was submitted by a pro-Romanian group in the Moldavian Writer's Union, proposed the full exclusion of the Russian language from the sphere of official society, as well as administrative and criminal penalties for officials who used any language other than Moldovan. The second bill, which was submitted by a working group in the Moldavian Supreme Soviet, was more moderate. It recognized Russian as the language of interethnic communication, and affirmed the right of Russian-speaking citizens to use Russian in dealings with government institutions. The debate on these bills was marked by alarming manifestations of ethnic hostility. Since both bills stipulated that all official business should be conducted in the Moldovan language and that anyone holding an official position in the republic should know that language, the monopoly of all important positions in the administration by the ethnic Moldovan bureaucracy was secured. Inasmuch as nationalist poets and writers played the leading role in the preparation of the bills, questions connected with use of the Moldovan language in industrial documentation, banking, and the entire sphere of economic activity had not been considered. The sudden introduction and broad scope of the proposed language requirements created major political and economic problems. Non-Moldovan ethnic groups naturally regarded these developments as threatening and hastened their own political consolidation and the formation of movements and public organizations to respond to the threat to their language rights.

The policy of replacing non-Moldovans in leading positions had not been implemented very successfully in the Transdniester region, where the leaders of many industrial enterprises were still predominantly of Russian and Ukrainian origin. By the end of August 1989, more than fifty factories and plants (in Kishinev, Bender, Rybnitsa, Komrat, and other towns) throughout the Transdniester region joined a strike that had started in Tiraspol against the adoption of the language law. A Union of Workers of Moldova was formed, uniting the workers' councils of 192 enterprises, and a national strike was called. According to official information, more than 80,000 workers from 116 enterprises in various branches of industry and transport went on strike over a period of three weeks, virtually paralyzing Moldavia's economy.[19]

At the same time, the pro-Romanian movement was gaining strength in Moldova. On August 27, 1989, pro-Romanian nationalists united in the People's Front of Moldova, and held a rally in the main square of Kishinev at which tens of thousands of people shouted "No to the Russian language!" and "Russians go home!"[20] This meeting received support from part of Moldavia's political elite, including Chairman of the Presidium of the Supreme Soviet, Mircea Snegur (former secretary of the Central Committee of the Moldavian Communist Party), who, in addressing the rally, called it "a great national assembly."[21] After this rally, the confrontation took on a more open and dangerous form.

---

19. "The Strike in Moldavia Spreads," ITAR-TASS, August 24, 1989. According to unofficial information, 202 enterprises were involved in the strike.

20. The People's Front of Moldova was officially registered as a political organization in October 1989 although it had been formed six months earlier. In reality, the People's Front was a national communist organization based on the principle of "Moldova for the Moldovans," and was financially supported by the Moldavian Communist Party. It encompassed a wide spectrum of ethnic Moldovan social groups, with a large representation among urban government workers and people in the service sector.

21. ITAR-TASS, August 28, 1989.

The September 1, 1989, session of the Moldavian Supreme Soviet ended with the adoption of the law "On the Use of Languages on the Territory of Moldova" and a decree on the order in which this law was to be implemented. During the session, the parliament building was surrounded by thousands of Moldovan nationalists shouting anti-Russian slogans. In an unauthorized procession organized by the People's Front, demonstrators carried a map of Moldova as part of Romania under the slogan "Reunite!"

The first violent clashes erupted during this demonstration. On November 11, 1989, around 6,000 supporters of the People's Front, armed with steel bars and stones, attacked and set fire to the republic's Ministry of the Interior. During widespread disorder, 83 militiamen and 46 demonstrators suffered injuries.[22] It is the author's opinion that these riots against the government were staged by the pro-unification faction of the Moldavian Communist Party (MCP) to demonstrate to Moscow the public pressure for reunification with Romania. Only part of the Moldavian party elite supported the People's Front and reunification, and the government could not openly support this position in the context of existing Soviet and CPSU structures.

At this time, nationalist movements across the Soviet Union were rising against the center. There were deep splits among the elites of the Union republics, with some supporting and some opposing independence. Moscow was increasingly unable to exert much control over the Union republics. Earlier in the perestroika period, Mikhail Gorbachev had essentially given the national *nomenklaturas* substantial freedom because he thought that they would be allies in the reform process. Meanwhile, the old guard conservative elites in the national republics resisted the changes proposed by Gorbachev. Thus, by 1989, central control over the Union republics was to a substantial degree only symbolic.

Five days after the clashes in Kishinev, old guard internationalists were removed from power and replaced by the national communists from the MCP and Pyotr Luchinsky was elected first secretary of the Central Committee of the MCP. When Luchinsky's group came to power, the result was not a lessening of interethnic tension in the republic, but rather the opposite. The government institutions and commissions responsible for defending the rights of ethnic groups in the Moldavian SSR completely failed in their task.[23] As previously

---

22. "The Situation in Kishinev," ITAR-TASS, November 11, 1989.

23. Particularly unhelpful was the Supreme Soviet's Committee on Inter-ethnic Issues, whose principal mission was "to legally enforce the freedoms and ensure

mentioned, the most active political force at that time, the People's Front of Moldova, was an organization of the bureaucratic *nomenklatura* established to facilitate the transition of the Moldovan government to a new ethnic and nationalist foundation of legitimacy. According to this new approach, Moldovans were the "host-nation" and other nationalities were "guests." One of the levers of this policy was the Republican Assembly of Voters, a mass organization of representatives of nationalist movements from various towns and districts organized by the People's Front and sanctioned by the authorities. Their principal demands were the political and economic independence of Moldova from the Soviet Union and the adoption of a new constitution and new laws on sovereignty, citizenship, immigration, and national emblems.

The campaign for January 1990 elections for the Moldavian Supreme Soviet heightened tensions.[24] In Kishinev, the People's Front and nationalist organizations close to it like the Republican Social Democratic Party and the Christian Democratic Women's League held unauthorized nationalist rallies and demonstrations and instigated mass disorder, violence, and intimidation against other ethnic groups and parliamentary deputies who opposed unification with Romania. In response, an international movement called Unity, the Gagauz movement Gagauz Khalky, and organizations of worker collectives from the Transdniester towns of Tiraspol, Rybnitsa, and Bender presented demands for a referendum on the formation of a Transdniester Autonomous Republic and a Gagauz Autonomous Republic.

In the January elections, national communists were elected to important leadership positions within the Moldavian Supreme Soviet, thus confirming the shift in official policy. Mircea Snegur, a leader of the national-communist group in the MCP, became chairman of the

---

respect for the interests of people of different nationalities, and to aid in defending their rights." This committee endowed itself with all the powers of a permanent commission of the Supreme Soviet, including the power to initiate legislation. Another organization that failed was the USSR Supreme Soviet's Commission for the Study of the Socio-Political Situation in the Moldavian SSR, headed by Deputy Chairman Auelbekov from the USSR Supreme Soviet's Council of Nationalities. This commission never went beyond traditional appeals for moderation, calling upon political and social groups to stabilize the situation by refraining from holding rallies and other events involving large groups of people. Striking worker collectives, enterprises, and other institutions were urged to return to work.

24. Unlike elections for the USSR Supreme Soviet, where roughly half of the candidates were hand-picked from Soviet social and professional organizations and official party lists, the elections in Moldova and other Union republics were much more of a political free-for-all in which nationalist parties played a significant role.

Supreme Soviet, and Ion Khadyrke, a writer and the leader of the People's Front, was elected as his first deputy. Both the general pool of candidates and the deputies ultimately elected did not represent a realistic cross-section of the republic's population. Instead, Moldovans were overrepresented, and there were disproportionate numbers of civil servants and members of the Communist Party.[25]

The first session of the new Supreme Soviet was held in an atmosphere of threats and physical intimidation of non-Moldovan deputies from the Transdniester and Gagauz regions. Nationalists picketed the Supreme Soviet. A group of 132 deputies from the Transdniester and Gagauz regions walked out of the session, and some of them left the capital in protest against the verbal and physical threats from the crowd surrounding the parliament building.[26] As a result of this government crisis, the extreme nationalist Mircea Druk was elected chairman of the Council of Ministers. A new Ministry for State Security was quickly formed, headed by another extreme nationalist, Ionu Kostashu. Druk and Kostashu subsequently played important roles in initiating the armed conflict in Moldova.

By the end of 1989, it was clear that the goal of the Moldovan nationalist elites was full control of the republic. However, in order to form a republic based on self-rule for ethnic Moldovans, they considered it essential to take over the valuable industry and property of the Transdniester region. This objective clashed with the political and economic interests of Transdniester's industrial elite. However, inasmuch as Moldova's main industrial work force came from the Russian-speaking population, industrial workers and elites both saw a real threat to their standard of living. Specifically, non-Moldovans feared the threat of dismissal and unemployment, the closing of enterprises, ethnically based limits on employment, the breakdown of economic

---

25. A total of 1,774 candidates competed for 380 parliamentary seats: 1,491 of these candidates were government officials, and 90 percent were members of the Communist Party. The ethnicity of the candidates was as follows: 1,285 were Moldavian, 187 were Ukrainian, 160 were Russian, 51 were Gagauz, 48 were Bulgarian, 20 were Jewish, and 23 were members of other ethnicities. By March 1990, 370 out of the 380 seats had been filled, and it turned out that of the 370 new deputies, 287 were government officials and 307 were members of the Communist Party. The ethnicity of the new deputies was as follows: 257 were Moldovan, 57 were Russian, 36 were Ukrainian, 12 were Gagauz, and 8 were Bulgarian. ATEM-TASS, January 26, 1990.

26. ATEM-TASS, May 24, 1990.

links with other republics of the Soviet Union—especially concerning the energy supply—and disruption of orders for merchandise and markets for industrial goods, all of which were coordinated by central planning structures. If these links were disrupted for political reasons—for example, by Moldova's declaration of independence and a boycott and other retaliatory measures from Moscow—industrial activity in the Transdniester region would shrink, creating a dramatic drop in production and an increase in unemployment. Big stakes were involved for the Transdniester region if Moldova became independent, or if it decided to unite with Romania. For the Gagauz and Bulgarians, who lived in compact settlements in the rural districts of the Black Sea region (including districts of the Odessa region of Ukraine), the claims of the Moldovan nationalists also posed territorial and linguistic threats. The greatest alarm was raised by territorial claims voiced by the People's Front of Moldova to districts in northern Bukovina, which had been given to Ukraine after World War II.

On July 27, 1990, the Moldovan Supreme Soviet issued a decree on the status of the Gagauz people which not only failed to recognize their right to autonomy, but even declined to recognize the Gagauz as a "people," labeling them instead as an ethnic group living among the Moldovans with no right to a national territory. The Gagauz decided to take matters into their own hands, and on August 19, 1990, the first full Congress of Gagauz People's Deputies met in Komrat, the capital of the Gagauz region, and proclaimed the Republic of Gagauzia as an independent entity within the framework of the Soviet Union (i.e., on the same level as the Moldovan Republic). The declaration "On the Freedom and Independence of the Gagauzian People of the Republic of Moldova" noted that the enactments of the Supreme Soviet of Moldova did not take into account the interests of the Gagauzians and other national minorities. The Congress formed a forty-member Provisional Committee of the Gagauzian Republic headed by Sergei Topal.

The Supreme Soviet of Moldova declared the Congress in Komrat and its decisions unconstitutional. Compliance with these decisions was considered tantamount to resisting Moldovan law. Moldovan law-enforcement agencies were ordered to establish the identities of the organizers of the Gagauz Congress among the leaders of Gagauz Khalky and to consider instituting criminal proceedings against them. Moldovan Prime Minister Mircea Druk signed a decree disbanding the Gagauz Khalky movement, charging that it had taken "unlawful decisions directed at undermining the state and social system of the Moldovan Republic along with its territorial integrity."[27]

Following these dramatic events in the Gagauz region, on September 2, 1990, an extraordinary session of deputies of all levels from the left bank of the Dniester met in Tiraspol and proclaimed the existence of the Transdniester Soviet Socialist Republic as another separate republic of the Soviet Union. The Transdniester Republic included the left-bank territories of the Kamensky, Dubossar, Rybnitsa, Grigoropol, and Slabodei districts and the towns of Tiraspol, Bender, Rybnitsa, and Dubossar. The session announced that all property in these areas formerly belonging to Moldova had passed into the possession of the Transdniester Republic. In response the Supreme Soviet of Moldova declared the nature and content of the decisions made in Tiraspol to be unconstitutional, unlawful in seeking to change the state system of Moldova, and in violation of Moldova's territorial integrity. Moldova declared the proclamation of the Transdniester Republic null and void.

Moscow did not react to the announcements by the Transdniester and Gagauz regions. No actions were taken to recognize these republics, nor was it announced that Moscow would deny recognition.

The formation of new republics in Transdniester and the Budzhak Steppe can be explained in part by the desire of their populations to protect themselves against the announced plans of some powerful members of the Moldovan government to reunite Moldova with Romania. The formation of these new self-proclaimed republics was an open attack on the main plank of the People's Front platform—reunification with Romania. The particular aggressiveness of the People's Front was exacerbated by the fact that reunification found little support, even among Moldovans. The People's Front had a support base in the cities, but the majority of the Moldovan population lived in rural areas and did not play much of a role in politics. According to the results of a 1990 nationwide sociological survey, only 4.1 percent of the respondents supported the idea of reunification with Romania, while 89.2 percent were against it.[28] At the same time,

---

27. ATEM-TASS, August 20, 1990.

28. In the period just before the dissolution of the Soviet Union, sociological surveys and opinion polls were used to circumvent the restrictions on conducting referenda in union republics and other, smaller political and administrative units on questions of autonomy and independence. See the chapter on Crimea in this volume for another example of this political tactic.

50 percent wholly or partly supported the demand of the People's Front for the return of the Moldovan territories ceded to Ukraine.[29]

Faced with two secessionist claims, a special session of the Moldovan Supreme Soviet decided to introduce presidential rule in the republic on September 2, 1990. President Snegur was given the right to suspend and dissolve the regional soviets as well as to declare a state of emergency. The Moldovan authorities first imposed a curfew in territories inhabited primarily by Gagauz and attempted to disarm the local militia. On September 4, 1990, Minister of the Interior Druk decided to form a special corps of 10,000 police under the direction of his ministry. This corps was to act as the principal assault force against the Gagauz and Transdniester separatists.

Almost immediately after declaring its independence, the Transdniester Republic began to form its own state institutions, beginning with a militia and ministries of the interior and security.[30] The Moldovan government proclaimed a state of emergency in the Komrat, Chadir-Lung, and Bessarabian districts, all inhabited by Gagauz, and on October 31, 1990, a detachment of 5,000 Moldovan nationalist "volunteers" approached the territory of the Gagauzian Republic, advancing on the settlement of Vulkaneshti. They were met by a detachment of local inhabitants roughly equal in number. A small unit of the internal troops of the Soviet Ministry of the Interior stationed in the area interposed itself between the two forces and a direct clash was avoided.[31]

---

29. ATEM-TASS, August 13, 1990.

30. Vadim Bakatin, Soviet Minister of Internal Affairs, refused to grant the request of the authorities in the left bank region to create a new post of Minister of Internal Affairs for the Transdniester Republic. Bakatin stated that the Soviet Union Ministry of Internal Affairs considered the decision to create a Transdniester Republic to be anti-constitutional, and that the ministry had no intention of creating any separate administrative structures in Tiraspol, the Transdniester region, or in areas with a large concentration of Gagauz. On the other hand, Moscow's attitude was evasive and ambiguous. In December 1990, Gorbachev issued a decree "On Measures to Normalize the Situation in the Republic of Moldova," Article 4 of which countermanded the declarations of independence of the Gagauz and Transdniester republics, their announcement of elections, and their intention to form their own supreme organs of power. Article 7 of the decree instructed the government of Moldova to disband its voluntary regiments and workers' defense regiments. However, no one intended to carry out Gorbachev's decree; he had lost control of events in the Soviet Union long before.

31. These interior troops were much like a form of national guard, and were routinely mobilized to keep public order by the Ministry of the Interior at the Soviet

However, in the Transdniester area of Dubossar, there was no garrison of Soviet internal forces to prevent events from spiralling out of control. On November 2, 1990, by order of the Moldovan prime minister, units of the Moldovan militia and detachments of nationalists moved into the Dniester districts, Bender and Rybnitsa, to reestablish government control. Armed clashes erupted between these troops and the Transdniester militias, and three people were killed and nine wounded. Events moved too quickly to bring in Soviet internal troops from other regions and although the 14th Army was permanently stationed in the Transdniester region, it had orders from the Ministry of Defense in Moscow not to intervene. In a meeting on September 5, 1990, President Snegur and Prime Minister Druk of Moldova met with President Gorbachev, who formally stated his approval of the desire of the leaders of the republic to take immediate steps to defuse the situation in Moldova and to preserve the integrity of Moldova within the framework of a new union of sovereign states.[32] Moscow's decision not to intervene in the clashes in Transdniester was consistent with Gorbachev's stance. Meanwhile, Transdniester prepared to defend itself. A detachment of about 4,000 workers occupied Dubossar and Grigoropol, while another group of around 6,500 men was on alert in Tiraspol. The Moldovan militias retreated at this show of strength, and during the ensuing armed standoff, both sides began to stockpile more weapons.

The War in Transdniester, 1991 through Spring 1992

In the spring of 1991, the Moldovan political elite suffered a serious internal crisis caused by a split among the nationalist groups. Two camps emerged: the upper strata of the ethnic Moldovan *nomenklatura* whose goal was an independent, ethnic Moldovan state; and various groups of mid- and lower-level civil servants who demanded immediate reunification with Romania. The formal pretext for the confrontation within the leadership was the government's proposal to replace local soviets (councils) with new administrative bodies.

---

and Moldovan levels, and their involvement was not a sign of an extraordinary situation or of any kind of intervention from the center.

32. "A Meeting with the Country's President," TASS, September 2, 1990. The signing of the agreement envisioned by Gorbachev for a reconstituted Soviet Union based upon sovereign states was preempted by the August 1991 coup attempt in Moscow and subsequently abandoned.

The proposed system mimicked the administrative and territorial units of Romania, under which the government would appoint prefects to supervise and guide local administrations. Although appearing to promote local self-rule, the prefect system was actually highly centralized and bureaucratically complex. The central government would have the power to repeal or suspend decisions of local councils and could prohibit regional administrations from taking political decisions or issuing protests. One of the key articles of the draft law was that Gagauz, Bulgarians, Russians, and Ukrainians residing in Moldova would be denied the right to defend their political interests if they contradicted the official political line; however, this draft law was not passed by the parliament.[33] At the same time, a deep economic crisis and rampant corruption in the cabinet of Mircea Druk led to many calls for the government's resignation and the transfer of executive power to President Snegur. President Snegur announced his resignation at a meeting of parliament, stating that a covert war was being waged against him and that it had become impossible to work with Prime Minister Druk. However, his resignation was not approved by the parliament.

A parliamentary crisis erupted in May 1991 when supporters of the People's Front provoked disorder near the parliament building to protest the failure of the legislature to act on their demands for reunification with Romania and administrative reform. They attacked the police who attempted to block access to the building, injuring twenty-six people. On May 22, 1991, the Moldovan Parliament overwhelmingly passed a vote of no confidence in Prime Minister Druk. Of the 228 deputies who took part in the secret vote, 207 voted against Druk. A new wave of demonstrations and violent disorders protested this action.[34]

The Moldovan Parliament passed another reform act in July 1991, "On the Foundations of Local Self-Rule," which replaced Moldova's fifty territorial districts with a number of new administrative units to be headed by prefects appointed by the president of the republic. This decision signaled the defeat of the reunification forces, since it effectively achieved territorial reorganization within an independent Moldovan state. It was announced that there would be a period of transition that would last until January 1, 1992, in order to allow the

---

33. "Local Self-Government in Moldova: Issues 1 and 2," TASS, January 16, 1991.
34. TASS, May 22, 1991.

new administrative and territorial system to be put into place. The Moldovan Parliament also passed a resolution stating that Moldovan state enterprises and organizations once subordinate to Moscow would henceforth fall under Moldovan jurisdiction. However, since the majority of these enterprises were located in the Transdniester region and staffed almost entirely by Russians and Ukrainians, this action was without practical effect.

The economic rebirth of Moldova, widely touted by the nationalists, turned out to be a hollow promise that only briefly disguised the disintegration of the national economy. Major reasons for this deterioration included the overt ethnicization of economic life, a general lack of expertise and professionalism in management, the contemptuous attitude toward Russian and Ukrainian administrative and technical personnel, and the dismissal of Russians and Ukrainians on ethnic and political grounds.[35] Under the Druk government, People's Front functionaries, who were generally inexperienced and incompetent, were appointed heads of various industries on the basis of their ethnicity and political leanings.

At the same time, the Moldovan nationalists continued to build up their armed formations. In November 1990, the Tiras-Tigin battalion was organized, and "volunteers" who had distinguished themselves in the October campaign against Gagauzia were invited to join. It was announced that there would be a national collection of funds for a future national guard, although according to Soviet law, such military groups were illegal. The Moldovan Parliament passed a "Law on

---

35. According to Petr Shornikov, a historian and deputy in the Moldovan Parliament, "ethnic cleansing was carried out in Moldova. The Presidium of the Parliament and its administration were filled almost exclusively with Moldavians and Romanians. Out of 30 ministers and division heads, only one was Russian. There were only three Slavs among the 143 judges confirmed by the Parliament. The Ministry of Internal Affairs lost 25 percent of its staff. In Kishinev in June 1991, 56 percent of research positions were empty. All the Russian and Ukrainian administrators in the medical institutions of the city were replaced. Out of the 1,500 workers at the National Television and Radio, only 30 Slavs were retained. 95 percent of workers laid off at the Statistical Office were Russians and Ukrainians, and 100 percent of those promoted were Moldovans. Dozens of research institutes and other organizations in which Russian speakers predominated were closed down. The only places where ethnic cleansing did not occur were the Transdniester and areas with a high concentration of Gagauz and Bulgarians, since it would have been politically impossible to have carried out ethnic cleansing there." Petr Shornikov, "Conflicts Over Language Policy in Moldavia, 1988–1993," in *The Transformation of Cultural Space and Civilization in the Former USSR* (Moscow: Soros Foundation, 1994), p. 182.

the Republican Guard," and the Department for Military Affairs began to organize new detachments. A vigorous effort was undertaken to supply these detachments with weapons, ammunition, technical equipment, and uniforms.[36]

The phases of the conflict in Moldova were directly linked to the development of the crisis in the Soviet Union's power structure. August and December 1991 were critical periods. Using the unsuccessful coup attempt of August 19, 1991, in Moscow as a pretext, Moldovan authorities arrested a number of Soviet officials and industrial managers, including many influential leaders of the Transdniester and Gagauz local administrations.[37] The arrests were carried out during the night of August 22–23, 1991, by special police teams sent from Kishinev to the towns and district centers of Transdniester and Gagauzia. These troops also occupied administrative buildings and other vital installations. Those who were arrested were supporters of the preservation of the Soviet Union and were opposed to Gorbachev and the new union agreement, but they had done nothing to support the coup. According to Valeriu Muravski, Prime Minister of Moldova, the support of the leaders of the Transdniester and southern Moldova for the coup in Moscow was demonstrated by the fact that they sent telegrams of congratulations to the State Committee for the State of Emergency. Muravski stated that those who supported the plotters would face criminal charges.[38]

---

36. A special resolution was passed by the Moldovan Council of Ministers requiring state enterprises and cooperatives to pay a portion of their profits into a fund for the national guard. The national guard and other military detachments were staffed by volunteers, who were rewarded with a number of material benefits; deserters from the Soviet Army, of whom there were hundreds in Moldova; and people who had refused to serve in the Soviet armed forces. The Moldovan leadership did not hide its purpose in creating these military detachments. In fact, the general director of the Moldovan Department for Military Affairs, Nikolae Kirtoake, remarked that the intention was not to create a national army, but rather to create a force capable of "cutting short any terrorist acts and other actions on the part of the Transdniester and Gagauz republics."

37. Among those arrested were Sergei Topal, the chairman of the Supreme Soviet of the Gagauzian Republic; his deputy, Mikhail Kendigelian; the department chairman of the Dubossar Municipal Soviet, G. Pologov; and the leaders of the joint councils of production collectives of Tiraspol and Grigoropol.

38. Moldova-Press, TASS, August 24, 1991. In fact, the indictment against the accused was political, and not juridical. If officials in Transdniester and Gagauzia had provided material assistance to putschists by sending weapons or other forms of support, there would have been a legal pretext for their criminal arrest. However, in merely sending telegrams to the State Committee for the State of Emergency, the accused violated no existing law, although many were, in reality, political supporters of the coup attempt.

On August 27, 1991, a week after the failed coup in Moscow, the Moldovan Parliament adopted a Declaration of Independence. President Snegur stressed that this historic act was based on the right of the people to national rebirth and future prosperity. He rejected Gorbachev's proposed new Union Treaty and asked the United Nations to accept Moldova as a new member. Snegur also expressed readiness to join the Helsinki Act and the Paris Charter.

In response to Moldova's declaration of independence, a congress of Transdniester deputies convened in Tiraspol on September 2, 1991, to consider the political and socioeconomic situation in the Transdniester Republic. The congress did not recognize Moldova's declaration of independence and affirmed its allegiance to the Soviet Union. The congress also adopted a constitution for the Transdniester Republic, along with a flag and coat of arms, and decided to form a national guard and to place the Directorate for Tiraspol Internal Affairs exclusively under the jurisdiction of the Transdniester Republic. Furthermore, the congress issued an ultimatum to the Moldovan government demanding the release of Igor Smirnov, chairman of the Supreme Soviet of Transdniester, and all the other arrested deputies, and threatened Moldova with economic sanctions—i.e., the interruption of gas and electricity and the obstruction of railroad travel to the right-bank districts of the Moldovan Republic. The inhabitants of Tiraspol and Bender did in fact stage a blockade at the bridge over the Dniester, stopping rail traffic in all directions and reducing the freight capacity of the Moldovan railroad by three-fourths. The most important freight line, linking the junctions of Razdelnaia, Tiraspol, and Bender, was completely blocked. On the following day, a congress of Gagauz deputies confirmed the August 1990 decision that proclaimed the Republic of Gagauzia and also demanded the release of Sergei Topal, chairman of the Gagauzian Supreme Soviet, and his deputy, Mikhail Kendigelian, both of whom had been seized by special teams of the Moldovan police.

Exactly one year after the first clashes in Dubossar, on September 25, 1991, armed confrontation broke out again between the municipal authorities of Dubossar, who supported the Transdniester Republic, and local law-enforcement agencies under the authority of the Republic of Moldova. The inhabitants of Dubossar and residents of the surrounding Moldovan villages faced each other on opposite sides of the barricades. When reinforcements for the republican police entered the town, armed clashes broke out, resulting in dozens of casualties.

The Moldovan authorities tried to impose a counterblockade of the Transdniester Republic, and set up a number of roadblocks on the main routes to the left bank of the Dniester in order to cut supplies to the region. This increased the risk of involving the population of the adjoining districts of the Odessa region of Ukraine in the conflict, because many people who worked in Transdniester lived in Ukraine. Road and rail links between the two republics were critical to the economy of the entire region.

On October 1, 1991, the leaders of Moldova and Transdniester signed two accords temporarily stabilizing the dangerous situation. The first envisaged normalization of the situation in Dubossar and the Dubossar districts, while the second addressed normalization in a number of other areas on the left bank of the Dniester. The deputies who had been under arrest, including the leaders of Transdniester and Gagauzia, were released. Under supervision by a group of observers from the Supreme Soviet of Russia and the Republic of Moldova as well as leaders of the Transdniester districts, the forces of the Moldovan Ministry of the Interior and the worker detachments were simultaneously withdrawn from the town of Dubossar and the Dubossar and Grigoropol districts. Arms were anonymously surrendered, and both sides agreed not to resort to force or the imposition of economic blockades.

Russia had sent observers to the region beginning in early 1991, following the election of the new Russian Supreme Soviet. Two parliamentary delegations from the Russian Supreme Soviet visited the conflict zone with differing objectives but neither of them represented the Russian President. The first delegation arrived in Moldova on September 15, 1991, at the invitation of the Moldovan leadership and with the aim of studying firsthand the treatment of ethnic minorities. It was headed by the well-known radical democrat Sergei Krasavchenko. Discussions centered on a new political accord, signed by Moldova and Russia, that dealt specifically with the rights of Russians living in Moldova. Ten days later fighting broke out in Dubossar. There is every indication that after meeting with Krasavchenko, the Moldovan authorities concluded that Russia would turn a blind eye to the use of force in the Transdniester, because its leaders were suspected of having supported the August coup.

The second Russian parliamentary commission, headed by Nikolai Medvedev, took a clearer position, one that was confirmed by a special announcement by the Russian leadership. The Russian deputies visited the areas of greatest sociopolitical tension, and reached an agreement with the Moldovan authorities regarding the improvement of conditions in a number of towns in the Transdniester. The Russians attended negotiations between the opposing sides that ended with the signing of agreements aimed at normalizing the situation. The clear distinctions between attitudes of the two commissions and the results they obtained were based on ideological differences.

The confrontation in Dubossar in 1991 revealed the instability of the political situation in Moldova. The economy was on the verge of complete collapse. Economic crime was on the rise, production was falling, corruption was flourishing, the pillage of public property had attained monstrous proportions, and there was little, if any, discipline in the workplace. Economic indicators demonstrated the extent of the crisis. The budget deficit stood at one billion rubles and was still growing, and the monetary system was on the brink of disintegration. There had been a sharp rise in inflation and living standards had fallen. Official statistics show that Moldova's gross national product (GNP) fell by 13.7 percent compared to 1990, industrial production fell by 7.3 percent, and food production fell by 16 percent. The economic chaos and social tensions in Moldova prompted members of ethnic groups not involved in the conflict to leave the republic.[39]

In light of these circumstances, the ruling circles in Moldova tried to introduce a plebiscitary presidency[40] like many nationalist regimes

---

39. During the first half of 1991, over 10,640 Jews emigrated to Israel from Moldova. This figure was twice that for the first six months of 1990. "The Country at This Hour," TASS, October 8, 1991.

40. This term refers to a regime based on a kind of raw presidential power. Although other branches of government may exist, formally providing the trappings of democratic government, in reality the executive branch has all the power. As a rule, such governments cannot remain stable, and tend to follow either a path of traditional rule, one of bureaucratization, or some combination of both. The principal reasons for this are the strong ideological and material pressures from the administrative staff, from workers newly promoted to management positions, and from party workers. In 1991, a plebiscitary presidency began to emerge in Moldova. It rapidly created its own structures—a mass party, legal justifications for the dominance of the executive over the legislative branch, a system of plebiscitarian elections to executive organs, and a new *nomenklatura*. The president's decrees were accorded the status of law. The control exerted by the plebiscitary presidency sharply increased tensions in relations with ethnic groups who did not have their own governmental institutions. All the post-Soviet republics wanted to institute a strong presidency. This was likely the result of the cultural legacy of the CPSU and the *nomenklatura* system of promotion. In the post-Soviet states, democratic institutions do not have any real power, though their existence appeals to Western observers.

in other republics of the former Soviet Union. The People's Front at once declared itself an opposition party as it was known that President Snegur opposed reunification with Romania, and at a national conference the People's Front decided to boycott the presidential elections scheduled for December 8, 1991.

Thus, three main forces had emerged on the Moldovan political scene. The first, headed by the People's Front and an alliance of parties and movements called the 16th of December, stood for immediate reunification with Romania. All of its activities were directed at achieving this objective. In the view of the Front's leaders, Mircea Druk and Y. Roshka, the process of reunification of Moldova and Romania was impossible to halt. Forces in both Moldova and Romania advocating immediate reunification formed a National Reunification Council at a meeting in the Romanian town of Iasi, and twenty-eight Moldovan and thirty-three Romanian parliamentarians became members. The alliance of trade unions known as Moldavia, the All-World Association for Bessarabia and Bukovina, and the Labor and National Liberal parties of Romania, all formed part of this Council. There was not much support in Moldova for the idea of reunification, but in Romania reunification had become a popular political issue, and all Romanian political parties saw it as their duty to reunite "their people."

The second main political force in Moldova was represented by pro-presidential parties and groups including the Agrarian Democratic Party (to which President Snegur belonged), the Social Democratic Party, and a group of independent deputies in the Moldovan parliament. All of these groups supported an independent Moldova and opposed reunification with Romania. The Agrarian Democratic Party, which was formed in October 1991, became the most powerful force opposing the People's Front. Its program declared that it would fight for the development of democracy, equality of all forms of property, and the gradual transition to a market economy in which the social rights of citizens would be guaranteed. The bulk of the party membership comprised agrarian deputies (the largest group in the parliament), directors of state and collective farms, and local officials. Nearly all were former members of the Communist Party.

The third force, which included the separatist movements in Transdniester and Gagauzia, strongly opposed the reunification of Moldova with Romania and preferred Moldovan independence as the best guarantee against any form of reunification. These groups decided to hold separate presidential elections for their republics on December 1, 1991, and not take part in the Moldovan presidential elections. In Gagauzia, the only candidate, Sergei Topal, became president, with 90 percent of the votes. In Transdniester there were two candidates, Grigori Marakutsa, chairman of the Supreme Soviet of Transdniester, and Igor Smirnov, Chairman of the Transdniester Republic. Smirnov was elected president, receiving 64.5 percent of the vote. In a referendum held simultaneously with the presidential elections, the majority of the inhabitants of these two republics voted in favor of independence as sovereign republics within the Soviet Union. These separate elections were declared unconstitutional by the Moldovan Parliament.

The election of the president in Moldova on December 8, 1991, coincided with the signing of the Belovezh Accords on the formation of the Commonwealth of Independent States. The breakup of the Soviet Union and the introduction of a plebiscitary presidency[41] in Moldova provided added impetus to the armed conflict in Transdniester. The heads of the Russian Federation, Ukraine, and Belarus appealed to all sides in the conflict to start negotiations on a peaceful settlement. On December 12, 1991, President Snegur met with President Yeltsin in Moscow, and both leaders agreed to give

---

41. The institution of a plebiscitary presidency reflects the interests of certain groups in the dominant ethnic *nomenklatura* who, while formally recognizing parliamentary democracy, use the president to establish a political order that promotes the interests of the dominant class. This is a transitional type of political regime (between the charismatic and rational-legal types, if we use the well-known typology of Max Weber), in which the central role falls to the president, who derives his legitimacy from the plebiscite.

The author defines the legitimacy of a ruling elite as its ability to induce its subjects to believe that the current social system is the very best of all possible systems. A loss of legitimacy by the ruling elite can cause it to lose control over society and can provoke political disorder. The ethnic *nomenklatura* hopes that during the period of transition the plebiscitary president will be able to integrate the country nationally and politically, and exert control over the administrative machinery of government while carrying out reforms of this very machine. To this end, the president endows himself with the personal authority (although in practice he acts on the advice of his advisers) to bypass representative democratic institutions and norms in order to make crucial national decisions in the name of the rather anonymous "will of the people." The authoritarian nature of this type of regime derives from the way in which it personalizes power while preserving a certain facade of parliamentarianism. In practice, a plebiscitary presidency will never attain its goals in full, and as a regime it will be racked by internal instability, since it is a hybrid mixture of two opposing tendencies—charismatic and bureaucratic—and embodies the weakest elements of each.

Because a plebiscitary president aspires to play the role of a "charismatic chief," the members of his administrative staff are recruited on the basis of their

particular attention to resolving questions connected with the protection of the rights and freedoms of citizens from one side when on the territory of the other. They also discussed measures to protect the rights of national minorities, but events developed according to their own logic and these pledges were not realized.

Armed conflict broke out in Bender on December 10, 1991, between Moldovan police and armed detachments from Transdniester. The municipal council of Bender demanded that the police forces be placed under its command and that Moldovan formations withdraw from the town. On December 13, fighting started in the streets of Dubossar between Transdniester detachments and columns of the Moldovan armed forces that had entered the town. The attack occurred after the Moldovan Parliament ordered the disarming of the Transdniester Guards within a period of ten days and the prosecution of the organizers of the elections and referendum in Transdniester. Armed clashes in the center of Dubossar resulted in a number of deaths both among members of the armed formations and civilians as well as the destruction of the economic infrastructure of the town.

After two days of fighting, President Snegur and the Transdniester leader, Igor Smirnov, met on December 15, 1991, and agreed to set up a joint commission to settle the crisis.[42] The next day, the armed formations of both sides were withdrawn from Dubossar, but the

---

personal devotion to him, and little attention is paid to their technical qualifications. What is lacking is a set of formal rules or abstract legal principles, a process of adopting rational legal decisions based on these principles, and a legal culture based on the idea of legal precedent.

Each action taken is begun anew, without reference to actions taken in the past, and as a result it is perceived as a revelation of the leader and his retinue. When such a ruling group comes into conflict with a competing group, the only solution for the conflict is violence, since only one of the sides can be in the right; the other is automatically labeled as "criminal," and as needing to "redeem itself" before the people. The events of 1991 in Moldova are a perfect example of this situation. President Snegur was originally elected by the parliament for a term of five years. Thus his legitimacy and the limits to his authority depended on the will of the highest organ of legislative power. However, Snegur then attempted to gain election on the basis of a national vote, as this would allow him personally to make decisions of national importance, referring simply to the anonymous will of the people. He was nominated as the leading candidate in the national campaign for the presidency of Moldova, and election day was set for December 8, 1991. In fact, Snegnur was the only candidate for this position, as all his potential rivals had withdrawn their candidacies.

42. It is important to remember that Snegur and Smirnov were both members of the same communist *nomenklatura*. Although they were adversaries, they came from the same political base, and it is highly likely that they had some communication throughout these events.

situation remained explosive. Tensions were high, but there was no fighting over the next month until shooting began again between the Moldovan police and Transdniester formations on January 13, 1992.

The Moldovan government linked its actions in Transdniester to the breakup of the Soviet Union[43] and seized the opportunity to abolish the independence of these regions, arguing that they claimed to be part of an entity (the Soviet Union) that no longer existed. However, in the period immediately following the Byelovezhsky agreement, there were many, including in Transdniester and Gagauzia, who refused to recognize the dissolution of the Soviet Union and hoped for its restoration. These groups were labeled neo-communists by their enemies and were effectively marginalized during subsequent events. The situation of Transdniester, however, illustrates that there were many non-ideological reasons for hopes of a revival of the Soviet Union.

The collapse of the Soviet Union and the agreement to form the CIS encouraged Moldova and Transdniester to seize weapons belonging to the former Soviet Army. Even before the collapse, the president of Moldova decreed on November 14, 1991, after the arrest of the top army leaders who had participated in the aborted Moscow coup, that the weapons and military technology that had once belonged to the Soviet army were now the property of the Moldovan Republic. After the disintegration of the Soviet Union, the newly independent republics reached an agreement granting them the right to create their own armed forces and to divide the military detachments of the former Soviet Army among them. During negotiations held in Kishinev, Moldovan Minister of Defense Ionu Kostashu and Colonel General Boris Piankov, the CIS Deputy Minister of Defense, agreed that a Moldovan national army would be created from the Soviet 14th Army. Ninety percent of the 14th Army's weapons became the property of Moldova. In addition, the Moldovan authorities demanded the return of weapons that had been transported from Moldova to Russia. In this way, modern weapons, including missile launchers, fell into the hands of the Moldovan nationalist leaders.[44]

---

43. The reason for this was indirectly disclosed by the director of the Department of Political Analysis of the Moldovan State Chancellery, Oazu Nantoy, who stated to a TASS correspondent that "the objective development of events in the Soviet Union removed the ground from under the feet of the Transdniester leadership." "Shooting Takes Place in Dubossar Again," TASS, January 13, 1992.

44. The Moldovan Army numbers approximately 15,000 troops, 210 tanks, 210 infantry transporters, 250 artillery units, 50 warplanes, and 50 military helicopters,

Another powerful armed force in the Transdniester conflict comprised Moldovan police brigades and volunteers who had been supplied with small arms, mortars, and armored personnel carriers by Romania and trained by Romanian instructors. Transdniester also took steps to arm itself, primarily by seizing weapons from depots belonging to the former Soviet army.

The Transdniester Republic continued to adopt measures that were in direct contravention to the Moldovan Constitution, including the laws "On the Defense of the Transdniester Republic," "On the Armed Forces," and "On Obligatory National Service in the Transdniester Republic." These laws provided that Soviet army units stationed on the territory of the Transdniester Republic would retain their former structures and would be financed by the republic. Officers and noncommissioned officers would serve under contract. The laws had no legal force and merely represented Transdniester's demands. The leadership of the 14th Army did not respond to these acts in any way, although individuals were successfully recruited from the ranks of the 14th Army to fight on the side of Transdniester.

The conflict in Transdniester coincided with the revival of the Cossack movement in this region and many other areas of the Soviet Union. While the ethnic and national conflict was developing in Moldova, the Cossacks had not yet grouped into a single organized body. Their attitude toward the government of the Russian Federation was contradictory and at times hostile. On December 14, 1991, the *ataman* of the Union of Cossacks chaired an extraordinary meeting of *atamans* from Cossack regions across the country in order to discuss the situation in the Transdniester. This council issued a statement addressed to the presidents of Russia, Ukraine, and Moldova that spoke of the "brutal violation of the rights and freedoms of the peoples of the Transdniester" and stated that if the presidents and parliaments of Russia and Ukraine abandoned these peoples to the whims of fate, the Union of Cossacks would take all possible steps to protect them. In the Cossack regions, volunteers began to sign up to defend the Transdniester Republic. Individual groups of volunteers from many different regions of Russia traveled to the Transdniester in response to the appeal by the *ataman* of the

---

according to Nikolai Osmokesku, First Deputy Foreign Minister and head of the Negotiation Working Group Session, "The Hague Roundtable Annotated Report," Cambridge, Mass.: Conflict Management Group, January 15, 1995, p. 68.

Transdniester Cossacks.[45] On February 25, 1992, the Ministry of Foreign Affairs of Moldova sent a note to the Russian Federation about the arrival of Russian Cossacks in Transdniester. (A detachment of Ukrainian nationalists from the Ukrainian self-defense organization was also sent to Transdniester.) Best estimates suggest that there were approximately 200–300 Cossack volunteers in Transdniester, and although this did not constitute a significant military force, the Cossacks had a considerable symbolic effect in raising morale and enthusiasm for the cause of "defending Russians abroad." Because of the high profile of these Cossack volunteers, the Moldovan side reacted strongly.

THE "CONFLICT" BECOMES A WAR

On March 2, 1992, after months of mounting tension, armed clashes again erupted in the city of Dubossar, resulting in a number of deaths. According to official information, between March 2 and

---

45. According to the chairman of the Democratic Party of Transdniester, Sergei Blagodarnyi, commenting on the presence of military detachments in Transdniester, in March 1992, there were 150 people in the Dniester battalion, around 1,000 in the national guard, and around 100 Cossacks who had come voluntarily from the Kuban and the Don. According to the *ataman* of the Don troops, Sergei Meshcheriakov, they were joined by independent Cossack volunteers from the Stavropol district, Siberia, the Baltic states, St. Petersburg, and Moscow. The Russian government had not been involved in the activities of these Cossack groups—in fact, since the Cossack movement tended to support a revival of the Soviet Union, the Russian government was against the Cossack movement—but in the chaotic circumstances surrounding the breakup of the Soviet Union and political instability in Russia, Moscow had little ability to control these groups. Measures could therefore only be taken against individuals, and there is no evidence that this was done. The actions of the Cossack movement were largely determined by its leaders, the *atamans*, who traditionally held a great deal of power. Different Cossack leaders have had different political orientations. The degree to which Cossacks have been involved in politics has depended on the political environment in the country and the region, and also on the relationship that emerged between the Cossack movement and the authorities. It was not until 1994 that Russian Cossacks began to form their own governmental structures, after the adoption of the resolution of the government of the Russian Federation (No. 355), dated April 22, 1994, "On Government Policy Regarding the Cossacks." This document defined the Cossacks in terms of "both their service to the state and their specific military-agricultural style of life." Tension in eastern and southern Moldova grew by the day as the number and intensity of armed encounters and incidents increased, and with it the migration from Moldova. One of the indicators of how dangerous conditions were was the mass migration from the republic. Statistics from the census show that in 1991, 64,700 people emigrated from Moldova, including 17,800 Jews, 14,900 Russians, 14,527 Moldovans, and 10,819 Ukrainians. During the first six months of 1992, 2,338 people emigrated from Moldova, including 900 to the United States, 897 to Israel, 463 to Germany, and 32 to Australia.

March 24, six Moldovan policemen were killed and thirty-seven injured in the confrontation with Transdniester guards and Cossack detachments, and seven people were killed and eighteen injured among the civilian population of the town. In the fighting in the Dubossar district, approximately thirty people were killed and one hundred injured. President Snegur characterized the situation in Transdniester as "an attempt to cover up the military-communist nature of the Transdniester pseudorepublic."[46] On March 5, 1992, Snegur stated on national television that the Moldovan government would not allow the genocide of the population of Transdniester and would find worthy and effective means of defending its people. Meanwhile, however, the situation continued to slide into war.

On March 24, 1992, the Moldovan armed forces advanced on the towns of Transdniester in an attempt to seize the main communication lines and to isolate the region's three main cities, Tiraspol, Dubossar, and Rybnitsa. In a decree of March 28, 1992, President Snegur proclaimed a state of emergency, and the Supreme Security Council introduced direct presidential rule to provide for the administration of the territories where the state of emergency was in force. Extraordinary committees were formed with full authority to take any action necessary. At this point, the plebiscitary presidential regime reached its highest level of development in Moldova. In a state of emergency, everything could be decided by presidential decree and local administrations had little power. As subsequent events in Moldova proved, this type of regime turned out to be highly ineffective and destructive.

Fighting continued over a period of three months along a front line that developed along the Dniester River. The fighting became especially bitter from June 1992 on, when the Moldovan armed forces, supported by police and volunteer detachments, advanced on the town of Bender with tanks that had once belonged to the 14th Army. These forces were opposed by the national guard of the Transdniester Republic, which also had arms and heavy weapons from the 14th Army garrisons. The Transdniester forces had either stolen these weapons or acquired them from officers who had left the 14th Army to join the Transdniester forces.[47] These military operations destroyed the town and its industrial infrastructure, and its inhabitants were

---

46. Moldova Press, TASS, March 5, 1992.

47. The fact that these officers could simply appropriate and transfer weapons is indicative of the disorder and lack of control in the 14th Army.

either killed or forced to flee. According to official data, the first days of the fighting alone saw more than 500 killed, 1,500 wounded, and roughly 80,000 inhabitants forced to abandon their homes. After three months of fighting, the material damage amounted to about five billion rubles (1992 prices).

During the fighting, units of the Moldovan Army and police attacked the 14th Army's military and housing facilities in Bender, creating casualties among the garrisoned troops. The 14th Army maintained an official position of neutrality under orders from the Minister of Defense of the Russian Federation, Pavel Grachev.[48] There were no orders either from Moscow or from the 14th Army's commander, General Netkachov, to take action. However, the 14th Army did become involved. Roughly 80 percent of the officer corps were from the Transdniester region, and some of them joined the Transdniester forces. At the same time, several sources have confirmed that soldiers, advisers, and equipment from the Romanian Army were involved in the military operations on the side of the Moldovans.[49] Moldova carried out massive artillery bombardment of the towns and populated areas using howitzers inherited from the Soviet army. Soviet MiG-29 aircraft, helicopters, tanks, mortars, and grenade-launchers were also utilized.

---

48. "Statement of the Russian Minister of Defense on the Situation of the 14th Army," ITAR-TASS, July 3, 1992.

49. According to data from the headquarters of the 14th Army, every day four to five railcars crossed into Moldova from Romania loaded with Romanian arms and ammunition. The Russian command had at its disposal many documents, film, and photo materials, which were shown at a press conference proving Romanian involvement in the armed conflict in Transdniester. See "The Situation in Transdniester According to Data of the Headquarters of the 14th Army," ITAR-TASS, July 7, 1992. Romanian military support for the Moldovan side was reported by a delegation from the International Society for the Defense of Human Rights who visited Transdniester in April 1992. (This organization unites the human rights organizations of 24 countries, and has its headquarters in Frankfurt.) The members of this delegation claimed to have received "absolute proof" that Romania was giving "full support" to the government in Kishinev, including weaponry, ammunition, and armed vehicles. According to the head of the U.S. office of this Society, it has documentary proof (including many photographs) to support these claims that the Moldovan government was using Romanian military advisers and security forces, and that there was evidence that Moldovan forces had received military and police training from the Romanians. On the basis of this evidence, the Society prepared a report that was distributed to the U.S. Congress and State Department, and to representatives of the CSCE. See "Human Rights Organization on the Situation in the Transdniester and Romania," ITAR-TASS, July 8, 1992.

While heavy fighting raged in Transdniester, no military operations were conducted on the territory of the self-proclaimed
Republic of Gagauzia, though in view of the continuing activities of
individual armed groups, the situation there remained tense. In districts settled mainly by Gagauz, roadblocks were set up to prevent
Moldovan sabotage groups from entering the territory. According to
the Gagauz authorities, such groups carried out attacks on local
functionaries and people's deputies. Administrative buildings,
industrial facilities, and houses were shot at and set on fire.[50] The
Gagauz seem to have managed to avoid violence on the massive
scale that occurred in Transdniester because Gaugazia was less
important to the Moldovan government.[51]

THE 14TH ARMY

The involvement of the Russian 14th Army in the Transdniester conflict deserves special attention. The 14th Army consists principally of
the 59th Mobile Rifle Division and several army detachments totaling
6,000 soldiers and officers. The administrative structure of the force
comprises more than 230 people, which is more appropriate for five
regular army divisions. Although the 14th Army consists of only one
division, it controls enormous arms depots that once belonged to the
Odessa military district of the Soviet Ministry of Defense, making it
a significant presence in the region. As noted above, 80 percent of its
personnel come from Transdniester, including 51 percent of its officers and 79 percent of its draftees.[52] The majority of these inhabitants
are indigenous Slavs, which explains their attitude toward the conflict. Some troops resigned from the army to fight for the
Transdniester Republic and occupy various positions of leadership.

---

50. On May 24, 1992, one of these groups, headed by an officer in the Moldovan
Ministry of State Security, was detained by the local police in the town of Chadir-
Lung. The group retaliated, killing one police officer and wounding another.
Gagauz deputies demanded that the Moldovan leadership punish the Moldovan
terrorists responsible for the Chadir-Lung incident. The parliamentary group
Budzhak, which includes Gagauz deputies, also demanded the resignation of the
Presidium of the Moldovan Parliament and of the Minister for State Security,
whom they held responsible for the tragedy. See "Gagauz Deputies Demand the
Resignation of the Moldovan Minister for State Security and the Leadership of the
Parliament," ITAR-TASS, June 10, 1992.

51. Consisting mostly of empty steppe, Gagauzia is not an economically valuable region and could easily be overcome by force if necessary.

52. See Alexander Lebed, "Life Obliges Generals to Get Involved in Politics,"
Izvestia, July 20, 1994, p. 4.

Most of them retain close links with their divisions and with the 14th Army as a whole.[53]

Both the independent Republic of Moldova and the unofficial Transdniester Republic have laid claim to the weapons and military equipment stored in the depots of the former Odessa military district. The loss of control over the troops of the former Soviet Army after the collapse of the Soviet Union and the lack of a legal basis for the division of its weapons and property among the former Soviet republics led to a chaotic situation in which weapons were transferred, illegally traded, or simply seized by whoever had the means to do so. Moldova and the Transdniester were no different in this regard. In response to a question from an ITAR-TASS correspondent on the transfer of military technology and weapons belonging to the 14th Army to the Moldovan Ministry of Defense, Major General Yuri Netkachov stated:

I personally did not transfer anything to anybody: the military technology was seized in accordance with a decree of the President of Moldova. At the summit meeting of leaders of the CIS states in Minsk, the decision was taken that the republics of the former Union would have the right to form their own armed forces, and Moldova was no exception. Our depot, in which we stored technology, property, artillery belonging to the army, and missiles, was located on the right bank of the Dniester. These weapons, which were seized by force [and included] self-propelled anti-aircraft installations, armored equipment, and high-caliber machine-guns, were used against the people of Transdniester.[54]

Most specialists can only hypothesize as to how the military detachments of the Transdniester Republic obtained their equipment. There is still no documented evidence of organized involvement of 14th Army personnel in military actions using this equipment.[55] Official Moldovan sources claim that between twenty and sixty T-64B tanks, as well as armored vehicles, artillery installations, and other pieces of equipment, were transferred to the Transdniester forces.[56]

---

53. See Vladimir Klimov, "Only the President of the USSR Can Dismiss the Commander of the Armies," *Rossiiskaia gazeta*, August 6, 1994, p. 1.

54. ITAR-TASS, May 26, 1992.

55. See, for example, Wilbur E. Gray, "The Chivalrous Republic: Intrarepublic Conflict and the Case Study of Moldova," Strategic Studies Institute, January 15, 1993, pp. 15–16; and Vladimir Socor, "Russia's Fourteenth Army and the Insurgency in Eastern Moldova," *International Relations*, September 11, 1992, p. 41.

56. Nedecivc, *The Republic of Moldova*, pp. 90–96.

The Russian Ministry of Defense repeatedly expressed the official view that the 14th Army was defending its neutrality in the Transdniester conflict. Its personnel were allowed to open fire only in response to a clear attack on military installations or compounds, attempts to seize arms, or when there was a real threat to the lives of army personnel and their families. According to the Ministry of Defense, accusations that the 14th Army had participated in aggressive actions against Moldova were completely unfounded, and direct, officially sanctioned participation of units of the Russian Army in military operations on the side of Transdniester had not occurred. However, the Ministry of Defense did concede that, during the attack on the town of Bender by Moldovan forces, some 14th Army officers took part in the defense of the town alongside the Transdniester forces, but insisted that they had acted as private individuals.[57] Since most of those who had fought for Transdniester were officers, they had the right to leave the Russian Army, and some did join the Transdniester National Guard.

On May 12, 1992, the president of Moldova demanded for the first time that President Yeltsin order the immediate withdrawal of the 14th Army, which he accused of interference in the internal affairs of Moldova.[58] Beginning on May 15, Moldovan forces attacked Dubossar, bringing units of the 14th Army under fire. On May 19, one day after the failed attack on Dubossar ended, President Snegur appealed to the member-states of the CIS for help, alleging that units of the 14th Army "had started open aggression against the Republic of Moldova and the forces of law and order."[59]

In response to these accusations, the Russian government issued a statement drawing the attention of the CIS and the world community to the fact that the Republic of Moldova was trying to solve a complex political conflict by force. This interpretation of events was completely different from that which the radical democrats around Yeltsin had put forth in the first months following the Soviet Union's collapse. This change in Russia's official position clearly demonstrated that the Russian leadership was gradually being disabused of

---

57. "The Chief of the Press Center of the Russian Ministry of Defense Stressed that the 14th Army Would Maintain Neutrality," ITAR-TASS, June 23, 1992.

58. "The President of Moldova Demanded of Boris Yeltsin the Immediate Withdrawal of the 14th Army," Moldova Press, TASS, May 20, 1992.

59. "The President of Moldova Addresses the People of the Republic," Moldova Press, TASS, May 20, 1992.

its earlier illusions regarding the democratic nature of the political regimes in the newly independent states.

The main (but not openly stated) challenge facing the Russian Ministry of Defense was to prevent the transfer of 14th Army personnel and equipment to the control of Transdniester. Since the Transdniester Republic repeatedly claimed ownership of all 14th Army military property, if the army were to attempt to remove it, there was a serious possibility of a mutiny in its ranks and a seizure of its stores by Transdniester. The task of controlling this explosive situation was entrusted in June 1992 to Lieutenant General Alexander Lebed, who replaced Yuri Netkachov as commander of the 14th Army during the most intense phase of the conflict when Netkachov had lost the confidence of his troops.[60]

Lebed is commonly perceived as having taken an openly pro-Transdniester position, but the role he played was much more complex, and in this author's opinion, included both open and hidden agendas. Lebed's initial actions were directed at two audiences. He addressed strongly worded statements to the Moldovan government demanding the cessation of their military activities in Bender, and carried out some demonstrations of force—maneuvers, deployment of heavy weapons, and the like—to show the Moldovan forces the fighting capacity of the 14th Army. The intended message was that the army's garrisons in the Transdniester region should not be attacked. The second audience for Lebed's actions, however, was his own officer corps, who were largely inhabitants of Transdniester whose homes had come under attack in the recent fighting, and who were increasingly difficult to control. Lebed had to demonstrate to his own officers his control over the army and his ability to defend their interests. Moreover, Lebed had another clear interest: to maintain Russian control over the 14th Army and its stockpiles of weapons. He succeeded in this objective, and in so doing, salvaged the authority of the Russian Army. Lebed's actions also did the Moldovan Army the favor of preventing Transdniester from gaining

---

60. Netkachov lost the confidence of his troops because he insisted upon fulfilling to the letter CIS directives that ordered the 14th Army to turn over its arsenals to the Moldovan government. In the early stages of this policy, the 14th Army, which was still quite large, was deployed across a wide swath of Moldova—not only in Transdniester. As the 14th Army's personnel was reduced as part of the general demobilization process, the army was increasingly concentrated in Transdniester and, as a result, less and less willing to hand over weapons and munititions to the Moldovans.

control of massive supplies of additional weaponry with which it could have intensified its fight for independence from Moldova.

Relative Stabilization of the Conflict, Mid-1992 to 1994

Only in the second half of 1992, when the Snegur administration finally began to realize that it could not solve the Transdniester conflict by force, did it decide to change course. Two factors played an important role in this decision. First, the social and economic crisis that engulfed Moldova made it increasingly difficult to conduct an expensive war. Second, there was the real danger of an assault by the 14th Army on the Moldovan armed forces, which by then had entered Transdniester.

ACHIEVING A CEASE-FIRE

At a summit meeting in Istanbul on June 24, 1992, the presidents of Russia, Ukraine, Moldova, and Romania initiated a diplomatic offensive to resolve the Transdniester crisis. A frank exchange of views on the situation revealed many similarities in the Russian and Ukrainian positions. Both emphasized the need to observe the territorial integrity, sovereignty, and independence of the Republic of Moldova and to resolve the conflict exclusively by political means, as well as the inadmissibility of military intervention or any kind of interference in the conflict by foreign forces.

The four presidents agreed that there should be an immediate cease-fire, along with the creation of safe zones for the unobstructed movement of civilians, medical personnel, and the delivery of humanitarian aid to the regions hardest hit. In the communiqué issued at the end of the meeting, all sides showed a desire for compromise. The presidents formally supported specific measures to be implemented by a parliamentary commission of representatives from Moldova and the Transdniester region, with the participation of a "Mixed Commission" of observers from each of the four countries. The Mixed Commission would observe the disengagement of forces, secure the neutrality of the 14th Army, develop measures to ensure the delivery of humanitarian aid to districts in need, and ensure that conditions were created to expedite the return of refugees. The status of the 14th Army and a timetable for its withdrawal were to be defined in negotiations between the Russian Federation and the Republic of Moldova in the near future. The four presidents appealed to the Moldovan Parliament to examine and determine the status of the left-bank regions of the Dniester, and requested that the Conference on Security and Cooperation in Europe (CSCE) advance the settlement of the conflict through its mediatory activity and human rights monitoring. They also welcomed a greater role for the United Nations in the political settlement process, and expressed satisfaction with the UN's decision to send a fact-finding mission to the region in the immediate future.[61]

In spite of the agreement reached in Istanbul, heavy fighting continued between the Transdniester forces and Moldovan Army and police. Exchange of gunfire continued along the entire front line, from Dubossar to Bender. Moldova's military and political failure to rein in the Transdniester region exacerbated the struggle within the Snegur regime between the radical pro-Romanian nationalists, who controlled the Ministries of Defense, Security, and the Interior; and the pragmatists, who controlled the president's office, parliament, and the administration. When it became clear that the radicals in the Moldovan government could not win the war, and in fact were inflaming the conflict, the groups that had advocated force most vocally became the government's scapegoats and were pushed out. Minister of Defense Ionu Kostashu and Minister of National Security Anton Plugary were dismissed in July 1992, and the government crisis ended with the resignation of the cabinet.

Meanwhile, tension between President Yeltsin and the Russian Parliament was mounting, and the fate of Russians abroad, particularly in Transdniester, was becoming an increasingly important issue in Russian domestic politics. Consequently, the Russian government was motivated to move quickly to try to reach a settlement in Transdniester. Talks on implementing the Istanbul agreements continued between Moldovan and Russian experts, culminating in an agreement called "On the Peaceful Settlement to the Armed Conflict in the Transdniester Districts of Moldova," signed in Moscow on July 21, 1992. This agreement played a decisive role in separating the armed formations, establishing a cease-fire, and creating conditions for the return of refugees and the restoration of the constitutional rights of the residents of the conflict zone. It also created real preconditions for a political settlement of the conflict. The document envisaged a stage-by-stage withdrawal of heavy weapons and Moldovan and Transdniester military forces from the conflict zone, after which security in the zone would be provided by military observers and

---

61. "Communiqué on the Meeting in Istanbul," ITAR-TASS, June 26, 1992.

limited peacekeeping contingents from all three sides. In order to coordinate these security measures, a Trilateral Control Commission composed of representatives of Moldova, Russia, and Transdniester was established in Bender.[62] To facilitate the return of refugees and protection of the civilian population, more than thirty control posts of trilateral peacekeeping forces were set up in various locations in Transdniester. These control posts were manned primarily by Russian observers under the auspices of CIS peacekeeping troops since the Trilateral Control Commission did not have actual monitoring or enforcement capabilities. Although in Moldova reaction to the accord was generally mixed, the People's Front and their supporters strongly opposed it.[63]

President Snegur lifted the state of emergency throughout Moldova on August 19, 1992. In early September 1992, agreement was reached on the introduction of the CIS peacekeeping forces into the conflict zone. At a meeting on September 4 with Deputy Supreme Commander of the CIS Armed Forces Colonel General Boris Piankov, President Snegur signed a protocol titled "On the Temporary Order for the Formation and Activities of Military Observer Groups and Collective Peace-Keeping Forces in Zones of Conflicts between States in the CIS," despite strong opposition from the People's Front and their supporters.[64] Under the agreement, political decisions on the

---

62. The various political factions within Moldova had different reactions to the accord on a peaceful resolution of the conflict. In an interview with the newspaper Respublika, Viktor Zhosu, secretary of the Moldovan Social Democratic Party, stated: "Despite the fact that the tragedy at Bender, which turned out to be a catastrophe for everyone, had a sobering effect on the authorities, it nonetheless failed to stimulate a search for a political solution to the Transdniester crisis." For Zhosu, what was most striking was "the surprising degree of irresponsibility with which political leaders on both sides of the Dniestr are attempting to extract themselves from this conflict." See "Moldovan Social-Democrats Believe Bender Tragedy to Have Been Catastrophic for All Concerned," ITAR-TASS, July 30, 1992. However, the Christian Democratic People's Front of Moldova publicly opposed the accord reached by Presidents Snegur and Yeltsin, and urged the Moldovan Parliament not to ratify it. *Moldova Suverana*, August 1, 1992.

63. "Communiqué of the Meeting of the President of Moldova Addresses the People of the Republic," Moldova Press, TASS, May 20, 1992.

64. In April 1992, the Moldovan side had rejected the idea of creating a CIS peacekeeping force and having Russian troops take part in peacekeeping operations. The commander of CIS armed forces, Evgenii Shaposhnikov, suggested to President Snegur that detachments of the Russian 14th Army could be used to separate the two warring sides, and that a system of military observers be set up in cooperation with military personnel from other CIS states. The Moldovan government immediately rejected this initiative, labeling it an attempt "to keep the forces of law and order of the Moldovan Republic from carrying out their constitutional

conduct of the peacekeeping operations would be taken on a consensus basis by the Council of Heads of State of the CIS at the request of one or more CIS member-states and with the consent of all parties involved in the conflict. In the event of a decision to carry out a peacekeeping operation—i.e., to actually use military force—the UN Security Council and the acting chairman of the CSCE were to be immediately informed, although nothing would be asked of either body. Every CIS state was obliged by the CIS Charter to provide military contingents, police personnel, and military observers for use in peacekeeping operations.[65] Ultimately, only Russian troops were included in these CIS forces, although some Moldovan and Transdniester troops also participated. Other CIS countries were invited to contribute, but no troops were forthcoming, ostensibly because none but Russia could bear the expense of providing these troops.

Some Western analysts argue that Moldovans viewed the deployment of the peacekeeping force as Russian imperial occupation and expansion under the guise of a CIS operation, and consequently insisted on the withdrawal of the force.[66] But the legal status of the CIS peacekeeping troops was not questioned by either Moldova's leadership or the CSCE and UN representatives who visited the republic at that time. No precise data exist regarding the reaction of the Moldovan populace to the introduction of CIS peacekeeping troops. The paucity of public demonstrations to compel the Moldovan government to protest this action may be interpreted as acceptance of, or indifference to, the measure, although there is no way of knowing for certain. The effectiveness of the peacekeeping operation received a favorable assessment from both the Trilateral Control Commission and observers from the UN mission. Although peacekeeping troops were fired upon from time to time by unidentified forces, these attacks were suppressed by the end of 1992.

---

duties, and also to open up the possibility of foreign military intervention in the republic, something that is completely unacceptable." The Sixth Congress of People's Deputies of the Russian Federation also called on the governments of the CIS to give immediate attention to the idea of setting up a CIS peacekeeping force to separate the two opposing sides, and forming a contingent of volunteers from the 14th Army to keep the two sides apart until a single peacekeeping force could be created. The Supreme Security Council of Moldova immediately stated that this constituted interference in the internal affairs of the Moldovan Republic and violated the principles of the United Nations Charter. See "Moldovan Government Rejects Marshall Shaposhnikov's Initiative," ITAR-TASS, April 5, 1992.

65. "President Snegur Meets with the Deputy Supreme Commander of the United CIS Forces, General Piankov," Moldova Press, TASS, September 4, 1992.

66. Hill and Jewett, *Back in the USSR*, p. 63.

INTERNATIONAL ORGANIZATIONS

All of these negotiations took place against a background of increasing involvement by international organizations in the Transdniester conflict. As early as the fall of 1991, the International Federation of Human Rights sent a group of representatives from the Helsinki Committees of Denmark, Switzerland, Norway, and the United Kingdom to Moldova to study "problems connected with the transition from a totalitarian society to a democratic society."[67] At the invitation of Alexandru Moshanu, chairman of the Moldovan Parliament, the group returned to Moldova in January 1992 to look into the situation of national minorities and ethnic and religious communities, and to study the impact of the new laws on relations among nationalities. The delegation visited southern Moldova, an area densely inhabited by Gagauz and Bulgarians. At a January 22, 1992, roundtable in Kormat, the question of turning Moldova into a federation of three republics was raised. The delegation also visited Tiraspol where a closed-door meeting took place with the president of the Transdniester Republic, Igor Smirnov, and the Chairman of the Supreme Soviet, Grigori Marakutsa. Meanwhile, President Snegur insisted that proposals for restructuring Moldova into a federation of three republics were unacceptable because eighty countries had already recognized Moldova as a unitary sovereign state. Snegur expressed the hope that the delegation's report would reflect "the real state of affairs in the Republic." The delegation considered it a positive development that people holding such different views were able to hold talks. This optimism was not confirmed by subsequent events, however. At that stage of the conflict, the Moldovan authorities viewed the activities of international organizations as a means of gaining political capital that would enable them to solve the problems of Transdniester and Gagauzia by force.

In mid-1992, as the fighting in Transdniester began to die down, the activities of international organizations in Moldova substantially increased. Gilberto Schlittler, director of the Political Department of the UN Secretariat, visited Moldova in June 1992 as the personal representative of the secretary general. Over the course of a few days, Schlittler planned to acquaint himself with the activities of the forces involved in the conflict and to submit his observations to the secretary general. His delegation met with the Moldovan ministers of Foreign

---

67. Moldova Press, TASS, January 17, 1992.

Affairs, Security, and the Interior, as well as with members of fact-finding commissions set up by the parties to the Trilateral Agreement on a settlement of the conflict. The UN group was generally very well treated, which was typical of all the former Soviet republics where ethnic conflicts had erupted since they sought to involve international organizations in the resolution of their difficulties.

Schlittler returned to Moldova on August 26, 1992, as head of a UN fact-finding mission that went to Bender to meet the commanders of the peacekeeping forces of Moldova, Russia, and Transdniester. The mission gave no official assessment of the conflict zone, but it was agreed that groups of UN experts and observers would participate in the verification of compliance with the cease-fire conditions and in settling any disputes that might arise.[68] In fact, this never occurred. The members of the mission were surprised to discover that, since their first visit, progress had been made in rebuilding Moldovan economic relations with Transdniester which would in time open the door to political contacts.[69]

On July 20, 1992, President Snegur received a delegation from the Parliamentary Assembly of the Council of Europe headed by David Atkins, chairman of the Assembly's Commission for Liaison with Non-member States. Snegur stated that Moldova was taking measures to prevent the infringement of anyone's rights, and again dismissed the idea of a federal republic as unacceptable.[70]

The CSCE dispatched a special mission headed by a special representative of the chairman-in-office, Adam Rotfeld, in September 1992. During its two-day visit, the mission met with representatives of the Moldovan government, the mixed control commission, and Transdniester authorities. Rotfeld wrote a detailed report, as a result of which the CSCE announced that it would send observers to Moldova if requested by the Moldovan government. The mission recommended granting special status to the left-bank districts allowing them to decide their own fate if Moldova were to reunite with Romania.[71]

---

68. "President of Moldova Meets with a UN Mission in Kishinev," Moldova Press, TASS, August 27, 1992.

69. Ibid.

70. "President of Moldova Meets with Delegation of the Parliamentary Assembly of the European Council," Moldova Press, TASS, July 20, 1992.

71. "The Interim Report on the Conflict in the Left Bank Dniester Areas of the Republic of Moldova by the Personal Representative of the Chairman-In-Office of the CSCE Council, Adam D. Rotfeld," Prague, November 5, 1992.

At its ministerial meeting in Prague in November 1992, the CSCE decided to establish a permanent mission in Kishinev with a mandate to help establish an enduring peace in Transdniester. Headed by Timothy Williams, the mission was to assist the Moldovan government in defining the status of the Transdniester districts and in verifying compliance with the agreement on the withdrawal of Russian forces from Moldovan territory. In addition, the CSCE mission was supposed to verify Moldova's compliance with its international obligations with respect to human rights and national minorities, and to ensure that the Transdniester conflict would be settled exclusively by political means. In May 1993, the Moldovan government and the CSCE mission signed a special memorandum on the mission's role in facilitating a settlement of the Transdniester conflict. The CSCE mission in Kishinev began to play a significant part in the negotiations between Moldova and Russia on the political status of Transdniester and the withdrawal of the 14th Army.[72]

POLITICAL NEGOTIATIONS AND DEVELOPMENTS

The July 1992 cease-fire agreement provided for joint meetings of Moldovan and Transdniester working groups charged with drafting principles for a peace settlement. At the first joint meeting, major differences were evident: the Moldovans proposed a draft that envisioned granting Transdniester local self-government, whereas the Transdniester working groups suggested establishing a Moldovan confederation and clearly defined the powers of the confederation's members.

In autumn 1992, the struggle intensified between President Snegur and his pro-independence allies, and the supporters of reunification with Romania. These two factions also held different views on the cessation of hostilities in Transdniester. While the pro-independence group considered the conflict a senseless massacre, the pro-unification faction called for war until victory was achieved. Snegur triggered a parliamentary crisis in January 1993 when he proposed a vote in parliament on holding a national referendum on unification with Romania. His intention was to embarrass the supporters of unification—including parliament—and kill the idea of unification once and for all. The outcome of such a referendum was virtually a foregone conclusion; several polls had shown that an overwhelming majority

---

72. "The Special CSCE Mission Intends to Help in Finding a Settlement to the Transdniester Conflict," ITAR-TASS, May 12, 1993.

of the Moldovan population opposed unification with Romania.[73] The leaders of parliament, who represented the pro-unification faction, tried to prevent a vote on the referendum proposal, but the majority of deputies supported it. Severely discredited as a result, the pro-unification parliamentary leadership was forced to resign, and Snegur's pro-independence faction received decisive support.[74] The referendum was not held because the goal of undermining the pro-unification parliamentary leadership had been achieved. Nevertheless, internecine struggles within parliament continued throughout 1993, provoking numerous parliamentary crises, and by the fall the deputies had split into two irreconcilable groups, paralyzing parliament. The majority of deputies, including the Agrarians, the Social Democrats, and others, considered Moldova to be a member of the CIS. The minority, which included the Members of Parliament (MPs) from the Christian Democratic People's Front, the Congress of the Intelligentsia, the Democratic Party, and the Labor Party, advocated Moldovan unification with Romania.

The government decided to deal with this situation by calling immediate parliamentary elections, which would be held in conjunction with a plebiscite on the national status of Moldova, on

---

73. A vast majority—83 percent—of respondents to a survey conducted in Moldova by the National Institute of Sociology stated that Moldova should be a sovereign, independent state. Only 9 percent of those who replied supported the unification of Moldova with Romania; 19 percent did not wish for unification; and 68 percent were absolutely opposed to the idea. However, 43 percent of those questioned opposed the entry of Moldova into the CIS, while 26 percent supported it, and 22 percent expressed specific objections to the idea. Fifty-six percent of those questioned supported Mircea Snegur's declaration of Moldova's independence, although 43 percent held the view that this announcement ought to have been made earlier. Moldova Press, TASS, January 20, 1993.

74. Relations between the two camps significantly worsened after the Ministry of Internal Affairs began to investigate a report published in the Chernovits (western Ukraine) newspaper *Bukovina* that representatives of the Christian Democratic People's Front, with the help of Romanian secret agents, were training terrorists in order to stage a coup in Moldova. The report stated that, beginning in 1992, the Romanian secret services had been providing training in terrorism to volunteers recruited in Moldova from among those who had fought in the Transdniester. The plan was that terrorist groups would become the chief weapon of the pro-Romanians, enabling them to violently overthrow the president and prime minister, seize power, and unite Moldova with Romania. Before this incident, in an interview with the newspaper *Molodezh Moldovy*, President Snegur had condemned the head of Romanian intelligence, Virgil Megurianu, openly stating that the Romanian secret services were doing everything possible to join Bessarabia to Romania. *Molodezh Moldovy*, January 8, 1993, p. 1.

February 27, 1994. The authorities in Transdniester did not allow elections to be held in the left-bank districts, but they did not prevent residents from traveling to Moldova to take part in the voting. The people of Gagauzia participated in the elections after reaching a special agreement with Kishinev. The Agrarian Democratic Party of Moldova (to which President Snegur belonged) came out on top in the elections and became the ruling party, with the right to form the government and executive bodies.[75] The outcome of the referendum also dealt a heavy blow to supporters of reunion with Romania.[76] The new parliament elected Andrei Sangeli, a deputy from the ruling Agrarian Democratic Party, Prime Minister, and another Agrarian Democrat, Mikhail Popov, became Minister of Foreign Affairs. These changes gave impetus to the efforts of the Moldovan government, both on the domestic and the international front, to resolve the Transdniester conflict.

Meanwhile, in Tiraspol the struggle intensified between the supporters of complete independence and those who regarded Transdniester as part of a confederative Moldova. In the Supreme Soviet of Transdniester, the supporters of secession demanded the resignation of Secretary of State Valery Litsky, who had proposed an arrangement whereby Transdniester would remain part of Moldova. Litsky had also headed the Transdniester delegation to the negotiations in Kishinev that had developed compromise proposals for a peaceful settlement of the conflict. At the same time, relations between Transdniester and the Moldovan government were strained by the trial in Tiraspol of a number of leaders of the People's Front who had been arrested in the summer of 1992 and accused of terrorist acts in Transdniester. The Moldovan government insisted that these individuals were being held for political reasons.[77]

---

75. Snegur's party won 56 out of 104 seats in parliament.

76. According to the official election results, the Agrarian Democratic Party received 43.18 percent of total votes cast. This gave the party the opportunity to independently form a government and other executive bodies. Twenty-two percent of the votes and 28 seats went to the electoral bloc consisting of the Socialist Party and the Unity movement. The bloc of peasants and intelligentsia, which had split off from the Christian Democratic People's Front before the elections, received 9 percent of the votes and 11 seats in the new parliament. The Christian Democratic People's Front received 7.5 percent and 9 seats. The remaining nine political parties and movements that competed in the electoral marathon failed to attain the 4 percent necessary to receive seats.

77. A wide-ranging anti-Russian campaign was launched in both Moldova and Romania to coincide with this trial. The Romanian Parliament and government,

Over the course of 1993 and 1994, a situation developed in Transdniester, which compelled Moldovan authorities to acquiesce to the de facto Transdniester and Gagauz republics and refrain from resorting to force. The Moldovan Republic remained separated from Transdniester by a security zone controlled by the Joint Control Commission of the trilateral peacekeeping force established by the July 1992 agreement. Meetings of the working groups drafting the main principles for the settlement of the conflict continued without any significant change in the initial positions of the parties and thus failed to make any progress.

The CSCE mission in Kishinev, however, began to play a significant role in the peace negotiations. In May 1994, the head of the mission, Timothy Williams, stated that in order to achieve an adequate solution to the conflict, support was needed from all countries.[78] The Russian side suggested that the mission's report dated November 13, 1993, should serve as the basis for the negotiations. This report contained a set of specific recommendations; in particular it asserted that the key to a peaceful settlement was recognition that the return of Transdniester to its former status as a subordinate part of a unitary Moldovan state was impossible, and recommended that Transdniester should be given a special status in the Moldovan Republic.[79] The importance that the UN and the CSCE attributed to the negotiation process was demonstrated by the autumn 1994 visits to Moldova of UN Secretary General Boutros Boutros-Ghali and CSCE High Commissioner for National Minorities Max van der Stoel.

In late 1994, a solution to the problem of the status of the Gagauz was reached. In negotiations between the Moldovan authorities and Gagauzia undertaken by an inter-parliamentary commission, both

---

submitting to pressure from nationalist parties, joined in this campaign, and issued anti-Russian statements to the president and the Supreme Soviet of the Russian Federation, the UN secretary general and Security Council, the Council of Europe, the CSCE, and various international human rights organizations. In February 1993, Boris Yeltsin and Mircea Snegur, desiring a rapid political resolution of the conflict in Transdniester, called upon the Transdniester authorities to show leniency toward certain individuals. In May 1993, the two presidents repeated their request, and asked that the case of these individuals be reconsidered by the Supreme Court of the Moldovan Republic. However, the "Ilashku group" remained in prison.

78. "The Special CSCE Mission Intends to Help in Finding a Settlement to the Trans-Dniester Conflict," ITAR-TASS, May 12, 1994.

79. Report No. 13 of the CSCE Mission in Moldova (in Russian), November 13, 1993, pp. 1–4.

parties agreed to a change in the terminology of the draft agreement: the term "national state autonomy," which the Gagauz had insisted on, was to be replaced by the term "national territorial autonomy," which was preferred by Kishinev. The provisions for the status of national territorial autonomy were set out in Article 111 of the new Moldovan draft constitution and included elements of self-government. Finally, on December 23, 1994, despite strong opposition from the Christian Democratic People's Front and the bloc of peasants and intelligentsia, the Moldovan Parliament passed a law, "On the Special Legal Status of Gagauzia," formally granting the region the status of an autonomous territorial entity. The details of the arrangement were as follows:

- the representative body of Gagauzia would be the Gagauz People's Assembly, which would have the right to legislate within the limits of its competence;
- by a decree of the Moldovan president, the head of Gagauzia (*bashkan*) would be a member of the Moldovan government;
- the Gagauz people were guaranteed the right to self-determination in the case of a change in the status of Moldova itself (i.e., if Moldova decided to unite with Romania);
- the official languages of Gagauzia would be Gagauzian, Moldovan, and Russian, while in Moldova itself, the only official language was Moldovan; and
- Gagauz symbols could be displayed in the area along with the symbols of the Moldovan state, and local elections would be the prerogative of the Gagauz People's Assembly.[80]

The Gagauz solution did not, however, influence negotiations over the status of Transdniester, as Transdniester had little interest in attaining this kind of special status. The dominant position of the Transdniester leadership was to gain formal independence and then enter into a negotiated relationship with the Moldovan government. The question of exactly what forms the special status of Transdniester should take became the subject of heated debate among various experts and politicians.[81] From the perspective of Kishinev, schemes

---

80. "The Parliament of Moldova Has Accepted the Law 'On the Special Legal Status of Gagauzia'," Russian Information Agency (RIA), December 23, 1994.

81. For example, specialists from the CIS Association of Lawyers argued that a federal, or confederal, structure for Moldova did not contradict the idea of preserving Moldova's cultural integrity. See Rais Tuzmukhamedov, "Economic

based on the concept of federalism were unacceptable. At the same time, the official position of the unrecognized Transdniester Republic came down to a demand for a confederal structure as the basis for any political agreement. This issue formed the primary stumbling block to solving the whole complex of problems connected with a peaceful settlement of the Transdniester conflict.

Due to growing instability in the Russian Federation and uncertainty over the outcome of parliamentary and presidential elections, set for December 1995 and June 1996, respectively, the Russian leadership was obliged to take a number of extraordinary measures regarding the CIS republics in order to ensure the support of their leaders. For example, during a visit to Moldova in April 1995, Vladimir Shumeiko, chairman of the Council of the Federation of the Russian Parliament, unexpectedly announced that Russia would withdraw the 14th Army from Transdniester in the very near future. Shumeiko argued that Russian forces in the Transdniester could no longer be considered a real army since, as of early 1995, there were only 6,000 soldiers and 85 senior officers from Russia, and the rest came from the local population. Although the 14th Army had shrunk to less than a full division, Shumeiko continued, it possessed a disproportionately large stock of weapons.[82] Arrangements were made to decommission these weapons.[83]

Although Shumeiko emphasized that the withdrawal of the 14th Army would take place despite the opposition of Transdniester leadership, Tiraspol nevertheless declared that it would not let the army leave and that the people of Transdniester would be allowed to protest its withdrawal. In fact, a majority of the residents of Transdniester had opposed the departure of the 14th Army in a referendum on March 26, 1995. Shumeiko maintained that, if Kishinev and Tiraspol could resolve the Transdniester conflict, then local opposition to the withdrawal could be defused.[84] However, an agreement on the

Problems are Forcing Kishinev and Tiraspol to Negotiate," *Nezavisimaia gazeta*, June 9, 1994. However, Ion Sofronie, press secretary of the Moldovan government, called this point of view a provocation and labeled the specialists defending it "theorists of separatism." See Ion Sofronie, "Unwelcome Advice: Kishinev Asks That Separatism Be Opposed," *Nezavisimaia gazeta*, September 3, 1994.

82. Over 50,000 small artillery pieces, approximately 300 armored vehicles, and almost 90,000 tons of ammunition.

83. "Vladimir Shumeiko States That 14th Russian Army Must Be Withdrawn from Transdniester," ITAR-TASS, April 4, 1995.

84. "Vladimir Shumeiko States that 14th Russian Army and its Weapons Will Be Withdrawn from Moldova Despite Opposition from Transdniester," ITAR-TASS, April 5, 1995.

resolution to the conflict would remain out of reach as long as the deadlock over Transdniester's political status continued.

Following Shumeiko's unexpected initiative, the Russian Minister of Defense issued a directive on April 19, 1995, which "reformed" the command of the 14th Army. The directive reduced the command of the 14th Army from over two hundred people to a supervisory commission composed of fewer than half that number. The justification for the cuts was the fact that although the 14th Army had shrunk to about the size of a small division, its command had not. These changes were to have been made by July 1, 1995.[85]

The Ministry's directive effectively resolved the issue of removing the 14th Army's commander, Lieutenant General Alexander Lebed. In a public statement, Lebed announced that he had been dismissed from his post and went on to criticize the Russian Ministry of Defense.[86] According to Lebed, reductions in the command of the 14th Army should not have been made until the Transdniester issue had been settled, and all obstacles obstructing an agreement between Russia and Moldova on the withdrawal of Russian troops removed. So far, Lebed argued, the proper arrangements had not been made for the reorganization of the army, and no progress was being made in settling the conflict between Kishinev and Tiraspol over the status of Transdniester. In fact, the most important requirements for an agreement on troop withdrawal were still lacking: Moldovan assistance in constructing apartments for troops forced to relocate, the division of army property, and an agreement on transporting weapons and ammunition across Ukraine.[87]

Lebed's dismissal was a direct result of his political activities and his criticism of the Russian military's high command, particularly its military failures in Chechnya. Lebed launched a particularly virulent attack on Russian political and military leaders on April 8, 1995, during a speech at the national convention of the Congress of Russian Communities, which called itself a new national patriotic organization. Lebed became a leader of this organization, increasing rumors of his possible nomination for the 1996 Russian presidential elections.

President Snegur, in a meeting in Kishinev with Russian Deputy Minister of Foreign Affairs Sergei Krylov, expressed his concern over

---

85. ITAR-TASS, April 25, 1995.

86. "General Alexander Lebed Announced His Intention to Leave His Post as Commander of the 14th Army," ITAR-TASS, April 25, 1995.

87. ITAR-TASS, April 25, 1995.

Russia's delay in ratifying the agreement on the withdrawal of the 14th Army. Krylov assured Snegur that all the agreements would be implemented and that Transdniester's efforts to determine the fate of the 14th Army would have no effect. At a press conference after the meeting, Krylov expressed his hope that the Russian Parliament would ratify the agreement on withdrawing Russian troops. He pointed out that although soldiers would have the freedom to choose where they would continue their service, the 14th Army's military technology and weapons would definitely be removed from Transdniester.[88]

Elizabeth Schredter, chairperson of the European Parliament Commission on Relations with Belarus, Ukraine, and Moldova, led a delegation to Moldova from April 14–19, 1995, and met with Transdniester leaders and General Lebed. According to Schredter, "a political solution to the Transdniester conflict must be reached in order to prevent the withdrawal of the 14th Russian Army and its weapons from creating a new wave of tension in Moldova." Furthermore, political and economic assistance from the international community would be needed for the withdrawal to take place, and Ukraine—as well as Russia and Transdniester—must be included in the negotiations since Russian troops and armaments would have to be transported across Ukrainian territory.[89]

Meanwhile, in Gagauzia, tensions remained high through mid-1995, despite the passage of the law on the legal status of Gagauzia. Shortly before the referendum on Gagauzia, which was held in March 1995, Gagauz leaders accused the Moldovan authorities of deliberately delaying a resolution on the referendum and attempting to sabotage the referendum in towns with mixed Gagauz and Moldovan populations. According to the referendum result, almost all settlements (twenty-nine out of approximately thirty-five) expressed their desire to join Gagauzia. (The results in one further town remained unclear due to suspected violations of the electoral procedure.) The next important steps were to elect a leader of Gagauzia and deputies to the Gagauz People's Assembly and then to select representatives for local councils. The law on the status of Gagauzia stated that local elections were the responsibility of the Gagauz People's Assembly, and the Gagauz Supreme Soviet requested the Moldovan Parliament

88. "Russian Deputy Foreign Minister Assures Moldovan President that Moscow Intends to Implement Agreements Reached with Kishinev," ITAR-TASS, April 25, 1995.

89. ITAR-TASS, April 19, 1995.

to alter Moldovan legislation to allow this. However, the Moldovan authorities insisted that elections had to be conducted in accordance with Moldova's law on local self-rule. But according to Gagauz leaders Mikhail Kendigelian, chairman of the Supreme Soviet, and Ivan Burgudzhi, a member of the Presidium of the Supreme Soviet, this would effectively negate the special status of Gagauzia. In their view, Kishinev wanted to delay the creation of Gagauz administrative structures and prolong the period of anarchy in Gagauzia so that dissatisfaction would mount and people would demand to exercise their legal right to leave Gagauzia.[90]

The Transdniester conflict has evolved against a background of changing economic and social conditions—features common to all of the former Soviet republics. In 1993–94, Transdniester moved toward a market economy no less quickly than Moldova; therefore, categorizing Transdniester as a stronghold of communism in order to explain the causes of the conflict was no longer a valid approach.[91] At the same time, rapid changes in the balance of political forces in the states involved in the conflict led allies and opponents to exchange positions on key issues and brought new actors onto the scene. For instance, whereas early in the conflict Kishinev hotly protested the introduction of CIS peacekeeping forces in Transdniester, by the end of 1994, the Moldovan leadership opposed reductions in these forces, and President Snegur even called General Lebed a guarantor of stability. Meanwhile, the confrontation between the pro-independence ruling party and the pro-Romanian opposition parties and movements grew more acute in Moldova. In Transdniester, the political conflict between the ruling group and the opposition also escalated.

The Neighbors: Russia, Ukraine, and Romania

Moldovia was surrounded by neighbors—Russia, Ukraine, and Romania—that had their own internal political complexities, problems, and agendas. Many of these have been played out in Moldova.

THE RUSSIAN FEDERATION

Much of the blame for the ethnic conflicts in the former Soviet states lies with the early mistakes of Russian politicians, especially the team

---

90. "Gagauzia Will Not Participate in Local Elections," *Nezavisimaia gazeta,* February 21, 1995.

91. See, for instance, Vladimir Socor, "The Creeping Putsch in Eastern Moldova," *RFE/RL Research Report,* Vol. 1, No. 3 (January 17, 1992).

of advisers who came to power with Yeltsin and stayed in office until early 1992. They are known in Russia as the radical democrats and include Gennadi Burbulis, Galina Starovoitova, Fyodor Shelov-Kovedaev, and others. In the first months after the breakup of the Soviet Union, this influential group of advisers viewed the new states that had emerged as aspiring democracies whose attempts at national self-determination should be encouraged. By contrast, they considered the republics of Transdniester and Gagauzia to be bastions of communism.[92] At the time they did not realize the dangerous consequences of this policy, which contributed to the outbreak of ethno-political conflicts all along the perimeter of the Russian Federation, as well as in Russia itself. This group of advisers was later widely blamed in Russia for taking an essentially ideological rather than pragmatic approach to politics and for encouraging the development of radical nationalist regimes in the new states with their rhetoric of national self-determination, stimulating conflicts like that in Transdniester. As the Transdniester case illustrates, minority regions in union republics had reasons to oppose the dissolution of the Soviet Union, including the economic consequences of the breakup, as well as the cultural divide that existed between them and the republics they had been made part of by Stalinist cartographers. By labeling Transdniester and Gagauzia communist strongholds, this group of advisers tacitly endorsed the Moldovan government's use of force to eliminate them.

In full accordance with this early Russian policy, the 14th Army was ordered to hand over part of its weaponry and equipment to Moldova and not to intervene in the Transdniester conflict. At that time President Yeltsin's entourage clearly miscalculated the course of the conflict. By the middle of September 1992, a split on the Transdniester problem had become apparent in the Russian leadership between the radical democrats and those who supported a strong state (*gosudarstveniki*), including former Vice President Alexander Rutskoi and presidential adviser Sergei Stankevich. This split was also reflected in the division between President Yeltsin and the leadership of the Supreme Soviet of the Russian Federation, which advocated the protection of Russians in Transdniester and

---

92. This position was partly ideologically motivated, since these people were the leaders in the nascent democracy movement in Russia, but it was also clearly part of the larger Yeltsin policy to undermine Gorbachev and the center by encouraging nationalist rebellion in the Union republics.

other enclaves in the "near-abroad." Yeltsin was forced to maneuver between these groups, which led him to make contradictory and inconsistent decisions on the question of the 14th Army.

The difference between Western and Russian views on the role of the 14th Army obscures a paradoxical situation: the Transdniester Republic no longer needs the 14th Army on its territory, whereas Moldova has attempted to slow its withdrawal. Transdniester has developed its own armed forces capable of repulsing the Moldovan Army, and, in the case of a rapid withdrawal of the 14th Army, the Transdniester authorities would seize control of the depots of the former Odessa military district, since they have already stated that this military property belongs to Transdniester. The Moldovan leadership has meanwhile begun to realize that if the 14th Army withdrew, they would alone face an extremist opponent over whom they have no influence.

Furthermore, the 14th Army under General Lebed was not an unflinching partisan of Transdniester. For example, on February 8, 1994, the military council of the 14th Army stated that a lack of political will was causing both sides to cling to irreconcilable positions and was seriously aggravating the situation in the region. In the event of a large military confrontation, the statement continued, regardless of who was responsible, the 14th Army would retain the right to "cool down the hotheads." The Moldovan Ministry of Foreign Affairs considered the announcement tantamount to direct interference in the internal affairs of the republic.[93] However, in the same announcement, the 14th Army accused the leadership of the Transdniester Republic of corruption and of having joined forces with a network of more than 200 criminal organizations in Transdniester.[94]

The Russian government's August 1994 attempt to reorganize the command of the 14th Army, and on this pretext to remove General

---

93. See "Moldovan Ministry of Foreign Affairs Accuses 14th Army of Destabilizing the Situation," RIA, February 11, 1994.

94. Even before this, Colonel Mikhail Bergman, the military commander in Tiraspol, had accused Aleksander Saidakov, minister for the Municipal Economy in the Transdniester Republic, of racketeering and collecting illegal payments from commercial consumer organizations. Bergman had also accused Boris Luchik, the chief prosecutor of Transdniester, and Nikolai Matveev, deputy minister of Internal Affairs, of sheltering mafia organizations. According to the commander of the 14th Army, almost all the organs of law and order in Transdniester were controlled by mafia organizations (Interfax, January 10, 1994). Relations between the 14th Army command and the staff of Igor Smirnov, president of the unofficial Transdniester Republic, significantly worsened after the crisis in Moscow in October 1994, during which, according to the Russian Ministry of

Lebed, ended in failure.[95] The Russian media reported that the Russian Counterintelligence Service had warned that if Lebed were removed, the 14th Army might stop obeying orders from the Ministry of Defense.[96] These circumstances, combined with Russia's internal instability (especially in the context of the Chechen conflict) and the resulting struggle for power within the Russian government created uncertainty around the status of Russian forces. Various Moldovan and Western officials commented on the need for international monitoring of the withdrawal, but the Russian side strongly resisted this, claiming that there were no provisions in any of the agreements for international monitoring of troop withdrawal.[97]

THE UKRAINIAN REPUBLIC

President Leonid Kravchuk stated Ukraine's position on Transdniester during a meeting with Yeltsin in Dagomys on June 24, 1992. Ukraine supported the right of Transdniester to become an autonomous republic of Moldova, in accordance with the expressed wish of its

---

Internal Affairs, an armed group from Transdniester took part in the defense of the Russian Parliament. Colonel Bergman demanded the immediate arrest of Vadim Shevtsov, the head of the Ministry of State Security, and Matveev, whom he declared responsible for organizing this armed group and sending it to Moscow. Bergman also accused Smirnov and his close advisers of sheltering mafia organizations.

95. Lebed became a prominent critic of the Russian government and a supporter of strong government and the introduction of order. Because of his growing popularity, the government would have liked to get rid of him. Lebed was a likely candidate for the Russian presidency in 1996, and entered into a public dispute with Pavel Grachev over the reform of the army and its activities in Chechnya.

96. "The Kremlin Has Decided to Avoid Open Confrontation with the Headquarters of the 14th Army," *Nezavisimaia gazeta*, August 30, 1994.

97. A representative from the Russian Ministry of Foreign Affairs stated on December 8, 1994, that following the October 21, 1994, signing of an agreement on the legal status, organization, and timetable for the withdrawal of Russian military detachments on Moldovan territory, various Moldovan and Western officials had commented on the need for international monitoring of the implementation of the agreement. However, the Russian Ministry of Foreign Affairs believed that this issue was the affair of the sovereign states of Russia and Moldova alone. At no stage of the Russian-Moldovan negotiations on the withdrawal of the 14th Army was there any mention or discussion of international monitoring of the withdrawal. The agreement and other related documents contained no clause allowing for the participation of foreign observers in monitoring the withdrawal of Russian troops. The mandate of the CSCE mission to Moldova never included monitoring the withdrawal of Russian troops. No allowance was made for the participation of the CSCE or of any other foreign observers. See *Nezavisimaia Moldova*, December 14, 1994, p. 1.

people, and in the case of a reunion of Moldova and Romania, Ukraine supported the right of the people of Transdniester to decide their own fate. Kishinev regarded Kravchuk's statement as interference in the internal affairs of Moldova. While officially Kiev avoided any mention of the fact that Transdniester had belonged to Ukraine until 1940, representatives of nationalist Ukrainian organizations, both in Transdniester itself (the Union of Ukrainians Povernennya) and in the western Ukraine (the Ukrainian National Union), demanded the return of Transdniester to Ukraine. The Ukrainian leadership had its own weak separatist currents to worry about; Kiev reacted negatively to any hints at the possibility of reincorporating Transdniester into Ukraine because extremist Romanian nationalists demanded the return to Moldova of southern Bessarabia and Bukovina, which were incorporated into Ukraine under Stalin.[98] In the mid-1990s, more than 450,000 ethnic Romanians lived in Ukraine, and their political organizations have addressed several appeals to the Romanian Parliament protesting the policy of "Ukrainization" of the Romanian population of these territories that began in 1940. They have pushed for an agreement among Ukraine, Romania, and Moldova, guaranteeing the rights of the Romanian population of Ukraine, including its "historic rights." Kiev thus had every reason to be concerned about the stability of its frontiers.

ROMANIA

The most critical factor in the development of the conflict in Transdniester has been the serious possibility of the reunification of Moldova with Romania, which was the axis of internal Moldovan politics from 1992 to 1994. Bucharest's stance on the Transdniester conflict was conditioned by strong domestic pressure from nationalist parties and movements that increased as the Transdniester conflict became more acute. The reunification of Moldova with Romania became a powerful populist slogan for all Romanian political parties because it afforded the opportunity to demonstrate patriotism. The visibility of this issue in Romanian politics increased fears in Transdniester that unification was imminent and exacerbated tensions in Moldovan politics. It was frequently stated in Romanian

---

98. On the Ukrainian position toward Moldova during the acute stage of the Transdniester conflict, see Bogdan Nahaylo, "Ukraine and Moldova: The View from Kiev," *International Relations* (Moscow), Vol. 1, No. 18 (May 1, 1992), pp. 39–45.

political circles that only a president who was determined to start negotiations with Moscow on the reunification of Bessarabia and northern Bukovina with Romania could garner popular support.

The United Democratic Convention, a union of fourteen Romanian political organizations, has the aim of restoring Romania's 1938 frontiers. It declared that any attack on the territorial integrity of Moldova should be regarded by Romania as an attack on its own borders and citizens, and demanded that, following the West German precedent with respect to East Germany, Romanian citizenship should be granted to the inhabitants of Moldova. The creation of a "Greater Romania" became a rallying cry for many Romanian organizations. This affected not only Moldova, where all political parties agreed on reunion, but also Ukraine and Bulgaria. Romania's more extreme nationalist movements demand the return of northern Bukovina and certain other districts of the Odessa region of Ukraine as well as part of Dobruzha, which belongs to Bulgaria.[99]

Romanian President Ion Iliescu was forced to maneuver among these demands and in March 1992, he was obliged to hold intensive consultations with the leaders of all the Romanian political parties to discuss the events in Transdniester. The National Liberal Party, the National Tserenist Party, the Christian Democratic Party, and others argued for raising armed volunteer formations and sending the Romanian armed forces to Moldova.

The official position of the Romanian government was that Moldova is a territory that has always been inhabited by Romanians and was annexed by the former Soviet Union as a result of the Molotov-Ribbentrop Pact. Romanian Minister of Foreign Affairs T. Meleshkanu expressed the view at the 38th session of the Assembly of the West European Union in Paris on December 4, 1992, that there were two aspects to the relationship between Moldova and Romania. The first was historical and concerned half the territory of Moldova,

---

99. Deputy Chairman of the Executive Bureau of the National Salvation Front Adrian Severin expressed the view that the preservation and restoration of Romanian nationhood should become the guiding principle of Romanian foreign policy. He claimed that in order to hasten the process of reunification, a joint custom, finance, and tax union should be negotiated with Moldova, as well as joint commissions to coordinate foreign policy and military cooperation. At the same time, the ministries for foreign affairs of Romania and Moldova should start negotiations with the Ukrainian government on the "liberation of other territories, unlawfully occupied by the former USSR" and their return to Romania. "Requirements of the Leaders of Some Political Associations in Romania," ITAR-TASS, March 12, 1992.

the Romanian province of that name, which was always Romanian and remained populated primarily by Romanians. That this province was part of Romania was not in doubt. The second aspect concerned that part of that historical province which became, as a result of the disintegration of the Soviet Union, the independent Republic of Moldova. The Romanian government acknowledged the existence of two independent Romanian states—Romania and Moldova—and established the following priorities: the creation of a common cultural space; the creation of an economically integrated zone; and gradual political integration.

Nevertheless, in the course of 1993–94, the attitude of the Romanian leadership towards Moldova underwent a marked change from the initial euphoria, which had been linked to the policies of the Druk government, to a more pragmatic assessment of the Snegur regime. Kishinev had gradually come to realize that the nationalist propaganda in Romania about the "Bessarabian question" (reunification of Soviet-annexed Bessarabia) had not brought them any benefits, and that the radical statements of the leaders of the Romanian parties, often inspired by domestic political considerations, did not help the Moldovan government solve its own problems. The initiatives of the Romanian nationalists put President Snegur in an embarrassing position and did him more harm than good. For example, Romanian organizations had urged Bucharest to disregard the results of Moldova's referendum on reunification because it had not taken into account the wishes of all the Romanian people—i.e., those living in Romania too.[100] The Romanian leadership was disappointed that the possibility of unification turned out to be illusory; it blamed not

---

100. Mircea Druk, former Prime Minister of the Moldovan Republic and candidate for the Romanian presidency in 1992, was now an opponent of Mircea Snegur, directing his campaign against Snegur's regime from Romanian territory. The Party of National Reunification, headed by Druk, became a fervent advocate of unification. Out of this party was created the National Council for Reunification, which announced that between June and September 1994 a census and survey would be carried out both within and outside Romania of those people who had been forced in 1940 to leave areas occupied by the former Soviet Union, and their descendants. Within Romania, district, city, and village commissions and centers were set up for this purpose. The organizers desired to "neutralize the consequences of the March 6, 1994, referendum in the Moldovan Republic," arguing that it had failed to take into account the opinions of the Romanian nation (which was taken to include both the population of Romania and the approximately 700,000 people who had left Moldova after 1940). See "Mircea Druk's Party Pursues Unification of Moldova with Romania," Moldova Press, TASS, April 4, 1994.

only Russia for this, but also the Moldovan leadership. In an interview in late 1994, President Iliescu stated:

Moldavia is a second Romania; it is a state that was artificially created following the Molotov-Ribbentrop Pact between the Soviet Union and Nazi Germany, and it consists of what was once Bessarabia and Walachia, which was "stolen" from the Romanian authorities. Today we recognize Moldavia as an independent state, but maybe, some happy time in the future, we will witness our full territorial, cultural, and historical reunification with these lands. On the other hand, since there were once two Germanys, why not two Romanias? Everything depends on Russia. Moscow still has its troops there.[101]

Moldova in turn reacted sharply to Romanian pretensions; thus the relative stabilization of the Transdniester conflict was accompanied by a marked cooling off in Moldovan-Romanian relations.

Bulgaria also expressed concern about the possible development of the situation in Moldova. On September 7, 1993, Bulgaria and Moldova signed a friendship treaty that contained a special section on Bulgarians living in Moldova. The Bulgarian authorities worried that the safety of these Bulgarians could not be guaranteed in an armed conflict. They also suspected that Romanian foreign policy reflected a desire to create a "Greater Romania," which implied a revision of the frontier in Dobruzha, the region between the lower Danube and the Black Sea coast that had repeatedly been the object of territorial disputes in the past. Since 1940, southern Dobruzha has belonged to Bulgaria and the northern part to Romania.

Conclusion

The main cause of the armed conflict in Moldova was the attempt to create a unitary, ethnic state with power concentrated in the hands of ethnic nationalists in what was actually a multiethnic society. One may passionately defend or oppose the principle of ethnic nationalism on the basis of very different ideological positions. Despite the merits of each argument, one thing is evident: if the growth of ethnic nationalism proceeds unchecked, sooner or later it will lead to a situation where the use of force becomes inevitable, especially if there are other groups who fear forced assimilation into the new nationalist

---

101. "Interview with President Ion Iliescu of Romania," ITAR-TASS, October 7, 1994.

program.[102] The armed conflict in Moldova was complicated by the existence of two strains of ethnic nationalism—Romanian and Moldovan. The disagreements between nationalists who considered themselves Romanians and those who considered themselves Moldovans aggravated the conflict and introduced a new split in society.[103] At the same time, the presence of Russian and Ukrainian minorities, ethnically related to the majority of the population in two large neighboring states automatically increased the tension in the region of conflict.

Adam Rotfeld, the personal representative of the acting chairman of the CSCE Council, reported that "the conflict in the Transdniester region of Moldova raises a question of a fundamental nature. Who in fact is legitimate to enjoy the right of self-determination: nations, ethnic groups or nationalities, or indeed anyone who claims it?"[104] Pal Kolsto, a researcher at Oslo University, commented, "Moldovan authorities consider Moldova a national state for the Moldovan nation in which some other national groups also happen to be living. Hence, ethnicity is the constitutive principle of this state. In contrast, the new Dniester republic was proclaimed a supranational state."[105] In the author's opinion, a referendum on national self-determination that provides the right to leave an ethnocratic state should be treated

---

102. Wilbur E. Gray has expressed the opinion that "discord centers around the power of ethnic nationalism. Once restrained by the Soviet state, it is now seemingly out of control in all corners of the former Communist Empire. If left unrestrained, the political power of ethnic nationalism could easily destabilize each and every one of the newly independent republics." Gray, "The Chivalrous Republic."

103. For example, fierce arguments arose over the issue of a new draft constitution for Moldova. Vlad Darie, head of the Office for Political Analysis of the president of Moldova, accused the Agrarians, the most powerful faction in parliament, of desiring to "halt the process of national revival and return the republic to its 1989 state." According to Darie, the Agrarians and the former Communist Accord group were attempting to introduce into the draft constitution fundamental changes regarding the definition of the language and ethnic origins of the people of Moldova, defining them as "Moldovan." However, in the draft Basic Law, prepared by a commission led by President Snegur, it was stated that the people and language of Moldova are "Romanian." As Vlad Darie insisted, this latter conclusion has been "the result of scholarly research and cannot be held up for vote." This point of view is contested by those who consider themselves Moldovans. See Moldova Press, TASS, April 1, 1993.

104. "Interim Report on the Conflict in the Left Bank Dniester Areas of the Republic of Moldova," Prague, September 16, 1992, p. 13.

105. Pal Kolsto and Andrei Edemsky with Natalia Kalashnikova, "The Dniestr Conflict: Between Irredentism and Separatism," *Europe-Asia Studies*, Vol. 45, No. 6 (November–December 1993), p. 983.

as a legal instrument in full accord with the UN and CSCE charters and international law.

The facts illustrate that the real causes of these conflicts have deeper roots than may appear from a formal or purely legal standpoint. Adequate norms for their evaluation and collective measures for their solution therefore cannot be developed on an ad hoc basis. A comparative analysis of the actions of the parties to the conflict at each of its stages, which is not limited to a study of legislation and official statements, is extremely necessary. It has been shown in practice that the governments of the new states that emerged on the territory of the former Soviet Union are ready to sign virtually any international document on respect for democracy and minority and human rights in their endeavor to obtain international recognition. But this does not assure that such rights will be protected. These states have no mechanisms for monitoring implementation of the agreements, and there is no effective way to enforce international commitments.

Not one of the constitutions of the former Soviet republics recognizes the right of nontitular ethnic groups to self-determination, which contradicts international legal principles, given the size of these groups and the fact that they live in densely populated clusters. The right to self-determination is affirmed by the UN Charter and other international laws.[106] Instead, their constitutions reinforce the superior status of the titular nationalities, employing a range of measures that underline the ethnocratic nature of these regimes. For example, the preamble to the Moldovan Constitution emphasizes "the unbroken historical and ethnic tradition of the Moldovan rule in the Moldovan lands." Other ethnocratic aspects of the Moldovan regime include the facts that the language of the titular nationality is the sole national language, disregarding the history and ethnic specificity of Transdniester and other regions; and that ethnic or religious parties are illegal.

The formalistic application of the principle of territorial integrity is inappropriate in these situations for at least two reasons. First, in breaking up the Soviet Union, the former Soviet republics themselves violated the principle of territorial integrity. Second, the ethnocratic regimes and their leaders have deprived peoples with whom they share territory of the freedom to choose a political status and manage their own economic, social, and cultural development. The actual

---

106. For example, Article 5 of the International Pact on Civil and Political Rights (1966), and Article 8 of the Helsinki Final Act (1975).

inequality of ethnic groups or the threat of the creation of inequality will inevitably lead to confrontation in a multiethnic society regardless of the legal, historical, or social arguments used to justify unequal treatment.

The work of international organizations in Moldova and elsewhere in the former Soviet Union must be evaluated in this context. The effectiveness of these organizations depends on how they deal with the fundamental issues of the origins of ethnic conflicts and the international laws governing them. This inevitably puts into question the legal framework of the CSCE's activities in the former Soviet Union, particularly in light of international law on national and human rights. Any objective analysis of the constitutions and governmental practices of the former Soviet republics, including Moldova, would undoubtedly reveal their ethnocratic nature. This raises the question of how their ethno-political programs correspond to international law and the UN and CSCE charters, to which these organizations are supposed to adhere when mediating conflicts.

Rotfeld provides the following interpretation: "Contrary to the widespread view, the issue between the Republic of Moldova and the Transdniester region is not so much ethnic or national as political and ideological. There is also an economic background. The leaders of the self-proclaimed Transdniester Moldovan Republic stand primarily for a system of values rooted in the Soviet-type mentality."[107] This assessment contains some truth, but not the whole truth. Rotfeld omits other important political and legal points, and effectively suggests that the CSCE should unilaterally support the Moldovan position in the Transdniester conflict. Again, to judge by the assessment of human rights specialists for the CSCE, the ethno-political conflicts in Transdniester and Gagauzia were primarily caused by the fact that certain parts of the population do not wish to learn Romanian and are afraid of Romanization. This extremely formal approach hinders an adequate analysis of the human rights situation in Moldova.[108] The effect of this one-sidedness and the ideological considerations behind it undermines, in the opinion of at least one of the two sides, the CSCE's status as a fair and independent mediator.

Often the arguments used by European representatives in support

---

107. "Interim Report on the Conflict in the Left Bank Dniester Areas of the Republic of Moldova," p. 14.

108. "Human Rights and Democratization in the Newly Independent States of the Former Soviet Union," Commission on Security and Cooperation in Europe, Washington, D.C., January 1993, pp. 86–87.

of the Moldovan position are extremely subtle. For example, Slavomir Dabrova, a CSCE representative in Moldova, argued that although the 1992 military conflict taught politicians a good lesson and was not likely to recur, the conflict was still far from resolved because "Moldova is going through a tortuous process, common in Eastern Europe, of systemic transition." According to Dabrova, the CSCE considered that the only way to resolve the conflict in Transdniester would be to give the region a special status within Moldova.[109] Miguel Ankhel Martines, chairman of the Parliamentary Assembly of the Council of Europe, speaking in the Moldovan Parliament on Moldova's possible acceptance into the Council of Europe, stated that the Council was "intrigued by the experience of Moldova, which has managed to make great progress towards constructing a democratic state." He went on to say that the continued delay in settling the Transdniester question would not prevent Moldova's entry into the Council, and in fact, Moldova's new allegiance to European standards "will have a positive effect on settling the Transdniester conflict."[110]

International organizations such as the United Nations and the CSCE that attempt to mediate in conflicts should not turn a blind eye to ethnocratic behavior by one of the parties to the conflict, regardless of the reasons for this behavior. Doing so not only contradicts their own charters and international law, but also dramatically reduces the likelihood that their mediation efforts will succeed. The actions of the UN and the CSCE in Moldova and Transdniester epitomized this tendency. Moreover, the failure of international organizations to condemn ethnocratic regimes indirectly encourages these regimes to repress minority ethnic groups and enables them to use the international organizations to justify their actions and to discredit their opponents. As a result, international organizations are usually able to do little more in ethnic conflicts than gather information and provide humanitarian assistance.

Ethnic conflict broke out in Moldova because the leadership of the republic resorted to the doubtful theory that an individual ethnic group constituted the only source of legitimacy in a state that had had a multiethnic structure for at least a century. The Moldovan cen-

109. "CSCE Supports Special Status for Transdniester Within Moldova," RIA, February 11, 1995.

110. "Moldova Will Soon Join Council of Europe," *Nezavisimaia gazeta*, February 25, 1995.

tral authorities considered resistance by other ethnic groups to the practical implementation of this theory a disturbance of law and order. Kishinev's attempt to enforce law and order by force, particularly using troops from the ruling ethnic group, was in turn perceived by minority groups as ethnic violence perpetrated by Moldovan nationalists. Inevitably, the conflict took the form of a civil war with ethnic undertones.

The idea that a single ethnic group can dominate a multiethnic society dooms that nation to ongoing conflict. Only by abandoning this concept will Moldova be able to create conditions for building a united community. Such a step implies the introduction of a federal structure and corresponding changes in the electoral system, political parties, political representation, and local self-government. Fortunately, this possibility remains open under Article 111 of the Moldovan Constitution, which permits a special status for the Transdniester and Gagauz districts.

Russia's massive use of force to solve the Chechen problem in late 1994 and 1995 disclosed the intensity of the struggle for power between various groups in the Kremlin. The victory of one of these groups could have a direct effect on the behavior of the Russian Army in Transdniester. The situation in Transdniester is much more complicated than the proponents of neo-imperialist theory suggest. Russia itself is in a state of disarray. While Yeltsin is no proponent of expanding Russian borders or defending the Russian populations in the near abroad, he has been compelled to respond to the importance of this issue in Russian domestic politics. In the context of such instability, further attempts to use ethno-political factors to redistribute power are likely in both the Republic of Moldova and Transdniester. That is why delays in the negotiation process on the political status of Transdniester can bring no benefit to any of the sides in the conflict.

Chapter 8

Commentary on Moldova

Brian D. Taylor

Edward Ozhiganov's stimulating, in-depth account of the conflict in the Transdniester region of Moldova is one of the most detailed available in English. He provides a wealth of new material on the origins and development of the conflict between the Moldovan government and the separatist, self-declared Transdniester Moldovan Republic (PMR).[1]

The primary contribution that Ozhiganov makes, however, is his analysis. In particular, his interpretation is a sharp departure from how the story of the Transdniester conflict is usually told in the West. In the standard Western account, blame for the conflict is placed on the hard-line Russian communist and nationalist forces leading the PMR. Moscow is faulted for siding with the separatists and surreptitiously arming them from the Russian 14th Army based in the region.[2] Ozhiganov, however, places primary blame on a hard-line

---

1. In Russian, the Pridniestrovian Moldovan Republic (PMR).

2. The main exponent of what I label here the "conventional view" is Vladimir Socor, who covered the conflict for Radio Free Europe/Radio Liberty (RFE/RL) and now writes for the Jamestown Foundation's *Monitor* and *Prism*. See, for example, Socor, "The Creeping Putsch in Eastern Moldova," *RFE/RL Research Report*, Vol. 1, No. 3 (January 17, 1992), pp. 8–13; Socor, "Russian Forces in Moldova," *RFE/RL Research Report*, Vol. 1, No. 34 (August 28, 1992), pp. 38–43; and Socor, "Russia's Fourteenth Army and the Insurgency in Eastern Moldova," *RFE/RL Research Report*, Vol. 1, No. 36 (September 11, 1992), pp. 41–48. See also Helsinki Watch, *War or Peace? Human Rights and Russian Military Involvement in the "Near Abroad,"* Vol. 5, No. 22 (December 1993), pp. 8–11; Fiona Hill and Pamela Jewett, *Back in the USSR: Russia's Intervention in the Internal Affairs of the Former Soviet Republics and the Implications for United States Policy toward Russia* (Cambridge, Mass: Harvard University, Kennedy School of Government, Strengthening Democratic Institutions Project, January 1994), pp. 61–65; and Gerald B. Solomon, *Peacekeeping in the Transdniester Region: A Test Case for the CSCE*, Draft Special Report, North Atlantic Assembly (November 1994).

Moldovan ex-communist and nationalist government. He faults Yeltsin's government for being naively pro-Moldovan in late 1991 and early 1992 and recklessly transferring weapons of the collapsing Soviet army to an unreliable Moldovan government.

Some readers may be tempted to dismiss Ozhiganov's account as the self-serving "view from Moscow." This response would be a mistake. Ozhiganov provides a valuable perspective on the conflict. Perhaps his most important contribution is a discerning account of the fears and interests motivating the non-Moldovan Transdniestrians (Russians and Ukrainians) as the crisis developed. His description of the "system of ethno-social stratification in Moldova" prior to independence and his emphasis on how "the political and economic interests of the national elite of Moldova clashed with those of the industrial *nomenklatura* of Transdniester" are significant contributions to our understanding of the conflict.[3]

Two major sticking points prevent a final resolution of the Transdniester conflict. First, the Moldovan government and the leadership of the self-declared Transdniester Republic are unable to agree on the degree of autonomy that should be granted to the PMR. The PMR leadership wants independence and a confederation agreement, while the Moldovan government favors PMR autonomy within a federal Moldova.

The second sticking point is the fate of the Russian 14th Army based in the PMR region. Ozhiganov's brief discussion of the role of Russia's 14th Army yields a telling insight, one almost always overlooked in other discussions of this complex issue. Ozhiganov argues that "the main, but not openly stated, problem for the Ministry of Defense of the Russian Federation was to prevent the transfer of personnel and equipment of the 14th Army to the jurisdiction or control of Transdniester." An understanding of why this was the main problem of the Russian military, and how this problem was solved, sheds light not only on the course of the Transdniester war of 1992 but on other ethnic conflicts in the former Soviet Union. By elaborating on

---

3.   Other articles making similar points include William Crowther, "Moldova after Independence," *Current History*, Vol. 93, No. 595 (October 1994), pp. 342–347; Charles King, "Eurasia Letter: Moldova With a Russian Face," *Foreign Policy*, No. 97 (Winter 1995), pp. 106-120; Charles King, "Moldovan Identity and the Politics of Pan-Romanianism," *Slavic Review*, Vol. 53, No. 2 (Summer 1994), pp. 345–368; and Pal Kolsto and Andrei Edemsky with Natalia Kalashnikova, "The Dniester Conflict: Between Irredentism and Separatism," *Europe-Asia Studies*, Vol. 45, No. 6 (November–December 1993), pp. 973–1000.

this crucial point in this brief commentary, I hope to demonstrate why the status of the 14th Army has remained a stumbling block in attempts to resolve the conflict long after the fighting has ended. The explanation is considerably more complex than simplistic notions of "Russian imperialism" would suggest.

The Russian 14th Army

By January 1992, the Soviet armed forces were facing the most serious crisis of their seventy-two-year existence. The country they were sworn to protect had collapsed, replaced by an ill-defined Commonwealth of Independent States (CIS). A massive and, from their perspective, humiliating withdrawal of thirty-four divisions and over one million military personnel and their families from Central and Eastern Europe was already under way. Many of the newly independent states, most importantly Ukraine, were "nationalizing" the forces based on their territory. The future for most officers, particularly those based outside Russia, was bleak and uncertain. From the point of view of the military establishment, chaos reigned throughout the territory of the former Soviet Union.

The position of the 14th Army exemplified the chaos faced by Soviet military units after the country's collapse. The 14th Army was based in two newly independent countries, Moldova and Ukraine, and there were four contenders for control over various parts of its equipment and personnel: Moldova, Ukraine, Russia, and the self-declared Transdniester Moldovan Republic. The 14th Army was headquartered in Tiraspol, the capital of the PMR. Fighting broke out between Moldova and the PMR in March 1992. The status of the 14th Army was very unclear, and many officers had ties to the local Transdniester population. Discipline was seriously undermined, and there was a real danger that the army would disintegrate, with most of its personnel and equipment coming under PMR jurisdiction. On April 1, 1992, Russian President Boris Yeltsin declared that 14th Army units based in the Transdniester region were under Russian jurisdiction. This declaration undoubtedly slowed, but did not stop, the leaking of 14th Army officers and equipment to the PMR.[4]

---

4. In January 1992, the PMR decided that it would form its own armed forces on the basis of units deployed in the republic, and that a loyalty oath would be sworn to the PMR by military personnel. The Commander of the 14th Army, Lieutenant General Gennadi Yakovlev, had thrown in his lot with the PMR in

Two separate and very difficult problems had to be resolved in the midst of a small-scale war. The first problem was the issue of the personnel, particularly the officers, of the 14th Army. More than half of the command personnel were local residents, and the percentage was even higher among mid-level and junior officers. Most sympathized with the local population, and many would have resisted either transfer to Moldovan subordination or withdrawal to Russia. The problem was more intractable than similar circumstances in the Baltic states, where the situation was peaceful, or in the Caucasus, where fewer officers had ties to the local population.[5]

The second problem was the large amount of equipment either based or stored in the region. It would take months, if not years, to withdraw all of this matériel, even under the best of circumstances. Already some of the 14th Army's hardware had fallen into local hands, whether it was given away, sold, handed over under duress, or stolen. If the army had been withdrawn hastily, even more of this equipment would have ended up with local armed units. Military equipment based in the Caucasus (Armenia, Azerbaijan, Georgia, and Chechnya) was "privatized" by a similar variety of means in 1991–92, or left behind when Russian troops hastily pulled out, and is still being used in the various conflicts there.[6]

December 1991, becoming head of its Defense and Security Department. Moscow replaced Yakovlev with Major General Yuri Netkachov. Yeltsin and the Russian Ministry of Defense acknowledged that on occasion 14th Army officers, sometimes with their equipment, were joining the Transdniester forces. See *Radio Rossii*, January 11, 1992 (*Foreign Broadcast Information Service* [hereafter *FBIS*] SOV-92-008, p. 54). Boris Yeltsin, interview, "Ia ne skryvaiu trudnostei i khochu, chotby narod eto ponimal," *Komsomolskaia pravda*, May 27, 1992, p. 2; and Sergey Nagaev, "The Conclusions We Select," *Rossiskaia gazeta*, May 27, 1992, p. 7 (*FBIS* SOV-92-108, pp. 20–21).

5.   Viktor Litovkin, "Vopros o vyvode 14-i armii iz Pridnestrov'ia reshen. No poka ne iasno, kak eto sdelat'," *Izvestia*, May 29, 1992, p. 1; Col. V. Gavrilenko, "14-ia armiia budet vyvedena iz Pridnestrov'ia," *Krasnaia zvezda*, June 4, 1992, pp. 1, 3; and Interfax, June 8, 1992 (*FBIS* SOV-92-111, p. 22).

6.   See Georgi Kondratev (Deputy Minister of Defense, Russian Federation), interviewed by Mikhail Leshchinskiy, "Topical Interview" television program, *Ostankino*, June 24, 1992 (*FBIS* SOV-92-125, pp. 8–12); Litovkin, "Vopros o vyvode"; Sergei Parkhomenko, "Bezhentsy s oruzhiem v rukakh," *Nezavisimaia gazeta*, June 30, 1992, p. 1; *Postfactum*, June 25, 1992 (*FBIS* SOV-92-124, p. 65); Pavel Grachev (Minister of Defense, Russian Federation), interview on *Ostankino*, May 31, 1992 (*FBIS* SOV-92-107, pp. 31–37); and Pavel Grachev, interview, "Vstrecha Ministra Oborony Rossii s zhurnalistami 'Krasnoi zvezdy'," *Krasnaia zvezda*, June 9, 1992, pp. 1–2.

The late May 1992 announcement that Yeltsin had decided to withdraw the 14th Army was arguably a mistake; if there had been a serious effort to implement this decision, a considerable portion of the 14th Army would have gone over to the side of the local PMR authorities. This point was conceded both by Russian Defense Minister Pavel Grachev and, more obliquely, by the commander of the 14th Army, Major General Yuri Netkachov.[7] It was clear that Netkachov had only partial control over his troops, and his explanations for their behavior seemed to vary daily.[8]

Moscow clearly had to do something if the 14th Army were to remain under Russian control. The most important step taken was the replacement of Netkachov with then-Major General Alexander Lebed, at the time a close associate of Grachev, in June 1992. Lebed reasserted Moscow's control over the 14th Army with a series of forceful press conferences in which he stated his determination to use the 14th Army against Moldova if the war continued; he backed up these words with an artillery attack on Moldova. Although General Lebed's statements and activities are often interpreted as the deeds of a rogue general, two things are clear about his activities in the summer of 1992: he acted under orders from Moscow, and his primary objective was to ensure that the 14th Army remained subordinate to Moscow and that it returned to the barracks. As Ozhiganov states, Lebed "succeeded in avoiding the loss of Russian control over the 14th Army."[9]

---

7.   On Yeltsin's decision and Netkachov's statement that he had no idea how the decision could be implemented, see Litovkin, "Vopros o vyvode." Grachev's statement is in "Vstrecha Ministra Oborony." See also the comments of General Nikolai Stoliarov, aide to General Shaposhnikov, Interfax, June 8, 1992 (*FBIS* SOV-92-111, p. 22).

8.   For example, Netkachov stated at various times that 14th Army soldiers fighting on the side of the PMR forces were acting against his orders, that he had ordered their activities, and that the soldiers in question were actually reservists who had seized army equipment. Ozhiganov puts the matter more delicately, stating only that Netkachov "had lost the confidence of the troops." The contradictory nature of Netkachov's statements was noted in Andrei Ostal'skii, "Vmeshatel'stvo voennykh v politiku dolzhno byt' prekrashcheno kak mozhno skoree," *Izvestia*, May 29, 1992, p. 7. See also ITAR-TASS, May 19, 1992 (*FBIS* SOV-92-098, pp. 51–52); Yuri Netkachov (Commander, 14th Army), interviewed by S. Fateev, *Ostankino*, May 20, 1992 (*FBIS* SOV-92-099, p. 87); and Viktor Litovkin, "Neuzheli vse-taki voina? Tanki 14-i armii v zone pridnestrovskogo konflikta," *Izvestia*, May 20, 1992, p. 1.

9.   The degree of control Moscow was exerting over the 14th Army is evidenced by the fact that on June 19–20, 1992, during the crucial battle of Bendery,

Lebed's achievement in ensuring the strict subordination of the 14th Army to Russia came at a cost, however. Ozhiganov never states the point explicitly, but the Moldovan government in Chisinau (Kishinev in Russian) does not control all of the territory that is legitimately Moldovan. This is regrettable and is the major reason for the protracted negotiations on the fate of Transdniester and the 14th Army. At the same time, the consequences of Russia's policy have not been all bad. The war in Transdniester has been over since 1992, and agreement has been reached on the withdrawal of the 14th Army, although Russia has shown little eagerness to implement this agreement.[10] Given the chaotic conditions of 1992, a Russian decision to withdraw the army immediately would have led to the same outcome as that experienced in the Caucasus: the transfer of large amounts of Soviet military equipment to local forces. Subsequent developments in that region suggest Moscow's policy in Transdniester was more effective at preventing bloodshed, albeit at the serious cost of an infringement of Moldovan sovereignty.

a situational staff headed by Vice President Alexander Rutskoi was established in the Kremlin. This staff was in close contact with all of the relevant parties. Even the possibility of bringing in Russian airborne troops to assist the PMR was discussed. This staff was aware of, and tolerated if not ordered, the use of 14th Army personnel to command PMR tanks during a key stage of the battle. See Pavel Fel'gengauer, "Bitva za Bendery—glavnoie voiennoe sobytie mesiatsa," *Nezavisimaia gazeta,* July 1, 1992, pp. 1–2.

On Lebed's actions, the fact that he acted under Moscow's orders, and that his mission was the reestablishment of Russian control over the 14th Army, see King, "Eurasia Letter," *Postfactum,* June 25, 1992 (*FBIS SOV-92-123,* p. 68); Alexander Kakotkin, "Ne sotvori sebe kumira," *Zhurnalist,* No. 7 (1994), pp. 8–11; Gennadi Sobolev, "General'skaia liniya," *Rossiyiskiie Vesti,* February 2, 1994, p. 2; Alexander Lebed, interview by Feliks Babitskii, "'Voiny Rossiia ne perezhivet!'" *Ogonek,* No. 32–34 (August 1994), pp. 9–13; Vadim Shevtsov (Minister of Security, PMR), interviewed by Nadezhda Garifullina, "Na levom beregu," *Sovetskaia Rossiia,* February 18, 1995, pp. 1–2; Lt. Gen. Alexander Lebed, interviewed by Yuliia Khaitina and Sergei Yastrebov, "'Favorit' Pridnestrov'ia, nazhivshii vragov," *Moskovskii komsomolets,* June 4, 1994, p. 2; and Pavel Fel'gengauer, "Nakanune 'reshaiushchikh srazhenii," *Nezavisimaia gazeta,* July 18, 1992, pp. 1–2.

10. Indeed, in 1995, Russia formally proposed that it be granted basing rights in Moldova, a proposal that Moldova rejected. On Russian-Moldovan negotiations since the October 1994 agreement on the withdrawal of Russian forces, see Pavel Fel'gengauer, "Sud'ba rossiiskoi armii v Moldavii poka ne reshena," *Segodnia,* June 28, 1995, p. 2; Aleksander Pel'ts, "Ministr oborony Rossii v Pridnestrov'e," *Krasnaia zvezda,* June 28, 1995, p. 1; Aleksander Pel'ts, "Reformirovannaia 14-ia armiia mozhet stat' osnovoi dlia sozdaniia rossiiskoi voiennoy bazi v Moldavii," *Krasnaia zvezda,* June 29, 1995, p. 1; and "Rossiia predlagaet izmenit' status voinskikh podrazdelenii v Pridnestrov'e," *Segodnia,* November 23, 1995, p. 1. For Western analysis of these developments, which tends to reflect the conventional view, see the articles in the special issue on "Moldova and Russia," *Transition,* Vol. 1, No. 19 (October 20, 1995).

That the 14th Army was now firmly under Russian control became even more evident after Lebed's resignation in the spring of 1995. Lebed and other commentators speculated that with his departure, the army would become unmanageable and its equipment would be acquired by the forces of the self-proclaimed Transdniester Republic or criminal elements. In fact, since Lebed's departure, Moscow's control over the 14th Army has become even stronger. The 14th Army has been downgraded to the Operational Group of Russian Forces and a new commander, Lieutenant General Valery Yevnevich, has exerted firm command. Old munitions have been destroyed, some equipment has been returned to Russia, and, most important, local officers and soldiers have been replaced by personnel from Russia, a move which substantially diminishes the problem of divided allegiances.[11]

Conclusion

Two major obstacles to a resolution of the Transdniester dispute were highlighted at the beginning of Ozhiganov's chapter: the fate of the Russian military based there, and the political question of the future status of the region. Real progress has been made since 1992 in normalizing the situation for the army units based there and avoiding a chaotic disintegration. Even the military problem is now under control; however, a political solution seems as far away as ever. With presidential elections scheduled in both Moldova and Russia in 1996, little progress can be expected soon. Among other obstacles, the Transdniester leadership is hoping that more sympathetic forces will come to power in both countries.

Ozhiganov's analysis is so valuable precisely because he reminds us of the complexity of the Transdniester situation. The conflict is not a simple case of Russian meddling and Moldovan victimization. I

---

11. On the alleged dangers of Lebed's departure, see Rodion Morozov, "Pridnestrov'e: gotovitsia prestupleniie," *Obshchaia gazeta*, No. 12 (May 18–24, 1995), p. 1; Interview with Lt. Gen. Alexander Lebed (Commander, 14th Army) by Aleksander Minkin, "V ozhidanii voiny," *Moskovskii komsomolets*, May 12, 1995, pp. 1–2; Mikhail Leont'ev, "Kapriznye deti generala Gracheva," *Segodniya*, May 11, 1995, p. 1; and Mikhail Leont'ev, "Chistka v 14-y armii," *Segodnia*, July 15, 1995, p. 2. For subsequent developments, see Fel'gengauer, "Sud'ba rossiiskoi armii," interview with Lt. Gen. Valery Yevnevich (Commander, Operational Group of Russian Forces in Moldova) by Aleksei Overchuk, "Lebed' uletel, i zatikhlo," *Moskovskii komsomolets*, August 16, 1995, p. 3; Interview with Lt. Gen. Valery Yevnevich by Lt. Col. Anatolii Stasovskii, "Ia ne ten' generala Lebedia," *Krasnaia Zvezda*, September 9, 1995, pp. 1–2; and Mikhail Shevtsov, ITAR-TASS, November 10, 1995 (*FBIS* SOV-95-218, p. 18).

believe Ozhiganov understates the inflexibility of the PMR leadership, which continues to insist on full independence. But he reminds us that, from the point of view of many Transdniester citizens, the 1992 war was caused by Moldova. Furthermore, they strongly believe that only the presence of Russian forces prevents their forced assimilation into a Romanian-speaking country.[12]

Given these entrenched attitudes, it will take more pressure than Russia has been willing to assert to force the PMR leadership to compromise. Although the lack of a settlement is regrettable, perhaps the real story of the Transdniester dispute has been the relative success in containing it, compared to the conflicts in the former Yugoslavia and other areas of the former Soviet Union such as Chechnya, Tajikistan, Georgia, and Armenia-Azerbaijan.[13] Ozhiganov's chapter is such an interesting read because he presents a viewpoint on the conflict rarely heard in Western commentary and calls attention to some of the deep-seated differences that make the dispute so intractable.

---

12. In a March 1995 referendum, 93 percent of Transdniester voters supported maintaining the 14th Army in the region. Sergei Kniaz'kov, "Itogi referenduma byli predskazuemy," *Krasnaia zvezda*, March 28, 1995, p. 3.

13. This point also is made by Crowther, "Moldova after Independence."

Chapter 9

Latvia: Discrimination, International Organizations, and Stabilization

Alexander Yusupovsky

The situation in Latvia and the Baltic states differs from the dramatic conflicts that have erupted in Georgia, Moldova, and Tajikistan. Unlike these tragic areas, separatism is not a serious concern in the Baltic states. Neither side has resorted to armed force to achieve its political objectives, and there is no imminent danger of civil war. There has been almost no overt violence between ethnic communities in the Baltic states, although the deep conflict over the status of the large Russian minority in Latvia and Estonia has manifested itself in other ways.

From the relative calm in Latvia it may be possible to conclude that there is no "conflict"—rather only a certain amount of tension and some problems in the relationship between Latvia's ethnic communities. This reading of the situation underestimates the real discontent and frustration felt by Latvia's Russian community. Relations have deteriorated between Latvians and Russians in the republic, as is evidenced by the growing strength of "radical nationalist" elements in various levels of the Latvian government, along with the radicalization of some in the Russian community. These developments, in combination with Latvia's difficult economic situation, make the status quo extremely unstable. In Russia, there is rising resentment of Latvian and Estonian policies toward Russian minorities, and these issues are used by politicians for domestic political advantage. The potential for more serious conflict remains. This chapter discusses how the changes in Latvia in particular, and also more generally across the Baltic states, have been perceived and received by the Russian communities in those states, and how these perceptions have resonated in the Russian public consciousness.

The status of non-Latvians in an independent Latvia has been the subject of intense political struggle in the period leading up to and following the disintegration of the Soviet Union. As long as the Latvian independence movement had as its goal the revival of Latvia as an independent nation, it was tolerant and ethnically inclusive. The population of Latvia included large numbers of non-Latvians (most of them ethnic Russians), who had been born and lived all their lives in the Latvian Soviet Socialist Republic (SSR). Many of them supported Latvian independence.

Once independence was achieved, however, the new Latvian government began to change its policies. In October 1991, the Latvian Supreme Soviet adopted a controversial strategy to restore the independent Latvian republic that had existed from 1918 to 1940, which had been destroyed following the incorporation of Latvia by the Soviet Union during World War II. Only citizens of this earlier republic and their direct descendants were automatically granted citizenship in the newly independent Latvia. In the official registration of citizenship status that took place in 1992, hundreds of thousands of citizens of the former Latvian SSR were registered neither as citizens of Latvia nor of any other state, and were transformed overnight into stateless persons. Ironically, a significant proportion of those who had elected the members of the Supreme Soviet were stripped of their citizenship by that body, and could only establish their eligibility for citizenship by meeting specified criteria. Under conditions of legal uncertainty and the continuing debate over a final law on citizenship, bureaucratic decisions on the categorization of individuals were taken by officials in the Department for Citizenship and Immigration, a stronghold of radical nationalists. Latvian authorities defended this policy as necessary to assure the predominance of Latvian interests and culture in the new state. The Russian minority, however, perceived it as a fundamental injustice and incompatible with the democratic values espoused by the Latvian government.

The Latvian government justified its citizenship policy as an "undoing" of the Soviet nationalities policy that settled large numbers of Russians and other non-Baltic nationalities in the region. In 1939, Latvians made up 75 percent of the population and Russians 10 percent, whereas in 1989, Latvians made up only 52 percent, Russians 34 percent, and Russian speakers 42.1 percent.[1] But Latvia was never

---

1.   Data from the bulletin of the All-Union Caucus of the Soviet Union, Moscow, 1991.

ethnically homogenous. A Slavic minority has lived in the region for many centuries. Ethnic Latvians have comprised more than half the population of Riga for only a few decades in the entire eight hundred years since its founding. The fact that currently more than 60 percent of the population of Riga are non-Latvian is not a recent phenomenon nor an anomaly.[2]

After 1940, the Soviet Union considered the Baltic states part of its national territory, and they were subjected to the same treatment as every other part of the Soviet Union. The influx of non-Latvians into Latvia reflected the standard Soviet policy at the time. The blending of various Soviet nationalities was achieved in part by moving large numbers of people to other republics as a labor force in developing industry. This practice was also ideologically motivated, since in the framework of proletarian internationalism, such blending was designed to facilitate *sblizhenie* (rapprochement) of the various Soviet nationalities. Big industrial projects were initiated in the Baltic states in the 1950s and 1960s, and often the entire work force was imported from other republics. Sometimes the condemnation of the Russian community in the Baltic republics seems to proceed from the assumption that Russians moved there voluntarily and opportunistically. In reality, there was little voluntary mobility within the Soviet Union. People moved and were moved primarily at the behest of the authorities. Internal demographic trends have reinforced the effects of Soviet-era migration policies; ethnic Latvians and Estonians have one of the lowest birthrates, the highest mortality rates, and the smallest average family size of all the nationalities of the former Soviet Union.[3]

In general, the Russian speakers tend to live in Latvia's urban areas, because they were brought in to work in industry and the service sector. As noted above, the majority of Riga's inhabitants are Russian. Ethnic Latvians, by contrast, have always formed the majority in rural areas. One exception is the region of Latgale, which borders on Russia, where ethnic Russians have historically been a considerable majority in both rural and urban areas.

---

2.   According to the 1897 census, for instance, the population of Riga comprised 46 percent Germans, 20 percent Latvians, 20 percent Russians, and 12 percent Jews. In another large town, Vindave (Ventspils), 38 percent of the population were Latvian, 32 percent German, 25 percent Jewish, and 4 percent Russian. See S.N. Yuzhakov, ed.,*The Great Encyclopedia* (St. Petersburg: 1905–08); and "The Port of Vindav," a publication of the Vindav-Moscow Railway Company (1908), p. 6.

3.   P.P. Zvidrinsh and M.A. Zvidrinya, *Population and the Economy* (Moscow: Mysl', 1987).

What is seen as a just solution to any problem depends on how the problem is defined. The Latvian authorities and the Russian population have almost entirely asymmetrical perceptions of the conflict and very different understandings of key problems and disagreements. Defining the problem has become a highly politicized question, subject to ideological struggle, propaganda, and polemics. The variance in the positions of the Latvian authorities and the Russian minority is perhaps best expressed by their choice of words: of being "denied" citizenship versus being "deprived" of it. Latvian authorities use the term "denial" of citizenship on the grounds that noncitizens did not have citizenship in the first place, and therefore could not be deprived of it. In this view, the fact that the state legitimately denies citizenship to certain people and then allows their naturalization with the fulfillment of specific conditions is reasonable. The Russian community, on the other hand, insists that Latvia's policy constitutes a deprivation of citizenship, a suspension of de facto equal rights, and the arbitrary division of Latvia's inhabitants into unequal categories with discrete packages of rights.

Since 1991, groups representing the interests of "noncitizens" have opposed this deprivation of citizenship, while at the same time they have demanded an easing of the naturalization criteria. However, even if naturalization is possible in the near term, the legal framework that governs economic and political life in Latvia excludes the bulk of Latvia's Russian community. The inability of ethnic Russians to participate politically greatly limits their future prospects in Latvia. But the impact of the policy goes far beyond the inability to vote. Noncitizens have the right neither to own land, nor to work in many fields. They are ineligible to receive state pensions or even to travel freely to visit relatives in neighboring Russian regions.

Ethnic Russians in Latvia demand that the world community recognize these restrictions as open discrimination on ethnic grounds and as violations of their civil and human rights. They claim that the aim of Latvia's policy is to force them out of Latvia. Official action is accompanied by constant psychological pressure in the mass media and in the statements of some public officials. Russian speakers who moved to the Latvian SSR and the other Baltic republics between 1940 and 1990 have been officially identified as "occupiers" and "colonizers"—people who have no rights or place in the new Latvian society. Inevitably such tactics have led to a radicalization of parts of the Russian community. The tenseness of the atmosphere has caused some to leave and has increased resentment among the vast majority who do not want to leave. According to the Russian Federation's Federal Migration Service, in 1989, 14,100 people migrated to Russia from Latvia, 9,500 of whom were ethnic Russians. In 1991, the number was 13,000, including 10,400 Russians. In 1992, the number rose to 27,300, including 22,500 Russians, and in 1993, 25,900 persons moved from Latvia to Russia, 21,000 of whom were Russians.[4]

The Latvian Constitution (*Satversme*) and the fundamental law, "On Human and Civil Rights," passed on October 12, 1991, guarantee equal civil rights for all nationalities. After many years of debate and numerous amendments, the final version of the law on citizenship was adopted on June 22, 1994, by the Seim, the highest legislative body in Latvia. Although some changes were later made in response to international pressures, the basic structure was not altered. The texts of these laws do not specify ethnic criteria for dividing the population of Latvia into categories possessing different levels of rights. The official difference is between rights accorded to citizens and noncitizens. The discriminatory impact is created by the fact that hundreds of thousands of citizens of the former Latvian SSR are now stateless. They fall outside the protection and many of the benefits of the new laws.[5]

Together with the demographic threat to the "indigenous" Latvian nation, the Latvian authorities have tended to stress military and foreign-policy aspects of disengagement from Soviet political and economic structures and the consolidation of new international relationships. Of particular concern have been the withdrawal of Russian troops from Latvia, the disposal of Soviet military installations on Latvian territory, and the campaign for membership in NATO.

By contrast, the Russian community in Latvia has focused on securing the observance of equal civil rights for non-Latvians, along with guarantees against discrimination on ethnic or other grounds and the removal of the threat of forcible repatriation to Russia. In general, their goal has been to create conditions in Latvia for a normal existence for the Russian minority, including the development of Russian-language education, Russian culture, and the easing of anti-minority

---

4.   Informational memo of the Federal Migration Service to the State Duma of the Russian Federation, dated June 24, 1994.

5.   In particular, ethnic Latvians are given preference over other groups in receiving citizenship. Thus, the Lithuanian Ministry of Foreign Affairs issued a note of protest at the beginning of 1995, expressing its concern over the problems arising in the registering of noncitizens of Lithuanian heritage. However, around 40,000 ethnic Latvians who are not direct descendants of citizens of the Latvian Republic, but are instead descendants of immigrants from Latvia to Russia between 1914 and 1918 who returned to Latvia after 1940, did not receive citizenship.

propaganda. From the perspective of Russians in Latvia, Riga's approach is punitive—forcing them to pay for the policies of the Soviet regime that brought them to Latvia in the first place.

The Latvian government has clearly won the public relations battle in the eyes of world public opinion. The voices of Russians in the Baltic republics are not heard, or if they are, they are not taken seriously outside Russia. International organizations involved in the debate over the citizenship law have helped to soften its provisions but have not challenged the Latvian government's dominant policy approach. In many ways the actions of international organizations are perceived, both internationally and inside Latvia, as legitimizing its discriminatory policies. Political exploitation of fears about Russian imperialism and a "Russian fifth column" in Latvia is also a factor. As in all of the other post-Soviet states, small-scale neo-communist elements exist in the Russian community in Latvia, but whether they constitute a real threat is questionable. However, Latvian authorities realized that, in claiming to feel threatened by Russia, they would secure support from the West, despite the fact that the Russian government was among the earliest and staunchest supporters of Baltic independence. Having raised the specter of a Russian threat, Latvian politicians are now hostage to these populist anti-Russian appeals.

This type of political rhetoric has also triggered a reaction in Russia. Antagonism toward the Baltic states has become a fixture in the rhetoric of Russian politicians. Inside Russia, the frustrations of the Russian communities in Latvia and Estonia strike a very strong chord among the public and increasingly among government and political elites. For Russians, world reaction to the "Russian question" in Latvia is perceived as a general indicator of a suspicious and hostile Western attitude toward Russia. High hopes that the international community and international norms of human rights would be applied and that such situations would not be tolerated by the West have been disappointed. Russians are now largely disillusioned with the ability and the will of the international community to uphold these norms. The intervention of international organizations, though softening some of the more extreme provisions of the citizenship laws, have not challenged the dominant approach of the Latvian government with regard to its treatment of ethnic minorities. In many ways, the actions of international organizations are perceived as legitimizing those policies both internationally and within Latvia. These perceptions have tended to strengthen the position of anti-

Western nationalist forces in Russia, who cite the situation in the Baltic states as evidence that the West applies gross double standards on human rights.

The Baltic states have traditionally been regarded as the link between Europe and Russia—an element that features prominently in the region's ethno-political situation. Developments in the Baltic states, including those concerning interethnic relations, should be considered not only as internal matters, but as issues having a disproportionately large and symbolic effect on the processes under way in Russia. If the symbolic role of the Baltic states is ignored, observers in the United States and other Western countries may misinterpret Russian reactions to events in the Baltics and republics may view them as excessive, irrational, and illogical.

The Origins and Evolution of Discord between Ethnicities

In order to fully understand the positions of the Latvian and Russian communities in Latvia, it is critical to grasp that each group operates with a radically different conception of the history of Latvia and its relations with Russia. The specific details of Latvian and Russian historical myths are not as important as the acknowledgment that they are interpreted from different angles and through different prisms of interests.

Ethnic Latvians in Latvia look primarily to the period of the independent Latvian Republic of 1918–40 to legitimize their authority, statehood, and policies. The declaration of May 4, 1990, "On the Restoration of the Independence of the Latvian Republic," proclaimed the restoration of the Latvian Republic and the succession to its rights. The declaration "On Latvia Joining the Union of Soviet Socialist Republics" of June 21, 1940, was proclaimed null and void. In accordance with this interpretation, the period up to 1918—which included several centuries when Latvia was part of the Russian Empire and the brief period of an independent Latvian Soviet government, and especially the period of the Latvian SSR from 1940–91—are looked upon as periods of occupation and colonial oppression that interrupted and deformed the development of the Latvian nation and Latvian statehood. In many ways this interpretation closely corresponds to the dominant image of the Baltic states in Western public opinion. The leading Western countries never recognized the Soviet incorporation of the Baltic states during World War II, and the Western media and politicians considered them "captive nations."

In the Russian public consciousness, the relevant history of the region stretches back much further than World War II to the centuries of Russian-Latvian cohabitation, when Latvia was part of the Russian Empire. The territories of contemporary Latvia and Estonia were incorporated into Russia as its Baltic provinces in 1721, following the Russian victory in the Northern War against Sweden. As part of the 1772 partition of Poland among Russia, Prussia, and Austria, Russia received the territory known as Latgale (present-day eastern Latvia) and, after the third partition of Poland in 1795, Russia obtained the Dukedom of Kurland in present-day western Latvia. Russians stress that at the end of the eighteenth century, no Latvian state existed and its territories were divided among a number of states. It was only after Latvian lands were gathered within the Russian Empire that the Latvian nation had the possibility to develop as a unified territory, eventually becoming one of its most developed economic regions.

During 1939 and 1940, the Baltic states were forcibly incorporated into the Soviet Union under dubious legal pretenses. Part of the Latvian population collaborated with the occupying German army during World War II. After the war, Stalin instigated massive repressions in the Baltic republics against nationalist groups accused of collaboration as well as purges of "nationalists" and "class enemies." As a result, tens of thousands of Balts fled westward or were exiled to Siberia. As noted above, the Soviet resettlement policy brought large numbers of workers and specialists from other Soviet republics to the Baltics, especially to Latvia and Estonia. These and other historical grievances against the Soviet government were among the many reasons why the Latvian nationalist movement that emerged under perestroika was directed against the Soviet authorities and the Communist Party of the Soviet Union (CPSU) and why it demanded secession from the Soviet Union and the restoration of Latvia's independent statehood.

To the Russian community in Latvia, however, frequent references to the history of the Latvian SSR as a period of occupation represent more than harmless propaganda. Rather, there are concrete legal ramifications in the post-Soviet period, including the withholding of citizenship and pension rights, the forced return of property to the "pre-occupation owners," and other similar measures.[6] If historical

---

6. The questionable nature of a divisive black-and-white approach becomes all the more evident if one recalls that many of the leading politicians in the Latvian

events are to be used to legitimize current claims, then representatives of the Russian minority opposition groups and the Russian community in Latvia cannot accept that arguments must be limited to the 1918–40 period. In their view, other historical periods are equally relevant. If, for instance, on the question of the Russian-Latvian state border, the official Latvian representatives refer to the Riga Peace Treaty of 1920, some irresponsible politicians in Russia refer to the Peace Treaty of Nistadt of 1721 as the starting point for a legal solution of the existing problems—a time when a Latvian state did not exist. In the end, reliance on historical arguments to establish the legitimacy of any new state is inherently problematic since competing historical justifications can always be found. Unfortunately Russians and Latvians have become trapped in this pursuit, and the net result has been to impede the process of working out a fair solution for the population of what was once the Latvian SSR.[7]

PERESTROIKA

Between 1988 and 1991, democratic movements against the domination of Moscow and the Soviet center emerged in all of the Baltic republics. In the early stages of the Latvian independence movement, what was most emphasized was the need for national unity among all inhabitants of Latvia. Appeals to purely national themes, such as protests against Moscow's (and in part Riga's) disregard of Latvian national interests, were important in this period, but not dominant. Slogans used during the initial stages of the movement—"For our freedom and yours," "Latvia our common home," "Not people against people, but together against darkness"—appeared in both the

---

Republic had extremely successful careers in the Soviet period, and thus participated in this repressive system of "occupation" at the highest levels. Yet the anonymous Russian population who came to Latvia as engineers, or soldiers posted with the Soviet Army, somehow bears responsibility for the crimes of the Soviet period.

7. The term "opposition" used throughout the chapter refers to an organized group of opposition parties that represent the interests of the non-Latvian population. The main group is *Ravnopravie* (Equal Rights), but the League of Stateless Persons, the Committee for Human Rights, and other social groups and cultural societies also oppose the citizenship policies of the new state toward non-Latvians. The majority of members of the opposition are noncitizens, though there are some who have become citizens of Latvia. There is also a sector of the politicized opposition, mainly ethnic Latvian parties, that approves of the framework on issues of citizenship but opposes the Latvian government on other grounds, but these groups are not relevant here; thus, the term "opposition" will signify only those opposed to the citizenship policies of the Latvian government toward non-Latvians.

Latvian and the Russian-language press in Latvia. They reflected the spirit of the movement in its early stage with appeals to democratic rather than ethnic or nationalist values.

During this period, a struggle emerged between the two main political coalitions—the nationalists and the pro-unionists—over Latvia's future political status. Substantively, the clash of opinions concerned whether Latvia should seek independence or whether it should opt to remain within the framework of a reconstituted Soviet Union. The divisions between these two groups did not correspond to ethnic divisions in Latvia. However, the seeds of future ethnic issues were already germinating. For example, the first program of the relatively moderate National Front of Latvia called for the allotment of the majority of seats in the legislature to ethnic Latvians, regardless of their proportion in the overall population.

The declaration on the restoration of the Latvian Republic adopted by the Supreme Soviet of the Latvian SSR on May 4, 1990, guaranteed "the citizens of the Latvian Republic and of other states who are permanently resident on the territory of Latvia social and cultural rights, as well as political freedoms, in accordance with generally recognized international standards on human rights. These rights and freedoms extend, in full measure, to the citizens of the USSR who desire to live in Latvia without taking up citizenship."[8] The chairman of the Latvian parliament, Anatolijs Gorbunovs, stressed this point in a May 4, 1990, statement to the Supreme Soviet in which he argued that "only if they are united will the people of Latvia be able to restore, in the general interest, an independent, democratic, European Latvian state."[9] The Latvian National Front, which won the elections in 1990, advocated granting citizenship to all those who expressed the desire to acquire it and who were resident in the republic at the time of the proclamation of independence. In the end, however, this approach was not carried out.

---

8. *Soviet Latvia*, May 9, 1990. Another expression of this prevailing approach was made by the much respected poet and public figure, Janis Peters: "We all understand perfectly well that to return to 1939 and start life again is impossible." "A family has the right to decide the order in its own house and also the place in it of its dear relatives, what is more, relatives not by nationality. In the family of Balts this distinction has never been predominant." Literaturnaia gazeta, June 7, 1989. A very influential figure in Latvia, Peters was at the time chairman of the Latvian Writers Union and one of the founders of the National Front of Latvia. He was elected people's deputy of the Soviet Union for Latvia and later appointed Latvian ambassador in Moscow.

9. *Soviet Latvia*, May 12, 1990.

Until the autumn of 1991, the Latvian authorities avoided taking a clear position on the citizenship question. The concept of a formal distinction between residents of Latvia and descendants of citizens of the Latvian Republic was put forward by one of the Latvian radical nationalist groups, the Movement for Latvian National Independence (MLNI). This organization's "Committee for Citizens" worked out concrete proposals for laws "depriving" or "denying" citizenship status to non-ethnic Latvians. After the August 1991 coup attempt in Moscow, this approach was formally adopted by the Latvian government.

In the initial stages, support for Baltic independence and secession from the Soviet Union came not only from the ethnic Latvian, Estonian, and Lithuanian parts of the population of these republics, but from Russians and other ethnic minorities as well.[10] In the spring of 1991, a referendum on independence was organized in Latvia. Of the 87.6 percent of the population who took part, 64.4 percent were for and 24.6 percent were against independence.[11] Where the proportion of Russians was considerably larger—in the capital, Riga, and in Daugavpils, the center of Latgale—support for independence was noticeably lower, in some places less than 50 percent. In Estonia and Lithuania, the results of similar referenda were much the same.

As the situation developed, ethnic themes began to dominate politics more and more, transforming the conflict from one with the Soviet center to one between Russians and Latvians. The unfavorable demographics of ethnic Latvians during the Soviet era was perceived as posing great problems for the creation of a state with Latvian cultural characteristics. On October 15, 1991, the Latvian Supreme Soviet passed a decree "On the Restoration of Rights of the Citizens of the Latvian Republic and the Main Conditions for Naturalization" that automatically granted citizenship only to direct descendants of the citizens of the Latvian Republic that had existed until 1940. The conditions for others to obtain citizenship include a period of residence of not less than sixteen years, a Latvian-language test and an examination on the Constitution of the Latvian Republic, and an oath of allegiance to Latvia.

The "nonindigenous" residents of both Latvia and Estonia were taken by surprise when it became clear that the process of

---

10. According to a poll conducted by the newspaper *Moscow News* on January 27, 1991, only 52 percent of the Russians claimed citizenship of the Soviet Union exclusively.

11. *Izvestia*, March 4, 1991.

independence would deprive them of citizenship in the countries they had struggled to free. They saw this as a betrayal by the "nationalist bureaucracy" and as an abandonment of democratic principles in favor of the greater political utility of nationalist appeals.

The failed coup in Moscow in August 1991 changed the balance of power in the Baltic republics by undermining the pro-Union coalition and strengthening the national and radical nationalist Latvian groups. This change was further consolidated by the subsequent breakup of the Soviet Union, the signing of the Belovezh Accords on the creation of the Commonwealth of Independent States (CIS), and the recognition of the independence of the Baltic states as subjects of international law both by Russia and the international community.

Throughout this period, the Latvian part of the population demonstrated its ability to organize and mobilize itself politically. The culture of state-centered political activity and the fact that with independence the Latvian nationalist groups had almost exclusive access to the state structures gave them a big advantage in mobilizing support. In contrast, the Russian community, which had always been weakly organized and loosely structured, proved to be completely disorganized. The relative passivity of the opposition groups in articulating the interests of the Russian minority is explained in part by the previous split within the Latvian Russian population between those who were for and against Latvian independence. The general lack of a culture of civic politics in the Russian community and its demonstrated inability to organize politically factored heavily into its passivity. In the fall of 1991, fifteen deputies in the Latvian Supreme Soviet, mostly pro-Unionist Russians, were deprived of their seats by a majority vote on the pretense that they had supported the coup attempt. This essentially decapitated the pro-union forces and almost completely eliminated them from the political life of the country.

The tactical alliance between Russia and the Baltic states to undermine Mikhail Gorbachev and the Soviet center further demoralized the Russian community in Latvia. In January 1991, Russian President Boris Yeltsin concluded treaties with the Baltic states, and after the August coup attempt, he formally recognized Baltic independence. This was viewed with alarm and dismay by a significant part of the Russian population in the region, who regarded it as supporting the Baltic nationalists and encouraging their anti-Russian policies.[12]

---

12. In the March 18, 1990, elections to the Latvian Supreme Soviet, 62.5 percent of the candidates were Latvian and only 26.6 percent were Russian. *Soviet Latvia*,

THE BREAKUP OF THE SOVIET UNION

The Soviet Union ceased to exist in December 1991. On March 31, 1992, a set of amendments and supplements to the Latvian law on languages eliminated the existing guarantee that Russian speakers could receive higher education in the Russian language. Later these amendments were applied to secondary education as well. More disturbing for the Russian community was an amendment that demoted Russian to the status of a foreign language like any other. Previously, although Latvian was the official language, Russian had been recognized as having a special status. Amendments to the language law also increased the number of spheres in which the use of Latvian was officially required and raised the minimum standards for competence in Latvian in a wide range of professional fields. The turnover of personnel as a direct result of the language legislation was particularly significant in higher-level positions. Although no surveys have yet documented this change systematically, the author has observed marked changes in the ethnic composition of various professional spheres in Latvia.

In the field of education, the Latvian government inherited the system of Soviet schools, which included Latvian, Russian, and mixed schools. It was mandated that, following a three-year transition period, education should be conducted exclusively in Latvian. But the state subsequently failed to provide existing Russian schools with adequately trained staff even for teaching the Latvian language, to say nothing of other subjects. Many Russian schools were closed. The *Ravnopravie* (Equality and Rights) faction sent an appeal to the heads of state and parliaments of the member-states of the Conference on Security and Cooperation in Europe (CSCE) on February 3, 1993, which noted that, with the passage of each law, conditions grew more unfavorable for preserving the right to education in one's own language.[13] In spite of recommendations from the Council of Europe, no exceptions to Latvia's language laws have

---

February 27, 1990. Subsequently, the predominance of ethnic Latvians in the administration increased to an even greater margin. In the Riga Municipal Soviet, 59 of the 120 deputies representing the interests of the non-Latvian population (who made up two-thirds of Riga's population) had been replaced. In the summer of 1992, a new city government body was appointed—not elected—by the Supreme Soviet and a law regulating self-government in Latvia was passed. As a result, non-Latvians, who comprised 67 percent of Riga's population, have only 10 percent representation in the city government. These data were gathered by Human Rights Committee activists, copies of which are in the author's possession.

13. A copy of the appeal was kindly supplied to the author by K. Matveev.

been allowed, even for regions where the Russian population has traditionally constituted a majority.

This exclusion of Russian language and culture has taken place by various means. Latvian authorities have reduced the number of Russian elementary and secondary schools, fired or demoted directors of Russian educational institutions, curtailed access to higher education, canceled Russian programs on state radio and television, and limited the circulation of Russian newspapers and magazines and the publication of Russian literature. At present, only one large Russian-language technical school, the Riga Institute for Civil Aviation Engineers, still functions, and its future is uncertain. Attempts to set up private alternative institutions for Russian-language higher education have so far met with little success due to lack of funds and staff and the withholding of financial support by the state. Teaching is a very poorly paid profession throughout the post-Soviet states, and the most competent people have left to work in commercial enterprises.

With respect to the general cultural atmosphere, the symbolic steps asserting a Latvian cultural renaissance that accompanied the independence movement were followed by actions perceived as openly insulting to the Russian community. For example, the Latvian nationalist movement characterized the Red Army's struggle against German Nazism during World War II as outright occupation and adopted a contemptuous attitude toward war memorials and veterans. Monuments to heroes of the Soviet era were pulled down by local councils, and in Riga a handful of cemeteries were designated as Latvian historical sites. The struggle against what the radical Latvian nationalists labeled "cultural occupation" turned into an effort to uproot all traces of Russian cultural influence, even to the point of removing monuments to Yuri Gagarin, the first cosmonaut. These activities were not only orchestrated by the Latvian national government, but in large measure were the result of the independent activities of local councils, individual public figures, and social groups. But the fact remains that the Latvian government took no action to stop the destruction, which generated deep resentment among the Russian population and created the potential for serious political repercussions.

Open attacks on Russian cultural values and symbols alienated the Russian intelligentsia in Latvia from the goals of the new government and increased the polarization between ethnic Latvians and Russians. The alienation intensified when Latvians who had collaborated with the Nazis during the war, including some who had been in the SS, were transformed in the Latvian public consciousness into heroes of national resistance against the regime. In general, the Russian community considered that the Latvian government was dominated by radical anti-Russian feelings. The new government did not make national unity and reconciliation a priority, but instead emphasized the establishment of an ethnically defined state, regardless of how many of its inhabitants did not fit the definition.

The elections to the Seim on June 5–6, 1993, consolidated the emerging balance of forces. Moderate nationalist blocs retained their majority position, but radical nationalist groupings made a strong showing. Following the election, representation in the parliament consisted of three main blocs. The first could be described as radical nationalists, also labeled "ethnic fundamentalists" in the Russian and moderate Latvian press. Radical nationalists want to build a Latvian state responsive to the interests and development of ethnic Latvians that ensures their dominant position. The main parties in this bloc are Movement for Latvian National Independence and the *Tevzemnei un Brivabai* (To the Fatherland and Freedom) Association. Both parties have been influential in formulating the ethnic Latvian political agenda since 1989, and in the 1993 elections, they won twenty-seven out of one hundred seats in the Seim.[14]

The most influential bloc was comprised of pragmatists and relative moderates similar to those who dominated the pro-independence Latvian National Front before the breakup of the Soviet Union. The main party in this bloc, which won thirty-six seats in the 1993 elections, is *Latvia's Tzelsh* (Latvian Way) which emphasizes populist-nationalist themes but shies away from the use of nationalist mythology. Members of Latvian Way include many former Communist Party leaders, former bureaucrats, and members of the Soviet *nomenklatura*. As pragmatists, they are concerned about their image in the West. The Peasants' Union, which is primarily Latvian and quite pragmatic as well, formed the other leg of the governing coalition. Together the two parties controlled a total of forty-eight votes in the Seim and filled all the seats on Latvia's Council of Ministers.

The third main bloc, the liberal nationalists and liberal democrats, tried to arrest the growing ethnic polarization in Latvia. Among its members are moderate nationalist politicians, including most of the Russian-speaking politicians who supported the Latvian Popular

---

14. See *RFE/RL Research Report*, Vol. 2, No. 28 (July 9, 1993), p. 2.

Front and Latvian independence, and many economic managers from both state and commercial spheres. The bloc includes the Democratic Party and a movement called the Latvian Accord for Revival of the National Economy. Together they controlled around 20 percent of the votes in the Seim.

The only direct representation of the interests of noncitizens in the new parliament came from the Equality and Rights faction which had 5 to 7 percent of the seats in the Seim. Prior to the 1991 coup attempt, Equality and Rights opposed Latvian independence. Later it became critical of the government and began to focus on the question of equal citizenship rights for the Russian community. The bulk of ethnic Russians who have obtained Latvian citizenship support Equality and Rights, as do some Latvians who are critical of the government's policies.

Although the national political picture was to a certain extent balanced, local elections held on May 29, 1994, decisively favored the radical nationalist groups. In Riga, the radical nationalists from the Movement for the Latvian National Independence won twenty-two seats and the rightist national movement, To Fatherland and Freedom, got six out of a total of sixty seats. The Latvian Way and the Peasants' Party, which formed the ruling coalition at the national level, ended up with only two and three seats, respectively.[15]

At the end of 1993, two-thirds of Latvia's Russians—nearly one-third of the total population of Latvia—still had no rights as citizens. Many of those affected had been born and raised in Latvia, paid taxes, and had contributed in many other ways to Latvia's development. At the end of 1994, of Latvia's 2.4 million inhabitants, 72 percent had managed to acquire citizenship, 80 percent of whom were ethnic Latvians. Of the 673,400 people who in 1994 did not have citizenship, 85 percent were Russian-speaking.[16]

The exclusion from the political process of tens of thousands of permanent residents of Latvia cannot be explained merely by reference to some kind of pathological Russophobia, although some Russians claim this to be the case. A more persuasive explanation is that some Latvian politicians cannot escape the political situation they themselves created. Before the Soviet breakup, Latvian nationalism

---

15. Approximately 739,000 (or 58.5 percent) of those having the right to vote took part in the local elections. Thirty-four percent of Latvia's inhabitants were disenfranchised. *RFE/RL Daily Report*, No. 102 (May 31, 1994).

16. *Opponent*, No. 14 (December 1993).

fulfilled an important function in mobilizing the Latvian population politically. Anti-Russian phraseology and arguments were effective in the struggle against the union center. But later, the impact of political mobilization along such lines maintained its momentum, making any reversal or compromise difficult.

Citizenship and Language: The Law and Its Implementation

Citizenship issues have driven the polarization of Latvian politics and increased the alienation between the ethnic communities. As mentioned above, the Latvian government defends its authority to grant or deny equal rights and responsibilities to its permanent residents as the right of a legally competent, independent state guided by security and other considerations. In explaining their position, Latvian leaders, including President Guntis Ulmanis, have repeatedly referred to the disloyalty toward the Latvian state of those who arrived in Latvia after 1940. This presumption of disloyalty on the part of non-Latvians is one of the most widely stated reasons for the deprivation of citizenship.[17] Yet most noncitizens regard Latvia as their homeland and refuse to leave voluntarily. Despite the unfavorable development of the situation, only an insignificant number of people have opted for Russian citizenship.[18] By mid-1994, only forty thousand out of approximately one million ethnic Russians permanently residing in Latvia had applied for Russian citizenship.[19]

Discrimination against noncitizens is not restricted to the deprivation of voting rights, as some Latvian officials have insisted. It affects all aspects of living. Only citizens have the right to hold government posts, to work in the state bureaucracy, or to hold diplomatic or consular offices.[20] Noncitizens do not have the right to work in the police or as private detectives or as armed guards or even as heads of any enterprises using armed guards.[21] They cannot hold judicial offices

---

17. This has become a self-fulfilling prophecy, however, since official Latvian policy provokes feelings of extreme vulnerability among the nonethnic Latvian population, which, in turn, stimulates disloyalty.

18. Information supplied by the Russian Ministry for Foreign Affairs during Federal Assembly hearings attended by the author.

19. ITAR-TASS, July 1, 1994.

20. The law "On Rights and Duties of Citizens and People," Article 8; the law "On State Public Service," Article 6.1; and the law on "Diplomatic and Consular Service to the Latvian Republic," Article 2.

21. The law "On Police," Rule No. 19, Clause 1.5; and the law "On Operational Activities," Article 25.3; amendments to "The Statute on Detective Activities and

or work as notaries or assistant notaries, nor are they allowed to work on the crew of commercial ships or to be engaged in teaching or scientific activities, for example, in the Latvian Medical Academy.[22] Moreover, some local councils, like the Vidzeme suburb of Riga, prohibit the employment of noncitizens by persons or firms who rent housing or office space there.[23]

In terms of property rights, only citizens have the right to own land and other natural resources[24] and to buy apartments in state-owned buildings or repatriated buildings, i.e., buildings that have been returned to the persons who owned them under the Latvian interwar republic.[25] Only noncitizens who have been residents for more than sixteen years can buy apartments that have been privatized.[26] Noncitizens were also shortchanged in the larger privatization process. In many former socialist states, shares of state property were allotted to residents in the form of privatization certificates redeemable for stock in enterprises. In Latvia, citizens—including newborn children—were issued fifteen privatization certificates over and above the "standard" allotment.[27]

In the sphere of private enterprise, only citizens and noncitizens who have been residents for more than sixteen years can privatize small service sector enterprises.[28] Noncitizens with less than twenty-one years residence in Latvia cannot found joint-stock companies.[29] Citizens

---

Licensing in the Latvian Republic," Decree of the Ministry of Internal Affairs No. 74.

22. The Law "On Judicial Authority," Article 51.1; the Law "On Restoration of the Latvian Republic's Law of 1937 on Notary Office and the Changes and Amendments to it of June 1, 1993," Articles 9.1, 147.1; and the law "On Aviation," Article 35. The restrictions on medical teaching and research do not apply to highly skilled specialists who have been invited to hold such offices on the basis of an agreement. Constitution of the Medical Academy approved by the Supreme Soviet on February 23, 1993, Article 5.3.

23. Decision of the Vidzeme Suburb Council No. 818, Clause 2.

24. The constitutional law "On Rights and Duties of Citizens and People," Article 9.

25. The constitutional law "On the State and Self-Government Institutions' Assistance in Settling Housing Problems," Article 3.

26. The law "On Privatization of Cooperative Apartments," Article 7.

27. The law "On Privatization Certificates," Article 4, clauses 2 and 4.

28. The law "On Privatization of Minor Trade, Public Catering and Consumer Service Facilities that Are the Property of Self-Government Institutions," Article 11.

29. The law "On Joint Stock Companies," Article 10.1.1.

must constitute the majority of the governing body of commercial banks.[30] And only citizens can obtain a permit to pilot air vehicles.[31]

On social issues the provisions are similarly restrictive. Only citizens can obtain land to build a freestanding house or obtain preferential loans and other assistance to liquidate communal apartments.[32] Only citizens have the right to own firearms for the purpose of self-defense,[33] and police operations are regulated only as they affect citizens with no restrictions on how they affect noncitizens.[34] Noncitizens do not have the right to take part in local elections, and the March 1994 amnesty for some categories of prisoners did not apply to them.[35] Only citizens are guaranteed the right to freely choose their place of residence and the right to return freely to Latvia after being abroad.[36] Only citizens can travel to certain countries (Hungary, the United Kingdom, and the Czech Republic) without a visa. Noncitizens cannot, for example, apply for a visa at the British Embassy in Riga, but must travel to Moscow, even though they are not Russian citizens, an expensive trip that must be made without a guarantee of readmittance to Latvia. Finally, only citizens have the right to work in Germany on the basis of a German-Latvian bilateral agreement.[37]

Such provisions have created a clear line between the rights and protection extended to citizens and noncitizens. Although they have been billed as a strategy to restore the independent Latvian Republic, the fact that neighboring Lithuania chose to adopt another path, the "zero option," in effect granting citizenship to all permanent residents of the country, demonstrates that Latvia had more than one possible route to accomplish this goal. Thus the decision to deprive a substantial portion of former citizens of the Latvian SSR of citizenship cannot be seen as merely political necessity, as its defenders maintain. Rather

---

30. Decree of the Latvian Bank Council No. 10/7.

31. The law "On Aviation," Articles 78 and 79.

32. The law "On State and Self-Government Institutions' Assistance in Settling Housing Problems," Article 3; and the law "On the Procedure for the Registry of Persons (Families) to Obtain State and Self-Government Institutions' Assistance in Settling Housing Problems," No. 17.

33. The law "On Firearms and Special Means of Self-Defense," Article 3.4.

34. The law "On Operational Activities," Article 23.2.

35. The law "On Amnesty," Clauses 4 and 5.

36. The constitutional law "On Rights and Duties of Citizens and People," Article 10.28.

37. Based on the Agreement between the German and Latvian Governments of June 2, 1992.

it represents a deliberate political choice. The approach to this problem reflected the priorities of the Latvian leadership and is ironically reminiscent of Soviet logic, according to which human and civil rights derive from the "higher" interests of the state. And if the government's decision not to recognize the citizenship of people is accepted, the right of the government to deport noncitizens is, in principle, also recognized. Although the second proposition does not follow logically or legally from the first, a strong link between noncitizenship and susceptibility to deportation was forged early on and is not questioned by the vast majority of those involved. The rationale of political expediency, coupled with the need to further the interests of the state, is no more legitimate in the case of Latvia than similar arguments justifying racial discrimination or apartheid. Repressive and discriminatory societies can be created in ways that do not directly clash with the provisions of international law.

Why did the authorities choose the confrontational variant on the citizenship question? First, the controversy over the status of noncitizens gave Latvian authorities additional leverage in their political negotiations with Russia. Second, by enacting and subsequently softening some aspects of the decision, the Latvian government managed to maintain the full support of the United States and Europe. Every small concession to noncitizens was presented to European public opinion as evidence of "evolution in the right direction" that should be encouraged. Another plausible interpretation is that these actions opened up vast possibilities for the Latvian national movement to institutionalize and consolidate power and to neutralize its political opponents by denying them representation in Latvian political institutions.

The implementation of the citizenship law was even harsher than the legislative language. The Department of Citizenship and Immigration did not permit people who had been working in the Soviet Union for an extended period (e.g., those who had left temporarily to earn high salaries working in the northern regions of Russia) to return and be registered in Latvia, though they had permanent Latvian addresses and apartments. During registration procedures, the department regularly registered people as having lived in the Latvian SSR for less time than was actually the case. Moreover, some bureaucrats refused to register persons who had worked at Soviet defense facilities. This restriction was applied not only to military and technical personnel, but to cleaning staff, caretakers at Defense Ministry housing facilities and health centers, clerks in

Defense Ministry shops, and others holding service jobs. Such persons and all members of their families were categorized as "service staff of the Soviet army of occupation." Not only were these people denied the right to register for citizenship, but Latvian officials also refused to count hours spent working at defense facilities toward pension rates or to include that time in the tally of years of residence in Latvia. Persons living in dormitories and hostels—a common long-term arrangement for workers in industry, especially for laborers brought in from other areas—were refused registration under the pretext that they were not fully "legal" residents. Furthermore, the Department of Citizenship and Immigration in many cases simply refused to implement decisions of other government bodies, including parliament and courts, regarding citizenship, residence permits, and the violation of registration procedures.[38] These injustices were rarely opposed.[39]

Radical nationalists were able to secure key administrative posts, such as director of the Department of Citizenship and Immigration, giving this faction a measure of influence in deciding the citizenship question quite out of proportion to its level of political support in the country as a whole. Thus, in reality, the situation was determined not solely by the new laws, but by the nature of their implementation based upon particular decisions and the personal qualities of individual officials. Observers who live outside the post-Soviet republics find it difficult to understand the subtleties of bureaucratic-administrative harassment perfected in the Soviet period. For anyone who has lived in the Soviet Union, however, it is all too clear how a language test or an application for a residence permit can become a

---

38. According to unpublished documentation in the author's possession collected by the Latvian Human Rights Committee, this has been the case. The Latvian government attempted to establish criteria for determining the eligibility for citizenship of all groups living in Latvia. However, even these criteria—as arguable as they may be in their own right—were regularly ignored by the Department of Immigration and Citizenship. For example, the Department established a special category for the relatives of military officers. Thus, a woman who satisfied all of the residence and other background requirements would still be denied citizenship if she had married an officer in the Soviet Army.

39. One exception is the case of Olaf Bruveris, a fervent Baptist, who for a short period held the post of Minister for Human Rights. Guided by his personal sense of Christian morality, he tried to correct gross acts of injustice committed by other government departments, particularly the Department for Citizenship and Immigration. His activities earned him the praise of many, but were not appreciated by the establishment, and it has been suggested that he was forced to resign.

refined instrument of mental torture.[40] These types of hurdles can be effective means of forcing people out, and those whom they affect consider them, with full justification, as trampling on human dignity and national feelings. A group called Citizens of Russia and Ethnic Russians Permanently Living in Estonia articulated in an appeal to the Russian leadership precisely this evaluation of similar procedures in Estonia. The situation in Latvia is not better.[41]

A new law on citizenship adopted by the Latvian Seim on June 22, 1994, was badly received both by the leaders of many noncitizen organizations and by Moscow. Despite some largely cosmetic amendments, the law retained its major defects and confirmed the deprivation of Latvian citizenship for hundreds of thousands of permanent residents. In so doing, the new law also preserved the grounds for continued social conflict.

The citizenship law was not the only issue that divided the Latvian and Russian communities and created ethnic strife. State control of many spheres of public life that was a key feature of Soviet society has continued in the post-Soviet states. The governments of the new states still act as powerful sociocultural agents. Their support of cultural and educational institutions or, on the contrary, the refusal of their support for economic or ideological reasons has the power to ease or intensify the tensions between ethnic communities. The state authorities support and sometimes even widen existing splits in the ethnic Russian communities which, like that in Latvia, are already very fractionalized and badly organized. The creation of various categories of residents, each possessing different rights, stimulates discord in the community and pits one group of Russians against another (the integrated versus immigrants, and so forth).

Even in Estonia, which also implemented a very harsh policy toward "foreigners," attempts were made to hold nonbinding consultations with representatives of the noncitizen organizations. These roundtables were prompted by the CSCE and organized by the Estonian government with participation from the Russian community.[42] The Latvian authorities, however, did not make similar symbolic overtures or attempt to institutionalize a constructive dialogue.

---

40. Often such documents require innumerable references, the collection of which is paid for by the applicant. Statements are gathered to testify to the absence of mental illness, AIDS, syphilis, and other afflictions—even from war veterans and survivors of the Leningrad blockade.

41. See *Nezavisimaia gazeta*, March 18, 1994.

42. In Estonia, it was difficult to say if the reasons for the different outcome were the result of 1) a more rational policy by the government; 2) the influence of the

Language requirements have been another major bone of contention. The law on the status of the Latvian language, introduced by a decree of the Supreme Soviet of the Latvian SSR of October 6, 1988, recognized the Latvian language as the only official language in the republic. The status of the Latvian language was confirmed in the May 5, 1989, language law. At the time of Latvia's independence, only about 20 percent of the non-Latvian population spoke Latvian with any competence. Although the majority of ethnic Latvians supported the law, it was greeted with alarm by the Russian-speaking part of the population.

The tension in relations between the ethnic communities over the language requirements continued to grow. With the introduction of Latvian competency tests, the Russian community saw its worst fears confirmed. Many viewed the tests as potential means to settle political accounts with opposition activists from the Russian community and to force non-Latvians from prestigious, well-paid positions and, ultimately, from the republic altogether. These suspicions were further confirmed when, once having adopted the law, the government took no steps to make it easier for those who did not know the Latvian language to learn it. Indeed, the state began a campaign to remove the Russian language from all public places, from street names to price tags in shops, which formerly had been in both languages.

Thus, what was seen as a renaissance of Latvian language and culture by ethnic Latvians was seen by Russians as a policy to exclude Russian language and culture and an attempt to create a monolingual environment.

Evolution of Russian Policy toward Latvian Nationalism

Within a few years, Russian support for Latvian independence became tempered by its critical concern for the Russian population that was systematically excluded from full participation in Latvia. Unsurprisingly, domestic politics of both Russia and Latvia and relations between the two new nations were deeply affected by consequent changes in policy.

CSCE on the process; or 3) the fact that the Russian community in Estonia was better organized and more able to defend its interests, making the Estonians wary of an open confrontation.

BALTIC INDEPENDENCE AND THE END OF THE SOVIET UNION

Before the breakup of the Soviet Union, the Russian leaders supported the struggle of the Baltic republics against the Soviet center, and in January 1991, they signed bilateral agreements with the Baltic republics. These were not agreements between sovereign states, but between republics of the Soviet Union. Nevertheless, they provided crucial Russian political support during a difficult period for Latvia, when the Soviet leadership tried to halt forcibly the centrifugal tendencies in the Soviet Union by provoking armed incidents in Riga and Vilnius.

The ratification of the first treaty between Russia and Estonia on December 26, 1991, by the Russian Supreme Soviet serves as an indicator of the political idealism, naiveté, and euphoria of Russia's early policies toward the Baltic countries. The Latvian and Lithuanian treaties were similar. Article 3 of the treaty with Estonia stated the obligation of the parties to "guarantee persons who are resident at the time of the signing of the present treaty the right to retain or acquire the citizenship of either the Russian Socialist Federated Soviet Republic (RSFSR) or the Estonian Republic in accordance with their own freely expressed wish." For "citizens" of either country living on the territory of the other as well as persons without citizenship, Article 4 of the treaty recognized "[their] civil and political rights and freedoms as well as [their] social, economic and cultural rights, in accordance with generally recognized international human rights norms." It was stipulated that the choice of citizenship was to be based on the legislation of the country of residence and the provisions of the treaty.

No sooner was the treaty signed than the Estonian government took measures making it clear to ethnic minorities that the government was inclined to carry out discriminatory policies toward the Russian population.[43] Unfortunately for the Russians and other minorities living in the Baltic republics, the treaties they concluded with Russia were worded in very general terms. They stipulated that specific questions, including those involving citizenship and property rights, would be settled in subsequent side agreements—which were never concluded. When the Russian Ministry of Foreign Affairs tried

---

43. The general character of the treaty left the Estonian government a free hand to develop its nationalities and citizenship policies without the immediate threat of rupturing relations with Russia. The fact that the Estonian government was so loath to stipulate specific guarantees for the status of non-Estonians was interpreted as a foreboding sign among Russians and other minority nationalities.

to negotiate the side agreements, the Baltic countries avoided any concrete commitments.[44] Issues left unresolved included questions on the rights of ethnic minorities, the provision of military pensions, and the schedule for the withdrawal of the former Soviet Army, as well as questions of transit, trade, and cooperation. In hindsight, the Russian Foreign Ministry should have sorted out these questions ahead of time. Russia was not wary enough, and the Foreign Ministry was not far-sighted enough, to ensure that the provisions were clear and concrete. The government preferred instead to overlook the details in order to maintain an alliance with the Baltic states during the volatile period of the breakup of the Soviet Union.

In spite of the treaty's vagueness, 56.3 percent of the deputies of the Russian Supreme Soviet voted to ratify the treaty with Estonia.[45] The signing of treaties with Estonia and the other Baltic states prompted protests throughout these former republics in which people carried signs saying, "This is Yeltsin's Munich" and "You Have Betrayed Us." Boris Yeltsin's advisers at the time, including Galina Starovoitova, his adviser on nationality issues, called the protesters neo-communists.[46] The legitimacy of the ethnic Russian protesters in Latvia was undermined as a result. The reaction of Yeltsin's government to these protests was remembered two years later, when large numbers of Russian citizens living in the Baltic states voted in support of Vladimir Zhirinovsky.

The interpretation of these treaties raised contentious issues. For example, Estonians claimed that in the treaty the term "citizen" referred to citizens of the RSFSR and the Estonian SSR, and thus was no longer valid in the context of an independent Estonia. Russians consider Estonia's interpretation as a refusal to comply with their commitments and as a case of unscrupulous subordination of treaty obligations to political expediency. Similar tactics were used in Latvia to get around the terms in its treaty with Russia.

---

44. Latvian officials felt a great deal of pressure from their domestic constituencies. However, the radical nationalist presence both in the government and in the population at large made it infeasible for a Latvian politician both to appear to acquiesce to Russian demands on Latvian internal policy and to remain in power.

45. Bulletin of the Supreme Soviet of the Russian Federation, 4th Session, No. 26 (1991), pp. 47–48.

46. Although Starovoitova did not hold an overwhelming sway over Yeltsin or his policies, she was very popular among the mass media, and her ideas came to symbolize for many Russians the unrealistic nature of Russian policy toward the former Soviet republics in the months following the dismantling of the Soviet Union.

Russian recognition of Latvian independence in a presidential decree of August 24, 1991, was in many ways dictated by short-sighted political considerations, including attempts to gain international recognition for Russia's own independence.[47] Russia's unconditional recognition of Latvia and the other former Soviet states came at the expense of ethnic Russians living outside the borders of the Russian Federation. It now seems clear that Russian officials did not fully appreciate the legal consequences of this act. The advisers who had negotiated Russia's agreements with the Baltic states were forced out of the Yeltsin government and were widely seen as political neophytes who failed to understand the need to clarify the treaty conditions. With the arrival of the Yeltsin-Gaidar government, the Russian community in Latvia believed that Moscow was no longer disposed to protect the interests of Russian communities outside Russia. Among the Gaidar government's first actions concerning Latvia was to extradite, at the request of the Latvian Procurator's Office, a Russian officer in the Soviet military to stand trial in Latvia.[48]

Subsequent diplomatic attempts by the Russian Ministry of Foreign Affairs to obtain Latvian and Estonian compliance with the treaties as Russian negotiators understood them, including direct appeals to the Baltic governments, met with no success. Latvia refused to consider Russian interests and requests on a number of specific questions, including the introduction of dual citizenship for part of Latvia's population, even as a provisional measure.[49] Rather

---

47. Russia, unlike Latvia and certain other republics of the former Soviet Union, did not declare itself to be based on any specific ethnic foundation. However, there has clearly been pressure to do so as a result of deep blows to Russian national self-esteem, the deepening economic crisis, the breakup of the Soviet Union, and the real threat of an outburst of Russian nationalism represented in the person of Vladimir Zhirinovsky. The growth of Russian extremism could be fed by the increasing flow of refugees and migrants from conflict zones in the former Soviet Union. This is all the more likely since Russia has no serious programs for refugee settlement.

48. The officer, Sergei Parfenov, was part of the Latvian Special Militia (OMON). He was accused of having committed crimes on Latvian territory during the armed OMON attack on the Latvian Ministry of the Interior and the television broadcast tower. The attack, which occurred at the beginning of 1991, resulted in a shoot-out in the center of Riga. Most of the accusations against Parfenov could not be substantiated, and he was sentenced to a short jail term. After completing his sentence, Parfenov returned to Russia and was pardoned by President Yeltsin as a gesture of goodwill by the Russian government. But, by this time, the message had already been transmitted that the Russian government would not protect ethnic Russians abroad.

49. While the Latvian government has refused to accept dual citizenship with Russia, a form of dual citizenship has been envisaged for members of the Latvian diaspora living in the United States, Australia, Germany, and other countries.

than moving toward a closer relationship with Russia, Latvian authorities instituted a visa regime, making contacts between non-citizens and their relatives in Russia especially difficult.[50] This stood out all the more against the background of agreements between the Baltic states and a number of European countries that abolished visa requirements for travel. Moscow considered anti-Russian prejudice on the part of the Latvian authorities as the driving force behind these measures.

Noncitizen groups defending the interests of those made stateless by Latvian legislation tried, albeit without much success, to involve the Russian government in their deliberations. Before the 1993 elections to the Seim, a written appeal, supported by ninety-eight thousand signatures, to rewrite the election rules so as to allow the participation of noncitizen residents was submitted to the Supreme Soviet of the Russian Federation and the Latvian Committee for Human Rights and International Humanitarian Cooperation.[51] The effort yielded no tangible results.[52]

RUSSIAN DIPLOMACY

As information on the policies toward the Russians in the Baltic states accumulated, and as public opinion inside Russia began to change, Moscow's position toward the Baltic states (especially Latvia and Estonia) also began to change. Indeed, as early as December 26, 1991, the Supreme Soviet of the Russian Federation adopted a decree calling for active negotiations with the Baltic republics on the protection of the citizenship rights of Russians. The call to defend the rights of Russians abroad was actively taken up by Yeltsin's opponents. In response to this pressure, the Russian government was forced to modify its approach to the problem.

Since it proved impossible to obtain concessions on the question of citizenship through bilateral negotiations with the Baltic states,

---

50. According to this new regime, the visas required by noncitizens could only be obtained with hard currency. The visas were also expensive—sometimes costing one-third of an average monthly salary.

51. The committee was headed by Vladimir Bogdanov, who was a defender of human rights even before Latvian independence and had become popular through his fights with the Soviet bureaucracy.

52. Following the appeal, observers from the Russian Federation were invited to observe the election in Latvia, but they refused on the grounds that Russian observers would only legitimize what was an inherently discriminatory undertaking.

Russia began to appeal to international organizations in order to reach a satisfactory solution. On April 12, 1992, a statement protesting discrimination against ethnic Russians was sent to CSCE member-states. On the same day, the "Memorandum on the Violation of Human Rights in the Baltic Countries" was given to the Committee of Ministers at the Council of Europe in Strasbourg. The Russian Ministry for Foreign Affairs undertook a number of other diplomatic demarches, but none of the initiatives was successful in persuading any of the European countries that the integration of the Baltic countries in Europe should be linked to a just settlement of the citizenship question regarding Russian minorities. Russian attempts to make Latvia's acceptance into the Council of Europe contingent upon liberalization of its ethnic policies did not succeed. From the perspective of the Russian government as well as mainstream Russian public opinion, Russia had demonstrated its inability to use the leverage of international organizations to end discriminatory practices against Russians and other non-Balts. Thus, despite Russian efforts and the still-unresolved citizenship issue, Estonia became a member of the Council of Europe in 1993 and Latvia was admitted on January 31, 1995.

By the middle of 1993, the cause of defending Russians in the former republics of the Soviet Union had become a frequently used and effective method of appealing to populist feeling and achieving political support in Russian politics. In 1993, President Yeltsin issued a number of strongly worded statements warning the governments of Latvia and Estonia of the need to change their position on citizenship. Again after the adoption of the Latvian law on citizenship in 1994, Yeltsin branded the political course of the Latvian authorities as "a dangerous drift toward militant nationalism," and charged them with "turning a young independent state into a hotbed of national intolerance, and elevating [that intolerance] to the rank of official policy." "Russia," he stated, "cannot reconcile itself to the fact that, in a neighboring country, hundreds of thousands of ethnic Russians have been placed in an essentially degrading position."[53]

A July 1, 1993, resolution of the Supreme Soviet of the Russian Federation charged Estonia with grossly violating "not only the corresponding articles of the 1948 Universal Declaration on Human Rights, the 1966 Covenant on Civil and Political Rights and other international documents on human rights, but also articles of the

---

53. ITAR-TASS, August 4, 1994.

Treaty on the relations between the RSFSR and the Estonian Republic signed on January 12, 1991." Estonia was further accused of operating "in direct contravention of documents from the Helsinki, Copenhagen and Moscow Conferences on security and cooperation in Europe."[54] The Supreme Soviet gave instructions to inform the UN, the CSCE, the Council of Europe, and the member governments of these organizations about the discriminatory policies of the Estonian Republic. The Russian Ministry of Foreign Affairs was ordered to secure the "defense of the Russian population," though that ministry had been the principal advocate for ratification of the original 1991 treaty.

These sometimes unjustifiably harsh declarations by Russian leaders did not contribute to constructive solutions, and in some ways made the situation worse. Yeltsin's rhetoric, designed primarily for domestic political consumption, was assessed, even by interested observers in Latvia itself (including the group "Civil Concord") as inflammatory and propagandistic and as "playing into the hands of the Latvian radical nationalists." Manifestoes and veiled threats from the Russian government did nothing to ease the situation of noncitizens in Latvia. Russian pronouncements were used by Latvian politicians to stir up support for stringent policies and as weapons in domestic political battles. Moreover, harsh Russian statements were exploited diplomatically, with the help of Latvians abroad, to gain the sympathy of the mass media and public opinion in the West. Latvia and Estonia were presented as two small countries on the road to democracy, threatened by an aggressive and undemocratic Russia. The image of a small David, Latvia, struggling against a massive Russian Goliath turned out to be of considerable propaganda value and seemed to take root in Western public opinion.

Aside from the rhetorical offensive, the Russian government adopted two strategies to counter discriminatory legislation in Latvia: economic pressure and the refusal to withdraw Russian troops left over from the Soviet era. Announcements by Yeltsin and by the Russian Foreign Ministry stipulated that if harsh measures continued against the ethnic Russian population, the schedule for withdrawal of Russian troops would be reconsidered. The policy was widely condemned by international public opinion and ultimately proved ineffective. The decision to emphasize the ethnicity of stateless persons was motivated by Russian internal politics and attempts

---

54. ITAR-TASS, July 1, 1993.

by individual politicians to mobilize internal populist support. Little sympathy was generated in the international community by the Russian government's portrayal of the problem as an ethnic issue, though sympathy was mobilized for the cause of "small and oppressed" Latvia. In retrospect, emphasizing the human rights and citizenship elements of the issue would likely have been a more productive strategy from an international legal standpoint.[55]

Corruption in both the Russian and Latvian government structures may well be another major reason for the limited effectiveness of Russian pressures. News analysis suggests that powerful organizations in Russia are engaged in the export of raw materials (not always legally) through the Baltic republics to the West. These groups have influential contacts in the higher echelons of the Russian administration, and they did not want to see relations with the nationalist governments of Latvia and Estonia worsen to the point that it would begin to interfere with their business interests.[56]

The clear beneficiary of the Russian strategy was, ironically, the Latvian government. It could now claim to have evidence for the international community of Russia's slide toward imperialist policies, and proof that Russia represented a threat to the security of the Baltic states and to Europe as a whole. The shift in the official Russian position toward greater concern for the problem of noncitizens was christened by Vitautas Landsbergis, the ex-President of Lithuania, as "the Kozyrev-Zhirinovsky doctrine." Estonian President Lennart Meri, many Latvian politicians, and the mass media constantly warned of growing "imperialist tendencies" in Moscow's policies.

In the eyes of international public opinion, the Russian Foreign Ministry lost its diplomatic battle. Russia failed to effect any change in internal Latvian policies toward the Russian minority. Its primary goal was to push for a more inclusive notion of citizenship, like the zero option adopted in Lithuania. Russia neither achieved this aim nor made its position understood. If Russia had been more effective in articulating its side of the story, it would have been more successful in mobilizing outside countries and international organizations to influence Latvia. The troop withdrawal policy attracted greater attention to

---

55. The author has frequently heard residents of Latvia who have been deprived of their citizenship complain bitterly that, in spite of all their shortcomings, international organizations have done much more to protect their rights than have Russia and Russian diplomacy.

56. *Obshchaia gazeta*, November 4–10, 1994.

the situation in the Baltic countries on the part of international organizations. Nevertheless, disappointment with Russian foreign policy toward the Baltic states was widely felt not only among the Russian communities in the Baltic states, but in Russia itself.[57]

RUSSIAN DOMESTIC POLITICS

From a Western perspective, it may seem that concern shown by Russian politicians for civil rights in Latvia and Estonia is nothing more than Russian nationalist propaganda. However, the fact is that the issue of Russians abroad, which was formerly kept carefully in the political background, became a central issue in Russian public opinion. Political organizations including Zhirinovky's Liberal Democratic Party, the Russian Communist Party, and the Congress of Russian Communities[58] have called for Russians to regard themselves as a "divided people," implying a refusal to recognize the breakup of the Soviet Union and portraying the current borders of the Russian Federation as temporary and unnatural. Yeltsin is seen by many Russians as the person who bears the primary responsibility for the dissolution of the Soviet Union. This opinion is especially common among those who, after the breakup, found themselves stranded in a foreign country as national minorities or stateless persons with no recourse against discrimination. Yeltsin is also viewed an anti-national leader who bears responsibility for the accession to power of anti-Russian politicians in the Baltic states. Even Russian politicians who can in no way be accused of chauvinism have been forced to review their positions. There has been a general shift in public opinion, giving more priority to the defense of national interests and expressing more critical and negative views about Russian-Baltic-Western relations. Georgi Arbatov, former director of the Institute of the USA and Canada, is an influential and strongly pro-Western analyst who cannot be lightly accused of an anti-Western agenda. However, in evaluating the prospects for the development of Russian-American relations, Arbatov expressed the hope that, "in the West, they will finally understand correctly, and will not mistakenly interpret a turn to normal policies which defend

---

57. *Segodnia*, July 12, 1994.

58. The Congress of Russian Communities is headed by Yury Skokov and former commander of the Russian 14th Army in Moldova's Transdniester region, Alexander Lebed.

one's interests as a change of the whole political course; and at the same time, that they on their part will show respect for our lawful, national interests and will not provoke (even unintentionally) an excessive hardening of our policies."[59]

The growing radicalization in the Russian community is evidenced by the strength of radical nationalist populists of Zhirinovsky's ilk, for whom the idea of a Russian national restoration is popular, and who have received a significant percentage of votes among the Russian community in the Baltic states. The several thousand Russian citizens residing in the Baltic states who voted in the Russian general elections in December 1993 generally supported radical candidates.[60] Among Russian citizens voting in Estonia, for example, Zhirinovsky received 47.7 percent of the vote, and twice as many people voted against the Yeltsin Constitution as for it.[61] The results in Latvia were similar, with Zhirinovsky receiving roughly one-third of the votes cast.[62]

---

59. *Nezavisimaia gazeta*, April 14, 1994. See also statements by Mikhail Gorbachev in *Nezavisimaia gazeta*, January 13, 1994. Andranik Migranian, an influential adviser to President Yeltsin, evaluated Russia's hasty decision to recognize the independence of the Baltic states as "a serious mistake," and the result of the "naiveté and dilettantism" of the new Russian leadership. "Forcing the establishment of ethnocratic governments, especially in Latvia and Estonia, and excluding from citizenship more than a million and a half of the nonindigenous population," he argued, "at once complicated relations between Russia and the Baltic republics and threatened to affect relations between Russia and the United States and other Western countries." Migranian stressed in particular that "the human rights problem and adherence to the principle of respect for these rights was apparently not a universal principle for the West and was only used against the Soviet Union as an ideological weapon." He concluded that "the acceptance of Estonia as a member of the Council of Europe was seen as spit in the face of Russia." "Russia and the Near Abroad," *Nezavisimaia gazeta*, January 18, 1994, pp. 4–5.

60. Clearly the voting behavior of people who had already chosen Russian citizenship was not indicative of all Russians in the Baltic states. Because taking Russian citizenship would prevent someone from acquiring Latvian citizenship, this group represented those who had already firmly decided that their interests lay with Russia. This was a very small number in total. Nevertheless, the radicalization of this group was not a good sign. The opposite view has also been expressed, though it has been the exception, in Russia. "Understanding" for the position of the Baltic republics and a readiness to justify deportation and discrimination against noncitizens managed to find its way into the Russian newspapers. For example, a February 1994 article in *Nezavisimaia gazeta* stated: "The well-known disloyalty shown by certain groups of the nonindigenous population toward the laws of the Latvian Republic make their further residence there and their continued role in the public and political life of [Latvia] impossible." *Nezavisimaia gazeta*, February 16, 1994.

61. "LDPR Representative in Estonia Comments," *Foreign Broadcast Information Service Central Eurasia* (hereafter *FBIS*) SOV-93-238, December 14, 1993, p. 35.

62. In Latvia, the Communist presidential candidate received the highest number of votes (1,855 out of 3,762) and Zhirinovsky came in second with 1,226 votes. However, in Latvia, the lack of support for the new Constitution was even more

The World Outside

Ironically, attempts by the international community to ameliorate the situation have been regarded by Russians as legitimizing discrimination. Numerous visits to Latvia by representatives from international organizations and various countries have prompted no serious criticism of the situation of noncitizens. The Latvian government's rationale for exclusionary measures in the cultural, educational, economic, and political spheres has not been challenged by the international community. Latvia's definition of citizenship and of the criteria for naturalization that disenfranchised one-third of the population at the critical formative stage of the new Latvian state has not been contested.[63] This response from outside observers has been interpreted as international approval of Latvia's policy of neutralizing its political opposition and of the general direction of Latvian policies. It has further undermined the legitimacy of the ethnic Russian opposition movement in the eyes of Latvians and has thus helped enhance domestic support for the government's policies.

INTERNATIONAL ORGANIZATIONS

Numerous international delegations and missions have come to Latvia in connection with the citizenship law and the observance of human rights. Many have noted problems with civil rights in Latvia and made observations about Latvia's draft law on citizenship. Notably, CSCE High Commissioner for National Minorities Max van der Stoel was critical of the intended yearly quotas for naturalization and other conditions for granting citizenship, including unrealistic standards for knowledge of the Latvian language.

Many of Van der Stoel's observations were considered, if only formally, before the decision to admit Latvia into the Council of Europe. Experts from the Council proposed that the extraordinarily high residence requirement in the draft law should be shortened. The Council also proposed eliminating ethnic background as a criterion in the naturalization process. However, these suggestions did not

---

pronounced than in Estonia, with only 691 out of 3,042 favoring its implementation. See "Further on Latvian Vote," *FBIS* SOV-93-238, December 14, 1993, p. 3.

63. It is well understood by both the Latvian government and the Russian community that even those individuals who could eventually acquire citizenship through language training will be unable to participate in Latvian politics for many years.

result in significant changes to the draft of the citizenship law that passed the Seim on June 22, 1994. The law continued to preserve the long residency requirement, the high standards of proficiency in the Latvian language, and the onerous system of examinations. After the passage of the law, representatives of international organizations concentrated on convincing the Latvian government to pass a law on the naturalization of noncitizens and to create a special agency for naturalization. It was recommended to entrust this role and other measures to integrate noncitizens to the infamous Department of Citizenship and Immigration.[64]

The efforts of international organizations and a handful of countries did help to soften the worst laws and to improve the situation of the Russian community in Latvia. Initially, outside observers looked only at the letter of the law and met only with government officials. However, after the increased activism of the Russian community, international organizations changed their approach, met with a wider range of groups, and investigated how these laws were actually implemented. Special criticism was directed at the activities of bureaucrats in the Department of Citizenship and Immigration. An October 1992 UN human rights mission headed by Ibrahima Fall and a 1993 delegation from Helsinki Watch criticized the activities of this department. The well-argued reports of Helsinki Watch were instrumental in convincing Latvian authorities to remove Maris Plyavinieks as the director of the department. Plyavinieks not only interpreted the existing laws arbitrarily, but also routinely ignored decisions handed down by the courts in favor of noncitizens. The scandal acquired international proportions and, in the middle of December 1993, this detested individual was replaced.

Missions from international organizations such as the Organization for Security and Cooperation in Europe (OSCE, formerly the CSCE) have not succeeded in inducing the acceptance of international norms, nor have they served as a legal instrument to relieve internal ethnic tensions in Latvia. Instead of questioning the fundamental decision on citizenship, international organizations have only tried to soften its effects. Although the High Commissioner for National Minorities and others have helped to ease some of the worst criteria for naturalization, their activities have so far been only a palliative. Even Van der Stoel's recommendations focused on secondary aspects of the situation, such as the obligatory period of residence and the

---

64. See, for example, CSCE Mission to Latvia, Activity Report No. 10.

unfair preference given to ethnic Latvians and Livonians in the natu-ralization process. Despite Ibrahima Fall's critical remarks on Latvian policies and the large amount of good work he has accomplished in resolving specific questions to ease the regime for noncitizens, even he has stated that "Latvia is not in breach of international law in how it determines its criteria for citizenship."[65] Other recommendations from international organizations have been directed at mitigating the consequences of Latvia's language legislation. These include recom-mendations to institute a dual language regime in districts with high Russian populations, as well as to impose less stringent requirements for language examinations, especially for certain categories of citizens such as the elderly. The recommendations actually implemented by the Latvian authorities have, almost without exception, concerned such secondary aspects of the situation.

In the opinion of the Russian public, the international organiza-tions never seriously questioned the justification, expediency, and legality of the key decision that created the problem—the deprivation of citizenship of non-Latvian residents. Council of Europe reports treated this decision as a purely internal affair and not a matter of human rights. The international organizations did not see the conflict in Latvia in terms of fundamental infringements of civil rights, but rather as a problem of the "democratization process," the formation of an "ethnically tolerant democracy," and the need to ensure politi-cal and social stability.[66] The choice of terms used to describe the sit-uation in the reports of international commissions is indicative. For example, the term "immigrants after 1940"—a far from politically neutral term—is used to refer to the portion of Latvia's population that has been deprived of citizenship. The reports also employ the Latvian government's distinction between the status of citizens and inhabitants without ever questioning whether it constitutes a viola-tion of civil or human rights, which is how the Russian population sees it. International organizations, in tacitly accepting the Latvian version of events, have not taken a neutral stance. They have failed to question the justice of collectively denying citizenship to non-Latvian

---

65. "Summary of the Report on the Fact-Finding Mission to Latvia," UN Document No. A/47/748, December 2, 1992, p. 4.

66. It is ironic that the general framework for the West's relationship with the Baltic states is predicated on the assumption that these states are undergoing democratization. Yet the deprivation of citizenship of so many people goes against the spirit and the norms of democracy.

minorities, and then granting it on a case-by-case basis. On the other hand, Western nongovernmental organizations (NGOs) such as Helsinki Watch have been more attentive to the civil rights situation and less diplomatic toward Latvian authorities.

For ethnic Russians in Latvia, correcting the difference in status between citizens and noncitizens is important, but so too is the means by which this goal is achieved. The most likely path is a compromise between nationalist-minded Latvian authorities and European standards of civil rights. Under pressure from international organizations, particularly the OSCE and the Council of Europe, Latvia has accepted that it must bring its citizenship law more into line with international standards. But the naturalization process has been preserved and can still be used as an instrument of reprisal.

THIRD-PARTY STATES

The international community has a strong interest in the Baltic states, perhaps more than in the other former Soviet states. The Baltic states have always been seen as part of Europe. The link between Baltic domestic problems and the potential for Russia's integration into Europe is also part of the picture. And the "Russian question" in Latvia has acquired a symbolic significance for ordinary Russians as a barometer of the West's attitude toward Russia.

Russia has tried to make it clear that Latvia's treatment of Russians has the potential to affect Russia's relationship with the West. Viacheslav Kostikov, Yeltsin's former press secretary, in describing the development of relations between the Latvian and Russian communities in Latvia, thought it necessary to point out that "the international community, the CSCE, and European public opinion have come to realize that they too cannot divest themselves of the responsibility for finding a solution to this problem."[67] At a meeting between Russian Foreign Minister Andrei Kozyrev and CSCE High Commissioner for National Minorities Max van der Stoel, Kozyrev argued that the West's attitude toward the problem of national minorities and concern for the treatment of Russians in the former Soviet Union could become the litmus test for the partnership with Russia.[68]

From the point of view of Russians in the Baltic republics, European countries and the United States have placed a higher priority on smoothing the path for quick integration of the Baltic states

---

67. *Izvestia*, September 17, 1994.
68. *Nezavisimaia gazeta*, March 30, 1994.

into Europe than on ensuring respect for civil rights.[69] Seen from Russia, a pro-Baltic position enhances European security by establishing a *cordon sanitaire* around Russia, which the West still fears as a potential aggressor. In this interpretation, the Baltic states help weaken Russia and the Russian Army. The Russians further consider that the Baltic governments would not have been so courageous without Western backing, and that the West does not care that its policies have had a detrimental impact on Russia's relations with the Baltic states.

The Russian government, after coming under much criticism domestically for its initial policy toward the former Soviet states, has begun to conduct a foreign policy that attempts to defend its interests. However, Russian policymakers are frequently met by outside actors with what appears to be a presumption of Russian guilt and aggressiveness. The tendency in Russia is to interpret such Western reactions as evidence of the desire to keep Russia as weak as possible. Conceptually, the presumption of malevolent Russian intent is rooted in a continuation of balance-of-power thinking, which, in the words of Zbigniew Brzezinski, supports the maintenance of "a Russia, that, *democratic or not*, is encouraged to be a good neighbor to states with which it can cooperate in a common economic space, but which [Russia] will not seek or be able, politically or militarily, to dominate."[70] To Russians, such a presumption implies that democracy alone is not a dominant value for the West: the first concern is stability. In the last few years, Russian vulnerability and the perceived infringement of its interests have been extremely painful for Russians.[71] In the end, "teasing Russia," as many policies of the Baltic

---

69. The *Washington Post* characterized the position of the new Baltic states in regard to citizenship as "an extraordinarily liberal position in regard to citizenship and minority rights," which is why "the alarm and apprehensions of the Russians can be seemingly attributed to the loss of the privileges which they enjoyed and the fear of reciprocal persecution by the oppressed minorities which have now come to power in those countries." *Washington Post*, July 19, 1992.

70. Zbigniew Brzezinski, "The Premature Partnership," *Foreign Affairs* (March–April 1994), reprinted in *Nezavisimaia gazeta*, May 20, 1994.

71. Infringements of Russia's interests include, in particular, preventing the sale of rocket engines to India and submarines to Iran. In Russia, the opinion is increasingly widespread that Russia does not need assistance from the West, but rather requires a good dose of fair competition. Yet Russia cannot compete if it is prevented from selling those products for which it is already a world competitor, in particular, arms and weapons. See Konstantin Sorokin, "Russia's 'New Look' Arms Sale Strategy," *Arms Control Today*, Vol. 23, No. 8 (October 1993), p. 11. The

countries are increasingly regarded in Russia, is not good for the peace and stability of the region.

So far no Western political decision has taken serious account of the Russian position. Thus, in spite of all the reservations expressed by both individual politicians and representatives of international agencies, the integration of Estonia and Latvia into European organizations has gone ahead—a precedent that can be interpreted as having an anti-Russian bias. Now that Estonia and Latvia have been admitted to membership in the Council of Europe and the OSCE without having complied with international recommendations on citizenship issues, the opportunity for these organizations to effect a change in their discriminatory policies would seem to have been lost. It is far more difficult to expel a member than to set conditions for admission.

Latvian politicians have continually and with some success used the Western powers and organizations as allies for both internal political purposes and as leverage in relations with Russia. Certain Baltic politicians have proposed that Russian acknowledgment of the Soviet occupation of the Baltic states should become a precondition for Russian membership in the Council of Europe. A similar proposal to make all forms of Western aid to Russia contingent upon Russia's conduct toward the Baltic states has even found support among some U.S. analysts, publicists, journalists, and politicians.[72]

Attempts by the Latvian authorities to involve Western states in financing the repatriation of certain categories of noncitizens provides an example of how humanitarian activity can become an accomplice to radical nationalist policies. Eighty percent of those classified as noncitizens want to stay in Latvia.[73] However, the radical nationalists have not hidden their intention to create an atmosphere that would stimulate "voluntary" repatriation. A program for voluntary repatriation could easily turn into an instrument for deportation if authorities were not well monitored and were permitted to threaten those noncitizens who did not wish to participate. To help

---

growing perception is that Russia is constantly being asked to subordinate its own economic interests to the political and economic priorities of the United States and Western Europe.

72. *Washington Post*, June 4, 1992. This position is most fully set out in The Heritage Foundation, "Russia and its Neighbors: The Formation of US Policy Toward Russia," *Analytical Bulletin*, No. 4 (December 10, 1993).

73. These figures were cited at a press conference held by the Chairman of the Russian Presidential Commission for Citizenship Questions, Abdullah Mikitaev.

finance such an undertaking would be counter to the declared aims of many of the international organizations involved.

The participation of the Latvian diaspora in the political struggle in post-Soviet Latvia has helped to shape international views of post-Soviet politics, especially in the United States. For example, the Congress of Latvian Citizens, the radical nationalist organization that spearheaded the policies toward noncitizens, carried out its actions through a prominent émigré organization, the All-World Union of Free Latvians.[74] Many émigrés played, and still play, an active role in domestic political struggles in the Baltic republics. An indication of their influence is the composition of the government of Latvian Prime Minister Maris Gailis, formed in mid-1994. Of the twenty-six members of the cabinet, seven are émigrés and four—including the Minister for Defense, Janis Trapans—are dual citizens of Latvia and the United States.[75] It would be fair to say that the émigré groups have contributed to the radicalization of the situation in the Baltic republics.

Latvian policies, as well as those of the other Baltic republics, attempted to focus the attention of the United States and European governments on the problem of Russia's military presence on their territories. Equally important were requests for security guarantees and support for the integration of the Baltic states into NATO. Western pressure for the withdrawal of Russian troops was viewed in some circles as anti-Russian. Russia was compelled to give up military bases that may well go to NATO, and its troops were forced to return to Russia where no housing or jobs were available. In the view of many Russians, insistence upon a hasty withdrawal failed to take Russia's interests into account. Moreover, the Baltic states' clear desire for early military integration with Europe arouses little enthusiasm among Russian politicians, and even less among the military, especially since these states have openly rejected a neutral military status.[76]

For Latvia to become formally integrated into European institutions, it must satisfy a number of basic conditions, including the conduct of democratic elections. However, Latvia was not censured for excluding

---

74. *Yurmala*, July 30, 1992.

75. *Izvestia*, September 17, 1994.

76. "In the future we want to become a demilitarized zone, but this does not mean that Latvia will become a neutral state. We are not rich and strong enough to be neutral," stated the former Deputy Chairman of the Latvian Supreme Soviet Andreis Krastynsh in an interview in 1991 (*Izvestia*, September 19, 1991). Such a position on the part of a Baltic leader was clearly not looked upon as enhancing Russian security.

one-third of its resident population from participation in elections although this would seem to fall short of European standards for free and fair elections. Former Latvian Prime Minister Vladis Birkavs stated in an interview that "many international bodies have established that there is virtually no violation of human rights in our country. There are, it is true, stupid and ill-disposed bureaucrats, but one finds those in any country in the world and we are, unfortunately, no exception to this." Birkavs claimed that "when preparing the law 'on citizenship,' we took into account the recommendations of the Council of Europe."[77] In the Russian view, international public opinion was persuaded to show tolerance for what in fact were the undemocratic, discriminatory policies of the Baltic regimes, and in essence to chalk them up to difficulties inherent in the transition from authoritarianism.[78]

Nevertheless, the Latvian government is extremely concerned about the republic's image in Western public opinion, and reacts quickly to any statements addressed to it. For instance, on March 2, 1994, when U.S. Secretary of State Warren Christopher was quoted as saying that "in Latvia live nearly one million Russian-speakers who are deprived of their voting rights," the Latvian Foreign Ministry responded that Christopher had confirmed the right of Russia to "encourage the Latvians to widen the circle of citizens and to grant voting rights to those Russians who wanted to live in Latvia." In other words, Chistopher's statement accomplished what Russian officials alone could not—it prompted the Latvian government to bow to outside forces on an issue that Latvians considered wholly an internal affair. On March 15, 1994, the Latvian Foreign Ministry received a reply from Christopher in which he expressed understanding for the painful problems that Latvia was confronting as well as hope that Latvia would find a "politically and morally well-considered solution

---

77. *Nezavisimaia gazeta*, May 14, 1994.

78. Radical nationalists attempt to subsume the situation under the norms of international law and argue that all migration to Latvia was illegal. "Latvia is a state which is endeavoring to restore its independence by legal succession and not as a republic seceding from the Soviet Union. Among those who arrived during the period of occupation and their descendants, the Latvian Republic can legalize the residence in the country of two main groups—ethnic Latvians and spouses of Latvian citizens. The arrival and residence of these colonizers cannot be considered legal on the basis of Article 49 of the Geneva Convention of August 12, 1949, which prohibits the settling of part of one's civilian population on occupied territory." Such was the position on the question of citizenship of twenty-seven radical nationalist deputies of the Seim, as formulated in their letter to the Council of Europe and the member-states of the CSCE. *Diena*, May 21, 1994.

to these problems."[79] In the letter's conclusion, he assured Latvia of the friendly sentiments and support of the United States.

When President Bill Clinton made critical remarks about the human rights situation in Latvia during his visit to Moscow in January 1994, they were rapidly countered by Latvian President Guntis Ulmanis: "Human rights violations as depicted [by Clinton]," he stated, "do not exist in Latvia."[80] Ulmanis added, "I do not want to concede the thought that two superpowers have between themselves decided the fate of a small country." In his view, "a law on citizenship must be enacted as soon as possible that precludes any further speculation on violations of human rights."

Thus, there are still opportunities for international organizations and Western governments to influence events in Latvia. Outside prodding from valued allies allows the Latvian government to explain certain concessions to noncitizens as the result of "pressure" coming from Europe. This gentle pressure from the West will continue to be critical in softening the effects of the citizenship law as long as the Latvian government must answer to the radical nationalists and their primarily ethnic Latvian electorate.

THE BORDER QUESTION

Another element of the Latvian situation is the territorial dispute between Russia and Latvia over the Pytalovo-Abrene district, which has been on the Russian side of the border since the 1940s but is claimed by Latvia. The borders between Russia and Latvia, established in the Riga Peace Treaty concluded on August 11, 1920, on the basis of which Latvia became an independent state, allotted the disputed district to Latvia. However, in the border adjustments that followed the 1940 Soviet annexation of the Baltic states, Pytalovo-Abrene was transferred to Russia.[81] Latvian officials claim that

---

79. ITAR-TASS, April 15, 1994.

80. The statement was made in a press briefing on the effects of the U.S. President's visit to Russia and the NATO program "Partnership for Peace."

81. It is important to remember that when the original transfer of the territories to Latvia took place in the tsarist era, it was not considered particularly significant, because the transfer occurred within the borders of a single state. In essence, the transfer of Pytalovo-Abrene was tantamount to a change in administrative borders, nothing more. The same can be said of the border adjustments that occurred in the 1940s within the Soviet Union. Now, however, the issue is much more complicated since the territory is disputed by two sovereign states and therefore subject to international law. In the Russian view, the territory never

Pytalovo-Abrene should be returned to Latvia.[82] The Russian side insists that the 1991 treaty between Russia and Latvia recognized those borders, including the status of Pytalovo-Abrene, as part of Russia. Latvian authorities cite ambiguities in the 1991 treaty that leave open the question of the Russian-Latvian border. A second line of argument posits that Russia should "compensate for the damage done by Stalinism and the Soviet Union, including in terms of territory," as Latvian diplomats have put it. This can only further destabilize a situation that is already far from stable. The Baltic states do not have a unified approach to border issues, however, because unlike Latvia and Estonia, the Lithuanian government has no interest in raising border questions. Each state champions different historical arguments and legal documents to back its territorial claims.[83]

The international element to this question is that European countries and the United States have formally recognized the restoration of the 1918–40 Baltic republics. Latvian authorities argue that international recognition logically extends to the borders as they existed in those years.[84] Ambiguity on this question could be dangerous for European security. Sporadic incidents have already occurred in disputed districts on the borders of Estonia in which radical Estonian nationalists moved the border posts eastward and tried to encourage the population on the Russian side to apply for Estonian citizenship. Russian military installations in the Baltic states came under attack, Russian military depots were seized, and, in January 1994, Russian generals in Latvia were arrested on the charge that they did not have the right to live there. Russians are alarmed when they see Latvia and Estonia—states that have not abandoned their territorial claims

---

really belonged to Latvia and was originally transferred to Latvia merely to simplify the administration of a Latvian railroad line, one corner of which was located in the Pytalovo-Abrene district.

82. The selective appeal to legalism on the border issue is set out in Latvian official documents and supported by the Latvian press and most political parties. The official position is that Pytalovo-Abrene is Latvian. Attempts to legitimize and add weight to Latvian claims to the districts occasionally reach a farcical level. For example, a document dating from 1210 was circulated in the Latvian Supreme Soviet in which Pope Innocent III mentioned Abrene as part of the lands of Albert, the Bishop of Riga. So far, even the most ardent nationalists have not claimed the right of succession to the bishopric of Riga or the Teutonic or Livonian Orders.

83. See Dzintra Bungs, "Seeking Solutions to Baltic-Russian Border Issues," *RFE/RL Research Report*, Vol. 3, No. 13 (April 1994), pp. 25–35.

84. The U.S. and European position on the Vilnius region and Kleipeda which were de jure part of Poland and Germany before World War II is not at all clear.

against Russia—becoming more and more integrated in both the Council of Europe and NATO.

Conclusions and Recommendations

Latvians blame the "unfavorable ethnodemographic situation" in their country on the Russification policies of the Soviet authorities, which brought large numbers of non-Latvians to the republic. Available sociological research does not support the idea that Russians had a privileged position, either in terms of education or economic status.[85] Statistics compiled in 1987 on the representation of various ethnic groups in prestigious, high-paid positions in the Latvian SSR show that non-Latvians, who constitute almost half of the population of Latvia, were disproportionately represented in low-status, poorly paid fields. Non-Latvians made up 61.9 percent of those engaged in industry and construction, 66.2 percent in transport, and 54.7 percent in housing and municipal services, in contrast to only 25 percent in culture and the arts and 16 percent in traditionally Latvian enterprises such as forestry and agriculture. Russians made up 41.2 percent of those employed in education and 46.6 percent of those engaged in health and social services. Non-Latvians were not well represented in high-ranking administrative positions; only 23 percent of the representatives on municipal and district administration executive committees were ethnic minorities, as were 17 percent of the ministers and chairmen of state committees and 35 percent in the cabinet offices. These figures illustrate that the Soviet regime in Latvia did not bear marked ethnic characteristics—and still fewer Russian ones—and that Russians were not a privileged group in the Latvian SSR.[86]

Nor does the Russification thesis look convincing in light of indicators such as the composition of students in institutions of higher education, especially in the very prestigious spheres of culture and the arts. In 1984 and 1985, for instance, 31 percent of the students at the University of Latvia were Russian. At the Academy of Arts,

---

85. In the opinion of the author, the fact that there was a second secretary in every Soviet republic (who was in almost every case a Russian) is not proof of a Soviet policy of Russification or that ethnic Russians enjoyed a privileged position in the Soviet Union.

86. These statistics have kindly been provided by Tatiana Zhdanok, one of the leaders of the *Ravnopravie* (Equal Rights) movement. See also *Soviet Latvia*, November 4, 1989.

Russians comprised a mere 8 percent; at the Conservatory, 16 percent; and at the Liepa Pedagogical Institute, 22 percent.[87] Because of the passage of the language law in 1989, admission of Russian students to the State University of Latvia was reduced from 31 to 18 percent,[88] and this downward trend continued in subsequent years. Russian enrollment at technical, engineering, and military institutes, where Russian was often the primary language of instruction, was much higher. However, graduates from these types of institutes did not receive high-status jobs and became the poorly paid mainstay of the Soviet military economy. The point is not that Latvian national culture was undamaged by the Soviet period. It clearly was. It is rather to illustrate that ethnic Latvians (and Balts in general) were not as severely disadvantaged by the Soviet system relative to other nationalities as some have claimed.

In the Soviet Union there was no ruling "imperial nation." Political and ideological considerations were much more important than ethno-national ones. The principle of national representation played an ornamental role in all the republics. But the guiding creed of the CPSU was "national in form, socialist in character," and in reality nothing that threatened the unity of the state was permitted. It remains an open question whether Russification—official bilingualism with Russian as the *lingua franca*, and the dominant role of Russian culture in the multinational Soviet Union—was the result of the "natural" development of a multiethnic society or the result of deliberate CPSU policies. In any case, it is extremely difficult for the Russians in Latvia to agree with the thesis that they occupied a privileged position and that Latvians in the Latvian SSR were oppressed.

Nevertheless, ethno-demographic arguments are a key element in the ideology of national renaissance in Latvia. The former leader of the National Front of Latvia, Romualdas Razhukas, is of the opinion that "a people can only develop in a country where the number of foreigners does not exceed a given critical level. That is why every effort should be made to enable citizens of other countries, who want to leave Latvia, to be repatriated."[89] In emphasizing historical causes of the current ethno-demographic situation, Latvian authorities are able to justify policies that exclude Russians as a natural, defensive

---

87. Statistics on the composition of the student bodies of the higher education institutions in *Soviet Latvia*, November 4, 1989.

88. *Soviet Latvia*, January 11, 1990.

89. *Soiuz*, No. 50 (December 1991).

reaction to the Russification policies of the Soviet era.

In the year since Latvia regained its independence, Russians have been virtually excluded from government bodies in Latvia. Three years after regaining independence, there was not one Russian minister in the cabinet, and the presidium of the parliament was entirely Latvian, as was the state control department. Russians are rarely appointed judges, and Russian directors of enterprises have been replaced by Latvians. This type of treatment may seem entirely justified to many Latvians. However, from the Russian perspective, exclusionary moves represent a form of apartheid and an attempt to turn non-Latvians into second-class citizens.

To understand the Russian interpretation of the situation in Latvia, it is important to consider not only the legal ramifications, but also the moral and psychological consequences of Latvian policies. Deprivation of citizenship has meant that people who were born and raised in Latvia must bear the burden of historical guilt for real and imagined crimes committed by political forces and organizations beyond their control. The imposition of collective guilt on individuals, simply because they are members of a particular group, is regarded as akin to the policies of the Third Reich toward the Jews, and to Stalin's regime, which inhumanely deported whole nations on the charge of treason against the Soviet regime.[90]

The Baltic states and all states of the former Soviet Union are striving to build democratic societies based on the rule of law and respect for human and civil rights. Policies of exclusion and nationalist xenophobia are incompatible with the spirit of democracy and a poor foundation for democratic development, no matter how injured the nation considers itself to be historically. The problems of inter-ethnic stability in Latvia carry a disproportionately large potential for conflict. In the worst-case scenario, the problems presented in this chapter would be capable of undermining the stability of the relations not just between Russia and Latvia, but between Russia and the West as well. Resurrecting undemocratic and exclusionary policies in order to achieve immediate political goals is dangerous and short-sighted.

In this context, problems involving violations of civil and human rights are of particular consequence since, in the eyes of public opinion, they constitute one of the most important criteria for evaluating the policies of any government. Internal political conditions in

---

90. Democratic countries have resorted to comparably harsh practices only in extreme circumstances such as, for instance, the internment of ethnic Japanese in the United States during World War II.

Latvia combined with its difficult socioeconomic situation make it unlikely that Latvian authorities will alter the political course and subordinate nationalist values to democratic principles without the active participation and influence of foreign governments and international organizations.

Russia has only limited possibilities to play a constructive role in the process for a number of political and historical reasons, including anti-Russian prejudice and the tight coupling of Russian foreign policy with internal Russian political struggles. The governments of the Baltic states no longer trust Russia to act fairly. However, it is also the case that without efforts to remedy the serious deformations in the relations between communities that have arisen in Latvia, long-term stability and democratic development within Latvia may be problematic.

The fact that the disintegration of the Soviet Union has meant the deprivation, in independent Latvia, of the political and civil rights of hundreds and thousands of citizens of the former Latvian SSR has created an international precedent with consequences that are difficult to predict. The international community's tacit approval of Latvian policies on citizenship has already done incalculable harm to the prospects for democratic development in both Latvia and Russia, and has seriously complicated Russia's relationship with the West. Western policies toward the Baltic states have undermined Russians' faith in the sincerity of the West's interest in democratic development in the republics of the former Soviet Union. Fears abound in Russian communities that Western leaders have responded to their own citizens of Baltic origin for domestic political gain, or that the West wants to weaken Russia by allying with the Balts and by expanding NATO to the borders of Russia. However, in the end, it is Russian politicians themselves who bear most of the responsibility for the deterioration of Russia's relations with the Baltic states.

Representatives of the OSCE, the Council of Europe, and human rights NGOs could act as mediators in negotiations between Russia and Latvia on questions connected with the future of the Russian community in Latvia and monitor the observation of human and citizenship rights. The activities of specialized organizations, such as UNESCO, could provide indispensable support to the process of reconciliation by providing Latvian-language instruction to members of the Russian community and developing programs for the preservation and development of Russian cultural and educational institutions in Latvia.

International organizations could also participate in the repatriation of these people, with the understanding that organizations representing stateless persons would also be involved, such as organizations representing former military personnel. In order to be successful, there would have to be guarantees that repatriation would occur only in cases where sufficient funds were available to provide for normal living conditions in the country of intended destination. To leave it to the bureaucratic structures of the Latvian government to carry out these operations would lead to catastrophic results, given that the Latvian government may actually be interested in deportation under the guise of repatriation.

It would be advisable to make further integration of Latvia into international organizations and European economic and security structures contingent upon progress in its treatment of noncitizens. One option might be to create a supranational institution to facilitate cooperation between Latvian authorities and representatives of the opposition, including Russian organizations, the Organization of Stateless Persons, international human rights organizations, and representatives of concerned departments and organizations in Russia. For the long term, the zero option is the only real solution to the problem of Russians in Latvia. Even if the zero option is not pragmatically feasible in the short term, this does not mean it should not be vigorously proposed for the future.

Latvians may rightly ask, "When will you Russians integrate?" The question of longer-term integration is a valid one, but agreement must be forged on the terms of that integration. Integration at the individual level is possible. But if integration is demanded at a societal level at the price of giving up the culture, language, and history of the collective, then the price is likely to be too high for Russians in the Baltic states. Ethnic characteristics are seen as a mark of loyalty in Latvia, which does not bode well for tolerance and multiculturalism. There is no question that Latvian authorities have faced difficult choices in trying to reestablish independent statehood. In choosing a confrontational approach to ethnic issues, however, they have alienated a large portion of the population, the majority of whom would have contributed to a prosperous independent Latvia.

Russians in Latvia hold up as the ideal a "Switzerland scenario," in which local governments can express a multidimensional identity, where one can be both a loyal Latvian and culturally Russian, and in this way contribute to the development of a prosperous, democratic state.

Chapter 10

Commentary on Latvia

Brian J. Boeck

When the Baltic republics began to push for independence from the Soviet Union, several Western commentators assumed that the Russians living in the region would bitterly oppose independence. Since these populations were believed to be an amorphous group of "colonists," "occupiers," and "immigrants" irrevocably hostile to local national aspirations, it was believed by many in the West to be inevitable that they would form some type of fifth column within these republics and actively mobilize against independence. As one journal stated in late 1988, "physical violence cannot be excluded, and it is not inconceivable that Riga or Tallinn could be metamorphosed into Soviet Belfasts or Beiruts."[1]

The fact that interethnic conflict has been avoided in Latvia is clear evidence that the situation in the Baltic republics, for various reasons, is qualitatively different from that in other areas of the former Soviet Union such as Georgia or Moldova. Indeed, there seems to be little possibility that an armed conflict will soon arise in Latvia. This does not, however, mean that a conflict does not exist. It simply means that "conflict" in the Latvian context exists at a different (for the moment lower) level of intensity, though it nonetheless permeates every level of day-to-day interaction.

In discussing the dynamics of interethnic relations in Latvia, it is necessary to keep in mind that a deep divide separates Russian and Latvian views on most of the important issues of recent history and contemporary life. Many Russians find it difficult to acknowledge the fact that Latvia was at the same time "liberated" by the Soviet Army and ruthlessly occupied by a foreign power espousing an

---

1. "Editors' Note," *Baltic Forum*, Vol. 5, No. 2 (Fall 1988), p. 17.

alien ideology. For their part, many Latvians cannot understand why the Russians do not simply pack up and go "home" now that the Party is over (conveniently forgetting that Latvia is the only home that most have ever known).

The most dangerous approach for outside observers is to accept blindly the perceptions and prejudices of one side against the other. Regardless of what happened in 1721, 1918, 1940, or 1991, the fact is that today Latvia has a sizable Russian-speaking minority. Former Soviet citizens constitute a significant portion of Latvia's population, and, if present trends continue, they likely will for some time to come.

Alexander Yusupovsky's chapter adds a previously unheard or misunderstood voice to the debate over Latvia's Russian question. Although many Western readers may not agree with Yusupovsky's thoughts on certain issues (for example, the question of Russification), if the Western view does not take into account the Russian perspective (as seen from Moscow) on events taking place in the post-Soviet territory, it tends to be one-sided and thus distorted. Russia and Latvia must live side by side, and therefore it is in the interest of both countries to resume normal relations as soon as possible.

In considering the current interethnic situation in Latvia, one cannot lose sight of the fact that the Latvian side has many true grievances, which cannot and should not be forgotten. Their country was occupied for half a century. Burgeoning national institutions were destroyed and countless numbers of Latvians were killed or exiled by the Soviet regime. Most Latvians view the events of 1940–91 as a national tragedy, and rightly so. It will take several generations for Latvia to overcome the effects of the Soviet occupation (psychological as well as economic, social, and political) and fully restore Latvian sovereignty as it existed in the interwar period.

By accepting a confrontational approach to the "Russian problem" in which Soviet-era settlers are denied citizenship and, more important, various other civil and economic rights, the current Latvian leadership has decided to gamble in an attempt to fully restore Latvian statehood as it existed from 1918–40. As a short-term measure aimed at compensating for injustices done to the Latvian nation by the Soviet regime, this policy might seem reasonable; as a pragmatic state-building project, however, its long-term implications seem less sensible or immediately predictable. As Yusupovsky notes, the Latvian fear of a hostile Russia and an angry fifth column of Russians within Latvia could (though it need not) become a self-fulfilling prophecy.

The nature of current interethnic tension in Latvia is not simply a product of policies pursued since Latvia gained independence. Its origins must be sought in the past as well as the present. If we examine the historical patterns of interethnic relations in the Latvian Soviet Socialist Republic (SSR), the extent to which the two main population groups (Russian-speaking and Latvian-speaking) were alienated from meaningful contact with one another is striking. This was both a result of Soviet policy and the sum total of countless thousands of conscious individual decisions (both Russian and Latvian) not to interact.

From the inception of Soviet rule in Latvia, the educational system perpetuated bifurcation of the population along linguistic lines and created life-long insular patterns of interethnic contact. A segregated environment developed in Latvia as a product of the initial confrontation that occurred as the interests of settlers and locals clashed in the immediate postwar period. In effect, low-intensity interethnic conflict existed among Russians and Latvians for many decades in the Soviet period due to competition for scarce resources (housing, educational opportunities, consumer goods, jobs, and political influence). Latvian independence has not eliminated this conflict; in fact, it has in some cases aggravated it and in other cases channeled it in new directions.

Both sides view events of the Soviet period (and beyond) as a zero-sum game. Any decision that seemed to favor one group over the other (and these matters often tended to depend less on reality than perception) caused hostility and suspicion. Presently, each side can muster arguments and statistics to prove that the other side had it better in the Latvian SSR. With the restoration of the independent Republic of Latvia, however, it becomes more and more difficult to blame Moscow for the vicissitudes of interethnic relations in Latvia.

It is safe to suggest that integration has not occurred because neither Russians nor Latvians have worked to promote it. It is commonly assumed that Russians were and continue to be simply unwilling to integrate. But the converse is also true: due to the huge psychological and social implications of Soviet rule, the Latvians were and continue to be equally adverse to integrating them.

The present political debate has therefore, in my opinion, focused too much (and at times exclusively) on the question of citizenship for the Soviet settler population of Latvia and its descendants. Even if Russians are granted citizenship, plus full civil and economic rights, the issue of the social alienation and de facto segregation of the two main population groups will continue to dominate the situation in

Latvia well into the twenty-first century. Even if the rubicon of the citizenship issue is crossed, obstacles to full integration (such as prejudice, self-segregation, and lack of trust) will remain in place. As long as the two main population groups are segregated and continue to pursue divergent goals, the potential for escalation of ethnic conflict will exist.

The fact that the two major ethnic communities remain captive to an "us-versus-them" mentality does not further the cohesion of society. If Russians remain alienated and disenfranchised, with no stake within the system, they will literally have nothing more to lose and may seek to redress their grievances through some kind of drastic measures. Although this does not seem likely, it remains a possibility if conditions worsen. Latvians must be willing to set aside past grievances and recognize that ultimately, future Latvian security and stability may depend more on winning the hearts and minds of the country's Russian population than on NATO, the CSCE, or any other external alliance.

There has been little conclusive evidence that societal integration has been taking place in Latvia since it regained its independence. If anything, the policies pursued since 1991 have tended to further reinforce segregation and ethnic prejudice to some degree, since the population has been divided into groups of citizens and noncitizens whose interests are in competition. What the Latvian side perceives as fair and perhaps even generous treatment is viewed by the Russians as an attack upon their civil and human rights. The converging ethnic agenda that was hailed from 1988–90 appeared in 1995 almost as divergent as it probably was in 1975.

The Russian community in Latvia has been slow to adapt to its new situation and is struggling with symptoms of postimperial denial. Russians in Latvia have not been able to mobilize to defend their interests ("interests" rather than "rights," which can be a politically loaded term) because of internal divisions among them. While apathy, denial, and resignation seem to characterize the feelings of many, mere survival under new economic conditions is the primary preoccupation of most.

With one foot in the past and one foot on the doorstep to the future, the Russians in Latvia are in legal, social, and psychological limbo. They can become either enemies of the Latvian state or some of its staunchest defenders. The policies that the Latvian government pursues in the next few years will largely determine the outcome. While it is in the long-term strategic interests of the Latvian state to do everything possible to speed the integration (both political and cultural) of those Russians who want to stay (up to 80 percent, according to opinion polls) and expedite the repatriation of those who desire to leave (possibly through generous housing and "separation settlements") since their very presence is a destabilizing factor, such a course of action is not politically realizable in Latvia today. The "Russian problem" will not simply go away by itself, and, as Yusupovsky demonstrates, radical attempts to resolve it are prone to exacerbate the situation and might even threaten the future of the Latvian state by upsetting the delicate political situation in Russia.

While Latvian government policies have directly and adversely affected the social and economic position of many Russians, more often than not government policy alone is not responsible for their plight. Poor integration in the past (self-segregation and poor knowledge of Latvian) as well as the difficulties of self-integration in the current political climate mean that Russians will be at a distinct political and economic disadvantage *vis-à-vis* the Latvians in the coming years. This is sure to increase the level of interethnic tension.

Until Russians become truly bilingual (not merely functionally bilingual), their position in Latvia will continue to be marginalized; attempts to set up special language regimes in areas of compact Russian settlement would probably only prolong the period (and perhaps also the pain) of complete transition to Latvian in the public sphere. Only through integration will Russians be able to seriously compete with Latvians on an equal basis for jobs, public office, etc., which in turn would lead to an improvement in their economic situation.

Russians in Latvia (and their supporters in Moscow) have spent considerable time and energy arguing for the "right" to receive Russian-language secondary and higher education in Latvia.[2] However, a linguistically segregated educational system did much to create (and to this day perpetuate) societal divisions in Latvia. The continued existence of a segregated system of higher education would mean that Russian youths would continue to be sheltered from total immersion in Latvian and meaningful contact with their Latvian peers (and vice versa). Even if Russian-language higher educational institutions were to devote significant time to the study of Latvian, their graduates would still be ill-equipped to compete head-to-head

2.   Elementary education should and must be bilingual. This, however, does not necessarily have to be achieved through segregated schools.

with Latvians for the best jobs. Only by becoming, in effect, better speakers and writers of Latvian than the Latvians themselves will the Russians be able to combat discrimination (in both its official and unofficial forms) and claim an equal role in the new Latvia. At the same time, Russians in Latvia must also be encouraged to discover and preserve the rich Russian cultural heritage of Latvia that was largely destroyed and neglected under Soviet rule.[3]

In post-Soviet Latvia the politics of identity are very important. The Latvian government must recognize that labeling Russians as "non-Latvians," "colonists," and so forth only creates animosity and does nothing to reinforce a positive identity (or self-image) among Russians. Only an inclusive vision of Latvian identity will serve to reduce interethnic tension. Rather than "forcing out" Russian culture, the Latvian government should devote resources to selectively promote a local variant of Russian culture in Latvia that is democratic and Latvia-oriented. By not spending money (investing) in promoting "local" Russian culture, the Latvian government concedes the initiative to other forces, which may in the long run be hostile to Latvia.

Whether or not Russians will be able to claim a role in the new Latvia ultimately will not be decided by them. If the Latvian population and government decide to perpetuate segregation, either through legislation or unofficial discrimination, they have the political power to do so. It must be stressed that reconciliation and integration are not the exclusive burden of the Russian population; reducing interethnic tension will require an attitude adjustment on the part of both major population groups, and even in the best of scenarios will take generations to complete. By not integrating its Soviet-settler and Russian-speaking population in an efficient and dignified manner, the Latvian government further opens the door to escalation of interethnic tension and future foreign interference in Baltic affairs.

---

3. The government of the Russian Federation could play a constructive role here by providing financial support for the development of Russian cultural institutions in Latvia.

Chapter 11

Kazakhstan: How Long Can Ethnic Harmony Last?

Vladimir Barsamov

Both Western and Russian researchers who study Kazakhstan are struck by its political stability and ethnic harmony relative to the other states that emerged after the breakup of the Soviet Union. It is even more puzzling that this harmony exists in the context of a volatile population mix—almost equal numbers of Kazakhs and Russians (or more accurately Slavs, since there are a large number of Ukrainians)—and government policies that appear to be focused on safeguarding the dominant position and interests of only one of these groups, ethnic Kazakhs.[1]

Until recently this unexpected stability was explained by the fact that both the Kazakh and Russian groups supported President Nursultan Nazerbaev, who was viewed as an advocate for market reforms, democratization, and human rights. Kazakhstan was even seen as a development model for the Central Asian republics and an example of how to implement post-Soviet democratic reforms while maintaining stability in a multiethnic society. Other accounts referred to the specific nature of the Russians in Kazakhstan, who, as some Western scholarly works affirm, "support the idea of sovereignty for

---

1. See, for instance, Martha B. Olcott, "Kazakhstan: A Republic of Minorities," *Nations and Politics in the Soviet Successor States* (New York: Cambridge University Press, 1993); Jan Bremer, "Minority Rules," *New Republic*, April 11, 1994, p. 26; Philip S. Gilette, "Ethnic Balance and Imbalance in Kazakhstan's Regions," *Central Asia Monitor*, No. 3 (1993); Alexandra Dokuchaeva, "In Defiance of Traditions: Why Information on Migration in Kazakhstan Was Kept Secret," *Rossiiskie vesti*, August 10, 1993, p. 7; and "Interview with N. Nazerbaev," *Caravan*, April 9, 1993.

Kazakhstan" and "are happy to live as citizens of Kazakhstan as long as their basic rights are protected."[2]

Recent events, however, have raised doubts about this optimistic view. A number of fundamental questions have emerged as to Kazakhstan's future development: how long can the ruling elite continue to maneuver between Kazakhstan's ethnic groups while relying for its legitimacy almost exclusively on its representation of the interests of ethnic Kazakhs? Will the Kazakhstani government be able to maintain the present course, preserving relative stability and realizing its idea of Kazakhstan as a bridge between Europe and Asia? Can some form of "Eurasian Union" incorporating Kazakhstan, Russia, and other former Soviet republics be created? Or is the breakup of Kazakhstan a possibility, as seems to be the case in Moldova, Georgia, and Azerbaijan?

Kazakhstan's complex geography, demography, and history have only recently begun to be studied by scholars outside the former Soviet Union. Contemporary Kazakhstan is an immense country of largely open steppe land, hemmed in by the Tian Shan Mountains to the east and the beginnings of the Hindu Kush to the south. The bulk of the population is concentrated either in the traditional oasis towns in the south and southwest or in the largely Russian-inhabited lands in the northern and northeastern territories. Situated on the interface of Europe and Asia and facing Russian civilization to the north, Chinese civilization to the east, and Muslim civilization to the south, the peoples of this region have been heavily influenced by all of these forces throughout their history. Today, the influence of the international business community and international political culture is equally strong, as a result of President Nazerbaev's active efforts to build strong ties with the world community.

The borders of khanates and, later, states in this region have changed frequently over the centuries, most recently in December 1991, when the Kazakhstan Soviet Socialist Republic, one of the fifteen constituent Union-level republics of the Soviet Union, declared its independence as the Republic of Kazakhstan. Although numerous border changes in the Soviet period have caused some groups in neighboring countries and within Kazakhstan to question existing

---

2. Such opinions are frequently met with among American authors. See Olcott, "Kazakhstan: A Republic of Minorities"; and Roland Dannreuther, *Creating New States in Central Asia*, Adelphi Paper No. 288 (London: International Institute for Strategic Studies [IISS], March 1994), p. 44.

borders, the conflicts in modern Kazakhstan are more about managing the demands of a multiethnic polity in the post-Soviet context than serious proposals for border changes, which are not welcomed by any of the states in the region.

Kazakhstan's ethnic composition is complex. It is composed of roughly 40 percent ethnic Kazakhs, 40 percent ethnic Russians, with the remaining 20 percent a mixture of Germans, Ukrainians, Uzbeks, Tatars, and Uighurs. Maintaining a manageable equilibrium among these groups, and especially among Kazakhs and Russians, is essential to Kazakhstan's stability. But today the possibilities for such equilibrium-oriented policies face major obstacles in the legacy of clan-based power structures, divisions among ethnic Kazakhs themselves, and the poor representation of the interests of the non-Kazakh groups.

The distribution of ethnic groups over the territory of Kazakhstan is very unequal. Kazakhs primarily inhabit three groups of regions, which coincide approximately with the borders of the Youngest (western Kazakhstan), Middle (northern Kazakhstan), and Eldest (southern Kazakhstan) *Zhuzes*, or Hordes.[3] In the southern regions, up to half the population is Kazakh, more than one-third is European, and about one-fifth is other Central Asian peoples; in the west and west central regions, more than half and up to two-thirds of the inhabitants are Kazakhs and the remainder mainly Europeans; in the north, east, and central regions only about one-quarter are Kazakh and the remainder European, mainly Russian and Ukrainian, both in the towns and rural districts.

The essence of the problem for Kazakhstan is that after the breakup of the Soviet Union and the independence of Kazakhstan, the new state's large Slavic population was transformed into a national minority facing new restrictions on attaining positions of political power, securing their property rights, and fulfilling their cultural interests. For example, the sphere of Russian-language use and the right to Russian-language education were increasingly limited. These restrictions turned the ethnic Slavic community in Kazakhstan into potential opponents of the official goal embodied in the 1993 Kazakhstani Constitution to build a state based on Kazakh national self-determination. Nevertheless, the conflicts in Kazakhstan have remained at a very low level in comparison to events in other post-Soviet states. The

---

3. The history of *zhuzes* (major contemporary clans) dates back to 1456, when a number of feudal tribal *ordas* (hordes) split from the Golden Horde to form three distinct *ordas*.

few violent incidents that have occurred have been sporadic and localized. It would be a mistake, however, to think that the problems in Kazakhstan are only of a legal nature—a matter of language rights in the official sphere, or education choices for the Russian population, although these are the key immediate issues. The legal instruments that Western analysts and observers have emphasized are of course important, but more important in this period is the inertia of traditional relations between people and the structures of power, the predominant role of the state in daily life, and therefore of the political elites who control the state.

Tensions began to rise when ethnic divisions coincided with other issues involving social stratification, economic disparities, and differences in opportunities for political representation. A central problem has been the disproportion in certain areas between the majority of the population and their political representation in government structures. In the north and east, for example, there is a Russian majority, but the Kazakhs have become the political elites since independence. Since the government still plays a large role in all spheres of life, including the organization of new commercial enterprises and ventures, ethnic criteria and an ethnic agenda for the state become important elements in the new economic life as well.

The sharp decline in the standard of living throughout Kazakhstan as a result of the breakup of the Soviet Union and the socioeconomic policies of the Kazakhstani government gave rise to additional social tensions: between rural and urban areas, between various regions of the country, and between the new *nomenklatura* (ruling elites) and the mass of the population. The growth of interethnic tensions not only generally, but within the Kazakh ethnic group and among Kazakh elites themselves, suggests that the political strategy since independence of balancing Kazakh nationalism and a modernization drive has exhausted itself. The dissolution of the Kazakhstani Parliament discussed below and the growing power vested in the office of the president do not bode well for the ability of the people of Kazakhstan to resolve how to coexist in such a complex multiethnic state. These heightened tensions make it clear that the Kazakhstani government will be forced to change course or that circumstances will bring about change. Why this is so and how events will likely unfold in Kazakhstan are the subject of this chapter.[4]

---

4.   Note to readers on terminology: the current understanding of certain terms used in Russian, Western, and Kazakhstani mass media and daily speech are not

A Historical Survey of Interethnic Relations

In order to grasp the complexities of Kazakhstan's multiethnic society and the political, economic, and social dynamics that drive it, one must begin with an understanding of the society's origins and historical developments over the centuries.

THE INCORPORATION OF THE KAZAKH HORDES INTO THE RUSSIAN EMPIRE

Over the last four centuries, what is now Kazakhstan was host to the Dzhungar Khanate, and the Youngest, Middle, and Eldest *Zhuzes* of the Kazakhs. Part of the territory belonged to the Khiva, Kokand, and Volga-Kalmykia khanates and was home to numerous Cossack settlements. The Kazakh Khanate was formed in the fifteenth century, though it is difficult to consider it a singular entity. The tribes and clans that made up the horde belonged to different ethnic groups of Mongol and Turkic origin. Furthermore, much of contemporary Kazakhstan was traversed by routes traveled by nomadic tribes. At the beginning of the eighteenth century, Russian settlements—largely fortresses built by Cossack groups—appeared on the right bank of the river Irtysh, in modern northeastern Kazakhstan. In 1731, the Youngest *Zhuz* in the west and somewhat later the Middle *Zhuz* in the north voluntarily became Russian subjects to gain protection against hostile neighbors like the Dungans, the Chinese, and others. The Russians continued to advance southward right up to the middle of the nineteenth century, building fortresses and towns along the way,

---

adequate to fully describe and understand the issues surrounding ethno-national conflict in Kazakhstan. As a result, some terms have become weapons of sorts in the ideological struggle between ethnic groups. For example, in Kazakhstan, the term "indigenous nation" (*korennoi narod*) is often used to describe a people who have lived in Kazakhstan for many centuries—in this case, ethnic Kazakhs versus peoples considered nonindigenous "newcomers" such as Germans, Ukrainians, and Russians who do not possess any historical land rights. Many ethnic Russians, particularly those living in the northern and eastern regions of Kazakhstan and whose families have resided there for several centuries, consider themselves indigenous and dispute this point. There is also confusion surrounding the term "Russian speaker." Most ethnic Kazakhs are indeed themselves Russian speakers, while a segment of this same population does not speak the Kazakh language. Therefore, the term "Russian speaker" does not necessarily mean "ethnic Russian," as might be inferred or implied. Therefore, in this chapter, the term "Kazakhstani" refers to *all* citizens of Kazakhstan, independent of their ethnic origins. The term "Kazakh" refers exclusively to members of the Kazakh ethnic group.

including the town of Verny, present-day Almaty. The Eldest *Zhuz* in the southern territories was incorporated into the Russian Empire in the course of its conquest of Central Asia in the 1860s and 1870s.[5]

The tsarist government and the local administrations conducted a policy of redistributing land in the sparsely populated new regions to colonists and Cossack settlers, and by the middle of the nineteenth century, there was a massive flow of Russian and Ukrainian peasants into present-day Kazakhstan. Because free land was abundant, there were few serious clashes in the early stages. Later, however, there were several significant conflicts, such as the widespread clashes in 1837–41 in the northern regions over the distribution of land between the Kazakh population and the new settlers. The most serious ethnically based conflict erupted in 1916 in Kazakhstan as well as in other Central Asian regions. Groups of Kazakhs formed armed bands and attacked colonial settlements and Russian garrisons. The official pretext for the revolt was to protest a tsarist order to mobilize Kazakhs aged 19 to 43 to work in the rear of the Russian Army in World War I. However, this antigovernment and, in part, anti-Russian revolt was really a reaction by some Kazakh groups to the redistribution of land in favor of the Russian population and official corruption.[6]

The first attempts to form a Kazakh autonomous territory took place in 1917, during fighting over the territory of Central Asia, then known as Turkestan. At an All-Kazakh Congress, the Alash-Orda autonomous interim government was formed,[7] which lasted only through the period of the civil war. With the victory of the Bolsheviks, a few members of the Alash-Orda government joined the Soviet power structure set up to govern the territories of the Southern Urals, Siberia, and Turkestan, including part of contemporary Kazakhstan.

THE NATIONALITY POLICIES OF THE SOVIET PERIOD

With the end of the civil war in 1920, the Kyrgyz Autonomous Soviet Socialist Republic (ASSR) was created on the traditional territory of the Youngest *Zhuz* as part of the Russian Socialist Federated Soviet

---

5.   See, for instance, Ermukhan B. Bekmakhanov, *The Incorporation of Kazakhstan into Russia* (Moscow: Academy of Sciences of the Soviet Union, 1957), pp. 128–133.

6.   See F.N. Kireev and Sh. Y. Shariro, eds., *The Revolt in Kazakhstan in 1916* (Alma-Ata: Academy of Sciences of the Kazakhstan SSR, 1947).

7.   The government was mainly formed from members of the Alash Party, who were close to the Russian Kadets. During the civil war, Alash supported the Whites.

Republic (RSFSR). This marked the beginning of a Soviet Kazakhstan.[8] The lands of the Elder *Zhuz* became part of the Turkistan ASSR. In 1925, the Kyrgyz ASSR was renamed the Kazakh ASSR and was expanded to include the territories of the Middle Zhuz and the lands of the Ural, Orenburg, and Siberian Cossack formations, which had been within the Russian Empire and are now parts of modern-day northern, eastern, and western Kazakhstan. Additional territories belonging to the Elder *Zhuz* and the Semirechi Cossacks in the south of present-day Kazakhstan were also included. In 1936, the Kazakh Soviet Socialist Republic was established in the present borders of Kazakhstan. This was an entirely new entity that included territories taken from the RSFSR. Since the internal frontiers of the Soviet Union were primarily administrative in nature, these changes were not seen as conflict-generating. But when Kazakhstan acquired independence at the end of 1991, the situation changed drastically and the borders suddenly acquired new importance. During the years of Soviet power, the policies pursued in Kazakhstan did not differ greatly from those implemented across the Soviet Union. However, ethnic and nationalities policies were frequently contradictory and in flux, often depending on ideological divisions and pure power struggles among elites both in Moscow and Alma-Ata.

In the 1920s, the Bolshevik leadership tried to consolidate its power by granting privileges to the rural Kazakh population, as opposed to the Cossacks who had supported the Whites during the civil war. Thus in 1921–22, in the course of land reforms directed at "equalizing the rights of the indigenous and the Russian population," a number of Russian villages and farms were liquidated.[9] A policy of *korenizatsia* (indigenization) was also initiated at this time, filling much of the Soviet administrative apparatus in Kazakhstan with native Kazakhs. This policy also specified that in locations with a Kazakh population, all business would be conducted in the Kazakh language; administrative bodies were to be staffed by ethnic Kazakhs; Russians were to be taught the Kazakh language; and Kazakhs were to be sent to

---

8.   Up until the 1920s, the term "Kyrgyzian" was used in literary references to Kazakh tribes. During the period of Kazakhstan's formation, local authorities of the Akmolin, Semipalatinsk, and Uralsk districts, as well as certain districts of the Kustanai government, expressed their doubt and opposition to the inclusion of these territories. See A.G. Sarmursin, ed., *About the Past for the Future* (Alma-Ata: s.n., 1990), pp. 171–176.

9.   See V. P. Voshchinov, "Kazakhstan," in *The Soviet Union by Districts* (Moscow: Gosizdat, 1929), p. 11.

administrative bodies in Russia for training.[10] Enthusiasm for the provisions for Kazakh language waned, however, and these goals were not fulfilled, largely because many of the people in the central and local governments were Russian-speaking and had little interest in this program.[11] Nevertheless, starting with the second half of the 1920s, an ethnic Kazakh intelligentsia developed at a rapid rate. Institutions of higher education were founded, a campaign to end illiteracy among ethnic Kazakhs was mounted, and a Kazakh written language was developed.

At the end of the 1920s and beginning of the 1930s, collectivization of agriculture was carried out in Kazakhstan. The rapid, forced transition of nomadic peoples to settled agriculture resulted in a serious famine from 1931–33. The whole population suffered irrespective of ethnic origin, but as nomadic peoples, the ethnic Kazakhs suffered the most. Some Kazakh clans were forced to flee to Mongolia and China. Revolts by the mainly Kazakh population broke out in the Semipalatinsk, Syrdarinsk, and Aktiubinsk regions in 1929 and 1930.[12] Since the collectivization campaign was undertaken by both Russian and Kazakh party leaders, however, it is not clear that these protests had ethnic motivations. At that point, class—not ethnicity—was the central factor in politics. In subsequent years, there was a large influx of non-Kazakhs into the republic. Kazakhstan's vast unpopulated regions served as a place of both economic opportunity and political exile for many Soviet citizens: for the Cossacks in 1921, the kulaks (rich peasants) in 1929, and for Koreans, Poles, Kurds, Germans, Karachaevs, Chechens, and others during World War II. In the course of industrialization in the 1920s and 1930s, large industrial enterprises were set up in Kazakhstan, many specializing in metallurgical processing, including the Chimkent lead plant and a huge copper

---

10. See G.T. Taimanov, *The Development of Soviet Statehood in Kazakhstan* (Moscow: Gosiurlit, 1956), pp. 46–48.

11. A witness of that period, Karatleev, a provincial bureaucrat and participant in the conference of the Central Committee of the Russian Communist Party, commented: "Regarding the introduction of the Kyrgyz language, it must be said that in spite of the orders and directives, not one worker has either thought about or tried to study the Kyrgyz language." See *Secret Nationalities Policies of the Central Committee of the RCP: Fourth Conference of the Central Committee of the Russian Communist Party with senior officials of the National Republics and Oblasts in Moscow* (Stenographic account, June 9–12, 1923, Moscow; reprints, Moscow Insan Publishers, 1992), p. 128.

12. See M.K. Kozybaev, *History and the Present* (Alma-Ata: Gylym, 1991), pp. 221–223.

smelter in Balkhash. In wartime, many people and even factories were evacuated from the European part of the Soviet Union to safety in Kazakhstan. The last major wave of settlers came in the 1950s with Nikita Khrushchev's plan for opening up uncultivated and fallow lands in northern Kazakhstan, Siberia, Altai, and the Southern Urals to solve the Soviet Union's growing food problem.

In the cultural sense, the Soviet center viewed Kazakhstan as a semi-Russian, semi-Kazakh republic. Since there was considerable Russian participation in the development of education and culture, all things Russian had a high status in the republic. The decision to heighten the role of the Kazakh language in the 1920s had been forgotten by the 1930s. The economic and political needs of the Soviet Union required a common language, and the only available candidate was Russian. Moreover, the traditional Kazakh language was based on nomadic and traditional ways, and lacked the vocabulary for the transition to a new industrial way of life. In daily life and in social and professional spheres dominated by Kazakhs, the Kazakh language was predominant. However, in the sphere of state administration and heavy industry, the backbone of the economy, Russian was almost universally used. Interethnic relations during this period were quite peaceful and there were many intermarriages. Even today in urban areas, a large percentage of Kazakhs are Russified, especially the younger generation and many of the intelligentsia.

NATIONALITY POLICIES DURING PERESTROIKA

With the installation of Mikhail Gorbachev as the new General Secretary of the Central Committee of the Communist Party of the Soviet Union (CPSU) in 1985 and the introduction of his new policy of perestroika, Kazakhstan's administrative apparatus was reshuffled.[13] One of the first leaders to be "retired" was Leonid Brezhnev's close friend, Dinmukhamed Kunaev—the first secretary of the Central Committee of the Communist Party of Kazakhstan, an ethnic Kazakh, and a politburo member—at the age of 74. Kunaev was removed in the traditional Soviet way: in December 1986, a new candidate was sent from Moscow to the Plenum of the Communist Party of Kazakhstan and was duly elected. The new first secretary was

---

13. In the Soviet Union, elites were always the key political actors, a fact inherently connected with the rigid political hierarchies. To understand events in the post-Soviet countries, this key role for political elites, and its corollary, the very low development of a civil society, must be kept in mind.

Gennadi Kolbin, a close associate and protégé of Gorbachev and an ethnic Russian from the Russian Federation.

After the announcement of Kolbin's confirmation, groups of Kazakh youth began to gather in Alma-Ata and other towns to protest the replacement of the ethnic Kazakh Kunaev with a Russian from Moscow. When the demonstrations turned into riots, they were suppressed by the authorities with the help of squads of largely Slavic workers (*rabochie druzhini*), which were created to help the militia keep public order. There were many injuries and some deaths, though there has been much controversy over the exact numbers.[14] This was an extraordinary event for both the Soviet Union and the Communist Party, which had long affirmed that "the nationality question, inherited from the past, has been successfully solved in the Soviet Union."[15]

In the power struggles that followed, the interpretation of the December 1986 events became a bone of contention between the two main groups of elites, the *tsentristy*—originating from the party's central power structures in Moscow—and locals who rose within local Kazakhstan structures. Although the centrists included more Slavs and the locals included many more Kazakhs, it would be mistaken to assume that ethnic origins were a critical factor in Soviet politics of this period. The centrists, exemplified by Gennadi Kolbin, looked upon the Alma-Ata disturbances as manifestations of "nationalism," while the locals, with Kunaev and Nursultan Nazerbaev as the most prominent representatives, described these events as a spontaneous protest by the masses against "dictates from the center." Later, with

---

14. There are still controversies over how many people were killed in these disturbances. According to official data of that time gathered from eyewitnesses and participants, including the militias, *druzhiniki*, and Kazakh youth, two people were killed and 1,233 received treatment for injuries received during the incidents. See Alexander Samoilenko, et al., "Alma-Ata, December 1986: Then and Now," *Literaturnaia gazeta*, December 20, 1989. See also *Alma-Ata December 1986: A Book of Chronicles* (Alma-Ata: Altynorda, 1991).

15. *Materials of the 27th Conference of the Communist Party of the Soviet Union* (Moscow: Politizdat, 1986), p. 156. It is typical that any mention of ethno-nationalism is absent, as, for example, in the summary report of D. Kunaev to the conference of the Communist Party of Kazakhstan of March 6, 1986. See D.A. Kunaev "Summary Report of the Central Committee of the Communist Party of Kazakhstan to the Conference of the Communist Party of Kazakhstan," 1986. The decree of the Central Committee of the CPSU "On the Work of the Kazakh Republican Party Organization on Internationalist Patriotic Education of Working People" noted the presence of "chauvinism, nationalism and localist tendencies." From *The CPSU on Perestroika* (Moscow: Politizdat, 1988), p. 188.

the adoption of an increasingly nationalist position by ethnic Kazakh elites, these same events were characterized as struggles against colonialism and empire.

One of the main causes of the riots was the perception that the existing balance of appointments to the highest posts had been violated. In the pre-Gorbachev period, a fairly strict system of appointments for representatives of specific ethnic groups to the highest posts had been developed, especially for the Communist Party of Kazakhstan, but also for local administrations. In districts with a mixed population, if the first secretary was a Kazakh, the second secretary was a Russian, and the third secretary a German, or the other way around. However, in the south and west and part of central Kazakhstan, where the population was mainly ethnic Kazakh, these proportions were often violated, and Kazakhs sometimes occupied all the most important posts in local administrations. The disproportion also occurred in the capital region, Alma-Ata.

The resolution on *korenizatsia* of the administration and government by national cadres adopted in the 1920s remained in force up to the 1980s. There were two basic methods of creating elite cadres: to recruit from the local population and to recruit from the central power structures in Moscow. During the Kunaev era, the predominant method was the recruitment of local elites. The two resulting general categories of elites looked to different ethnic groups, the locals to the Kazakhs and the centrists to the Russian (Slavic) population for support. During this period, however, there was no great difference in the possibility for upward mobility between Russians, Kazakhs, Germans, and others.[16] The evaluation that ethnic Russians enjoyed a hegemonic position is not accurate for a considerable

---

16. In studying Central Asian internal conflicts, we are confronted with a situation in which it seems that the long-forgotten pre-Soviet borders of khanates *(zhuzes)* and emirates have once again become important. In Kazakhstan these are the borders of the Eldest, Middle, and Youngest *Zhuzes,* and the frontiers of settlement of the Ural Cossacks. In Tajikistan they are the Emirate of Bukhara and the borders of the medieval khanates. Two groups of factors affected the development of this situation: first, after the dissolution of the Soviet Union, the search for identity among elites was conducted in the pre-Soviet past of the territories of newly formed regions (states), and since a majority of the republics of Central Asia were created only in Soviet times, this sharply increased tendencies toward regionalization. Second, the infrastructure (roads, telephone, postal, and other communication links) created in the Soviet period began to deteriorate rather quickly because of the disruption of the traditional forms of upkeep and the outbreak of armed conflicts, as in Tajikistan. Barriers such as mountains and

period of Kunaev's regime or, later, that of Nazerbaev,[17] certainly for the state and party apparatus, where Russian-speaking Kazakhs held a preeminent position. Disproportionate representation of Kazakhs in government was especially marked in the predominantly Russian capital, Alma-Ata.[18] In industry, by contrast, the overwhelming majority was of Slavic origin, and in the mining and metallurgical

---

rivers, which traditionally divided people, have once again begun to play a large role. In Central Asia, the post-Soviet states are juridically constituted, but in reality not one can claim to be united and consolidated in the sense of a modern state. This is due not only to the fact that these states are populated by different ethnic groups (which was the norm for all Asian states), but more importantly because the territorial entities themselves are a product of Soviet policies, and were to a large degree maintained by those policies. Therefore, difficulties arise for elites who seek identity with the pre-Soviet past, and special difficulties arise among those elites who seek ethnic legitimacy by concentrating their efforts on criticizing the Soviet period. The result is identification with the pre-Soviet period of Central Asia and, accordingly, increasing aspirations among local elites, who are the heirs of pre-Soviet and pre-Russian principalities, hordes, and khanates. There were many such entities and in practically all the new republics (Tajikistan, Kyrgyzstan, Kazakhstan, Uzbekistan), conflicts of interest between elite groups belonging to the different clan structures of Tajiks, Kyrgyz, Kazakhs, and Uzbeks are numerous. Attempts to redistribute power in republics and regions where those who were in power during the weakening of the Soviet center and the acquisition of independence were not representative of local (titular) ethnic groups with a local ethnic orientation has become one of the main causes of conflict in Central Asia. In Kazakhstan and Tajikistan, ethnic "aliens" or elites oriented toward other "unpure" groups had important positions in the republic's power structure. In Tajikistan, "Uzbekified" Leninabad clans under strong Uzbek and Russian influences held power; in Kazakhstan, significant power in the north was concentrated among Slavs and Germans, and, in addition, Kazakhstan was the only republic where the titular population did not have a majority. Even historically, Kazakhstan was formed from Russian autonomous regions and Tajikistan was formed out of Uzbekistan. This is why the main conflict in Tajikistan was between Tajik groups of differing ethnic orientation, but in Kazakhstan conflict is developing between Kazakhs and Russians. Therefore, the relative ethnic stability in Uzbekistan, Turkmenistan, and Kyrgyzstan is understandable, since those who are in power in both the center and regions are ethnic "insiders"—representatives of an ethnic majority. In these three republics, the main contradictions and conflicts are localized in a given region (in places where other ethnic groups reside) or are interclan conflicts. An example of this is the clashes that took place in late 1990 in the Osh region of Kyrgyzia between Kyrgyz and Uzbeks (who constitute up to one-third of the population in that district). This conflict could hardly spread to the rest of Kyrgyzstan. The conflict in the Fergana Valley of Uzbekistan between Uzbeks and Meskhetian Turks was of similar character.

17. Gilette, "Ethnic Balance and Imbalance in Kazakhstan's Regions," p. 22.

18. It has been noted that "Kazakh participation in the government has also increased. Whereas in 1964 only 33 percent of the members of the Council of Ministers were Kazakhs, by 1981 Kazakhs held 60 percent of the posts, and the Kazakh share of ministerial and state chair positions increased from 39 to 61 percent." Martha Brill Olcott, The Kazakhs (Stanford, Calif.: Hoover Institution Press, 1987), p. 244.

industries there were hardly any Kazakhs at all. There was no consistent correlation between status and ethnicity, with Kazakhs disproportionately represented among political elites, and Slavs disproportionately represented in industry. However, the existence of stratification in a local context and the rapid progress of urbanization led to growing tensions in towns and settlements between people who came from poor, agricultural Kazakh regions and the relatively well-off population of industrial towns, mostly of Russian origin. With the arrival of Gennadi Kolbin, a campaign was started to replace leaders who had worked under Kunaev for many years to correct the disproportionate representation of Kazakhs in the party leadership, the militia, and the student population, and to root out corruption and bribery. Soon after his appointment, Kolbin initiated a series of trials of members of the Kazakh *nomenklatura* accused of bribe-taking, which was fairly common in Kazakhstan. This met with strong protests from newly created independent social organizations. To consolidate its position, the Kolbin group started to replace the leading officials in the regions, and in a short time many first and second secretaries of regional party organizations were replaced, especially in the predominantly Kazakh south. In the period from November to December 1988 alone, the secretaries of the Chimkent, Taldy-Kurgan, and Dzhambul regional party organizations were replaced. In the Soviet hierarchy, first secretaries of regional and district party committees were the most powerful personalities in their regions or districts. Although there were some ethnic elements to these changes, since the old *nomenklatura* had been closely allied with Kunaev and were mostly from the "local" group, the replacements were primarily motivated by Kolbin's desire to bring in a new leadership elite loyal exclusively to him.

NAZERBAEV'S POLICIES

In June 1989, Gennadi Kolbin was unexpectedly appointed to a high-ranking post in Moscow. In his place, Nursultan Nazerbaev, a Kazakh belonging to a clan from the southern region (the former Elder *Zhuz*) who had headed the Kazakhstan SSR Council of Ministers since 1984, was elected first secretary of the Central Committee of the Communist Party of Kazakhstan at a plenum at the end of June.

The accession of the new leader meant the victory of the "local" party group. The harsh measures aimed at the informal social organizations that had emerged during the Kolbin period were rescinded and the Kunaev era was rehabilitated. With the arrival of Nazerbaev, virtually all criminal proceedings against former regional leaders were halted.

Within a fairly short time, power was concentrated in the hands of the new first secretary. On February 22, 1990, Nazerbaev was elected chairman of the Supreme Soviet of the Kazakh SSR. At his instigation the post of president was created, to which he was elected on April 24, 1990, followed by a wave of elections of new regional leaders. The new head of state was fairly flexible and followed a good-relations policy with the existing Kazakh *nomenklatura*, the central authorities in Moscow, and the new public organizations that were then starting to emerge.

Up to 1991, the situation with respect to interethnic relations was under complete control of the authorities under Nazerbaev. The 1989 "Law on the Languages of the Kazakh SSR" was designed to make Kazakh the official state language. It required that, as of July 1, 1995, officials of state bodies and administrations, law-enforcement agencies, social services, educational institutions, cultural and health services, trading enterprises, repair and other services, postal and telegraph services, and transport and municipal services communicate with the public in the local vernacular.[19] The article came to be interpreted as meaning that officials were required to know two languages, which gave rise to controversy and the demand by the Russian ethnic group that Russian should become the second state language. At that time as well, historical themes were openly discussed for the first time, claims were openly made to certain territories on a historical basis, and open evaluations of controversial historical figures appeared in the mass media. For example, there was much controversy about the famous Cossack, Yermack. Russians saw Yermack as a heroic figure who opened up Siberia in the sixteenth century, while Kazakhs saw him as a conqueror. The Nazerbaev government opposed both the extreme Kazakh nationalist organizations, as well as the Cossack and Russian movements in a number of northern regions. In October 1990, the Declaration of Sovereignty of Kazakhstan within the framework of the Soviet Union was adopted. A decree of the Presidium of the Supreme Soviet of the Kazakh SSR officially rehabilitated the Kunaev regime and the participants in the events of December 1986.[20] At the same time Nazerbaev defended the unity of the Soviet Union, and in the March

---

19. *News of the Supreme Soviet of the Kazakh SSR*, No. 40–41, September 22, 1989.

20. A decree of the Presidium of the Supreme Soviet of the Kazakh SSR "On the Conclusions and Recommendations of the Commission on the Final Assessment

1991 all-Union referendum, 94 percent of Kazakhstan's voters answered yes to the question: "Do you consider the preservation of the Soviet Union as a union of equal sovereign states necessary?" President Nazerbaev also supported the ideas of democracy and market reforms. By carefully balancing these somewhat contrasting policies, Nazerbaev secured the loyalty of all the major political actors and movements.

After the victory of Boris Yeltsin's supporters in the August 1991 coup attempt in Moscow, Kazakhstan's leadership took a series of measures to consolidate its power and strengthen its political control. This was necessary in order to fill the vacuum that emerged from the paralysis of the Soviet power structures in Moscow and the transfer of real power to Russian Federation structures.[21] In a short time the Kazakhstani central state apparatus was reorganized, a national guard was formed, and new management took charge of the mass media, part of which was on the brink of bankruptcy. Nazerbaev announced his withdrawal from the politburo of the CPSU, and steps were taken to halt the activities of party organizations in government institutions. Henceforth it was forbidden to combine party and state appointments. The Communist Party of Kazakhstan was abolished and the test range at Semipalatinsk closed down.[22] On December 1, 1991, presidential elections were held in Kazakhstan, and Nazerbaev, who ran unopposed, was elected president with 98 percent of the votes. The purpose of the elections was to strengthen the institution of the presidency. Thereafter Nazerbaev appointed regional heads of administration and invested them with considerable powers. Again,

---

of the Circumstances Connected with Events in the City of Alma-Ata on December 17–18, 1986" was adopted on September 24, 1990. *Alma-Ata December 1986: A Book of Chronicles*, pp. 3–5.

21. The participation of members of the Cabinet of Ministers in the State Committee for the State of Emergency (GKChP) and the cessation of activities by the CPSU paralyzed all union organs. Thus an August 24, 1991, decree of the Supreme Soviet of Kazakhstan stipulated that "additional measures for strengthening the state sovereignty of the republic" would be adopted. It was established that leaders of organizations directly subordinate to the Union and located on Kazakh territory would be held responsible for obeying directives that contradicted Kazakhstani laws. In addition, the authority of the Kazakhstani Cabinet of Ministers over the activities of organizations and enterprises subordinate to the Union was established. Finally, the necessity of concentrating all state-centralized credit resources in a National State Bank of the Kazakh SSR was noted.

22. The ecological movement to close down the Semipalatinsk polygon, one of the most important nuclear test sites during the Soviet years, played a mobilizing role in the formation of the Kazakh national movement.

ethnic criteria for these appointments were not particularly significant. This further consolidated Nazerbaev's power base and made the presidency the strongest element in the political system of Kazakhstan.

THE ETHNIC FACTOR

During this period, tensions grew between the central Kazakh elite and the Russian regional elite (mainly in the northern and eastern regions) who feared the approaching end of the Soviet Union, the increasing independence of Kazakhstan, and what they saw as the ethnocentric policies of the Kazakh leadership. The first confrontation between political organizations based on ethnic principles dates from this time. The incident occurred in September 1991 in the town of Uralsk in the course of celebrations connected with the 400th anniversary of the founding of the Ural Cossacks in which representatives from the Don, Kuban, Northern Caucasian, Southern Ural, and Siberian Cossacks took part. The celebrations were held even though they had been prohibited by the local authorities and were therefore regarded as illegal. Local Kazakh students and representatives of Kazakh public associations from Alma-Ata, Chimkent, and Dzhambul got involved in fistfights with representatives of the Cossack groups, but the authorities intervened early and succeeded in averting a more serious clash.

As elsewhere in the Soviet Union, informal, independent political organizations began to emerge in Kazakhstan only in the second half of the 1980s. By the end of 1990, more than one hundred political associations were active in the republic.[23] The main political organizations were grouped into four informal blocs. The first was the ruling Communist Party of Kazakhstan, members of which occupied all state posts. As in other Soviet republics, all ethnic groups in the republic were represented in the Communist Party. At least formally there was no discrimination on ethnic grounds, and in fact Kazakhs were actively promoted through party structures.

The second bloc could be characterized as moderate Kazakh nationalists and was made up of organizations that received the support of official authorities. It has been said that "the nationalist

---

23. See *New Public-Political Organizations, Parties and Movements* (Moscow: Department for Contacts with Public-Political Organizations of the Central Committee of the CPSU, 1991). V. Ponomarev, *Independent Public Organizations of Kazakhstan and Kyrgyzia 1987–1991* (Moscow: Asia Publishing House, 1991).

agenda in Kazakhstan came, as elsewhere in the Soviet Union, from outside the Communist Party structure."[24] This is only true in that nationalism did not originate directly within the Communist Party structure; nevertheless, it found support and protection in the higher strata of the party among the "local" group. This ethno-nationalism was of a moderate nature and was compatible with the demands of the second bloc of political parties and even the *Azat* (Freedom) movement, which was part of the third bloc, discussed below. Among the leading groups in the second bloc were the anti-nuclear movement Nevada-Semipalatinsk, which was headed by the secretary of the Union of Writers of Kazakhstan, Olzhas Suleimenov, and the *Kazakh tili* (Kazakh language) movement. Nevada-Semipalatinsk demanded the prohibition of nuclear tests on the Semipalatinsk test range and control over the use by Union agencies of nuclear materials in Kazakhstan. *Kazakh tili* was founded to support the implementation of the law on languages in the Kazakh SSR. Neither organization initially pursued any clear political aims, but as they increased their activities and with the support of the leadership of the republic, they began to formulate political demands. By the end of 1990, the Nevada-Semipalatinsk movement had turned into a mass movement of the ethnic Kazakh population. Many of its regional branches were made up of supporters of the third and most radical bloc in the political spectrum, which was composed of radical Kazakh nationalists along with parties and movements upholding the ethnic claims of the Kazakh part of the population. All the parties in this bloc were in favor of an independent state (when the Soviet Union was still intact) and migration control, including restricting the entry of non-Kazakhs into the republic and improving conditions for the return of Kazakhs. The *Azat* movement demanded an independent, democratic republic, the laws of which would be paramount throughout the territory of Kazakhstan. Among its leaders were many Kazakh writers, academics, and former high functionaries. The national democratic party *Zheltoksan* (December) demanded the rehabilitation of the participants in the December 1986 events, the formation of national armed forces, and, ultimately, secession from the Soviet Union. The Alash Party (the party for the National Independence of Kazakhstan) formed the strongest opposition to communism and consequently to the leadership of the Communist Party of Kazakhstan. The principal goal of this party

---

24. Dannreuther, *Creating New States in Central Asia*, p. 15.

was the renaissance of Greater Turkestan as a common Turkic state uniting all of Central Asia.[25]

The fourth bloc was pro-Unionist and anti-Kazakh nationalist. It held an internationalist position, supporting the preservation of the Soviet Union and opposing separatism and privileges on ethno-national grounds. This bloc consisted mainly of organizations representing the Russian population. Of these, the most important was the *Yedinstvo* (Unity) movement. Formally advocating harmonious relations between ethno-nationalist groups and stressing its nonpolitical nature, Yedinstvo first emerged in August 1990 and was based in large industrial enterprises. But it was only a weak response by the Russian population to the formation of the second and third blocs of ethnic Kazakh organizations.

Regional Cossack associations were also formed—*Vozrozhdenie* (Rebirth), the Movement for Political Autonomy of the Ural Cossacks, and the Association of Siberian Cossacks in the northern Kazakh regions—which stood for the renewal of the Cossacks as a social-ethnic group, along with their culture, traditions, and Cossack self-government. The demands of the Cossacks and Russians were little known, since these groups were concentrated in the northwest and northeast far from Alma-Ata, and both the Kazakh and Soviet leadership were reluctant to make them public.

Ethnic German groups in Kazakhstan had been quite active as early as the 1960s and 1970s. Originally they had lived in the Volga region of Russia, and had been deported and resettled in the northern and central regions of Kazakhstan during World War II to prevent their anticipated collaboration with the German armies. In the 1960s and 1970s, decrees were issued rehabilitating this group and restoring their rights, which catalyzed the activities of the ethnic German community in Kazakhstan.[26] Revival, a social-political and cultural-

25. In tsarist Russia, Turkestan comprised the Central Asian lands inhabited by Turkic peoples. In 1918, during the revolution, the Turkestan ASSR was formed. It was then abolished in 1924 during the course of the redefinition of national territories in Central Asia and the creation of the union and autonomous republics there.

26. Decree 2829 of the Presidium of the Soviet Union Supreme Soviet (August 29, 1964) stated that the accusation made in 1941 that led to the resettlement of Germans from the Volga region "was a manifestation of the arbitrariness characteristic of the Stalinist personality cult." In the resolutions of this decree, it was also stated that "the German population had put down roots in their new places of residence on the territories of the republics, krais, and oblasts and that the districts of their previous residence had been settled. The goals of the future development of the districts with a German population charge the Council of

educational society of Soviet Germans, was founded in the spring of
1989 at a conference in Moscow. It was the first social organization in
the Soviet Union founded according to national principles. Despite
its all-Union political activism, the ethnic German community in
Kazakhstan never realized its main demand for the creation of a
national autonomous territory. The question of German autonomy
was transferred to the Soviet level and focused on a proposal to
restore the Volga German Republic in Russia, which had been
liquidated during World War II. The German organizations directed
most of their activism toward this goal. With the easing of exit restrictions and the improvement in relations between the Soviet Union and
the Federal Republic of Germany, part of the German population
began to emigrate from Kazakhstan and other republics of the Soviet
Union to Germany. According to the data of Alexander Dederer,
chairman of the Council of Germans of Kazakhstan, in 1994 alone,
121,000 ethnic Germans emigrated from Kazakhstan. He also claimed
that "the majority of Kazakhstan's Germans willingly rejected the
opportunity to build a sovereign Kazakh state. The overwhelming
majority of them did not participate in the political, economic, or cultural life of the country."[27] As a result of the massive departure of the
German population for Germany, the "German problem" in
Kazakhstan began to disappear.

Ministers of the Union Republics henceforth to provide assistance in their economic and cultural projects . . . to the German population living on the territories
of their republics, taking into consideration their particular national characteristics and interests." The unpublished decree of the Presidium of the Soviet Union
Supreme Soviet of November 3, 1972, eliminated "the restrictions in choice of
place of residence that had existed in the past for certain categories of citizens."
An appendix to the decree of the Presidium of the Soviet Union Supreme Soviet
of January 9, 1974 (No. 5333), publicly repealed Article 2 of the decree of the
Presidium of the Soviet Union Supreme Soviet of December 13, 1955, "On The
Removal of Restrictions on the Legal Status of Germans and Members of their
Families Located in Special Settlements," including the ban on the return of the
Germans to the areas from which they had been exiled.

27. He cited the discrimination and the negative attitude toward those who were
leaving: "Take for instance the special letter to the Ministry of Interior of the
Republic, which forbade those leaving to take their 'work documentation books'
[trudovie knizhki, in which each person's place of work, positions, and length of
employment is specified] to Germany. Apparently they contain some kind of
'government secrets.' However, Germany will only accept newcomers with these
'work documentation books.' Is it really possible after all this to respect such a
government and seriously expect the possibility for civilized relations between it
and the rest of the world?" Victor Verk, "Suitcase, Train Station, Germany:
Interview with Chairman of the Council of Germans of Kazakhstan Alexander
Dederer," *Caravan*, February 24, 1995, p. 7.

To sum up this period, there were a number of causes for increased tension on the eve of the proclamation of an independent Kazakhstan:

• the general crisis in the administration of the Soviet Union created a power vacuum in Kazakhstan;

• the ethnic composition of the population, with two large groups, almost equal in numbers, concentrated in different regions and living mostly in different territories;

• the opposition that developed between the Unionist-communist elites and the local communists, who had shifted to a more Kazakh nationalist position in the late 1980s;

• the growing resentment at the disproportionate representation of some ethnic groups in Kazakhstan's social and professional spheres;

• the perception of some Russian groups that they had been unjustly transferred to another state, aggravated by the fact that some regions mainly inhabited by Russians previously had been part of the Russian empire and the Soviet Union; and

• the fact that throughout the Soviet period, ethnic considerations were subordinated to economic priorities, such as collectivization and industrialization, and did not play an important role in the way policies were implemented, resulting in damage to the interests of the indigenous group.

Independent Kazakhstan: A Country of Kazakhs or Kazakhstanis?

On December 16, 1991, after the leaders of Russia, Ukraine, and Belarus signed the Belovezh Accords proclaiming the dissolution of the Soviet Union and the formation of a Commonwealth of Independent States (CIS), the Supreme Soviet of Kazakhstan passed a law on the independence of the republic. The complexities that independence revealed were only realized gradually.

In practice, Kazakhstan's dependence on Russia as the largest constituent of the Soviet Union had been considerable, especially in economic terms. In the Soviet period, as is now well understood, the economic links between many Soviet industries did not correspond at all with the administrative political divisions between republics. In the Soviet division of labor, individual republics specialized in certain sectors and did not produce all the goods necessary for self-sufficiency. In Kazakhstan, the predominant economic activities were the metallurgical industries, processing of raw materials, coal extraction, and agricultural products. The electricity and fuel needed to run these processes came from other republics, generally from the RSFSR. The main mining enterprises were located in the center and the north of the republic, in the cities of Karaganda, Ust-Kamenogorsk, and Pavlodar. These major extraction enterprises were oriented toward processing plants in the Urals region of the Russian Federation; part of the region received its energy from Siberia and the Volga region. The Russian-speaking population of the northern, eastern, and central regions suffered most from the disruption of economic links because they were the most industrially developed regions of Kazakhstan, and had been integrated to the greatest degree in the Union-wide division of labor. The same difficulties arose in Russia in the southern Urals and Siberia, where the population and industries suffered from insufficient supplies of coal from Kazakhstan.

It was inevitable, given the links between the two countries, that Kazakhstan would closely follow the economic reform policies of Russia, especially in the early years following independence. In the words of academician A. Koshanov of the National Academy of Sciences of the Republic of Kazakhstan, Director of the Institute for Economics, "for a number of objective and subjective reasons, treading in the footsteps of Russia, the liberal shock model of reform of the national economy was widely followed in Kazakhstan."[28] The financial dependence resulting from Kazakhstan's membership in the ruble zone was another factor that forced it to follow in the wake of Russian economic policies. In January 1992, the presidential decree "On the Liberalization of Prices" entered into force, as a result of which retail prices of the main consumer goods rose several times in Kazakhstan as well as in Russia. The liberalization of prices seriously affected the peasants and the strata of the urban, ethnic Kazakh population who had recently come from rural areas and worked in the lower levels of industry. Modernization was designated a priority task, but it bore mainly a propagandistic character. Kazakhstan's leadership emphasized rapidly developed natural resources—questionable from a

---

28. A. Koshanov, "Problems of Market Reform in the Economy of Kazakhstan," *Voprosy ekonomiki,* No. 3 (1994), p. 90.

strategic point of view but enabling the authorities to consolidate their power—attracting investments, increasing employment, and focusing on economic rather than political and social problems. Beginning in early 1992, a number of large contracts for the joint development of natural resources were signed with Western firms, including Chevron, the French firm Elf-Aquitaine, British Petroleum, and with Turkish, Iranian, Chinese, and Japanese firms for the construction of oil and gas pipelines. In this connection the president frequently visited countries viewed as potential investors. An agreement with Germany on economic and cultural contacts can be explained by German interest in halting the mass emigration of Germans from Kazakhstan.[29] In the three years following independence, the Kazakhstani leadership was unable to halt the drastic drop in production, the closing down of factories, the growth in unemployment, the fall in the standard of living, and rising inflation. In 1993 prices increased by twenty-three times, while personal income only increased by fourteen times. The national currency introduced in October 1993 lost five-sixths of its value in the course of six months. The general economic policies decreased contracts for the products of government enterprises, so that by the beginning of 1994, 732 factories with a total labor force of 350,000 people had completely or partly closed down.[30] According to the Kazakhstani State Committee for statistics, on a minimal income of 100 tenge one could buy daily, in April 1994, 200 grams of bread and milk, 30 grams of butter and beef, and 100 grams of potatoes and pasta. By June, only half these quantities could be bought for this sum.[31] The sharp discrepancy between the optimistic promises of the government, which stimulated high expectations about a coming

---

29. Similar considerations motivate China, which is interested in trade relations with Kazakhstan, but at the same time fears a mass exodus of Uighurs that would increase the numbers of ethnic Uighurs in the Sinthizian-Uighur frontier region. The Uighurs, like the Kazakhs, come from the Turkic group of the Altai family of peoples. Approximately 180,000 Uighurs live in Kazakhstan, concentrated in the eastern border regions. Altogether, Uighurs make up one percent of Kazakhstan's population. In China there are seven million Uighurs, the majority of whom live in the Sinthizian-Uighur autonomous region in northeastern China, which lies on the eastern border of Kazakhstan. Extremist Uighur organizations in China aspire to create an independent state of Uighuristan, but this does not seem to have aroused much support among the Kazakh Uighur population.

30. V. Ardaev, "The New Kazakhstani Parliament: Drama or Farce," *Izvestia*, May 12, 1994, p. 4.

31. "The Social and Economic Situation in Kazakhstan: January–June 1994," *Committee for Statistics of the CIS Statistical Bulletin*, No. 32 (September 1994), p. 87.

economic upturn as a result of the market reforms, and the reality of the dramatic decrease in the standard of living was an additional cause of the increase in political and social tension.

THE SHIFT IN NATIONALITIES POLICY AFTER INDEPENDENCE

The nationalities policy of the Kazakhstani government since 1991 has generally served the interests of the Kazakh ethnic group. Although the government opposes the extreme Kazakh nationalists by organizing campaigns in the press, preventing demonstrations, and sometimes arresting the party leaders, in fact many of their demands have been satisfied by the political leadership and administration. Towns and villages with Russian names were given Kazakh names. For example, the town of Guriev was renamed Atyrau; Tselinograd was changed to Akmolu; the Ural region became West Kazakhstan; and the Chikmen region is now South Kazakhstan. Local administrations were replaced and some redrawing of administrative lines occurred to give certain districts a more Kazakh orientation. The appointments policy of the president favored naming ethnic Kazakhs to leading positions, which resulted in a marked disproportion between the bulk of the population and the new Kazakh local elites, especially in the northern and eastern territories largely populated by Russians.

An important element in the ethnic policy was the support given to Kazakhs returning from abroad to settle permanently. A program of assistance was initiated for Kazakhs emigrating from other republics of the former Soviet Union, Mongolia, and China. Thanks to the new immigration law and with the aid of the local authorities, a considerable number of families from Mongolia were resettled in the central and northern regions. Among them were descendants of the nomads who had migrated there as a result of the famine in the 1930s. The government gave the settlers cattle, transport, furniture, and other necessities and provided them with work. This program was viewed by the Russian population as an attempt to change the demographic structure of the population in regions mainly inhabited by Russians. Against a background of departing Russians and Germans and general material shortages, it sometimes led to conflicts, especially with the rural Cossack population in these areas, who resented the newcomers and the privileges given to them as well as the competition they posed in the markets.

The frequently proclaimed equality of all national groups was considered by many members of the Slavic groups, particularly the Russians, as a screen behind which the real policy, directed at securing a dominant position for the ethnic Kazakh population, was being implemented. Nazerbaev repeatedly affirmed that "if the Russians in the republic are worried about their future, this is because of events in other parts of the CIS—people draw parallels. We have complete equality before the law. We have no people who are discriminated against because of their nationality."[32] But in reality relations between ethnic groups during this period were marked by a growing suspicion of the others' actions and policies. An important factor was the adoption of legislation that was not balanced in its ethnic orientation or consequences. The 1992 "Law on the State Independence of the Republic of Kazakhstan" contained a number of articles that were especially troubling to the non-Kazakh population. It provided that the Republic of Kazakhstan came into being as a result of the realization of "the right of the Kazakh nation to self-determination" and, as a result, citizens of the republic belonging to other nationalities are united "in a common fate with the Kazakh nation." Furthermore, it declared that the republic of Kazakhstan enjoys territorial integrity; and "all Kazakhs who were forced to leave the territory of the Republic and reside in other states have the right to Kazakhstani citizenship at the same time as citizenship of other states." The law also stated that "the rebirth and development of the culture, traditions and language, the strengthening of the national dignity of the Kazakh nation and of the representatives of other nationalities living in Kazakhstan, is one of the most important obligations of the state."[33]

After the passage of the Law on Independence, a draft constitution was submitted for broad discussion by the population in the summer of 1992. In the ensuing debate, the Kazakh- and Russian-speaking populations took different positions on the provisions concerning ethnic groups. The principal disagreements concerned questions of the status of the Russian language; citizenship and the right to dual citizenship; the state structure of Kazakhstan; and higher representatives bodies.

The draft constitution contained a clause establishing the Kazakh language as the official language of the state. Supporters of this clause argued that "in the 70 years of Soviet rule, the Kazakh language, on its historic territory, has been reduced to a language used

---

32. Nursultan Nazerbaev, "The Commonwealth Should Be Strengthened: The People Want It," *Kazakhstanskaia pravda*, September 2, 1992, p. 2.

33. "The Law on the State Independence of the Republic of Kazakhstan" (Alma-Ata, 1992).

only in the family and everyday life." Therefore "it is necessary to create a preferential regime for it in order to overcome the backwardness to which it was condemned by the discrimination to which it has fallen victim in the past." Moreover, "a people has the right to the official status of its language."[34] An "Appeal by the group of deputies [of] 'Civil Peace'," various proposals by Russian associations, and a number of municipal soviets demanded that Russian be given official status alongside the Kazakh language. They argued that the majority of the population of Kazakhstan knows Russian and that having one official language, Kazakh, which is spoken by only a minority, would lead to sociolinguistic discrimination. On the matter of citizenship, the authors of Kazakhstan's draft constitution proceeded from the premise that the granting of dual citizenship to Kazakhs abroad was a question of rendering historical justice to those "who were forced to leave their homeland against their will." At the same time, when members of the Russian ethnic group proposed that dual citizenship should also be granted to ethnic Russians, the request was rejected on the grounds that dual citizenship is a "rare occurrence in world practice" and "can only be applied to a restricted number of people."[35] The draft constitution proposed to create a unitary state. It was argued that "a unitary state would ensure the unity of the legal system" and the "coordination of the activities of all government organs" and "would help avoid conflict as democratic processes become entrenched in society."[36] The opponents of such a form of statehood—mainly Cossack organizations— wanted either autonomy to be granted to the north and east or a federal state. These proposals were also supported by *Vozrozhdenie* (Rebirth), the association of ethnic Germans. In accordance with these ideas, organizations of Russian speakers argued for a bicameral parliamentary system. The interests of various ethnic groups would be represented in a Chamber of Nationalities, as had been the case in the parliamentary structures of the Russian Federation until 1993.

---

34. Speeches of the chairman of the Committee for Nationality Policies and the Development of Culture and Language, A. Kikilbaev, and deputy Alexander Kniaginin, at a session of the Supreme Soviet. A. Kikilbaev and A. Kniaginin, "In the Interest of Peace in the Common Home," *Kazakhstanskaia pravda*, June 9, 1992, p. 2.

35. Serikbolsan Abdildin, "Speech Of The Chairman Of The Supreme Soviet Of Kazakhstan: Through National Concord To A Democratic State," *Kazakhstanskaia pravda*, August 7, 1992, p. 2.

36. Ibid.

The new constitution, adopted in January 1993, rejected all these counterproposals.[37]

The Russian part of the population was equally concerned with subordinate enactments, the regulation of government and other state bodies, and, in particular, the way individual laws were to be implemented. For instance, the implementation program for the constitutional clause on the state language gave rise to heated debate. After many months of discussion, at the end of 1993, a number of the provisions of this program most disputed and disliked by the Russian-speaking group were removed. The Kazakh language and literature test was no longer obligatory for everyone who wanted to take the entry examination for higher education institutions teaching in Russian, or for confirmation of appointments of government personnel. Regional soviets (local administrations) were given discretion to decide the length of the transition to conducting all government business in the Kazakh language, with an outside limit of 1995.[38] The policy of favoring the Kazakh ethnic group continued, however, albeit at a somewhat slower pace. According to the weekly *ABV* (Shareholders and Stock Exchange News), in the beginning of 1994,

---

37. The following is parts of the preamble and articles of the Constitution of the Republic of Kazakhstan that spell out the nationalities policy of the Republic of Kazakhstan:

Foundations of Constitutional Order: The Republic of Kazakhstan is a democratic, secular, and unitary state. The Republic of Kazakhstan, formed from the self-determination of the Kazakh nation, guarantees equal rights to all of its citizens. In the Republic of Kazakhstan, the state language is Kazakh. The Russian language is the language of communication among nationalities. The state guarantees the preservation of spheres of use for the language of communication among nationalities and other languages, and insures their free development. Limitation of the rights and freedoms of citizens on the basis of non-fluency in the state language or language of communication among nationalities is forbidden. Article 1. Citizens of the Republic of Kazakhstan are guaranteed equality of rights and freedoms regardless of race, nationality, gender, language, social position, material wealth, professional position, social position, place of residence, relationship to religion, personal beliefs, membership in organizations, and also previously completed criminal punishment. Any form of discrimination against citizens is forbidden. Article 4. All citizens of the Republic who are forced to leave its territory, and also Kazakhs who live in other states, are reserved the right to have citizenship of the Republic of Kazakhstan and the citizenship of other states, if this does not contradict the laws of the states in which they are citizens.

See *Constitution of Kazakhstan* (Almaty: Kazakhstan Publishers, 1993).

38. "The Government Makes Amendments to the Government Program for the Implementation of the Law On Languages, An Interview with the Head of the Department of Internal Policy of the Apparatus of the President and Council of Ministers, Bazar Damitov," *Kazakhstanskaia pravda*, December 4, 1992, pp. 1–2.

the ratio between Kazakhs and non-Kazakhs in the President's Office was about 6:1 and in the Ministry for Economics 7:1. In a number of regional administrations in the north and east with a predominant Russian population, ratios ranged from 2:1 to 4:1.[39] The ethnic disproportion continued to grow, most noticeably in the northern and eastern regions, between the predominantly Kazakh authorities and the main part of the population. Resentment over these policies led to the growth of independent organizations of non-Kazakhs in these regions, each with their own political demands.

THE CONSOLIDATION OF PRESIDENTIAL POWER

After the passage of the new constitution in 1993, power continued to concentrate in the hands of the president and the powerful groups around him. After the Constitutional Court became more active and altered the government's legislation on guaranteed minimum income and the municipal courts had acquitted strikers accused of striking illegally, their functions were restricted or changed. The heads of local administrations were appointed by the president and were subordinated to him. Under Article 92 of the Constitution, the head of the oblast executive body was to be appointed and discharged by the president. The Kazakhstan Supreme Soviet had, under pressure from the president's office,[40] passed a law "On the Temporary Delegation of Additional Powers to the President of the Republic and the Heads of Local Administrations," which gave the president power to issue decrees with the force of law. In February 1993, a pro-presidential association, the Union for People's Unity of Kazakhstan, was founded; it presented itself as a centrist organization, openly working to strengthen the position of the leadership and its control over economic processes. Other aims of the Union were consolidation of state sovereignty, support for the reforms initiated by the president, and ensuring stability and progress. The party's leadership included

---

39. See S. Kozlov, "Democratic in Form, Nationalist in Essence," *Nezavisimaia gazeta*, April 2, 1994, pp. 1–2.

40. In an interview, the former chairman of the Supreme Soviet, Serikbolsan Abdildin, stated that he knew that administration heads received a directive to induce the pro-Communist local Soviets to dissolve themselves and that *Kazakhstanskaia pravda* had received an order to organize criticism of the Supreme Soviet. Furthermore, Abdildin stated that "there were open discussions about the fact that the heads of administration were pressuring chairmen of the Soviets, to assemble in session and to dissolve itself within 10–15 minutes." Interview with Serikbolsan Abdildin, *ABV* (Alma-Ata Exchange Herald), April 29, 1994.

a considerable number of representatives of the Kazakh elite. President Nazerbaev spoke at the charter meeting.

In November and December 1993, the majority of the deputies of soviets at all levels began to leave their posts on the ground that elections should be held for a more "professional" parliament to replace the Supreme Soviet, which was a holdover from before independence. On December 10, legislation was enacted "On the Dissolution, Before the End of its Term, of the Supreme Soviet of Kazakhstan." Since many deputies were also members of executive organs and thus directly responsible to the president, many experts considered that the move was stage-managed by the president's administration in order to consolidate its power.

Before its dissolution, the Kazakhstan Supreme Soviet passed an Election Code specifying the regulations for the parliamentary elections. For a political organization to take part in these elections, it had to register with the Ministry of Justice. There were a variety of bureaucratic means to prevent registration, and many organizations—particularly those that the government did not want to participate—were unable to take part in the elections because they were not registered or reregistered by the Ministry of Justice. For example, radical Kazakh nationalist organizations and some of the more radical Russian and Cossack organizations were ineligible, although Lad, the strongest moderate organization representing Russian speakers, did participate. Once an organization had registered, candidates emerged in several ways: they were nominated by public organizations; those who could collect enough signatures from supporters could present themselves as individual candidates; and some were on a list of candidates put forward by the president personally, to be voted on by the whole population.

Of the total of 177 seats, 42 were elected from the presidential list. The majority of the elected deputies were officials of various ranks who supported the president's line. Overall, the March 1994 elections strengthened the position of the presidential group and the Kazakh representation in this body. Until May 1990, 47 percent of the members of parliament were Kazakh; after May 1990, this increased to 54 percent; and after elections in March 1994, to 58 percent.

The elections were observed by representatives from outside countries, including Russia. Observers from the parliamentary assembly of the Conference on Security and Cooperation in Europe (CSCE) noted that the elections in themselves represented a positive element, but that, according to Western standards, a considerable number of violations had occurred. The principal shortcomings identified were that

- the election campaign was too short;

- the registration system of candidates was extremely complex, and the election commissions arbitrarily disqualified candidates;

- a presidential list of candidates existed;

- many people voted not only on their own behalf but also on behalf of numerous relatives;

- observers were not admitted to some polling stations;

- the control system of the ballot papers was ineffective;

- independent candidates were not able to campaign for themselves in the mass media; and

- there was financial support for some candidates and restrictions on others.[41]

The observers concluded that the main reason for these irregularities was the electoral traditions of the Soviet period.

These observations by the election observers caused considerable furor, and precipitated a wave of meetings and publications in both Kazakhstan and Russia regarding the elections and the general situation in Kazakhstan. The Kazakhstani authorities did not agree with the evaluation of the CSCE observers and considered the elections a success. The chairman of the Central Election Commission, Karatai Turysov, responded, calling on the observers to evaluate the elections in terms of the situation in Kazakhstan. He pointed out that "the existence of the presidential list of candidates had been sanctioned by the Election Code passed by the previous [Kazakhstani] Supreme Soviet which dissolved itself in December 1993."[42] Nazerbaev stated that

---

41. According to the head of the Central Election Committee, there was no basis for the rejection of the parliamentary election results. *Inter-Review* (electronic data), February 10, 1994. "Konstantin Zatulin Has Ambivalent Feelings about Election in Kazakhstan," *Postfactum Official Chronicle* (electronic data), March 11, 1994.

42. "The Organization and Course of the Elections," *Soviets of Kazakhstan,* March 10, 1994, p. 1.

"accusations of gross violations of the standards of international law in the course of the elections in the Republic are not leveled by all the members of the CSCE delegation," and that "far reaching conclusions have been drawn from individual cases."[43] In spite of this, it can be said that the elections had some positive effect in clarifying the stances of all sides and in enabling the positions of the various groups to be more clearly understood, not only by one another, but also by the election observers.

On March 13, 1995, President Nazerbaev dissolved the newly elected Supreme Soviet of Kazakhstan. The official reason for this action was the decision of the Constitutional Court holding that there had been illegitimate methods of counting the votes and improper demarcation of borders of voting districts during the elections. Thus the Supreme Soviet itself was declared to be illegitimate. The parliament attempted to contest the Constitutional Court's decision and to remain in the Supreme Soviet building. Many deputies signed an appeal to the United Nations to send independent observers to Kazakhstan to evaluate the situation. All these efforts were rejected by statements from the president and by the action of the militia. The legislative function was automatically transferred to the president, who would have to reaffirm the judgment of the Constitutional Court on the election of the parliament and form a Central Election Commission, which would develop regulations for new parliamentary elections. A few days later, on March 18, President Nazerbaev, speaking at a conference of representatives of the law-enforcement organizations, announced that Kazakhstan should become a full-fledged presidential republic and that since the existing constitution and laws did not correspond to this need, constitutional reform would be carried out, as well as changes in the distribution of powers.[44]

A week later in Almaty, an Assembly of Peoples of Kazakhstan, created on Nazerbaev's initiative, was convened as a consultative body to the president. The Assembly declared in a resolution that "the coming to power of people who lacked sufficient knowledge and ability to govern could undermine the process of economic stabilization and Kazakhstan's establishment as a sovereign government." Therefore the Assembly, "in order to avoid a split in society in the

---

43. "The Kazakhstanis Rose to the Occasion," *Soviets of Kazakhstan*, March 12, 1994, p. 1.

44. "Kazakhstan Should Become a Full-Fledged Presidential Republic—Nazerbaev," *Interfax*, March 18, 1995.

struggle for presidential power in the absence of fit alternative candidates to Nursultan Nazerbaev, urgently recommend[ed] the President of the Republic to conduct in the nearest future a nationwide referendum on extending his term to December 2000."[45] The Russian organizations in Kazakhstan proposed to include one more question in the referendum: "Do you agree that the Republic of Kazakhstan should have two official languages: Kazakh and Russian?" However, this did not meet with the president's approval and was not included.

By presidential decree the nationwide referendum was held on April 29, 1995. Confirming the widely held predictions of observers, it was clearly in Nazerbaev's favor.[46] By Central Election Committee data, approximately eight million people, 91.2 percent of those eligible, took part in the election. Of these, 95.5 percent supported prolongation of Nazerbaev's presidential term.[47] On June 30, 1995, a draft constitution prepared by the president's administration was presented to the Assembly of the Peoples of Kazakhstan in which a unitary state with a "strong form of presidential power" was proposed. According to the draft, the state language of Kazakhstan would remain Kazakh, but also included was the idea that "the use of the Russian language will be officially acknowledged as being on the same level as Kazakh." The draft was completed following the Assembly's evaluation and debate, and the new constitution was adopted by referendum on August 30, 1995. Following the referendum, Nazerbaev issued a law regarding new elections to parliament, establishing a bicameral legislature.[48]

---

45. Resolution of the First Assembly of the Peoples of Kazakhstan, "On a Nationwide Referendum," press release, Almaty, March 2, 1995.

46. The chairman of the newly appointed Central Election Commission of Kazakhstan, Yuri Kim, confirmed this when he stated: "President Nursultan Nazerbaev has sufficient authority with the people that there is no doubt about the results of the scheduled referendum [on April 29] on the extension of his term." See "Nazerbaev should not doubt the results of the Referendum—Chairman of the Central Elections Commission," *Interfax-Vestnik*, March 31, 1995.

47. "The Central Election Committee of Kazakhstan Announces Results," *Postfactum*, May 15, 1995.

48. "Constitution Proposes the Establishment of a Strong Presidential Power and Minister of Justice," *Interfax-Vestnik*, June 29, 1995; and "The New Draft Constitution of Kazakhstan in Conformity with the Core Interests of Kazakhstanis and Solves Fundamental Problems that Disturb Society and President Nazerbaev," *Interfax*, August 2, 1995.

THE EVOLUTION OF ETHNIC POLITICS UNDER NAZERBAEV

The balancing act between the ethnic ideology and the objective of economic modernization generated opposition to the government, not only among non-Kazakhs, but also among some Kazakh groups.

KAZAKHS. During Soviet rule, the segmentation along clan and *zhuz* divisions had been pushed to the background. The theme of clans and their influence was considered taboo and was strongly condemned by Kazakh authorities and academic circles. After independence, appeals for a return to the Kazakh past and the revival of "precolonial" traditions led to a renewed and strengthened interest in these matters. Descriptions of the clan structure of Kazakh society and its influence on the powers that be stirred considerable interest among the reading public. Most researchers, however, go no further than to establish the existence of the clan structure among the Kazakh portion of the population[49] and to note the strong position of the representatives of the clans of the Elder *Zhuz* in the power structure. The official Kazakh position denies the existence of any such influence, which in any case would be of a hidden nature and inaccessible to "strangers." Experts studying the conflicts between Kazakh political organizations are inclined to ascribe them to certain interests of the *zhuzes*. Loyalty to the Kazakh organization Parasat, which is so far not widely known, was linked to the interests of the Younger *Zhuz*. The interests of the Middle *Zhuz* are thought to be represented in part by the People's Congress of Kazakhstan and in part by the Socialist Party of Kazakhstan, led by Anwar Alimzhanov.[50] Originally, these two parties more or less reflected the position of the authorities on most questions and enjoyed the protection of the president. However, with the worsening of the social situation, the partial abandonment of modernization policies, and the growth of ethnic conflict, these parties adopted more critical positions and lost their presidential support. At the same time, because of the different clan bases of the Kazakh nationalist organizations, they have occasionally entered into temporary coalitions, even with Russian associations toward which in principle they are hostile.

---

49. See James Critchlow, "Letter from Alma-Ata," *Central Asia Monitor*, No. 2 (1994), p. 11. This article includes interesting insights into and assessments of Kazakhstan's political, social, and organizational "subterranean forces."

50. See, for example, Sergei Kurginian, "The Contents of the New Internationalism," *Nezavisimaia gazeta*, July 7, 1994, p. 5; Nur Erige, "The Kazakh Zhuzes," *Kazakhstanskaia pravda*, October 6, 1992, p. 4; and Dmitry Trofimov, "In Kazakhstan the Grandsons of the Khans Have to Be Reckoned With," *Izvestia*, July 6, 1994, p. 3.

RUSSIANS. The political organization of the Russians took some time but gradually spread to most of the regions. An influential Russian political organization, the Russian Community of Kazakhstan, led by Yuri Bunakov, was formed in 1993–94. It has branches in seventeen regions of Kazakhstan and provides the foundation for the Slavic republican movement Lad, led by Alexandra Dokuchaeva. Lad espouses moderate views and has succeeded in uniting various organizations of the Russian-speaking population. After the 1993 elections, Lad issued an appeal in the name of the deputies from eastern Kazakhstan demanding elected rather than presidentially appointed regional heads of administration and broader self-government. In a number of regions in the northeast, the Russians obtained an electoral majority in the local, regional, and municipal councils, which enabled them to present their demands at an official level to the government in Almaty. One demand was for the right of groups within Kazakhstan—particularly in the northern and eastern regions with an ethnic Russian majority—to attain political and territorial autonomy.

At this time, the Party for the Democratic Progress of Kazakhstan was formed on the basis of the earlier *Yedinstvo* movement, which had represented the interests of the wider Russian population and supported the unity of the Soviet Union. Its leader, Alexandra Dokuchaeva, was simultaneously the leader of the Lad movement.[51] The goals of the new party were much narrower than those of the Lad movement and came to play a concrete role in Kazakhstani politics. The party stood for defense of civil equality and human rights. As a result, the Russian population started to make use of the theme of human rights and democracy. A sign of this is the recent formation of yet another new party, the Party for the Legal Development of Kazakhstan, under the leadership of Vitali Voronov and Andrei Peregrin, which calls for the development of a law-based state that protects human rights.

COSSACKS. Three Cossack associations operate in locations in Kazakhstan where Cossacks have traditionally lived: the Ural Union of Cossacks in the west (Alexander Kachalin, hetman); the Association for the Support of Semirechi Cossacks in the south and central region (Nikolai Gyunkin, hetman); and the Union of Cossacks

---

51. It was not uncommon for one person to start up several movements and parties, in the event that one or more might be banned. Often these movements would strive for slightly different goals.

of the Gorki line in the north and east (Victor Achkasov, hetman). These organizations and others in the adjoining southern Siberian regions had traditionally maintained strong ties within a larger Cossack movement and preserved their traditional political, economic, and social structure. After 1992, the activities of the Cossack organizations intensified. They demanded the rehabilitation of the Cossacks repressed under Soviet rule, the granting of official status to Russian as a state language, the restoration of the historical names of the Cossack settlements, "the restoration of all their rights," and provisions for the traditional forms of Cossack self-government. It was also suggested in government legislation and official speeches that the term "indigenous population" should not be used, as this was understood to mean exclusively the Kazakh population. Among Cossacks, the desire for, and expectation of, a revision of the borders of Kazakhstan were particularly strong because their historical traditions were promoted to a certain degree by Russian government statements, which I discuss in greater detail below.

The Cossack movement met with strong opposition from the authorities in Almaty. The main problem was the tension between the Cossacks' historical tradition of service to Russia and their position in Kazakhstan as inhabitants of a foreign state. Cossacks see themselves as a separate ethnic and social group, but they have been looked upon by the Kazakhstani government as a "privileged military caste" and their organizations as "paramilitary formations," without the right to be registered or active. Cossack meetings were prohibited, and their hetmans detained. Confrontations between the Kazakh and Cossack populations became frequent. In April 1994 alone, clashes over the prohibition of meetings were narrowly avoided in two villages in southern Kazakhstan. Cossack newspapers were repeatedly banned. In March 1992, the *Cossack News* published in Uralsk was forbidden and *Gubernia*, published in Ust-Kamenogorsk, was refused reregistration. Both publications were accused of "stirring up strife between nationalities" and "encroachment on the sovereignty and territorial integrity of the republic."[52]

EMIGRATION. Migration out of Kazakhstan has considerably increased in recent years as a result of economic and nationality policies. The Kazakh population has grown, while that of Russians, Ukrainians, and Germans is declining. According to the State

---

52. Z. Yesimkulov, "It Isn't Worth Violating the Law," *Kazakhstanskaia pravda*, May 22, 1992, p. 3.

Committee for Statistics, the number of Russians living in the republic in 1994 had fallen by 200,000, of Ukrainians by almost 40,000, and of Germans by 344,000 since Kazakhstan gained its independence in 1992.[53] In 1990, 306,000 people left the republic; in 1991, 255,000; in 1992, 369,000; in 1993, 333,000; and in the period from January to April 1994, 132,000, contrasted with only 25,000 new arrivals. The number of Russians who emigrated totaled 38,000 in 1990; 26,000 in 1991; 82,000 in 1992; and 87,000 in 1993.[54] As with any significant phenomenon, migration became a subject of contention and mutual accusations. The Kazakhstani authorities explained it as a result of the withdrawal of Russian army units and the closing down of scientific space facilities and settlements. Members of the Russian population, however, attributed it to the government policies based on ethnic principles.

THE CURRENT STATE OF ETHNIC RELATIONS

By 1993–94, Kazakhstan's initial nationalities policy had exhausted itself. This policy had been based on a combination of internally contradictory objectives: first, to privilege the leading Kazakh clans and the Kazakh population; second, to secure the support of the Slavic population by trying to preserve the Soviet Union and, later, to create a Eurasian Union; and third, to modernize and form a national state for Russian-speaking Kazakhs and Slavic technocrats. On the one hand, the Nazerbaev government's economic modernization policy was undermined by the appeal to clan loyalties and the ethno-nationalist mobilization of the masses. On the other, Russians constituted the main part of the technically educated population, and the hope that this group would remain loyal was constantly receding as the prospect of some kind of territorial-political union with Russia faded.

On the whole, in 1993 and especially in 1994, the presidential group alternated between granting concessions to and putting pressure on the leaders of Russian and Cossack organizations. Thus, at the suggestion of UN High Commissioner for Refugees Peter van Krieker, the law on immigration, which to that point had applied only to ethnic Kazakhs and allowed ethnic Kazakhs to join relatives in Kazakhstan, was amended to allow all citizens of Kazakhstan the same rights of immigration and reunification of families. A presidential decree

---

53. INFO-TASS, July 25, 1994.

54. Official statistical figures are from the ABD.1.S. computerized data bank, version 6.50, of the State Committee for Statistics of the Russian Federation.

allowed close relatives of other ethnic groups, in addition to Kazakhs, to settle in Kazakhstan. Another decree supplemented the law on citizenship to extend the period for acquiring Kazakhstani citizenship until March 1995. A few members of the Russian community obtained ministerial posts, and a Russian was appointed chairman of the Supreme Court.

In the summer of 1994, the government also made efforts to find common ground with the Cossacks. In June, the Ministry of Justice registered the Association for Support of the Cossacks of Semirechi. The main emphasis on this occasion was that the Cossacks in Kazakhstan should not constitute a military formation and that the aim of the movement was the revival of historic traditions, feasts, and customs. But more far-reaching ideas were also expressed. In the view of the Councillor of State, Kairbek Suleimenov—a Nazerbaev man—"the Cossacks could serve as border troops on the frontiers with China, Iran and on the Caspian Sea. They could also form part of the Republican Guard, which guards the president, and a separate Cossack unit as a part of the Kazakhstani army could be formed."[55] At the same time, the parliament approved the president's proposal to transfer the capital from Alma-Ata to Akmola, formerly Tselinograd. When there is tension between groups, any important event is likely to be given different interpretations. The official motivation for the move was that the present capital is situated in the very south of the republic, while Akmola is located virtually in the center. It would be easier and more convenient to govern the country from the new capital. Some of the Russian population interpreted this measure as a attempt to move a considerable part of the Kazakh population to the north and thus change the ratio between the Kazakh and predominantly Russian population. Yet some Kazakh radicals saw it as an attempt to strengthen the Slavic element in politics. The real purpose was probably an attempt by Nazerbaev to weaken the outwardly unapparent influence of the clans of the Elder (southern) *Zhuz*. Nazerbaev was himself a member of the Elder *Zhuz*, and this clan structure was his primary base of support. Nevertheless, he also wanted to weaken its direct influence on his policies, which now emphasized modernization, and the stronger Kazakh nationalist position of the Elder *Zhuz* might lead to open conflict with the Russian population.

---

55. "The Cossacks of the Alma-Ata and Taldy-Kurgan Regions Have Been Granted Official Status," INFO-TASS, June 6, 1994.

In contrast to these conciliatory actions, in April 1994, one of the leaders of the Russian community of northern Kazakhstan, the Russian citizen and journalist Yevgeni Supruniuk, who was well known for his criticism of the Kazakhstani government, was arrested. In September he was sentenced by a court to two years, provisional imprisonment for "having stirred up strife between nationalities." His arrest and trial led to mass protests by the Russian movement in Kazakhstan and protests by the Russian Ministry of Foreign Affairs and organizations in Russia. The authorities kept a close watch on the press. Undesirable publications had their telephones cut off or, under various pretexts, were refused printing services.[56]

Through the winter of 1994, the confrontation between Russians and Kazakhs in the northern and eastern regions grew to such a pitch that virtually any event was interpreted as malice on the part of the other ethnic group. Cases of provocation became more frequent, such as the October 1994 kidnapping of Fedor Cherepanov, the hetman of the Cossack community of Old Believers, chairman of the Council of Hetmans of the Verkhne-Irtysh line, and deputy of the Municipal Council. In November 1994, by order of the Ministry of Justice, the Association for the Support of the Cossacks of Semirechi had to suspend its activities for six months. The Ministry charged that the Cossack organizations in Kazakhstan considered themselves a branch of the political structures of the Russian Cossacks, claimed to be paramilitary organizations, did not recognize existing administrative-territorial divisions or the changes to the names of localities without authority, indulged in activities tending to "stir up strife between nationalities," and organized illegal meetings and other events. The leaders of the Cossacks in Alma-Ata, Taldy-Kurgan, and Petropavlovsk were arrested. The Lad movement and other Russian social and political organizations took up the defense of the Cossacks. Tensions increased further in December, when it became known that the leaders of *Azat*, one of the most powerful Kazakh nationalist organizations, demanded the death sentence for the writer Alexander Solzhenitsyin for his statements on Kazakhstan. In response, the leaders of the Russian community asked the Procurator's Office to cancel *Azat's* registration with the Ministry of Justice for stirring up strife between nationalities. Also in December, the government made

---

56. Sergei Kozlov, "The Office of the Public Prosecutor Accused Newspaper of Inflaming Interethnic Discord," *Nezavisimaia gazeta*, November 22, 1994, p. 3.

massive arrests of the Cossack leadership on charges of holding illegal meetings. The leadership of the Ministry of the Interior publicly announced the suspension of all Cossack activities.

However, after the dissolution of the parliament in 1995 and the evident choice to establish a regime based on the personal power of the president, the government's attitude toward Russian organizations seemed to change again, and was determined more by their degree of loyalty to the state than the ethnicity of their members.

To summarize, growing ethnic tension in Kazakhstan seems to stem from a combination of the following factors:

- general instability linked to the formation of a new, independent state;

- the fall in the standard of living;

- the rapid change in the social status (representation in political bodies, confidence about their position in Kazakh society) of the Kazakh and Russian ethnic groups;

- the indigenization of the main political institutions by replacing ethnic Russian officials with Kazakhs;

- the priority that Kazakhstan's founding legislation gives to the Kazakh people and Kazakh statehood;

- ambiguity and uncertainty caused by the balancing act between favoring the Kazakh ethnic group and the creation of a "national civilian state";

- the uncertain future of the Russian population in political, cultural, and economic terms; and

- uncertainty about the border between Kazakhstan and Russia in the consciousness of the Russian ethnic group.

External Factors

The foreign policy of the Kazakhstani government has been almost entirely subordinate to the task of stabilizing the internal situation. It has looked eastward with respect to culture, in accordance with the traditional values of the more conservative part of the Kazakh population; westward on questions of finance and technology, consonant with the wishes of the technocratic part of the population; and, finally, toward Russia in the political and economic spheres, following the hopes of the Slavic population. It has emphasized its role as "a natural link between East and West."[57]

These multiple orientations prevented Kazakhstan from embracing such proposals as the formation of Turkestan as a Central Asian confederation, advanced by Alash, one of the Kazakh nationalist organizations, and supported by similar groups in the other Central Asian countries. These same tendencies, together with the Kazakh tradition of opposition to emirates with a strong Islamic influence, also point to extremely unfavorable conditions for the growth of Islamic fundamentalism in Kazakhstan. The Kazakhstani government has repeatedly pointed to Turkey and Korea as models for its development. Even in the north and east, where the situation is fairly tense, the religious factor hardly plays a role, though mosques are being built in Kazakhstan and close links are maintained with the Islamic world.

KAZAKHSTANI-RUSSIAN RELATIONS

From 1990–1992, relations between Kazakhstan and Russia were dominated by the crisis and demise of the Soviet Union and the search of ways to exist independently. Tension between the Russian and Kazakh elites was very great at this time. Nazerbaev and some deputies from Kazakhstan in the Supreme Soviet of the Soviet Union hotly defended the preservation of the Soviet Union. They strongly opposed proposals by the government of the RSFSR to create a one-channel tax system, where the republics, rather than Moscow, would collect the taxes and forward a portion to the center,[58] with corresponding cuts in traditional subsidies from the Soviet center. Many Kazakh representatives openly criticized the policies of the RSFSR leadership. During the period of confrontation between the Russian and Union authorities, relations between Boris Yeltsin and Nazerbaev became strained. To the very last, Nazerbaev supported President Gorbachev.

---

57. See the article by Kazakhstan's Minister for Foreign Affairs, T. Suleimenov, "On Certain Directions in the Foreign Policy of Kazakhstan," *Mezhdunarodnaia zhizn'*, No. 1 (1994), p. 33.

58. The RSFSR recommended that all taxes be paid directly to republican governments, which would then forward a portion of the proceeds to the central government. Under a system in which republics could decide whether to pay or not, republics and republican leaders would gain valuable leverage and a way to weaken central structures. The Soviet government opposed the scheme for obvious reasons.

THE BORDER QUESTION. The most serious problem from 1990–92 was the Russian-Kazakh border in northeastern Kazakhstan, a region that had been separated from the RSFSR and included in the newly formed Kazakh Soviet Socialist Republic in 1936. By the end of August 1991, after the fiasco of the putsch in Moscow, Pavel Voshchanov, Boris Yeltsin's press secretary, stated that there was a frontier question, "the resolution of which will be possible and conceivable only with the existence of a firm corresponding agreement on relations within the union. In the case of a dissolution of these relations, the RSFSR retains for itself the right to raise the question of a review of the borders."[59] This statement provoked a number of mass demonstrations by Kazakh political organizations and protests by the Kazakhstani government. Urgent talks in Alma-Ata with a Russian delegation headed by Alexander Rutskoi, vice president of the RSFSR, did not produce results. But the two sides confirmed their adherence to former agreements and their obligations with respect to the rights of citizens and territorial integrity contained in the November 1990 treaty between the Kazakh SSR and the RSFSR. In addition, they expressed the intention of creating new, joint state formations. In December 1991, Gorbachev also raised the territorial question. In addition, many Russian politicians of differing stripes touched on the problem of the northern and eastern "Russian" regions of Kazakhstan.[60] According to one report, "in the beginning of 1992, Yeltsin repeated three times at the talks in Alma-Ata that

---

59. Pavel Voshchanov, "Statement by the Press Secretary of the President of the RSFSR," *Rossiiskaia gazeta*, August 27, 1991, p. 2.

60. Anatolii Sobchak, mayor of Saint Petersburg and an active participant in the democratic movement, and acclaimed film director, now deputy to the State Duma Stanislav Govorukhin have both addressed the issue in television interviews; Svetlana Goriacheva, a deputy of the Supreme Soviet of the RSFSR when she was member of the Russian Communist Party, brought up the ethnic regional issue in a speech to a Conference of Deputies of the Supreme Soviet; Alexander Solzhenitsyin has also addressed the issue in numerous interviews and in his work, *How to Rebuild Russia* (Paris: YMCA Press, 1990). The discussion of the territorial question was so heated that representatives of both ethnicities and numerous political groups exchanged angry statements. For example, Gorbachev incensed the public when he misstated that during Khrushchev's Virgin Lands Campaign Russia (allegedly) transferred five northern regions to Kazakhstan. In fact, territories were not transferred during the Virgin Lands Campaign, and the one transfer of a region with a Russian population to the Kazakh SSR occurred in 1936—not during the 1950s. The reaction of the Kazakhstan Soviet to Gorbachev's misstatement matched the public outcry; Gorbachev's assertion was declared "intolerable, neither expediting the improvement of the situation nor strengthening tradNgmal friendship

Russia has certain territorial claims on Kazakhstan and raised the question of the eastern regions of Kazakhstan."[61] However, Nazerbaev rejected attempts to discuss the issue. A period of even greater coolness in Russian-Kazakhstani relations followed. Despite the visit of Russian State Secretary Gennadi Burbulis in March 1992, which was mainly devoted to economic questions, relations remained distant. The Russian government ignored Nazerbaev's political initiatives for greater integration. Information on Kazakhstan, and especially on the situation in the northern and eastern regions, began to disappear from the Russian official press. Discussions were limited primarily to economic links between the countries, the grain supply, the continued use of military and space facilities located in Kazakhstan, and the division of Soviet property. In May 1992, the two countries signed a treaty on friendship, cooperation, and mutual aid that established a common military-strategic space and provided for the common use of military bases, test ranges, and installations. In exchange, Russia confirmed the inviolability of existing frontiers and the territorial integrity of Kazakhstan. In addition, the parties undertook "to proscribe and terminate on their territory the formation and activities of groups and organizations, as well as of individuals, directed against the independence and territorial integrity of both states or toward the exacerbation of relations between nationalities."[62] These provisions were invoked against a number of (mainly Cossack) organizations in Russia. Thereafter the question of frontiers was no longer touched upon at an official level. Later the idea became prominent among democratic circles close to the Russian government that Russia should have little interest in incorporating Kazakhstan's northern territories because these regions would likely come under the influence of the Southern Ural region and Siberia, which they considered quite conservative, with

---

and understanding among peoples." Citing the Constitution, the Declaration on State Sovereignty, the agreement between the RSFSR and Kazakhstan signed on November 21, 1990, and the communiqué of August 20, 1991, regarding results of negotiations between delegations, the Kazakhstan Soviet declared the Republic "one and indivisible." "Statement of the Kazakhstan Supreme Soviet No. 1005-XII," passed at the seventh session of the Supreme Soviet of the Republic of Kazakhstan, December 13, 1991.

61. "The National Doctrine of Russia," *Obozrevatel* (1994), p. 312.

62. "The Treaty On Friendship, Cooperation and Mutual Assistance Between the Republic of Kazakhstan and the Russian Federation" (signed May 25, 1992), *Kazakhstanskaia pravda*, July 23, 1992, p. 2.

Russian-nationalist and communist orientations. They thought that if these territories joined Russia, they would strengthen the forces opposing their own policies.

ECONOMIC ISSUES. Apart from the border question, the main efforts of Moscow and Alma-Ata continued to focus on economic ties. Considerable interest was expressed in establishing regional contacts. By April 1992, private enterprises established an interregional unified trade system for goods and raw materials between the Urals, Siberia, and northern Kazakhstan. In December 1992, Russian Prime Minister Victor Chernomyrdin signed a treaty in Alma-Ata on mutual supplies of raw materials and goods and the mutual payment of debts by enterprises. In January, May, and August 1993, the heads of administration of the Russian and Kazakhstani border regions held talks and signed a number of agreements related to economic questions. Chernomyrdin, Kazakh Prime Minister Sergei Tereshenko, and President Nazerbaev took part. But despite numerous meetings between highly placed officials, major political problems, including those connected with new forms of union, the ruble zone, and the use of the Baikonur space complex (which was the heart of the former Soviet space program and crucial to Russia), continued unresolved. Nor were border problems or interethnic relations addressed. Controversies between Russia and Kazakhstan and between the Kazakh and Russian populations of Kazakhstan were passed over in silence in the official press. Russia concentrated its efforts on seeking closer relations with Ukraine and Belarus, while Kazakhstan developed its links with the other Central Asian republics. Nevertheless, these meetings helped the regional elites of northern Kazakhstan to adapt to the new conditions in an independent Kazakhstan and had the intangible psychological effect of creating links with Russia. There was little open tension between the Kazakh and Russian populations in these territories. The overriding need was to maintain economic links and the supply of energy and oil to the industries in Kazakhstan that were heavily dependent on them.

In the second half of 1993, the Russian Central Bank accelerated Kazakhstan's transition to its own currency, the tenge. Although the relationship between the two countries again cooled, they continued to cooperate on economic issues and to undertake some new joint projects. The breakup of the ruble zone, while a necessary step in the consolidation of the economic independence of all the post-Soviet states, increased the difficulties of trade between centers in northern Kazakhstan and southern Siberia. The Russian interest was primarily in the development of oil projects in Kazakhstan. In August 1994, Chernomyrdin visited the town of Uralsk, where he met again with Kazakh Prime Minister Sergei Tereshenko. The main subject of the talks was the exploitation of the Karachaganak oil field. In November 1994, Chernomyrdin and the directors of the Chevron Corporation discussed the conditions under which the company would take part in the project to build an oil pipeline through Russian territory from the Tengiz oil field in Kazakhstan. Russia also participated in the repair and reconstruction of oil wells on Kazakhstani territory on the basis of agreements between Rosneft of Russia and Minneftgas of Kazakhstan.

From 1994 to the first half of 1995, further rapprochement developed between Kazakhstan and Russia. The Kazakhstani side touted this as a realization of its conception of a Eurasian Union. However, despite the numerous meetings and agreements during this period, rapprochement was slow and full of difficulties. The basic area of agreement was the accord reached on cooperation in the processing and transport of Kazakhstani oil to outside countries using Russian pipelines.

In October 1994, a CIS summit meeting in Moscow approved agreements on greater economic integration within the CIS, including "The Basic Direction of Integrated Development of the Commonwealth of Independent States" and the "Future Plan for Integrated Development of the Commonwealth." In January 1995, during high-level negotiations between Russia and Kazakhstan, a declaration on the widening and deepening of Russian-Kazakhstani cooperation was signed, along with a decision on the formation of joint armed forces and the establishment of a general military-strategic space. Documents were also signed on the creation of a customs union, a free-trade regime, and currency convertibility. A treaty on the joint protection of external borders and the establishment of a united command of forces abroad was also signed.[63] However, in February 1995, the leaders of CIS countries did not pass Russia's proposal to create a joint system of defense and a common external border. Consequently, two tracks of cooperation have emerged between CIS countries, with Kazakhstan and Russia moving the most quickly.[64]

Throughout this period, the Kazakhstani government's attitude toward the nuclear weapons it inherited from the Soviet Union was

63. "Russia and Kazakhstan Proceed to Establish United Armed Forces," *Postfactum Official Chronicle* (electronic agency), January 20, 1995.

64. "On the Summit Meeting in Alma-Ata," ITAR-TASS, February 11, 1995.

directly subordinated to economic interests.[65] Beginning with the 1991 announcement of the retention of the nuclear weapons on Kazakh territory under dual Kazakhstani-Russian control until Kazakhstan signed the Nuclear Non-Proliferation Treaty in 1993, transferred the weapons to Russia, and declared its non-nuclear status, the Kazakhstani position on the nuclear question became more flexible in proportion to the amount of credits, assistance, and political concessions it received. That is not, however, to imply that the Kazakhstani authorities were unambivalent about what to do with Kazakhstan's nuclear inheritance, or that their intentions were always transparent. As late as January 1994, Kazakhstan's ambassador to Iran was quoted as saying that Kazakhstan would not eliminate or transfer its nuclear weapons out of its territory.[66] However, at the December 1994 CSCE meeting in Budapest, Kazakhstan formally agreed to eliminate all of its nuclear weapons by 1996. Built into this agreement were a number of security assurances for Kazakhstan and other former Soviet signatories, including the security of their independence and territorial integrity, guarantees against unfair economic pressure, and security against attack from outside states.

ETHNIC QUESTIONS

Moscow did not begin to pay serious attention to the problem of interethnic tension in Kazakhstan until the end of 1993. At that point, the Russian Ministry of Foreign Affairs confronted the Kazakhstani government on two main issues: dual Russian-Kazakh citizenship for ethnic Russians and the status of the Russian language in Kazakhstan. As discussed above, the Kazakhstani side did not accept dual citizenship on the grounds that this was not current world practice and that it would create difficulties in defining the duties of citizens. In the autumn of 1993, Nazerbaev was "unable" to receive Russian Minister of Foreign Affairs Andrei Kozyrev, who had come to Kazakhstan to discuss the problem of the ethnic Russians. The common interpretation of this action is that Nazerbaev was quite unhappy about the public references of Russian politicians to the problems of "Russians abroad" and deliberately snubbed Kozyrev.

---

65. Kazakhstan inherited 104 SS-18 10-warhead silo-based intercontinental ballistic missiles (ICBMs). Amy Wolf, *Nuclear Weapons in the Former Sovier Union: Issues and Prospects,* a report from the Congressional Research Service, (Washington, D.C.: Library of Congress, 1992), p. 1.

66. "Statement of a Kazakhstani Representative," ITAR-TASS, January 28, 1994.

The Kazakhstani side denied the existence of any problems connected with the Russian population. "The problem of the Russian-speaking population does not exist in Kazakhstan," stated Kazakhstani Minister for Foreign Affairs Kanat Saudabaev, speaking to journalists.[67] After the Kazakhstan parliamentary elections in early 1994, President Nazerbaev visited Moscow at the end of March and signed twenty-three accords with Russia, including one concerning the Russian leasing of the Baikonur space center and another that provided citizenship to individuals of any ethnic group who move to Kazakhstan to take up permanent residence. Even after the March 1994 agreements, Moscow remained generally uninvolved in the problems of the Russians in northern and eastern Kazakhstan. The Russian Ministry of Foreign Affairs supported the Kazakhstani position on the regulation of citizenship in Kazakhstan, and abandoned its previous proposal to introduce dual citizenship for ethnic Russians in Kazakhstan. During the high-level negotiations in January 1995 discussed above, a treaty was signed on the legal status of citizens of the Russian Federation permanently residing on the territory of Kazakhstan, and citizens of Kazakhstan living on the territory of the Russian Federation. At the same time, the presidents also signed an agreement on the simplification of the procedure for the acquisition of citizenship for citizens of the Russian Federation who move to Kazakhstan to take up permanent residence, and for citizens of Kazakhstan who move to the Russian Federation. It is worth noting that Russian organizations in Kazakhstan have expressed a negative attitude toward these agreements, considering them half-measures that permit the governments of Kazakhstan and Russia to drop the problem from their agendas. Instead, they continue to lobby for dual citizenship, which ethnic Kazakhs already have.[68]

It was more often individual Russian journalists and "nationalist patriotic" social organizations, rather than the Russian government,

---

67. The 1994 conclusion on the citizenship question was that an individual should be able to acquire citizenship from the government of the territory of permanent residence. The goal of the Kazakhs is simply to try to deny the existence of a problem with the Russian-language population. See Kazakhstani Minister of Foreign Affairs Kanat Saudabaev quoted in "Problems With Regard to the Russian-Speaking Population Do Not Exist in Kazakhstan," INFO-TASS, June 3, 1994.

68. See the appeal to the State Duma of the Federal Assembly of the Russian Federation from the leaders of the organizations Lad, Russian Community, Russian Center, the Semirechi Cossacks, and a group of deputies of the Supreme Soviet of Kazakhstan, February 4, 1995.

who drew attention to the situation of the Russian-speaking community and organizations of ethnic Russians in Kazakhstan. The most active in this respect was the Congress of Russian Communities, based in Moscow and representing the Russian-speaking populations in the former Soviet republics. This organization supports Russian autonomy in northern Kazakhstan or its legal incorporation into the Russian Federation.[69] The growing support from such organizations in Russia, as well as the increased pressure from the Kazakhstani leadership on the ethnic Russian associations in Kazakhstan discussed above, led to an intensification of the activities among ethnic Russians. The new Russian Federal Assembly elected in December 1993, unlike most other official bodies, paid a certain amount of attention to the problem of interethnic relations in Kazakhstan—primarily because its members represented constituencies that were concerned with the interests of Russians abroad. Thus, at a press conference held by the Committee on CIS Affairs of the State Duma, Russian observers of the Kazakhstani parliamentary elections maintained that the government's policy of defending the rights of the Russian population was correct as far as it went, but that not enough was being done in this respect and that Russia's aim in relation to Kazakhstan should be integration in a closer union than the CIS in order to jointly meet the challenges posed by the outside world.[70] Deputy Anatoli Dolgopolov, a Russian Cossack, drew attention to the situation of the Cossacks and the Russian population in Kazakhstan and noted with regret that the absence of a positive Kazakhstani government program reduced the possibility of finding a peaceful solution to the problems confronting the two states—a fact that was fraught with "most serious consequences for Russian-Kazakhstani relations," which should be avoided. He also noted that the tendency toward radicalism among the Cossacks might increase in these conditions.

---

69. The Congress of Russian Communities and the chairman of the Executive Committee, Dmitri Rogozin, are headquartered in Moscow. Members of the Congress include organizations and representatives of the Russian-speaking population in the republics of the former Soviet Union. "Bullets are Flying," *Glasnost*, April 15, 1994, p. 2.

70. Material from the chairman of the Commission for CIS Affairs and Links with Fellow Countrymen in the Russian State Duma, Konstantin Zatulin. "On The Results of the Visit of a Group of Deputies of the Federal Assembly, Observing the Elections to the Supreme Soviet of Kazakhstan," press release, March 11, 1994, p. 5.

In Russia there are several approaches to the issue of the Russian population of Kazakhstan, ranging from the official position, which notes the existence of problems regarding the status of the Russian language and citizenship of ethnic Russians; to the position of the Cossack organizations seeking recognition of autonomy for the Russian-populated regions; to demands (also by Cossack organizations) for the formation of a Federal Republic of Kazakhstan; and even to proposals, mainly raised by the national patriotic and communist opposition, for a Kazakhstani state within the frontiers of a reconstituted Soviet Union.[71] There is no public opinion polling information on how the majority of Russians in Russia consider the question of the Russian population of Kazakhstan. It is certainly an issue that many people believe needs to be settled, but it is not clear in what manner. These are seen as matters that will be decided by political elites, and there are few channels through which the public can express opinions.

THE KAZAKHSTANI POSITION ON REGIONAL RELATIONS

While many military, economic, ethnic, and cultural issues were discussed in the framework of the CIS, and a number of agreements were reached, many Russians in Kazakhstan considered the CIS insufficient as a unifying organization because it had no means to handle issues of

---

71. In general, the Russian leadership is unconcerned about the problems of Central Asia. According to Anatolii Adamishin, a famous Soviet and Russian diplomat who knows the upper echelons quite well, the Soviet elite experienced "a fear of the Central Asian republics." Anatolii Adamishin, "Evreiskii Anekdot" (A Jewish Anecdote), *Nezavisimaia gazeta*, September 15, 1994, p. 5. It is obvious that the Russian elite inherited this quality. In contrast to many other republics of the former Soviet Union that declared their independence once Soviet central power began to weaken, the republics of Central Asia were forced into statehood by the Soviet Union's collapse, and denied the continuation of the intimate political relationship they had shared with the Russian Federation. Only in 1993–94 did a representative of official circles, Presidential Council member Andranik Migranian, support "involving Kazakhstan in close economic and political relations with Russia." Migranian did so in an article in which he cited the opinions of various Russian politicians and academics. "Russia and the Near Abroad," *Nezavisimaia gazeta*, January 18, 1994, p. 5.

Discussion of the proposed Eurasian Union evoked similar responses. Thus, Chairman of the Russian State Duma Ivan Rybkin noted in a meeting with Kazakhstani Foreign Minister Kanat Saudabaev that Nazerbaev's idea of forming a Eurasian Union was well received in Russia "and in spite of the fact that not all states of the CIS are ready to reunite on that basis, we are ready for such a Union." ("Chairman of the State Duma Met with the Minister of Foreign Affairs of Kazakhstan," INFO-TASS, June 2, 1994.) A similar position is held by one of the

importance to ordinary people. Despite the existence of the CIS, it remained difficult to post parcels to relatives abroad because of the different postal systems, to send money because of constant fluctuations of the exchange rate, and to visit relatives in other republics. The differing currencies also made trade difficult between the southern Ural region of Russia and Western Siberia and northern Kazakhstan. Indeed, many politicians and analysts considered that the CIS, through 1992 and even 1993, was more a civilized divorce than a new form of union of the former Soviet republics.

In general, CIS decisions have wide resonance in the mass media, but largely go unrealized. It is sufficient to remember the inconsequence of the decision to preserve the single ruble zone and common armed forces. The same may be said about many mutual Kazakhstani-Russian agreements. For example, after concluding the agreement in January 1995 between Kazakhstan and Russia, the customs border between the two countries was removed, only to be reinstated in March 1995, since the treaty was not adequately implemented.

President Nazerbaev tried to compensate for the policies of "Kazakhization" that his government pursued by actively supporting greater integration within an inter-state entity that would be stronger than the existing CIS. As the internal situation worsened, the external proposals of the Kazakhstani government became more unambiguous, culminating in Nazerbaev's April 1994 proposal to create a

---

authors of the Belovezh Accords, Vice Premier of the Russian Federation Sergei Shakhrai, who believes that there are no alternatives to reintegration and that any consideration of such action should be on a voluntary and equal basis with preservation of political sovereignty of the states. (Sergei Shakhrai, "There Are No Alternatives to Reintegration," INFO-TASS, July 6, 1994.) Finally, at a roundtable discussion on "Eurasian Space: The Potential for Integration and its Realization," hosted by Nazerbaev, none of those invited from the Russian leadership took part. Sergei Shakhrai was "virtually forbidden" to attend by Chernomyrdin. Victor Kijanitsa, "Nazaerbaev Against a Good Backdrop," *Moscow News*, September 25–October 2, 1994, p. 10.

The Russian public is also discussing the issue of how close and how strong the possible union between Russia and Kazakhstan should be. In a 1994 television interview, Alexander Solzhenitsyin proposed that Russia and Kazakhstan not be limited by Nazerbaev's proposals, but pursue all forms of cooperation that, together with Kazakhstan, would secure Russia's southern borders. Meanwhile, communist and patriotic opposition has adopted a harsher position supporting a wide range of approaches from voluntary restoration of the Soviet Union to the use of economic pressure on the new states or gradual restoration of one state.

The Liberal Democratic Party of Vladimir Zhirinovsky advocates the consolidation of the Russian state within the Soviet Union's 1977 borders and considers the founding of so-called independent states within its territory to have been unlawful.

Eurasian Union as not only an economic union, but also as some form of political union. The proposed union was to include supranational bodies to coordinate economic, defense, and foreign policies, a Council of Ministers of Defense and Foreign Affairs, a single parliament, and common citizenship. In the absence of serious support for the union among CIS leaders, it was proposed that interested states could join individually. However, the Russian leadership was very reserved in its response to this idea, and supported instead the creation of a common economic space, which was already under discussion within the framework of the CIS. It is difficult to know if the Eurasian Union was a serious proposal by the Kazakhstani leadership, since Russia had never indicated genuine interest. It is possible that the proposal may have had more domestic political utility for Nazerbaev, gaining support for him from the Russian population in Kazakhstan. There was no mention in this proposal of the status of the Russian language or territorial autonomy for certain areas.

By 1994, a close alliance with powerful states was officially viewed as harmful to Kazakhstan in the context of its envisioned role as a link between the East and the West. For example, academician A. Koshanov, director of the Institute for Economics of the Kazakhstani Academy of Sciences, argued that "Kazakhstan, for instance, or any other Central Asian state cannot and should not hurry to join some kind of economic union or artificial confederative formation with more developed states since its obvious fate would be to again serve as a source of cheap raw materials and a market for stale goods."[72]

The formation of a Central Asian Economic Union comprising Kazakhstan, Kyrgyzstan, Turkmenistan, Tajikistan, and Uzbekistan was more compatible with the above conceptualization of Kazakhstan's interests than a union with Russia. This economic union was created in spite of the rivalry between Kazakhstan and Uzbekistan for regional leadership, the cautious attitude of Turkmenistan to any kind of union, and the continuing internal conflict in Tajikistan. Kazakhstan, Kyrgyzstan, and Uzbekistan have already moved much further among themselves in creating an economic union stronger than the CIS, having established a supranational body, the Interstate Economic Committee, designed to set up a unified economic space and facilitate free trade among the republics. These economic accords

---

72. A.K. Koshanov and B.K. Kazbekov, "The Structure of the Economy of Kazakhstan in the New System of Integration of the States of Central Asia," *Obshchestvo i ekonomika*, No. 3–4 (1994), p. 29.

and decisions do not seem to have had any real political impact in Kazakhstan and on its various peoples. The economic value of these ties was much less than the economic value of securing Russia as a trading partner. The Islamic factor, which might have been a point of concern for the Slavic population, did not in fact materialize. The influence of religion in Kazakhstan remained quite low, and so closer ties with the Central Asian countries were generally not seen as a threat.

THE ROLE OF INTERNATIONAL ORGANIZATIONS

The material presented in this section is based exclusively on reports from the Russian-language mass media in Kazakhstan and Russia. Materials from the international organizations themselves were not used. This approach makes it possible to show how the Russian-language mass media have evaluated the activities of international organizations, which reflects their perception of the importance of visits and speeches by members of delegations from international organizations. There is very little analysis of the effect of these visits, which reflects the belief that these organizations have only a marginal impact on the politics of the new states and can have little direct effect on the situation.

While Kazakhstan was establishing itself as an independent state, international organizations engaged primarily in exploratory activities, acquainting themselves with the general situation. Their initial evaluations were largely based on information obtained during meetings with political leaders and government representatives in Alma-Ata, and thus were not very representative of the situation in the country as a whole. In July 1992, the Kazakhstani press reported that Western experts had assessed the interethnic situation in Kazakhstan as satisfactory.[73] During this initial stage in 1992–93, the visits of representatives of international organizations had no visible impact on interethnic relations. As time went on, the post-Soviet

73. In the opinion of this author, the following INFO-TASS report, reproduced below in full, fairly well characterizes the dominant trend in media reportage on the ethnic situation in Kazakhstan. According to Kazakh Telegraph Agency correspondent Tatiana Zhurbenko: "A delegation of the Council of Europe, led by its chairman, the Minister of Foreign Affairs of Turkey, Hikmet Chetin, and the General Secretary of the Council, Catherine Lalumiere of France, is in town. The representatives of this influential intergovernmental organization were received by Vice President of the Republic Erik Asanbaev who noted that 'Kazakhstan is going to structure its state on ethnic principles.' Asanbaev also stated that Kazakhstan is the only republic in the CIS where the indigenous population numbers fewer than the Russian-speaking population. Therefore the concern of the

Kazakhstani leadership, and particularly President Nazerbaev, devoted much attention to international organizations in an endeavor to raise its status both within Kazakhstan and in the eyes of the world community and to obtain economic assistance from the West. Between 1993 and 1994, the activities and evaluations of international organizations played an active role in the political life of Kazakhstan. This was largely because President Nazerbaev was trying to preserve his image as a reformer and a modernizer and to encourage Western investment in the economy. For Nazerbaev, his external image was very important, since the future prospects of Kazakhstan depended on his finding new ways to develop Kazakhstan's wealth in raw materials, and he needed outside help and links in order to do so. Thus, a critical part of his policy was to build up the image of Kazakhstan as a fruitful and prosperous place. In this, as in all his policies, Nazerbaev had to be careful to manage all three of his political audiences—inside Kazakhstan, among the CIS countries, and in the West.

The Kazakhstani government's attentiveness to international organizations was also strengthened by its desire to gain the support of influential member governments as a way of reinforcing Kazakhstan's internal and external security. President Nazerbaev emphasized this point in his comments after attending the CSCE summit in Budapest in December 1994. He stated that the memorandum signed there on guarantees for the security of the republics of the former Soviet Union, in addition to the Nuclear Non-Proliferation Treaty, resolved "today's most important task—the preservation of the sovereignty of Kazakhstan."[74]

The CSCE and the United Nations have been the most active and influential organizations in Kazakhstan, but the Council of Europe has also made a number of visits.

---

government and parliament about protecting the language and culture of the Kazakh people is perfectly natural. But at the same time he emphasized that the interests of representatives of other peoples will be taken into account. A law has already been passed which gives Russian the status of language of communication among nationalities. Catherine Lalumiere expressed satisfaction with the delicate way in which the language question is being resolved in Kazakhstan. In her opinion, the republic can set an example for the world. Speaking of the republic's economic problems, members of the delegation affirmed their intention to further the consolidation of Kazakhstan's position in the world arena." "Representatives of the European Union Expressed Satisfaction with the Method of Resolving Nationalities Problems in Kazakhstan," INFO-TASS, July 17, 1992.

74. "The President of Kazakhstan Praises the Memorandum on Guarantees of Security for the Republics, Signed in Budapest," *Interfax*, December 9, 1994.

CSCE/OSCE. The CSCE's most important activity in Kazakhstan was sending observers to the March 1994 parliamentary elections. As discussed above, the CSCE observers made a number of serious criticisms of the electoral process, which had important political repercussions. The CSCE's significance in relation to security issues has also been mentioned. Beyond that, there have been a variety of visits and delegations under CSCE auspices, primarily related to problems of ethnic relations and human rights.

In April 1992, a group of experts from the CSCE visited Alma-Ata to acquaint themselves with the political and economic life of the republic and to report to the CSCE. This group met with representatives of various parties, organizations, and movements based in Alma-Ata. At a meeting with journalists, the delegation made inquiries about the publication of periodicals, problems with the financing of newspapers, the publications of various "national" groups, and the language problem in Kazakhstan. They also had separate meetings with Deputy Prime Minister Yevgeniy Grigoriyevich Yezhikov-Babarkhanov.[75]

Soon after, the U.S. ambassador to the CSCE, John Maresco, visited Kazakhstan, mainly to discuss Kazakhstan's participation in the CSCE. He met President Nazerbaev, who told him that Kazakhstan's policies were in full accord with the CSCE principles.[76] In the same month, while the Swedish foreign minister was serving as the president of the CSCE, a delegation from the Swedish Ministry of Foreign Affairs visited Alma-Ata in the capacity of official representatives of the organization to study the observance of human rights and democratic freedoms in the republic on the eve of Kazakhstan's confirmation as a full member of the CSCE. They also saw as part of their task informing the Kazakhstani public about the general structure and activities of the CSCE, including how human rights are understood and how democracy functions in a law-based society. The delegation explained that the CSCE saw the resolution of acute conflict situations as its priority task, and evaluated the situation in Kazakhstan as "transitional" and "complex," concurring with the evaluation of the

---

75. "The OSCE Delegation Meets With Journalists," *Kazakhstanskaia pravda*, April 4, 1992, p. 1.

76. Leila Tylebaeva, "Minister of Foreign Affairs of Kazakhstan Receives the US Ambassador to the CSCE," INFO-TASS, May 5, 1992; and Murat Buldekbaev, "President of Kazakhstan: The Principles of the CSCE Are in Full Harmony with Kazakhstan's Existing Policies," INFO-TASS, May 6, 1992.

mission that had visited the country in April. According to these evaluations, serious steps were being taken to ensure the rights of individuals and to create better living conditions. Various independent organizations and associations had been founded in Kazakhstan, meetings were freely held, there was no censorship, and a new constitution was being drafted. Overall prospects for the development of Kazakhstan were evaluated as good. However, at a meeting with journalists, Nina Shumilkina, a member of the Association for the Defense of Human Rights in Kazakhstan, made a statement that strongly differed from the evaluations of the CSCE representatives. She said that no mechanism for the defense of human rights existed in the republic and offered to meet separately with members of the CSCE delegation. She expressed the opinion that only the presence of a permanent representative of the UN in Kazakhstan could ensure accurate information on the situation.[77]

Later that month, a CSCE working group made up of three Americans visited Kazakhstan to study the human rights problem and reached a less sanguine conclusion. In Alma-Ata, the group met with the representatives of various public movements and parties, including those of the opposition. In the course of these meetings, the CSCE representatives expressed the opinion that the preconditions existed in Kazakhstan for a repetition of the Yugoslavia scenario. This possibility was further aggravated by the fact that extremist parties, movements, and individuals were using the new conditions of free speech to further their aims, and that parties with fundamentally opposed tenets could divide society and lead to a schism. The members of the group stated that the government of Kazakhstan was not yet democratic and that there was no indication that this would happen soon. They offered to help search for areas of common interest between the various parties and groups if they were prepared to live in one state. They also suggested that it was essential that the Russian language be given the status of a second official language, since less than half of the citizens knew Kazakh, while Russian was known by the overwhelming majority. In their view, this step could lower the possibility of conflicts.[78] As noted above, this recommendation was not adopted by the Kazakh government, although the

---

77. T. Kostina, "Yet Another Visit: But There Is Swedish Interest," *Kazakhstanskaia pravda*, May 15, 1992, p. 1.

78. N. Zhorov, "They Know What They Want," *Kazakhstanskaia pravda*, May 28, 1992, p. 1.

1993 constitution did recognize Russian as the language of interethnic communication, which was a symbolic concession since this designation had no legal meaning.

In February 1994, CSCE General Secretary Wilhelm Hoynck paid a working visit to Kazakhstan. During the visit, he discussed Kazakhstan's desire for greater integration in the CSCE and the problem of ending the conflicts in Central Asia, in particular the conflict in Tajikistan.[79]

In April 1994, the CSCE High Commissioner for National Minorities, Max van der Stoel visited Kazakhstan and held a seminar on the "human dimension."[80] According to press accounts, van der Stoel praised Kazakhstan's policies on relations between nationalities and voiced his support for its position on human rights for its citizens.[81]

THE UNITED NATIONS. A UN delegation first visited Kazakhstan in June 1992 and reached an agreement with President Nazerbaev on the opening of a UN mission in Alma-Ata. The Kazakhstani side expressed its desire that the mission should serve simultaneously as a central office for all of Central Asia and operate in the neighboring states as well.[82] The UN was represented in Kazakhstan by the coordinator of the UN Development Programme, Nigel D. Ringrouz, who in 1993 had developed a plan of support for the Kazakh government's program to reform the economy, which envisaged granting technical aid and expert advice to various organizations working in promising areas. In February 1993, a UN diplomatic mission opened in Kazakhstan, headed by the permanent UN representative in Alma-Ata, Julian de Wette. This office monitors activities in all of Central Asia.[83]

COUNCIL OF EUROPE. In July 1992, a delegation from the Council of Europe visited Alma-Ata to investigate the general political situation. It was headed by the chairman of the Council of Europe, Turkish

79. Ivan Zaharenko, "The Visit of the General Secretary of the CSCE, William Hoynck, to Almaty," INFO-TASS, February 23, 1994.

80. The CSCE has embraced a human dimension policy, based on the respect for and promotion of economic, social, cultural, civil, and political rights. In recent years this has led to the creation of the office of the High Commissioner for National Minorities (HCNM) and the Office for Democratic Institutions and Human Rights (ODIHR).

81. "CSCE High Commissioner for Refugees and National Minorities Conducts a Seminar," Interfax, April 25, 1994.

82. Murat Buldekbaev, "President Nazerbaev of Kazakhstan Receives a UN Delegation," INFO-TASS, June 16, 1992.

83. Gennadi Kulagin, "The UN Representative in Kazakhstan States Readiness to Support Nazerbaev's Initiatives to Ensure a Degree of Confidence in Asia," INFO-TASS, February 16, 1993.

Minister of Foreign Affairs Hikmet Chetin, and Council Secretary General Catherine Lalumiere.[84]

In March 1995, a delegation from the European Parliament, headed by Carlos Robles Pique, visited Almaty and called for the speedy convening of parliamentary elections. The delegation's visit was part of an agreed program to strengthen cooperation between the European Parliament and the Supreme Soviet of Kazakhstan. Pique commented that the Partnership and Cooperation Agreement between the European Parliament and Kazakhstan, which Nazerbaev had signed on January 24, 1995, in Brussels, could not be ratified since it was impossible to abide by Article 7 of the agreement, which envisioned the cooperation of the European Parliament and the parliament of Kazakhstan—because Kazakhstan now lacked a parliament. Pique expressed confidence that the government of Kazakhstan would address the increasingly complicated situation and speed up the conduct of new parliamentary elections. He passed on the information that the Council of Ministers of the European Union had issued a statement on the political situation in Kazakhstan; it expressed concern at the crisis and the blow to the democratic foundations of the country. The EU Council of Ministers urged Kazakhstan to quickly hold new elections with the participation of international observers. At the same time, members of the European Parliament delegation announced that they would respect the decision of Kazakh judicial and executive powers to recognize that the old parliament was illegitimate, and to appeal for new parliamentary elections.

To sum up the role of international organizations in Kazakhstan, the bulk of their activities has focused on reviewing legislation enacted by the government and suggesting correctives in line with international standards. They could, however, have been more energetic in supporting democratic institutions. In a regime based on personal presidential power, the external factor has a certain influence in leveling out the situation of the various ethnic groups because, as mentioned earlier, the president is very sensitive to external pressures.

Nevertheless, these kinds of activities are inherently not very effective because Kazakhstan, like most of the states that emerged from the breakup of the Soviet Union, is not a law-based society. Rather, it is a society where traditional types of social relationships dominate, and where laws regulate only a small portion of the social relationships;

---

84. Zhurbenko, "Representatives of the European Union Expressed Satisfaction with the Method of Resolving Nationalities Problems in Kazakhstan."

the *nomenklatura* politics established during the Soviet period, and perhaps more significantly the clan structures and hierarchies that survived the Soviet period, play a much more important role. Since these deeper social patterns are beyond the influence of international organizations, their activities so far have been useful but somewhat marginal to the development of the situation. In a place as remote as Kazakhstan with such strong internal forces, it is difficult to imagine outside forces like international organizations having much impact. At the margin, however, the activities of international organizations were certainly useful. The monitoring of the 1994 election in particular was viewed by the non-Kazakh population as having had a positive effect since it gave an audience to those dissatisfied with the conduct of the elections.

Conclusion

It seems that the end of 1995 was a turning point for Kazakhstan. The Kazakhstani government too will have to decide its further political course. Developments in the rest of the 1990s and beyond will depend almost entirely on the policies of President Nazerbaev, since parliament will not function until future elections. Kazakhstani authorities predict that economic reform will speed up, that this coming period will not be easy for Kazakhstan, and that the time and the possibility for the achievement of social concord is receding.

For the longer range, there are several possible scenarios for the development of relations between Kazakhs and Russians in Kazakhstan.

MAINTENANCE OF THE STATUS QUO

The status quo is not likely to persist. The principal challenge for independent Kazakhstan is building a national state that gives "the right to self-determination to the Kazakh nation" in conditions where the ethnic Kazakhs do not constitute a clear majority. But Kazakhstan will continue to confront difficulties in preserving its unity. On the one hand, the growing nationalistic mood that is increasingly evident in Russia will increase support for the ethnic Russian groups in Kazakhstan, whether officially from the Russian government or otherwise. On the other hand, the group associated with President Nazerbaev that is trying to play the role of the patron of the center is now meeting with growing opposition from the Kazakh elite. The former political balance has already been disrupted and now all political forces are engaged in the search for a new balance. Trying not to lose the initiative, Nazerbaev has taken the first step by disbanding parliament and securing by referendum the extension of his term through December 2000.

CIVIL WAR BETWEEN ETHNIC RUSSIANS AND ETHNIC KAZAKHS?

Unfortunately, the possibility cannot be ruled out that the situation may degenerate into a serious armed conflict. Isolated conflicts between various groups in Kazakhstan are, however, unlikely to acquire the dimensions of a full-scale civil war: there are few areas of mixed population, and the centers of the Russian north and east and the Kazakh south and west are separated by great stretches of territory in central Kazakhstan, most of it very harsh and uninhabitable. Moreover, estimates by military specialists suggest that in the event of such a conflict, the army would not be able to participate since most of its officer corps and higher command are ethnic Russians, while most soldiers are ethnic Kazakhs.

TERRITORIAL CHANGE

There are three possible forms of territorial change that could take place in Kazakhstan. First, a federation with increased independence for all regions, including for Russians in the northern and eastern territories, could be established. Second, autonomous territorial entities in the north and east could be set up for the Russian (Slavic) population. Finally, the northern and eastern territories predominantly inhabited by Russians could separate from the rest of Kazakhstan in a relatively peaceful manner.

All three variants are completely unacceptable to the Kazakhstani leadership and to the Kazakh population as a whole. However, among part of the Russian population they have steady supporters, although most do not show their support publicly, and it often must be read between the lines in Russian-language publications. If the ethnic problems are left unresolved, the more extremist options will become more popular, and there is some possibility that the most extreme scenario—secession—could occur. There is a small chance that some of the northern and eastern territories could secede without a full-scale civil war—through a referendum, for example—but this would inevitably involve localized standoffs and serious armed conflict.

EMIGRATION OF THE RUSSIAN POPULATION FROM KAZAKHSTAN

Although the flow of Russian emigration from Kazakhstan has grown considerably in recent years, it is difficult to imagine that all the militants of the ethnic Russian movement will leave the areas now densely inhabited by Russians. Paradoxically, this could be one of the most dangerous scenarios, since the existing emigration of Russians from Kazakhstan actually strengthens the chances of the separatism. Many of the émigrés are leaving regions where a considerable part of the population are ethnic Kazakhs. Thus areas of mixed population— the links between the "Russian" north and the "Kazakh" south—are disappearing, and each group is becoming more concentrated. Because these areas of mixed populations and a roughly fifty-fifty ethnic balance exists in Kazakhstan, each side has a vested interest in reaching a mutually acceptable resolution. It is possible that as the population balance between the two groups is disrupted, the Russians who remain will feel themselves increasingly surrounded and weakened, and their hopes that the situation will improve in the foreseeable future will fade. Along with this would grow the desire to resolve their situation more quickly, using more radical measures in the territories where Russians form a majority. It is arguable that the large numbers of the Russian community and the possibility of effecting change through protests and legislation have a moderating influence. But if the Russian community's numbers begin to decline sharply, those remaining could become more defensive and radicalized.

NATIONAL-CULTURAL AUTONOMY FOR THE RUSSIAN POPULATION
Russian proposals to create national cultural autonomy are regarded even by their proponents as a half-measure and not a real solution. Such an autonomy would follow the common Soviet model of political and administrative unity, giving the Russian population control over the sphere of language and culture. This result could only be realized, however, where there is a strong civil society, and where individuals would have the initiative and ability to open private educational institutions, cultural organizations, and the like. But in the post-Soviet republics, the role of government in these spheres is still very large, and it is not clear how such a project would be realized without government involvement. So far, such proposals have been met with resistance from leaders at various levels in the Kazakhstani government.

RUSSIAN ASSIMILATION IN THE KAZAKH COMMUNITY
Even in the very distant future, assimilation of the non-Kazakh population does not seem possible, since the majority of non-Kazakhs are

city dwellers working in industry and the service sector. Almost all urban areas in Kazakhstan remain primarily Russian-speaking. The cultural and social setting in which the Russian-speaking population lives does not present a clear necessity to learn the Kazakh language, the introduction of which is seen as forced by the government. Forcing such a changeover in language will be very difficult.

A CONFEDERATE STATE BETWEEN KAZAKHSTAN AND RUSSIA

The establishment of a confederate state including Russia and Kazakhstan could also be considered a potentially favorable scenario. Until now, however, such proposals have met with strong resistance from the Russian government. The organization of such a union would call into question the actions of the Russian leadership which, in 1991, helped break up the Soviet Union, and thus deliberately ruptured the link with Kazakhstan. Establishing a new entity would inevitably require new elections and a reorganization of the entire state structure. Russia is completely unprepared to do this. The difficulties connected with the formation of such a confederated state are simply too great, especially taking into account the differences in the economies of the two countries, which, though once compatible in the context of the command system, have developed very differently in the last few years.

CREATION OF A CIVIL STATE IN WHICH ETHNIC KAZAKHS AND ETHNIC RUSSIANS ARE EQUALLY REPRESENTED IN ALL SPHERES OF LIFE

This seems to be the strategy of the Kazakhstani government: to build a multiethnic state with equal rights for the two largest ethnic groups that also takes into account the interests of smaller groups. So far this has not been achieved. It faces strong opposition from powerful representatives of the Kazakh clans, and a significant part of the Russian-speaking population perceives the formal position of the Kazakhstani government—reflected in legislation and speeches by the leadership on "the equality of the two groups of the population" and "striving for interethnic accord"—as pure rhetoric. Nevertheless, this is clearly one of the more acceptable scenarios. The issue is whether the existing tensions and the extreme mutual suspicion between Kazakhs and Russians can be overcome so that it can be brought into being.

Chapter 12

Commentary on Kazakhstan

Henry Hale

As ethnically charged violence has broken out across the former Soviet Union, Kazakhstan shines as a model of peace and concord in the eyes of many outside observers. Yet split nearly across the middle between Russians in the North and Kazakhs in the South, Kazakhstan might seem to be a prime candidate for the eruption of deadly ethnic violence. Russian demands for ties to the "motherland," the scenario goes, ignite patriotic passions as they strike calls for Kazakh independence. Indeed, Slavs in the former Soviet republic of Moldova took to arms in order to join their sliver of land to Russia. How then can we explain peace in Kazakhstan?

Russian sociologist Vladimir Barsamov takes up this challenge in his chapter, rigorously explicating sources of tension between ethnic Kazakhs and Russians in Kazakhstan.[1] His answer is the nimble politicking of Kazakhstan's prudent President Nursultan Nazerbaev, and perhaps the forbearance of the republic's Russian population. He contends, however, that both of these sources of stability are encountering their limits, especially as they are being dashed against the unresponsiveness of the Russian Federation to its own neighboring co-ethnics. Events, he implies, are hurtling toward the rise of a strong secessionist movement in northern Kazakhstan, and the changes in Russian and Kazakhstani policy that could prevent this appear unlikely.

Barsamov's account represents an important step in improving our understanding of the ethnic dynamics of collapsing empires, particularly the problems irredentas pose. His chapter represents one

---

1. "Russians" may be more appropriately called Slavs, since as Barsamov points out, there are also many Ukrainians involved.

of the first works published in the West that systematically examines ethnic politics in Kazakhstan, a task capably managed. Further, as Barsamov is an analyst for the Russian Parliament's upper chamber, his interpretation is important as a perspective from the region's most powerful national actor. He also puts forth views not often encountered in standard Western analyses, examining the implications of what he sees as a state structure based on ethnic rather than civic ideals.

Indeed, there is a certain logic to post-Soviet irredentist politics that has important implications for relations between these states and suggests certain policy options for the concerned international community. While this logic may have application in other areas of the world, it is particularly powerful in the aftermath of the Soviet collapse, which was sudden and unexpected, in which the hegemonic nation was the one to leave large numbers of its co-ethnics across its own border, and where the hegemonic state came to enjoy a higher standard of living than most of its "new" neighbors.

The main problem is that, despite rhetoric proclaiming a unified national interest, the two groups involved (Russians and the "titular" ethnic group, the term often used to refer to the ethnic group for which the republic is named) have different interests in relations between the new state and Russia.[2] If one takes a materialist perspective, each group has an interest in securing for its own members a competitive advantage (both political and economic) in as wide a region as possible, and this involves expanding the domain in which one's own language and culture are dominant, *ceteris paribus*.[3] Indeed, in the Soviet era, ethnic Kazakhs had to bear the cost of learning Russian before they could move up the economic and political ladders, giving Russians a competitive advantage. This advantage is magnified when, as Donald Horowitz argues, the dominant group tends to be more associated with the skills of urban, industrialized society, while the other tends to be more rural, as is often the case in empires.[4] Russians in the new states also tend to have significant

---

2. Due to space considerations, I do not explore here the many problems involved in talking about "group interests," such as group diversity or collective action dilemmas.

3. This draws on the logic of Ernest Gellner, who writes about the nationalist imperative associated with industrialization in his *Nations and Nationalism* (Ithaca, N.Y.: Cornell University Press, 1983).

4. For more on what Horowitz calls "backwards" and "advanced" groups in the politics of secessions and irredentas, see Donald L. Horowitz, *Ethnic Groups in*

familial or economic ties to the "motherland." When one throws in strong emotive attachments to one's culture, as politicians often do, these preferences become intensely felt and politically potent. From this perspective, then, Russians have an interest in maintaining the old union. Titulars, on the other hand, have an interest in breaking these ties, creating affirmative action programs to redress the competitive disadvantages they have faced and, perhaps, making their own culture dominant in their "own" state.

How does a state leader balance such divergent demands? Assuming (s)he wants to keep the country together, this logic implies (s)he will tend to push for a loose confederation with Russia, actually favoring the Russian side on this issue. This might seem counterintuitive, since most leaders of such post-Soviet states are themselves of the titular ethnic group. Yet if these leaders do not want to end up presidents of "rump" titular states, they must weigh the strengths of their two constituencies' positions, and the Russian population can make the most credible threats.

Faced with a real or perceived decline in status and competitive opportunities, a Russian irredenta can threaten to secede. This threat is backed up by the lingering fear that mighty Russia itself might intervene. In retaliation, the titular group cannot similarly threaten the leader, since their nationalist ideology tends to be founded on the maintenance of territorial integrity. They can, of course, threaten civil war if the state's independence is at risk, yet this costly act is unlikely to be undertaken unless the leader goes so far as to agree to the absorption of the new state into Russia.[5] In short, the leader is likely to believe that the titular nationalists will bend further than the Russians, despite threats to the contrary. Leaders are thus likely to press for a loose confederation with Russia.[6] Such an arrangement would include enough ties with Russia to satisfy Russians' interest in

---

Conflict (Berkeley: University of California Press, 1985), especially pp. 229–288. In some cases, these two sets of incentives may offset each other to some degree, as with "advanced" groups operating in another group's cultural domain.

5.   They might also threaten civil war if Russians actually try to secede; but Russians convinced that the Russian Army will come to their aid are unlikely to be deterred by this threat alone. This does, of course, go into Russian calculations of the costs of rebellion, meaning they will not do so unless they feel severely wronged.

6.   For the present time I am saying nothing about whether the Russian Federation will accept such proposals and terms.

expanding their sphere of opportunity (i.e., free trade, an absence of border restrictions, easy currency convertibility or even a single currency, and perhaps mutual agreements on the provision of pensions and other transfer obligations). It would not go so far, however, as to alarm a large number of titular nationalists, avoiding, for example, a unified presidency, and preventing Russia from being able to make key policy decisions unilaterally.

Reality is more complex than any model, of course, and leaders in fact have many other options available. Most obviously, they can crack down on the Russians, making it much more difficult for them to organize. Leaders can also exploit the range of other preferences these groups have; for example, they might offer Russians complete symbolic and linguistic equality domestically in hopes that this will assuage feelings of deprivation. Perhaps more appealingly, but more unrealistically in many cases, leaders can try to raise their state's prosperity to the point at which the Russians will be so materially satisfied that they will not care about formal ties with Russia and may even agree to keep other Russians (competitors) out. Perhaps through such policies, leaders can try to lessen passions involved by trying to shape the identities of their Russians, fostering the development of civic notions of citizenship rather than ethnic ones, or at least encouraging them to view themselves as culturally distinct from Russia's Russians.[7] The real world is also much more uncertain, and much of the violence involving irredentist communities has involved misperception of motivations and misjudgment of relative strengths.

Despite the caveats, these dynamics go a long way in explaining Nazerbaev's ethnic tightrope act. Before the Soviet collapse in December 1991, Kazakhstan was known as one of the most "unionist" Soviet republics, although at the same time, as Barsamov points out, it also made Kazakh alone the official state language of the republic. During Kazakhstan's first eighteen months of independence, Nazerbaev had a relatively easy time maintaining ethnic peace. Formally independent, Kazakhstan's borders were effectively trans-

---

7. The latter possibility has been suggested by David D. Laitin; see his "Identity in Formation: The Russian-Speaking Nationality in Estonia and Bashkortostan," monograph in the series "Studies in Public Policy," Centre for the Study of Public Policy, University of Strathclyde, Glasgow, 1995. The former distinction is drawn by Roman Szporluk in "Introduction: Statehood and Nation-Building in Post-Soviet Space," in Roman Szporluk, ed., *National Identity and Ethnicity in Russia and the New States of Eurasia* (New York: M.E. Sharpe, 1994), pp. 3–17.

parent and it remained in the ruble zone, which meant Russians suffered little real loss from the collapse. There was even talk that an
independent Kazakhstan would do better economically than Russia
by avoiding controversial "shock therapy" reform efforts.[8] Formal
independence, however, was quite important to Kazakh nationalists,
as were Nazerbaev's efforts to promote their language and culture.
Nazerbaev continued to champion integration with Russia and, partly
as a result, enjoyed a long national honeymoon.[9]

Russia effectively pushed Nazerbaev off his tightrope, although his
own government's economic failings removed any cushion he may
have had upon landing. In July 1993, the Russian Central Bank suddenly declared pre-1993 ruble notes invalid. For the supply of new
rubles, Russia eventually demanded not only that Kazakhstan give
Russia a deposit worth half the value of the new rubles, but that it surrender complete control of economic policy to Moscow.[10] Although
Nazerbaev toyed with acquiescence, these terms proved too tough to
accept, and Kazakhstan introduced its own currency unit, the tenge,
that fall. This event more than any other since independence seems to
have set off Russian discontent in the north. Suddenly, Russians in
Kazakhstan had to buy a foreign currency before visiting relatives or
conducting business in Russia, a task rendered more upsetting as the
tenge began to plummet in value. These events came on top of a general decline in Kazakhstan's economy relative to that of the Russian
Federation, making associating with Russia increasingly expensive.
Nazerbaev's popularity in the north began to drop, although it was
his prime minister who took most of the heat in 1994. In the March
1994 elections, one of the more radical northern cities elected an all-
Russian local legislature determined to struggle for reintegration.
Feeling increasingly cut off from Russia, Russians also focused on
what they saw as discrimination at home. One Russian member of the
Kazakhstani Parliament elected in March 1994 staked out a radical
position, arguing, "There are different kinds of unity. There is the
unity between a horse and rider, and there is the unity between two
riders. We are for equality." For their part, Kazakh cultural activists

---

8.   This point was made by Lara Olson.

9.   Martha Brill Olcott emphasizes the popularity Nazerbaev enjoyed during
this period in "Kazakhstan: A Republic of Minorities," in Ian Bremmer and Ray
Taras, eds., *Nation and Politics in the Soviet Successor States* (New York: Cambridge
University Press, 1993), pp. 313–330.

10.   *Moscow Times*, November 4, 1993, pp. 1–2.

stood by efforts to promote their culture and language, viewing them as necessary to counteract decades of subjugation during the Soviet period. They also claimed that the Russian language continued to be used in most official capacities, including the president's major international addresses. In short, they asserted, Russians were just upset over losing their dominant status, a claim that Barsamov disputes. Nazerbaev thus found himself in a bind in 1994.

As the logic outlined above would lead us to expect, in March 1994, Nazerbaev launched an even more comprehensive proposal for integration with Russia: the creation of a "Eurasian Union," which would include not only free trade, but common citizenship and economic institutions.[11] Moreover, it would be open to many states and involve joint control over central institutions. Realistic or not, this proposal met with rejection by Russia as well as other former Soviet states. More recently, in March 1996, Kazakhstan became one of three former Soviet republics to join Russia in a quadripartite economic union in the framework of the Commonwealth of Independent States (CIS). In "future stages" of integration, the treaty envisages a common currency, among other things. From the start, however, Nazerbaev's opponents have accused him of making empty proposals to appease the Russian population, harboring no intention of actually forming such unions or carrying through with such pledges. Whatever the reality, he has been able to buy time with such proposals; but stability may not be long-lived in the absence of results.

Just as Kazakhstan's Russian irredenta has driven Nazerbaev to pursue close ties with Russia, concentrated Russian populations in other former Soviet states have exerted similar pulls, though not always successfully. In Moldova, the titular population ended up with civil war before realizing the seriousness of the Russian minority's intentions. With the Russian 14th Army hanging over it like the sword of Damocles, Moldova began to react more favorably to integration within the CIS. In Ukraine, President Leonid Kuchma was elected after campaigning for closer economic ties with Russia, arguably partly due to Crimean threats to secede if these ties were not strengthened. In Estonia, Russians were effectively disenfranchised temporarily, but the relatively strong economy suggests that potentially restive Russians have been placated. In any case, violence in Moldova and

---

11. For a description of his London speech introducing this idea in a rudimentary form, see Liz Fuller, *RFE/RL Daily Report*, No. 57 (March 23, 1994). See also the article by Bess Brown, *RFE/RL Daily Report*, No. 201 (October 21, 1994).

even Yugoslavia has undoubtedly demonstrated the deadly serious-ness with which irredentist threats can be made.

In such situations, what role is there for international actors? As the regional hegemon and the "mother state" of the irredentas in question here, Russia is clearly the most important actor. Initially, it has the pas-sive power either to accept or reject offers of integration when its neighbors make them. Since the Soviet collapse, Russia has wavered in its willingness to subsidize the "near abroad." While refusal may be fiscally sound economic policy, it can have serious ethno-political consequences, as was the case with Kazakhstan and the ruble zone. Barsamov's interpretation is that Russian President Boris Yeltsin is not interested in integrating with Kazakhstan; but another possibility is that Russia is holding out for integration on its own terms, denying Nazerbaev the kind of loose confederation he could use to satisfy both his Russian and Kazakh constituents. This would be a dangerous game. A third interpretation holds that Russia is primarily worried about its own domestic economic stability, and that integration is a weak secondary concern to be raised only if it has few negative eco-nomic consequences. Clearly, Russia also has the power to intervene directly in the conflict, openly supporting or working to moderate the claims of Russian activists in Kazakhstan. Barsamov argues that pri-vate individuals rather than the Russian state have been the most active supporters of irredentism, although official Russian pressure in 1994 for Kazakhstan to implement dual citizenship did not ease eth-nic tensions there. But Russians, Barsamov implies, tend to feel these demands are just.

The logic laid out here is largely based on economics, and accord-ingly it suggests several ways that Western countries and interna-tional organizations might help alter economic incentives so as to promote ethnic conciliation. Initially, if Kazakhstan can catch up with Russia in its standard of living, Russians there will not resent the Kazakhs so much for what they consider deprivation. The problem is that rapid growth can lead to social dislocations and hence aggravate ethnic tensions.[12] Thus Western help in establishing a social safety net could be crucial during market reforms. This is especially true to the extent that layoffs and plant closings will hit Russians the hardest, since they are more concentrated in the state's heavy industrial jobs.

---

12. This reflects Samuel P. Huntington's maxim: "modernity breeds stability, but modernization breeds instability." Huntington, *Political Order in Changing Societies* (New Haven, Conn.: Yale University Press, 1968), p. 41.

Inflation also creates psychological and economic barriers between Russians in Kazakhstan and the Russian Federation, and the International Monetary Fund can play a role in eliminating it. The international community can also help guarantee the legitimacy not only of elections, but of the privatization process, "certifying" (and ensuring) that property does not unfairly end up in the hands of a single ethnic group, as rumors sometimes have it. They can also champion certain policies sought by Russians in Kazakhstan that coincide with generally accepted economic goals. These include free trade (at least within the former Soviet space) and efficient, accessible currency convertibility, making the split with Russia less costly. In some ways, good economic policy is good ethnic policy.

Politically, international actors should of course counsel conciliation, encouraging each side to know the other's language. Accordingly, they should guarantee the fairness of elections and support the development of a strong legal infrastructure that is not perceived as being controlled by any one group, as may be increasingly the case. While the West may have missed its chance to help design state institutions in a way that promotes ethnic moderation, it should be ready to do so should the opportunity arise.[13]

Barsamov is correct that Kazakhstan has been peaceful because of President Nazerbaev's moderate politics. Moldova provides the counterexample: rash (and credible) talk of unification with Romania prompted Slavs in Transdniester to make good on their (more credible) threat to rebel with at least tacit support from the Russian 14th Army. While both sides have come to see the depth of the other's convictions, much blood was shed in the process. As even the Moldovan case shows, the logic of post-Soviet irredentas eventually pressures even nationalist leaders toward measured integration with the motherland, although they may seek (and find) other ways out. Nazerbaev has sought such integration as a way of compensating Russians for domestic affirmative action programs for Kazakhs. He was successful until he began to meet Russian unwillingness to agree to his terms, and a crisis developed in his own economy. With Nazerbaev's balancing act so delicate, much may depend on the international community, especially Russia.

---

13. Donald L. Horowitz, "Democracy in Divided Societies: The Challenge of Ethnic Conflict," *Journal of Democracy*, Vol. 4, No. 4 (October 1993), p. 35.

Chapter 13

The Republic of Georgia: Conflict in Abkhazia and South Ossetia

Edward Ozhiganov

Measured by their scale and intensity, the conflicts in Abkhazia and South Ossetia in the Republic of Georgia are closer to war than the other nascent conflicts in the former Soviet Union described in this volume.[1] Like the others, the situations in Abkhazia and South Ossetia emerged and developed against the background of the disintegration of the Soviet Union in 1989–91. The main parties to these "internal wars" are the secessionist authorities in the Autonomous Republic of Abkhazia and the Ossetian Autonomous Region, on one side, and the "ethno-nationalist" regime in the Republic of Georgia, on the other. The Georgian regimes of both Zviad Gamsakhurdia and Edward Shevardnadze, who was installed as head of state by the military coup that deposed Gamsakhurdia, were based upon principles of ethnic nationality.[2] The immediate causes of armed confrontation were differences of opinion over the political and administrative status of

---

1.   See footnote 1 in the chapter on Moldova in reference to the PIOMM rating system for conflicts.

2.   Contemporary scholarship allows for two different definitions of nationality: ethnic nationality and civic nationality. According to Jack Snyder, a political scientist at Columbia University, "ethnic nationality is based on the consciousness of a shared identity within a group, rooted in a shared culture and a belief in common ancestry. Civic nationality, by contrast, is inclusive within a territory. Membership in the national group is generally open to everyone who is born or permanently resident within the national territory, irrespective of language, culture or ancestry. Today, Serbian, Armenian and Azeri nationalists advance ethnic criteria for group membership. Russian President Boris Yeltsin and [former] Ukrainian President Leonid Kravchuk generally argue for civic criteria." Jack Snyder, "Nationalism and the Crisis of the Post-Soviet State," *Survival*, Vol. 35, No 1 (Spring 1993), p. 7.

Abkhazia and South Ossetia. The leadership of these former autonomous entities announced the creation of independent, national states and expressed the desire to become sovereign republics as part of the Russian Federation. However, Georgia regarded them as its provinces, where the Abkhazians and Ossetians might at most be granted the right of cultural autonomy.

The conflicts in Abkhazia and South Ossetia highlight issues raised in the other chapters in even more intense form. Both conflicts have been bitter and have led to heavy material damage and loss of life. In the South Ossetian conflict alone, between 1989 and 1992, 1,000 people were killed, more than 1,800 wounded, and 120 disappeared without a trace. The industrial infrastructure of the South Ossetian Autonomous Region was completely destroyed. In Tskhinvali, the South Ossetian capital, more than 80 percent of the dwellings and all important installations were laid to waste. One hundred fifteen Ossetian villages were destroyed and more than 100,000 Ossetians became refugees. Similarly, in Abkhazia more than 10,000 people were killed in fighting and punitive expeditions, and material damage amounted to more than 500 billion rubles. More than 140,000 people had to flee their homes.[3]

Georgia's policies turned out to be disastrous for its own national economy and for the social infrastructure of the republic. Once one of the wealthiest republics of the Soviet Union, Georgia seemed to have a bright economic and political future after independence, but conflicts in South Ossetia and Abkhazia, as well as the civil war in western Georgia conducted by supporters of ex-President Gamsakhurdia, have dealt a catastrophic blow to the country's infrastructure. According to official statistics and indicators such as the gross volume of industrial and agricultural production, the median standard of living has been thrown back thirty years. The disintegration of the monetary and credit system after the introduction of Georgia's own currency, the acute deficit of energy resources, the impoverishment of

---

3. See Russian Vice President Alexander Rutskoi's account of the situation in South Ossetia in ITAR-TASS, June 19, 1992; "The Situation in South Ossetia: Ten Days Without War," ITAR-TASS, July 24, 1992; and *The White Book of Abkhazia: 1992–1993* (Moscow: Z.S. Khalvash, R.A. Khagba and TOO "Vnekom," 1993), pp. 143–213. It should be noted that the statistics regarding human and material destruction submitted by parties to the conflict are not complete. From examining particular cases, it seems evident to the author that these statistics do not reflect the true scale of losses as a result of the violence, which has created social disorder and economic catastrophe.

the population, and the unprecedented growth of crime are just some of the problems facing Georgia today. Georgia has become financially insolvent. From 1992–1994, Georgia's external debt amounted to $800 million, $200 million of which was expired credit. Georgia will not be able to pay this debt in the near future.[4] Furthermore, Georgia has no international weight of its own and is in a position of political dependence on either Russia, Turkey, or Iran. In part because of the simultaneity of the two conflicts, not one of the objectives of Georgia's ethno-nationalist regime has been achieved. The net result is de facto independence for both Abkhazia and South Ossetia.

Abkhazians and Ossetians have distinct histories, although they share the same region; the Abkhazians occupy a fertile strip of land on the Black Sea coast, and the South Ossetians inhabit the harsh slopes of the Georgian side of the Great Caucasian Range. They share a political connection, however, in that both reacted sharply to the xenophobic nationalism that appeared in Georgian political circles after Georgia attained independence, although the Abkhazian and South Ossetian separatist movements arose independently of one another. Georgian nationalism threatened to eliminate the limited autonomy Abkhazians and South Ossetians had enjoyed under the Soviet system and to force their assimilation within Georgia.

A close analysis of the Abkhazian and Ossetian conflicts shows that the concepts of "historic enmity" or "communist restoration" are not adequate to explain these conflicts although both ideas were frequently advanced as reasons for the interethnic wars in Abkhazia and South Ossetia in their early stages.[5] Although each conflict

---

4. "Georgia is Now an Insolvent Country," POSTFACTUM, September 28, 1994.

5. The idea of "historic enmity" was implanted into the consciousness of the Georgian people by nationalist groups who cultivated the concept of the Georgians as a "host people," with the other ethnic groups in the republic as "guest peoples." As Olga Vasileva writes, "During the first conflict between Georgia and Abkhazia in 1989, a number of stereotypes crystallized in the Georgian national consciousness. The first and most important of these was the belief that the Georgian nation had a 'historic past' which predetermined that it would flourish as an independent, united nation in the future. The clearest manifestation of this stereotype was the idea of the 'historical right of Georgians to Georgian lands' and the related concept of 'guests,' who should know their place, as opposed to 'hosts'." *Georgia as a Model of Postcommunist Transformation* (Moscow: s.n., 1993), p. 45. Svetlana Chervonnaia's book *Abkhazia 1992: A Postcommunist Vendee* (Moscow: MGPU "Mosgorpechat'," 1993) is a classic example of the theory of "communist restoration." Chervonnaia explains the events in

developed in its own way, the potential for intensification and abatement is linked to several key factors. First, in both cases, infighting between factions in the ethnic Georgian Communist Party and government elites (*nomenklatura*) affected the scale and intensity of the conflict. The change of regime after the ouster of President Zviad Gamsakhurdia by Edward Shevardnadze, former Foreign Minister of the Soviet Union and a former head of the Georgian Communist Party, was particularly important.

Second, political struggles within the Russian leadership on which the Shevardnadze regime depends economically and militarily played an important role. The Abkhazian and South Ossetian conflicts arose in the context of intense political struggle both within Georgia and within the Soviet Union. Mikhail Gorbachev courted the leaders of the union republics in his search for allies to reform and maintain the Soviet system, but at the same time he threatened the position of the union republic leaders and undermined the stability of the political status quo by creating institutions and mechanisms—including the Congress of People's Deputies—that gave equal status to representatives from union republics, like Georgia, and representatives from autonomous entities within those republics, such as Abkhazia and Ossetia. With its many layers of units based nominally on national attributes, the ambiguous relationships forged by this quasi-federalism were galvanized and politicized in a struggle for real power as the Soviet center began to dissolve.

In both Abkhazia and South Ossetia, the conflict was aggravated by the participation of kindred ethnic groups from the neighboring North Caucasus republics and the presence of units and installations of the former Soviet Army, which became the armed forces of the Commonwealth of Independent States (CIS) and later of the Russian Federation. Both conflicts were also marked by the deep concern and involvement of Russia.

The conflict in Abkhazia attracted much more attention from international governmental and nongovernmental organizations (NGOs) than the South Ossetian conflict; the United Nations, the Organization for Security and Cooperation in Europe (OSCE), NATO, and the

---

Abkhazia and South Ossetia as the result of the machinations of "communist reactionaries plotting to restore their power," who, she argues, "are in alliance with the darkest, wildest fascist and nationalist forces, as well as the mafia and other groups" (p. 91).

Organization of Non-represented Peoples all became involved. Consequently, the events in Abkhazia are better known and documented than those in South Ossetia. Various organizations have made considerable efforts to bring about a peaceful settlement of the conflicts and to organize negotiations with the participation of all parties to the conflict. However, the definition of the political status of Abkhazia and South Ossetia has remained the main stumbling block.

The Historical Context

The following is a brief account of a number of pivotal events in the history of the Georgian, Ossetian, and Abkhazian peoples from which all sides draw their historical justifications. Because history is so complex and varied that it may be used to buttress any political claim,[6] ethnic nationalists have resorted to historical arguments to substantiate their claims to domination. Often newly independent groups turn to history to assess the danger posed by potential opponents, asking, "How did the other group behave the last time it was unconstrained?" and "Is there a record of offensive military activity by the other?" Unfortunately, the conditions under which such assessments occur predispose groups to conclude that their neighbors are more likely to be dangerous than not.[7] Historical argumentation can serve as a powerful means to mobilize ethnic feelings that later lead to acute conflicts,[8] and the conflicts in Georgia are no exception. The use of

---

6.   Askold Ivanchik, "History—The Teacher of Life: The Bitter Fruits of a Lesson. The Historical Background to Ethnic Conflicts," *Segodnia*, No. 213 (1994), p. 10.

7.   Barry R. Posen, "The Security Dilemma and Ethnic Conflict," *Survival*, Vol. 35, No 1 (Spring 1993), p. 30.

8.   For example, the ethnic disturbances in Abkhazia in 1978 were directly inspired by publications and scholarly discussions on the history of the eastern Black Sea region between the third and first centuries B.C. As historian Askold Ivanchik comments, "Georgia's military campaign against South Ossetia in 1990 began with the stated purpose of returning to Georgians lands which rightfully belonged to them. The Ossetians were referred to as guests who had overstayed their welcome. They had originally been given shelter in Georgia at a time of urgent need (the Mongol invasion of the 13th century during which the Alan state had been destroyed). Now, the argument ran, it was time that the Georgian land be cleansed of these people who had overstayed their welcome by 700 years. The Ossetians countered with a similarly absurd argument, namely that, since the first Scythian invasions of South Ossetia took place in the seventh century B.C., the lands in question rightfully belonged to them (the Ossetians are the descendants of the ancient Scythians and Sarmathians), whereas no one really knew when the Georgians had arrived." Ivanchik, "History—the Teacher of Life," p. 10.

historical justification by all parties is important to an understanding of the Georgian political situation.

SOUTH OSSETIA

The Ossetians are a traditionally tribal people whose area of settlement includes both North Ossetia (on the Russian side of the Caucasus Mountains) and South Ossetia on the Georgian side. The immediate ancestors of contemporary Ossetians were the Alans, who from the ninth to the thirteenth century formed a tribal union called Alania on the territory of the western and central Caucasus in the contemporary Russian Federation. This state converted to Christianity and maintained close political and trade links with Byzantium, Kievan Rus', and Georgia. The thirteenth century Mongol Tatar invasion destroyed this union and drove the Alans (Ossetians) into the mountains of the central Caucasus. Some of the Alans crossed the mountains and settled on the territory of what is now South Ossetia, joining a large ethnic Georgian population that had already lived in the region for many centuries. Over the course of the following centuries, the two peoples lived separately as this region came under the political control of feudal Georgia and was ruled by the Georgian princely dynasties.[9]

In 1801, Georgia was incorporated into the Russian Empire, and for the next 127 years, South Ossetia and North Ossetia were both under Russian rule. Although South Ossetia remained part of the Georgian province of the Russian Empire and the lands inhabited by South Ossetians were owned by the Georgian aristocracy, the administrative border between North and South Ossetia had little significance. This period of Ossetian unity fostered the development of a national high culture and increased national self-awareness. The tsarist government's policy of recruiting local elites contributed to the rise of an Ossetian intelligentsia.[10]

The creation of the independent Democratic Republic of Georgia in 1918 drastically altered the situation of the Ossetian people. During the Russian Civil War (1918–21), Georgia staked its claim on South

9.   See G. Kokiev, *Essays on the History of Ossetia* (Vladikavkaz: s.n., 1926).

10.   See Mark M. Bliev, *Russo-Ossetian Relations: From the 1740s to the 1830s* (Odzhonikidze: "IR," 1970); Z. Bliev, "Ossetia in the System of Administration of Russia at the End of the Eighteenth to the First Three Decades of the Nineteenth Century," in *The Role of Russia in the History of Ossetia* (Ordzhonikidze: s.n., 1989), pp. 43–56.

Ossetia. The Ossetians had announced the creation of a Soviet republic and expressed their desire to remain part of Russia, but in June 1920, Georgian armed forces launched large-scale punitive actions that left 5,000 Ossetians dead and forced 50,000 to flee to North Ossetia. During this flight another 15,000 Ossetians died of cold and hunger.[11] In 1921, the Democratic Republic of Georgia was defeated by the Bolshevik army and became the Georgian Soviet Socialist Republic (SSR). A year later, the South Ossetian Autonomous Region (*aftonomnaia oblast*) was created as part of the Georgian SSR. This status gave some limited autonomy to the South Ossetians, including the right to use their indigenous language and to preserve some cultural symbols. But the differences within and between union republics were largely formal; almost everything was decided by the centralized Communist Party structures in Moscow. Union republics like Georgia had independent authority over their internal regions, which meant that the policy of *korenizatsia* (indigenization) of the local government apparatus was implemented much less thoroughly in these areas.

In the Soviet period, relative stability prevailed in the Caucasus region, attributable in good measure to the overwhelming control exerted from the center. It was also important that, as had been the case under imperial Russian rule, the borders between the North Ossetians in the Russian Socialist Federated Soviet Republic (RSFSR) and the South Ossetians in Georgia were largely formal. Maintaining links was not difficult and Ossetians did not feel divided. In addition, the ethnic composition of South Ossetia remained quite stable during the Soviet period, with approximately 50 percent Ossetians and 50 percent Georgians. Because South Ossetia's territory is mountainous and harsh, and not especially desirable for industry, there was no influx of industrial workers and migrants as in other areas of the Soviet Union.

ABKHAZIA

Abkhazia, at the eastern edge of the Black Sea, has a subtropical climate and its inhabitants have always lived well. The land is excellent for agriculture and fruit orchards, and renowned for its natural beauty. In the Soviet period, Abkhazia became a popular and valuable resort area.

---

11. *South Ossetia: Blood and Ashes* (Vladikavkaz: Assotsiatsia tvorch i nauch intelligentsii, "IR," 1991), p. 47.

The Abkhazians, like the Ossetians, have a very long history in the Caucasus region and close historical links with the Georgian people. Abkhazians and Georgians share many elements of a common culture. Controversy has emerged over whether the Abkhazians belong to the same national group as the Georgians or constitute a separate nation. This question has become highly politicized and has contributed to an increase in the influence of radical nationalists who attempt to deny the existence of a separate Abkhazian ethnic group.[12] Georgian historical sources identify Abkhazians as members of the Iberian-Caucasian family of peoples, of which Georgians are the principal branch, and this position has been frequently cited in defense of Georgia's policies toward Abkhazia.[13] The Abkhazians see this as a politically motivated historical falsification. They assert that the Abkhazian people are the original inhabitants of the region and a separate ethnocultural community.[14] Ethnically, the Abkhazians claim membership in the larger western Caucasian (Abkhazo-Adygean) family of peoples, which includes other groups in the Caucasus.

---

12. The Western Caucasian (Abkhazo-Adygean) family is made up of two branches: 1) the Adygean (Cherkessian)—the Adygean and Kabardinian peoples; and 2) the Abkhazian—the Abkhazian and Abasinian peoples. See the seminal work by Shalva Inal-ip, a well-known Abkhazian ethnographer, entitled *On the Ethnocultural History of the Abkhaz People* (Sukhumi: s.n., 1976). In his preface to this book, Mikhail Korostovtsev writes: "The Abkhazian and related Adygian tribes were the original, ancient inhabitants of the eastern Black Sea region, which includes Abkhazia proper; they did not come from anywhere else, and it was here that they evolved into a separate ethnic community. Cultural infiltration, tribal migration and other ethnic changes took place in a context of many tribes but only one ethnic and geographical environment. The Abkhazian ethnic group evolved over a period of several dozen centuries, from earliest times to the present. The fact that the Abkhazians were the aboriginal people of this region in no way implies that they lived in ethnic or cultural isolation. On the contrary, over the centuries they had close relations with other peoples living in the western Caucasus and adjacent regions. Yet the Abkhazians and the Georgians are separate ethnocultural communities who have, however, shared a history together and influenced each other in a great variety of ways over more than a millennium" (p. 4).

13. *Bloody Separatism: What Happened in Abkhazia* (Tbilisi: s.n., 1993), p. 5. The most openly pro-Georgian position can be found in Avtandil Menteshashvili and Georgii Pandzhikidze, *The Truth about Abkhazia* (Tbilisi: s.n., 1990).

14. Both Stalin and Beria were ethnic Georgians.

Abkhazians concede, however, that for the past one thousand years they have a shared a historical relationship with the Georgians in which each influences the other. Abkhazians note that throughout the centuries, Georgians have continually encroached upon and expanded into Abkhazian territory.[15]

Abkhazian political identity has a long history stretching back to the first century A.D., when feudal principalities of ancient Abkhazian tribes emerged on the territory of present-day Abkhazia. By the sixth century, Christianity had been established in these regions, and in the ninth century, an Abkhazian kingdom was founded. In the tenth century, Abkhazia became part of a united feudal state of Abkhazians and Kartvelians, but under pressure from the Mongol invasion in the thirteenth century, this state broke up into separate kingdoms and principalities and Abkhazia again became independent. Georgian sources disregard the independence of the ancient Abkhazian kingdom, however, and refer instead to a history of Georgian-Abkhazian statehood with varying degrees of integration.[16]

From the sixteenth to the eighteenth century, Abkhazia was a quasi-independent vassal state of the Ottoman Empire. During this interval the Abkhazians, an ancient Christian people, converted to Islam. At the beginning of the nineteenth century, Georgia became a province of the Russian Empire, and in 1810 Abkhazia voluntarily incorporated itself into the Russian Empire while retaining its autonomous structures. During the great Caucasian War (1830-64), the Abkhazians, like the other peoples of the Abkhazo-Adygean group in the Caucasus, received military support from Turkey, which was seeking to curtail Russian expansion in the Caucasus. Georgia sided with the Russians and fought along with the regular tsarist army. Following the Russian victory in 1864, Abkhazia came under direct Russian rule. Later, after two unsuccessful Abkhazian revolts and Russia's defeat of Turkey in 1878, Russia expelled huge numbers of Abkhazians to Turkey and settled Georgians, Armenians, Russians, and Greeks on Abkhazian lands, significantly changing the region's ethnic

---

15. The most pro-Abkhazian position is found in Stanislav Lakoba, *Essays on the Political History of Abkhazia* (Sukhumi: s.n., 1990).

16. Zurab Anchabadze, et al., *The History of Abkhazia* (Sukhumi: Alashara, 1976), pp. 98–99.

composition and forever decreasing the population of ethnic Abkhazians in the region.[17]

During the Civil War after the February 1917 revolution in Russia,[18] Abkhazia found itself in the center of a struggle between the Bolsheviks, the tsarist White Army, and the Democratic Republic of Georgia. On June 8, 1918, Georgia concluded a treaty with Abkhazia providing that Abkhazia would have autonomous status within Georgia. However, Georgian leaders did not respect this autonomy and, suspecting the Abkhazian Soviet of disloyalty, twice dispersed it by military force. When the Red Army eliminated the Democratic Republic of Georgia in 1921, the Abkhazian Bolsheviks declared independence and proclaimed the establishment of the Soviet Socialist Republic of Abkhazia—a union-level republic directly subject to Moscow with no formal links to the newly created Georgian SSR. The union agreement provided that Georgia was comprised of two independent republics, Georgia and Abkhazia.

This situation lasted until 1931, when the status of Abkhazia as a union republic was suddenly revoked and the region was turned into an autonomous republic within Georgia, probably as the result of

17. Changes in the demographic composition of the population of Abkhazia between 1886 and 1989:

	1886	1897	1926	1939	1959	1970	1989
Abkhazians	58,963	58,697	55,918	56,197	61,193	83,097	93,267
Georgians	4,166	25,875	67,494	91,967	158,221	213,322	239,872
Russians	971	5,135	20,456	60,201	86,715	79,730	74,913
Armenians	1,049	6,552	30,048	49,705	64,400	73,000	76,541
Greeks	2,149	5,393	27,085	34,621	9,111	13,600	14,669

The White Book of Abkhazia, p. 30. See also Olga Vaslieva, Georgia as a Model of Post-Communist Transformation (Moscow: s.n., 1993), p. 58.

According to the 1886 census, the total population of Abkhazia was 68,000, of whom 34,000 were Georgians and 28,000 Abkhazians. Since then the share of ethnic Abkhazians in the population has constantly decreased; they are now only about one-third as numerous as the Georgians.

18. The provisional government in Moscow formed a Special Caucasian Committee, which had its own local administrative body in Abkhazia. In November 1917, the Abkhazian People's Council (which did not support the Bolsheviks) was established as the supreme national authority, but it was overthrown by the Soviet authorities, who established control over Abkhazia during April and May 1918. They in turn were defeated by forces loyal to the Georgian National Council and the self-designated government of the Transcaucasus. In May 1918, following the collapse of the government of the Transcaucasus, the Democratic Republic of Georgia declared its independence.

power struggles within the Communist Party of the Soviet Union (CPSU). Abkhazia lost its independence and the Abkhazian political elite was eliminated. Abkhazians believe that this act marks the beginning of a deliberate policy to annihilate the Abkhazian people that reached its zenith in the late 1930s during the period of the Stalinist personality cult. Nearly the entire Abkhazian intelligentsia was repressed, the use of the Abkhazian language was restricted, and a policy of mass resettlement of Georgians was undertaken in an attempt to further alter the demographic structure of Abkhazia.[19] Between 1937 and 1956, approximately 100,000 new settlers arrived in Abkhazia and the resettlement policy continued long after the Stalin era—as recently as August 3, 1976, an agency was set up in accordance with Decree No. 533 to resettle 60,000 Georgians in Abkhazia by 1980, and 160,000 by 1990.

THE PRELUDE TO INDEPENDENCE

Historically Georgia is a multiethnic society made up of Georgians, Abkhazians, Ossetians, Russians, Ukrainians, Armenians, Greeks, and Jews. In the thirty years between Khrushchev's 1956 denunciation of the Stalin personality cult and the beginning of Gorbachev's perestroika in 1985, social and economic developments in South Ossetia and Abkhazia reflected tendencies common to all Soviet autonomous regions. These tendencies included the arbitrary location of production capacities, the mass migration of the labor force to follow industrial production, and the granting of only nominal independent powers to local administrations.

From the Georgian perspective, Abkhazia occupied a privileged position during the Soviet period not only within Georgia, but within

---

19. A decree of the Supreme Soviet of the Abkhazian SSR, dated August 25, 1990, and entitled "On Legal Provisions for Protecting Abkhazian Independence," states the following: "In the mid-1930s a series of repressive acts were carried out against the Abkhazian people with the aim of dissolving the Abkhazian people and merging Abkhazia with Georgia. The actions taken were: closing Abkhazian schools and forcing Abkhazian children to attend Georgian schools; making Georgian the official language of business; replacing Abkhazian place-names by Georgian ones; organizing mass settlements of Georgians in Abkhazia, and constructing special villages for them; expelling Abkhazians from positions in government institutions and the Party and replacing them by Georgians; favoring Georgians in matters of personnel recruitment and distribution of apartments, land etc.; doing everything possible to stifle independent Abkhazian popular culture; and falsifying the history of Abkhazia and the Abkhazian people, who were declared to be a Georgian tribe."

the Soviet Union as a whole. Abkhazia had a relatively higher rate of growth in per capita income, a disproportionate share of the state budget, and a larger than average number of publications in the Abkhazian language, to cite but a few examples.[20] By contrast, many Abkhazians take the view that the rights of the Abkhazian people were continuously restricted throughout the Soviet period, although the discrimination took less obvious forms. Sporadic instability was not unknown in the region, and the Abkhazians held mass demonstrations against Georgian authorities in 1957, 1965, 1967, and 1978.

The political crisis that led to the 1991 collapse of the Soviet Union began to take shape in 1988–89, when the central government in Moscow gradually became less effective. In the vacuum that emerged, ethnic-Georgian ruling elites initiated a political campaign aimed at making Georgian ethnicity a criterion for political legitimacy.[21] Beginning in mid-1988, a media campaign was mounted on the theme of "the rebirth of the Georgian nation" that was based on the permanent rights of the Georgian people over the other nationalities living in the Georgian SSR, like the Ossetians and Abkhazians, who were said to pose a threat to Georgian culture and statehood. Even those who openly support the Georgian point of view admit that public discourse in Georgia during this period was highly chauvinistic.[22] An atmosphere of ethnic intolerance developed, and the hypernationalism that arose in Georgia provoked the mobilization of nationalist sentiments among the Abkhazians and the South Ossetians[23] and increased resistance to Georgian independence. This in turn solidified Georgian perceptions of minorities as traitors, thereby furthering the spiral of reactive nationalism.

---

20. *Bloody Separatism*, pp. 14–17.

21. For discussion of the creation of ethnic *nomenklaturas* in the national republics of the Soviet Union, see the chapter in this volume on the ethno-national conflict in Moldova.

22. Svetlana Chervonnaia, whose book was strongly endorsed by the Shevardnadze administration, writes: "The Georgian press, mass media and journalists, as well as ethnologists and political scientists, are definitely to blame for having aggravated interethnic tensions and caused ethnic minorities in Georgia to be terrified of Georgian nationalism: Ossetians, Abkhazians, Russians, Armenians, Azeris and others." *Abkhazia 1992: A Postcommunist Vendee*, p. 58. Vendée is a province in France where a counterrevolutionary revolt of monarchists occurred in 1793.

23. John Mearsheimer defines the psychological ground of "hypernationalism" as the belief that other nations are "both inferior and threatening and must

The centrifugal tendencies that accompanied the collapse of the Soviet political system manifested themselves early in Georgia. There was a strong movement for independence under the leadership of Zviad Gamsakhurdia and others in the Georgian Communist Party (GCP). The leadership of national autonomous institutions in South Ossetia and Abkhazia had always feared the growth of Georgian nationalism in the event that Georgia were to secede from the Soviet Union. Sensing the political current, on November 10, 1989, the South Ossetian Autonomous Region proclaimed itself an autonomous republic within the Georgian SSR and moved to set up its own parliament. The South Ossetian leadership gave assurances that it did not seek changes in the boundaries of the Georgian SSR if Georgia remained part of the Soviet Union. If, however, the Republic of Georgia were to secede from the Soviet Union, the South Ossetian leadership would ask the Supreme Soviet and the president of the Soviet Union to uphold the constitutional right of South Ossetia to self-determination and allow it to join the Soviet Union directly. The Georgian parliament immediately overrode these decisions.

On December 16, 1990, the leaders of the Georgian SSR announced that they would not sign the new union treaty being prepared by Gorbachev, which was tantamount to secession from the Soviet Union. Upon declaring its independence, Georgia reinstituted the 1921 Constitution of the Democratic Republic of Georgia, annulled all Soviet decrees and actions, and juridically reinstated both South Ossetia and Abkhazia as territories within an independent Georgian state. Even within the limited context of Soviet history, this action was highly problematic, for while it is true that South Ossetia and Abkhazia had been territories within independent Georgia for a very brief period before the Soviet army subdued Georgia, Abkhazia had existed as an independent republic from 1918–1920, and South Ossetia had been an independent republic for a short time in 1920 until it was crushed by the Georgian Army. In August 1990, the Soviet of People's Deputies of South Ossetia opted to abandon South Ossetia's status as an autonomous region and declare it the South Ossetian Soviet

---

therefore be dealt with harshly." Mearsheimer, "Back to the Future: Instability in Europe After the Cold War," *International Security*, Vol. 15, No. 1 (Summer 1990), reprinted in Sean M. Lynn-Jones and Steven E. Miller, eds., *The Cold War and After* (Cambridge, Mass.: MIT Press, 1991), p. 157. For details of this period, see *South Ossetia: Blood and Ashes*, pp. 49–55; and *The White Book of Abkhazia*, pp. 12–15.

Socialist Republic, a direct subject of the Soviet Union. From this point on, the two conflicts developed quite independently and will therefore be discussed separately in the following sections.

The Conflict in South Ossetia

"Georgia for the Georgians" was the slogan of the Roundtable bloc headed by Zviad Gamsakhurdia in 1988–90 and became the central theme of an intensive ideological propaganda campaign directed against non-Georgian ethnic groups, including Ossetians. In 1988, Ossetians began to form their own national political movement, *Adamon Nykhas* (People's Assembly), which at that time worked mainly for the improvement of socioeconomic conditions in South Ossetia, where the standard of living of ethnic Ossetians was considerably lower than the Georgian average.[24] After South Ossetia proclaimed itself an autonomous republic on November 10, 1989, Gamsakhurdia announced at a mass meeting in Tbilisi that his supporters were advancing on Tskhinvali, the capital of South Ossetia, to take over the region. On November 23, 1989, about 30,000 Georgian nationalists, including illegal armed formations from an organization known as the Legion of Georgian Hawks, approached the town,[25] but the demonstrators were stopped by Ossetian picketers. After a 24-hour-long confrontation, the majority of the Georgians retreated, but

---

24. According to information from the State Committee for Statistics of the Soviet Union, in 1979, 160,497 Ossetians lived in the Republic of Georgia. The population of South Ossetia itself is about 100,000 people, of whom 68 percent are Ossetians. South Ossetia was the least developed region of Georgia from an economic and social point of view, and all economic indices, including average income and budget expenditure per capita, were considerably lower than the Georgian average. *South Ossetia: Blood and Ashes*, p. 53.

25. This group was headed by Gamsakhurdia and the former first secretary of the Georgian Communist Party, Givi Gumbaridze. The fact that Gumbaridze, a top Georgian Communist Party boss, took part in organizing and leading the campaign against South Ossetia demonstrates the significant role played by the Georgian *nomenklatura* in unleashing ethnic and political conflict. Dzhumber Patiashvili, who was replaced by Gumbaridze as first secretary of the Central Committee of the Georgian Communist Party after the events in Tbilisi in 1988 and who later became a member of the Georgian Parliament, stated at an October 1994 meeting of parliament on the possible resignation of Shevardnadze that the destruction of Georgia began with the emergence of the national movement, as the leadership of the time "was unable to act flexibly." *Gruzia*, No. 7 (October 1994), p. 2.

several armed formations stayed behind and organized a prolonged blockade. Six people were killed and approximately five hundred were wounded. In spite of repeated agreements between Gamsakhurdia and the Ossetian leaders on the withdrawal of the armed formations from the region, the armed conflict lasted from the end of November 1989 until January 1990. In an interview, Gamsakhurdia later stated: "Yes, [the Tskhinvali] campaign was organized by me. We wanted to persuade the Ossetians to give in. They took flight, which is quite logical since they are criminals. The Ossetians are an uncultured, wild people—clever people can handle them easily."[26]

There was relative stabilization in the Ossetian-Georgian conflict in early 1990, which can be explained in part by differences that emerged within the Georgian nationalist movement over the course of the Georgian parliamentary election campaign. Specifically, a dispute arose between Gamsakhurdia's Roundtable and the National Democratic Party, whose members were not enamored with the personalized leadership of Gamsakhurdia.

On December 9, 1990, South Ossetia held elections for its new Supreme Soviet. The following day the Georgian Supreme Soviet declared these elections invalid and voted to abolish South Ossetia's autonomy altogether. At that point, the South Ossetian leadership appealed to Mikhail Gorbachev and the Supreme Soviet of the Soviet Union for protection of the rights of South Ossetia and its people. The appeal included a request to send a commission of deputies and representatives of the Soviet government to study the situation and to ensure that the rights of the South Ossetians were being respected. However, Gorbachev's administration pursued a policy of noninterference and essentially ignored the tensions between the Georgians and the South Ossetians. Meanwhile, the North Ossetians became involved in the conflict. The North Ossetian leadership, headed by Askharbek Galazov, issued a strong protest to the Georgian Parliament. Georgia's blockade of the South Ossetia region left North Ossetia as the South's only source of food and fuel. It is difficult to verify completely, but it seems clear that North Ossetia also supplied arms and fighters.

---

26. Zviad Gamsakhurdia, "We Have Chatted Too Long with the Separatists: A Conversation with the Chairman of the Georgian Supreme Soviet," *Moscow News,* December 2, 1990, p. 11.

GAMSAKHURDIA'S WAR

In January 1991, under the pretext of enforcing law and order, the Georgian government decided to introduce a special detachment of 3,000 Georgian Interior Ministry troops into South Ossetia. Interior Ministry helicopters transported armed fighters from Georgian nationalist organizations to South Ossetia, and a bloody drama ensued in the environs of Tskhinvali. Barricades were thrown up in the town and clashes broke out between the Georgian militia and Ossetian fighters, and the main victims were civilians. At this point, Soviet President Gorbachev passed a decree "On Certain Enactments Adopted in December 1990 in the Georgian SSR," ordering the withdrawal within three days of all armed formations from South Ossetia. The decree was ignored.

On January 22, 1991, heavy street fighting again broke out in Tskhinvali between Ossetian self-defense groups and the Georgian militia and the Georgian National Guard. At the same time, paramilitaries called the Mehedrionis and a group called White Georgy began to gather forces nearby. These forces were not direct parties to the conflict, but illegally formed armed bands constituted primarily of radical nationalists and criminals who spontaneously organized to support the Georgian government. The official Georgian position was very clear: Tbilisi did not recognize the Republic of South Ossetia; thus any peace initiatives concluded by the Georgian leadership were doomed to failure. The blockade of Tskhinvali continued for several months. There was no water or electricity, all industrial enterprises were closed, and municipal services ceased to function. The section of Tskhinvali seized by the Georgians was plundered and destroyed. Aid from North Ossetia ceased during the winter months as the roads through the Caucasus became impassable. Two months after the confrontation had begun, more than 20,000 people had fled to Georgia and North Ossetia. According to official information, 53 people had been killed on the Ossetian side and more than 230 injured. More than 50 Ossetian villages had been pillaged and burnt, and the whole economic and social structure of South Ossetia had been destroyed.[27]

On March 6, 1991, Gamsakhurdia, as chairman of the Presidium of the Georgian Supreme Soviet, outlined his program for resolving the crisis in South Ossetia. One of its key points was that "rightful"

---

27. "Telegram to the President of the Soviet Union," TASS, March 26, 1991.

authority should be established in Tskhinvali—in other words, the administrative structures of the formerly autonomous region would cease operation. In exchange, the Ossetians were guaranteed what was termed "cultural autonomy." As part of an administrative reform, municipal elections were to be held in South Ossetia, prefectures were to be created, and a prefect appointed in Tskhinvali. These prefectures were set up in Georgia at the personal initiative of Gamsakhurdia and were directly answerable to him. Prefects held unlimited power in their jurisdictions; they had the authority, for instance, to override the decisions of local municipalities and suspend verdicts of district and municipal courts. The Tskhinvali prefect differed from the others insofar as he only made appointments for Tskhinvali and did not exercise regionwide authority.

Increased tension in South Ossetia was directly linked to the decision by the Georgian leadership to take steps toward secession from the Soviet Union. In response to these actions, a group of Soviet People's Deputies and representatives of the administrative organs of South Ossetia made the following announcement at a session of the Soviet Union Supreme Soviet:

The people of South Ossetia firmly protest the announcement made by a representative of the Georgian leadership at yesterday's session of the Soviet Union Supreme Soviet in which the Georgian government was urged not to sign a new Union treaty, effectively removing Georgia from the Soviet Union and transforming the political structure of the republic. The people of South Ossetia repeat that it is only as a result of the Soviet authorities and the Soviet Union that the Ossetian people have been able not only to preserve but also to develop their language, national culture, and science. The people of South Ossetia firmly declare their socialist orientation and their desire to continue to live in the family of peoples of the Soviet Union. If the Georgian Republic decides to leave the Soviet Union, we will ask the president and Supreme Soviet of the Soviet Union to uphold our constitutional right to self-determination and to arrange for us immediately to enter the Soviet Union as subjects of the Federation.[28]

Despite the explicit prohibition by the Georgian authorities, the Councils of People's Deputies of Abkhazia and Ossetia decided to hold the Gorbachev referendum on the preservation of the Soviet Union on March 17, 1991. Gamsakhurdia vowed that only those who boycotted the Gorbachev referendum and voted for the restoration of

---

28. TASS, November 17, 1990.

the independence of Georgia would be given land and citizenship,[29] and on March 31, 1991, a referendum was held throughout Georgia on the following question: "Do you agree with the restoration of the independence of Georgia in accordance with the Act of independence of May 26, 1918?" This meant an independent state that included both South Ossetia and Abkhazia. Only a portion of the population in Abkhazia participated in the Georgian referendum, the results of which will be discussed in the section on the Abkhazian conflict.[30]

On March 24, 1991, Boris Yeltsin, chairman of the Supreme Soviet of the Russian Federation, and Gamsakhurdia met for talks. At this stage of the South Ossetian conflict, Yeltsin supported Gamsakhurdia because he saw him as an ally in his fight to undermine Gorbachev and the Soviet center. Yeltsin's policy was also determined by the orientation of his key advisers at the time, a group known in Russia as the radical democrats who looked upon South Ossetia as a communist stronghold. The Ossetian leadership continued to uphold the socialist system and support the preservation of the Soviet Union. Both positions were patently unacceptable to Gamsakhurdia and Yeltsin. Although there was little Yeltsin could do openly given that the Soviet structures still existed, in the course of talks, the Russian Federation recognized the abolition of the South Ossetian Autonomous Region.[31] The text of the protocol, which referred to "the former South Ossetian Autonomous Region," was disseminated in North and South Ossetia the following day, and the Ossetian population reacted very negatively. Convinced of Yeltsin's support, the Georgian leadership moved reinforcements to the area of conflict on March 30, 1991, with the intent of attacking Tskhinvali and the Dzhav district, both controlled by the Ossetians. The Georgian Parliament abolished the Tskhinvali and Znaur districts of South Ossetia and joined these territories to the Rorii and Kareli districts of Georgia. As

---

29. "Warning to the Abkhazian People," TASS, February 12, 1991.

30. "Preliminary Results of the Referendum Across the Soviet Union," TASS, March 18, 1991.

31. On March 25, 1991, in a speech on Georgian television, Gamsakhurdia announced that Yeltsin had approved the abolition of the South Ossetian Autonomous Region. He also announced that an agreement had been reached to establish working groups that would spend April 1991 preparing a draft treaty on intergovernmental relations between the Russian Federation and the Republic of Georgia. "After Gamsakhurdia's Negotiations With Yeltsin," ITAR-TASS, March 26, 1991.

a result, the confrontation again intensified; discrete clashes grew into full-scale military operations in which automatic rifles, heavy machine guns, mortars, and rockets were used. Tskhinvali was closely surrounded by well-armed forces numbering over 12,000. However, no decisive attack was carried out because, on orders from the Soviet Union Council of Ministers, Soviet Interior Ministry troops normally stationed in the region warned Georgian forces against attacking the town. In Russia this step taken by the central authorities was perceived not so much as an action in support of the South Ossetians than as part of the routine procedure of Soviet internal troops to suppress mass disorders in any republic. The center had no interest in a full-scale civil war erupting in the region and undermining what order remained.

The Russian Congress of People's Deputies intervened separately with a resolution on the situation in South Ossetia that seemed to have a deterrent effect.[32] The resolution called on the Supreme Soviet of the Republic of Georgia to restore the status of South Ossetia as an autonomous republic, lift the blockade, return refugees to their homes, and stabilize the region. It expressed a willingness to establish treaty relations with Georgia once these conditions were met. The Congress of People's Deputies also called on Gorbachev and the Council of the Federation of the Soviet Union Supreme Soviet to take immediate measures to intervene politically and, if necessary, militarily in South Ossetia.[33]

These events led to a temporary lull in the conflict that allowed the Russians to partially lift the blockade of Tskhinvali and to open up the main road from Dzhav to Tskhinvali in order to transport food, medicine, and fuel. After some months, however, events in Russia encouraged the Georgian leadership to reactivate the conflict. After the unsuccessful coup attempt in Moscow in August 1991, the Georgian Prosecutor General Vakhtang Ramadze signed a warrant for the arrest of a number of leading officials in South Ossetia, accusing them of "stirring up conflict between the Georgian and Ossetian peoples" and lending support to the coup plotters, though there seemed to be no evidence to support the charges.[34] The arrests were

---

32. The Congress of People's Deputies by that time was superior to the Supreme Soviet.

33. ROS-TASS, March 31, 1991.

34. "The Situation in South Ossetia," ITAR-TASS, September 5, 1991.

not carried out, however, because the accused were protected in the still heavily armed city of Tskhinvali.

Early September 1991 saw an escalation of military activities stimulated by the weakening of the Gamsakhurdia regime inside Georgia. An opposition group led by Tengis Kitovani, head of the National Guard, Djabaa Ioseliani, leader of the Mehedrioni, and Prime Minister Tengis Sigua demanded Gamsakhurdia's immediate resignation. In the course of the next two months, bitter fighting took place in the neighborhood of Tskhinvali and the Znaur district, which was virtually destroyed by rockets and artillery. The 29th helicopter and 37th engineer regiments of the Soviet Army, which were normally stationed in the region of conflict, were ordered by the Ministry of Defense in Moscow not to intervene. These forces tried to maintain neutrality until they themselves came under attack, and then acted only in self defense. Their commanding officers asked the Soviet Minister of Defense and the commander of the Transcaucasus Military District to take urgent measures to protect the lives of the military personnel and their families and to evacuate these units to Russia.

On December 20, 1991, with the Soviet Union in its death throes, armed clashes erupted in Tbilisi between the presidential forces and armed detachments of the opposition. Gamsakhurdia called in his supporters from detachments besieging South Ossetia, and an unexpected lull set in around Tskhinvali. The Military Council of the Georgian opposition forces, led by Kitovani and Ioseliani, finally succeeded in seizing control of Tbilisi, and on January 4, 1992, addressed an appeal to the warring sides in South Ossetia, calling for a cease-fire and negotiations to end the conflict. Criminal proceedings were instituted against former President Gamsakhurdia, who was accused of "stirring up discord between nationalities" and "provoking and escalating the conflict in South Ossetia," but he escaped to his base in western Georgia where he continued to harass the new government.

The dissolution of the Soviet Union prompted the South Ossetians to reevaluate their situation as well. They put their hopes in the Congress of People's Deputies of the Russian Federation, which had supported them earlier in the conflict. South Ossetia again made an appeal for acceptance as a republic of the Russian Federation, which would mean reunification with the North Ossetian Republic. On January 19, 1992, the South Ossetians held a referendum to decide two questions: 1) Do you agree to the independence of the Republic of South Ossetia? and 2) Do you agree with the decision of the

Supreme Soviet of the independent Republic of Ossetia to reunite with Russia? An overwhelming 98.2 percent voted in favor of an independent South Ossetia as part of the Russian Federation. In response, the Georgian interim government issued a statement reinforcing the notion that the Republic of Georgia did not intend to cede any of its territory and would prevent the reunification of South Ossetia with Russia. South Ossetia's desire to reunite with North Ossetia put President Yeltsin's advisers in an embarrassing position since they had earlier labeled South Ossetia a communist stronghold, and a fifth column committed to reviving the Soviet Union. The Yeltsin government issued no formal response to this declaration, but instead called for a review of the legality of the South Ossetian referendum.[35] Meanwhile, in Russia the response was mixed. Under the leadership of Ruslan Khasbulatov, the Russian Parliament, which was still quite powerful in 1992, championed the South Ossetian cause, in part as a way of undermining President Yeltsin.

The depth of the gulf that separated the two sides was illustrated in a debate on the November 1991 draft union treaty presented by President Gorbachev as the legal basis for a "renewed" Soviet federation. At the Congress of Russian People's Deputies, the leader of South Ossetia, Askharbek Galazov, argued that the treaty should be signed as soon as possible, stressing that any delay would "push the country into an abyss." Representing the Democratic Russia bloc, Galina Starovoitova, who later became an adviser to Boris Yeltsin on ethnic issues, called the proposed document "a cosmetic makeover of the 1922 treaty." Starovoitova was convinced that Gorbachev's proposed Union treaty would "do nothing for Russia," and would "certainly not transform the empire into a free and equal association of states."[36]

---

35. Galina Starovoitova, who at that time advised the Russian President on interethnic relations, proposed that an evaluation be made of the "legality and legitimacy" of the referendum. First Deputy Minister of Foreign Affairs of the Russian Federation, Fyodor Shelov-Kovedaev, argued that events in Georgia should be closely monitored so that a "considered decision" could be made on the issue. In any event, according to Znaur Gassiev, one of the South Ossetian leaders, South Ossetia did not plan to raise the issue of withdrawing from Georgia, although in return the people of South Ossetia needed a reliable guarantee that they would not be the target of any sort of discrimination. "Russian Government Leaders on the Issue of South Ossetian Reunification with Russia," TASS, January 21, 1992.

36. TASS, December 8, 1990.

CEASE-FIRES AND RELATIVE STABILIZATION

The January 1992 appointment of Edward Shevardnadze as chairman of the Georgian Council of State engendered hope for a peaceful settlement of the conflict. On May 13, 1992, a trilateral meeting took place in Tskhinvali between delegations from the North Ossetian SSR, the Republic of South Ossetia, and the Republic of Georgia to discuss a settlement. Agreements were reached on a cease-fire in the zone of military operations. Nevertheless, on June 8, 1992, heavy fighting erupted between detachments of the Ossetian Guards and armed Georgian formations in the vicinity of Tskhinvali, and the Shevardnadze regime began a massive attack on South Ossetia. Georgia had obtained heavy weapons in accordance with the CIS agreement that divided up the military property of the Soviet Union. On June 20, 1992, Georgian troops, supported by armored vehicles, broke through to the left-bank district of Tskhinvali, and defenders and inhabitants of the town were told to leave by evening or punitive action would follow. The ensuing assault virtually destroyed the city, since the attacking Georgian forces had the strategic advantage and were able to bombard the town from the surrounding heights with mortars, guns, and rocket launchers. More than 80 percent of the dwellings and administrative buildings were burnt down, and all important industrial and social facilities were damaged. Nevertheless, the Georgian troops did not succeed in seizing Tskhinvali.

At the start of this campaign, the Georgian leadership completely denied any military involvement. Speaking at a June 17, 1992, press conference at the Georgian Mission to Moscow, Georgi Khaindrava, a member of the Georgian State Council, affirmed that the Georgian leadership would do everything possible to end the bloodshed in South Ossetia and bring the warring sides to the table for negotiations. Any statement implying that the council was involved in the escalation of violence, he said, was "a provocation designed to destabilize the region." Khaindrava stated that the council was not able to control all Georgian armed groups and thus was not responsible for their actions. Clearly the Georgian leaders were hoping for a swift military resolution of the conflict. Only three days later, however, Shevarnadze was forced to admit that the attack on Tskhinvali was not being led by "detachments out of the control of the Georgian government," but by elements of the Georgian National Guard—an admission that placed Boris Yeltsin and his advisers in an embarrassing position.[37]

The war in Transcaucasia also contributed to the destabilization of the situation in North Ossetia, where a conflict erupted between the Ossetians and Ingush. Some South Ossetian fighters assisted the North Ossetians, and the flood of refugees from South Ossetia aggravated economic conditions in North Ossetia. There was a real danger of military activities spreading to North Ossetia if the North Ossetians mobilized to aid their ethnic kin in the south. Forced to take urgent action, the Russian government issued a strongly worded statement accusing the Shevardnadze government of mounting a "large-scale disinformation campaign" and carrying out "military action designed to drive the non-Georgian population out of South Ossetia."[38] On June 20, 1992, the government of the Russian Federation, noting that the escalation of armed conflict in the region had reached a crisis point, issued the following statement:

The acts of violence aimed at driving the non-Georgian population out of South Ossetia are a flagrant violation of human rights. A growing number of refugees are pouring into North Ossetia, a part of the Russian Federation, which poses a direct threat to Russian national security. The Georgian leadership has conducted a vast campaign of disinformation aimed at deceiving its own people and the world as a whole. We reject Georgia's accusations of Russian aggression. . . . Russia proposes that negotiations begin immediately involving representatives from Georgia, South Ossetia, Russia and North Ossetia in order to find a political solution to the South Ossetian problem. If the various sides involved in the conflict ignore these justified demands, which are founded on generally accepted international principles, the Russian Federation will take all action necessary in order to protect the human rights, lives and dignity of the inhabitants of the region, and to restore peace and order. The government of the Russian Federation intends to inform the UN Secretary General of the situation in South Ossetia, which poses a threat to international peace and security, and if necessary, to call upon the UN Security Council for help. The citizens of Russia can be confident that the national leadership will act sensibly and decisively so as not to allow the conflict to develop any further.[39]

On June 24, 1992, Yeltsin, Shevardnadze, and representatives of North and South Ossetia met in Dagomys (Sochi) and signed an

---

37. ITAR-TASS, June 17, 1992.

38. "Statement of the Russian Government," ITAR-TASS, June 20, 1992.

39. Ibid.

agreement on the principles to govern a settlement of the conflict. Practical steps were agreed upon during a further meeting of representatives of the four parties in Tskhinvali on July 3, 1992. Troops from Russia, Georgia, and Ossetia were used to establish a joint peacekeeping force of four battalions numbering 2,000 troops and 1,000 reserves. A mixed control commission comprising one representative of each of the four governments and one military expert from each party was organized with full powers to make decisions affecting the zone of conflict.[40] The commission's purpose was to verify compliance with the cease-fire, control the withdrawal of armed formations and the disbanding of the defensive forces, and monitor security in the conflict zone. At the Dagomys meeting it was also decided to form mixed observer groups, establish a multilateral press center, and establish joint command of the local peacekeeping forces that would create a safety corridor.

Mixed detachments of Russian, Georgian, and Ossetian armed forces began to carry out their peacekeeping mission in the Tskhinvali area not only in the 15-kilometer-wide neutral corridor, but in the entire region where military actions had occurred. In the view of Chairman of the Council of Ministers of North Ossetia, Sergei Khetagurov, the 1,500-person peacekeeping contingent should remain in the Tskhinvali region until the status of South Ossetia, was settled.[41] The OSCE mission, discussed below, began to operate in South Ossetia at the end of December 1992 and also contributed to the relative stability of the region.

These joint peacekeeping forces were able to prevent further serious fighting even though the situation in the zone of peacekeeping operations continued to be extremely difficult. In February 1993, the North Ossetian government adopted a "Declaration on the State Independence and Sovereignty of the Republic of South Ossetia," which formally recognized the South Ossetian Republic.[42] The action was only symbolic, however, since as a constituent republic of the

---

40. The Mixed Control Commission was headed by three co-chairmen: Sergei Shoigu, a member of the Russian government; Tengis Kitovani, a member of the Georgian Council of State and Minister of Defense; and Sergei Khetagurov, chairman of the Council of Ministers of North Ossetia.

41. "Press Conference of the Leadership of the Peacekeeping Forces in Tskhinvali," TASS, July 14, 1992.

42. "Ossetia: The Situation in the Conflict Zone Has Not Changed," ITAR-TASS, March 6, 1993.

Russian Federation, North Ossetia did not have the authority to recognize other states. The South Ossetian Parliament adopted a new
constitution in November 1993, and the State Council (Nykhas) was
made the supreme legislative body of South Ossetia. Both actions
were declared illegal by the Georgian authorities, which continued to
insist that the Georgian Supreme Soviet had abolished the South
Ossetian Autonomous Republic in December 1990 and that these
enactments represented unlawful attempts by the province of Shida
Kartli (the Georgian name for South Ossetia) to break away from the
Republic of Georgia.[43]

Following the withdrawal of Georgian troops in 1992, South Ossetia
achieved de facto independence, since in the following two years, the
Georgian leadership was preoccupied with the situation in Abkhazia.
The situation of "no peace, no war" continues and could shift in either
direction. However, some hope for a positive change was contained in
a statement by Edward Shevardnadze, who declared in a March 24,
1995, interview on Georgian radio that the best administrative structure for Georgia would be a federation, and emphasized that a federation would allow for a swift and peaceful solution of the conflicts in
Abkhazia and South Ossetia.[44] Until Shevardnadze's announcement,
the official Georgian position was that any political status for South
Ossetia was completely out of the question; his statement marked an
abrupt change in the Georgian position. However, many political
groups in Georgia opposed the idea of a federation, and no full-scale
settlement of the conflict has been achieved.

THE ROLE OF THE RUSSIAN FEDERATION

The conflict in South Ossetia has direct ramifications for the situation
in the Russian Federation. Various opposition groups have used the
South Ossetian conflict in their campaign against the Yeltsin government, accusing it of being incapable of defending Russian interests in
the region. North Ossetia's proposed assistance to South Ossetia
threatened to destabilize Russian control over the whole North
Caucasus region.[45] North Ossetia was itself unstable and has been

43. "CIS Today and Tomorrow," ITAR-TASS, March 31, 1994.

44. "Eduard Shevardnadze Announces that a Federation in Georgia Will Ensure
a Swift and Peaceful Political Settlement of Conflicts in Abkhazia and the
Tskhinvali Region," ITAR-TASS, April 24, 1995.

45. A special session of the Supreme Soviet of North Ossetia decided to respond
to Georgian actions. The Georgian military road was blockaded, and gas supplies

inundated with refugees from the fighting. Potential frictions with the North Ossetians are worrisome to Moscow, since North Ossetia has traditionally been a Russian ally in the volatile North Caucasus.[46] The official Russian position on the conflict was that Georgian territorial integrity should be maintained, but it was unwilling to stand by while South Ossetians, close ethnic kin of its own citizens, were killed.

In the final two years of the Soviet Union's existence, the Gorbachev administration used the prospect of South Ossetian secession to pressure Georgia to remain within the Soviet Union. Boris Yeltsin, who was at the time Chairman of the Supreme Soviet of the Russian Federation, was waging a struggle against Gorbachev and the Soviet center and was prepared to ally himself with any forces that supported his agenda, including the Gamsakhurdia regime. His team of advisers characterized autonomous entities looking to the union center for guarantees against assimilation as communist enclaves. The Russian leadership's actions toward South Ossetia thus reinforced Gamsakhurdia and gave him, however unintentionally, confidence that he could pursue his policies toward South Ossetia unimpeded. It should be stressed that this was not the intention of the Russian government, but the net effect of its policy; initially the Georgians were cautious in dealing with the separatist region, but when they saw that there would be no reaction from Moscow, they became bolder.

Growing struggles inside Yeltsin's government gave his opponents, led by Chairman of the Russian Supreme Soviet Ruslan Khasbulatov and Vice President Alexander Rutskoi, the opportunity to take strong stances against Georgian actions in South Ossetia in the hopes of undermining the Russian leadership. As noted above, in October 1991, the Russian Supreme Soviet passed a resolution condemning the Georgian actions and demanding that Russia apply

---

to Georgia were cut off pending stabilization of the situation in South Ossetia. In Vladikavkaz, volunteers and Cossacks were recruited into a republican guard. The North Ossetia Defense Committee issued a statement from Vladikavkaz appealing to the Russian government to supply the new national guard with weapons and military equipment, and warning that in the case of a refusal, North Ossetia would take over the military property and armaments belonging to the Vladikavkaz garrison and the other military divisions and units in the republic.

46. See Olga Osipova's chapter on North Ossetia and Ingushetia in this volume for more on this (Chapter 3 of this volume).

severe economic sanctions against Georgia.[47] Rutskoi sharply criticized Shevardnadze's policy toward South Ossetia, calling it a genocide against the Ossetian people "conducted not by groups out of the control of the Georgian State Council, but by detachments of the national guard."[48]

These political pressures forced Yeltsin to change course several times. At first he had condoned Gamsakhurdia's efforts to eliminate the self-proclaimed independent entities, but when the conflict affected Russian security by provoking strong reaction and threatening instability in North Ossetia, he reversed his course and staunchly opposed Gamsakhurdia's policies. Similarly, Yeltsin had initially been a strong supporter of Shevardnadze, but later turned against him. These shifts may also have been linked to the growing problem that the self-proclaimed Republic of Chechnya posed for Russia. The need to counter the Chechens added to the importance of North Ossetia as a strategic ally in the North Caucasus and reinforced the need for a harsh policy against Georgian actions in South Ossetia.

Thanks to the presence of the Russian peacekeeping contingent and representatives of the OSCE, the armistice in South Ossetia has endured since 1992. Officially the Russian Federation seeks progress toward a settlement of the conflict and has attempted to affirm its role as an active mediator. In an official statement, the Russian

---

47. In October 1991, the Supreme Soviet of the RSFSR passed a resolution "On the Situation in the North Ossetian SSR," which stated: "As a result of human rights violations in the Republic of Georgia, a growing number of refugees from South Ossetia and other areas of Georgia are pouring into the North Ossetian SSR. So far, over 85,000 have arrived, and the result has been that social conditions in North Ossetia have significantly worsened and tensions have increased. The leadership of the Republic of Georgia has ignored the appeal of the Third (Extraordinary) Congress of People's Deputies of the RSFSR on the situation in South Ossetia. Continuing tension in the North Ossetian SSR and failure to resolve the conflict in South Ossetia may have disastrous consequences. With the aim of promoting the normalization of the situation in the North Ossetian SSR and the region as a whole, the Supreme Soviet of the RSFSR decrees that: "The President of the RSFSR will take all possible steps, including severe economic sanctions against Georgia if necessary, in order to ensure a swift resolution of the conflict in South Ossetia and restore respect for human rights, and will provide additional material assistance to the North Ossetian SSR." ITAR-TASS, October 26, 1991.

48. Rutskoi continued: "What is infuriating is when instead of averting the killing of innocent Ossetian people, a man who is recognized as a peacemaker starts a squabble and takes it to the UN, the OSCE and other organizations." ITAR-TASS, June 20, 1992.

Deputy Minister of Defense, Colonel General Georgi Kondratev, maintained that the Russian Federation was the only force capable of separating the various groups fighting in the former Soviet territories and bringing them to the negotiating table. No other international organization or group of governments, he said, could do this.[49] The agreement signed in Sochi on June 24, 1992, continues to be looked upon as the basis for a solution. The official position of the Russian Federation has remained unchanged: support for the independence and territorial integrity of the Republic of Georgia, but with effective guarantees for the autonomy of the Ossetians and other peoples.[50]

THE ROLE OF INTERNATIONAL ORGANIZATIONS

The international organization most heavily involved in the South Ossetian conflict has been the OSCE. In November 1992, following a fact-finding visit to Georgia by Ishtvan Garmati in his capacity as personal representative to the Chairman-in-Office, and at the request of both parties for mediation, the OSCE Committee of Senior Officials dispatched a "mission of long duration," which arrived in Tbilisi on December 3, 1992.[51] According to the mandate and subsequent memorandum, the mission was to identify and seek to eliminate sources of tension, create a visible OSCE presence in the region, uphold the existing cease-fire, and help create a broader political framework for a lasting resolution of the conflict based on OSCE commitments.[52] The nine-person mission was led by Ambassador Garmati, and included military officers from the Federal Republic of Germany, Sweden, Hungary, Poland, and France.

The composition of the mission reflected its purpose. It included military observers, whose role was to create "a visible OSCE presence" and "to uphold the cease-fire," as well as diplomats, who were

49. In the words of Kondratev, who is in charge of Russian peacekeeping forces, "peacekeeping in Russia has become an issue of government policy, and peacekeeping issues are now part of our national military doctrine." According to Kondratev, in 1993 the Ministry of Defense spent over 26 billion rubles on financing peacekeeping operations. ITAR-TASS, March 22, 1994.

50. "A statement by the Ministry for Foreign Affairs of the Russian Federation on the Decision of the Supreme Soviet of North Ossetia," ITAR-TASS, February 22, 1993.

51. The mission's mandate is extended every six months. In September 1995, it was extended to June 30, 1996.

52. See the mandate of the CSCE Mission to Georgia, adopted at the CSO Meeting in Prague, November 20, 1992.

to organize negotiations between the Georgian government and the South Ossetian authorities. In accordance with its mandate, the mission monitored the cease-fire declared in the Sochi Agreement and tried to promote dialogue between Georgian officials and South Ossetian representatives. It conducted negotiations with the leaders of Georgia, South Ossetia, and North Ossetia, and facilitated extensive talks between experts on both sides in the conflict. Of particular importance was the first round of Georgian-Ossetian negotiations in Tskhinvali, beginning on January 26, 1993, in which the first steps to a settlement of the conflict were defined. As a result of these negotiations, three joint intergovernmental commissions were created: one to help refugees, one to deal with human rights, and one to facilitate economic and financial activity.

The mission organized a number of meetings in Vladikavkaz, the capital of North Ossetia, among representatives of Georgia, South Ossetia, North Ossetia, and the OSCE to continue the search for reconciliation.[53] According to the head of the mission, whereas the military observers had some success, the mission's attempts at negotiation ran aground on the sheer incompatibility of Georgian and South Ossetian positions. As the mission reported,

both sides declare their full readiness to negotiate without preconditions, but interpret this [readiness] differently: the Georgian understanding of "without preconditions" is that we accept that Southern Ossetia is part of Georgia, nothing but cultural autonomy would be offered to the Ossetians and only its details would be subject of political negotiations. The Ossetians, for their part, understand "without preconditions" as the recognition of an independent South Ossetia, and the negotiations should accordingly be aimed at the elaboration of the peaceful coexistence of Georgia and the Republic of Southern Ossetia.[54]

Meeting again in Vladikavkaz in June 1994, the representatives of Georgia, South Ossetia, North Ossetia, and the OSCE mission issued a joint statement on means to promote reconciliation in Georgia. In addition, the Mixed Control Commission established two years earlier renewed its attempts to find a permanent settlement to the conflict.

Characteristic of these types of negotiations is the tendency of each side to defend its version of the application of OSCE principles. The

---

53. The OSCE meetings were located in Vladikavkaz because the capital of South Ossetia was completely devastated.

54. OSCE Communication No. 41, Prague, February 2, 1993.

Georgian leaders continually referred to the principle of territorial integrity and insisted that no OSCE requirement obliged them to grant South Ossetia anything beyond cultural autonomy.[55] The South Ossetian authorities, for their part, pointed to the principle of ethnic and national self-determination and asserted that basic individual rights and freedoms should have precedence over the principle of territorial integrity.

By declaring its aim "to identify and seek to eliminate sources of tension," the OSCE mission inevitably ran into the problem of how to apply international law to the complex issues involved in the conflict while adhering to OSCE principles of national and human rights. For example, Georgia's Constitution and administrative laws clearly reveal the ethnocratic nature of the Georgian political system. Article 52 of the Constitution unequivocally states that power belongs to the Georgian nation, and Article 129 limits the rights of so-called "national minorities" to "managing their own cultural development."[56] Moreover, since the late 1980s, Georgian public discourse has been imbued with the ideology of the Georgians as the "host people" in Georgia, with all others as "guests"—an ideology that still prevails. The contradiction between the ethno-political claims of the Georgian state, on one side, and the OSCE Charter and international statutes on national and individual rights, on the other, created a problem for the OSCE and other international organizations attempting to mediate the conflict. In these circumstances the OSCE could not overcome the impasse and mediate a solution. It could do little more than monitor compliance with a cease-fire, keep tabs on general developments, provide information, and help in the procedural aspects of relations between the two sides.

---

55. Although some Georgian officials have recently been more willing to discuss the possibility of a federal state structure, this phenomenon is still only a tendency—not official policy.

56. EDITORS' NOTE: In contrast with the interim Georgian Constitution of 1992, which was a slightly modified version of the 1921 Constitution of Georgia, Article 5 of the new Georgian Constitution adopted on August 24, 1995 states that "the people are the only source of state power in Georgia." This provision strongly suggests that Georgian authorities have opted for civic, territorial nationalism as opposed to ethnic nationalism. Moreover, the Article of the Constitution dealing with the state structure of Georgia is an open clause stipulating the definition on the resolution of conflicts in Abkhazia and South Ossetia. Article 2 of the new Constitution reads: "The internal territorial state arrangement of Georgia is determined by constitutional law on the basis of the authority demarcation principle effective over the whole territory of Georgia at such a time when there is the full restoration of the Georgian jurisdiction."

Although a fundamental settlement eluded them, the parties were able to reach agreement on joint action to stabilize the situation in the zone of conflict—combating organized crime, which had arisen in the chaotic conditions of the breakdown of law and order; restoring road and rail communications between Tskhinvali and other towns; and cooperating on economic, agricultural, and social reconstruction. In particular, they agreed to take joint action against the drug trade, which has been an important source of support for the independent militia groups of mixed Georgian and Ossetian ethnicity that terrorize the local population.[57] At the same time, the absence of a solution to the conflict itself made it difficult to deal with the problem of the return of refugees and deported people, although at the end of February 1995, a joint supervisory committee began assisting in the repatriation of refugees to South Ossetia. Although the issues were far from resolved, it appeared that the OSCE was the only international organization whose activities produced results in the South Ossetian conflict.

The issue of who would command and finance peacekeeping activities in the conflict zone was discussed in Moscow during several rounds of negotiations between Russia, Georgia, South Ossetia, and North Ossetia, with the participation of the OSCE mission. On March 1, 1995, a roundtable was organized in Vladikavkaz with the OSCE mission to discuss future relations between Georgia and South Ossetia, as well as establishing and financing a united command for peacekeeping.

The Conflict in Abkhazia

As described above, the status of Abkhazia within Georgia has been contested for several centuries, including throughout the Soviet period, when sporadic outbreaks of violence were easily suppressed by the Soviet authorities. From 1988–90, a power struggle developed within the leadership of the Georgian Communist Party between the old guard and the national communists.[58] Unlike the old guard,

---

57. In early 1995, the Georgian and South Ossetian authorities took part in a joint crackdown on criminal militias in the Tskhinvali region and confiscated their weapons. "Georgian and South Ossetian Authorities Take Part in Joint Crackdown on Criminal Militias in Tskhinvali Region," ITAR-TASS, January 18, 1995.

58. For more on the national communist movement in the communist parties of the union republics of the Soviet Union, see Edward Ozhiganov's chapter on Moldova in this volume.

which held to the official party line of internationalism—i.e., preservation of the Soviet Union—the national communists looked upon autonomous entities within the territory of Georgia as superfluous formations. For example, Anzor Totadze, head of the Interethnic Relations Department of the Central Committee of the GCP, wrote:

The creation of an Abkhazian SSR was a mistake from the very start. Abkhazia did not deserve this status, for two principal reasons. First, the large indigenous Georgian population in Abkhazia is larger than the Abkhazian population. Second, Abkhazia never achieved the minimum population threshold of one million required to attain the status of autonomous republic under the Soviet system.[59]

Calls for the abolition of Abkhazian autonomy predated the rise of tensions in South Ossetia and were heard for the first time at the end of 1988 during meetings organized in Tbilisi by Georgian nationalists. Georgia's anti-Abkhazian campaign reached its climax in Tbilisi on April 9, 1989, when, after five days of anti-Soviet demonstrations by supporters of Georgian independence, a clash broke out between demonstrators and troops in the square adjacent to the government building; eighteen people were killed and many injured. The most common slogans at the rally were: "End discrimination against Georgians in Georgia!" "Go home, Russian invaders!" and "Abolish the Abkhazian Republic!" Soviet Interior Ministry troops and the army were brought in ostensibly at the behest of the Georgian leadership, but clearly the real initiator of this decision was Mikhail Gorbachev and the politburo in Moscow, who feared that the nationalist opposition might seize power in Georgia.[60] Although the decision was supported by many leaders in Georgia, decisions of this nature could not yet be taken by the party leaders of a republic without the direct approval of the politburo of the Central Committee of the CPSU.[61] Gorbachev, speaking to Georgian communists a few days after the Tbilisi events, said:

---

59. *The White Book on Abkhazia*, p. 14.

60. A collection of documents, including the conclusions of commissions of inquiry on the clashes on April 9, 1989, in Tbilisi, was published in *April 9: Documentary Materials on the Tbilisi Tragedy* (Tbilisi: s.n., 1990).

61. "E. Shevardnadze's Speech to the Plenum of the Central Committee of the Georgian Communist Party April 14, 1989," in *April 9: Documentary Materials on the Tbilisi Tragedy*, pp. 41–52.

What happened in Tbilisi was undoubtedly a blow to the campaign to restructure, democratize and revive the country. The decisions and actions of certain irresponsible people have led to heightened tension in the republic. . . . Working people have nothing to gain from those who attempt to destroy the ties of friendship and cooperation that bind our peoples together, to dismantle the socialist system in the republic, and to push Georgia into the vortex of ethnic hatred. Those who advocate these actions have time and again been reminded of the dangers of the path they are following, and onto which they are summoning others, and [warned] of the extreme harmfulness of their actions.

An investigation into the Tbilisi events was later conducted by a special commission of the Soviet Union Supreme Soviet, but the commission failed to clarify who was responsible for the tragedy.

On July 16, 1989, the first clashes of the Abkhazian conflict erupted in Sukhumi, the capital of Abkhazia, and continued for several days before being brought under control. The spark was a disagreement between Abkhazians and Georgian residents over the establishment of a branch of the Tbilisi State University in Sukhumi. According to official information, twelve people were killed and about two hundred injured.[62] This incident provoked widespread disorder throughout Abkhazia and part of western Georgia. The government and Supreme Soviet of the Georgian SSR and the Abkhazian authorities asked the Soviet Interior Ministry to send troops to Abkhazia to reestablish law and order.

The new first secretary of the Central Committee of the GCP was Givi Gumbaridze, who rose to power with the national communists, and whose advisers lacked a clear policy on interethnic relations. However, they plainly opposed Abkhazian autonomy. Georgian political elites shared the view of the ethnic nationalist groups that the Georgian people were the "host" people and the sole legitimate source of power. The indifference of the ruling *nomenklatura* toward the ideology of ethnic superiority and the ethnic attacks motivated by it were interpreted by Georgian ethnic nationalists as a tacit sign of approval for organized violence against minority groups.

Mikhail Gorbachev and his close advisers provided both ideological and practical support to the Georgian communist *nomenklatura*. In the Soviet Union Supreme Soviet, which Gorbachev chaired, Abkhazian deputies proposed the establishment of a commission to

---

62. "The Supreme Soviet of the Soviet Union: Information on the Situation in Abkhazia," TASS, July 17, 1989.

study interethnic relations in Abkhazia and hold public hearings and debates by specialists. They also proposed the creation of commissions on ethnic groups and minorities at both the central and republic levels. These suggestions were not adopted. Gorbachev indicated after the events in Sukhumi that a constructive dialogue was under way, but in fact the ethnic crisis in Georgia was worsening. The ambiguous and vacillating policy of the Soviet elites in Moscow gave mixed signals; it emboldened the Georgian nationalists and undermined the confidence of the leaders of Abkhazia and South Ossetia in the central Soviet authorities.

In March and June 1989, the Supreme Soviet of the Georgian SSR passed resolutions restoring Georgian independence and declaring that Soviet control in Georgia had been imposed in 1921 after the overthrow of the Georgian Democratic Republic and military occupation by Russian (Bolshevik) forces, and that consequently all government structures created after February 1921 were illegal. The logical implication was that the creation of the Abkhazian Autonomous SSR by the Soviet authorities was null and void and that the status quo of February 1921 should be restored in Abkhazia.[63] The Abkhazian leadership further claimed that in order to facilitate Georgia's exit from the Soviet Union, the Georgian leadership changed the electoral rules so as to deny representation to autonomous regions, which were treated as administrative districts of Georgia.

From July 1989 to July 1990, the situation in Abkhazia remained relatively calm. Troops from the Soviet Interior Ministry were a continuous presence and managed to maintain order in the region, though outbursts of violence did occur, including attempts to seize weapons depots. No progress was made toward solving any of the interethnic problems or addressing the status of Abkhazia. (At this point, Georgians constituted a majority of the population of Abkhazia and occupied many key positions in the local administration.[64]) With the rise of separatist aspirations among the Abkhazians,

---

63. This logic parallels that used in Moldova and Latvia—i.e., the attempt on the part of republican authorities to return to the pre-Soviet status quo, at least juridically.

64. According to the Soviet Union Central Statistical Committee, Georgians comprised 45.7 percent of the population of the Abkhazian ASSR. Ethnic Abkhazians made up 17.8 percent; Russians, 14.2 percent; Armenians, 14.6 percent; and other ethnic groups, 7.7 percent.

support for Gamsakhurdia among ethnic Georgians grew. The Georgians in Abkhazia were virulently opposed to Abkhazian independence and their involuntary separation from the rest of Georgia. They coalesced around the Abkhazian branch of the Roundtable bloc, which supported Gamsakhurdia. Meanwhile, the Abkhazians consolidated into the People's Forum of Abkhazia (*Aidgilara*).

A decree of the Presidium of the Supreme Soviet of Georgia dated August 20, 1990, proclaimed that Georgian would be the sole language spoken in the Supreme Soviet of Georgia. From this legislation the Abkhazians concluded that the Georgian leadership had recognized the status quo existing before February 1921. Five days later, the Abkhazian Supreme Soviet adopted a Declaration on Sovereignty and a decree "On Legal Guarantees for the Defense of Abkhazian Statehood." The Georgian leadership regarded these documents as attempts to change the territorial structure of the Georgian SSR and a gross violation of the Georgian Constitution as well as those of the Abkhazian ASSR and the Soviet Union, and the Abkhazian decrees were declared invalid.

Out of a total of 140 deputies, the Supreme Soviet of the Abkhazian region included 57 ethnic Abkhazians, 53 Georgians, and 14 Russians. An Abkhazian and a Georgian party emerged in the local administration, each of which claimed to represent the lawful authority in Abkhazia. The session of the Supreme Soviet that passed the act to restore Abkhazian statehood was boycotted by the ethnic Georgian deputies in order to make it impossible to gather the necessary quorum to pass legislation. Later, Georgian deputies insisted that the Abkhazian sovereignty acts were passed as a result of violations of procedure. They convened on August 31, 1990, and declared an extraordinary session of the Abkhazian Supreme Soviet, at which they rescinded all the enactments passed at the August 25 session, declaring them contrary to the constitutions of the Abkhazian ASSR and the Georgian SSR. From this point on, the ethnic Georgian and ethnic Abkhazian political deputies divided formally and with great enmity.

All-Georgian parliamentary elections were held on October 28, 1990. The bloc of political parties called the Roundtable for a Free Georgia, which brought Gamsakhurdia to power, became the dominant political force in Georgia, gaining considerably more seats than the GCP and marking a shift in Georgian state power from the national communists to Gamsakhurdia's openly nationalist group. This new government was more prepared to resort to force to solve the separatism problem.[65] When Gamsakhurdia became head of state, the aggressive policy he had instituted against South Ossetia while leader of the informal national movement was still in place, and the Abkhazians interpreted this as a clear demonstration of what they could expect in the foreseeable future. At the first session of the new Georgian Parliament, national communist deputies overwhelmingly passed, over the opposition of communist deputies from Abkhazia and South Ossetia, a series of laws and resolutions enabling Georgia to leave the Soviet Union. On November 16, 1990, the new Supreme Soviet of the Republic of Georgia sent an appeal to the Paris Conference on Security and Cooperation in Europe (CSCE), stating Georgia's intention to restore its independence and placing special emphasis on the relevance of principles of international law to Georgian territorial integrity. These particular principles were emphasized because the Councils of People's Deputies in Abkhazia and South Ossetia clearly did not share Georgia's desire to leave the Soviet Union.[66] In February 1991, the Georgian Parliament abolished the system of local Soviets on the territory of Georgia and introduced prefectures headed by prefects with unlimited powers, who acted as Gamsakhurdia's personal representatives. In Abkhazia, as in Ossetia, a personal representative of Gamsakhurdia was introduced, with no responsibility to the Supreme Soviet or to either of the two self-proclaimed Supreme Soviets that existed at that time.

Gorbachev had announced a nationwide referendum scheduled for March 17, 1991, on whether the Soviet Union should be preserved as a federation of states. Gamsakhurdia refused to allow the referendum to be held in Georgia, and the leaders of the Abkhazian Autonomous Republic who planned to hold it anyway were accused of being separatists and agitators. Nonetheless, on March 17, Abkhazia participated in Gorbachev's referendum, providing 245 voting sites and lists with some 340,000 voters. The Georgian government was able to prevent the referendum in Gali, a primarily Georgian region of Abkhazia where approximately 20 percent of the total voting population resided. Disregarding such procedural irregularities, more than 60 percent of the total population of

65. "Statement of the Chairman of the Georgian Parliament," TASS, February 10, 1991.

66. "The Preference of the Georgian Parliament," TASS, November 16, 1990.

Abkhazia voted, and 97.65 percent of them supported the preservation of the Soviet Union.[67] In response, the Georgian leadership moved to file criminal charges against referendum organizers in Abkhazia, and Gamsakhurdia stated at a press conference in Moscow on July 3, 1991, that ethnic minorities in Georgia should be content with cultural autonomy. This included Abkhazia, which was planning to sign the new union treaty that Gorbachev was then preparing.

Georgia held its own referendum on the question of restoring the independence of the Georgian state on March 31, 1991. Gamsakhurdia announced that since votes would be cast by secret ballot, the results would be the chief test of the loyalty of various ethnic groups in districts with large non-Georgian populations. The results were overwhelming—90.5 percent of the electorate participated in the voting, and 98.93 percent of the votes supported Georgian independence.[68] The only places where the referendum was not held were Tskhinvali and the Dzhav and Kornis districts of South Ossetia. In Abkhazia, 59.84 percent of the voting-age population supported Georgian independence, although turnout as a whole was only 61.2 percent.[69]

While the two referenda were under way, Gamsakhurdia's main forces initiated military operations in South Ossetia. In order to safeguard against a probable Georgian invasion, the Abkhazian leadership began to look for allies and became increasingly involved in the Confederation of Mountain Peoples, a transnational sociopolitical organization of the North Caucasus republics of the Russian Federation with the ultimate aim of creating a Confederative Union whose relationship to Russia was not clearly specified. On November 10, 1991, this group held its third congress in Sukhumi and accepted Abkhazia as a member. Later, as discussed below, the Confederation established its own military forces, which fought on the side of the Abkhazians against the Georgians although they were officially citizens of Russia.

Gamsakhurdia's overthrow by the forces of the Interim Military Council in December 1991 and January 1992 confronted the

---

67. TASS, April 1, 1991.

68. "The Results of the Referendum in Georgia Are Summed Up," Sakinform-TASS, April 5, 1991.

69. Of those who turned out, almost 98 percent voted for Georgian independence. "Preliminary Results of the Referendum Across the Soviet Union," TASS, March 18, 1991.

Abkhazian authorities with a real threat. Gamsakhurdia's supporters had retreated to western Georgia, and the conflict among the Georgian factions could have spread to Abkhazian territory. The new Georgian leaders appealed to the Abkhazian leadership and tried to make allies of them. At the end of March 1992, the worst fears of the Abkhazians were realized when armed bands of Gamsakhurdia's supporters seized key district centers in western Georgia. The Abkhazian authorities were determined not to allow the military activities to spread to Abkhazian territory, and the idea of asking for military assistance from the Confederation of Mountain Peoples gained increasing support among the Abkhazian leaders.

Once again, the local authorities and public institutions of Abkhazia began to split up into ethnic Georgian and ethnic Abkhazian groups, which created a kind of dual authority in the republic. On June 24, 1992, the Abkhazian National Guard, under orders from the long-time chairman of the Abkhazian Supreme Soviet and leader of the ethnic Abkhazian faction, Vladislav Ardzinba, seized the Abkhazian Interior Ministry, which was headed by ethnic Georgians. The ethnic Georgian members of the Supreme Soviet—the Democratic Abkhazia faction headed by Tamaz Nadareishvili—blamed separatist elements for raising tensions in the region and called for a massive strike by the Georgian population of Abkhazia.[70] On July 23, the ethnic Abkhazian members—thirty-five of the sixty-five deputies—abrogated the constitution and restored the 1925 constitution of the Abkhazian Soviet Socialist Republic—i.e., the constitution of the Abkhazian Republic before its incorporation into Georgia. Abkhazia proclaimed itself a sovereign state and declared its intention to conduct its relations with Georgia on the basis of negotiations between two sovereign states. The Abkhazian Parliament also selected a coat of arms and a flag and declared its official name to be the Republic of Abkhazia.

The new Georgian leader and chairman of the Council of State, Edward Shevardnadze, called this decision a serious mistake on the

---

70. At a press conference in Moscow, on June 4, 1992, Nadareishvili argued that it was necessary to pass a new election law in Abkhazia inasmuch as the existing law envisaged the election of deputies according to nationality: thus, of the 65 seats in the Abkhazian Supreme Soviet, 28 were allotted to Abkhazians though only 93,000 lived in the republic, while the Georgian population numbering 239,000 controlled only 26 seats. He accused the Abkhazian leadership of increasing tension and of "gross violation of the constitution of the republic by passing various unconstitutional enactments," TASS, June 4, 1992.

part of the ethnic Abkhazian leadership. "I am afraid," he said, "that the consequences may be serious. We must look for a way out of this dead end."[71] The way out proved to be war. On August 14, 1992, Georgian Army units invaded the territory of Abkhazia. According to Colonel General Valeri Patrikeev, the commander of Russian forces in the Transcaucasus Military District, Russian armed forces in Georgia did not support either side.[72] However, there is no doubt that the heavy weaponry used by the Georgian troops to attack Abkhazia was of Russian origin. In an address to the parliaments of the world, Ardzinba stated: "Shevardnadze publicly admits that his greatest source of support against Abkhazia and its allies has been the commander of the Transcaucasus Military District, General Patrikeev."[73] A communiqué from the press department of the Cossack Association of Abkhazia dated August 16, 1992, also asserted that "in the Sukhumi region there are as many as 50 tanks and 40 artillery units that have been supplied by the commander of the Transcaucasus Military District."[74]

SHEVARDNADZE'S WAR IN ABKHAZIA

At a meeting of the Georgian Council of State in Tbilisi on August 15, 1992, the day after the attack on Abkhazia, Shevardnadze stated: "We have done the right thing." He explained that the military operations were necessary to defend the interests of the Abkhazian Autonomous Republic against banditry and to protect important road, rail, and communications links in western Georgia.[75] Shevardnadze went to great lengths to present this justification of the decision to the world community. For example, a UN mission that visited Georgia from September 12–20, 1992, substantially adopted Shevardnadze's account. Section V of its report states:

When it became clear to the Georgian government in mid-1992 that the police were unable to prevent the ongoing sabotage and robbery,

---

71. Edward Shevardnadze denounced the decision of the Abkhazian Parliament to revert to the 1925 constitution. ITAR-TASS, July 25, 1992.

72. ITAR-TASS, August 14, 1992.

73. G. Amkuab, ed., *Abkhazia: Chronicle of an Undeclared War*, Part I (Moscow: Luch Publishing House for the Press Service of the Supreme Soviet of Abkhazia, 1992), p. 37.

74. Ibid.

75. "The Georgian Council of State Discusses the Situation in Abkhazia," ITAR-TASS, August 15, 1992.

the government decided to send around 2,000 Georgian soldiers to Abkhazia for the purpose of protecting railroads and other means of communication. Mr. Shevardnadze stated that the Republic of Georgia had a sovereign right to move troops within its territory. He told the mission that he had telephoned Mr. Ardzinba and had informed him of these measures.

The Georgian armed forces, with the use of heavy armor and helicopters, attacked the Abkhazian towns of Sukhumi and Gali, and Georgian forces seized the Council of Ministers headquarters and other Abkhazian administrative buildings in Sukhumi.[76] The Abkhazian population and other non-Georgian inhabitants were terrorized, leading to an exodus of refugees from Abkhazia to the adjoining territory of the Russian Federation.[77] On August 14, 1992, the Abkhazian leadership ordered the mobilization of the entire adult population and the issue of weapons to the units of the internal troops. The next day they demanded that a nearby Russian air defense unit stationed in the town of Gudauta hand over its weapons and munitions to the Abkhazians. The commanding officer refused to comply, but a large number of weapons were taken from the depot by force.[78]

At this point, the government of the unrecognized Republic of Chechnya within the Russian Federation dispatched a note to the Georgian Council of State, which demanded "an immediate halt to the aggression against Abkhazia." Dzhokhar Dudaev, former Chechen President and rebel leader, in an order to the Chechen armed forces, stated that the action against Abkhazia "represents a direct threat to the security of the Republic of Chechnya and all the republics of the Caucasus."[79] The leaders of the Supreme Soviets of the Adygan, Dagestani, Kabardino-Balkarian, and Karachaevo-Cherkessian republics in the Russian North Caucasus, along with the heads of the Soviets and administrations of the Krasnodar and

---

76. Evidence of the attack on Sukhumi by Georgian troops is presented in the book by IMA press correspondent Anna Broido, *The Road to Temple is Shelled Every Day* (Moscow: 1994), pp. 2–11.

77. Detailed documentary evidence on the destruction of the civilian population and the pillage and destruction of the material and cultural infrastructure of the Abkhazian Autonomous Republic can be found in *The White Book of Abkhazia*, pp. 143–213.

78. "The Abkhazian Leadership Demands Weapons from Military Unit," ITAR-TASS, August 15, 1992.

79. "Dzhokhar Dudaev Denounces the Actions of the Georgian Council of State in Respect to Abkhazia," ITAR-TASS, August 15, 1992.

Stavropol regions, called on all sides for an immediate halt to military operations, the withdrawal of Georgian troops from Abkhazia, and the pursuit of a peaceful settlement. The Confederation of Mountain Peoples sent an ultimatum to the Georgian government demanding the withdrawal of all Georgian troops from Abkhazia by August 21 and the payment of compensation for the damage caused. The Confederation threatened military operations against Georgia if Abkhazia continued to be occupied.[80] Such a possibility posed a serious threat to the Georgian government, but it made no official response. At the same time, the Georgian State Council issued a statement pointing out that the restoration of the 1925 constitution by the Abkhazian Parliament was tantamount to the "self-dissolution of its autonomy." This same logic had been applied to South Ossetia before the war was unleashed there.

By August 19, 1992, four days after the fighting began, it became clear that there would be no quick Georgian victory, and the military confrontation between the two sides rapidly evolved into a guerrilla war. According to information supplied by the Abkhazians, at this point the Georgian armed forces had already suffered one hundred casualties and lost nine tanks.[81] Volunteer detachments continued to be formed in the republics of the North Caucasus and sent to Abkhazia. Local Abkhazian Cossack organizations, which supported the Abkhazian bid for independence because it offered the possibility of reunification with Russia, sent an appeal to the Union of Cossack Troops in southern Russia requesting help, including military intervention.[82] Fighting became especially bitter in late August and early September, when Georgian army units started operations near Sukhumi and Gagri.[83] Entire quarters of these towns came under fire along with Russian Army units stationed there.

---

80. For more on this extraordinary session of the Parliament of the Confederation of Mountain Peoples, see "The Situation in Abkhazia and the Repulsion of the Aggression of the Georgian Council of State Forces," in *The White Book of Abkhazia*, pp. 55–56.

81. *Abkhazia: Chronicle of an Undeclared War*, Part I, p. 58.

82. "Appeal by the Association of Cossacks of Abkhazia to the Union of Cossack Troops of Russia," in *Abkhazia: Chronicle of an Undeclared War*, Part I, p. 106.

83. On August 24, 1992, following the initial setbacks, a new commander of the Georgian forces in Abkhazia was appointed. The man chosen was Georgi Karkarashvili, who had been commander in chief of the national guard, and had directed military operations in South Ossetia and western Georgia (the previous commander of military operations in Abkhazia had been Tengis Kitovani, one of the junta leaders). Speaking on television in Sukhumi, Karkarashvili announced

On September 3, 1992, the Russian government, worried by the turn of events, organized a meeting in Moscow between the ethnic Abkhazian leaders and the Georgian government. The Russian position was based on the principle of the territorial integrity of states and the inviolability of their frontiers, and protection of the interests and lawful rights of all national minorities living on their territories. The conference ended with the signing of a total cease-fire. But the agreement did not contain precise provisions for the redeployment of the Georgian troops in Abkhazia or for the disbanding and return home of the volunteer detachments from the North Caucasus. Nor did it specify conditions under which the Abkhazian administrative departments, located in Gudauta, could function. Also, there were no provisions for peacekeeping forces, like those in Ossetia, without which it would be difficult to monitor or assure compliance with the cease-fire. Article 12 of the final document contained an appeal to the UN and the OSCE to uphold the principles on which a settlement could be based and to assist in their implementation, including sending a fact-finding mission and observers.[84] Ten days later, the Control Commission that had been established according to Article I of the final document of the Moscow meeting on September 3, 1992, concluded that the agreement was not being upheld, in terms of either the withdrawal of Georgian troops or the dispersion of the illegal bands of volunteers.

The activities of the Confederation of the Mountain Peoples also intensified, and the leaders of the North Caucasus republics understood that their credibility depended on their attitude toward the Georgian-Abkhazian conflict. President Yeltsin found himself in a difficult position: if he intensified his contacts with the Georgian State Council, he might lose the whole North Caucasus, since the leaders of the North Caucasus republics, who were Yeltsin's own people, would be undermined.[85] But without Yeltsin's active support,

---

that enemy soldiers would be shot on sight and that he was calling on all armed groups in Georgia, whatever their political orientation, to fight in Abkhazia. In addition, he promised to annihilate all 97,000 Abkhazians, "who all support Ardzinba." "Commander Karkarashvili, the Commander of the Georgian State Council's Troops, Speaks on Sukhumi Television," in *Abkhazia: Chronicle of an Undeclared War*, Part I, pp. 127–128.

84. "The Final Document of the Moscow Meeting," in *Abkhazia: Chronicle of an Undeclared War*, Part I, pp. 244–246.

85. See, for instance, an interview with the vice president of the Confederation of the Mountain Peoples, Gennadia Alamia, in *Nezavisimaia Gazeta*, October 6, 1992.

the cease-fire was likely to be short-lived. On October 2, 1992, Abkhazian detachments supported by volunteers from the Confederation of the Mountain Peoples attacked Georgian troops guarding the approaches to Gagri and captured the town. This defeat caused considerable alarm among the Georgian leadership, and the Council of State ordered the mobilization of 40,000 reservists and issued a declaration blaming separatist Abkhazian leaders and the parliament of the Russian Federation for the breakdown of the cease-fire agreement and the escalation of military conflict in Abkhazia.[86] Shevardnadze stated that the Control Commission was incapable of coping with its task in Abkhazia and had made the situation worse. He said that the events in Gagri were "the result of a vast plot against Georgia" encouraged by the September 25, 1992, resolution of the Russian Parliament condemning the Georgian leadership.[87] At this time, Georgian officials demanded that a session of the UN Security Council be called to discuss the situation in Abkhazia.

The bombardment of Gagri demonstrated not only the capabilities of the Abkhazian forces, but also that they possessed Russian-made military equipment similar to that used by the Georgian forces, with the exception of aircraft. The former Soviet Army had left vast amounts of armaments in the Chechen Republic, including hundreds of armored units and a variety of artillery and missile systems, and transporting these weapons was not an impossible task given the chaotic situation in the Caucasus. The weapons could also have been obtained from arms traders in the Transcaucasus Military District who were supplying both sides of the conflict.

The fact that the troops from the former Transcaucasus Military District lacked a clearly defined legal status created danger for Russian personnel stationed in what had become a conflict zone. Russian soldiers had received orders from the Russian Ministry of

86. Deputy Commander of the Transcaucasus Military District Sufeian Beppaev, who had been invited to this session of the State Council, stated: "Not one soldier or officer from the district is in the conflict zone, and not one piece of armored equipment has been given to the Abkhazian militias." ITAR-TASS, October 2, 1992.

87. The Supreme Soviet of the Russian Federation passed a resolution "On the Situation in the North Caucasus and Events in Abkhazia" condemning the Georgian leadership, which had "attempted to resolve complex interethnic problems with the use of violence," and demanding that Georgian forces be withdrawn from Abkhazia. The Supreme Soviet also recommended that President Yeltsin and the government of the Russian Federation cease transferring weapons from the Russian Army to the Georgians.

Defense to refrain from shelling or otherwise attacking if Georgians were to hit Russian military targets. The first time Russian troops actively took part in the fighting in Georgia was on October 27, 1992, when two Russian Su-25 bombers stationed in Georgia participated in the Georgian bombardment of the garrison in the town of Eshery in Abkhazia.

In a speech at a Tbilisi rally in November 1992, Shevardnadze agreed that Russian troops withdrawing from Georgia should be prevented from taking their military equipment and weapons with them. A spate of incidents followed in which Russian military equipment and weapons were seized by Georgians. General Karkarashvili, speaking on Georgian television, said that "the confiscation of weapons and ammunition is being conducted in the interest of Georgia and is necessary to ensure the support of the Georgian people." He also revealed that the parts needed to assemble a MiG-29 warplane had been seized from a Russian military depot in Tbilisi.[88] A series of terrorist attacks were carried out against Russian soldiers in Tbilisi and other cities. According to a communiqué from the press office of the Transcaucasus Military District, "there are grounds for assuming that these attacks are being carefully planned and executed with the approval of top Georgian leaders."[89] During this period, twenty-one Russian soldiers were killed and thirty-five wounded. Finally, on December 31, 1992, a meeting took place in Moscow between Russian Defense Minister Pavel Grachev and Georgian Defense Minister Tengis Kitovani, at which Grachev expressed Moscow's anger at the illegal attacks on Russian troops in Georgia and asserted that any similar attacks in the future would be dealt with in a severe manner. Grachev also stated that the transfer of Russian military equipment located on Georgian territory should be discussed by the two governments rather than by their defense ministers. Throughout the rest of the conflict, the Russians restricted their military involvement to retaliatory air and artillery strikes against Georgian troops who attacked Russian military targets. Georgian attacks continued, and the presence of Russian military forces in Abkhazia became a serious issue of contention between Russia and Georgia.

It is poorly understood in the West why Russian forces got involved in the fighting in Abkhazia in the first place. When hostilities between Georgia and Abkhazia first erupted into exchange of fire, garrisons of

88. ITAR-TASS, November 3, 1992.
89. ITAR-TASS, November 18, 1992.

Russian troops were still located on Abkhazian territory between the Georgian and Abkhazian forces. Georgian troops continued to shell the region, and the Russian troops began firing on the Georgian forces in self-defense. Georgian Minister for Foreign Affairs Georgi Khaindrava, speaking on Georgian radio on October 28, 1992, stated that "Georgian guns are aimed at all Russian military targets, and if necessary we will open fire. We will not be talked down to."[90]

The Georgians suspected Russian military forces of supplying Abkhazian detachments with weapons and ammunition. Although this may have occurred on a small scale by members of the Russian armed forces acting on their own initiative, such transfers were not official and should not be considered part of a coordinated policy to support Abkhazian separatists. Abkhazia was uncomfortably close to Transdniester, where Moldovan forces had already attacked the Russian garrison in the town of Bender—a fact which may have increased the willingness of some Russians in the area to disregard official orders. Georgia's refusal to join the Commonwealth of Independent States (CIS) following the dissolution of the Soviet Union caused a certain amount of tension in Russian-Georgian relations, but distress over Georgia's decision was hardly universally shared inside Russia's ruling circles. For this reason, explanations of events in 1992–93 in Georgia and Abkhazia that see behind every Russian move the desire to break the back of Georgia's resistance and force it to join the CIS vastly oversimplify a situation in which military, governmental, parliamentary, and uncontrolled social forces all contributed.

In May 1993, the Russian Ministry of Foreign Affairs entered the picture. After extended negotiations on July 9, 1993, Boris Pastukhov, Deputy Foreign Minister and special representative of the Russian president, succeeded in arranging a temporary cease-fire. Pastukhov summarized the positions of all sides at a Moscow press conference on July 12, 1993. The agreement was reached with the mediation of the Russian Federation. Pastukhov stated that "within ten days of the cease-fire, all armed groups subject to the Republic of Georgia, all volunteer groups, and all other armed groups and individuals in the conflict zone must be withdrawn from Abkhazian territory." A multi-national police force, whose constitution, size, and management would be agreed upon by the Georgian and Abkhazian representatives, was to be formed to enforce the cease-fire and preserve law and order, as would the Russian military contingent temporarily stationed

90. ITAR-TASS, October 28, 1992.

in the conflict zone. Pending approval by the UN, which had been monitoring the dispute for several months, the Russian force might assume the status of an international peacekeeping force. International observers would patrol the dividing line along the Gumista, Psou, and Inguri rivers. However, the Abkhazians insisted that a clause be added mandating the restoration of the Supreme Soviet of Abkhazia and other rightful institutions. The Georgians rejected this request and stated that they reserved the right to reconsider the agreement. Thus, the draft agreement was never signed. The Russian side stressed that "the most urgent task is to arrange a cease-fire and a reliable means of monitoring it using international observers.[91] Negotiations were initiated on mechanisms to implement measures such as the separation of forces and the withdrawal of heavy weapons.

As is common in cease-fires, both sides continued hostilities in violation of the agreement. It was impossible to assign one side blame for the breakdown. After some initial setbacks, Abkhazian troops began to advance in the middle of July 1993. Fighting was renewed along several lines, and the Georgian forces seemed to be falling back. At a meeting of the Georgian Parliament, Shevardnadze unexpectedly declared that Russian involvement was the key to stabilizing the situation in Abkhazia and reaching a settlement. International organizations, which had been involved since September 1992, should not be ignored, Shevardnadze said, but so far they had proved unable to influence the situation.[92]

Once more, thanks to Pastukhov's continuing diplomatic efforts, an agreement was signed in Sochi on July 27 in which the two sides agreed to return to strict compliance with the cease-fire. Temporary control teams comprised of Georgians, Abkhazians, and Russians would verify compliance as of July 29, 1993. Agreement was also reached on the formation of a joint commission of Abkhazian and Georgian officials to settle the conflict on which both UN and OSCE representatives would also serve. Both sides agreed to initiate a phased demilitarization of the conflict zone. It was stipulated that within ten to fifteen days after the cease-fire came into force,

---

91. This withdrawal would be monitored by the Joint Commission, and a plan for demilitarizing the conflict zone would immediately come into effect. ITAR-TASS, July 12, 1993.

92. ITAR-TASS, July 13, 1993.

Georgian troops should be withdrawn from Abkhazia and all other armed groups disbanded and expelled from Abkhazia.[93]

By the end of August 1993, the trilateral working group on military and security questions attached to the Joint Commission had to deal with the fact that the Georgian side had not kept to the timetable. They needed to find a way out of the situation, since Georgian violations of the agreement could lead to countermeasures by the Abkhazian side. In early September, the working group again noted that Georgian weaponry had not been fully withdrawn from the zone.[94] Meanwhile, during the end of the summer of 1993, the civil war between the Shevardnadze government and forces loyal to Gamsakhurdia was at its peak. The situation was further complicated when, on September 7, 1993, an armed detachment of two hundred Gamsakhurdia supporters entered the Abkhazian town of Gali, occupied administrative buildings and installations, and captured heavy weapons from the Georgian forces. The Abkhazian side asserted that the Georgians were transferring military equipment and artillery systems to local Georgian armed detachments in the region on the pretext that these materials had been captured by Gamsakhurdia's supporters. The Abkhazians stated that they could only continue to take part in the work of the Commission on the condition that they received guarantees that the Georgians would comply with all Commission decisions in accordance with the Sochi cease-fire agreement.

Several days later bitter fighting again erupted on several fronts. Each side accused the other of having violated the Sochi agreements, and both began to prepare for large-scale military operations. When it became clear that the situation was catastrophic, Shevardnadze himself went to Sukhumi and tried to provide moral support for the defense of the city. On September 27, 1993, Abkhazian forces captured Sukhumi. The military defeat of the Shevardnadze regime opened the door for all of Abkhazia to come under control of Abkhazian forces. After this crushing defeat, Shevardnadze accused his Defense Minister, Tengiz Kitovani, of betraying the Georgian forces because his troops had refused to fight in Sukhumi. The consequences of the Abkhazian victory turned out to be tragic for the ethnic Georgians living in Abkhazia who fled their homes from fear of reprisals. Ethnic revenge and violence returned to the territory, but

---

93. ITAR-TASS, July 27, 1993.
94. ITAR-TASS, September 7, 1993.

this time the roles were reversed and ethnic Georgians were harshly treated. More than 140,000 refugees fled the region—nearly the entire Georgian population in Abkhazia.[95] Approximately 20,000 of these refugees were accused by the Abkhazian forces of direct participation in the military operations on the side of the Georgian forces and in the reprisals against the Abkhazian population.

THE RELATIVE STABILIZATION OF THE CONFLICT

Until the fall of Sukhumi, Shevardnadze had pursued an independent line toward Russia, keeping his distance from the Yeltsin regime. He demanded the withdrawal of Russian troops from Georgian soil and, despite pressure from Yeltsin, refused to join the CIS. Shevardnadze was in direct confrontation with the Russian Parliament, which sided with the separatist forces in Abkhazia and South Ossetia. Within two weeks of the fall of Sukhumi, Shevardnadze went to Moscow, ostensibly to attend a meeting with Yeltsin and the leaders of Azerbaijan (Geidar Aliev) and Armenia (Levon Ter-Petrosian). The four heads of state agreed on the need for collective action to stabilize the situation in the Caucasus. In his speech at this meeting, Shevardnadze agreed to join the CIS and argued that Russia and the other CIS states should help the Caucasus countries maintain their collective security. Although Shevardnadze very much wanted the introduction of peacekeeping forces to stabilize the situation in Georgia, he was unenthusiastic about having those forces supplied primarily by Russia, even under CIS auspices. However, by this time it was apparent that no peacekeeping forces

---

95. The Georgian side cites the following statistics: "When the Sochi Agreement was signed on 27 July 1993, there were over 140,000 people in Georgia who had been forcibly displaced from Abkhazia. There were also several thousand refugees in the Russian Federation, the overwhelming majority of them Georgians. Ardzinba was conducting ethnic cleansing on the territories under his control, and Georgians were being deported. More than 500 Georgians have been deported from the Gudaut district and the area around Gagra alone since the Agreement 'On a Ceasefire in Abkhazia and a System for Monitoring its Implementation' was signed on 27 July, and there have been many other such incidents. At an August 10 session of the Joint Commission on the Abkhazian conflict, it was confirmed that acts of looting and robbery were being committed against Georgians in the village of Bzyb in the Gudaut district, that people were being scared away from their homes, and that the village administration had helped to organize an exodus of Georgians from the village. Less than 200 of the 3,100 Georgians originally living in Bzyb are now left. Similar acts have been committed across the whole territory controlled by the separatists." *Bloody Separatism*, pp. 64–65.

would be forthcoming from either the UN or the OSCE, so Shevardnadze conceded to the introduction of Russian peacekeeping troops at the Moscow meeting, forced by both the disastrous military situation and the wider failure of the entire ethno-nationalist political course in Georgian domestic politics. Another reason for Shevardnadze's decision was Yeltsin's destruction, in October 1993, of the Russian Parliament that had opposed Shevardnadze's policies in Abkhazia.[96]

In his address to the Georgian people, Shevardnadze outlined Georgia's two aims in joining the CIS. Politically, Georgia would now have "a real chance of keeping Abkhazia—which we nearly lost— within Georgia" since "the conflict in this autonomous republic was initiated by reactionary forces within Russia and led by rebellious elements in the [Russian] White House." On the economic front, he stated that joining the CIS would help to revitalize Georgia's economy by restoring its economic ties with other former Soviet republics.[97] Shevardnadze maintained that his efforts had always been directed at a peaceful settlement of the Abkhazian conflict and that Georgia suffered defeat in spite of support from the world community. He cited Georgia's break with Russia as the reason for this turn of events, and called it "the greatest mistake made by Georgia since the breakup of the Soviet Union." "Much has now changed in this respect," said Shevarnadze, "we are for friendly and good-neighborly relations with Russia. Georgia has become a member of the CIS and the Council for Collective Security which guarantees the integrity and inviolability of the frontiers of our country."[98]

On February 3, 1994, the "Treaty on Friendship, Cooperation and Peaceful Coexistence between the Russian Federation and the Georgian Republic" was signed in Tbilisi. On April 15, 1994, Georgia,

---

96. "The Leaders of the Three Caucasus Nations Meet," ITAR-TASS, October 8, 1993.

97. "Eduard Shevardnadze Demonstrates to Georgian Society the Need for Georgia to Enter the CIS," ITAR-TASS, October 14, 1993. According to Valerian Advadze, the Georgian ambassador to Russia, Georgia's change in attitude toward the CIS was a dramatic shift in Georgian foreign policy, ending what had been a destructive two-year absence of Georgia from the CIS. Advadze argued that "the danger that Gamsakhurdia's regime will return has passed," and that with his departure "fascism and biological nationalism" are being replaced by "constructive nationalism" in Georgia. "Georgian Ambassador Valerian Advadze is Optimistic About Georgia's Entry into CIS," ITAR-TASS, November 9, 1993.

98. ITAR-TASS, June 20, 1994.

as a new member of the CIS, signed a "Resolution on the Sovereignty, Territorial Integrity and Inviolability of the Borders of Nations Belonging to the Commonwealth of Independent States." On April 4, a quadripartite agreement on the voluntary repatriation of refugees was signed, and a commission consisting of Georgian, Abkhazian, Russian, and UN representatives was established.[99] The commission encountered many difficulties that slowed the return of Georgian refugees to their homes; Georgian sabotage in the Gali district of Abkhazia, the absence of guarantees for the safety of returning refugees, and problems with the supply and processing of registration forms were all to blame for these delays. According to representatives of the UN High Commissioner for Refugees (UNHCR), about two hundred people a month were returning.[100]

Georgian-Abkhazian relations again worsened at the end of November 1994 after the Supreme Soviet of Abkhazia (sitting in Sukhumi) elected Speaker of the Parliament Vladislav Ardzinba as the first president of the reconstituted Abkhazian Republic and adopted a constitution in which the sovereignty of the Republic of Abkhazia was affirmed on the basis of historical precedent and the right of the people to self-determination. Shevardnadze characterized the proclamation of Abkhazian sovereignty as "an attempt by the separatists to set up an independent state." He asked the UN Security Council, the OSCE, the heads of CIS states, and the government of the Russian Federation to react immediately to "this new, irresponsible and provocative step by aggressive separatists" and to adopt measures, including sanctions, spelled out in the UN Charter and the basic documents of the OSCE and CIS.

THE ROLE OF THE RUSSIAN FEDERATION

Russia's role in these events was unclear. Ideologically and politically, Russia has always supported the territorial integrity of Georgia. However, Russian arms were in fact given to the Abkhazians. Undoubtedly there was assistance from at least one part of the Russian political spectrum, including members of parliament and some local commanders; because of a lack of a uniform official policy, such things were possible. The attitude of the Russian Federation toward the Georgian-Abkhazian conflict was inconsistent, and

---

99. *UN Chronicle* (June 1994), p. 37.

100. Between October and November 20, 1994, 233 Georgian refugees returned to the Gali district. *Interfax*, November 23, 1994.

reflected the fluctuations of internal policy struggles and the complex mix of actors on the Russian political scene. Different assessments of the conflict appeared within Russian ruling circles. The elites and advisers around President Yeltsin responsible for formulating foreign and nationality policy, Foreign Minister Andrei Kozyrev and Yeltsin's adviser on nationality questions, Emil Pain, took a pro-Shevardnadze position. Ruslan Khasbulatov, who was then speaker of parliament, was suspicious of the Shevardnadze regime. On September 25, 1992, the Russian Supreme Soviet issued a statement that attributed the main cause of the conflict in Abkhazia to the introduction of Georgian forces into Abkhazia, and it denounced the policy of violence conducted by the Georgian leadership and demanded the immediate cessation of all military activities, the withdrawal of all military formations from Abkhazia, and strict compliance with all international agreements on human rights. It also adopted a resolution that halted the transfer of all arms, ammunition, and equipment to the Georgian Army as part of the ongoing division of Soviet military assets.[101] This reaction reflected the concern of deputies from the North Caucasus republics, where the situation had sharply deteriorated as a result of the war in Abkhazia. They quite rightly feared a loss of control over the situation.

To make matters worse, by late 1992, relations between President Yeltsin's administration and the Russian Supreme Soviet had become strained, and in an attempt to tip the balance of forces in the region in their own favor, each side was pursuing its own policy toward the North Caucasus republics. Renewed fighting in Abkhazia coincided with the September–October 1993 climax of Yeltsin's confrontation with the Russian Parliament. Shevardnadze's plans for a blitzkrieg in Abkhazia were probably known to Yeltsin's entourage since, without massive supplies of Russian arms from the Transcaucasus Military District, Georgia could not have implemented them. Heavy weapons used by Georgian forces in the Abkhazian invasion were without question of Russian origin. As a rule, Western analysts argue that Russian weapons acquired by the Abkhazian side were a destabilizing factor. But they forget that without massive Russian arms supplies, many—but by no means all—of which were obtained entirely legally as part of the post-Soviet division of the Soviet armed

---

101. "Resolution of the Supreme Soviet of the Russian Federation on the Situation in the Northern Caucasus in Connection with the Events in Abkhazia." *The White Book of Abkhazia*, pp. 121–123.

forces,[102] the Shevardnadze regime would never have initiated military operations against Abkhazia.[103]

Although Russian troops were stationed in Georgia throughout the period and participated in a number of the tripartite military efforts to monitor the series of abortive cease-fires, they first appeared as official peacekeeping forces in accordance with the Russian-mediated agreement signed in Moscow on May 14, 1994. The plan was to use about 2,500 troops in the operation, who would serve on a voluntary contractual basis at an estimated cost to Russia of two billion rubles a year. Operational arrangements were confirmed in negotiations between Russian Defense Minister Grachev, Shevardnadze, and Ardzinba in June 1994. The peacekeeping forces in Abkhazia were to comprise the Russian 345th parachute regiment, which was stationed in Gudauta, and three battalions of the Russian Army Group in the Transcaucasus. The main force—three battalions made up of troops from the Leningrad and Volga military districts—was to take position in a separation zone along the Inguri River. On June 9, 1994, President Yeltsin signed a decree "On the Participation of the Russian Federation in the Peacekeeping Operations in the Zone of the Georgian-Abkhazian Conflict," which states that the operation would be carried out "with the support of the member-states of the CIS," but the majority of these forces turned out to be Russian. While other former republics made token contributions, as newly independent states they had difficulty providing even minimal funds for maintaining these forces.

The leaders of Georgia and Abkhazia had repeatedly requested the urgent deployment of peacekeeping forces. The commanding officer of Russian peacekeeping forces, Major General Vasili Yakushev, expressed his conviction that the mandate of his forces would be extended until such a time that they would have completed their

---

102. It should be recalled that the Russian Parliament had attempted to freeze the legal transfer of arms and arms depots to Georgia. Nevertheless, Russia's executive authorities did not second the freeze, and in any case, numerous semilegal and illegal channels for the acquisition of Russian weapons and other military supplies existed in the region.

103. See, for instance, Fiona Hill and Pamela Jewett, *Back in the Soviet Union: Russia's Intervention in the Internal Affairs of the Former Soviet Republics and the Implications for United States Policy toward Russia* (Cambridge, Mass.: Harvard University, Kennedy School of Government, Strengthening Democratic Institutions Project, January 1994), pp. 54–55; and *Report on Ethnic Conflict in the Russian Federation and Transcaucasia* (Cambridge, Mass.: Harvard University, July 1993), pp. 105–106.

mission: to create conditions for the return of refugees, to prevent renewed fighting, and to demobilize armed formations and military equipment on both sides.[104]

Russia's dominant role in the peacekeeping effort evoked criticism by the Georgian opposition, which particularly attacked the unsuccessful courting of Western powers. In a debate in the Georgian Parliament against Deputy Teimuraz Zhorzholiani, who started a hunger strike to force Shevardnadze to retire, Shevardnadze defended his policies, including the signing of the CIS treaty. He stated that Russia's influence on Georgia was so important that "if Boris Yeltsin were to ask me to retire, I would go tomorrow because if a person constitutes an obstacle to his country, that person should go."[105] Since the UN and the Western powers were unwilling or unable to form a multinational contingent under UN auspices, Russian troops remained Shevardnadze's only option for enforcing peace in this region.

THE ROLE OF INTERNATIONAL ORGANIZATIONS

The April 1994 Quadripartite Agreement on Repatriation of Refugees was the product of complex negotiations and almost two years of UN involvement in Georgia and Abkhazia.[106] The military defeat of Georgia was the main reason for internationalizing the search for a peaceful settlement. Many international government and public organizations joined in this process, including unofficial mediating groups and missions from nongovernmental organizations (NGOs) in Russia, the United States, France, Germany, and the United Kingdom. But nothing came of the NGO missions, which were largely of a fact-finding or academic nature. Of more practical importance were several rounds of meetings held in Geneva over the course of 1994 at which

---

104. *Interfax*, November 10, 1994.

105. *POSTFACTUM*, November 9, 1994.

106. The OSCE seems to have agreed to allow the UN to take the lead in the Abkhazian situation, whereas it concentrated most of its efforts on Ossetia. As the February 2, 1993, report of the OSCE Mission to Georgia underlines, "the [OSCE's] mechanisms are too slow to react to the challenges, and rivalry between organizations makes things even more difficult. In this conflict both sides seem to be confused by the great number of organizations appearing on the scene and offering their services to find a solution to the conflict. This matter is further complicated by the fact that newly independent states and, even less, the conflicting sides which do not have the status of states, do not know the actual role and possibilities of the different organizations." *OSCE Communication*, No. 41, Prague, February 2, 1993.

problems connected with the deployment of peacekeeping forces in Abkhazia and the status of Abkhazia were debated.

The United Nations became involved in Abkhazia in September and October 1992, when UN goodwill missions visited Georgia for the first time in order to meet with the main parties to the conflict. On September 15, 1992, a UN mission arrived in Tbilisi; the visit was arranged by Shevardnadze and UN Secretary General Boutros Boutros-Ghali. The mission's purpose was to become acquainted with the situation in Abkhazia and to assist in finding a solution to the conflict.

In their initial fact-finding missions to Georgia, members of the UN delegation were monopolized by the Georgian leadership and were not adequately exposed to the Abkhazian side. This was reflected in the mission's final report, which gave a one-sided version, inspired by Shevardnadze, of the origin of the conflict.[107] Abkhazian leader Vladislav Ardzinba noted in a September 16, 1992, letter to Boutros-Ghali that the UN could be accused of applying double standards in its approach to the Georgian-Abkhazian conflict.[108] The UN essentially took a pro-Georgian position and was not neutral in its evaluations of the conflict, frequently accusing the Abkhazian side of excesses, but never Georgia. Another source of contention was the decision to locate the headquarters of the UN mission in Tbilisi, allegedly because of poor conditions in Abkhazia.

The Georgian side made active use of the possibilities offered by international organizations to try to turn the situation to its advantage. Once international organizations become involved in a conflict, there is always the possibility that one or both sides can use them to appeal to a wider international public. In order to be effective as mediators, international organizations must be seen as absolutely neutral. If not, their involvement can be counterproductive and actually reduce the chances for conflict resolution. In the second half of 1992, several UN and OSCE fact-finding missions visited Georgia, but the nature of their activities and the content of their reports were perceived as biased. The representatives of these organizations, it has

---

107. First Deputy Minister of Foreign Affairs of Georgia Tedo Dzhaparidze, speaking on Georgian television on the results of the UN mission, admitted that he had personally participated in composing the mission's final document. *The White Book of Abkhazia*, pp. 33–36.

108. Vladislav Ardzinba, "Letter to the UN Secretary General of 16 September 1992," in *Abkhazia: Chronicle of an Undeclared War*, Part II, pp. 17–18.

been argued, were inclined to accept the Georgian point of view and did not give sufficient weight to the Abkhazian position. The Organization of Unrepresented Peoples was one organization that tried to call attention to this bias. Michael van Walt van Praag, the general secretary of this organization, stated at a November 1992 press conference in Moscow: "Groups from the UN and the OSCE have visited this region. It is now apparent that they have not devoted sufficient attention to the Abkhazian point of view. What is needed right now is an active and effective process of mediation. All areas of Abkhazia should be made accessible to humanitarian and human rights organizations." According to van Praag, Europeans still knew little about this region, and the Western press had long been exclusively presenting the Georgian perspective; only recently had more objective information begun to appear. West European governments needed to change their attitude toward the conflict and understand that the goal of the Organization of Unrepresented Peoples is to get Abkhazian representatives involved in all negotiations addressing the conflict. Van Praag also recommended that UN representatives in Tbilisi should visit Abkhazia regularly in order to ensure that their information was objective.[109]

On January 4, 1993, Shevardnadze sent a letter to the UN Security Council "urgently requesting that UN peacekeeping forces be sent to Abkhazia." No troops were sent, but an agreement was signed in Tbilisi in February 1993 to establish permanent UN representation there. On the basis of UN Security Council Resolution No. 858, a UN observer mission in Georgia (UNOMIG) began operation in late August 1993. The mission's tasks were defined as: maintaining contacts with both sides in the conflict and with troops from the Russian Federation; and monitoring the situation and presenting reports to UN headquarters, with particular attention to any signs that movement was under way toward a general settlement of the conflict.

On July 1, 1993, UN Secretary General Boutros-Ghali recommended that the UN Security Council send military observers to Georgia,[110] and on August 8, 1994, the first group of nine UN observers arrived in Georgia to monitor the cease-fire.[111] However, as

---

109. "Statement of the General Secretary of the Organization of Unrepresented Peoples (OUP) M. Van Praag," *The White Book of Abkhazia*, pp. 41–43.

110. See the report "On the Situation in Abkhazia," S/26023, July 1, 1993.

111. The decision was made on the basis of UN Resolution No. 854, passed on August 6, 1993.

noted above, Abkhazian troops had already resumed activities in July. Shevardnadze and his foreign minister tried to clarify their situation at the UN and protest what they saw as the destruction of the cease-fire by Abkhazian forces. Shevardnadze sent a letter to the UN on October 12, 1993, urgently requesting that a special UN Security Council meeting be convened. On October 19, 1993, the UN Security Council reaffirmed "its strong condemnation of the grave violation by the Abkhaz side of the Cease-fire Agreement of July 27, 1993, and subsequent actions in violation of international humanitarian law."[112]

From November 30–December 1, 1993, the first round of direct negotiations in the Georgian-Abkhazian conflict took place in Geneva under the supervision of the United Nations, and with the participation of the Russian Federation. One of the most complex issues was the future status of Abkhazia. The Georgians stated that they would continue to take part in direct negotiations only if Abkhazia acknowledged the territorial integrity of a Georgia that included Abkhazia. Thus, the nature and extent of Abkhazian autonomy in any subsequent settlement became an essential question. On December 1, 1993, the Georgian and Abkhazian delegations signed a memorandum of mutual understanding pledging not to use violence or the threat of violence during negotiations. In addition, progress was made on the refugee issue, and it was agreed that beginning on December 20, there would be an unconditional exchange of prisoners of war. Finally, it was also agreed that a joint consultative body would be established to produce proposals on future governmental relations between Georgia and Abkhazia.

From January 11–13, 1994, a second round of direct negotiations between Georgia and Abkhazia was held in Geneva. Refugees were high on the agenda of this round, and a draft agreement drawn up by the UN High Commissioner for Refugees laid down detailed procedures for the voluntary return of refugees and displaced persons to their homes in Abkhazia beginning in February 1994. A decision was reached to establish a special commission for refugees that would include representatives from Georgia, Abkhazia, the UNHCR, and the Russian Federation. The group also expressed the wish that an international commission be established no later than February 15,

---

112. United Nations Security Council, S/RES/876, 1993, p. 1; see also "Shevardnadze Goes to the United States and Speaks at a Session of the UN Security Council, March 9, 1994," Security Council 3346th Meeting PM Summary, SC/5803, March 9, 1994.

1994, to help in the economic reconstruction of Abkhazia, particularly with the rebuilding of vital infrastructure such as transportation arteries, airports, bridges, and tunnels. Other topics of discussion included humanitarian aid, political issues, and the possibility of deploying peacekeeping forces along the Inguri River. During this round, it was also reported that the memorandum of mutual understanding was for the most part being implemented, and both Georgia and Abkhazia asked for UN and Russian assistance to ensure that the process would continue.

In early February 1994, difficulties arose in the negotiation process. At a Moscow meeting of experts on the future of Abkhazia's political status, the Georgian side announced its intention to reconsider the earlier decision to grant Abkhazia wide-ranging autonomy while preserving the territorial integrity of Georgia. The Abkhazian side responded with a demand for complete independence. Later in the month, from February 22–25, a third round of UN-sponsored negotiations between Georgia and Abkhazia took place in Geneva. The two sides failed to reach a compromise, and postponed signing of both the Declaration on the Political Regulation of the Georgian-Abkhazian Conflict and the Quadripartite Agreement on the Voluntary Repatriation of Refugees. On March 7, negotiations resumed, but ended in failure two days later. Speaking at a meeting of the UN Security Council later in the month, Shevardnadze presented a plan to establish international rule in Abkhazia and to hold internationally supervised elections on the basis of which new administrative bodies would be established.

In early April, progress was again evident as the Quadripartite Agreement on the Voluntary Repatriation of Refugees and the Declaration on the Political Regulation of the Georgian-Abkhazian Conflict were signed. The implementation of both agreements was made contingent upon the introduction of peacekeeping forces into the zone of conflict. The four sides also established a committee chaired by a UN representative to set up a timetable for efforts to reestablish diplomatic relations between the two sides. The committee was to include representatives from both the OSCE and the Russian Federation and would meet alternatively in Moscow and Geneva. In mid-April, in the midst of discussions on the possibilities for introducing peacekeepers, Georgia rejected a plan that would have established a demilitarized zone that included the banks of the Inguri River. In May and June 1994, an agreement was reached among Georgian, Abkhazian, UN, Russian, and CIS representatives on the introduction of Russian and CIS peacekeeping forces into the region, with the participation of the UN on an administrative and monitoring basis. The UN increased the number of permanent observers from 22 to 55, and in July 1994, it increased them to 136.[113] The mandate for keeping the forces deployed in the region continued to be extended, but the conflict between Georgia and Abkhazia did not show any clear signs of a political resolution.

By the end of 1994, there were already ten UN Security Council resolutions on a settlement of the Georgian-Abkhazian conflict, which, in the view of UN Secretary General Boutros-Ghali, constituted an adequate basis for a solution to the problem. But these resolutions failed to specify all the necessary steps. They primarily addressed questions of refugee return, yet concrete measures addressing the painful question of the future status of Abkhazia were not proposed. International organizations have had the potential to greatly influence the stabilization and resolution of the conflict in Abkhazia through the involvement of peacekeeping troops, and it would be difficult to deny that the introduction of Russian peacekeeping forces under the auspices of the CIS had an effect on the situation in the region. However, a more interesting question is whether this would have occurred in the absence of UN and OSCE involvement. It is quite likely that Russian or CIS peacekeeping forces would have come to play the same or a similar role in the stabilization of the conflict in Abkhazia even without the efforts of these organizations.[114]

Conclusion

The policy of ethnic nationalism pursued in Georgia proved a powerful instrument for the destruction of the socialist political system while at the same time preserving the power of the ruling bureaucratic *nomenklatura* in a disintegrating society on the basis of ethnic

---

113. *UN Chronicle*, September 1994, p. 35.

114. The peacemaking activities of NGOs were not effective in Georgia for several reasons. First, in the majority of cases conflict resolution activities were conducted by social and academic organizations located in Moscow. The effectiveness of these organizations was limited by the fact that their conflict resolution models were too formalized and did not take into account the effect of the Soviet legacy. Second, peacemaking efforts were primarily declarative and did not touch upon the social and political issues that generated the conflicts. Finally, a number of these organizations were not at all neutral and functioned as propaganda tools supporting one side or the other in the conflict.

legitimacy and popular support. Georgian nationalism, like Moldovan, Latvian, and other post-Soviet nationalisms, represents a combination of ethnocentrism and features inherited from the communist system. The myth about the building of communism has been replaced by the myth of building an ethnic nation, and, as in the Soviet era, this myth is used to justify the imposition of serious restrictions on the political and social rights of individuals. Ethnonationalist concepts of the state envision a single, dominant, populous, "historic" nation. Although the rights of other ethnic groups in Georgia are formally recognized and proclaimed, in reality these groups—Abkhazians, Ossetians, Armenians, Greeks, Russians, Jews, and others—are regarded as "guests." The Georgian nation state may adopt a tolerant policy toward them on the condition that its demands are fulfilled. This concept is openly or covertly embodied in legislation and administrative practice and decisively affects the everyday life of individuals belonging to the various ethnic groups, even if they have been granted formal citizenship. Other ethnic groups are treated as suspect and must prove their loyalty.

This brand of post-communist ethno-nationalism became dominant in Georgia because it initially raised the banner of the struggle against the Russian-dominated communist empire, and articulated the desire to build a liberal, democratic state. Georgian nationalists received support from various levels of society both inside the country and in the democratic West. Nevertheless, during its struggle for power, the Georgian nationalist movement contained clearly defined elements that represented a threat to political pluralism, human rights, and the rights of ethnic minorities. Nationalist political parties and movements formed that excluded "foreigners" from participation. It is clear that in a multinational state such as Georgia, the identification of political programs with specific ethnic groups does not pass unnoticed. The politicization of ethnicity creates insurmountable barriers between parties and prevents the emergence of a pluralistic party system. Political coalitions become impossible, and in a society with a strong legacy of resolving conflict through force—in this case, the legacy of Soviet society—political parties may turn into paramilitary organizations and engage in armed warfare with each other. As struggles become more bitter, all social and political organizations are subjected to the test of patriotism. The political process becomes increasingly primitive because other participants are no longer looked upon as normal political opponents, but as traitors or enemies.

The growth of intolerance and ethnic threats in Georgia led the ethnic minorities to form ethno-political movements and organizations of their own, which then adopted the very same principles and tactics to organize their own resistance. These political movements also acquired mass support, both among their ethnic kindred within their home regions and among the ethnic diaspora in neighboring states, first and foremost in the North Caucasus republics of the Russian Federation. The violation, or the clear threat of violation, of the fundamental human rights—the right to life; the right not to be subjected to torture, arbitrary arrest, or discrimination; the right of free association, political activity, and freedom of speech; and the right to nutrition, health, education, and work—made it easy to gather mass support.

The change of regime in Tbilisi from Gamsakhurdia to Shevardnadze did not lead to any significant changes in this model. Thus, Georgia's transition from a socialist multinational state to a post-communist mono-national state gave rise to two ethno-national conflicts that turned into local wars in South Ossetia and Abkhazia.

A range of factors characterizes ethnic conflict, including historical relations among peoples in the region, the nature of ethnic stratification, the balance of interests of neighboring states, and economic crises. The behavior of all sides, particularly during military activities, hardly differs. A report by the UN fact-finding mission that visited Abkhazia from October 22–30, 1993, noted that responsibility for human rights violations in Abkhazia lay equally with the Georgian government forces and the Abkhazian formations. The paradox of the Georgian-Abkhazian and Georgian-Ossetian conflicts is that the bitter and destructive struggle has returned the sides to the positions from which the increase in ethno-political tension started. In South Ossetia and Abkhazia the same distribution of political forces exists, but their material and ideological resources are almost completely exhausted. Both Abkhazia and South Ossetia still demand independence, and Georgians still insist that autonomy is the most they will ever be granted. All the violence has accomplished nothing and has left enormous material and human damage in its wake. Future developments will greatly depend on the internal politics of Russia, on whose stability the whole region depends.

Chapter 14

Commentary on Georgia

Arthur G. Matirosyan

Edward Ozhiganov's chapter on the conflicts in South Ossetia and Abkhazia in the Republic of Georgia exhibits a perspective to which Western readers on developments in one of the most volatile and conflict prone regions in the world today—the Caucasus—are unaccustomed. Most Western interpretations of the origins and dynamics of conflicts in this region draw an immediate and yet often unsubstantiated correlation between these conflicts and the Russian search for neo-imperialist domination in this strategically important region where East meets West. Thus, William Odom and Robert Dujarric in their monograph *Commonwealth or Empire?* maintain that "Russia successfully executes its policy of imperial reassertion" in the region.[1]

Counterpoised to this thesis, Ozhiganov's analysis of conflicts in Georgia is replete with details and ample evidence in support of his proposition that, more than any other factor, Georgian nationalism and the fighting among various Georgian elite groups are responsible for the genesis and escalation of these conflicts.[2] However, when it comes

---

1. William Odom and Robert Dujarric, *Commonwealth or Empire? Russia, Central Asia and Transcaucasus* (Indianapolis, Ind.: Hudson Institute, 1995), p. xv.

2. Despite overall accuracy of the data presented by Ozhiganov, there are some imprecisions in his text. For instance, Ozhiganov writes, "The disintegration of the monetary and credit system after the introduction of Georgia's own currency...are just some of the problems facing Georgia today. Georgia has become financially insolvent." However, the most recent economic data from Georgia indicates that the European Union resolved the looming problem of $141.7 million owed by Georgia by covering this debt in the form of a grant for macroeconomic assistance. The grant enables Georgia to remain current in its payments to the International Monetary Fund (IMF), World Bank, and the European Bank for Reconstruction and Development (EBRD), which normally do not reschedule debt. On February

to the role of Russia in those conflicts, Ozhiganov focuses predominantly on the positive aspects of the Russian involvement. He does criticize Russian policies in the region, but only for the political naiveté that led Boris Yeltsin and his associates to trust first nationalist (read, anti-communist) Zviad Gamsakhurdia and then the former First Secretary of the Communist Party of Georgia, Edward Shevardnadze.

The existence of different narratives of the same conflicts poses an interesting methodological problem. While dealing with such complex social and political phenomena as ethnic conflicts, it would seem misguided to try to distill a certain group of "objective" factors in order to identify the genesis and dynamics of conflicts. Moreover, in analysis of protracted conflicts, often the initial causes are replaced by problems generated at a later stage.

A narrative of a conflict presented by a "neutral" party, unless it is a mere chronology of events, cannot be neutral if only because it is aimed at an end result. As Ozhiganov himself notes, "history is usually so complex and varied that an objective full account can provide arguments to any of the sides involved in conflict." However, from the very beginning Ozhiganov's sympathy with the underdogs of these conflicts—the South Ossetians and Abkhazians—has been explicit.

The historical context of Ozhiganov's chapter is by and large based on Ossetian and Abkhazian sources, which inevitably reveals the author's anti-Georgian predisposition. While relating the history of Georgian-Ossetian relations during the civil war in Russia (1918–21), Ozhiganov puts full faith in secondary Ossetian sources. Furthermore, he extensively quotes from a contemporary book published in Vladikavkaz (North Ossetia) in 1992, at the height of this conflict's tension. Ozhiganov writes that, "during the Civil War Georgia *staked* its claim on South Ossetia" (emphasis added). At that time Georgia was recognized as an independent state, even by Bolshevik Russia. In 1919, Shida Kartli, then part of the Georgian Democratic Republic, and later, under the Bolsheviks and Soviets, known as the Soviet Socialist Autonomous Region (SSAR) of South Ossetia, was the scene of a rebellion instigated by Bolsheviks (includ-

---

23, 1996, the IMF approved a ten-year $246 million loan to Georgia under its extended structural facility program. The exchange rate for the Lari against the U.S. dollar has barely moved from 1.25 Lari per U.S. dollar at its introduction in October 1995 to 1.258. Georgian Gross Domestic Product (GDP) was projected to grow by 8 percent in 1996. See Michael Wyzan, "Georgia's Economy in First Quarter 1996: Solid Improvement from a Low Base," *OMRI Analytical Brief*, No. 173, June 17, 1996.

ing such Georgian Bolsheviks as Sergo Ordzhonikidze and Josef Stalin) against the social democratic (Menshevik) government of the Georgian Democratic Republic.[3]

Following the rhetoric of current Abkhazian and Ossetian leaders, Ozhiganov writes:

The return of Georgia to its Constitution of 1921 and the abrogation of all enactments of the Soviet authorities juridically reinstated the status of both South Ossetia and Abkhazia to that which they had before that date. In August 1990, at a session of the regional Soviet of People's Deputies of South Ossetia the decision was taken to change status from that of an autonomous region to that of the South Ossetian Soviet Republic.

However, as noted earlier, an administrative unit based on ethnicity, the SSAR of South Ossetia, was established by the Bolsheviks in 1924.[4]

It was the history of uneasy relations that was politicized and mythologized by nationalists on both sides on the eve of the collapse of the Soviet empire. This mythologized history has become part of these conflicts by reinforcing—nearly petrifying—the positions of each side. Hence it is important to know the historical accounts of both sides to better understand their positions. However, it is hardly possible to present an "objective" historical narrative without further locking the sides into their positions. In that case, either side finds its history unrecognizable and unacceptable. As Joseph Brodsky put it, "Whenever one pulls the trigger in order to rectify history's mistake, one lies. For history makes no mistakes, since it has no purpose . . . No man possesses sufficient retrospective ability to justify his deeds— murder especially—in extemporaneous categories."[5]

---

3. The most authoritative account of these events can be found in a book by Sanakoev and Kozaev, Ossetian Bolsheviks, and participants in the events, who interpreted the rebellion as a "heroic class struggle of Bolsheviks against Mensheviks" rather than as a plea for self-determination. See Nikolai Siukakaev, *Dve tragedii Iuzhnoi Osetii* (Vladikavkaz: North Ossetian University Press, 1994), p. 7.

4. By an interesting twist, the rhetoric of the Abkhazian leader, Vladislav Ardzinba, was very similar to this one until the end of 1991. Ardzinba, then a strong proponent of preserving the Soviet Union, used this argument to blackmail leaders of the Georgian independence movement, and only gave it up after the collapse of the Soviet Union. He shifted his emphasis from becoming part of the Soviet Union to union with Russia, and eventually to sovereignty and independence for Abkhazia.

5. Joseph Brodsky, in Zlatko Dizdarevic, ed., *Sarajevo: A War Journal* (New York: Fromm International, 1993), pp. ix–x.

The structure of Ozhiganov's chapter—chronological narrative and analysis of events—necessitates catching up with more recent events and predetermines an open ending. Thus, some of the most important recent developments could not possibly find their way to the pages of his chapter; his narrative ends somewhat abruptly in November 1994, just before the Supreme Soviet of Abkhazia adopted a new constitution that proclaimed Abkhazia an independent and sovereign state, and just before the conflict in Chechnya turned into a large-scale war and diametrically changed the approaches of key Russian policymakers to the Georgian-Abkhazian conflict. However, it is not so much the absence of important recent developments from Ozhiganov's analysis as the way the author treats some consequential variables that leaves a lot to desire.

One of the keys to the Georgian-Abkhazian conflict and ensuing impasse in the negotiations is demography. Ozhiganov does speak about forced migration, but again, only from the Abkhazian historical perspective. And by doing so he dwells in detail on the Abkhazian historical justification of the current *modus operandi* and only in passing mentions the plight of Georgian refugees from Abkhazia. The simple truth, however, is that both sides are trying to change the demographic situation. While Georgians are striving to return to the prewar distribution of the population, Abkhazians hope to significantly increase the proportion of Abkhazians by encouraging repatriation of Abkhazians from abroad. Thus the Abkhazian Parliament is preparing legislation on citizenship that may allow diaspora Abkhazians in Turkey, Syria, Jordan, Germany, the Netherlands, and some other countries to return to Abkhazia. The diaspora Abkhazians are mostly descendants of the *muhacirs* who fled from the North Caucasus to the Turkish Ottoman Empire in the second half of the nineteenth century. In October 1994, the Second World Congress of the Abkhazian and Abazian Peoples held in the village of Lykhni, the cradle of Abkhazian civilization, estimated that there are some 500,000 Abkhazians throughout the world.[6]

The Abkhazian leaders have stated on numerous occasions that "the process of political stabilization in Abkhazia cannot successfully develop without the repatriation of Georgian refugees to the Galskii district of Abkhazia."[7] However, to justify their reluctance to sign a

---

6. Taras Shamba in an interview in *Abkhazia*, Vol. 29, No. 1 (1994), p. 14.

7. See, for example, Enver Kapba in *Segodnia*, November 25, 1994, p. 4. According to the proposed schedule of repatriation, 35,000 refugees were to return to the Galskii district by October 1995.

new schedule of repatriation, the Abkhazian leadership has also argued that Abkhazia does not have means and resources to expedite this process;[8] a significant number of Georgian refugees participated in the military activities and atrocities committed against civilians of the Republic of Abkhazia; and the problem of repatriation can be resolved only after Georgia and Abkhazia reach an agreement on the political settlement of the conflict. Vladislav Ardzinba, president of Abkhazia, put forward yet another precondition for repatriation of Georgians to the Russian parliamentarians visiting Sukhumi in January 1995: "Russia should lift the economic blockade," i.e., open the border along the river Psou. Obviously, this condition further complicates the negotiations because the Abkhazian side has indirectly linked the process of repatriation to the conflict in Chechnya.

The conflict in Chechnya has some very important consequences for Abkhazia. The Abkhazian side never made secret the fact that the bulk of the Abkhazian military comprises paramilitary groups from the Confederation of the Peoples of the Caucasus, predominantly of Chechen origins. Now that Russia faces the challenge of Chechen separatism, Moscow seems to be less inclined to support secessionist movements in the CIS;[9] the Abkhazian leaders now face the dilemma of either getting back to the negotiating table with Georgia (the more likely scenario), or openly defying Moscow by supporting the Chechens. In this sense, the Chechen crisis reinforced the position of Tbilisi *vis-à-vis* Moscow by revealing the strong Abkhazian sympathy with the Chechen cause.

Ironically, back in 1993, Edward Shevardnadze warned the Russian leadership that the Russian support for the Abkhazian separatists not only destabilized Georgia internally, but would result in the spread of separatist movements in the Northern Caucasus. The best trained and most experienced group of Dzhokhar Dudaev's fighters is known as the "Abkhazian Battalion." This group of about four hundred fighters, under the notorious Chechen commander Shamil Basayev, formed the core of the Abkhazian advance on Sukhumi in the fall of 1993. Shevardnadze was the first to support the actions of

---

8.   Ibid.

9.   As evidence, one can cite statements by Vladimir Shumeiko and Victor Chernomyrdin made during their visits to Georgia in the fall of 1995. In fact, Shumeiko went so far as to compare Vladislav Ardzinba with Dzhokhar Dudaev, and Chernomyrdin asserted that Russia and Georgia shall take "joint steps against aggressive separatism." OMRI Daily Digest, September 18, 1995.

Moscow in Chechnya, while President Ardzinba protested the introduction of Russian troops in Chechnya. Shevardnadze stated that the
Chechen conflict was "an internal affair of the Russian Federation. If
the conflict were to spread, it could result in the disintegration of the
Russian Federation with some serious negative consequences for the
entire world."[10] Furthermore, the Russians had to seal the border
with Abkhazia in order to prevent movement of Abkhazian and
Chechen fighters to and from Chechnya via Karachaevo-Cherkessia
and Kabardino-Balkaria.

Under pressure from Moscow, Abkhazian leaders have retracted
their demand for sovereignty and independence. Sokrat
Dzhindzholia, speaker of the Abkhazian Parliament, reiterated his
earlier March 1995 statement that Abkhazia is no longer seeking
independence. It is important to emphasize here that shortly before
the Russian incursion in Chechnya, in November 1995, the
Abkhazian Parliament adopted a constitution declaring Abkhazia's
independence. Thus it turns out that one of the factors that
Ozhiganov links to the intensification and abatement of the conflicts
in the beginning of his chapter on Georgia—"the struggle within the
Russian leadership on which the Shevardnadze regime economically
and militarily depends"—works both ways. That is to say,
Ardzinba's regime is also highly dependent on Moscow. The current
impasse in negotiations can be explained by what Boris Pastukhov,
Russian envoy to the talks, called "the Abkhaz lie-in-wait tactics."
While Shevardnadze's efforts have been aimed (quite successfully) at
gaining the support of key Russian decision-makers[11] and democrats
in the Russian Duma, Ardzinba's plans revealed stark dependence on
the outcome of the December 1995 parliamentary elections in the
Russian Federation. Oddly enough, Ardzinba's strongest political
ties are to both the left (communists) and the right (Congress of
Russian Communities, Derzhava, et al.) on the spectrum of the
Russian opposition. On several occasions Ardzinba has threatened to
conduct a referendum on becoming part of the Russian Federation in
Abkhazia. Results of this referendum in the absence of the Georgian

---

10. Reuters, January 18, 1995.

11. Shevardnadze's efforts culminated in agreements on three Russian military
bases (Vaziani, Akhalkalaki, and Batumi), signed on September 18, 1995. At a
press conference that followed the signing ceremony, Shevardnadze stated that
Russia "resolutely supports Georgia's territorial integrity and words will be followed by action." Russian NTV News, September 18, 1995.

majority in Abkhazia are quite predictable. Only if the Russian left and right, whose geopolitical thinking often converge, gain control of the executive branch of power, may the results of Abkhazian referendum then acquire the necessary support and weight.

This brings us back to an earlier point. Without an explicit statement of his premises, Ozhiganov's chapter acquires a touch of one-sidedness. True, his text does explain some of the initial causes of the conflicts in Georgia—Georgian nationalism and the power struggle in Russia. But strangely, Ozhiganov fails to apply the same proposition to the Abkhazians and South Ossetians, although they too have been successfully seeking support in Russian corridors of power; they too have not been immune to the ills of the retroactive utopia called nationalism.

Part III
What Will the Future Hold?

Chapter 15

Russian Security Interests and Dilemmas: An Agenda for the Future

Alexei Arbatov

Profound international and domestic changes have in recent years presented Russian policymakers and the Russian public with dilemmas and choices of truly historic consequence.

It is now universally recognized that Russia's greatest external challenge is its political environment—relations with the fourteen other former Soviet republics that became independent states when the Soviet Union was disbanded in December 1991, some for the first time in their history. Only recently did these states constitute a highly integrated totalitarian empire. The newly independent states of the former Soviet Union (FSU) form a zone of vital interest for Russia, not unlike Mexico and Canada for the United States. Russia's relationships with its closest neighbors transcend economic, political, ethnic, security, and other ties. They affect the prospects of Russia's success for democratic, political, and economic reform; in fact, they affect the course of its internal evolution. The reverse is equally true: Moscow's successes and failures in domestic reform greatly affect its relations with other former Soviet republics.

Russia's policy toward its former colonies is also an important factor in its relations with other regional and global powers, including the United States and Western Europe, the Muslim world, and more indirectly, China and Japan. Historically, Moscow's empire-building was both defensively and offensively motivated. Russia was a rival, and often the main enemy of other great powers. The historic opportunity to change this paradigm of relations and forge genuine partnership and cooperation, particularly between Russia and the West, is also predicated on Moscow's policy toward the new states of the FSU, as well as on domestic developments in Russia. It almost goes without saying that relations between Russia and the West are crucial to progress in arms control and nuclear non-proliferation, as well as conflict resolution and peacekeeping outside the post-Soviet space. And again, the reverberations are very strong: in the post-communist world, Russia's relations with the West, and particularly Europe, are a primary factor in Moscow's policy toward its neighbors.

This enormous web of interrelated problems has presented Russian democrats and Western policymakers with a challenge of historic dimensions. Since 1991, policymakers on all sides have been desperately trying to cope with the complex problems that have emerged since communism's collapse. Notwithstanding some significant achievements, it has to be acknowledged that Russian, U.S., and European leaders have largely proved unequal to the task. The unique opportunity to make a break with traditional patterns—of Russia's domestic system, of imperial expansion in the zone surrounding Russia, and of adversarial relations with the West—may have already been lost. The war in Chechnya should provide indisputable proof to even the staunchest optimists that all of these old patterns are being revived.

The main question in the late 1990s is not whether the tide of positive changes is receding, but rather how long, comprehensive, destructive, and dangerous this ebb will be. It is unclear how many of Russia's genuine internal and external achievements will survive the change. This is not an unimportant issue, since Russia will remain a transregional, if not a truly global, state. Russia is a great power with nuclear weapons and vast natural, human, and intellectual resources. Its evolution over the next several years, whatever its character, will strongly affect world developments. And sooner or later, with new leaders in Moscow and other countries, the time will come for another attempt to reform Russia domestically and to introduce major foreign and security policy revisions. What happens in the meantime will be of critical importance for future developments.

This chapter is designed to illuminate the complex and contradictory interaction of Russia's domestic situation, its policies toward neighboring countries, and its relations with the West during a period of great change. In the first section, the main geopolitical, economic, and security realities that ensued from the disintegration of the communist world are analyzed. The conclusion is that, although Moscow has suffered severe setbacks in a classic geopolitical and balance-of-power sense, it also has unprecedented opportunities that, if used wisely, could enhance Russia's security and facilitate democratic reforms. The second section explores the dialectics of Russia's domestic developments and its relations with other former Soviet republics and the West. The ill-conceived and even more poorly implemented domestic reforms of 1992–93 predictably failed, leading to the weakening and disintegration of the Yeltsin administration's political base. The regime lost its policy orientation, indulged in unprecedented corruption, and shifted to increasingly authoritarian methods of rule, including reliance on force and military power. As a consequence, imperial policies toward other post-Soviet states were revived, prompting the growth of mutual suspicion, controversy, and lack of cooperation in Russia's relations with the West.

The third section discusses the principal issues of Russia's relations with its neighbors, criticizes its neo-imperial propensities of 1993–95, and suggests alternative policy concepts. In the fourth section, these general criticisms and alternatives are applied to particular post-Soviet republics and regions. The former republics are subdivided into several groups, and policies tailored to each group are elaborated. The fifth section deals with the emerging pattern of Russian and Western policies toward conflict areas in Central and Southern Europe and in the FSU, and assesses the role, opportunities, and deficiencies of international organizations in these conflicts. It addresses the dangers stemming from the new division of Europe, the authoritarian trends within Russia, and renewed confrontation between Russia and the West, and makes some suggestions for damage limitation. In particular, expanding the involvement of international organizations in European and post-Soviet peacekeeping and conflict-resolution activities could put a brake on Moscow's unilateralism and limit the divergence of Russian and Western security strategies.

New Realities: The View from Moscow

The Soviet empire has disintegrated. Its outposts near and far as well as its colonies and semi-colonies are lost. The centrifugal force created by the breakdown even threatens to split the Russian nucleus, as evidenced by the December 1994 bloodbath in Chechnya. After the Soviet Union was disbanded at a secret meeting of Russian, Ukrainian, and Belarusan leaders in the Belovezh Forest in December 1991, the Russian Federation, as was to be expected, received by far the largest portion of the Soviet legacy: 60 percent of the population, 65 percent of the industrial capacity, 76 percent of the territory, and about 90 percent of the energy resources of the Soviet Union. Russia also acquired approximately 60 percent of the Soviet Union's conventional military forces and 80 percent of its strategic and tactical nuclear weapons.[1] Moscow also inherited the core of the highly centralized administrative, monetary, and banking system; the bulk of the information, management, communications, and energy infrastructure; and the best available cadres in all spheres, including those previously recruited from the provinces, as well as virtually all Soviet property abroad.

Nevertheless, the Soviet collapse left Russia much weaker than its still impressive size and resources would imply. It is plagued by deep economic, social, and political crises and paralyzed by the disintegration and corruption of its state structures. Russia's decision-making mechanisms are in shambles, its armed forces are demoralized and suffering from failures of maintenance and modernization, and its foreign policy lacks any sense of direction, priorities, or values.

The economic crisis that underlies these calamities is the result of three overlapping factors: first, the degradation of the socialist economy and management system inherited from the Soviet era; second, the effects of dividing the once highly integrated Soviet economy and infrastructure; and third, the failure of the economic and political reforms undertaken since 1992. Although these factors are largely internal, they are closely intertwined with Russian security policy. Economic dependence on the West for financial aid and credits is humiliating to Russian national pride and has provoked a nationalistic anti-Western backlash, which is a growing factor in Russian domestic politics.

No less significant than the shrunken perimeters of its political power is the new security environment that lies beyond Russia's borders. In the past, territories belonging to, or controlled by, the Soviet Union were directly contiguous to territories belonging to, or protected by, the United States and China. With few exceptions, the lines were drawn quite clearly and fortified by high levels of military force. At present, the Russian Federation borders on former union republics to the west, to the southwest, and to the south. These states are marked by a high degree of internal instability and are open to influence from outside. Many are in conflict with each other and with Russia.[2]

---

1.   See Grigori Yavlinsky, *The Lessons of Economic Reform* (Moscow: EPI Center, 1993); and Alexei Arbatov, ed., *Nuclear Weapons and Republican Sovereignty* (Moscow: Mezhdunarodnaia Otnosheniya, 1992).

2.   P. Felgengauer, "Are We Entering the Caucasus War?" *Nezavisimaia gazeta*, November 7, 1992; E. Pain and A. Popov, "The Flame of the Caucasus War Is the

Russia formally recognizes these states as foreign countries. They are all members of the United Nations and the Organization for Security and Cooperation in Europe (OSCE), and many are parties to the Strategic Arms Reduction Talks (START I), the Conventional Forces in Europe (CFE) Treaty, and the Nuclear Non-Proliferation Treaty (NPT). However, they remain closely bound to Russia by a comprehensive web of vital economic, ethnic, cultural, personal, and psychological ties, as well as historic grievances and outstanding territorial and property claims. Conflicts and problems afflicting the new republics are rarely confined to the borders of these states, and often expand to involve other states, including Russia. More than sixty million people in the territory of the FSU are living outside of their ethnic homelands, including roughly twenty-six million Russians. According to various assessments, about 100,000 Russian military personnel are still deployed at various defense facilities in the "near abroad" with control over huge stockpiles of weapons.[3]

The Russian term "near abroad" has acquired a definite neo-imperial flavor, and its use is often condemned in other former Soviet republics. Whatever its use and abuse at present, the initial meaning of the term was quite neutral, without any imperial connotations. It is in this spirit that the term "near abroad" is used in this chapter. Whether the former Soviet republics like it or not, Russia is part of their near abroad, just as they are part of Russia's. Russia's relations with other former Soviet republics, from Estonia to Turkmenistan, have a number of distinctive features that do not enter into its relations with other states, whether the United States or Sudan. To debate the semantics of the issue is to miss the point. The problem is not which term to apply, but rather how to develop policies in Russia, in the other FSU states, and in the West that will do away with the distinction between the "near" and "far" abroad.

Russia's first major dilemma regarding its policies in the near abroad is how to find the right balance between treating the other former Soviet republics as independent, and cultivating some kind of "special relationship" with them. In concrete terms, the question

---

Price of Juridical and Political Mistakes," *Izvestia*, November 5, 1992; and A. Khanbabian, "Myth-making as a Cause of National Tragedy," *Nezavisimaia gazeta*, February 3, 1993.

3.   I. Serebraikov, "Russia's Military Doctrine," *Nezavisimaia gazeta*, February 8, 1994; and A. Zhilin, "Yellow Trident on Rusty Armor," *Moscow News*, No. 5 (January 30–February 6, 1994), p. 9

encompasses such issues as whether Russia should demand payments in hard currency for energy, the arrangements governing the status of Russian military personnel and civilians abroad, and the use of industrial and defense facilities located outside the Russian Federation. Obviously, there is room for a great deal of political disagreement on these issues, and the parties involved often end up supporting contradictory aims.

Another great dilemma is how to minimize the hostility of Russia's immediate external environment. It is clearly in Russia's interest to prevent the emergence of a *cordon sanitaire* of newly independent states between Russia and the world beyond, and to prevent them from falling under the political and military influence of either adjacent regional powers or distant global ones. An isolationist stance would abandon the former republics—not all of which may prove to be viable states—to economic collapse, territorial and ethnic conflict, civil wars, and general chaos. Instability in these states could invite intervention from outside and might expose Russians and other ethnic minorities to oppression or even genocide. Moreover, chronic instability in the states along Russia's largely transparent borders could penetrate Russia, either directly or through other states.

Conversely, attempts to guarantee a benign near abroad through Russian economic blackmail, coupled with political and military domination, might provoke resistance and involve Russia in multiple wars along its perimeter. Such an outcome would exhaust Russia's resources and undermine its democratic reforms. Russians living abroad could become hostages to local radical nationalists. However, an effort to forcibly annex territories inhabited by ethnic minorities[4] would serve to create precisely the hostile *cordon sanitaire* Moscow wishes to avoid. Moreover, it would likely invite outside intervention in support of resistance to Russian encroachments, bring confrontation with the West and the Muslim world, and engender spillover violence in Russia itself. An attempt to create a benign international political environment in the surrounding states by providing economic and political assistance would certainly overburden Russia's economic, financial, and administrative resources at a time of severe

---

4.   Enclaves densely settled by Russian minorities are found in southern Latvia, eastern Estonia, Crimea and eastern Ukraine, the Dniester region of Moldova, Georgian Abkhazia, South Ossetia, Ajaria, Azerbaijan's Lezgin area, and Baikonur and Semipalatinsk in northern and eastern Kazakhstan. Other, smaller enclaves also exist.

crisis in Russia, with few tangible results. Such an altruistic policy would not gain support at home, especially since Russians do not feel guilty about past Soviet and Russian imperial rule. On the contrary, they see the newly independent states as thoroughly ungrateful for the freedom Moscow granted them in 1991, and often gloat over the economic and political turmoil these states are enduring "without Russian rule." More to the point, it is not at all clear that Russia can, based on its own experience, claim expertise in economic and political reconstruction.

Russia's relations with the near abroad deeply affect its relations with the far abroad. In reality, the two spheres are indivisible, and, as will be shown below, Russia's relations with other post-Soviet states are a decisive element in a broader post–Cold War, Euro-Atlantic, Middle Eastern, and South Asian security framework. The dissolution of the Warsaw Treaty Organization (WTO) and the breakup of the Soviet Union dismantled the stable Cold War strategic framework and distorted the well-proportioned disarmament structures of the 1990 Treaty on Conventional Forces in Europe, the 1991 START I Treaty, and the 1993 START II Treaty. The reshuffling of political power also aggravated problems with the 1969 Nuclear Non-Proliferation Treaty on the eve of its 1995 review conference, later solved. As for the CFE Treaty, agreements were reached on individual national ceilings for former Warsaw Pact countries, and the 1992 Tashkent Agreement divided the military assets of the Soviet Union among Russia and other former Soviet republics in a manner deemed consistent with the CFE Treaty. The nuclear issues were addressed in the 1992 five-party Lisbon Protocol to START I and the January 1994 trilateral U.S.-Russian-Ukrainian Agreement on nuclear forces, but they have thus far failed to resolve important problems concerning the control, maintenance, and reduction of the former Soviet nuclear forces. In addition, the ambiguities of the situation created an acute threat to the international nuclear non-proliferation regime.

Together with the economic crisis and disintegration of defense cooperation among the former Soviet republics, these developments were deeply detrimental to Russia's strategic posture and its negotiating position. They created a gaping disadvantage for Russia that will continue into the next decade in terms of the balance of conventional forces in Europe and the U.S.-Russian balance in strategic and theater nuclear forces. Whereas in the past, the Soviet Union and WTO enjoyed almost three-fold conventional superiority over NATO in Europe, after 1995, Russia's force was reduced to about one-third the size of NATO's and one-fifth the combined power of the Western states.[5] Taking into account the effects of economic crisis and the disorganization of the Russian armed forces, Russia's conventional inferiority will be much greater than CFE arms allocations may indicate.

Moreover, the dissolution of the Warsaw Pact created a new geostrategic situation with the withdrawal of Soviet military power to 1,500 km from the center of Europe from Magdeburg and Prague to Smolensk and Kursk. For the previous forty years, Soviet strike armies stood within a two-week advance of the English Channel. Now, for the first time in three hundred years during peacetime, the Moscow Military District has been transformed from the deep rear into Russia's advanced western defense line. The unstable and unpredictable geopolitical conglomerate of East European states and former Soviet republics has created a barrier effectively isolating Russia from European security affairs. These developments threaten to bring a not clearly friendly military alliance within a fifteen-minute jet flight from the Kremlin.

In the Transcaucasus and Central Asia, widespread economic and social turmoil, wars, and a rising level of violence directly involve Russia with Turkey, Iran, and Afghanistan, and indirectly with Iraq and Pakistan. Moscow's relations with these countries have a major impact on developments in this region, which is often referred to as Russia's "soft underbelly," not least because of the approximately ten million Russians living there. Escalating instability in this area has already spilled over into the North Caucasus in the Russian Federation, which has always been culturally and politically more a part of the Caucasus than of Russia. The "dirty" war in Chechnya is equally the result of the failure of Russia's policy in the Transcaucasus and of its inability to devise a viable federal system within the Russian Federation. The conflict in Chechnya raises the threat of spreading domestic turmoil, particularly among the twenty million Muslim-Turks inside the Russian Federation.

In the Asia-Pacific region, although the near abroad is not a factor, Russia's vulnerability is not significantly less, and it compounds Russia's weaknesses to the west and south. To the east of Lake Baikal, Russia borders directly on the two rising Asian giants, China and Japan. Both have a long history of territorial disputes with the Soviet

---

5. Dorn Crawford, *Conventional Armed Forces in Europe (CFE): A Review and Update of Key Treaty Elements* (Washington, D.C.: United States Arms Control and Disarmament Agency, December 1995).

Union and, earlier, with the Russian Empire. At present neither country represents a clear military threat to Russia, and both are more fearful of each other than of Russia. In the future, though, their growing economic and possibly military superiority to Russia will have serious security implications, particularly in light of the vulnerability of Russia's enormous Siberian territory. Although uniquely rich in resources, Siberia is sparsely populated, paralyzed by developments in Russia, and slipping from Moscow's control. It is protected only by demoralized and badly supplied armed forces and populated by numerous non-Slavic ethnic groups, including growing numbers of Chinese and Korean immigrants.

These unfavorable changes and prospects are not without counterbalancing advantages. For the first time in many centuries, Russia is not threatened by military aggression. This in itself is unique in the history of fallen empires. Moreover, Moscow's political, military, and economic relations with the West changed dramatically for the better from 1985–93. Despite the changes in the military balance, Russia remains one of the most powerful states in the world. In 1995, the number of active-duty personnel in the Russian armed forces dropped to about 1.7 million, and further reductions to 1.5 million were planned for 1996. As of mid-1997, these levels have not been attained; when they do, they will be roughly equivalent to U.S. force levels, and three to four times larger than the next largest European army. In addition, there are approximately 800,000 uniformed and armed personnel in the border guards and internal troops, and 600,000 civilian personnel employed by the Ministry of Defense. In the principal categories of conventional arms, Russia is superior to all but the United States, and in some catagories it remains ahead of the United States.[6] In the nuclear field, after ten years under the START II Treaty, Russia will be able to maintain parity with the United States at a ceiling of about 3,000–3,500 warheads, a force that is many times greater than that of any other nuclear power.

To summarize, compared to the Soviet Union and the former socialist camp, Russia today is weaker and more unstable due to its domestic problems, drastic shifts in the military balance, and new geostrategic vulnerabilities. Nevertheless, it remains a great power

6.   See Jonathan Dean and Randall Forsberg,"CFE and Beyond: The Future of Conventional Arms Control," *International Security*, Vol. 17, No. 1 (Summer 1992), pp. 86–87, 110–121; and Alexei Arbatov, "Empire or Great Power?" *Novoe Vremia*, No. 49 (November 1992), pp. 18–19.

by European and world standards, and by the scale of its geopolitical presence in Europe and Asia. Most of the problems that plague Russia are self-inflicted and should not be blamed on bad advice from abroad or on so-called "objective circumstances." The absence of threats to Russian security from the major world powers provides Moscow with a unique window of opportunity for domestic reforms, deep reductions in defense efforts, and the development of a new military and foreign policy. However, good relations with both the West and China from 1991–1993 were largely predicated on Russia's complete preoccupation with domestic problems and its passive foreign policy, which consisted largely in following the U.S. lead in world affairs. But for a country as large as Russia, this state of affairs cannot continue indefinitely. A subservient policy is doomed to provoke—and has already provoked—a counterreaction in Russia in the form of nationalism and anti-Western posturing. Besides, Russian passivity would deprive the world community of a powerful and resourceful player with the potential to fill an important, even crucial, role in post-communist, post–Cold War affairs.

Thus, the great security dilemma facing Russia, along with the other great powers, is how to adapt to these profound changes in the nature of Russia's relations with the West and China while maintaining its national foreign policy identity, its international role, and respect from other nations without reviving tensions, mutual fears, and rivalries with other great powers. The great challenge is to find a new Russian place in the international environment that neither looks like a scaled-down version of Soviet imperialist geopolitical expansion, nor reverts to self-contained isolationism. The former would be certain to provoke resistance in the near abroad and a new containment policy from the far abroad. And the latter would deprive Russia of the benefits of political, economic, and security cooperation with the West and leave other post-Soviet states to disintegrate in violence and chaos, with dire consequences for Russia and the rest of the world.

Domestic Factors in Russian Foreign Policy

The Soviet Union was not defeated by the West in the Cold War. The Soviet Empire, from the end of the 1920s on, was built for war—economically, politically, ideologically, and militarily. It proved its resilience in the terrible test of 1941–45, and was geared for a never-ending confrontation with the West and China during the four subsequent decades. The Cold War was the Soviet Union's natural milieu, allowing it to advance when opportunities appeared or retreat when resources were overextended. It was the internal dynamics of the economic, social, and psychological evolution of Soviet society—the inability of the system to satisfy the growing demands of the people generated by the development of technology and mass information—that, by the early 1980s, had worn down the fabric of the Soviet regime.

Boris Yeltsin rose to power on the waves of agony that accompanied the demise of the centralized and highly militarized Soviet economy and the loss of purpose, legitimacy, and efficiency of the huge state-party bureaucracy. He was propelled by the mass democratic movement in Russia and the national-liberation wave in other Soviet republics. However, upon coming to power, Yeltsin and his team committed a fatal strategic blunder: they did virtually nothing to create a solid political and institutional foundation for their authority and for the democratic reforms they envisioned.[7] The autumn of 1991 was exactly the right time for a referendum on the new constitution, for elections in all branches and levels of Russian state institutions, for the reorganization of governmental structures, and for a revision of relations between the center and the regions of the Russian Federation. Finally, every effort should have been made to consolidate the political base of the new leadership by creating a broad coalition of liberal to moderate-conservative forces supporting democratic transition and market reforms. But no significant steps in this direction were taken.

Nor did Russia make enough of an effort to comprehensively revamp its relations with other Soviet republics, apart from the hastily concluded first agreements establishing the Commonwealth of Independent States (CIS) in Minsk and Alma-Ata in December 1991. Economic reform was initiated in Russia without regard to future political, military, or economic-financial relations with the other CIS states. Decisions were made on the erroneous assumption that disbanding the Soviet Union would liberate Russia from the burden of subsidizing other republics. The Russian oil that had formerly supported the economic activity of these areas was to be sold to the West to finance reforms. The other republics would link up with the

---

7.   I. Timofeev, "The Big Waste," *Izvestia*, February 26, 1993, p. 4; see also the report of the "RF-Politika" Center: "The Unfinished Coup d'Etat," *Izvestia*, October 30, 1992.

system later. In fact, however, Russia could not isolate itself from its neighbors. For one thing, Russia did not possess real administrative or economic borders. Some 40 percent of the highly integrated subsidiaries of the Russian economy were stranded outside the Russian Federation. Russia's currency, in cash and checks, was shared by one hundred million people in fourteen other sovereign states, each with its own independent central bank.[8] All of these basic economic, financial, defense, humanitarian, and legal problems were addressed *after*, not before, disbanding the Soviet Union.

No attempt was made to thoroughly review CIS or Russian defense requirements in view of the new economic, political, and security situation. The Russian military was not placed under firm political control by the appointment of a civilian minister of defense with a civilian staff and by vesting the parliament with real authority in this area. Instead, President Yeltsin relied on the personal loyalty of top military officers, a strategy that almost failed him in October 1993. The armed forces were reduced and withdrawn from deployment abroad largely on a haphazard basis. Military reform was primarily a bureaucratic cover for preserving the traditional ways of the Soviet Army. Defense industries were simply left without defense contracts and without aid for conversion, marketing, or exploring export options.

Instead of realistic and careful revision of political and security relations with the West, the predominant emphasis was put on getting Western economic aid and credits. Russian foreign policy and security strategy were largely subordinated to this goal, resulting in a long sequence of unilateral concessions on various international and security issues in 1992 and 1993. Foreign assistance and International Monetary Fund (IMF) credits very quickly became not means in themselves for economic reform, but ends to which economic reform was merely the instrument. An evaluation of Yegor Gaidar's economic reform efforts is beyond the scope of this chapter. Suffice it to point out that in a democracy, which Russia longed to become, no idealized economic reform program (even if approved by the World Bank's top experts) could ever work if it were not adapted to Russian conditions, elaborated with the participation of the major pro-democratic political parties, and based on cooperation among all three branches of power. Instead, the Gaidar program was imposed on an unresponsive and non-participating society. The program

---

8. Yavlinsky, *The Lessons of Economic Reform*, pp. 51–56, 64–69.

quickly disintegrated, and the conditions it created brought Russian society to the verge of civil war. The October 1993 massacre in Moscow and the results of the December 1994 elections were indisputable signs of the failure of the first phase of market reforms and democratic innovations in Russia. The unconstitutional and indiscriminately violent suppression of Chechen rebels initiated in December 1994 can be viewed as a milestone on the road to the restoration of an authoritarian regime in Moscow.

During most of 1993–94, a major realignment of the parties in foreign policy debates took place, which prepared the ground for a significant shift in Russian foreign policy. This shift had several facets, all pointing in one direction. First of all, there was a growing popular mood in favor of Russian self-assertiveness—finding clear-cut Russian national interests and defending them with all available instruments, including military power. There was also an increasing aversion to "universal" values, international law, and other "idealistic" principles as guidelines for policy. Anti-Western sentiments became more prominent in the public mood and political debates. Finally, Russian relations with the "near abroad" came to the foreground of theoretical debates and practical policymaking, leaving all other international issues far behind. All these above factors came together in increasing support for what was labeled Russia's "Monrovsky Doctrine."[9] This doctrine was articulated officially and at the highest level for the first time in early 1993 in President Yeltsin's appeal to the United Nations and Conference on Security and Cooperation in Europe (CSCE, precursor to the OSCE) to delegate to Russia the mission of ensuring stability and conducting peacekeeping operations on the territory of the former Soviet Union. This line was further elaborated by Russian Foreign Minister Andrei Kozyrev at ministerial sessions of the CSCE, the Group of Seven Industrialized Nations (G-7), the CIS, and the Baltic states.[10]

There are a number of reasons for this profound shift. The fundamental explanation is the deterioration in Russia's economic and social situation and the growing popular dissatisfaction with the

---

9. The "Monrovsky Doctrine" is a play on the U.S. Monroe Doctrine, proclaimed in 1823 by the young and vulnerable United States to prevent attempts by European empires (in particular Spain and Russia) to regain their colonies in the Western Hemisphere.

10. Alexei Arbatov and B. Makeev, "The Kuril Barrier to Russian Diplomacy," *Novoe Vremia*, No. 40–41 (November 1992).

results of the reforms. Russia's political leadership became increasingly vulnerable to nationalist and aggressive moods, emanating not only from the public and the Supreme Soviet, but also from within the bureaucracy, the military and security establishments, industrial groups, and the new private entrepreneurs. The support of the military and security institutions assumed new importance to the contestants in the political conflict between the executive and legislative powers. Rival factions of the new ruling elite attempted to attract support through neo-imperialist appeals.

The deficiencies of Russia's 1992–93 foreign policy continued to haunt the Yeltsin administration. Having failed to formulate palpable and imaginative new Russian national priorities, the foreign policy leadership began to succumb to superficial, primitive, "non-idealistic" impulses calculated to appeal to insulted national pride. Such appeals resonated perfectly with both traditional Russian insecurities and the general dissatisfaction with the new circumstances, easily transforming current discontents into nostalgia for past advantages. Most of the professional staff of the Foreign Ministry shifted even further to the right than Kozyrev. A still harder stance was adopted by the central bureaucracy of the Ministry of Defense, while the vast majority of field officers supported radical nationalist views. Even the democratic and liberal factions of the new parliament, to say nothing of conservatives, communists, and nationalists, coalesced on the side of neo-imperialism to oppose the Foreign Ministry.[11] Salient examples include the Duma's condemnation in February 1994 of the Russian-Georgian treaty of friendship and good neighborliness and its enthusiastic support for the newly elected pro-Russian president of Crimea.[12]

Nevertheless, no grand design for a new imperialistic expansion lurks behind Russian foreign policy. The Monrovsky Doctrine is a policy by default, not an elaborate long-term strategy. Its meaning is vague and subject to various interpretations, ranging from the endorsement of benign mediation among parties in post-Soviet conflicts[13] to an aggressive call for the restoration of the Soviet (Russian)

---

11. See P. Felgenhauer, "Everybody in Russia Wants to Sell Arms," *Nezavisimaia gazeta*, October 1, 1992.

12. A. Mikadze, "The Georgian Treaty 1994," *Moskovskie novosti*, No. 5 (January 30–February 6, 1994), p. A–10.

13. V. Portnikov, "Andrei Kozyrev Defines Priorities," *Nezavisimaia gazeta*, (January 20, 1994), pp. 1–3.

empire by force.[14] Its implementation proceeds by way of ad hoc decisions in a generally disorganized administration, achieved by tugging and pulling within the turbulent new political elite.

As the Yeltsin administration's military action bogged down in Chechnya, the political situation in Moscow grew less and less stable. There are two important aspects of the Chechen tragedy that should by no means be confused. One side of "Chechen coin" is the unacceptable situation in Chechnya, its infectious effects in Russia, the outrageous nature of Dzhokhar Dudaev's regime, and the existence of an illegal army on Russian territory, which would be intolerable for any sovereign state with self-respect. The same goes for the Chechen claim of independence, which was historically and legally dubious and had only limited political appeal in the republic. The secession of Chechnya would have triggered further disintegration of the Russian Federation and encouraged separatists in other post-Soviet republics, turning the former Soviet space into one large Yugoslavia. This malignant tumor had to be removed sooner or later, and under the circumstances, spilling some blood was probably unavoidable.

But the other aspect of the Chechen problem is the real motives and goals of the Kremlin, which resulted in a totally illegal application of force, caused greatly excessive casualties and destruction, led the real policy and its consequences far from its stated noble and legitimate goals, and broadened the cleft between the Russian leadership, on the one hand, and the public, mass media, and democratic movement, on the other. In this perspective, if Chechnya had not existed, it would have had to be invented. Alternatively, Russia would have intervened with massive military force elsewhere in the former Soviet Union, which could have been an even greater disaster.

The failures of domestic economic and political reforms in Russia, the growing autonomy of the regions, and the declining authority and popularity of President Yeltsin and his disorganized and corrupt administration all seemed to call for some decisive action to show who was in charge in Russia. Especially after the crisis of October 1993, popular disenchantment with Yeltsin's management of domestic and foreign affairs and expanding support for the communist and nationalist opposition made Yeltsin rely more and more on authoritarian rule and military force, without regard to laws, constitutional procedures, and the division of powers, instead of changing policy and advisers to gain greater democratic support—hence the seemingly

---

14. Mikadze, "The Georgian Treaty 1994."

deliberate arrogance and arbitrariness of the decision on Chechnya and its impudent neglect of the constitution, federal laws, the position of the parliament, the sentiments of the mass media, and public opinion. In the regime's calculations, widely perceived humiliations and mishaps in dealing with both the near and far abroad required some major forceful act of self-assertion to rally public support for Yeltsin and his team, for the armed forces and internal troops, and for suppressive forceful methods.

In this sense, the functional purpose of the Chechen operation was to intimidate the political opposition, parliament, and disobedient regions and to enhance the transition to authoritarian rule—allegedly for the sake of democratic reforms, but in fact to retain power for the incumbent regime, which was unable and unwilling to rule by democratic methods. As might have been expected, the character of the operation was condemned by the democratic parties and mass media and enthusiastically supported by nationalists and outright fascists. The Western reaction was dichotomized: the governments emphasized the first side of the "Chechen coin" while Western public opinion and opposition parties stressed the second.

Finally, all the familiar features of Yeltsin's administration were more conspicuous than ever in the preparation and conduct of the Chechen war: incompetence, reliance on fragmented and false information, lack of any long-term strategy or centralized control, numerous broken promises, slander of all opponents. At the highest level, decision-making was dominated by egocentric political and career considerations with little consciousness of the disastrous policy results: the human losses and suffering and the vast destruction in Chechnya. If all the preceding evidence was not enough, the war in Chechnya presented a horrified Russian public and the world at large with convincing proof of the profound decomposition and transformation of the regime itself.

The political situation in Moscow remained highly unstable throughout 1995. On the one hand, for the first time in Soviet or Russian history, democratic liberal opposition to a war waged by the government has acquired great momentum and partially hamstrung the actions of the armed forces. A free press has reasserted itself in Russia, and the population has proved quite immune to nationalist moods. On the other hand, an embryonic and weak Russian democracy failed to prevent this illegal and unpopular war, directed not so much against the Dudaev junta, but against Russia's own people, foremost among them the ethnic Russians in Chechnya.

If the war continues even in a new guerrilla form, large-scale violence will eventually expand into the rest of the North Caucasus and other regions, provoking Moscow to suppress political opposition and the free press, and to ignore the other branches of government. This would effectively be the end of Russian democracy and the final restoration of authoritarian, militarized, and chauvinistic rule. During the ten years of the war in Afghanistan, the Soviet Army inflicted about 1.2–2 million fatalities. For Chechens, this would mean the total annihilation of the ethnic group. Such an outcome cannot be completely excluded, but it would certainly be incompatible with Russia's democratic development or partnership with the West.

However, if pressure within Russia and from world public opinion leads to a stable and peaceful settlement (with all those responsible for the illegal and indiscriminate use of force removed from power), succeeding generations of Russian politicians will learn the lessons that political methods are preferable to the use of force, that the application of force must be strictly based on law, the cooperation of other branches of government, and public support, and that methods of warfare should not contradict the war's stated goals.

As of early 1996, the domestic political implications of the Chechen tragedy were not clear. However, it was clear that the Yeltsin administration was unable either to win the war politically or to stop it. Winning politically, in contrast to succeeding operationally, means gaining administrative control over the territory, establishing local authorities supported by the population, and providing for the economic and social revival of the region. Actually, no one had ever doubted the capability of the Russian armed forces to suppress in open combat the resistance of the Chechen troops. But the time it took to do so, the human losses incurred, and the collateral damage inflicted by the federal forces were all far greater than any forecasts. Political victory is likely to remain out of reach as long as the Yeltsin administration is in power since it bears responsibility for the losses, the destruction, and the massive violations of the law and human rights. At that time, stopping the war implied negotiating with the Dudaev regime and thus recognizing the failure of the operation and the futility of its enormous cost. This would effectively undercut Yeltsin as well.

As for Russian relations with the near abroad, the disaster in Chechnya made Moscow much more politically and morally vulnerable and thus more cautious in its policies toward other post-Soviet states. This was reflected in its mute reaction to Kiev's decision in

April 1995 to put an end to Crimean semi-independence.[15] At the same time, Russia, by relying on brute violence instead of ongoing negotiations, has provided other republics with a bad example of how to deal with such problems. If others follow this example, ethnic tensions could steeply escalate in the near abroad, inadvertently drawing Russia into the hostilities, as is apparently happening in Tajikistan.[16]

As with many other uncertainties and alternative possibilities, the major impact of the war in Chechnya on Moscow's relations with the near abroad will be further domestic political evolution in Russia, on which the Chechen phenomenon is certain to have a profound effect. Russian internal developments will determine whether the Chechen suppression was the first open military counteroffensive of the reviving authoritarian nationalistic regime—or the last convulsion of the dying empire, the last desperate effort to defy the imperatives of changing centuries-old traditions of oppressive arbitrary rule.

Russian Vital Interests in the "Near Abroad"

Russia's situation today is not at all comparable to that of the young United States, protected by vast ocean barriers, that proclaimed the Monroe Doctrine in 1823 against attempts by European empires, particularly Spain and Russia, to regain their colonies in the Western Hemisphere. But mistaken historical analogy is not the main deficiency of the Russian "Monrovsky Doctrine." According to advocates of this doctrine among former pro-Western liberals, centrists, and conservatives, Russia is entitled to a "special role" in the post-Soviet space. They cite Russia's size, its historic influence and central economic position, the need to protect the millions of Russians living there, as well as unique out-of-area strategic and political interests. Preserving and, wherever needed, reinstating Russia's dominant role throughout the former Soviet Union is the principal goal of this version of Russian foreign policy.[17]

Specific Russian "pragmatic interests" (as some U.S. scholars label them) to be safeguarded by such a policy include securing access to warm water ports in the Black and Baltic seas; maintaining a buffer

---

15. V. Portnikov, "Evgeniy Marchuk Has Left in a Good Mood," *Nezavisimaia gazeta*, No. 71 (April 20, 1995), pp. 1–2.

16. A. Dubnov, "Does Russia Have a Tajik Policy?" *Novoe Vremia*, No. 16 (April 1995), pp. 12–14.

17. See A. Zubov, "CIS: Civilized Divorce or New Marriage?" *Novoe Vremia*, No. 36 (September 1992), pp. 8–9.

zone between Russia and the European powers, as well as between Russia and Turkey, Iran, and China; retaining control over raw materials in other former republics; ensuring access to industrial facilities and control over defense assets and military bases; and guaranteeing markets for Russian products.[18] But these are not central. The principal goal of this version of Russian foreign policy is to avoid being left isolated and alone, without satellites or allies, and to regain recognition of Russia's status as a great power. This objective is deemed impossible without a defined geopolitical Russian "sphere of interest." Nuclear weapons alone cannot achieve this status, and the Russian economy is still too weak to ensure it.

Various means are to be used to reassert Russia's great-power status according to the situation in particular FSU states: economic dependence in some republics; the continued presence of ethnic Russian populations and Russian armed forces in others; ethnic and political tensions within the newly independent states; and territorial conflicts among them. But there is one common thread: according to this logic, the weaker and less stable that the other former republics are, the stronger and better off that Russia will be.

President Yeltsin's 1994 foreign policy agenda stated that "unconditional emphasis . . . will be placed on the defense of Russia's national interests, and the defense of the rights of Russians and Russian-speaking populations, within the guidelines of international law and proceeding from the idea of all-national solidarity."[19] Foreign Minister Kozyrev, in his notorious January 1994 speech at the conference of CIS and Baltic ambassadors, claimed that "the CIS and the Baltic states constitute the area in which Russia's principal vital interests are concentrated . . . [and] from which the main threats to its interests emanate." "I think," he went on, "that raising the question about complete withdrawal and removal of any Russian military presence in the countries of the near abroad is just as extreme, if not extremist, as the idea of sending tanks to all the republics to establish some form of imperial order."[20]

---

18. See the interview with K. Zatulin, "To Become our Satellites or Perish," *Nezavisimaia gazeta*, No. 83 (May 5, 1994), p. 3.

19. V. Chernov, "The National Interests of Russia and Threats to its Security," *Novoe Vremia*, April 29, 1993, pp. 1–3.

20. See Fiona Hill and Pamela Jewett, *Back in the USSR: Russia's Intervention in the Internal Affairs of the Former Soviet Republics and the Implications for United States Policy toward Russia* (Cambridge, Mass.: Harvard University, Kennedy School of Government, Strengthening Democratic Institutions Project, January 1994), p. 3.

Proponents of this policy believe that preserving Russia's ability to keep developments in the FSU states under control and constraining the inclination of the smaller republics in the Russian Federation to seek independence will in due time result in the decline of local nationalism. Then reintegration will regain momentum. On this subject, the principal difference between former liberals and moderate-conservatives, on one side, and radical nationalists on the other, does not involve the main thrust of the policy, but rather its scope and methods, the time frame envisioned, and the accompanying attitude toward the West. Unlike radical hard-liners, moderates would prefer economic and political instruments to military ones, and they would exclude the Baltics. They also consider it important that Russia's "special responsibility and authority" in the FSU should be recognized by the United States and sanctioned by the UN. They do not want Russian policies to become an apple of discord and a source of confrontation with the West.

This new dominant strand of Russian policy thinking underestimates the power of nationalism and the scale of historic grievances in the smaller republics of the Russian Federation. Equally, it overestimates Russia's resources and Moscow's ability to keep extreme nationalists at bay and to control the escalation of ethnic conflicts. Ironically, the "democratic" ruling elite, who came to power as a result of the disintegration of the Soviet empire, has completely forgotten the lessons of the Soviet downfall. They wrongly assume that the collapse was caused by the actions of Mikhail Gorbachev and Edward Shevardnadze, who were driven from power. They mistakenly believe that the complete independence of the other republics will bring greater economic, political, humanitarian, and defensive losses to Russia than will large-scale efforts to keep those states under Russian control. And they misjudge the outside world's level of tolerance for Russian neo-imperialist policies, in particular the routine use of force that would be required.

Another deficiency of this approach is that the goal of ensuring stability under Russian dominance across the entire territory of the former Soviet Union undermines Moscow's ability to rationally and pragmatically select among national interests and priorities. Neither the time and scope of Russian involvement would be fully under the control of Moscow. Russian involvement and intervention would be automatically triggered by local troubles, particularly involving Russian ethnic minorities or military deployments that are the legacy of perished Soviet and tsarist empires. Local players would be able to draw Russia into their conflicts, either directly or through independent actions of local institutions, including military and security forces, groups of irregulars or "volunteers," or Cossack units.[21] In short, actions of opposition forces could determine the dynamics of Russia's involvement.

In light of these many shortcomings, the policies advocated by moderate-conservatives (let alone the aggressive nationalist visions of empire restored) may create conditions that actually undermine the realization of the stated goals. Russia might become bogged down in local civil or ethnic wars, suffer large numbers of casualties, an influx of refugees, increased expenditures, and possibly retaliatory terrorist strikes in Russian cities. Some smaller republics might be motivated to join together to oppose Russia economically, politically, and militarily. Eventually opposition forces might receive outside support from the West, the South, or the East; political and economic sanctions might be imposed on Russia; and the Cold War could revive—putting Russia in a much less favorable position than it was in the 1940s.

Developments along these lines would be inimical to Russia's democratic reforms. They would lead, if only for a relatively short time before the final catastrophic collapse, to the revival of a besieged, militarized, authoritarian state complete with central economic planning and rationing. As we have seen, radical nationalists and communists would not object to such an outcome, which would be quite consistent with their avowed or implied domestic and foreign policy. But this possibility is denied by moderate and centrist conservatives, who suggest that it is precisely Russian neglect of developments in the near abroad and their destabilizing consequences that might eventually bring nationalists to power in Russia.

Russia's real national interests require a policy very different from the "Monrovsky Doctrine." There are indeed strong economic, humanitarian, cultural, and security forces of attraction among the former Soviet republics, foremost among Russia, Ukraine, Belarus, Kazakhstan, Georgia, and Armenia. But these ties should not be forced by one state upon another. A consistent policy of respect that recognizes the sovereignty and territorial integrity of other states, combined with fair and equal cooperation in various spheres, would be the best way to arrest the centrifugal forces at work throughout the former Soviet Union.

---

21. A. Dubnov, "This Great World Solidarity," *Novoe Vremia*, No. 2 (January 1994), p. 10.

Small states are especially sensitive to any signs of dominance by others. Therefore, genuine economic reintegration may begin only on the basis of the independence and free choice of the states involved. Only in this case will economic ties be founded on mutual economic interests and facilitate economic reform, instead of being merely a foil for reviving a centralized and militarized economic system in the service of a unitary state.

Likewise, using economic and financial levers to extract political and security concessions would not serve the purpose of genuine reintegration. Such deals would place additional burdens on the Russian economy and once again compel Russians to sacrifice their well-being and prospects for affluence to satisfy the imperial ambitions of the ruling elite. If economic pressure is the only tie binding smaller states to Russia, then those states will revoke their concessions as soon as the economic situation changes, or other sources of aid become available. Economic assistance should be provided to states in the near abroad only in exceptional cases, on the basis of well-defined political, security, or humanitarian needs. The transfer of resources and credit should not become a neocolonial paradigm for defining relations between Russia and the post-Soviet republics. Republics seeking special treatment, privileges, or subsidies from Russia should reciprocate with economic concessions of their own—for example, Russian access to natural resources, communications, or banking and financial systems.

The first priority of Russia's foreign policy should be to support the emergence of independent, stable, peaceful, and neutral new states in place of the former Soviet colonies. If they are weak and militant, they may fall under the influence of other states potentially hostile to Russian interests. To prevent this, Russia would have to establish its own dominance over the former Soviet geopolitical space. The first alternative would be highly detrimental to Russian foreign interests and security. The second would draw Moscow into unwanted imperial wars, undercut its resources, and destroy its economic and democratic reforms.

However, many of the new states are inherently unstable, caught in conflict with Russia and with each other. Thus, Russia's primary goal should be to help these states to achieve at least a minimum of stability and to resolve outstanding conflicts without overextending its own diminishing resources. Toward this end, it would be desirable to involve the industrialized West in coordination with Russia, to provide economic and political assistance to the newly independent states on a coherent and consistent basis. This would require new political and security frameworks to facilitate Russian interaction with the CIS and transatlantic organizations.

Much of the tension and conflict in Russia's relations with other republics stems from Moscow's ambivalence on a basic issue: territorial integrity. There are strong groups in the Russian elite and in the foreign policy and security bureaucracies that do not want to recognize the viability of other former Soviet republics as sovereign states. They have been willing to use local separatist movements and the Russian military presence in Estonia, Latvia, Ukraine, Moldova, Georgia, and Kazakhstan to dismember those states, or to subjugate them to Russian dominance.[22] Understandably, these ideas foster fear in these and other republics and undercut the possibility for genuine and fair economic, political, and military cooperation with Russia.

There is no shortage of official documents and declarations at CIS summits and ministerial conferences on the subjects of territorial integrity and the rights of ethnic minorities.[23] However, the inherent tension between the two concepts has not been resolved, either in principle or in particular cases. Moreover, the Yeltsin administration's practical policy on this subject has been highly inconsistent. The Russian government has not acted decisively to refute nationalist actions at home, including those coming from the military or parliament. The president, reluctant to pick a fight on this issue, has never introduced a single agreement concluded with other CIS states for ratification by parliament.[24]

Nonetheless, Russia's highest national interest has been, and should remain, maintaining the Helsinki principle regarding the inviolability of national frontiers to change by force as the basis for relations between the new states of the former Soviet Union. Border revisions should occur only through peaceful negotiations. Ethnic separatism within individual republics should be discouraged. Military support by one state for ethnic separatists across the border should be prohibited. Only two exceptions to this rule should be allowed. The first would be if an individual republic initiated a revision of its own frontiers, for instance, by deciding to unite with

---

22. Interview with K. Zatulin, "To Become our Satellites or Perish."

23. L. Minasian, "Cossacks Want to Guard Russia's Borders and Do Not Recognize the Borders of the Commonwealth," *Nezavisimaia gazeta*, No. 32, February 18, 1994, p. 3.

24. See the interview with K. Zatulin, "To Become our Satellites or Perish."

another state as may occur between Moldova and Romania. When a state initiates the change of borders itself and does not want to recognize the right of ethnic minorities to choose whether to live in that new state or not, the armed resistance of the national minorities is justified. Moreover, international involvement, including military intervention, is warranted to support minorities in such situations. The second exception would be if a state initiated a policy of genocide against a national minority that was not checked by domestic authorities, as happened with Armenians in Azerbaijan. In either case, a demand by the ethnic minority in question for secession or unification with some other state would be legitimate.[25] In protecting the rights of minorities, various sanctions should be permissible to stop pogroms or to evacuate civilians from a dangerous situation, including as a last resort the use of military force. To preclude any abuse of these norms (such as provoking ethnic conflicts to justify military intervention), all the necessary rules and mechanisms of a coherent policy should be established in advance at CIS forums and submitted for international recognition to the UN and the OSCE.[26]

One of the key dilemmas of the post–Cold War world is finding the proper balance between the principles of state sovereignty and integrity, on the one hand, and the right to self-determination, on the other. Obviously there is no neat solution to this dilemma. Each case requires individual study and an individual solution. Only a very general principle can be articulated, namely, that it should be the duty of a state to accommodate, insofar as possible, the interests of all ethnic minorities living within it. This principle clearly implies high economic, democratic, and moral standards not universally prevalent in today's world. If violence is initiated by a state to suppress its ethnic minorities, it is usually an indication of its inability or unwillingness to solve the problem by political or legal means.[27] The use of

---

25. Seccession should be a viable response to genocide (not just any violence) initiated by a state—which makes Azerbaijan, Turkey, or Iraq different from Ulster. Thus, the Armenians in Nagorno-Karabakh and Kurds in Iraq had the right to stage armed revolt, while the Russians in Estonia and Latvia do not, however deplorable and unacceptable the violations of their civil rights.

26. See I. Rotar, "Russian Neo-Imperialism," *Nezavisimaia gazeta*, May 18, 1994, p. 4.

27. Russia's conduct in the war in Chechnya will not soon be forgotten or forgiven by the Chechens. Large numbers of civilians—ironically, mostly Russians—were killed by bombing and shelling, as well as torture and looting. Following the events of the winter of 1994 and the spring of 1995, the only possibility that

force to settle internal problems should be discouraged by the international community and may call for sanctions and, in some cases, even outside multilateral military intervention.

However, armed secession should be discouraged, as well as efforts from abroad to inspire such actions. Changes in existing borders are acceptable as a result of negotiations, preferably under the supervision of an international organization or with international mediation to prevent blackmail or threats by armed separatist movements. Such negotiations must also resolve problems among subminorities living in the seceding territory. The question is not whether peaceful secession and change of borders are possible (they certainly are), but whether violent secession is permissible at all as a last resort. It was in this regard that the two exceptions permitting violent secession were suggested above.

The borders dividing the former Soviet republics are arbitrary. But is it possible to make them less arbitrary by changing them in any way other than through peaceful negotiations? In reality, all borders are to some degree arbitrary, and violent redrawing makes them still more disputable and unjust. Western Europe learned this lesson and stopped redrawing its borders forcibly only after two thousand years of war, including two world wars. Provoking violence to justify violent suppression or secession should be prevented through monitoring by international organizations entrusted with this mission. Likewise, there is no unequivocal right to self-determination. Independence and justice gained by one nation may mean injustice and loss of freedom for its subminorities—as with Serbs in Croatia and Bosnia, Russians in some former Soviet republics, and Georgians in Abkhazia. Here, too, negotiations under international auspices are the only acceptable solution.

There is no question that international organizations have not been sufficiently effective in balancing a state's right to territorial integrity and sovereignty with a people's right to self-determination. The issue is whether major states will choose to coordinate their policies in order to enhance the efficiency of these organizations—first and foremost the UN and the OSCE—or to rely on unilateral actions to achieve

---

Chechnya would stay within the Russian Federation would be if all persons responsible for the war resigned from the Kremlin, and if those implicated in military crimes were brought to justice. The damage and fatalities caused by the war must be compensated, and the population must be given the freedom to choose their own leaders and national status.

policy goals, thus dividing the world into de facto spheres of influence and responsibility governed by the geopolitical balance of power.

This analysis applies in full measure to the roughly twenty-five million Russian speakers living outside the Russian Federation, whose fate is inseparably intertwined with Russia's vital foreign interests. Defending the rights of these people is a sacred duty of all Russians, particularly the Yeltsin administration, whose accession to power in 1991 was, in part, paid for by the millions of Russians left abroad. These Russians have often been the victims of discrimination, deprivation of rights and property, and sometimes even physical threats. Unfortunately Russia has not been able to protect them effectively or to mobilize the support of world public opinion on their behalf. What is worse, Russians abroad have in some cases become a card in the domestic political games of Russian nationalists, or used as a lever to put pressure on other republics (in Estonia, Latvia, Lithuania, Moldova, Ukraine, and Crimea). In other cases, Russian minorities have become hostages to local elites in an effort to affect Moscow's policy (in Turkmenistan and Tajikistan).

The situation is complicated by the presence in several republics of armed forces under the jurisdiction of the Russian Federation. Their slow withdrawal exacerbates anti-Russian sentiments, thereby aggravating the situation of the Russian-speaking population. This, in turn, has led to demands to retain troops in the former republics to protect the Russian population, thus creating a vicious circle. Morale and discipline in Russia's armed forces are collapsing. Russian troops have become mercenaries, sold weapons, and taken their own position in local affairs, independent of Moscow (in Moldova, Crimea, Abkhazia, and Tajikistan).

In early 1994, Russia's highest officials, including the president,[28] the minister of defense, and the minister of foreign affairs,[29] espoused using Russia's foreign military presence to protect the rights of Russians abroad. The plight of Russian minorities in the near abroad has fed neo-imperialist tendencies in official Moscow policy and in the general attitudes of the political elite. It has become politically detrimental to question the orthodox perception of the situation or to call for an unbiased investigation of the real state of affairs. The problem has been aggravated by real cases of mistreatment of Russians in

---

28. See the interview with V. Gustov, chaiman of the Committee on CIS Affairs of the Russian Federal Assembly in *Nezavisimaia gazeta*, May 25, 1994, p. 2.

29. See Arbatov, "Empire or Great Power?" pp. 20–21.

the near abroad and discriminatory naturalization laws adopted by some post-Soviet republics (Latvia, Estonia). Provisions that are normal elements of naturalization laws—such as the requirement of elementary knowledge of the indigenous language—have become humiliating instruments of discrimination, contributing to tensions that are regularly stirred up by local nationalists on both sides as well as by neo-imperialists in Russia.

By contrast, in the Russian Federation, with very few exceptions citizenship has been automatically provided to any former Soviet citizen residing in Russia or the near abroad who wants it.[30] There is no concern whatsoever about individuals of non-Russian ethnicity from other former Soviet republics living in, or visiting, Russia, with the exception of people from the Caucasus and Central Asia. It is widely assumed that peoples from these regions are associated with both organized and random crime and with trafficking in weapons and drugs.

However important the issue may be for Russia's political elite, the rights of ethnic Russians abroad are a matter of minor significance for Russian public opinion at large, lagging far behind domestic problems such as the economy and crime. This is not something to be happy about, since this apathy largely reflects the underdeveloped state of Russian civil society and general indifference toward gross violations of civil rights and democratic freedoms in Russia itself—including those committed by federal and local authorities.

Russians abroad often end up looking more like a lever than a genuine motive of Russian policy. The degree of importance attributed to the situation tends to depend on the state of relations between Moscow and particular states—not the other way around. Moscow gives greater attention to Russians in the Baltics than to those in the loyal Central Asian republics, where Russians are much more frequently abused and physically threatened. After the secession of Transdniester, all talk of discrimination against Russians in Moldova stopped, although only a small fraction of ethnic Russians in Moldova live in the "Dniester Republic." Russia's largest military commitments outside its own territory are in Georgia and Nagorno-Karabakh, where ethnic Russians are not an issue. Russian involvement in Tajikistan was initially justified as necessary to defend the Russian minority there. All Russians able to leave Tajikistan have

---

30. One exception is persecution of "persons of Caucasian nationalities" after the October 1993 crisis in Moscow.

now done so, but Russian operations continue under other pretexts. The shameful neglect and the lack of funding for accommodating Russian refugees in Russia reveal a great deal about Russian attitudes toward co-ethnics abroad, to say nothing of the lack of any policy to protect the rights and security of Russians caught in dangerous zones within Russia itself (Chechnya, Tuva). In some cases, Russians have been simultaneously threatened by the indigenous population and ignored by local authorities.

Changing the conditions for Russians in the near abroad and altering domestic perceptions of their plight will require joint efforts by moderates both in Russia and in other former Soviet republics. But the initial impulse must come from and be sustained by Russia. The main dilemma in protecting the rights of the Russian diaspora is, paradoxically, that unless and until Russia truly and unequivocally recognizes the new states as sovereign countries with inviolable frontiers, it will be impossible to make them observe the rights of Russian minorities. As long as these states are treated as disobedient semi-colonies, enclaves of Russians and other ethnic minorities will be perceived as Trojan horses. These Russians are more likely to be feared as aliens, or even used as hostages, than treated as fellow-citizens. World public opinion usually sympathizes with the position of newly independent states and tends to disregard violations of the rights of minorities affiliated with the former colonial power, as was the case during the decolonization in Africa.

Of course, the perception of the situation on the part of international organizations and the Russian political elite may differ. Coming to agreement on basic issues would seriously test the ability of Russia and other post-Soviet states to cooperate. It would also test the West's ability to treat the issue fairly through international organizations and to put humanitarian issues ahead of other political considerations. With good-faith efforts on all sides, it should be possible to achieve a consensus among the parties concerned. Otherwise the issues will have to be submitted to international organizations—principally the UN and the OSCE—for decision. Cooperation largely depends on the willingness of the United States and its allies to grant these organizations greater authority, and to go along with their decisions in cases directly affecting the interests of the West. Russian nationalists, like nationalists elsewhere, are impossible to convert or persuade. But it might be possible to marginalize and isolate them politically by achieving unbiased and effective cooperative policies implemented by international institutions.

Last, but by no means least, a state program for resettlement of immigrants and refugees from the near abroad should be a Russian national priority. Depending on how resettlement is handled, Russians and Russian speakers who choose to immigrate to Russia will either contribute to Russia's prosperity and help to reverse its negative trend in demographic growth,[31] or they will become a social base for extreme fascism and revanchism that could demolish democratic reforms. If organized and funded properly (hopefully with foreign aid), resettlement programs would greatly alleviate tensions in Russia's relations with other republics and remove this fertile soil for nationalist activities on all sides.

Within this general framework, Russia's relations with individual republics should be adapted to particular circumstances. Indeed, the very attempt to formulate a single policy toward the near abroad as a whole reflects imperial biases, in effect treating all those states as former Russian colonies. Recognizing them as independent states would imply bilateral relations with each republic, as is the case with Moscow's policy in Europe, the Middle East, and the Asia-Pacific region.

Russian Policy in Post-Soviet Subregions

Without addressing all the republics individually, it is possible to define four principal groupings posing roughly comparable problems for Russian foreign policy and requiring comparable reactions.

UKRAINE AND BELARUS

Ukraine and Belarus are by far the most important focus of Russian policy in the near abroad.

Russia's vital interests dictate that a consistent policy of recognizing and respecting Ukraine's independence and territorial integrity is the best way to revive fair and mutually beneficial cooperation, facilitate economic integration, and enhance human contacts and deep cultural ties. There are virtually no ethnic problems between Russia and Ukraine. The two states' controversies and conflicts have largely resulted from the mismanagement of their difficult "divorce" process. Despite some historical grievances, the two countries have so much in common and are so deeply intertwined that only impudent

---

31. G. Cherkasov, "There May Be 6 million Refugees in Russia," *Segodnia*, June 15, 1994, p. 2.

neo-imperialist policies on the part of Russia or extremist actions by Ukrainian nationalists could hinder the natural development of a close and genuine relationship, not unlike that between the United States and Canada. Nevertheless, problems between Russia and Ukraine are often played up for effect in domestic political games in both states. Leonid Kuchma's victory in Ukraine's 1994 presidential elections and his subsequent policy course should teach Russia two important lessons. First, the idea of Ukrainian independence and statehood has an overwhelming nationwide appeal in Ukraine. Ukrainian independence is a political reality that serves as a political baseline for even the most pro-Russian leaders in Kiev. Second, all policies and actions that threaten this idea only push Ukraine farther from Russia and undercut Ukrainian political groups advocating close economic, political, and other relations with their neighbor to the east.

Although Russia and Ukraine are close to each other economically, socially, and culturally, Russian-Ukrainian reintegration in a federation or confederation is quite unlikely in the foreseeable future. Kiev's fear of domination by Moscow is justified by a legacy of historical examples. Ukraine, by European standards, is a large and developed country with a growing sense of national identity. Like the United States and the British Empire in the period following America's war of independence, Ukraine and Russia cannot be closely linked. A military alliance is hardly possible for the same reason, especially in the absence of a common enemy.[32] However, diplomatic cooperation on security is quite feasible under the auspices of the UN, the OSCE, and the North Atlantic Cooperation Council (NACC), or a successor acceptable to both, as are united peacekeeping operations, integrated defense-technology programs, and joint military exercises.

The main thrust of Russian policy toward Ukraine should be for full-scale economic integration. If Moscow were to consistently promote economic integration and the legal, social, and political relations needed to achieve it, most of the controversial issues in bilateral relations would be much easier to resolve. In the distant future, economic and social integration may naturally evolve into more permanent supranational structures, as the European Union (EU) and security alliances like NATO promise to become.

A policy of economic cooperation and Russian and U.S. security guarantees and financial aid to Ukraine are the preconditions for the

---

32. Turkey may fill this niche in the future, thereby changing the situation.

final elimination of nuclear weapons on Ukrainian territory as stipulated by the 1992 Lisbon Protocol and the January 1994 Trilateral Agreement between the United States, Russia, and Ukraine.[33] Deep reductions in conventional forces on a bilateral or multilateral basis (like a CFE follow-on treaty) would be perfectly in line with the security interests of all the countries involved. Russia should clearly recognize Crimea and Sebastopol as part of Ukraine, regardless of the style of relations between Kiev and Simferopol, provided, of course, that this involves no violation of human rights or recognized OSCE norms. As for the Black Sea Fleet, neither Russia nor Ukraine can support it financially, and neither needs it strategically at its present force levels and composition. Radical unilateral reductions of the fleet by Russia would remove most of the problems of sharing it with Ukraine, including the issue of allocating base facilities.[34]

Instead of this policy, Moscow has exerted consistent pressure on Ukraine. It has exploited Ukraine's vulnerabilities on Crimea by testing the loyalty of the Black Sea Fleet and contesting the ownership of the Sebastopol port facilities; it has exacerbated tensions between western Ukraine and the pro-Russian, industrial eastern region; it has manipulated the supply of energy for political goals; and it has tried to discredit and isolate Ukraine in the West—all of which undercuts Russia's security interests. The argument that Ukraine is not viable as an independent state, and that its economic and social destabilization and disintegration are highly likely, is designed to encourage this policy of active Russian intervention in Ukrainian affairs "to take care of Russian economic, humanitarian, and security interests."[35] At best, an interventionist policy would result in Ukraine's growing estrangement from Russia. This in turn would lead Kiev to seek support from Germany, Poland, or Turkey, or to intensify its drive for NATO membership in order to gain protection against Russia. At worst, there could be serious social and political destabilization in Ukraine, secession of Crimea, armed clashes, and possible Russian military intervention. This could initiate a Bosnia-type scenario in a country with nuclear weapons and numerous nuclear power stations.

---

33. Alexei Arbatov, "Nuclear Missiles: Prestige or Real Security?" *Moskovskie novosti*, No. 49 (December 5, 1994), p. 4.

34. For a detailed discussion of the Black Sea Fleet controversy, see the chapter on Crimea in this volume.

35. V. Razuvaev, "The Crisis in Ukraine and Russia," *Nezavisimaia gazeta*, December 17, 1993, p. 5.

The consequences for Ukraine, Russia, Europe, and the entire world would certainly be disastrous. In the immediate future, the possibility of military conflict with Ukraine is the single greatest threat to Russian national security.

Belarus is culturally and economically as close to Russia as Ukraine, but in every respect is much smaller, more vulnerable, and dependent on Moscow. The idea of national independence was historically much weaker in Belarus and presently has relatively little public appeal. The government in Minsk never really strove for independence; it was imposed on Belarus in 1991 by Russian and Ukrainian leaders when they disbanded the Soviet Union. As with Ukraine, Russian national interests require economic and social integration with Belarus, along with its political cooperation on all CIS issues. There is no need for a formal security alliance or a mutual defense treaty, at least as long as there is no military threat to the two states from the west or the north. Permanent political and security structures can wait until a more distant future and could perhaps evolve in a trilateral format with Ukraine. The existing burden of the Russian armed forces and defense industry is too heavy for the Russian economy, and it would be unable to support those of Belarus as well.

In the case of Russia and Belarus, it is the smaller of the two republics that is pressing for maximum economic, political, and military integration. Russia cannot completely reject overtures from Minsk for both moral and historical reasons, including the consequences of Chernobyl disaster. The ongoing economic reintegration of Belarus, although resisted by some Russian governmental agencies for budgetary reasons, will probably be followed by political reintegration in some type of confederation or federation. In principle, there is nothing wrong with reunification if it occurs without Russian pressure. But in this case the right thing is happening for the wrong reasons. In Minsk, the old communist elite has largely remained in power and has not moved forward with economic and political reforms. The character of the government was reinforced by the results of the 1994 Belarusan presidential elections.

With the failure of economic reforms in Russia and the curtailment of democracy in Belarus since 1994, Minsk began the process of returning to the federal fold by appealing to neo-imperialists in Moscow. What is occurring is not reintegration on a new economic and political basis, but an attempt by Minsk to avoid democratic reforms altogether. From the Russian viewpoint, reintegration with Belarus would represent an economic sacrifice for political and military goals. If reintegration proceeds on these terms, relations between Russia and Belarus will not be equal, natural, or mutually beneficial. Rather, it will contribute to the restoration of authoritarian power in both states. It is no coincidence that after Yeltsin's visit to Minsk in early 1995 and Russia's extension of 150 billion rubles in credit, Belarusan President Alexander Lukashenko announced a freeze on the arms reductions mandated by the CFE Treaty.[36] Soon afterward, Russian Minister of Defense Pavel Grachev, during a meeting with U.S. Secretary of Defense William Perry, threatened the same if NATO expanded eastward.[37]

If Russia's democratic reform process is resumed in earnest, an increase in internal tensions in Belarus would be unavoidable and might create serious problems in its relations with Russia. Coordinated economic innovations and democratic reforms would be best for both states, and are a precondition for rapid reintegration in a federal state if that is in fact what Belarus wants.

GEORGIA, ARMENIA, KAZAKHSTAN, AND KYRGYZSTAN

The economic, social, and political integration of these four states with Russia, as distinct from trade relations, capital investment and the like, is hardly possible because of the great differences in their cultural values, histories, and economic and political development. But these countries need Russian security guarantees in the form of a Russian military presence to protect their outer borders against foreign threats. For Armenia, the threat emanates from Turkey and Azerbaijan, and to a smaller degree from Georgia. In the case of secular Kyrgyzstan, the rise of Muslim fundamentalism in Tajikistan and Uzbekistan represents a political threat.

Georgia likewise needs an alliance with Russia to forestall challenges to its integrity from Abkhazian, Ossetian, and (potentially) Ajarian secessionists. These movements in Georgia receive support from Muslims in the North Caucasus and other militant autonomous republics inside the Russian Federation. These groups directly threaten Russia's territorial integrity, a threat that has been intensified by Russia's war in Chechnya. Moscow's security commitments and military presence would enable it to monitor the safety and autonomy of Georgia's national minorities. Restoration of stability in

---

36. See *Nezavisimaia gazeta*, April 6, 1995, p. 2.

37. Press conference of Russian Minister of Defense Pavel Grachev on April 3, 1995.

Georgia would help Russia to control its North Caucasus republics and ensure the security of the Stavropol, Krasnodar, and Kalmyk regions in southern Russia, which are located dangerously near Tatarstan and Bashkortostan. If properly implemented, the Russian-Georgian friendship treaty signed in January 1994 should serve the interests of both nations and enhance regional stability.[38]

The independence of Nagorno-Karabakh and the security of Armenia—including its full control over the strategically important Megrin Corridor—are crucial to Russian efforts to contain potential Turkish economic, political, and military expansion in the Transcaucasus, the Black Sea region, and Central Asia. As for Kyrgyzstan, as long as it remains a secular state and the home to almost one million Russians, its security will matter to Russia. Kyrgyzstan's long border with China, which is mountainous and easily defended, and its frontier with Kazakhstan, which is absolutely transparent, make this state strategically important to Russia. An agreement concluded in early 1995 by Russia, Kyrgyzstan, and Kazakhstan on joint border protection was a move in the right direction. It created a continuous defensible border between Russia and its allies, on the one side, and China, on the other.

In 1994, Russian mediation in the conflict between Armenia and Azerbaijan and in the Georgian-Abkhazian conflict was the right policy, as was the introduction of Russian peacekeeping forces in both regions. This is not to deny that Moscow's position on Nagorno-Karabakh prior to May 1992 and its tacit support of the Abkhazian offensive after the July 1993 cease-fire agreement exacerbated both conflicts and led to a general socioeconomic and political collapse. Making the preservation of a Russian military presence in the Transcaucasus the goal rather than the means of policy may backfire in the future, particularly in Georgia. Moscow's weak political control over the military is an obvious reason for these policy aberrations, especially in the wake of the October 1993 events in Moscow. Another Russian mistake was downgrading the role of the OSCE and the UN in Georgia and Nagorno-Karabakh.[39] However, the blame must be shared by these international organizations themselves, which have taken a low profile in the area and offered policies that are generally too little too late.

---

38. For a detailed discussion of Russia's interests in Georgia, see Edward Ozhiganov's case study on Georgia in this volume.

39. See L. Minasian, "Pavel Grachev: We'll Fix It As I Suggest . . . ," *Nezavisimaia gazeta*, May 17, 1994, p. 2.

In its importance to Russia, Kazakhstan is second only to Ukraine (and in some sense to Belarus). Its natural resources (oil, gas, uranium, gold), its 6.2 million Russian residents, and its highly developed industrial, scientific, and military infrastructure[40] make Kazakhstan an area of vital Russian interest for ethnic, economic, and security reasons. Nonetheless, there is a fundamental difference between Russia's relations with Ukraine and Belarus, on the one hand, and its relations with Kazakhstan, on the other. Politically, Almaty—in contrast to Kiev—is one of the most active supporters of reintegration, either within a CIS framework or within a Eurasian alliance.[41] The reasons for this are economic decline and national tensions between Russians and Kazakhs, who make up only 40 percent of the population in their own country. Both of these factors threaten the integrity of Kazakhstan and the authority of the ruling clan. But in terms of economics, social and cultural composition, and political development, Russia and Kazakhstan are too diverse to reintegrate into one state on an equal basis. Even if the Kazakh leadership were to insist upon confederation or federation with Russia, it would hardly be feasible without a revival of Moscow's domination, which would provoke resistance by Kazakh nationalists, which in turn would lead to harsh attempts at suppression. To create such a federation, Russia would have to pay dearly both economically and militarily, and Kazakhstan would have to forfeit its sovereignty. Russia's democratic development and market reforms and Kazakhstan's national independence and integrity would both be sacrificed to the reinstitution of Russian hegemony over Kazakhstan.

However, if the two states drift further apart, ethnic tensions will rise in the areas of concentrated Russian population in northern and eastern Kazakhstan. This would be certain to ignite dormant Kazakh nationalism and Muslim fundamentalism, which would be fatal to Kazakhstan's integrity and tragic for the Russians living there. Ethnic violence and the forced partitioning of Kazakhstan would certainly involve Russia militarily, and might even lead to large-scale war with Kazakhstan. If confronted with the prospect of a war

---

40. Among the most important of Kazakhstan's industrial, scientific, and military facilities are the Baikonur space test range, the Sarishagan ABM test-range and radar station, numerous strategic weapons deployment sites, and the Semipalatinsk nuclear test range.

41. See "Interview with Nursultan Nazerbaev," *Nezavisimaia gazeta*, June 11, 1994, p. 1.

with Russia, Kazakhstan would likely ally itself with Islamic regimes in Central Asia and the larger Muslim world. In spite of Russia's military superiority, such a war would be bloody, drawn out, and exhausting—like Afghanistan on a larger scale. The sympathies of China and the West in such a scenario are unpredictable. Ethnic conflict in Central Asia involving Russians could provoke ethnic and religious turbulence inside the Russian Federation. In the medium term, this is the second greatest threat to Russian security interests, after destabilization in Ukraine.

At the same time, there is a profound mutual interest in the normalization of economic cooperation with Kazakhstan, including Russian investment, financial aid, and technological assistance. Kazakhstan might also be interested in Russian security guarantees against potential threats from China or Muslim fundamentalism from the south. Kazakhstan would like to avoid three dangerous developments: a massive exodus of its Russian-speaking population, the secession of its Russian-populated regions, and the creation of a Russian-Kazakh confederation, which could trigger Muslim fundamentalist resistance.

Almaty is conscious of its precarious domestic economic and ethnic situation, and desires relations with Russia to be as close as possible without compromising the political sovereignty of Kazakhstan and the rule of its national elite. This largely coincides with Russia's national interests. Mutually beneficial economic and military cooperation with Kazakhstan stopping short of confederation could, at least in the short term, be broader than cooperation with Ukraine. But this desirable evolution in the relations between the two countries is predicated on Russia refraining from trying to take advantage of Kazakhstan's economic, ethnic, and territorial fragility in an attempt to reimpose Russian rule. Thus certain policies should be strictly avoided, including denying Kazakhstan the right to exist as a legitimate state, putting its territorial integrity into doubt, and blaming the Kazakh leadership for abusing the rights of Russians in Kazakhstan and for increasing emigration to Russia.[42] Sophisticated tactics are required on the part of Moscow in support of a long-term strategy aimed at splitting Kazakhstan from the rest of Central Asia and the Muslim world without destabilizing it.[43] Policies that could help to

---

42. The problem of Russian emigration exists despite the efforts of President Nazerbaev.

43. The West achieved this with regard to Turkey.

improve the situation include providing economic and financial support for Kazakhstan, instituting dual citizenship for Russians, and providing assistance to those who emigrate. Claiming unilateral Russian control over Kazakhstan's industrial and military assets should be avoided, with the exception of nuclear weapons, which are in any case slated to be eliminated in accordance with the Lisbon Protocol and the NPT. Baikonur and the city of Leninsk should be leased by Russia for commercial and military purposes, as postulated by the bilateral treaties of July 1994 and April 1995.[44]

Despite the wishes of many Russians, some Kazakhs, a few Ukrainians, and Alexander Solzhenitsyin, full reintegration of the three largest, most advanced, and closely related republics of the former Soviet Union is not feasible in the foreseeable future. In the case of Russia and Ukraine, economic, ethnic, social, and cultural factors are favorable, but political and security considerations are not. In the case of Russia and Kazakhstan, the opposite is true: political and security interests bring the two states together, but ethnic, social, and cultural differences place stringent limits on the degree of closeness that can be achieved. To push forward with reintegration without regard for these objective obstacles would be a recipe for disaster for all three states.

As noted above, the right choice for Russia would be to cultivate economic integration with Ukraine and Belarus on an equal basis without political or military provisions while simultaneously striving for "mature partnership" within a broader European security framework. This would open up possibilities for building broad-based human and cultural ties and achieving closer interaction of democratic institutions and public movements. Eventually conditions may ripen for some form of political integration among these three states. As for Kazakhstan, a political and security alliance as well as economic cooperation with Russia should enable Almaty to maintain a satisfactory status for ethnic Russians living in its northern and eastern regions.

MOLDOVA AND THE BALTIC STATES

Neither Moldova nor any of the Baltic states—Estonia, Latvia, and Lithuania—wants to return to Russia's fold, and none would reintegrate voluntarily. Instead, these countries naturally gravitate to the neighboring cultures and economic environments outside former

---

44. *Sobranie zakonodatelstva Rossiiskoi Federatsii* (Journal of laws of the Russian Federation), No. 21 (May 22, 1995), pp. 3, 5.

Soviet territory from which they were separated by force on the eve of World War II. Once Russian troops are withdrawn from these states and their internal ethnic problems (i.e., the contested authority in the Transdniester and enclaves in Moldova, and the civil rights of the Russian minority in Estonia and Latvia) are alleviated, Moscow will be able to restore normal economic and political relations with them. For example, Russia could negotiate special agreements on the use of port facilities and communication lines. Ideally Russia could develop security relationships with these states much like those it now maintains with Romania, Poland, and Finland—i.e., based on their neutrality. Political cooperation within the framework of the OSCE and subregional security structures would also be possible. As long as Moldova and the Baltic states refrain from associating too closely with any military alliance with a potentially anti-Russian orientation, Russia poses no security threat to them. However, should any of these states join in such an alliance, Moscow will interpret this move as a major threat to its national security.

AZERBAIJAN AND THE CENTRAL ASIAN STATES

Azerbaijan will align with Turkey, Russia's regional rival, and will always be on less than friendly terms with Armenia, Russia's natural ally in the Caucasus. Russia should make its best effort to mediate peace, but not at the expense of the independence and security of Armenia and Nagorno-Karabakh. The Central Asian states— Tajikistan, Turkmenistan, and Uzbekistan—are rigidly traditional states. Some of them are willing to be closer to Russia on a number of levels—as participants in a ruble zone or a more integrated economic unit, as members of the CIS, and as part of a collective security organization complete with Russian troops and border guards on their territories. But the reasons why the Central Asian states desire integration are hardly compatible with Russian interests. The former communist regimes, now semifeudal, are trying to secure Russian military support against local opposition movements by labeling them Muslim fundamentalists, hoping thereby also to draw support from outside states that perceive Islamic extremism as a threat. With this tactic, the leaders of Central Asian states are in fact pushing their domestic oppositions toward religious extremism, which threatens to involve Russia in pointless neocolonial wars that are against both its foreign interests and its domestic political preferences.

Apparently this is what is now happening in Tajikistan, where the Russian army is fighting to keep a repressive regime in power against internal opposition groups allied with Afghani *mujahidins*.[45] Russia's intervention was initially prompted by Uzbekistan's leaders. Interestingly enough, in mid-1995 Tashkent started to back away from the Tajik regime, and established contacts with the opposition in an attempt to acquire greater freedom of maneuver. By contrast, Moscow, strongly impelled by the semi-autonomous actions of its armed forces and border guards, has become more deeply involved in fighting on behalf of the ruling regime. This has created new tensions in Russia's relations with UN representatives, as well as with the Uzbek leadership.[46]

Russian military intervention in Tajikistan is all the more wrong because Tajik and Uzbek leaders have intervened in the Afghan civil war without any consideration of Moscow's preferences.[47] Russia cannot control these policies and is more a pawn in a regional game—in which Pakistan and Iran are also involved[48]—than an active player. Russia's direct military involvement, apart from being costly and bringing losses, will inevitably transform the conflict from local tribal infighting into a transnational, religious, anti-Russian, and anti-colonial *jihad*. As with the war in Afghanistan, Russia could not win such a war. If it continued, it would eventually cause the collapse of the regimes in Uzbekistan and Turkmenistan, destroy the former Soviet border leaving the Russian Federation without a defensible frontier, and place the Russians remaining there under threat of massacre. Eventually it would also destabilize Kazakhstan.

Russia should avoid direct military intervention in this region under the guise of opposing the expansion of Muslim fundamentalism—a pretext that was adopted by Andrei Kozyrev when he was Russia's Foreign Minister.[49] In fact, despite the arguments of Russian conservatives and nationalists to the contrary,[50] Central Asia is the least important subregion for Russian interests in the

---

45. O. Panfilov, "Russia Sends Another Battalion to Tajikistan," *Nezavisimaia gazeta*, April 29, 1992, p. 3.

46. Dubnov, "Does Russia Have a Tajik Policy?" pp. 12–14.

47. A. Dubnov, "Russia Again Has an Afghan Headache," *Novoe Vremia*, No. 5 (February 1994), pp. 24–27.

48. A. Umnov, "Who Needs Peace in Tajikistan?" *Nezavisimaia gazeta*, June 11, 1994, p. 3.

49. K. Egert, "Moscow Puts the Brake on Muslim Extremism in Central Asia," *Izvestia*, September 11, 1993, p. 4.

50. Ya. Plais, "Russia and Central Asia," *Nezavisimaia gazeta*, January 19, 1994, p. 3.

entire former Soviet geopolitical space. If democratic reforms in Russia continue, Tajikistan, Turkmenistan, and Uzbekistan will most likely move away from Moscow and become integrated in South Asian economics, politics, and security affairs. Of course, Russia should not instantaneously withdraw from Central Asia. At least several years will be needed to resettle the roughly three million Russians who live in the region, to redeploy troops, to build a new fortified border (hopefully, jointly with Kazakhstan and Kyrgyzstan), to train and supply local governmental forces, and to normalize relations with the Tajik opposition and rival Afghan groups. Russia's policy should clearly be a phased military withdrawal, not open-ended involvement. Cooperation on protecting the border against drugs and weapons traffic, agreements on the use of defense facilities (like the Nurek space tracking station), and investment in natural resources would be possible and effective with stable, popularly supported local governments.

The Euro-Atlantic Security Framework

Russia's relations with the near abroad are an integral element of a much broader security landscape that encompasses conflicts in the former Yugoslavia and the rest of Central and Eastern Europe. The stability of post–Cold War international relations is contingent upon building a new multilateral security system that incorporates the whole of Europe, including the post-Soviet space. In the period spanning the late 1980s and early 1990s, the world witnessed a tectonic shift in the international landscape. The disintegration of the Soviet communist empire and Yugoslavia triggered a chain reaction of political, security, and economic events across the entire world comparable in scale to those that occurred after the first and second world wars. With each major shift, international security changed drastically to accommodate the realignment of major powers and the revision of their national priorities and international agendas.

The current revolution has thus far unfolded without world war. At the end of the Cold War, there were no winners or defeated states in the traditional sense. The Soviet Union disintegrated primarily for internal reasons, with foreign affairs playing only an indirect role. In the Euro-Atlantic or western Eurasian security zone where the principal changes took place, nothing has emerged to supersede the previous security system based on opposing political and military alliances.

The continued absence of a new security system to incorporate new relationships and address new international agendas is the principal problem facing both Russia and Western Europe. If not resolved, new tensions and old hostilities could revive and feed into a more traditional pattern of imperial disintegration—one involving major wars.

From a historical point of view, there is nothing new about tension in relations between a large power and the smaller countries around it. In principle, there are two main paradigms in such a situation. In one, the large power establishes its domination over the smaller ones and extends its perimeter of security until constrained by natural boundaries or the military-political resistance of surrounding states. In the other paradigm, the smaller states unite to oppose the large power, often with support from larger outside regional or global powers playing balance-of-power politics. Often the possibility or fear of one pattern of development provokes the other, and a dialectical interaction is established between the two. In other words, the large power may develop a propensity for domination out of fear of hostile surroundings and the involvement of outside powers in its vulnerable periphery. This possibility may be sufficient to induce smaller states to create opposing coalitions and to appeal for outside support from a strong patron. Difficulties could also occur the other way around: small countries can start the interaction out of fear of the large power's domination and thus provoke it to make aggressive encroachments.

Of course, a third model of relations is also possible: friendly political relations and mutually beneficial economic integration between the large power and its smaller neighbors. After a long history of confrontation, this model has worked for most of the twentieth century for the United States, Canada, and Mexico. The same hopefully will be true of Germany in the European Union. Relations of this type are feasible between Russia and some other post-Soviet states, provided democratic developments in Russia continue.

With the exception of the Baltic states, none of these paradigms has yet become predominant in the post-Soviet context. Traditional economic dependencies, along with human and other ties among the former Soviet republics, have combined with the benign attitudes of the West, China, Iran, and Turkey toward Russia and with democratic development within Russia itself to contain the vicious dynamics of the first two models. Nonetheless, these circumstances may be changing for the worse. Benign post-Soviet relationships and cooperative relations between Russia and the West should not be taken for granted. The first two paradigms pose major threats in the near term.

Russian attempts to secure Western recognition of its "special rights" and to receive a UN mandate and funding for peacekeeping operations in the former Soviet Union should be neither rejected out of hand nor accepted unconditionally. Until the summer of 1994, Russia's record as a peacekeeper in Transdniester, Abkhazia, Nagorno-Karabakh, Tajikistan—and even on its own territory in Ingushetia and Chechnya—was extremely dubious in terms of motivation, effectiveness, and ability to control events. The one exception has been Russian peacekeeping efforts in South Ossetia, which have worked reasonably well. There can be no objections to Russian diplomatic activity directed toward resolving conflicts in the area, including mediation between warring parties. But military actions in support of one side or the other, or supplying arms and "volunteers" for direct participation in combat actions are altogether a different matter.

On the other hand, Russia's isolation from conflicts in the post-Soviet space would undoubtedly lead to their proliferation and escalation. It could also lead to the involvement of other regional powers, increased fatalities, material destruction, and refugees and other social dislocations spilling over into Russia, constituting a threat to international peace and security. Western powers and international organizations like the UN and the OSCE have been unwilling to take on the expensive, dangerous, and controversial responsibilities of large-scale peace enforcement and peacekeeping operations throughout the enormous post-Soviet space. Even Yugoslavia, so much smaller and closer to Europe, has overburdened Western peacekeeping capabilities.

Since 1992, there have been several missions from international organizations seeking to prevent or resolve conflict on former Soviet territories. The UN and the OSCE have sent missions to Abkhazia and Tajikistan. There have been OSCE missions in South Ossetia, as well as in Moldova, Estonia, Latvia, Ukraine (a sanctions assistance mission relating to Yugoslavia), and Tajikistan. A large OSCE Monitoring Mission of 500–600 persons is preparing to go to Nagorno-Karabakh under the auspices of the OSCE Minsk Conference on peaceful settlement. However, these efforts have been superficial and have not played a serious role in mediation, nor any role in peace enforcement, or peacekeeping in post-Soviet clashes. Part of the reason is the complicated and inefficient decision-making procedures at the UN, and especially at the OSCE. Their resources are limited, and the major powers are unwilling to get involved on a broad scale or to incur the attendant human losses, large expenditures, and potential complications in relations with Moscow and regional regimes. This attitude greatly affected Western involvement even in Yugoslavia, to say nothing of the post-Soviet vortex.

As it has turned out, there is no real or effective alternative to the Russian military presence in FSU conflict areas. Russian border guards, in accordance with CIS agreements, are involved (sometimes overwhelmingly) in patrolling the borders of Belarus, Kazakhstan, Kyrgyzstan, and Tajikistan.[51] Apart from Russian regular armed forces stationed in Belarus (Strategic Forces), Ukraine (Black Sea Fleet), Kazakhstan (Strategic Forces and Baikonur test range), Georgia, Armenia, Moldova (14th Army in Transdniester), and Tajikistan, there are about 10,000 Russian military peacekeepers serving under the banner of CIS peace operations. Specifically, these include 600 military personnel in Transdniester, 500 in South Ossetia, 2,000 in Abkhazia, and 6,000 in Tajikistan.[52]

The other side of the coin is Russia's reluctance to allow foreign states, the UN, and the OSCE to become involved in conflict management on a broad scale while continuing to place all operational burdens on the Russian armed forces and federal budget. Moscow could not be enthusiastic about the prospect of UN or OSCE involvement when these organizations promise no alleviation of Russia's material or financial burden. Instead, their involvement will mean political and operational constraints on the actions of Russia's military command, perhaps leading to greater losses. A still more hostile reaction from Moscow would be provoked by the prospect of NATO involvement in the security affairs of the former Soviet Union.

Russia's involvement in these conflicts has been messy and controversial even without other players joining the game. As a former imperial state, Russia naturally possesses national ambitions of its own. Given its domestic political pressures and overwhelming military power, Russia cannot be an impartial broker and a purely altruistic peacekeeper. It is biased in favor of Russian-speaking minorities and the interests of Russian armed forces deployed in or near zones of conflict.

Moscow is also partial to ethnic secessionist movements and local ruling regimes loyal to Russia—regardless of their political and legal character. Its preferences have depended on the extent to which these

---

51. Russian border guards are also operating in Turkmenistan on a commercial basis.

52. A. Dubnov, "The Case of Lukashenko," *Novoe Vremia*, No. 9 (March 1995), pp. 14–15.

parties have recognized Russia's leadership in the post-Soviet space. First Soviet and then Russian authorities lent various kinds of support to local secessionists and opposition groups in other republics seeking, ironically, to escape Moscow's control. This was the case with the popular fronts in the Baltics, the Crimean movement in Ukraine, the Transdniester secessionists in Moldova, and the South Ossetian and Abkhazian movements in Georgia. Once the separatist movements became a threat, the states in which they were operating had no choice but to recognize Russian supremacy. Russia then switched sides to help its "loyal allies" crush their domestic opposition. Events unfolded in this way in both Tajikistan and Georgia. Likewise, when Armenia withdrew from the Soviet Union, Moscow sided with Azerbaijan and opposed Nagorno-Karabakh's liberation. Soon thereafter, Armenia joined the CIS's collective security organization, and requested that Russian military bases remain on its territory. While Azerbaijan dragged its feet on joining the CIS, Russia changed sides to support Armenia. Similar motives explain why Moscow has turned a blind eye to violations of human and ethnic rights in places like Kazakhstan and Kyrgyzstan. Of course, there is nothing new about such biases in the foreign policy of great powers. The United States and many other highly advanced democratic states have on numerous occasions demonstrated a preference for "our son-of-a-bitch" over abstract considerations of international law, justice, human and ethnic rights, and democratic ideals, which have often served as noble justifications rather than the true motivations for policy choices.

Whether such interventions are really in the Russian national interest and promote the stability of the region as a whole is a different matter. Too active and open manipulation of secessionist movements to reestablish Russian dominance over other post-Soviet republics has hampered the development of joint CIS principles and policies to deal with the spread of volatile and destructive ethnic conflicts. This policy has deprived Russia of a powerful means of gaining the trust and loyalty of smaller states, and it has backfired in Russia itself, leading to the disastrous Chechen war and the destabilization of the entire North Caucasus. Moscow's skepticism toward prospects for cooperation between Russia and the West on conflict resolution and peacekeeping in the post-Soviet space is easy to understand in traditional "sphere of influence" terms. But on the other side of the equation, all the burdens and frustrations of unilateral interventionism are borne by Russia, yet in return Russia has not been rewarded with reliable allies, political-military control capable of impressing the far abroad, or genuine stability along its borders.

The Western proposal to base the new Euro-Atlantic security system primarily on NATO and the European Union has a number of fundamental defects. NATO is an alliance conceived and structured for collective defense against a common enemy, and it is not designed to resolve conflicts among its members. The reason for its continued existence is the hypothetical possibility of a renewed Russian threat. Indeed, it would be difficult to find another justification for maintaining such a deeply integrated and powerful defensive alliance. By definition, therefore, Russia cannot become a full member of NATO: If Russian policy continues to be seen as presenting some dangers to the West, its membership in NATO would be inconsistent with Western security. As soon as there are no more security threats emanating from Russia, there will be no need for NATO, at least in its present incarnation.

The possibility of NATO's eastward expansion has provoked a strong negative reaction in Russia and strengthened the hand of hard-liners in Moscow, who argue for an end to military reductions and a buildup of military deployments and facilities in western Russia. Such steps would increase tensions with the former Soviet republics and raise new fears in Eastern Europe. Instead of one new security system, there would be at least two—one based on NATO, and the other on the CIS—and a very high probability that tensions and confrontation would arise between them.

Despite the UN's disappointing performance, it might provide an alternative basis for a new Euro-Atlantic security organization. The UN is potentially capable of rising to this role, although it is in need of serious reforms of its own. The end of the Cold War made the UN, and the Security Council in particular, much more important to conflict resolution and peacekeeping than was previously the case. But the UN's potential to become an effective European collective security organization is quite doubtful. The United Nations is a global organization. Its seventeen peacekeeping operations, involving 80,000 people and annual expenditures of U.S. $3.6 billion, already overtax its resources.[53] In addition, the UN's ability to take quick and decisive actions, especially those involving the use of force on a large scale, is highly constrained. The composition of the Security Council and the UN General Assembly does not correlate with a European or

---

53. Cited by S. Lodgaard in *UNIDIR Newsletter*, No. 24 (December 1993), p. 7.

extended-European zone, which makes Western powers and Russia reluctant to delegate too much decision-making authority to these bodies. Even in the former Yugoslavia—which is much less of a priority for Russia than the near abroad, and is less important for the West than maintaining good relations with Russia—the UN has played a rather marginal role. Real decision-making on the use of force and conflict resolution has been left to the Contact Group comprising the United States, France, the United Kingdom, Germany, and Russia. Nevertheless, the UN has proven to be more effective organizationally in authorizing legal actions in Yugoslavia than either NATO or the Western European Union.

By process of elimination, the only existing organization capable of providing a new European security framework is the OSCE. First, the OSCE has the advantage of already including all of the European states among its fifty-three members. Another advantage is that Russia's say in the OSCE is equal to that of the United States and the major West European powers. But there are obvious deficiencies as well. First, the OSCE mandate, based on the Helsinki Final Act, does not provide the OSCE with sufficient authority for effective peace enforcement or peacekeeping. Second, OSCE decision-making requires the consensus of all fifty-three member states, and is so slow and inefficient as to make the organization less an operational body than a forum for policy discussion. Third, the OSCE lacks a policy implementation apparatus, as well as sufficient financial, material, and personnel resources.

A profound reform of the OSCE would be needed to transform it into a real European security system. Its mandate would have to be adjusted to bring it into line with Chapter VIII of the UN Charter, which deals with regional security arrangements. Peace enforcement and efficient peacekeeping decision-making procedures would need to be elaborated, and the OSCE structure would have to be reformed to invest the general secretary with political rather than purely administrative functions. Most important, a body similar to the UN Security Council would be needed to make and enforce major OSCE decisions. The various OSCE institutions (Senior Council, Conflict Prevention Centre, High Commissioner on National Minorities) should be transformed into executive institutions and supplemented by other structures. Additional funding would also be needed. The OSCE's yearly budget is U.S. $18 million—less than the cost of a single fighter plane.[54]

---

54. B. George and J. Borawski, *Reflections on the CSCE: Consultations or Collective Security?* (London: House of Commons, 1994), p. 7.

Unfortunately, serious obstacles to the creation of this ideal OSCE emanate from the United States, NATO, Russian conservatives, smaller European states, and even from the UN bureaucracy and OSCE officials. Nations, institutions, and individuals all have a natural propensity to oppose major changes in the way things are done and to prefer small adjustments and incremental improvements.

It may be that Europe will once again miss its chance to build a genuine multilateral security system in place of balance-of-power mechanisms, spheres of influence, opposing alliances, and the unilateral use of force. International organizations and regional and subregional structures will play a greater role than before, as will economic, technological, and cultural cooperation among states. Nonetheless, crucial issues such as the inviolability of borders, national self-determination, peacekeeping, and conflict resolution in Eastern Europe and the former Soviet space will probably continue to be addressed more on the basis of traditional power politics. International organizations will participate only partially and peripherally to supplement national decisions and unilateral force applications. The idea of the UN or the OSCE "subcontracting" national (in particular Russian) peacekeeping operations looks more like a damage-limitation exercise or a middle-of-the-road alternative than either a genuine multilateral security system or a traditional "spheres of influence" arrangement. It does not solve the fundamental problem of finding the proper balance in the division of authority and obligations between Russia and international organizations. For Russia, the years 1991–95 were punctuated by many more failures than successes in this endeavor.

In order to find a balance, Russia and the West need first of all to elaborate wise and far-sighted formulas for calculating their national interests in the vast and unstable Eurasian region and to devise strategies for securing these interests. This task will not be made easier by the rapid transformation of Russia itself, which implies an element of volatility and unpredictability in the ideas of its political elite. If the tragic test of Chechnya is passed without major setbacks, it can only be hoped that the interests of Russia and the West will turn out to have broad areas of overlap and allow for shared responsibility in post-communist conflict management. This would be in contrast to both the stark juxtaposition of Soviet and Western interests that prevailed during the Cold War, and the false Russian identification with those interests that arose out of the euphoria of 1992–93. After all, NATO, the European Union, the UN, and the OSCE are only policy mechanisms of the states that comprise them. These mechanisms—however important in their own right—may, in the final analysis, be only as effective as the sum of the national policies that they are supposed to implement.

Chapter 16

Horror Mirror: Russian Perceptions of the Yugoslav Conflict

Nadia Alexandrova-Arbatova

History does not allow for the subjunctive mood, but in dealing with the conflicts that have arisen in the former Yugoslavia and the former Soviet Union since the disintegration of these multiethnic states, one may ask whether these events were inevitable. In all probability, both the Yugoslav Federation and the Soviet Union were doomed to collapse after the defeat of the dominant ideologies of "Yugoslavism" and "Sovietism," which had suppressed the nationalistic aspirations of the individual republics that had comprised those unitary states. But perhaps the painful process of disintegration could have been more gradual and more civilized.

In the case of Yugoslavia, the international community should not have waited to intervene politically until the outbreak of armed conflict in mid-1991. If other states or international organizations had become engaged much earlier, such as after the 1990 Yugoslav elections, or even in 1989 when Slovenia adopted a new constitution that allowed its secession from the Yugoslav Federation, they might have helped to facilitate a "velvet divorce."

Is it possible to conclude that there was an alternative to the Yugoslav tragedy and the impotence of the international community in the face of the conflict that developed? The greatest democracies seemed to be wedded to policies that they themselves knew were likely to lead to catastrophe. Yet these states could not agree on strategies that would avoid the tragedy. Why was this the case?

Russia and the West: Partners in Failure

One possible explanation may be that few in the West, and especially in Europe, accepted the dimensions and seriousness of the Yugoslav conflict, even though it was the first in the post–Cold War era on

European soil. West Europeans did not consider it a threat to their national security or to their economic and political interests. No resources such as oil were involved. Ironically, when conflict erupted near its borders, even Italy did not appreciate its seriousness, even though it had been preparing to counter a hypothetical threat from the northeast for forty years.

The West considered the Yugoslav problem an internal conflict with only local significance. That was a major reason why no Western countries or relevant security institutions made a serious or early effort to become sufficiently engaged in attempts to resolve the Yugoslav problem and prevent escalation, and instead responded only to *faits accomplis*.

It may be useful to review the main events that led to the violent disintegration of Yugoslavia so as to understand the course of the negative developments that occurred.

The results of the December 1990 elections in Yugoslavia predicted the end of the Yugoslav state. However, when Western governments became engaged in efforts to prevent the violence in Yugoslavia (e.g., U.S. Secretary of State James Baker's visit to Belgrade in June 1991; the Brioni Accords of July 1991), they urged the republics to stay together. Ironically, this was the very goal of Serbian President Slobodan Milošević, and helped strengthen his hand. Apart from the evident impossibility of such an objective in 1991, it should be noted that the very idea that the West would support the integrity of the former Yugoslav state provided the Serbs with the illusion that their efforts to hold the Yugoslav republics together would be approved and supported by the international community. Milošević never made a secret of his plans, and after fruitless attempts to define a new relationship in the spring of 1991, he threatened that, in the event of secession by Slovenia and Croatia, Serbia would incorporate Serbian minorities living in other republics. What is even more striking is that the West was aware of the communist, totalitarian nature of the Milošević regime, but that was not an obstacle to supporting a Yugoslav Federation that would be Serb-dominated and upheld by the Yugoslav National Army. One wonders why this ideological aspect of the Yugoslav problem arose only several months later.

There may be several explanations for the inconsistencies in Western strategy.[1] First, the West was trying to steer a course that

---

1. Of course, it would be an oversimplification to discuss the West as one undif- ferentiated mass. The differences between the European Union (as well as

both encouraged nascent democracies and discouraged separatism. Yet this dual strategy was bound to create dilemmas and inconsistencies in policy responses.[2] The second explanation is no less important. The West had to take into account the Soviet factor, which comprised two discrete elements: the threat of a repetition of the Yugoslav scenario in the Soviet Union; and the Soviet posture on Yugoslavia, which was unequivocal. On several occasions the Soviet leadership had proclaimed its stance: "The USSR wants to see Yugoslavia as one whole and prosperous state; it supports the territorial integrity of the country and the principle of inviolability of its borders; the Soviet Union is against any international interference in Yugoslav affairs; the republics of Yugoslavia should agree upon the new relationship between them without any external intervention."[3]

The underlying reasons for this position were quite evident. In the struggle between the Soviet leadership and the Soviet republics seeking independence from the center, 1991 was a peak year. It was also a peak in the personal confrontation between Soviet President Mikhail Gorbachev and President of the Russian Federation Boris Yeltsin. Gorbachev was trying his best to maintain the unity of the Soviet Union, whereas Yeltsin was encouraging national liberation movements throughout the Soviet republics—especially in the Baltics. On the eve of the August 1991 coup d'état, which only accelerated the demise of the Soviet Union, the main spokesman for the Soviet leadership published the following declaration of the Soviet government on Yugoslavia:

Many aspects of the Yugoslav crisis depend on the position of the international community. The balance between offering its good offices and interference in internal affairs (which cannot be accepted either from the point of view of international law, or from the point

---

between its members) and the United States over concrete aspects of the Yugoslav conflict (e.g., on disintegration of Yugoslavia, recognition of the former Yugoslav republics, lifting the embargo on arms deliveries to Bosnian Muslims) were quite evident from the earliest beginnings of the conflict. Nevertheless, when reduced to a common denominator, all these differences appeared as a unified strategy in the UN Security Council and in NATO, since it was involved to protect the UN Protection Force (UNPROFOR). But what is more important is that Russian public opinion did not differentiate between the United States and Western Europe in this conflict.

2. See John Zametica, *The Yugoslav Conflict*, Adelphi Paper 270 (London: International Institute of Strategic Studies [IISS], 1992), p. 60.

3. See *Vestnik MID*, No. 8 (April 30, 1991), p. 13; No. 16–18 (August–September, 1991), p. 33.

of view of the possible consequences), is very unsteady. Those who think that the problem may be solved by recognizing the secession of Slovenia and Croatia cannot but know that it would not only pro-long, but also aggravate, the national tragedy. Those who now sug-gest sending international military forces to Yugoslavia in all probability have miscalculated the possible outcome of this step.[4]

This position is very revealing of Soviet concerns about the prece-dent of international interference in Yugoslavia. The Soviet leader-ship was afraid that it could be applied to the Soviet Union if Moscow decided to suppress national liberation movements in the most intractable republics. After the August 1991 coup, during the last months of his presidency, Mikhail Gorbachev was desperately trying to maintain the Soviet Union in any form whatsoever. These aspirations were reflected in the Soviet position on the Yugoslav cri-sis, an obvious parallel to the Soviet Union. A September 16, 1991, dec-laration of the Soviet Ministry of Foreign Affairs acknowledged the necessity "of new forms of coexistence and cooperation for the former Yugoslav republics in one and the same economic and legal space."[5] In October 1991, President Gorbachev tried to play the role of media-tor during an official visit by Serbian President Slobodan Milošević and Croatian President Franjo Tudjman to Moscow, confirming the readiness of the Soviet Union to contribute to the negotiation process between the two parties. In November, one month before its demise, the Soviet Union joined the declaration of the European Community (EC) and the United States in the Hague to support the EC taking the lead in attempts to resolve the Yugoslav crisis.

The leadership of the newly independent Russian Federation, headed by President Yeltsin, entered the international community after December 1991 with a pronounced desire to become "part of the family." The Russian leadership declared its readiness to implement market economic reforms and to establish a functioning democracy. It never lost an opportunity to demonstrate to the West that it was more attached to Western democratic values than the former Soviet leader-ship, and that Russia was a more reliable partner than the Soviet Union. There was a very strong personal motivation behind this Russian eagerness to join "the civilized world." Yeltsin had to com-pete with Gorbachev in the West, where, although his star was fading, Gorbachev remained popular. Russian Minister of Foreign Affairs

---

4.   *Pravda*, August 7, 1991.

5.   *Vestnik MID*, No. 19 (October 15, 1991).

Andrei Kozyrev presented a set of foreign policy initiatives just before the demise of the Soviet Union, such as a new Strategic Democratic Initiative[6] and Russia's desire to become a member of NATO,[7] that competed with the New Political Thinking of Gorbachev and his foreign minister, Edward Shevardnadze, and their cautious rapprochement with the West. Unfortunately, in focusing on integration with the West, the Russian leadership failed to formulate a distinctive foreign policy and failed to examine its own security priorities based upon its geopolitical position and transitional domestic situation.

THE EVOLUTION IN BALKANS POLICY

Soviet policy in the Balkans had been part of Moscow's overall Mediterranean policy, with long historical traditions. Imperial Russia and then the Soviet Union took an understandable interest in the closest warm-water ports. "Imperial Russia's numerous clashes with Turkey almost invariably raised the Bosphorus and Dardanelles as an important problem, while the major powers of Europe were concerned about not letting Russia gain a major outlet into the Mediterranean."[8] There was no radical change with the advent of the Soviet Union, which lacked the capability to penetrate the region before World War II.

After World War II, with East-West confrontation spreading to the Mediterranean, the Soviet Union seriously began to consider the possibility of expanding its influence in that region. After its clash with Yugoslavia in 1947, Soviet policy was directed toward Albania, with the goal of having a presence there. In 1950, the Soviet Union started to use the strategically important island of Saseno and the port in Valona as bases for Soviet submarines. Soviet policy after

---

6. Alexei Arbatov, "Empire or Great Power?" *Novoe Vremia*, No. 49 (November 1992), p. 16. Kozyrev called for Russia and the West to defend democracy and human rights all over the world. In view of events in Chechnya, this initiative in retrospect looks like a cynical joke.

7. See Andrei Kozyrev, "Russia is Doomed to be a Great Power. . . ," *Novoe Vremia*, No. 3 (January 1992), p. 23. In this interview, Kozyrev could not explain why, for three days, no high-ranking official had refuted the well-known misprint in President Yeltsin's speech: "Russia is [not—alleged to be omitted by a typist] going to be a member of NATO." He confirmed Russia's objective to become a member of NATO by saying, "I have been asked whether we really pose a question of Russia's membership in NATO. I answer, yes, we pose this question, but not right now, later."

8. Radovan Vukadinovic, *The Mediterranean Between War and Peace* (Zagreb: s.n., 1987), p. 55.

Stalin evaluated the world and the Soviet Union's place in it differently. On the one hand, Moscow demonstrated its interest in normalizing relations with some countries in the region, particularly Yugoslavia and Turkey. On the other, it wanted to gain access to the Mediterranean with a view to demonstrating its naval potential and competing with the West. From the 1960s, when the Soviet Union established its presence in the Mediterranean region on a permanent basis, Moscow's policy objectives combined support for strongly anti-American and anti-Western regimes and efforts to weaken U.S. influence while strengthening Soviet military objectives. Specifically, these objectives included: offsetting the presence of the U.S. Sixth Fleet and restraining its operations in crisis situations; creating the ability to defend naval and air bases, industrial centers, and other shore targets from nuclear and conventional strikes by the U.S. Navy and from amphibious assaults; and creating the capability to interrupt or close Western sea lines of communications.[9] These aims, which were not linked directly to the Balkans, could be considered the "maximum task" of the Black Sea Fleet. However, even the "minimum task" would have affected that region: blockading the Black Sea Straits; establishing maritime control in the Black Sea; and providing support for land operations against Turkey and Greece.[10] The Soviet Balkans policy was distinguished by competition with the West on its southern flank and the Soviet goal of maintaining the unity of the socialist camp in view of the Yugoslav factor.

Post–Cold War Russian policy in the region has developed in an entirely new context and taken an entirely new direction. First, the Yugoslav conflict became a test for the post–Cold War European security system and posed the question of Russia's place in that system. Second, post-communist developments in the Balkans catalyzed political and ideological infighting between Russian democrats and nationalists. Third, Turkey, having emerged as a strong regional power, challenged Russia in the Black and Caspian Sea regions. Fourth, some of the post-Soviet conflicts that affected Russia's interests and increased regional interdependence also involved some of

---

9.   Nadia Alexandrova-Arbatova, "Naval Arms Control in the Mediterranean: A Soviet Perspective," in A. Furet, V. Heise, and S. Miller, eds., *Europe and Naval Arms Control in the Gorbachev Era* (Oxford, U.K.: Oxford University Press for the Stockholm International Peace Research Institute [SIPRI], 1992), p. 196.

10.   Ibid., p. 200.

the Balkan states. For example, the Transdniester conflict affected the interests and concerns of Russia, Moldova, and Romania.[11]

It is important to emphasize that there was no continuity between Soviet and Russian post-communist Balkans policy. The new Russian leadership was confronted with the need to formulate its own foreign policy interests and objectives. Unfortunately, it did not understand that achieving better and more stable political and strategic relations with the West did not mean that Russia could not have different foreign policy objectives than the United States or other Western states. The simple goal of rapid integration with the West substituted for a well thought out foreign policy strategy based on careful analysis of Russian interests.

One of Russia's central foreign policy challenges in the new geopolitical situation was posed by the emergence of regional centers of power—i.e., Germany, Turkey, and Iran—capable of expanding their influence over the unstable zones of the former Soviet Union. All these countries became involved, although in different ways, in the Yugoslav conflict. Turkey, a main actor in the Balkans, began to look toward reestablishing influence in the region and expanding it to the Muslim republics of the former Soviet Union. In Russia's view, this was a Turkish attempt to profit from Russia's relative economic, political, and, in some respects, military weakness.[12] For post-unification Germany, the Yugoslav conflict presented an opportunity to play a major role in European politics. Iran, now competing with Turkey in the former Soviet Muslim republics, became involved because of its ambitions in and commitments to the Muslim world. Furthermore, Iran (as well as several Arab countries) provided extensive military support to the Bosnian Muslims. It is quite logical that these states should also define their interests in the context of the conflict in the former Yugoslavia and take positions consistent with those interests. But there is no logic to Russia's failure to formulate its own objectives in the region.

---

11. The Transdniester conflict and other ethno-national conflicts in Moldova date from 1989, when economic depression and the failures of the Gorbachev program of perestroika catalyzed a national movement for independence. Even before Moldova declared independence in 1991, the national movement took on a clear Romanian tinge as expressed in the Popular Front slogan of reunification with Romania. This slogan and the idea of the priority of the indigenous nation supported by Romanian nationalists provoked strong opposition from the Russian minority.

12. Turkey's attempt to review the article of the Montreux Convention on the Black Sea Straits is quite revealing.

The hyper-Westernism of the Yeltsin-Kozyrev group was based on the sincere, even naive, opinion that the West, having won the competition with the East, was in a better position to set policy in the post-bipolar world. Ironically, both this hyper-Westernism and the anti-Westernism of the opposition in Russia's executive and legislative bodies stemmed from the same inferiority complex. The outcome of these miscalculations was that the vacuum in Russia's foreign policy priorities and objectives was gradually being filled by different forces, including the military, who still maintained the old "foot-in-the door" policy in this region.

There is another important factor that should be taken into account in the analysis of Russian policy toward the Yugoslav crisis: the parallel between Russia's role in the former Soviet Union and that of Croatia or Slovenia in the Yugoslav Federation. There was a very short period in its history when Russia could not be accused of imperial ambitions. In his crusade against the center, Yeltsin had encouraged national liberation movements in the Soviet republics, and had even promised greater independence to the subjects of the Russian Federation with his now famous slogan, "take as much sovereignty as you can." At that time Yeltsin could not imagine that after the collapse of the Soviet Union he would be confronted with a similar problem of the disintegration of the Russian Federation. The trends he blessed in his struggle against the monster of the centralized system later became the main threat to the integrity of Russia itself. Tatarstan, Chechnya, and even economic regions (subjects of the federation like Sverdlovsk oblast) indicated that they were ready to take an amount of sovereignty that was in fact unacceptable to President Yeltsin. These problems only emerged later; Russia abandoned the Soviet Union free of old commitments. This may help to explain why in 1992 and 1993, almost without hesitation, Russia joined the bandwagon on all decisions on Yugoslavia taken by the West and the principal international organizations.

Having accepted the role of obedient follower of the U.S.-EC position on the Yugoslav crisis, Russia must share responsibility with the West for the ensuing disaster. Furthermore, taking into account the significance of the Yugoslav crisis for European security and Russian national interests, and given the potentially unique role Russia might have played in preventing and reducing violence in the region, Moscow bears heavy responsibility for the mistakes made in Yugoslavia. In particular, Russia carries heightened responsibility for not taking a stronger position on the manner in which the international community recognized the independence of the former Yugoslav republics.

RECOGNITION POLICY

Leaving aside the controversial recognition policy of the EC and German arm-twisting, it should be noted that, at that stage, the West and Russia together might have prevented the violence in Yugoslavia not only by applying clear principles of self-determination, as the Arbitration (Badinter) Committee attempted to do, but by insisting upon the implementation of necessary preconditions for recognition. The legal basis for recognition is of great importance because it affects such serious issues as territorial integrity, self-determination, secession, and human rights of national minorities, all of which are closely intertwined. Russia should have been interested in the elaboration of such principles because it had (and still has) similar problems in the former Soviet territory. In all probability, the Helsinki principle of the inviolability of frontiers, with two clearly formulated exceptions, could have formed the basis for resolving this problem. The first exception is if an individual republic initiates a revision of its own frontiers, for instance by deciding to unite with another state (e.g., Moldova with Romania, Azerbaijan with Turkey, Tajikistan with Afghanistan). The second exception is if a republic engages in outright genocide against a national minority, and this is recognized and classified as such according to international law and by impartial (e.g., UN) observers. In these cases, secession or unification with a neighboring republic would be legitimate.[13]

The international community did require guarantees from Slovenia, Croatia, and Bosnia-Herzegovina to assure protection of national minorities living on their territories. In December 1991, while war was raging in Croatia, the EC acknowledged criteria for recognition of the new states in Eastern Europe and the former Soviet Union, "in particular, guarantees of the rights of ethnic and national groups in accordance with the commitments adopted by the CSCE and respect for the inviolability of borders which cannot be changed except by peaceful means with unanimous consent."[14] Milan Babic, president of Srpska Krajina, expressed his astonishment that he and other leaders of Srpska Krajina had not been consulted by Cyrus Vance on the peace plan.[15] These criteria were the basis of the

---

13. See Arbatov, "Empire or Great Power?" pp. 20–21.
14. *Diplomaticheskii vestnik*, No. 1 (January 15, 1992).
15. *The Observer*, February 16, 1992, p. 20.

Arbitration Committee's determinations. Yet those determinations were not followed by the very nations that created the Arbitration Committee. Even after the bloodshed in Croatia, the EC, followed by the United States and Russia, repeated the same mistake in Bosnia by recognizing its independence without enforcing the criteria it had announced, and without regard for the position of the Bosnian Serbs. The deliberate boycott by the Bosnian Serbs of the referendum on independence in Bosnia-Herzegovina, held from February 29–March 1, 1992, should not have been a pretext for the West to neglect Serbian aspirations, but a clear warning against hasty irreversible steps. In the words of John Zametica, "by seemingly ignoring the fears and wishes of the Serbian population in Bosnia and Herzegovina, something that seems with hindsight a grave but understandable mistake, the Muslim population in particular, along with the EC, made war in the republic a distinct possibility."[16]

Many voices in the international community predicted catastrophe, just as they had during the six months preceding the 1991 declarations of independence by Croatia and Slovenia. Why the European and the Muslim communities both joined in the headlong rush to recognition, and thus toward war, remains a mystery for historians to solve.[17] It is also puzzling why other members of the international community—particularly Russia—failed to make a strong effort to prevent such a woeful decision. In all probability, having taken the road to integration with the West, Russia was reluctant to complicate the relationship with objections and criticism of its Western partners.

The ill-conceived recognition of Bosnia-Herzegovina made inevitable not only war in the republic, but also the future demise of the state. Having ignored the will of one ethnic group in Bosnia, the international community doomed the new state to collapse. And although the West has continually encouraged Bosnian Croats and Muslims to coexist in one state and continues jointly with Russia to try to pressure the Bosnian Serbs to take part in a federation, the fabric of this federation is artificial, and few believe in its viability. One may argue whether Russia, which blessed the independence of the former Soviet Union (FSU) republics in 1991, could have prevented

16. Zametica, *The Yugoslav Conflict*, p. 37.

17. Stephen Iwan Griffiths, *Nationalism and Ethnic Conflict: Threats to European Security*, SIPRI Research Report No. 5 (Oxford, U.K.: Oxford University Press, 1993), p. 48.

the hasty recognition of the former Yugoslav republics.[18] The question is not whether the international community should have recognized the former Yugoslav republics, but whether, had recognition been achieved in a different way, much of the violence would have been avoided. And by March–April 1992, Russia already had its own experience with the partition of the former Soviet heritage.[19]

The premature recognition of the newly born independent republics unfortunately became the substitute for exhausting (and, perhaps in some circles, unpopular) negotiations to reach compromise among all the parties in Yugoslavia, the only real alternative to war. The ultimate irony is that the international community had to return to the very same type of negotiations that should have taken place initially—but, after bloodshed and destruction occurred, in an environment boiling with hatred and mistrust.

SANCTIONS

Sanctions must be addressed as an important issue in the analysis of Western and Russian policy toward Yugoslavia. In November 1991, the first economic sanctions were applied to Serbia and Montenegro, against which the international community invoked Article 41 of Chapter VII of the UN Charter. Sanctions are considered part of the system of collective security and a significant instrument against aggression. Yet both before and after World War II they failed to be effective "as there were always two confronting groups of powers, one of which did everything it could to enforce sanctions, and the other to nullify them."[20] Only after the end of bipolarism did sanctions become at all feasible as a means of achieving a measure of effectiveness, but even then, only after a long period of time.

Economic sanctions are only the means to achieve a certain goal. Thus, if they do not work as intended, or have a counterproductive

---

18. Here it is important to underline the way the Soviet republics declared their independence: they did so during the August 1991 coup, when Moscow became the main arena of the fighting between the communist center and the newly born democracies. Nobody could imagine during those days that problems like Crimea or Transdniester would emerge in the near future. By contrast, the process of disintegration in Yugoslavia brought on problems with national minorities from the very beginning.

19. See M. Shakina, "The Hour of Partition," and V. Zhitmirsky, "Reefs Near the Crimean Shores," *Novoe Vremia*, No. 3 (January 1992), pp. 4–7.

20. Ranko Petkovic, "International Impact of the Crisis in the Former Yugoslavia," *Review of International Affairs*, Vol. 14 (April 1, 1994), p. 2.

effect, it is more expedient to consider other possibilities of dealing with the issue. Sanctions cannot be a substitute for resolute measures of peace enforcement. Nor can the international community abuse their implementation without the risk of discrediting its role in the conflict resolution process.

As Stephen Iwan Griffiths has written, "the initial phase of sanctions imposed against Yugoslavia resulted in losses of $650 million, although this figure did not include an estimate of the impact of the cessation of raw materials, semi-finished products and spare parts from abroad. The sanctions hit harder than expected because Yugoslavia had spent the past decade orienting its trade toward the European Community."[21] While they undoubtedly had economic impact, the sanctions were a blunt instrument and operated against all Serbs regardless of guilt or innocence. This bluntness, in the view of many observers, led to counterproductive results. "The fact is that sanctions hit a great many innocent people—which is not the objective—while, at the same time, they considerably reinforce the positions of the regime against which they were imposed—which also cannot be the objective."[22] It may not go too far to argue that the sanctions policy stems from a very strong, perhaps even unconscious, desire to punish Serbia for initiating the conflict. This may be understandable emotionally, but it is unacceptable politically. The preconceived policy of the international community toward Serbia gave Serbs the impression that the entire world was against them and that they had nothing to lose.

Russia supported all UN Security Council resolutions on sanctions, except in April 1993, when Russia abstained from supporting new sanctions against Serbia and Montenegro. That case represents an important illustration of the relations between the West and Russia. By the end of March 1993, Bosnian Croats and Muslims had signed all four agreements of the Vance-Owen plan, whereas Bosnian Serbs had signed only two and rejected the map of Bosnia and the agreement on the temporary organization of the Bosnian state. When the question of new sanctions against Yugoslavia was raised in the UN Security Council, Russia convinced the Western partners to postpone the vote on sanctions until April 26, 1993.

It was a time of new tensions around the city of Srebrenica: the Serbs declared that they were ready to admit the International Red Cross into

---

21. Griffiths, *Nationalism and Ethnic Conflict*, p. 50.
22. Petkovic, "International Impact of the Crisis in the Former Yugoslavia," p. 2.

the city but not UN troops, because they feared that UN soldiers would become the target of provocations that could lead to military intervention against the Bosnian Serbs. Russia initiated negotiations on this subject with Slobodan Milošević and finally succeeded in persuading the Serbs to let UN troops into the city; on April 17, a Canadian battalion entered Srebrenica. However, the UN Security Council received misinformation and immediately put the question of sanctions to a vote without verification of the facts of the situation. This violated the agreement with Russia not to raise the sanctions issue until April 26. As Russian Deputy Foreign Minister Vitalii Churkin[23] pointed out during a press conference on April 19, it was not the first case when important questions were put to a vote on the basis of unreliable information.[24] Revealing the widening gulf between Western and Russian perceptions of the conflict, he also stated:

I'll repeat the same, I have said many times to my foreign colleagues: if the international community had responded in an adequate way to the firing on the Italian aircraft carrying humanitarian aid . . . which was shot down in the fall 1992, obviously not by the Serbs; if the international community had responded in an adequate way to the murder of French soldiers of the UN contingent in Sarajevo, killed obviously not by Serbian sharpshooters . . . we would have avoided encouraging the other belligerent parties to continue the bloodshed.[25]

How then did it happen that Russia did not veto the Security Council decision that violated the gentlemen's agreement and was, in Russia's opinion, unjust? When asked this question at a press conference, Churkin said there were two reasons. The first was that Russia had already twice succeeded in postponing the vote on new sanctions by promising, in exchange, not to impose a veto if it were put to a

---

23. Vitalii Churkin is a key figure in Russian policy toward the former Yugoslavia, along with Foreign Minister Andrei Kozyrev and Yulii Vorontsov, head of the Russian Mission to the UN. Due to his high authority, Churkin has enjoyed the confidence of all parties involved in the Yugoslav conflict. After the solution of the first crisis in Sarajevo in February 1994, Churkin's popularity in Russia was higher than that of Kozyrev. He was sent to negotiate with the Serbs during the crisis in Gorazde in the spring of 1994, but this mission was a failure. Churkin ended his visit and returned to Moscow infuriated by the Serbian position. The unexpected defeat of "invincible" Churkin generated rumors that he had been forced to cut short his visit by jealous colleagues in the foreign ministry. Several months later Churkin became Russian ambassador to Belgium, a curious position: as Russian ambassador he is still involved in the Yugoslav negotiations.

24. *Diplomaticheskii Vestnik*, No. 9–10 (May 1993), p. 23.

25. Ibid., pp. 23–24.

vote. The second reason was, as he explained it, that Russia had its own foreign policy priorities and must not quarrel with the international community simply because the parties in Bosnia-Herzegovina could not agree upon the proposed borders for a settlement. Trying to encourage the Serbs, Churkin said at this same press conference that "economic sanctions do not mean the end of the world." And a journalist from Belgrade parried with, "But they mean the end of peace."[26]

This example highlights many of the deficiencies of the partnership between Russia and the West and its policy on the Yugoslav crisis. It reveals the preconceived position of the Western governments toward the Serbs; the West's readiness to punish them by all means regardless of the consequences of such measures; and the inclination of Western governments until 1995 to seek easy solutions instead of engaging in hard bargaining and agile political maneuvering to reach agreements. Russia's servile and low-profile policy, on this issue as well as others, cannot be justified by its foreign policy priorities, especially taking into account its ability to influence the Serbs.

PEACE OPERATIONS

The third point in the analysis of the Western-Russian partnership addresses peacemaking, peacekeeping, and peace-building.[27] Originally the UN Protection Force (UNPROFOR) was intended as a buffer force between Serbs and Croats in Croatia. Subsequently it was redeployed and expanded to undertake essentially humanitarian missions in Bosnia-Herzegovina. Lieutenant General Satish Nambiar, the first force commander of UNPROFOR, was quoted as saying, "Looking back at what is happening in former Yugoslavia, nine months after leaving the scene, and from a distance of many thousands of kilometers, one is still struck by the futility of the UN operations, given the fact that they are being conducted under a cloud of hypocrisy on the part of the international community."[28]

The international community did not provide a preventive deployment to Bosnia, as it had in Macedonia, although the spread of violence in connection with Bosnian independence was predictable. Some Russian and Western experts suggested deploying peacekeeping

---

26. Ibid., p. 24.

27. See Sverre Lodgaard, "In Defence of International Peace and Security: New Missions for the United Nations," *UNIDIR Newsletter*, No. 24 (December 1993), pp. 5–11.

28. Ibid., p. 18.

forces along the perimeter of Bosnia's borders to assure the necessary conditions for cease-fire and further steps in the conflict resolution process. Such a step would have demanded larger contributions of UN peacekeeping contingents from the international community—and greater risks. As bloodshed increased in Bosnia-Herzegovina, it became clear that some form of peace enforcement was badly needed in the region. In this respect, Moscow's May 1993 initiative to introduce a massive contingent of U.S., European, and Russian troops under the auspices of the United Nations to ensure the implementation of the Vance-Owen Plan was a bold step in the right direction. However, the West, which was not inclined to deploy large ground forces for effective peace enforcement, did not support it. Instead, the West sought a substitute for such a risky and politically unpopular measure (but the only one that might have been effective), and settled upon NATO air strikes against Serb positions. Whereas the possible outcome of such measures will be analyzed in the last part of this chapter, here it is only necessary to underline that at a certain stage, when conflict could not be forestalled by diplomatic means, and however unpopular and risky it might have been, some sort of enforcement effort had been the only option to avoid further escalation of the conflict, which would have saved lives and money in the later stages of the war.

There may be another reason for Western reluctance to accept Russia's proposal. "As UNPROFOR operations proceeded, it soon became amply evident that shared responsibility between the United Nations and the European Community (with NATO coming into the picture later for Bosnia-Herzegovina) was an unsatisfactory arrangement. Regional organizations should either handle such operations on their own, or the operation must be completely under the United Nations."[29] NATO, in fact, did provide the headquarters. However, the United States, especially after the mishap its Rangers suffered in Somalia in October 1993, was increasingly reluctant to commit ground forces as well as increasingly supportive of NATO control over any military operations in Bosnia.[30]

The new relationship between NATO and the UN in the former Yugoslavia in 1993 affected not only the conflict resolution process of

29. Ibid., p. 20. "The UN was being criticized by NATO for lacking the capability to set up a Force Headquarters with the required degree of cohesiveness, communications and operational effectiveness," p. 21.

30. It is noteworthy, however, that the U.S. Rangers were not under UN control. Ibid., p. 18.

the post-communist period, but also the conceptualization of the broader issue of a new security system. The combination of NATO policy enlargement eastward and a growing role for NATO enforcement operations against the Serbs was interpreted in Russia as an attempt to isolate Russia in an emerging NATO-centered security system, and as a shift away from partnership with Russia.[31] This strategy became a catalyst for a political and ideological dispute within Russia and attracted criticism not only from Russian nationalists and moderate conservatives, but also from a small group of liberals. In contrast with the anti-Westernism of the former, the latter pointed out that these policies threatened to revive the past East-West confrontation and create a new division of Europe. The West was probably not aware of the fact that even Russia's limited participation in UNPROFOR (nine hundred Russian blue helmets were assigned to UNPROFOR in 1993) was a subject of intense domestic debate in Russia. The Russian military initially did not want to participate at all in peacekeeping operations in the former Yugoslavia.[32] In 1993 it became clear that the period of unconditional partnership with the West was over.

The Turning Point in Russia's Balkans Policy: Putting on the Serbian Costume

The events of October–December 1993 in Russia created a clear turning point in Moscow's policy toward the Yugoslav conflict, as well as in its entire foreign policy. The major reason for this shift was the domestic and foreign policy failure of the Russian leadership during the previous two years. Domestically, the Russian leadership failed both to implement market economy reforms by "shock therapy" and to establish a functioning democracy. In foreign policy, the Kremlin's idealistic pro-Western course was discredited domestically when the

---

31. See Sergei Karaganov, "NATO's Expansion Leads to Russia's Isolation," *Moscow News*, No. 38 (December 17, 1993).

32. On several occasions, Russian Minister of Defense Pavel Grachev stated that he opposed Russia's participation in UNPROFOR using the argument of the Afghanistan syndrome. Deputy Foreign Minister Vitalii Churkin, during one of his press conferences, mentioned that high-ranking Russian military officers did not want to take part in UNPROFOR because they were against personal contacts between Russian and Western soldiers and officers. Only the Ukrainian decision to support UNPROFOR and sophisticated efforts by the foreign ministry made Grachev change his position.

public realized that Russia had not become "part of the family," and had lost its inherited superpower prestige. The well-known Russian politician Vladimir Lukin wrote in the *Washington Post:* "A wave of infantile pro-Americanism brought about its opposite—infantile anti-Americanism" (and in a broader sense, anti-Westernism).[33]

Of course, the Russian leadership is responsible for its own fail-ures, and it would be dishonest to look for a scapegoat abroad. But for all their good intentions, the United States and Europe, as well as Western-dominated international institutions, contributed to the evo-lution of Russian domestic and foreign policy by their arm-twisting efforts to promote economic reforms; by insisting on taking the lead in international affairs; by introducing double standards; and by unconditional support of the so-called "government of reforms" (regardless of the growing unpopularity of their measures), and later of the concept of "enlightened authoritarianism" in Russia. In fact, inside Russia, the unpopular "shock therapy" was associated not only with the government of Yegor Gaidar but also with the West, which many believed had forced Russia to follow this approach. But wherever the blame lies, these strategic failures had serious conse-quences for Russia's foreign policy, including its posture *vis-à-vis* the Yugoslav conflict.

By the end of 1993, Russian public opinion had moved toward a more self-assertive and Russia-centered policy, which was cemented by the parliamentary elections in December 1993. This shift was a reaction to policies of the previous years, which many Russians con-sidered a policy of national humiliation. This public sentiment was heavily exploited by a variety of political parties and their leaders, from Nikolai Travkin to Vladimir Zhirinovsky, in the 1993 election campaign.

The right-wing opposition capitalized on government mistakes and grew stronger. Having accepted the lead of the West at the early stage of the Yugoslav crisis and having ignored Russian interests, the gov-ernment then tried to distance itself from the Yugoslav issue. But the policy initiative was picked up by both moderate conservatives and the right-wing group of "red-browns" who used the Balkans issue to encourage Russian separatists in the Baltics, Crimea, and Moldova and to raise public awareness in Russia, which became very sensitive to the Russian minority issue in the former Soviet republics. Having

---

33. *The Implications of the Yugoslav Crisis for Western Europe's Foreign Relations,* Chaillot Paper No. 17, WEU Institute for Security Studies (October 1994), p. 37.

stumbled on the path toward democracy, the Russian leadership assumed a nationalistic tinge and became responsive to ideas of Russia's "special rights and responsibilities" in the post-Soviet territory. In September and December 1993, Foreign Minister Kozyrev tried to convince the UN and the Conference on Security and Cooperation in Europe (CSCE) to provide formal legitimacy and financial support for Russia's peacemaking interventions in the "near abroad."

However, it would not be sufficient to analyze the shift in Russian foreign policy, including its Yugoslav dimension, as stemming from growing nationalist sentiment in Russia. Rather, the main question should be: why did Russia, which started on its own path to independence like a "Croatia" or "Slovenia" within the former Soviet Union, identify more with Serbia after the Soviet Union disintegrated, not only in its sympathies, but also in its policy stance?

There is a strong temptation to offer an easy answer to this question and to explain it by "the call of the blood" (according to Samuel Huntington's paradigm), but that would be both wrong and superficial. There is a certain Russian predisposition toward Serbs based on the historical ties between the two peoples. The old generation of Russians cannot forget, for example, that the 1941 Belgrade uprising delayed the German Army from reaching Moscow until late autumn, when the weather created insurmountable difficulties for the Wehrmacht. Nevertheless, at the same time, however, these ties should not be overestimated. The same generation also remembers the Cold War hostility between Russians and Yugoslavs under Josef Stalin and Josip Broz Tito, when there was no place for sentimental feelings. Nor should the Orthodox factor and the cultural ties between Russians and Serbs be exaggerated. The Orthodox Church has never played an independent role in Russia, and Russia's historical and cultural ties with France or Italy have been of no less importance than those between Russians and Serbs. The 1993 shift in Russian policy was highly political. It cannot be explained merely by ethno-cultural elements or historical ties. The ethno-cultural factor may be part of the foreign policy background, but it does not figure prominently in foreign policy practice.

PARALLELS BETWEEN THE NATIONALIST EXPLOSIONS IN THE FORMER YUGOSLAVIA AND IN THE FSU

The Yugoslav case has provided Russia with many parallels. Although some of the similarities may seem superficial and of little importance, others were consciously perceived and therefore cannot be ignored for an understanding of the evolution of Russian foreign policy. There is a similarity between the role of Yugoslavism and Sovietism in creating fertile soil for nationalism in both states:

In the nineteenth and twentieth centuries, Yugoslavism was closely intertwined with Croatian, Serbian, and Slovene nationalism. Immediately after the two world wars Yugoslavism overshadowed these particular nationalisms, but did not eliminate them. In the 70 years after the formation of a southern Slav state, Yugoslavism proved to be a durable idea, especially when it was combined with Titoism in the second Yugoslav state after World War II.[34]

The Soviet parallel is clear. Sovietism combined with Stalinism suppressed local nationalism in the Soviet republics, but did not eliminate it. After the collapse of the ruling ideologies in both multi-ethnic states, there was an outbreak of local nationalism. Although Croatian nationalism was constantly suppressed throughout the Tito period, the rise of Milošević in Serbia in 1987 helped fuel a new nationalist cause that brought the right-wing Croatian nationalist party, Hrvatska Demokratska Zajednica (HDZ), to power following elections in the republic in April 1990.[35]

Anti-Serbian and anti-Russian moods inside the former "empires" have similar origins. The bulk of responsibility for all the sins of the communist regimes in these multinational states have been put on two of the component nations—Russia and Serbia. This may partially be explained by the fact that Moscow and Belgrade, the embodiments of imperial power, were the capitals not only of the Soviet Union and Yugoslavia respectively, but also of the Russian Federation and Serbia. In response to these accusations, Russians always say that they have been the most suppressed nationality in the Soviet Union; that they have always been "robbed" by the center for the sake of other nationalities of the Soviet Union; and that Russian territories were given away to other republics by Soviet leaders, regardless of the will of Russian people.[36]

It is important to note that the economic factor played a very important role in the turn toward nationalism both in the former Yugoslavia

---

34. See Griffiths, *Nationalism and Ethnic Conflict*, pp. 39–40.

35. Ibid., p. 47.

36. It is true that in both the FSU and the former Yugoslavia the party *nomenklatura*, recruited from different nationalities, represented the "ruling nation." But it should also be also noted that in the FSU the second secretary of the Communist Party in each republic was Russian.

and in the FSU. A dramatic decline in the Yugoslav economy after the death of Tito sowed unrest. In the FSU, the economic depression and failures of Gorbachev's program of perestroika became a catalyst of national movements for independence.

Russian grievances about the anti-Russian behavior of the former Soviet republics, particularly the Baltic states, were intensified by the fact that most of the Russian minorities living in these republics, and the Russian government itself, had supported national liberation movements. Yet after the victory of the national fronts, these minorities were betrayed by the new leadership. The simple truth is that communism was defeated everywhere not by democracy but by nationalism. But this is difficult to explain to those Russians who, at the risk of their own lives, supported democracy and independence in Vilnius or Riga, regardless of the warnings of Russian nationalists from pro-Russian international fronts. Leaving aside the fact that Russia contributed to the problem of Russian minorities by contradictory and even provocative policies and by maintaining a military presence in the Baltics, it should be recognized that the posture of the Baltic governments was counterproductive and short-sighted.

Even though Serbia's position on the disintegration of the Yugoslav Federation was the opposite of Russia's *vis-à-vis* the Soviet Union and cannot be considered a major cause of anti-Serbian grievances, there is a certain parallel between Russian minorities in the near abroad and Serbs in Srpska Krajina, where Franjo Tudjman had been supported earlier for the Croatian presidency. Of course, that fact was not well known in Russia, but other parallels were quite evident. Russian public opinion, which was far from taking sides in the Yugoslav conflict in 1991 and 1992, became increasingly sensitive to the anti-Serbian stance of Western policy and its implications for Western policy toward Russia beginning in 1993. In April 1994, after the first NATO air strikes against Serbian positions, a demonstration of Russian popular concern took place in front of the U.S. Embassy in Moscow in which people carried placards with slogans condemning the air strikes. One of them sums up their concerns: "First Serbs, then Russians!"

BORDERS, TERRITORIAL INTEGRITY, AND NATIONAL MINORITIES

The disintegration of the Soviet Union and Yugoslavia highlighted three interdependent problems: borders, national minorities, and territorial integrity. Almost all borders in the former Soviet Union, as well as in the former Yugoslavia, were artificial. Almost all have the potential to give rise to infinite territorial claims—it only depends on how far one is ready to delve into history. The best way out of the situation in the former Yugoslavia would have been to recognize the administrative borders as state borders but to permit some changes if they were found to be in the overall interest of the new states. This could have solved the painful problem of national minorities separated by new borders from their heritage and people. Ironically, after bloody conflict and destruction have taken their toll, such changes have been introduced and accepted in the difficult negotiations leading to peace.

The problem of national minorities appeared to have two dimensions: the rights of one's own minority outside a certain republic, and the rights of foreign minorities inside a republic. Serbia was confronted with both sides of this problem—in Srpska Krajina, the Serbian-populated area in Croatia, and in Kosovo, the Albanian-dominated autonomous province in Serbia. In post-Tito Yugoslavia, the Albanians who make up 90 percent of Kosovo's population had demanded a degree of self-determination. In Serbia this was considered a challenge to Serbian territorial integrity, and Milošević was thus determined to suppress the Albanian demands. In the autumn of 1989, violent demonstrations and riots were being ruthlessly suppressed by the Serbian military in Kosovo. In the spring of 1990, the Serbian National Assembly announced the dissolution of Kosovo's government and provincial assembly, and introduced new censorship laws.[37] The problem of Kosovo had a distinctive geopolitical aspect for Serbia, which feared that Albania was planning to build a Greater Albania by incorporating the former Yugoslav territories inhabited by ethnic Albanians, Kosovo and Macedonia.[38] Serbian

37. Griffiths, *Nationalism and Ethnic Conflict*, pp. 42–43.

38. A similar problem may appear for Russia in the future. In recent years, several million Chinese have illegally inhabited Russian territory in the Far East. In all probability this migration was encouraged or at least approved by the Chinese authorities. It may create tensions sooner or later between Russian and China similar to those in the Serbia-Kosovo-Albania triangle. See F. Stephen Larrabee's unpublished paper, "Russia and the Balkans: Toward Reengagement" (Russia in Europe: Emerging Security Agenda, SIPRI seminar, Moscow, March 11–13, 1995, p. 12, note 17) in which he states: "This reluctance [of Russia to support Albania] is all the more striking because the Albanian concern for the treatment of the Albanian minority in Kosovo has strong parallels with the Russian attitude toward the Russian minority in the Baltic states and the near abroad." The answer is that Russia, which had been a part of a large empire, like Serbia and other republics of the former Yugoslavia, could not see any Serbian minorities in Croatia or Bosnia (Russian minorities in the Baltic states, Moldova, and Crimea).

actions in Kosovo further harmed Belgrade's reputation in the international community. Paradoxically, however, the same international community said nothing in August 1990 when a similar incident occurred in Croatia. The Serb minority in the city of Knin in Srpska Krajina decided to hold a referendum on cultural autonomy. Just as in Kosovo, riots broke out and were suppressed by the Croatian leadership, which rejected the referendum as unconstitutional.[39] Even more important, there was no parallel strong international response when the Croatians took Srpska Krajina in mid-1995 and engaged in the same ethnic cleansing that had horrified the West in Bosnia.

This resurgence of nationalism was closely linked with the growth in national consciousness and the right to self-determination in the post-Soviet territory and in Russia itself. This confronted Russia with problems of national minorities in the Baltics, Ukraine, Moldova, and other republics and was perceived as a threat to the territorial integrity of the Russian Federation. The chain reaction of anti-Russian sentiments in the near abroad brought with it violations of the civil rights of the Russian-speaking minorities. As already mentioned, the greatest disappointment was the nationality policy of the Baltic states, which had traditionally been regarded in Russia as the most civilized republics and which were supported by Russian democrats in their struggle for independence. Russian public opinion was also disappointed by the attitude of the West, whose indifference to the rights of Russian minorities in the former Soviet republics was seen as representing both bias and a willingness to ignore the standards it had been instrumental in creating.

The problem of territorial integrity of the Russian Federation itself assumed new meaning after the disintegration of the Soviet Union with "the parade of sovereignties" in Tatarstan, Tuva, and Chechnya. President Yeltsin—having declared to the subjects of the Russian Federation shortly before the demise of the Soviet Union, "take as much sovereignty as you can"—could not imagine that many would

---

This does not mean that Russia, also like Serbia, always chose the right way to deal with the problem of Russian minorities in the near abroad; on the contrary, it often provoked and blackmailed other republics, using its military presence on their territories or their economic dependence on Russia.

Following Larrabee's logic, it would be no less appropriate to ask why the United Kingdom does not support Serbia because the problem of Kosovo has strong parallels with that of Ulster. This example illustrates the superficiality and relativity of such speculations.

39. Griffiths, p. 43.

actually make use of the offer. Fortunately, the Russian leadership succeeded in resolving the issue with the president of Tatarstan and in postponing the issue in Tuva, but completely failed to settle it with the authoritarian regime of General Dzhokhar Dudaev in Chechnya. Similar problems may well arise after a settlement is reached in the former Yugoslavia, continuing the parallel.

THE LEGACY OF COMMUNISM

The numerous border changes within both the Soviet Union and the former Yugoslavia during the communist period were directed toward balancing power among republics. The Yugoslav Federal Constitution of 1974, created by Tito, was seen as protection for Croats, Slovenes, and the Albanians of Kosovo who were fearful of Serbian hegemonic ambitions. It divided Serbia into three constitutional units, allowing Vojvodina and Kosovo to become de facto republics and to have a say in Serbian affairs, and it ensured that Serbia could not interfere in the affairs of its former provinces. "The constitution prompted the development of a sense of a real grievances among Serbians that was not addressed effectively until Milošević rose to power in 1987."[40] Within Yugoslavia, the 1974 Constitution was considered discriminatory against Serbia and became a prime target of the Serbian intelligentsia after Tito's death.

With the demise of the Soviet Union and growing tensions between Russia and some of the FSU republics, particularly Ukraine, Russians began to entertain similar feelings, however ungrounded they may seem. The transfer of Crimea, once part of Russia but given to Ukraine in 1954 by Nikita Khrushchev, became a bone of contention between the two independent states. Famous for its seaside resorts and health spas, Crimea has traditionally been a favorite destination for millions of vacationing Russians. But this was not the only reason for Russian grievance. The Crimea problem was aggravated by disputes between the Russian and Ukrainian military over the division of the Black Sea Fleet and the naval base at Sebastopol, "the city of Russian glory," as Edward Ozhiganov's case study in this volume describes.

Communist-era border changes also led to unequal levels of regional economic and industrial development in both the Soviet Union and Yugoslavia. In the context of one unified economic space, various areas specialized in manufacturing, raw materials, or agriculture. With the

---

40. Griffiths, p. 41.

threat of dissolution, it suddenly became evident that agricultural regions had been disproportionately subsidizing the industrial development of the Baltics or Slovenia, allowing these industrialized areas to achieve a greater standard of living and self-sufficiency and a higher potential for integrating into the world economy. These emerging facts heightened the sense of historic grievance and represent a further parallel.

RUSSIAN PERCEPTIONS OF WESTERN PREJUDICE AGAINST SERBS

The perceived policy of the West toward Serbs had a negative impact not only on the situation in the former Yugoslavia, but on Russia as well. Awkward attempts by Russian diplomats to "correct" anti-Serbian bias in the Western policy toward the former Yugoslavia seemed to fall on deaf ears in the West. In late 1992 and early 1993, Russia raised questions in the UN Security Council about the Croatian violations of the Vance-Owen Plan. The Croats had instigated several military clashes in Srpska Krajina, and in September 1993, fifty Serbian civilians were killed. In another incident, after disrupting a UN-organized meeting to discuss the problem of Krajina, Croats attempted to blow up a hydroelectric power station in Serbian territory. In response to these violations, the UN Security Council issued a declaration that merely stated that that it would "continue to study this question in future, in particular, what further steps may be needed in order to assure complete realization of Resolution 802 and of the other corresponding resolutions."[41]

The same tolerance distinguished the attitude of the international community toward the Bosnian Muslims. The Bosnian Serbs were punished by economic sanctions when they refused to sign all the documents of the Vance-Owen Plan, but in September 1993, on board the British aircraft carrier *Invincible,* the Bosnian Muslims also refused to sign the new plan. In April 1994, the Bosnian Serbs were punished by NATO air strikes for attacks on Gorazde, which had been interpreted as a threat to UNPROFOR personnel. However, Russians believe that the Bosnian Serbs were provoked by Muslims. Encouraged by the tolerance of the international community, the Bosnian Muslims used the same tactics in Brcko, Tuzla, and other Muslim enclaves under UN protection. They tried to provoke a Serbian response by attacking their positions because they knew that it would be punished again by NATO air strikes. In Sarajevo, Bosnian

---

41. *Diplomaticheskii Vestnik,* No. 5–6 (March 1993), p. 16.

Muslims killed one man from the British battalion simply because he had no identification. Even though U.S. President Bill Clinton had proclaimed, "if only one soldier from UNPROFOR was injured. . . ," the West did not respond strongly to this incident.[42] Such imbalance illustrates attitudes that Russians felt would only harden Serb positions and drive them into a corner. Russians also interpreted these double standards as evidence of a generally hostile attitude toward Slavs. The impotence of the Russian leadership to change this policy was considered additional proof of Western disregard for Russia.

RUSSIA'S POLICY INDEPENDENCE

The crisis in Sarajevo that led to the first NATO ultimatum in February 1994 was a turning point in Russia's Yugoslav policy. With the help of Russia's mediation, the Bosnian Serbs agreed to withdraw their heavy artillery from Sarajevo. Yet the first evident Russian diplomatic success seemed to raise ambivalent feelings in the United States and other NATO countries. On one hand, the negotiated arms withdrawal was positive, and helped the West reach its goal of ending the attacks on Sarajevo without military intervention. On the other, it was a demonstration of Russia's more independent and active foreign policy, which irritated a United States accustomed to Moscow's low profile. As Jonathan Dean writes, "the Russian action provided a face-saving excuse for Serb compliance with NATO's order to withdraw the artillery or to hand it over to UN peacekeepers, and a pattern of sometimes disharmonious U.S.-Russian diplomatic collaboration began to emerge."[43]

Yet both Russian aspirations and Western concerns about Russian self-assertiveness were quickly overestimated and exaggerated. Soon after its diplomatic success in Sarajevo, Russia committed the mistake of trying, under Western pressure, to convince Bosnian Serbs to join the Bosnian federation of Croats and Muslims. In April 1994, Russia failed to solve the Gorazde crisis: Russian Special Envoy Churkin interrupted his mediation and returned to Moscow infuriated with the stubbornness of the Bosnian Serbs.

NATO's involvement in Bosnia contributed to Russia's assertiveness. NATO involvement was, and continues to be, interpreted by

---

42. Elena Martynova, "We and the International Community," in *Obshaia gazeta*, No. 16–41, April 22–28, 1994, p. 1.

43. Jonathan Dean, *Ending Europe's Wars: The Continuing Search for Peace and Security* (New York: Twentieth Century Fund Press, 1994), p. 146.

Russia as a strong Western move to establish NATO as the main instrument in the conflict resolution process in former Yugoslavia. The failure of the West to adequately consult Moscow strengthened this conclusion.[44] Beginning with the first NATO ultimatum, the West did not consult the Russian government in advance of NATO air strikes, which put the Russian leadership in a very difficult position. As a partner of the West, Russia was forced to share responsibility for policies it had never approved, nor been asked to approve. Not only did this increase tensions between Russia and its Western partners, but it created domestic political tensions within Russia. Vladimir Zhirinovsky used it to reinforce his aggressive image by calling on Russia to bomb NATO bases in Italy in response to the air strikes on Gorazde.[45] Even liberals like Churkin had to recognize after the first NATO ultimatum that the West "had started to use a language that we cannot accept."[46] Moreover, the "unilateralism" of NATO in the Balkans (as perceived in Russia) represented an additional argument for Russia's "special rights and responsibilities" for conflict resolution in the near abroad. This was another impact of the Balkan conflict and its "mirror effect" on Russia.

It could be argued that, apart from all the other causes of a pro-Serb stance, Russia was nudged into it by Western policy itself. With Austria strongly pro-Slovenia, Germany an advocate of Croatia, and the United States supporting the Bosnian Muslims, the international community had left only one side without support, almost guaranteeing that Russia would speak for the Serbs. At the London Conference in August 1992, which was designed to relieve the EC of some of its burden, it was decided to divide the mediation efforts, concentrating EC efforts on the Croats and Muslims and making Russia responsible for the Serbs.[47] But, as already discussed, during 1992 and 1993, Russia did not want to threaten its partnership with the West. Even after the Gorazde crisis, Russia did not violate the unity of the Contact Group in favor of the Serbs. Formal departure from that policy only occurred on December 2, 1994, when Russia

---

44. Andrei Baturin, "Serbian Immunity from the Ultimatums," *Nezavisimaia gazeta*, April 29, 1994, p. 4.

45. "Zhirinovsky Fans the Flames," *Financial Times*, April 12, 1994, p. 3.

46. Vitalii Churkin, "How the War Was Prevented," *Moskovskie novosti*, No. 8 (1994).

47. Pavel Baev, *The Impact on Relations between Russian and Western Europe*, Chaillot Paper No. 17, WEU Institute for Security Studies (October 1994), p. 41.

vetoed a UN Security Council resolution on new sanctions against Bosnian and Krajinan Serbs. This was Russia's first veto since the demise of the Soviet Union, and it represented a new discordant tone between the partners. Pro-Serbian resolutions of the Russian State Duma mirrored pro-Muslim resolutions of the U.S. Congress calling on the Clinton administration to lift the arms embargo, illustrating the strong domestic pressures at work in both countries.[48]

Even after Moscow began to steer a relatively independent course in its Balkans policy in 1994, it failed to formulate clear policy goals. Russian policy still remains inconsistent and largely reactive. Nevertheless, as a member of the Contact Group, Russia contributed to the search for compromise among the belligerent parties: it succeeded in securing the inclusion of "mirror rights" for all ethnic groups in Bosnia in the Bosnian peace plan. This means that the Bosnian Serbs have the same right to form a confederation with the rump Yugoslavia (Serbia and Montenegro) that the Bosnian Croats have with Croatia. Under pressure from Russia, Slobodan Milošević began to dissociate himself from the Bosnian Serbs. At the same time, Russia promoted the decision of the international community to review economic sanctions against Yugoslavia and to discuss greater involvement of Belgrade in the conflict resolution process. Moscow also succeeded in encouraging negotiations between Zagreb and Knin, which in spring 1995 were interrupted by the escalation of the Bosnian conflict, and later by Croat military action. In general, the shift in Russia's Yugoslavia policy was positive. The negative factor, however, was that it occurred because of pressure from conservative forces within Russia.

THE MIRROR EFFECT

The similarities between the Soviet Union and Yugoslavia and the problems of their disintegration not only had an impact on Russia's Balkans policy, but also heightened major concerns about the possible Balkanization of the FSU. The threat of a repetition of the Yugoslav scenario in Russia is evident when one considers the fact that during the last few years, Russia has come close to war with other former Soviet republics.

By 1994, Russia seemed to be on the verge of military conflict with Ukraine. Several clashes occurred between Russian and Ukrainian

---

48. Interestingly, neither Yeltsin nor Clinton supported their respective legislative resolutions.

military forces in Crimea (which increasingly began to resemble Srpska Krajina), and threatened to escalate into a real war. If this catastrophe had occurred, it would not only have been a tragedy for Russia and Ukraine, but would have involved the international community. Nor was the paradigm of the Croatian war ignored during the period of growing tensions between Moscow and Kiev in 1993 and the first half of 1994. It is entirely possible that the fighting in Croatia, by its example, put a brake on Russia and Ukraine's slide toward conflict.

Transdniester, the Russian-populated region in Moldova, was another area of potential violent conflict threatening to involve Russia. The situation in Transdniester was also similar to Srpska Krajina; open military clashes between Russians and Moldovans in this area in 1992 are actually referred to in Russia as "the war in Transdniester."

What was the "mirror effect" of the Yugoslav conflict for Russia? Was anything learned? It can be argued that for several years after the collapse of the Soviet Union, the Yugoslav conflict played a restraining role; Russia could see its own future mirrored in the bloodshed, destruction, hatred, and mistrust, and refrained from following this path in the FSU republics. The creation of the Commonwealth of Independent States (CIS) helped considerably in avoiding a repetition of the Yugoslav scenario. And while the CIS turned out to be an inefficient and loose structure for economic cooperation, it played an important role as a vehicle for a relatively civilized divorce of the former Soviet republics. Unfortunately, an institution of this kind was not established in the former Yugoslavia because of the resolute insistence of Croatia and Slovenia on immediate and complete sovereignty.

Citing the restraining role of the Yugoslav example is valid in discussing Russian policy before the war in Chechnya. The war in Chechnya, which Russia started in December 1994 in an attempt to quash the separatist rebellion led by General Dudaev, created new uncertainties over the Balkanization of the post-Soviet territory. One could argue that Russia's anti-constitutional military operation in Chechnya was "inspired" in part by the events in the former Yugoslavia. The use of force may have been viewed as the only way to halt the disintegration of the Russian Republic itself, a far more threatening prospect than the breakup of the Soviet Union. It is possible that international acceptance of violent conflict in the former Yugoslavia and the unwillingness to take the steps that might end it made the use of force somehow more acceptable elsewhere. This is the second aspect of the Yugoslav mirror effect for Russia. During the first four years of the Yugoslav conflict, people became used to bloodshed. The corrosive effect of this tolerance may be seen in Chechnya, where Russian leadership overcame a psychological barrier—the fear of massive bloodshed. It was the first war started by Russia on its own territory, and it dramatically affected its own people.

What is most worrisome about Chechnya is whether Russia, by taking the action it did, contributed to the acceptability of violent action as a means of solving the problem of separatism in the former Soviet territory, rather than leading the way toward peaceful, negotiated solutions. New serious tensions between Kiev and Simferopol (the capital of Crimea) seemed to result from Russia's experience in Chechnya. And while all of this is speculative, one might even argue that Chechnya encouraged Ankara to engage in a decisive battle against Kurdish separatism. And the Croatian leadership, perhaps inspired by the Russian example, resumed military actions in Srpska Krajina in April 1995 after disrupting the negotiations with Knin, which had been prompted and promoted by Russian mediation.

The Yugoslav Conflict and Its Implications for the West and Russia

The importance of the Yugoslav conflict has transcended its subregional boundaries. Not only is it the first armed crisis on European soil since World War II, but it is likely to shape international relations not only in the Balkans and Europe, but throughout the world. Thus far, it is the most important event in the transition to a post-bipolar political relationship, and it may determine whether that relationship will be cooperative or will create a new division in Europe. Thus the former Yugoslavia continues to pose serious dilemmas for both Russia and the West.

THE WEST AND THE CONFLICT PROCESS IN YUGOSLAVIA

Although the very notion of a Western policy toward the former Yugoslavia is too monolithic because the European and U.S. positions on particular aspects have differed, it is possible to speak about the general approach of the West toward the conflict. The first dilemma concerns all the Western powers. Even though it is evident that the Serbs are responsible for a military conflict that might have been prevented, the war raged on for years. The West was trying to carry out two incompatible goals: assuring that the Serbs were punished, and trying to end the violence. David Gompert, a former U.S. State

Department official and vice president of the RAND Corporation, believes that any available peaceful settlement would reward aggression[49] and urged a "patient cold war against Serbia." He stated that "years, decades, if need be, of deprivation, isolation and misery should produce a democratic revolution and leaders eager to earn a place for the Serbs in the society of nations. . . . this war is terrible, but not so terrible or unstable as to justify a bad final settlement now, when the Serbs have the upper hand."[50] A war is terrible by definition, but it is likely to continue until the parties can accept a resolution that they consider less than ideal.

Fortunately Gompert's argument, though not dismissed, did not become U.S. policy, even though distaste for rewarding the Serbs is deeply held in the United States. Only a resumption of a normal life, without the hardships of war and international boycott, has a chance of changing Serbian attitudes. There is a democratic opposition and moderate nationalist opposition (DEPOS) to Milošević in Serbia, and both are quite critical and outspoken. One reason for Milošević's strength and the opposition's weakness has been the Serb's perception that the world is against them. Milošević skillfully played this card and strengthened his position. Moreover, it should be recognized that Western mass media were also partly responsible for reinforcing this besieged fortress mentality. After the air strikes against Serbian positions near Gorazde, President Clinton and UN Secretary General Boutros Boutros-Ghali declared that there was no anti-Serb sentiment in the policies of the UN and NATO. Yet this statement was not followed either by concrete measures or accurate information about the activities of all belligerent parties that would have provided world public opinion with a complete and balanced picture of the Yugoslav tragedy.

The decision of the international community to involve Belgrade more closely in the conflict resolution process was a step in the right direction, as was the review and conditional termination of sanctions. It would have been far more effective, however, to have exercised creativity earlier by finding ways to differentiate and separate the Belgrade Serbs from the Bosnian Serbs. Economic sanctions only slowed that process. If the United States had carried out the congressional mandate to lift the arms embargo, not only would it have

---

49. David Gompert, "How to Defeat Serbia," *Foreign Affairs* (July/August 1994), pp. 30–42.

50. Ibid., pp. 44, 46.

prolonged the war, but it would have provided Russian nationalists with a strong argument to help the Serbs in a more resolute way. [51]

THE YUGOSLAV CONFLICT AND RUSSIAN RELATIONS WITH THE WEST

The Western posture toward the former Yugoslavia has conveyed a message to Russian nationalists about Russia's foreign, domestic, and near abroad policies. It indicated, no doubt inadvertently, that all calls for building a new order in Europe are no more than beautiful words; that Americans do not consider Russia to be an equal partner in international affairs; and that the Cold War mentality still persists. That is why it is so important for Moscow to have a well thought out and coherent Yugoslav policy, as well as a well developed foreign policy in general so that Russia cannot be ignored in the future.

Given Russian assertiveness in the Balkans, it is no longer possible for the West to hope to deal with the Balkan crisis without Russia, nor to take for granted that Russia will follow the Western lead. Cooperation has proven essential in ending the Yugoslav conflict, and in implementing measures to ensure that a settlement endures and its terms are implemented. Cooperation implies mutual respect for divergent views and interests. Proposals like those of David Gompert would drop right into Russian domestic politics like a stick shoved into an anthill. Russian liberals have called for cooperative conflict resolution measures sponsored by Russia and the West, citing Serbia's failure to keep Yugoslavia together by unilateral military actions. Russian liberals believe that a Russian-Western partnership is the best way to deal with post-Soviet and other international problems. Conservatives, blaming the West for its unfair anti-Serbian policy and attempts to exclude Russia from the settlement process, propose to follow the same pattern in dealing with other former Soviet states and settling the problems of twenty-five million Russian ethnic minorities left there. They would tacitly acknowledge a Western domain in Eastern and Central Europe for the time being, in exchange for Western recognition of Moscow's version of the Monroe Doctrine in the former Soviet Union. This would certainly untie the hands of those in Moscow who are looking for a pretext to suppress and subjugate every state and faction they oppose in the former Soviet Union. However, this could trigger a chain reaction with unpredictable consequences, including for relations with the West.

---

51. Dean, *Ending Europe's Wars*, p. 148.

As for the outright nationalists, they point to Western policy in Yugoslavia as a manifestation of an anti-Orthodox, anti-Slavic crusade of the United States and its allies. In response to a one-sided anti-Serbian policy of the West, Russian nationalists advocated a one-sided pro-Serbian policy for Russia, including unilateral lifting of the UN embargo and massive supplies of oil and arms to the Serbs. If this had put an end to good relations and Western economic assistance to Russia, so be it. Nothing could be more conducive to their aspirations at home and in the near abroad, or as responsive to their calls for a renewed alliance with North Korea, Iraq, Libya, and China.

If such a result had occurred, one could imagine the impact it would have had on the precarious Russian domestic balance, on the messy conflicts in the former Soviet territory, and on U.S.-Russian relations, as well as its effect on European politics. A new chill, if not Cold War, might have inadvertently resulted, and one not confined to relations in the former Yugoslavia. Yet some political groups in Russia advocated a deliberate split with the West for the sake of defending the Serbs.

Internal developments in Russia will continue to be influenced by the attitudes and policies of the United States and Europe toward Russia's role in the Balkans and in international relations generally. Russia has its own interests and responsibilities with respect to the Balkans, based both on historical ties and its own precarious geopolitical situation. But one of the main questions remaining is whether Russia will stay involved as an indispensable partner of the West or will become its rival. This poses another dilemma for the West.

It is no longer a dilemma for Russia to decide whether to be a mere follower of the West or to pursue an independent foreign policy that takes into account its entire situation, domestically and internationally. Through its diplomatic activity in Sarajevo, in many other "flash points" in the former Yugoslavia, and in deliberations of the Contact Group, Russia has demonstrated that it can play an independent, important, and positive role. Russia's previous subservient policy was counterproductive and did not lead to international stability and security. As has become evident, this policy permitted exclusion and blocked Russia's capabilities to play an active and creative role in international relations of the post–Cold War era (the Yugoslav case is not the only example). It fueled Russian nationalists who capitalized on the government's mistakes. And now the expectations of the West, once accustomed to Russia's low foreign policy profile, have had to change.

Thus the main goal for the Russian leadership in the field of foreign policy is to define its own course—one that corresponds to Russia's national interests, but is compatible with general international policy trends of the civilized world. There is another lesson that Russia should draw from the Yugoslav case: it should learn to treat the other former Soviet republics not as its "near abroad" and the "post-Soviet territory," but as completely independent, sovereign states. That will be the best guarantee against the repetition of the Yugoslav disaster on the territory of the former Soviet Union.

The Yugoslav crisis has provided the international community with the opportunity to prove that a genuine new world order could be built by joint efforts, at least in post-communist Europe. There is still a chance to use this opportunity to bring final defeat to relapses into a Cold War mentality wherever they remain or may reappear.

Chapter 17

The Development
of U.S. Policy Toward
the Former Soviet Union

Abram Chayes, Lara Olson,
and George Raach

On December 8, 1991, Boris Yeltsin, the president of the Russian Federation, Leonid Kravchuk, the newly elected president of Ukraine, and Stanislav Shushkevich, the chairman of the Belarusan Supreme Soviet, met at a retreat in a forest near Minsk. The ostensible agenda was to convince Kravchuk to sign a new version of a treaty proposed by Soviet Secretary General Mikhail Gorbachev as the basis for a continuing Soviet Union. Instead, the three leaders signed a Joint Declaration that stated that "the objective process of secession by republics from the USSR and the formation of independent states have become a reality" and established "a commonwealth (or community) of independent states" consisting of the three states represented at the meeting but "open for accession by all member-states of the USSR." Within two weeks, the remaining member-states (with the exception of the Baltics, whose independence had already been recognized, and Georgia, which was bogged down in internal conflict) met with the original three in Alma-Ata, Kazakhstan, where they formally established the Commonwealth of Independent States (CIS) and declared that "the Union of Soviet Socialist Republics ceases to exist." Four days later, on December 25, Gorbachev resigned as president of the Soviet Union and the Supreme Soviet of the Soviet Union dissolved itself.

These astonishing events led to a rash of anguished self-questioning by Western pundits, Kremlin watchers, statesmen, diplomats, and intelligence officials: how was it possible that as recently as a few months before, even after the August coup, nobody predicted that the awesome Soviet empire would collapse like a house of cards? The sudden breakup of the Soviet Union was something for which the

United States and other Western diplomatic establishments were almost completely unprepared. The Soviet Union, a single, well-known, and moderately well-understood adversary, with which relations were conducted in accordance with relatively well-established and increasingly amiable ground rules, gave way to a gaggle of new states, extending from the eastern marches of Europe through the Caucasus and on to the reaches of Central Asia, each with its own interests, its own new government, its own politics, its own mélange of ethnic groups, and its own cast of characters—none of which was familiar in Western capitals.

Beyond this, 1992 was a presidential election year in the United States, and it was already clear that the campaign would be dominated by domestic policy concerns. In 1993, the new, inexperienced Clinton administration "focused like a laser beam" on the domestic economy, and was struggling to get its bearings in the field of foreign policy. U.S. policymakers were not only taken by surprise but had to formulate their responses to the Soviet dissolution in the shadow of these powerful domestic political developments. This chapter explores the policy they developed toward this new group of countries, and especially how they have dealt with ethno-national conflicts within them, all within the context of their continuing focus on Moscow.

Before the Fall

The initial response to the dissolution of the Soviet Union was heavily conditioned by U.S. policy toward the Soviet Union in the closing years of the Gorbachev period. Even though the superpower relationship had undergone a sea change, the United States remained focused on Moscow as it had been for forty years, supporting the person and power of Mikhail Gorbachev. The secretary general was the architect of glasnost and perestroika internally, and of the "new thinking" in foreign policy that fostered rapprochement with the United States. In the euphoria over the end of the Cold War, it is not surprising that little attention was paid to the fate of the fifteen Soviet socialist republics. For the United States, they remained peripheral to the center of power.

Even as centrifugal forces began to gather in 1991, U.S. support for the continuation of the union remained unwavering. On a visit to Kiev on August 1, 1991, U.S. President George Bush spoke out, in what became known as the "chicken Kiev speech," in support of Gorbachev's efforts to consummate a new union treaty in the midst of growing agitation for Ukrainian independence. Inertia, together with a strong preference for the familiar rather than the multiple risks and uncertainties of what might happen in the aftermath of a collapse, played an important role in assuring this continuity of policy. Washington was also concerned that successor republics might not move as quickly or in the same direction as the Gorbachev regime, slowing, if not halting, the pace of political and economic reform in their regions. More dangerous, and of still greater concern, was the possibility that nuclear weapons would end up in the hands of new governments that were less inclined to or unable to cooperate with the United States in the control and reduction of the nuclear arsenal.

The U.S. response to the declaration of independence by the Baltic states in August 1991 after the coup attempt in Moscow is an especially striking example of the commitment to the integrity of the Soviet Union. The United States had never recognized the validity of the Soviet annexation of these countries in 1940, and there were intense pressures for prompt diplomatic recognition from large U.S. co-ethnic constituencies. Yet even though the European Community (and indeed Yeltsin's Russia) extended recognition almost immediately, the United States waited until September, when the Soviet government itself had accepted the inevitable, to extend diplomatic recognition to Latvia, Lithuania, and Estonia.

Within the framework of this focus on Moscow and Gorbachev, U.S. policy in the closing years of Soviet rule and the Bush administration contained two main substantive strands: the reduction of the East-West military confrontation, and especially the nuclear threat—primarily through continuing pursuit of arms control; and support for the political and economic reforms of the Gorbachev regime.

The demise of the Soviet Union and Gorbachev's departure from the political stage placed the United States in an uncomfortable position. Washington now had to deal with Boris Yeltsin, with whom it had a relationship of uneven quality, and no prior support. Also, the United States was faced with a complex array of new governments in the former Soviet territory with which previous relations were virtually non-existent. There were few diplomats in the Moscow-oriented U.S. Department of State with the background and experience necessary to make a prompt start in developing meaningful associations with these new states.

When the Clinton administration came into power, it articulated new programmatic approaches, but the focus of U.S. policy was not substantially altered. Concerns about nuclear stewardship and avoiding proliferation intensified. Promoting the transition to democracy and a market economy was more energetically pursued. But the policy remained Moscow-centered. Only after the violent explosion and suppression of the Russian parliamentary opposition in October 1993, and the sweeping gains of nationalist and reactionary candidates in the elections at year's end, did U.S. policy broaden its gambit to encompass more serious attention to the non-Russian republics and in some degree to the implications of their ethno-national makeup for continued reform.

Opening Gambits

Russia remained central, and has continued to have the highest priority in the Clinton administration's stated foreign policy objective of enlarging the number of democratic free market societies in the world.[1] "We want to see a stable, democratic Russia being integrated into the international community,"[2] stated Secretary of State Warren Christopher in early 1995. The idea was to bring Russia into a larger partnership with the West, eliminate the lingering threat of the past, and in so doing establish economic relationships of benefit to all parties that would continue to underwrite ongoing political reforms. Although helpful in some ways in the transition to democracy and a market economy, the conflation of economic and political reform created unanticipated problems that complicated both types of reform efforts as well as Russia's relations with its near abroad and with the West.

An essential question in the aftermath of the breakup of the Soviet Union was how to treat the dozen new political entities, established in accordance with preexisting republican borders, in the space that had been occupied by the now-defunct Soviet Union. The general response was almost automatic. Like most other countries, the United States promptly recognized the constituent republics of the Soviet Union as independent states. However, for a few weeks

---

1. See A National Security Strategy of Engagement and Enlargement (Washington, D.C.: The White House, July 1994).

2. Warren Christopher, remarks at a press conference in Geneva, Switzerland, after meeting with the Russian Foreign Minister on January 18, 1995. Excerpted from U.S. Department of State, *Dispatch*, "The United States and Russia: A Maturing Partnership," Vol. 6, No. 4 (January 23, 1995), p. 48 (hereafter *Dispatch*). Dr. Paul Goble defined the objective as *stabil'nost' über alles* in testimony before the U.S. Congressional Commission on Security and Cooperation in Europe, January 19, 1995.

Washington tried to implement a more nuanced, two-tiered policy based on the U.S. perception of the progress these republics were making toward free markets and democracy. Thus full diplomatic relations were initially established with only six of the twelve republics: Russia, Ukraine, Belarus, Kazakhstan, Kyrgyzstan, and Armenia. For the others, diplomatic recognition was to be conditioned on demonstrating further progress toward democracy coupled with free market institutions, protection of human rights and ethnic minorities within their borders, and responsible behavior on issues of arms control and nuclear proliferation.[3]

This intended two-tier scheme broke down almost immediately. It was hard to see any clear-cut distinction in terms of democracy or human rights between many of the favored six and those in the second tier. It was equally difficult for the United States to establish criteria to determine success or measure progress, given the lack of diplomatic experience in these regions. Nor was the leverage of recognition a powerful tool for changing behavior in these matters, especially in the absence of meaningful incentives such as aid and security assistance programs. At the same time, the European Community was recognizing the former Yugoslav republics of Croatia, Slovenia, and Bosnia-Herzegovina without applying such criteria, with Germany eagerly in the vanguard and the United States only slightly behind. Washington and at least some of its allies were also discomfited by worries that a policy based on such distinctions would drive the new states away from the newly created CIS, an organization in which Moscow played a dominant role, and thus feed into centrifugal tendencies that could ultimately undermine the U.S. policy of expanding and consolidating the sphere of democratic states with market economies. Moreover, it seemed easier to insist that the new states were legally bound by the international obligations of their predecessor—of special importance with respect to the arms control treaties and the Helsinki norms—if they were accorded recognition as full-fledged members of the international community. Thus the initial two-tier policy was soon abandoned, and diplomatic recognition was extended to all the new republics, except, for a time, Georgia, where a civil war was raging.[4]

---

3. See U.S. Secretary of State James Baker III, "America and the Collapse of the Soviet Empire—What Has to be Done," address delivered at Princeton University, reprinted in *Dispatch*, Vol. 2, No. 50 (December 16, 1991), pp. 887–893.

4. *Dispatch* announced the opening of embassies in Moldova, Uzbekistan, Turkmenistan, and Tajikistan in its March 23, 1992, issue, p. 243.

However, new U.S. embassies in the Newly Independent States (NIS) were slow in coming. In the critical early period following the dissolution of the Soviet Union, personnel to staff the new missions were often seconded for only brief periods of time, which did little to establish personal associations or build a base of knowledge so important to effective diplomacy. At the same time, many of the new states did not have funds or personnel to establish embassies of their own, so their concerns and perspectives on the new political landscape were not heard in Washington. By contrast, Russia inherited the Soviet Embassy in Washington and much of the experienced diplomatic and foreign policy apparatus of the former Soviet Union, further emphasizing the Moscow focus.

By April 1992, all fifteen post-Soviet states had not only been recognized by the United States and its allies, but had been welcomed into the United Nations, the Conference on Security and Cooperation in Europe (CSCE), and the North Atlantic Cooperation Council (NACC), an advisory adjunct of NATO formed in November 1991. In April 1992, the United States, which in a reversal of earlier policy had begun pushing for special associate status for Russia with the International Monetary Fund (IMF) and the World Bank, endorsed full membership for all the new states as well.[5] However, many of the consequences within those states of accepting the boundaries of the old Soviet socialist republics as international borders—protected against modification by the UN Charter, the Helsinki Final Act, and a plethora of solemn international legal instruments—were not fully appreciated at the time.

Most significant to the United States, the dissolution of the Soviet Union left the vast Soviet nuclear arsenal scattered among more than a dozen new states, with governments of unknown reliability, experience, and intentions. Moreover, Soviet, and before that, tsarist, internal divisions had been a complex web designed to bind to the center a multitude of diverse and geographically concentrated groups, often by separating them administratively, guaranteeing their formal autonomy, and playing them off against each other. Ethnic groups, and especially Russians, in these republics, previously protected by the power of the center, were now exposed to possible domination by new majorities and forced integration into the new

---

5.   Secretary of State James Baker III, "Securing a Democratic Peace," statement before the Senate Foreign Relations Committee, Washington, D.C., April 9, 1992, published in *Dispatch*, April 13, 1992, p. 285.

states, many of them ruled by leaders with little commitment to democracy and not above mobilizing ethnic passions for political purposes. The ultimate risk, starkly realized in the former Yugoslavia, was that the existence of ethnic minorities stranded within the confines of the new and stridently nationalist republics might lead to violence that would be profoundly destabilizing not only to the country in which it occurred, but to the Russian Federation itself.

From Washington's perspective in the early years of the new dispensation, ensuring adequate safeguards for the scattered nuclear weapons of the former Soviet Union was the first priority. The second was the prompt establishment of democracy and a market economy in Russia. If the United States, in its concentration on Moscow, was aware of the potential for serious problems arising from real or perceived mistreatment of ethnic minorities in the new states, it saw no need to act or to help develop a concerted approach. Indeed, Russia itself seemed to neglect these issues in its preoccupation with its own gargantuan problems.

It is worth reviewing briefly the focus, activities, and accomplishments of U.S. policy in order to understand its slowness in responding to the turmoil and conflict that was developing in the rest of the former Soviet empire.

Nuclear Policy

As early as November 1991, two months before the dissolution of the Soviet Union, a group of analysts at Harvard University's Center for Science and International Affairs produced an alarming account of the potential dangers of the loss of control over the Soviet nuclear establishment. They argued that the "possibility of a devolution of control . . . from the center to a much more complex set of political forces" in the context of possible social disintegration would leave the destiny of 27,000 nuclear weapons uncertain.[6]

The study called for a wide range of actions designed to maintain Moscow's command and control over the arsenal; to assist in the dismantling and destruction of weapons in accordance with the START I

---

6. Kurt M. Campbell, Ashton B. Carter, Steven E. Miller, and Charles A. Zracket, *Soviet Nuclear Fission: Control of the Nuclear Arsenal in a Disintegrating Soviet Union*, CSIA Studies in International Security No. 1 (Cambridge, Mass.: Center for Science and International Affairs [CSIA], November 1991), pp. i–ii.

(Strategic Arms Reduction Talks); to help the Russian authorities prevent the theft of nuclear weapons or materials; and to prevent Soviet nuclear scientists from selling their knowledge to the highest bidders. This analysis struck a responsive chord in the U.S. Senate Armed Services Committee, where its Chairman, Senator Sam Nunn, and his Republican counterpart, Senator Richard Lugar, set about taking measures to assure that such nuclear loss of control would not occur. The study helped provide the impetus for the Nunn-Lugar bill discussed below for financing assistance for nuclear disarmament in the former Soviet Union.

Nor was Moscow unaware of the nuclear dangers attendant upon dissolution. During early 1992, the consolidation of tactical nuclear weapons from widely dispersed locations in at least eight of the new republics began, and by mid-1992, all of them had been transported back to Russian soil.[7] But when the dust of dissolution had settled, strategic nuclear missiles remained in Belarus, Kazakhstan, and Ukraine, as well as in Russia. These weapons were controlled from Moscow and guarded by the highly trained and disciplined Rocket Forces. The other republics never had the ability to fire the weapons. Nevertheless, it was within the range of possibility that at some point, a state on whose territory the weapons were deployed could gain physical control of them, and that over time, knowledgeable weapons engineers might be able to gain access to their firing systems. It was not inappropriate, therefore, to state that the breakup of the Soviet Union gave rise to the possibility of three new nuclear-armed states in the world.

U.S. policy was designed not only to ensure that this would not happen technically, but that these former republics would abide by the Soviet Union's commitments embodied in the START I agreement. The United States also wanted to assure their commitment to adhere to the Nuclear Non-Proliferation Treaty (NPT) as non-nuclear weapon states, and their agreement to eliminate all nuclear weapons as part of a denuclearization program applicable to all former non-Russian Soviet territory. For obvious reasons, the goal of reducing nuclear risks was widely shared by all European states, East and West, and all non-nuclear Soviet republics. This was the context of their initial foreign policy dealings with the United States.

---

7. Dunbar Lockwood, "Ukraine to Join START and NPT, All Tactical Nukes Removed," *Arms Control Today*, Vol. 22, No. 4 (May 1992), p. 16.

The three nuclear states did not seem to have a strong desire to become independent nuclear powers—at least not at first. At the same time, however, they believed, not without reason, that the nuclear presence they enjoyed was an asset that could give them leverage in their relationships with the West and with Russia. Dismantling the weapons, they argued, required funds that could not be made available from their budgets. Washington sought to provide incentives to offset this argument. The Cooperative Threat Reduction Program (CTR),[8] previously known as the Nunn-Lugar bill, was first enacted in 1991, with an authorization of $400 million in fiscal 1992 for various activities connected with the dismantling of nuclear weapons in Russia and the other three republics. Similar amounts continued to be authorized in subsequent years.[9]

When the Soviet Union dissolved in December 1991, Russia as the successor state formally accepted the obligations under existing arms control treaties and the NPT. Although the United States might have maintained that the three other republics were also successors and thus inherited the same obligations, it took the more pragmatic view that they should adhere to these agreements affirmatively in their own names. Throughout the spring of 1992, however, both Ukraine and Kazakhstan, believing that they should get something in return for giving up their newfound status as nuclear powers, were unwilling to subscribe to the NPT as non-nuclear states.[10] In April 1992, U.S. Secretary of State James Baker engaged in extensive telephone diplomacy to convince both countries to change their minds. On May 6, Ukrainian President Kravchuk made an official visit to Washington and gave his assent to the U.S. proposal. Kazakhstan also finally agreed during President Nursultan Nazerbaev's Washington visit in mid-May.[11] The stage was set for a long-planned summit in Lisbon, where all four successor states signed the Lisbon Protocol to START.

---

8. Cooperative Threat Reduction Act of 1993, 107 stat. 1777.

9. By early 1994, the total authorization for all former Soviet republics was just under $1 billion, although only about $130 million of this was obligated. Carnegie Endowment for International Peace and Monterey Institute of International Studies, *Nuclear Successor States of the Soviet Union: Nuclear Weapon and Sensitive Export Status Report* (May 1994), Table 1-F, pp. 19–20. The table also records additional assistance that was given as a reward for good performance in meeting the goals of U.S. denuclearization policy.

10. Kazakhstan even proposed that the weapons on its territory be under CIS or joint Kazakh-Russian control, an alternative that did little to assuage U.S. concerns.

11. Daniel Sneider, "Kazakhstan to Accept Phaseout of Nuclear Arms," *Christian Science Monitor*, May 19, 1992, p. 3.

Under the provisions of the protocol, Russia would be the only nuclear state. The three others states agreed to ratify START I and to transfer all their strategic nuclear weapons to Russia. They also pledged to adhere to the NPT as non-nuclear weapon states, prohibited from having any nuclear weapons.

Although the Lisbon meeting is widely regarded as a triumph of U.S. nuclear diplomacy, the implementation of the agreement was not wholly automatic. Kazakhstan ratified START I promptly, and Belarus somewhat later. The transfer of the missiles to Russia and the destruction of missile silos have been proceeding on or ahead of schedule.[12] NPT ratification took a good deal longer: July 22, 1993, for Belarus, and February 14, 1994, for Kazakhstan. Nevertheless, it can be said that these two states have carried out their Lisbon pledges in good faith.

Ukraine, however, continued to consider the weapons as an important counter in its not always amicable security relations with Russia. (See Alexei Arbatov's chapter in this volume, "Russian Security Interests and Dilemmas: An Agenda for the Future.") For the next year, Kiev made little progress toward implementing the Lisbon agreement. The United States applied continuous pressure on President Kravchuk to fulfill his commitments, often with apparent insensitivity to what Ukrainians saw as serious and legitimate security concerns. This led to resentment and further intransigence in Kiev. Only in late 1993, when the Clinton administration had taken hold, did the United States initiate a more comprehensive strategy toward Ukraine that ultimately resulted in the Trilateral Agreement among Russia, Ukraine, and the United States, which provided the needed reassurance.

It was not until after the immediate threat of nuclear proliferation within the former Soviet Union had been alleviated that Washington began to examine other issues within these and other republics.

---

12. As of July 1995, Russia had 6,833 treaty-accountable warheads under START I and had reduced the number of its strategic nuclear delivery vehicles to about 1,547—a level it is not required to reach until December 2001. (Transcript by Federal News Service of Arms Control Association Panel, October 20, 1995.) Additionally, according to U.S. Defense Secretary William Perry, 2,000 warheads have been destroyed and 750 missiles removed from launchers and bombers destroyed under the Nunn-Lugar program. (Speech by Dr. Perry at Pennsylvania State University Commencement, May 12, 1995.)

Democracy and Marketization

Beginning almost immediately after the breakup of the Soviet Union in 1991, Washington pressed toward its other primary policy objective, the rapid transformation of Russia into a society with a democratic government and a market economy. The conflation of democratic government and market economies became something of a mantra of immediate post–Cold War policy. The unstated assumption was that economic reforms would automatically result in political democracy.[13] The definition of "market economy" and economic reforms reflected the rigid orthodoxy of Milton Friedman's Chicago school, which prescribed what came to be called shock therapy. This consisted of a rapid transition to currency convertibility, an immediate end to controlled prices and subsidies on consumer goods, privatization, and rationalization of industry. These measures were to be accomplished simultaneously and with little regard for either the capacity of the system to absorb the changes or the provision of a social safety net for the millions who would lose incomes, jobs, security, and perhaps their enthusiasm for both reform and democracy in the transformation process. Shock therapy was embraced initially by some Russian democrats, who saw a short window of opportunity for Russia alone to make the leap to a market economy. These "radical reformers"—Yegor Gaidar, Suyatoslav Fyodorov, Anatoli Chubais, among others—achieved positions of power in the first years of the Yeltsin administration and allied themselves with the United States and the West, which in turn saw this group as the best hope for a quick transition to a market economy.

It should have been understood by U.S. policymakers, if not by their Russian counterparts, that rapid transformation to a market economy via shock therapy would not be so easy to reconcile with notions of democracy as government that listens and is responsive to its people. Nor, as the case of China illustrates, is it inevitable that political reform will automatically follow from market reform. Unlike some of the Central and Eastern European countries where the linkage seemed to

---

13. See also David Lipton and Jeffrey D. Sachs, "Prospects for Russia's Economic Reforms," *Brookings Papers on Economic Activity* (Washington, D.C.: Brookings, 1992), No. 2, pp. 213–284; Lipton and Sachs do not make the error of conflation. However, they make very optimistic assumptions about the pace and depth of political reform and of Western financial assistance to reach their conclusions that "shock therapy" would be sustainable without a crippling backlash (see especially pp. 249–261).

be working, Russia had no historical experience of either market practices or democratic government to draw upon. Moreover, Russia faced
some unique disadvantages in the effort to transform itself. Not only
was the Soviet Union a command economy, but it depended on a complex integration of the resources and assets of the Soviet Union's constituent republics that dissolved along with the Soviet empire. The
reformers' idea that Russia could underwrite its own economic transformation by selling goods and resources to its near abroad was unrealistic in light of their dislocated, struggling economies and the impact
of dissolution on the Russian economy itself. Moreover, the impact of
the economic distortions caused by the primacy of the military economy had not been fully appreciated by post–Cold War economic analysts. The drastic Russian reform efforts and the radical alteration in
economic as well as political relations with the republics affected not
only internal politics within Russia, but the dynamics of the political
struggles within the republics. U.S. policy, however, remained closely
focused on the Russian economic transformation, shutting out its
broader political effects.

Shock therapy began in Russia on January 2, 1992, only weeks after
the dissolution of the Soviet Union. Subsidies to farms and factories
were cut and consumer prices were decontrolled, except for a few
basic commodities such as bread, milk, and gasoline. The impact was
an immediate trebling in prices. By the end of the year, prices had
risen twenty-four fold.[14] There were growing concerns about the possibility of famine during the winter of 1991–92. In response, the
United States launched Operation Provide Hope, a hastily conceived
project, with goods often inappropriate to local needs in ill-conceived
distribution plans. The use of U.S. military officers to effect the distribution of this aid seemed to some local officials a way of granting
them access to once forbidden areas. A technical assistance program
was launched simultaneously, mustering advice from Western academics and business leaders with the knowledge and experience
required to overhaul the economy. However, meaningful financial
assistance was not available.

Through most of 1992, analysts were warning that massive
amounts of aid would be required to ensure economic and political
reform in the former Soviet Union. Both Congress and the executive
branch were reluctant to commit substantial funds, and Congress did

---

14. Marshall I. Goldman, *Lost Opportunity: Why Economic Reforms in Russia Have
Not Worked* (New York: W.W. Norton, 1994), pp. 106–107.

not support a "Marshall Plan" advocated by some Soviet experts. The administration did take the lead in convening a Conference on Assistance to the NIS in Tokyo in October 1992, where the United States pledged an additional $412 million for humanitarian assistance over the course of the winter. But in the end, the United States provided little direct financial aid, apart from the Nunn-Lugar initiative.

The Bush administration's cautious stance came under criticism from all sides. Even ex-president Richard Nixon weighed in, warning that the administration was losing Russia by failing to provide adequate economic support. In the 1992 presidential campaign, Clinton and other candidates strongly criticized the Bush administration for its lack of leadership and its minimalist policies toward the region. After the election, campaign oratory had to be translated into effective policy. The new strategy was not a real departure, but it was more energetic and designed to be more effective, with the United States acting as a forceful catalyst to sustain the necessary multilateral assistance program.[15]

At the Vancouver summit in April 1993, Presidents Bill Clinton and Boris Yeltsin worked out a new $1.6 billion package of bilateral programs to address key needs identified by Russian reformers and Western concerns. These included privatization, democratization, dismantling of nuclear weapons, housing for demobilized military personnel, people-to-people exchanges, upgrading of the energy sector, and measures to spur trade and investment.[16] U.S. Vice President Al Gore and Russian Prime Minister Victor Chernomyrdin were appointed co-chairs of a commission on cooperation in science and technology.

There were other promising early results. The Vancouver summit was followed by agreement of the Paris Club to reschedule $15 billion of Russia's foreign debt. At the Tokyo meeting of the Group of Seven industrialized countries (G-7), finance and foreign ministers pledged a $28.4 billion multilateral support package, primarily from international financial institutions. The G-7 package mirrored U.S. policy concerns—assistance to Russia and the Newly Independent States (NIS) to dismantle nuclear weapons, and a

---

15. U.S. Secretary of State Warren Christopher, "Assistance to Russia and the Foreign Affairs Budget," statement before the Senate Foreign Relations Committee, Washington, D.C., April 29, 1993, published in *Dispatch*, Vol. 4, No. 17 (April 26, 1993), p. 280.

16. Ibid.

Special Privatization and Restructuring Fund to ease the economic and social consequences of privatizing more than 20,000 medium and large-scale enterprises. The United States offered a challenge grant to stimulate other donors and pledged an additional $1.3 billion in new bilateral programs.[17] Although Russia and Russian reform were the primary focus of these efforts, a significant share of the grants and credits announced in Vancouver and Tokyo were to be directed toward the NIS.

In the end, however, very little of the pledged aid reached its intended destinations. The IMF was given the key role in channeling economic assistance to the new states, and this turned out to be a crucial factor in the operation of the program. The IMF was more than a convenient conduit through which to channel funds. It was charged with establishing and enforcing the free market principles on the basis of which the funds were to be advanced to reforming states. As an institution, the IMF had long espoused the monetary and fiscal orthodoxy that became the hallmark of reform. Its implementation of the Clinton administration's policy put post-Soviet reform in the hands of economists and technocrats. The conditionality imposed by the IMF on Russia included performance criteria that the Russian economy was in no position to meet. The Russian reaction was well expressed by Georgi Arbatov:

What concerns me the most is the [American] policy support for the ruinous pseudo-market reforms of...Gaidar. This support has produced suspicions in Russia that the entire reform program is a plot to undermine the economy, to de-industrialize the country, and to roll it back into the third world.[18]

The Russian economic decline continued. By August 1993, when the confrontation between Yeltsin and the parliament was reaching its climax, prices had risen by another 30 percent. Overall, the consumer price index rose 9.4 times in 1993.[19] Industrial output dropped almost 20 percent in 1992 and another 16 percent in 1993. Real

---

17. Secretary Christopher also announced that President Clinton would seek $704 million in Freedom Support Act funds in the fiscal year 1994 budget to continue current programs to dismantle nuclear weapons, deliver humanitarian aid, and promote democracy and privatization. Ibid., p. 281.

18. Georgi Arbatov, "Seeds of a New Cold War," *World Press Review*, Vol. 41, No. 7 (July 1994), p. 33.

19. Russian Research Center, Harvard University, *Economic Newsletter*, Vol. 19, No. 7 (March 25, 1994), p. 1.

incomes in 1993 were about half what they were in 1991. Gross domestic product (GDP) fell 19 percent from 1991 to 1992, and another 21 percent in 1993. Official unemployment figures remained at 2 percent, but the true level of unemployment was acknowledged to be much higher. One report estimated between 9 and 10 million people were unemployed in 1993—12–13 percent of the work force. Half of these were workers who nominally had jobs but were unpaid or partially paid.[20] Marshall Goldman reports that at one point, "Russian enterprises were in arrears for 220 billion rubles just for unpaid wages."[21] Defaults on debt repayment were routine for state enterprises (and incidentally provided a form of credit expansion that the Central Bank could not control, even if it had wished to do so). The state itself defaulted on its foreign debt service.

The effect on most of the Russian population was a dramatic departure not only from the conditions they had experienced in the Soviet era but from their expectations for democracy. The economic decline with its vast hardships for ordinary Russians was accompanied by a frightening increase in crime, both organized and unorganized. Beyond all the figures was a numbing sense of demoralization, disorientation, and alienation. And there were the beginnings of ethnic discord as authorities in Moscow began to forcibly expel many non-Russian citizens—who were singled out for blame as the economy continued to decline—from the city and its environs in the autumn of 1993.

Russian reformers had difficulty sustaining support for shock therapy early on, but the problem grew steadily worse throughout 1993. Old-line communists in parliament, chosen under the election laws of the previous regime, obstructed reform efforts. Members of liberal, reform-oriented factions, driven by the plight of the Russian population and the precariousness of democratic reform, urged more gradual alternatives.[22]

---

20. Russian Research Center, Harvard University, *Economic Newsletter*, Vol. 19, No. 13 (September 8, 1994), p. 1.

21. Goldman, *Lost Opportunity*, p. 110.

22. For examples, see speeches by Strobe Talbott in the spring of 1993. He repeatedly describes the struggle in Russia as one which "pits those who brought down the Soviet communist system against those who would like to preserve its vestiges if not restore its essence. . . . In short, it pits reform against reaction." Testimony of Ambassador Strobe Talbott before the House Appropriations Subcommittee on Foreign Operations and Export Financing, April 19, 1993; also in Testimony of Ambassador Strobe Talbott before the Foreign Affairs Committee, House of Representatives, April 21, 1993.

As resistance from parliament grew, President Yeltsin increasingly ruled by decree to continue the reformist course.[23] Unwavering U.S. support for Yeltsin and his reformers, duly reported by a newly liberated Russian press, backfired. It left this group extremely vulnerable to charges that they were betraying Russian interests for an agenda set by outsiders, and lent credence to accusations by opposition members from a number of factions that Yeltsin was attempting to impose a "primitive, savage and predatory capitalism" on an impoverished Russia, and "derailing Russia as instructed by western intelligence sources."[24] The United States found itself in the uncomfortable position of upholding the Yeltsin government's decision to decrease grandmothers' pensions, while the "communist reactionaries" held the moral high ground by espousing new policies to guarantee fundamental rights to a basic livelihood and human dignity.

By mid-1993, there were many signs that Russia's economic policies were in deep trouble. The IMF's release of the first half of a $3 billion package aimed at macroeconomic stabilization was followed by a resurgence of inflation. The confiscation by the Russian Central Bank of pre-1993 rubles in the summer of 1993 further undercut consumer confidence in the reform program, and the confidence of the IMF in the reformist government. The growing political power struggles resulting from different ideas for proceeding with reform between the Yeltsin government and the parliament created a dual power structure with no final arbiter. Democratically inclined advisers were replaced. The climax came in October 1993, when leaders of parliament led a violent revolt against the government. President Yeltsin responded by sending tanks to bombard the White House, the building where the parliament met. The revolt was suppressed, and the parliament was dissolved.

But the last word had yet to be spoken. In December 1993, new parliamentary elections resulted in a resounding defeat for the party of the reformers and even the centrist opposition. The Liberal Democratic Party, led by nationalist Vladimir Zhirinovsky, got the largest popular vote with 23 percent, while Russia's Choice, the party

---

23. Yeltsin increasingly succumbed to the appeal of special or emergency powers, ruling by personal decree. See William Bodie, "The Threat to America from the Former USSR," *Orbis* (Fall 1993), p. 516, for an account of how rule by decree has become common for the executive, which has been characteristic of the post-communist states.

24. Goldman, *Lost Opportunity*, pp. 114–115.

of the reformers, polled only 15 percent. Overall, the main anti-reform groups totaled 43 percent against 34 percent for the government. In the new parliament, the anti-reform groups had a substantial margin. Among the new parliament's first acts was to grant amnesty to members of its predecessor, who were awaiting trial for treason as a result of the October uprising. And in 1996, these same people were part of the anti-Yeltsin faction supporting neocommunist Gennadi Zyuganov.

After the Deluge

As the signs of growing dissatisfaction with the Yeltsin program increased, the United States began to reconsider and modify its own policies. Declaratory policy statements began to include references to the NIS as well as Russia.[25] Even before the dissolution of the parliament, Strobe Talbott, then President Clinton's special adviser for Russian affairs, laid out the new line in testimony to the Senate Foreign Relations Committee on September 7, 1993:

We begin from firm and unwavering support for the independence, sovereignty, and territorial integrity of all the New Independent States, including the Russian Federation itself. We do not support secessionism through armed struggle or the breakup of any of these states, nor do we seek to pit any state in the region against any other. In accordance with the United Nations Charter and the CSCE Final Act, the United States can accept changes of borders only if they are achieved by peaceful means and mutual consent.[26]

In the same speech, Talbott also voiced U.S. support for multilateral approaches to conflicts in the former Soviet Union. "The United States does not have pat solutions for these conflicts," he said.

Nor do we seek a formal role as mediator among the independent and sovereign states of the region… America's role will often be as an active participant in multilateral efforts through international bodies in which all the New Independent States are members—such as the

---

25. From this time on, there were few speeches on Russia that did not explicitly mention Ukraine and other NIS countries or put Russia in the context of one of many NIS states. "Our policy is intended to support reform throughout the NIS— that is in 12 countries, not just one." Statement before the Senate Foreign Relations Committee by Strobe Talbott, September 7, 1993. Talbott uses the metaphor of a "strategic alliance with post-Soviet reform" as opposed to the earlier formulation of a strategic alliance with Russian reform.

26. Ibid.

UN, CSCE, or the NATO Coordinating Council. The United States will also continue to use bilateral contacts with each of the New Independent States whenever our diplomacy can help resolve or prevent conflict. We will not act unilaterally, nor will we take sides. Our efforts will be undertaken openly and in close consultation with all the states of the region.[27]

In contrast to the earlier fixation on Yeltsin and Moscow, channels of communication were opened with a broader cast of prominent figures in the legislature and the government as well as with political and opposition leaders in Russia's regions and the near abroad. U.S. consulates were opened in St. Petersburg and Vladivostok and another was planned for Ekaterinburg. Without withdrawing support for President Yeltsin, U.S. officials began to broaden their contacts with legitimate groups and factions across the Russian political scene. The mandate of the Gore-Chernomyrdin Commission was expanded, first to economic and foreign policy issues, and ultimately to cover defense conversion, environment, and health.[28] Moreover, with nationalist sentiment on the rise in Russia and visions of ethnic conflict spreading across the policy horizon, the United States (and indeed the Yeltsin government itself) began to pay much more attention to the brewing conflicts in the NIS. James Collins, who had previously worked on developments in the CIS from his position as deputy chief of mission in Moscow, was appointed senior coordinator in the office of the ambassador-at-large for the NIS. In January 1994, Strobe Talbott, the administration's leading expert on the former Soviet territory, was designated deputy secretary of state.

In practice, however, Washington's "new" policy seemed to consist primarily of ad hoc reactions to crises, often in response to U.S. domestic constituencies. The denuclearization policy continued, though with increased emphasis on Ukraine. The well-kept secret of the purchase of 600 kilograms of highly enriched uranium from Kazakhstan beginning in 1993 and ending in November 1994 ("Project Sapphire") was a concrete accomplishment that received little attention in the United States, but nonetheless contributed to the policy of slowing proliferation.[29] Similarly, the implementation of the

---

27. Ibid.

28. See *Dispatch*, Vol. 5, No. 52 (December 26, 1994), pp. 843–846, for a partial listing of the Commission's agreements.

29. *CTR*, U.S. Department of Defense (April 1995). See also John D. Morrocco, "US Takes Charge of Uranium Cache," *Aviation Week and Space Technology*, Vol. 141, No. 22 (November 1994).

Conventional Forces in Europe (CFE) and START I treaties, which were considered preconditions for START II ratification, continued to be stressed. Concern about Russian economic reform was tempered by the evident political turmoil. U.S. support for the efforts of international organizations in the region was not energetic, and although the administration seemed concerned with ethnic problems in the near abroad, little attention was paid to incipient ethnic unrest in Russia itself.

As the 1990s progressed, ethnic conflict was increasingly on the international mind and conscience. The violence and bloodshed of the former Yugoslavia were inescapable as a "horror mirror" for the former Soviet Union, as Nadia Arbatova points out in her chapter in this book. The war between Armenia and Azerbaijan had already begun when Gorbachev was in the Kremlin. In the aftermath of the breakup, it seemed that there were many candidates for a like fate, particularly as some twenty-five million ethnic Russians now found themselves minorities in the new states, no longer able to count on Moscow for protection. Violence was avoided in the Baltic states, but it flickered along the southern rim of the old empire, in Moldova, Crimea, Georgia, and Tajikistan. In each case there were charges, and in some, there was evidence, that Russian troops, still deployed in the area, had interfered on behalf of the pro-Russian faction, but whether at the initiative of local commanders or at the behest of Moscow (and if so, who in Moscow) was not clear. There was also potential for violence to erupt in relatively placid states such as Kazakhstan, which had large Russian populations concerned about their treatment under new citizenship and employment laws in their places of residence.

In his rise to power and in his campaign for Russian independence, President Yeltsin, as many of the case studies in this volume attest, had encouraged separatist movements throughout the Soviet Union. The December 1993 elections that propelled Zhirinovsky's party into parliament produced an overhaul of this original stance, at least at the verbal level. Zhirinovsky had skillfully exploited the humiliation of the loss of empire and the plight of Russian compatriots in the new countries. Yegor Gaidar and the reformers were replaced by a new group of more conservative (and pragmatic) politicians headed by Prime Minister Chernomyrdin. Defense Minister Pavel Grachev and even Foreign Minister Andrei Kozyrev displayed a new truculence in their approach to their new neighbors and an attitude more protective of Russian speakers in local ethnic frictions. Soon the Russian government began to portray its objectives as protecting Russians abroad from persecution and deprivation of human rights, and securing its own frontiers against destabilizing foreign incursions, given the intermixture of the populations of Russia and most of the other former Soviet republics.

This new Russian attitude toward the near abroad provoked a spirited debate in the United States. On one side were what might be termed the neo–Cold Warriors, of whom Zbigniew Brzezinski, President Carter's national security adviser, was a leading example. This group warned against the dangers of Russian resurgence.[30] As they saw it, Moscow was resorting to deliberate destabilization to force the old tsarist colonies back into a new Russian fold. At one stroke, it was said, Russia would restore its lost superpower status, assure the safety of the Russian populations now stranded abroad, and undercut the nationalists in domestic politics who were assailing it for failing to protect Russia's national interests. These apprehensions were echoed by leaders in Ukraine and the former Soviet satellites in Eastern Europe, where history gave cause for a continuing concern about the emergence of the Russian bear from hibernation. Strobe Talbott came under heavy criticism, as did administration policy toward Russia in general. Talbott, as a representative of the administration, was charged with ignoring other NIS interests and being naive about the potential for Russian reform. Critics claimed that the "Russia first" policy failed to take into account the revanchist tendencies on display even among moderates like Foreign Minister Kozyrev.[31]

The State Department generally rejected the charges of Russian neo-imperialism. However, as early as April 1993, Talbott had warned:

We understand Russia's concerns for stability on her borders and for the well-being of millions of ethnic Russians in neighboring states. It is crucial, however, that Russia neither assert nor exercise any special role or prerogatives that would be inconsistent with the independence, sovereignty, and territorial integrity of any other state. We have made our position on this question clear in dialogue at all levels with Russia, as well as with the other New Independent States.[32]

---

30. See Zbigniew Brzezinski, "The Premature Partnership," *Foreign Affairs*, Vol. 73, No. 2 (March/April 1994).

31. See Fiona Hill and Pamela Jewett, *Back in the USSR: Russia's Intervention in the Internal Affairs of the Former Soviet Republics and the Implications for United States Policy toward Russia* (Cambridge, Mass.: Harvard University, Kennedy School of Government, Strengthening Democratic Institutions Project, January 1994).

32. Statement before the House Foreign Affairs Committee by Strobe Talbott, April 21, 1993.

In January 1994, this tougher tone intensified. In testimony before the House Foreign Affairs Committee explicitly addressing relations between Russia and neighboring states, Talbott expressed a new concern with instability and civil wars on Russia's periphery and criticized Russian conduct in several of the neighboring states, particularly in Transcaucasia. But he also noted successes—in the Trilateral Agreement and the Russian government's promise to participate in Partnership for Peace (PfP), discussed below, which had now become the keystone of U.S. security policy for NATO and the Central and East European states.[33]

The outcome of the debate as well as of developments on the ground was a more complex and differentiated Clinton administration policy toward Russia and the other former Soviet states. The central components continued to be denuclearization, support for Russian democracy and marketization, and a primary focus on Russia, in particular President Yeltsin. But in a growing number of cases, other U.S. policy goals came into conflict with real or perceived interests of Russia or the Yeltsin regime, and the United States was faced with a choice between them. We consider here four of the most important cases: support for the Baltic states, often involving sharp criticism of Russia, driven by strong ethnic constituencies in the United States; the evolution of the independent U.S.-Ukrainian connection stemming from denuclearization policy but extending well beyond it and showing increased understanding of Ukraine's importance for stability in the former Soviet Union (FSU); the problem of NATO expansion, reflecting the continuing U.S. interest in European security and the pressures for admission from Eastern and Central European (ECE) states, which worried about a future remilitarized Russia; and finally, the tragedy of Chechnya, where the plague of ethnic conflict in its most virulent form turned against the Russian Federation itself.

The Baltic States

The Baltic states were occupied by the Soviet Union in 1940 after a brief period of independence between the world wars. They represent

---

33. See Antonia Handler Chayes and Richard Weitz, "The Military Perspective on Conflict Prevention: NATO" in Abram Chayes and Antonia Handler Chayes, eds., *Preventing Conflict in the Post-Communist World: Mobilizing International and Regional Organizations* (Washington, D.C.: Brookings, 1996).

prime examples of Soviet policy on ethnic groups and population transfers. During the period of Soviet domination, large numbers of local residents were moved out; ethnic Russians moved in and, particularly in the major cities and in the heavy industrial sector of the economy, often became the predominant group. During the Soviet period, the region was heavily dependent economically on Russia, especially for power and petroleum products. Since the collapse of the Soviet Union, the Baltic governments have sought to divorce themselves from the Russian economy and become more fully integrated with the economies of Western Europe.[34]

The main focus of U.S. concern in the Baltics was the continued presence in 1991 of 130,000 Soviet troops stationed in the three countries.[35] These forces were almost entirely composed of ethnic Russians, and remained under the authority of the Russian Federation. The necessary forces were in place for rapid military action. The governments of the newly independent Baltic states feared (and perhaps expected) that Russia's imperial ambitions might be reasserted at any time.[36] In fact, according to newspaper accounts in the spring of 1992, a Russian invasion of the Baltics was one of the scenarios used by U.S. military planners to justify force structures and develop strategies. However, even as of January 1994, there were still more than 165,000 troops remaining elsewhere in the FSU[37] without raising significant issues for U.S. policy, suggesting that the urgency of U.S. insistence on Russian withdrawal from the Baltics owed much to the importance of their U.S. co-ethnic constituencies. Although Yeltsin insisted that the presence of Russian troops was not linked to the treatment of ethnic Russians resident in the Balkans and that the forces would be withdrawn, the deliberately slow pace of withdrawal and the sometimes shrill tone of Russian pronouncements seemed to be calibrated to the progress of citizenship legislation.

---

34. See Alexander Yusupovsky's chapter in this volume, "Latvia: Discrimination, International Organizations, and Stabilization."

35. See, for example, the statement of the North Atlantic Council, January 14, 1991. See also the remarks of Assistant Secretary of State for European Affairs G.H. Seitz before the CSCE Commission, Washington, D.C., January 17, 1991.

36. Jonathan Steele, "Clinton Appeals to Russian 'Greatness': US President Sells Democracy at TV 'Town Meeting'," *The Guardian*, January 5, 1994, p. 9. Also see Lech Walesa, "Expansionist Russia Could Blackmail Europe," speech reprinted by Agence France Presse, December 14, 1993.

37. See Bruce Porter and Carol Saivetz, "The Once and Future Empire: Russia and the Near Abroad," *Washington Quarterly*, Vol. 17, No. 3 (Summer 1994), p. 82.

When the Baltic states achieved independence in 1991, about one-third of the population of Estonia and 30 percent of Latvia were Russian. Only in Lithuania does the titular nationality have a clear majority. In his chapter in this book, Alexander Yusupovsky presents the details of the harsh citizenship laws that not only disenfranchised the Russian population in Estonia and Latvia after independence, but deprived them of many other elements of everyday existence. In part because of the belief that in the Baltics, as elsewhere in the FSU, the treatment of ethnic Russians could be a flash point that might lead Moscow to launch some form of military operation, and in part because of the obvious linkage with the Russian military presence, the citizenship laws became an object of U.S. interest.

The United States pressed on both fronts, insisting that Russia comply with agreed timetables for withdrawal, while at the same time trying to induce the governments of Latvia and Estonia to adopt more generous laws on citizenship and political and property rights for Russian residents.[38] The process of withdrawal continued in fits and starts until the garrisons were reduced by half in 1992, and by August 1993, there were only 20,000 Russian troops remaining in Latvia and 5,000 in Lithuania.

The endgame was played out on President Clinton's trip to Riga in July 1994, the first ever visit to the Baltics by a U.S. president, on his way to a meeting with Yeltsin and then to the G-7 summit. At that time there were still about 1,500 Russian troops in Estonia and another 2,500 in Latvia. Militarily the number was insignificant, but to Baltic nationalists, the presence of these forces was unacceptable. Little progress had been made on softening citizenship laws, and it did not appear likely that Russia would withdraw the troops unless and until progress occurred. Nevertheless, President Clinton said pointedly that he was "confident" that the troops would be withdrawn on schedule, and, to ensure there was no misunderstanding, a senior U.S. official reiterated how important it was that the troops be out by August 31—the withdrawal deadline set by the Russian government.[39] President Yeltsin, however, was not going to put himself

---

38. Lithuania, with its much smaller Russian minority, had already passed a law in December 1991 with a grandfather clause extending citizenship to Russians previously residing in the country. Perhaps as a result, the 22,000 Russian troops based there had departed by August 31, 1993.

39. Susan Cornwell, "Clinton Confident Russia to Withdraw from Baltics," Reuters, July 6, 1994.

in the position of having been bullied by the U.S. president. He responded that the exit from Estonia would not occur until that country granted citizenship rights to retiring officers who stayed on, a matter that was of great concern to the general staff of the Russian Army.[40] At that point, Clinton successfully urged the Latvian president to veto a restrictive citizenship law that had been enacted by the parliament, and all Russian troops were out of the three states on August 31.

The major U.S. policy goal in the Baltics had been met. But the United States cannot take much of the credit for the improvements, however incremental, in the situation of Russian minorities in the Baltics. Most of the work to relieve the harshness of the Latvian and Estonian citizenship policies was done by the Organization for Security and Cooperation in Europe (OSCE, the successor to the CSCE), in particular the High Commissioner on National Minorities and the Council of Europe.[41] The OSCE operates with ridiculously low funds.[42] The High Commissioner on National Minorities gets his $2–4 million annual budget from European governments, primarily the Dutch, augmented by support from private U.S. foundations. The U.S. government has been conspicuously absent.

Ukraine

Difficulties underlying the relationship between Russia and Ukraine—including nuclear issues, the status of Crimea, the terms on which energy will be provided, and ownership of the Black Sea Fleet and its support facilities—are discussed in Edward Ozhiganov's chapter in this book, "The Crimean Republic: Rivalries for Control." Until mid-1993, U.S. interest in Ukraine was driven primarily by its strategic goal of nuclear non-proliferation.[43] Interest in other problems

---

40. At talks between officers of the American Joint Staff and the Soviet General Staff in October 1990, the issue of the treatment of Red Army officers in the Baltics was brought up by the Soviets as a matter of grave concern. Notes in possession of the authors.

41. Diana Chigas with Elizabeth McLintock and Christophe Kamp, "Preventive Diplomacy and the Organization for Security and Cooperation in Europe: Creating Incentives for Dialogue and Cooperation," in Chayes and Chayes, *Preventing Conflict in the Post-Communist World*, pp. 59–63.

42. The OSCE's entire budget in 1994 was $27 million. Ibid., p. 71.

43. While the focus of the Clinton administration remained on the reform process in Russia, the prominence of denuclearization in U.S. policy toward

between the two neighboring states seemed predicated on how they affected Washington's nuclear goals. For example, the tensions between Russia and Ukraine over Crimea and the division of the Black Sea Fleet created instability and threatened the denuclearization agenda.[44] Washington's "Moscow first" policy and single-minded pressure on Ukraine to fulfill its agreement to get rid of its nuclear stockpile began to have perverse effects. It served to deepen the Ukrainian leadership's convictions that to eliminate its nuclear weapons would be to relinquish Ukraine's only source of influence and to dissipate its guarantee of territorial integrity in the face of rising Russian separatist movements in Crimea and eastern Ukraine. Continued Ukrainian waffling on the question of denuclearization led to an evolution of U.S. policy objectives to encompass a broader-based relationship with Ukraine, a turn that appears to have been a positive step for the long run.

As early as the summer of 1993, the Clinton administration began to make repeated references to a "strategic alliance with reform in Russia and Ukraine."[45] In late June 1993, Ambassador Talbott and U.S. Defense Secretary Les Aspin visited Kiev and announced a series of new U.S. measures focusing on Ukrainian concerns. In this instance, to encourage Ukraine to fulfill its promises to ratify START I and the NPT, the United States held out the hope of a U.S.-Ukraine Charter that would confirm the U.S. commitment to the independence and sovereignty of Ukraine and be signed at the highest levels,

---

Ukraine sent the message that its nuclear weapons were the most valuable political and economic assets Ukraine had. For discussion of this dynamic, see William H. Kincade and Natalie Melnyczuk, "Eurasia Letter: Unneighborly Neighbors," *Foreign Policy*, No. 94 (Spring 1994), pp. 84–104; and Dave McCurdy, "The Evolving U.S. Policy Toward Ukraine," *SAIS Review* (Winter–Spring 1994), pp. 153–169.

44. Independent negotiations between Ukraine and Russia were faltering over the division of the Black Sea Fleet and the questions of p ayments for resources. A comprehensive political agreement on the Black Sea Fleet, dual citizenship, and fuel and energy issues was signed by Presidents Yeltsin and Kravchuk at a June 17, 1993, summit meeting in Moscow, but subsequently broke down. McCurdy, "The Evolving U.S. Policy Toward Ukraine," p. 158.

45. For a full statement of new U.S. policy toward Ukraine, see testimony by Strobe Talbott on Ukraine, June 24, 1993, to the Senate Committee on Foreign Relations Subcommittee on European Affairs; for explicit reference to Ukraine in policy statements thereafter, see Strobe Talbott, statement before the Senate Foreign Relations Committee, September 7, 1993; and Strobe Talbott, statement before the House Foreign Affairs Committee, September 21, 1993.

once the Lisbon pledges of 1992 had been carried out.[46] The pilgrimage to Kiev continued with a visit by U.S. Secretary of State Warren Christopher in October 1993, when President Kravchuk agreed at last to submit the critical treaties to parliament. However, when he did, parliament attached so many conditions to its acceptance as to render it invalid.

This backing and filling took place against a background of economic decline in Ukraine that was perhaps the worst of any of the successor states. In 1992, inflation grew at the rate of 30–40 percent per month. Production dropped 15 percent. Ukraine's heavy dependence on Russia for petroleum and natural gas generated mounting bills that it could not pay. In mid-1993, Russia decided to eliminate the preexisting subsidy that moderated prices for Ukraine and began to charge market rates for these products.

A problem with almost equally serious domestic political ramifications was the contention between Russia and Ukraine over the future of Crimea, described in both Ozhiganov's case study and Alexei Arbatov's chapter on "Russian Security Interests and Dilemmas: An Agenda for the Future," in this volume. The peninsula, which was a part of the Russian Republic until 1954, was given by Nikita Khrushchev to Ukraine to celebrate the 300th anniversary of the union of the two countries. Two-thirds of the inhabitants of Crimea are Russian, and although many of them voted for Ukrainian independence, Russian nationalists among them dominated the Crimean Parliament. In 1992, this body declared the independence of Crimea from Ukraine, and the Russian Supreme Soviet tried to revoke Khrushchev's gift. In response the Ukrainian Parliament vowed to end the secession by all necessary means. Clearly the ante had been raised considerably. Cooler heads prevailed, however, and Yeltsin and Kravchuk, with some U.S. prodding, met at a June summit and temporarily defused the issue. Crimea was granted broad autonomy and a special economic status within Ukraine.

A similar flare-up occurred in mid-1993, when the Russian Parliament declared Sebastopol to be a part of Russia. This was smoothed over by another presidential meeting. Nevertheless, both presidents were vulnerable to the stridency of extreme nationalist factions at home, who did not hesitate to exploit Crimea for their own

---

46. On July 2, 1993, the Ukrainian Parliament passed a resolution by a vote of 226 to 15 that claimed ownership of all nuclear weapons on Ukrainian territory. See *Arms Control Today* (September 1993), p. 25.

political purposes. "What Kuwait is to Iraq," Zhirinovsky declaimed, "the Crimea is to Russia." To which the Ukrainian Deputy Foreign Minister replied, "If Russia takes Crimea, Ukraine will remain nuclear."[47] In Kiev it was hinted darkly that Russia was promoting secession, not only in Crimea, but in the eastern region of Ukraine bordering on Russia. In any case, Ukraine's history and geopolitical position gave it ample reason to worry about its larger neighbor.

Another six months of complicated maneuvering led to the signature in Moscow of the much-heralded Trilateral Agreement among Presidents Yeltsin, Kravchuk, and Clinton on January 14, 1994. Under the agreement, Ukrainian missiles were to be shipped to Russia, where the warheads would be dismantled and the fissile material sold to the United States for a purchase price estimated in the billions of dollars.[48] The United States offered a package of financial incentives, and Russia canceled the balance owed to it for oil shipments. Pledges on the NPT and START treaties were renewed. Both Russia and the United States solemnly recognized the existing Ukrainian borders and pledged themselves to respect the sovereignty and territorial integrity of Ukraine.[49] But the skeptical Ukrainian Parliament still responded equivocally.

In the Ukrainian elections of June 1994, President Kravchuk was defeated and many members of parliament were turned out in an election that reflected the population's dissatisfaction with the deteriorating economy. Kravchuk's successor, Leonid Kuchma, was a member of the pro-Russian faction, and the voters put many ex-communists back in office. As of August 1994, when Kuchma visited Washington, Ukraine had sent 200 missiles to Russia in return for about 100 tons of reactor fuel. The remaining 1,400 were to be transferred over the course of seven years in accordance with the START schedule. Ukraine ratified the NPT as a non-nuclear weapon state in November of 1994.[50]

---

47. Paula J. Dobriansky, "Ukraine: A Question of Survival," *The National Interest* (Summer 1994), p. 67.

48. "White House Press Briefing by Mark Geran in Minsk," *Newswire*, January 17, 1994.

49. For more on this agreement, see "Statement by Ukraine, Russia and the USA, Signed 14th January in Moscow," *BBC Summary of World Broadcasts*, January 20, 1994, Part 1, Special Supplement (English translation of Radio Ukraine World Service broadcast, January 15, 1994).

50. David Albright, "Jury-Rigged, but Working," *Bulletin of the Atomic Scientists*, Vol. 51, No. 1 (January 1995), p. 20.

Peace between Ukraine and Russia remains central to the stability of the entire region of the former Soviet Union,[51] and to a great degree peace hinges on the stability of Ukraine. It is not clear, however, that stability can be maintained simply by a U.S. commitment to Ukrainian territorial integrity. Economic conditions will play a large role in the stability equation, and there is much room for improvement at present. Bilateral and multilateral assistance is available, although how effectively that aid is used is open to question. Ukraine is said to be the fourth largest recipient of U.S. aid in the world after Israel, Egypt, and Russia, yet its economy continues to free-fall. For example, in 1994 Ukraine experienced a 23 percent drop in GDP, leaving it at less than half its 1989 level, and, by August of 1995, consumer prices were 434.4 percent above the level in February 1995.[52] Washington pledged $350 million to support Ukraine's economic reforms in 1994 and about an equal sum to help dismantle nuclear weapons.[53] Yet here is some reason for optimism. In late 1996, the ethnic fires are contained, though not extinguished. Since 1993, dangerous issues have been handled with a modicum of skill and considerable luck. Yet without an upturn in Ukraine's economic situation, it is unclear how long the calm can continue. It would not be the first time that economic despair has metamorphosed into fanatic nationalism and ethnic unrest. Until all nuclear weapons are removed from Ukraine, the U.S. concern on that score is warranted, but an economic strategy may be as important a tool of conflict prevention as security reassurance has been thus far.[54]

Eurasian Security, Russia, and the Expansion of NATO

An important element in the evolution of U.S. policy toward the former Soviet Union has been NATO expansion—another arena in which the West has come to engage the NIS apart from Russia. The evolution of European security exposed competing interests for the United States that have created tensions with Russia.

---

51. See Alexei Arbatov's discussion of the importance of amicable relations between Russia and Ukraine in his chapter in this volume.

52. "Ukrainian Numbers," *Financial Times Limited*, August 18, 1995.

53. Carole Landry, "Clinton Hails Kuchma as Ukraine's Renaissance Man," Agence France Presse, November 22, 1994.

54. General Volodymyr Mykhtiuk, a commander of strategic missile forces in Ukraine, stated that all nuclear warheads were to be removed from Ukrainian soil by the end of 1998.

The evolution of NATO has preoccupied security planners and analysts since 1989, as they wrestled with changing its missions in ways designed to maintain its relevance in the absence of the Soviet threat. The decision was made to transform NATO into an encompassing collective security arrangement—an alliance restructured not only for conventional defense but also for peace operations designed to prevent, contain, or ameliorate European conflict.[55]

A central element of this process has been the questions of whether and under what circumstances the ECE countries should be offered full NATO membership. Following the London summit in July 1990, NATO invited all former Warsaw Treaty Organization (WTO) members to establish diplomatic ties with the NATO Secretariat, and several did so within the next few months.[56] In November 1991, NATO's relations with the ECE countries deepened further with the creation of the North Atlantic Cooperation Council (NACC), which eventually included all WTO members, Albania, and the successor states to the Soviet Union, as a forum for relatively high-level consultations in a number of areas, including new missions such as peace operations.[57] However, NACC was not very satisfactory from the perspective of the ECE countries, the NIS, or Russia. The ECE countries, wary of Russia and perhaps Germany,[58] wanted a quick transition to full NATO membership. NACC gave them neither the security of the Alliance's defense umbrella nor transition to membership. Non-Russian members of the FSU, notably Ukraine and the Baltics, wanted protection that the NACC could not provide. Russia, with memories of more than forty years of confrontation with NATO, "wanted a withering away" of NATO to be replaced by "a new military organization for collective security and stability—something like a military adjunct to the OSCE, where [Russia's] voice was strong and [its] veto effective."[59]

From the NATO perspective, offering full membership to the ECE countries was not an attractive proposition, and admission of the NIS

---

55. Henry Kissinger, "Expand NATO Now," *Washington Post*, December 19, 1994, p. 27.

56. These included Bulgaria, Czechoslovakia, Hungary, Poland, and the Soviet Union.

57. See the discussion of NACC in Chayes and Weitz, "The Military Perspective on Conflict Prevention: NATO."

58. Kissinger, "Expand NATO Now."

59. Chayes and Weitz, "The Military Perspective on Conflict Prevention: NATO," p. 402.

was out of the question in the near term. Few members were then willing to accept either the risk or expense that such a course would entail. Admitting any ECE state on the same terms would require existing members to defray additional expenditures to bolster the incomplete or obsolete defense establishments of the new entrants. ECE military competency is low, and it will take time and resources before these states can make a positive contribution to collective defense. ECE countries had different equipment and operational doctrines that would make interoperability with NATO countries problematic. It had taken forty years for NATO to achieve a satisfactory degree of interoperability, and while it might take less than that for new members, the time would still be extensive. Finally, there was the risk that admitting them would provoke Russia to act unpredictably and perhaps upset the relative stability of Europe at a time when Western defense budgets were declining. Yet, despite these factors, it seemed clear that an additional step beyond NACC was required to preserve NATO, maintain European security, and, insofar as possible, further the course of reform in the ECE and the FSU. That step was the Partnership for Peace (PfP).

The Partnership for Peace originated as a way to address the concerns of the ECE states that felt threatened by Russia without provoking Moscow or initiating divisive arguments within the alliance. Seeking to balance the concerns of all countries involved (albeit without completely satisfying any) was like a Rorschach inkblot into which participants could read whatever suited them. Although not completely satisfying ECE concerns, PfP held out the promise of eventual integration into NATO by offering individual contractual relationships with NATO. Affiliation with NATO via PfP offers inducements to stay the course of reform, because only by doing so could applicants hope to obtain full membership. Although consultation in times of crisis is offered, NATO is not bound to come to the aid of PfP countries. Moscow saw the PfP for what NATO hoped the ECE countries would see in it—the next step toward full membership in the alliance, causing consternation instead of reassurance.

While U.S. policymakers may see the progression from diplomatic ties to PfP as a process of building confidence, sustaining reform, and revitalizing NATO,[60] Moscow views it as an effort to bolster a traditionally hostile alliance at Russia's expense. Despite attempts by

---

60. Statements by President Clinton and other statesmen as well as the communiqué issued by the NACC ministers at the end of their meeting in December 1994

Western leaders to provide reassurance, the view from the Kremlin is that at its core, NATO is an organization created, nourished, and maintained to oppose Moscow.[61] Defense Minister Pavel Grachev warned that NATO expansion would cause Russia to discard the restrictions imposed by the 1990 CFE agreement, and could lead to other "countermeasures." Policy executives and legislators have made clear that there is a linkage between NATO expansion and Russian ratification of the START II agreement.[62] For Moscow, NATO's presence on Russia's frontiers is provocative. Its WTO buffer was eliminated even before the demise of the Soviet Union. To include former WTO states, especially Poland, in NATO would bring the West to Russia's front door, increasing its sense of isolation. To contemplate membership of other NIS members is more threatening yet. Although the United States knows that it is not in the West's interest for Moscow to think of itself as isolated, PfP was formulated almost as an improvisation, without serious consultation with Moscow.[63]

The result could be a spiraling, self-fulfilling prophecy that contributes to neither regional stability nor continued reform in Russia.[64] Each time Russia expresses opposition, as President Yeltsin did in Budapest in December 1994, ECE states become more concerned for their security and agitate for more rapid assimilation into NATO. This in turn fuels additional Russian suspicions, leads to internal

---

make no secret of the eventual intent to expand NATO membership. See, for example, Kissinger, "Expand NATO Now," and Zbigniew Brzezinski, "NATO— Expand or Die?" *New York Times*, December 28, 1994, p. A–15.

61. As Russian Defense Minister Pavel Grachev made clear in an interview in May 1994, given its symbolism as an anti-Russian Cold War instrument, NATO can never be acceptable to Russia.

62. See Paul E. Gallis, *Partnership for Peace* (Washington, D.C.: Congressional Research Service, August 9, 1994) p. 8. See generally, Chayes and Weitz, "The Military Perspective on Conflict Prevention: NATO," pp. 381–427.

63. PfP came about without a great deal of deliberation within the alliance or with those concerned outside of NATO. The dilemma faced by the United States was that, while the absence of consultations would not sit well with the Russians, opening the matter to debate by the alliance members could have increased internal tensions.

64. Russian policymakers cannot be oblivious to the fact that one reason for their former allies' haste to cement relations with NATO is concern about Moscow's intentions. This concern has been brought into even sharper focus by events in Chechnya although that may be lost on Moscow decision-makers. Thus there is a requirement for Moscow to reassure East Central Europe (ECE) of its intentions as part of any effort to break the spiral.

political discord, and could unsettle the Eurasian security environment if it led to increased Russian military expenditures.[65]

Although the United States continues to take Russian concerns into consideration, it has not pursued European security and stability with a "Moscow first" approach—nor could it do so. But the Clinton administration has not considered it prudent to ignore Russian interests, and Russia has warmed to PfP somewhat. There have been opportunities for cooperation with Russia—exercises and missions that might make NATO less threatening to Moscow. The creation of the UN Implementation Force (IFOR) as a peacekeeping force for Bosnia with Russian participation in it has been a major step in NATO's transformation, and a first step toward a change in the Russian perception of NATO. Although Russian troops can play only a nominal role with one infantry brigade and a logistics operation group, NATO has worked out elaborate command arrangements to accommodate Russian insistence on autonomy and refusal to report through the NATO chain of command. A Russian colonel-general sits in Brussels as a deputy IFOR commander.[66]

The process of transforming NATO into an expanded collective security organization will require continued consultations and continued collaboration. IFOR has been a big step forward. Engaging Russia and the ECE states in the dialogue surrounding the creation of a new transcontinental security system is another area for cooperation.[67] Whether it is possible for Russia to gain enough confidence to work with NATO to engage in peace operations in the near abroad remains to be seen. However, NATO, through the Partnership for Peace, may well have a role in conflict prevention in the NIS, even if it would not be acceptable for Russia to perform peace operations. And NATO expansion is a further indication that U.S. policy, while tilting toward Russia, has a strong competing focus in the security arena.

---

65. For example, Michael E. Brown argues that expansion of NATO to include Poland, Hungary, the Czech Republic, and Slovakia would almost certainly trigger a nationalist backlash in Russia that could lead to an effort to rebuild the military and perhaps serious Russian efforts to intimidate Ukraine and the Baltics, among others. Such a turn of events would lead to exactly the sort of regional instability Washington and its NATO allies seek to avoid. Michael E. Brown, "The Flawed Logic of NATO Expansion," *Survival*, Vol. 37, No. 1 (Spring 1995).

66. Confidential interviews at U.S. Department of Defense, April 1996.

67. See, for example, Brzezinski, "NATO—Expand or Die."

Chechnya

Chechnya, which is about the size of Connecticut, is resource-rich, a crucial node in the transport route for oil from the Caspian deposits. Furthermore, it is a "tough neighborhood." Imperial Russia succeeded in bringing Chechnya to heel in the 1860s, but only after forty-seven years of war and insurgency and at the cost of maintaining a sizable permanent garrison in the region. Chechnya was the only region that refused to sign the 1992 pact establishing the Russian Federation. Muslim ethnic Chechens make up the overwhelming portion of Chechnya's 1.3 million population, followed by Ingush and a lesser number of Russians who arrived as colonists either during the tsarist period or between 1944 and 1957 when, like many inhabitants of the Baltics, most Chechens were in exile.

Although it is sometimes lost amid the current furor, the present round of tensions between Russia and Chechnya began prior to the disintegration of the Soviet Union. In October 1990, a convention of more than one thousand Chechen delegates declared independence. A year later, Dzhokhar Dudaev, who had been proclaimed president of Chechnya by the convention, petitioned the Russian government to negotiate the issue in accordance with the Helsinki principles.

From Moscow's perspective in 1994, a constituent region was attempting to change borders by means of secession, an act in contravention of the Russian Constitution and the international covenants that are the central pillars of the international order. Efforts to destabilize the Dudaev government began in mid-1994 and reportedly included support for a Russian-dominated internal resistance movement that attempted a coup in November 1994.[68] On December 11, 1994, Russian troops moved into Chechnya, only a week after President Yeltsin emphasized at the OSCE summit at Budapest that the primary objectives for the CSCE to aim at were, "first and foremost, . . . ensuring human rights, the rights of minorities, and . . . curbing aggressive nationalism."[69]

Moscow's immediate justification for the invasion of Chechnya was that it was necessary to uphold the Russian Constitution.

---

68. For a more complete discussion of Russian efforts to destabilize Chechnya, see the testimony of Mohammed Shashiani before the U.S. Congressional Commission on Security and Cooperation in Europe hearings, January 19, 1995.

69. Excerpted from *Vital Speeches*, Vol. 61, No. 6, pp. 164–165. At the time that Yeltsin spoke, the Conference had not yet changed its name to the Organization for Security and Cooperation in Europe.

Although Moscow has consistently proclaimed its concern for the fate of Russian minorities in the near abroad, the welfare of the Russian minority in Chechnya did not seem to figure heavily in pre-invasion calculations or post-invasion explanations.[70] A senior U.S. State Department official speculated that Yeltsin's "policy in Chechnya may well have been, in part, a misguided attempt to counter perceptions of weakness" of the central government, if not Yeltsin personally.[71] There is a ring of plausibility in this, given the embarrassing results of the Russian elections of 1993.

But Moscow had more objective considerations of national interest as well. Even more critical were the arguments of national integrity. It was not unreasonable to suppose that a successful Chechen secession would threaten the continued existence of the Russian Republic. Other autonomous regions of the Russian Federation might follow suit, contributing to the disintegration of the Russian state. Moreover, an independent Chechnya would be free to construct alliances that might undermine Russia's national security by allowing presumably hostile powers and ideologies into the region. In addition, in the years following 1991, Chechnya had become a safe haven for organized criminal elements in the new Russia. Yeltsin described the Chechnya operation as "a struggle against the most dangerous, powerful, and arrogant forces of the Russian and international criminal and extremist world," adding that "the threat of gangsterism on the Chechen land is a dangerous threat to our whole country."[72] Finally, there is the issue of oil and the overland oil pipeline between the Caspian and Black seas. Although Moscow did not use oil as a primary justification for the invasion, it seems reasonable that there was concern about the loss of oil supplies from Chechnya and the North Caucasus and the revenues from the pipelines that carry them.[73]

---

70. In fact, Russian residents of Grozny seem to have suffered more than resident Chechens during the siege because, while many Chechens could find sanctuary with friends and relatives in the countryside, the Russians had nowhere to run.

71. U.S. Department of State, Director of Policy Planning James B. Steinberg, "Dual Engagement: U.S. Policy Toward Russia and China," speech before the annual meeting of the Trilateral Commission, Copenhagen, April 24, 1995.

72. Boris Yeltsin quoted in Steven Erlanger, "Russia's New Budget Raises Doubt on a Stable Economy," *New York Times*, December 28, 1994, p. A–6.

73. For a more detailed discussion of the role of oil in the Chechnya crisis, see the testimony of Elena Bonner, Charles Fairbanks, and Paul Goble at the U.S. Congressional Commission on Security and Cooperation in Europe hearings, January 19, 1995.

Despite early indications that Chechnya was likely to be messy and civilian casualties substantial, U.S. policy in the immediate aftermath was neither strong nor consistent. On December 12, 1994, the day after the invasion, President Clinton was quoted as saying the invasion was an "internal affair."[74] An official elaborated that "showing any support for the [Chechen] insurrection could not only anger President Boris N. Yeltsin as an improper intervention in Russian affairs . . . but could also encourage rebellions elsewhere in Russia."[75] Deputy Secretary of State Talbott testified that the United States did not object to the use of force in discussing Chechnya with Russian decision-makers. It only "made the point that Moscow should limit the use of force to a minimum."[76]

Moscow, however, had badly underestimated the will, the tactical skill, and the endurance of the Chechen fighters, as well as the support of the Chechen people for their cause in the weeks prior to the invasion. And it badly overestimated the capability of its own armed forces.[77] As a result, decision-makers probably believed that not much force would be needed and that the operation would be over quickly. Soon the action had turned into a major war, with all-out artillery and air attacks on Grozny, the Chechen capital, and mounting civilian casualties. Once the operation was under way, however, Yeltsin faced the difficult choice of persevering or risking further erosion of his power and influence. In all likelihood, that fact was not lost on Clinton administration policymakers who were not in a position to withdraw support for Moscow.

U.S. administration officials began to criticize Russian action in Chechnya publicly some weeks after the initial assault. An unidentified senior official stated that the United States had "pointedly warned the warring sides to respect the Geneva convention regarding protection of civilians." But that source reaffirmed that the Clinton administration continued to believe that Chechnya was an internal problem and was willing to give Moscow a relatively free

---

74. Lee Hockstader, "Russia Tries Takeover of Breakaway Chechnya, Troops, Tanks Pour In," *Washington Post*, December 12, 1994, p. 1A.

75. Ibid., p. A-13.

76. Strobe Talbott, testimony before the Subcommittee on Foreign Operations of the Senate Appropriations Committee, February 9, 1995.

77. David Remnick quotes Defense Minister Grachev as saying that Chechnya could be brought to heel "in two hours by a single paratrooper regiment." David Remnick, "In Stalin's Wake," *New Yorker*, July 24, 1995, p. 55.

hand, saying, "the Administration still believes that Russia is entitled to impose order on the Republic."[78] Speaking on *Meet the Press* on January 15, 1995, U.S. Secretary of State Warren Christopher offered only "a modest change" in policy when he warned that Yeltsin could lose U.S. support if he strayed too far from democracy and free markets. Undersecretary Talbott testified in February 1995 that "last fall [autumn 1994] we repeatedly made the point that, although Chechnya is an integral part of the Russian Federation, Moscow should limit any use of force to a minimum and respect human rights."[79] Speaking before a Senate subcommittee, he stated, "We support the sovereignty and territorial integrity of the Russian federation. We oppose attempts to alter international boundaries by force, whether in the form of aggression by one state against another or in the form of armed secessionist movements. . . . At the same time, our policy holds that Russia has an obligation to observe international standards in the way it deals with internal problems."[80] In the same testimony, however, Talbott saw a bright side to the Chechnya incident: it showed how far Russia had come from its authoritarian past in its willingness to allow open criticism by the Russian press and Yeltsin opponents in parliament.[81]

The first criticism of the mounting carnage in Chechnya came from German Chancellor Helmut Kohl, who told Yeltsin on January 5,

---

78. The account concluded by attempting to put a positive spin on events by noting that "the Chechens bear considerable responsibility for the casualties, too, since their fighters are interspersed with civilians...," a line originally put forth by the Yeltsin government. Michael Gordon, "U.S. Warns Russia," *New York Times*, December 30, 1994, pp. A-6, A-12. For other instances in which administration officials passed on Moscow's explanations as to why the Chechens, not the Russians, were responsible for the misfortunes that befell them, see the report of the hearings of the U.S. Congressional Commission on Security and Cooperation in Europe, January 19 and 27, 1995.

79. Strobe Talbott, "Supporting Democracy and Economic Reform in the New Independent States," statement before the Subcommittee on Foreign Operations of the Senate Appropriations Committee, February 9, 1995. See the testimony of James Collins, one of Talbott's key subordinates and an old Moscow hand, before the U.S. Congressional Commission on Security and Cooperation in Europe hearings, January 27, 1995.

80. Strobe Talbott testimony, before the Subcommittee on Foreign Operations, February 9, 1995.

81. In at least one case, for example, it was stated that a newspaper editor, openly critical of the incursion, was threatened with death by a close adviser to Yeltsin. Elena Bonner testimony, U.S. Congressional Commission on Security and Cooperation in Europe hearings, January 14, 1995.

1995, that Bonn regretted that Moscow's military campaign to crush the Chechen rebels had claimed so many civilian lives.[82] It was not until March, however, that the Clinton administration publicly faced up to Yeltsin's Chechnya debacle. On March 22, almost two months after Sergei Kovalev, the chairman of the Russian Presidential Commission on Human Rights, publicly asked all Western governments to use the means within their powers to urge the Russian government to end hostilities in Chechnya,[83] Warren Christopher described the Russian invasion as "foolhardy and tragically wrong."[84] And Washington was also instrumental in crafting the final communiqué of the North Atlantic Council released on May 30, 1995, that said in part: "we call for an immediate cease-fire and urge the parties to pursue negotiations. We urge Russia to facilitate the free passage of humanitarian assistance and hold elections."[85]

In developing its response to the Chechnya crisis, the United States faced a serious dilemma. The sanctity of international borders was a cornerstone of U.S. foreign policy at least since World War II, and was a central principle of the UN Charter as well as countless international instruments in the succeeding years. On a practical level, the disintegration of the Russian Federation would not only spell the end of reform—economic and political—but could lead to dangerous chaos in the heavily nuclear state. Yet President Yeltsin was acting in ways incompatible with democracy, and the use of force was anything but minimal. Washington, like almost all other observers, was not prepared for the intensity of ethnic separatism within Russia itself. In any case, there had been little effort, before the military action, to help the Yeltsin government understand that it might be possible to make the kind of moves that both preserved the republic while giving due consideration to human rights issues in suppressing breakaway regions.

Paul Goble, a former State Department official and an expert on the FSU, testified in mid-January 1995 that "if Secretary Christopher had said on December 12 what he said yesterday, I have a feeling that the

---

82. See Craig R. Whitney, "US and Allies to Press Russia for Chechnya Peace Settlement; Kohl Cautions Yeltsin," *New York Times*, January 6, 1995, p. A8.

83. Transcript from U.S. Congressional Commission on Security and Cooperation in Europe hearings, January 19 and 27, 1995, p. 7.

84. Stephen Greenhouse, "U.S. Warns Russia on Chechnya," *New York Times*, March 23, 1995, p. A-5.

85. *Dispatch*, Vol. 6, No. 23 (June 5, 1995), p. 488.

course of events which now have so many tragic consequences would not have taken place. Now, however, we have less influence because we didn't speak up earlier."[86]

Mikhail Gorbachev, who, not surprisingly, was highly critical of President Yeltsin, also argued that it would have helped had the West made clear the zones of acceptable and unacceptable behavior. Although his views may be politically self-serving, they cannot be dismissed out of hand. In an interview he stated:

The reaction [of the West] was inadequate. Maybe at an early stage, when events are unfolding, it's possible to take the position that it's an internal affair. But . . . it becomes very clear that this is a policy of violence, when glasnost and information are restricted, when society is deprived of control, when parliament has no control either, and when we don't hear the voice of the West . . . this does not correspond to democracy. There are certain absolutes; there cannot be a double standard.[87]

Not only did U.S. policymakers lack public clarity, they made little effort to mobilize international support through the institutions designed to deal with such problems. Talbott told Congress that the administration "strongly supported the OSCE mission to Chechnya, including its call for a humanitarian cease-fire."[88] Yet when Moscow prevented a key Russian human rights advocate from accompanying that mission in January 1995, and when Moscow excluded human rights from the mandate of the mission, the protest from Washington was somewhat muted. In not acting more forcefully to enlist the aid of international organizations, the United States may have missed an important opportunity to orchestrate a coherent international response that might have been persuasive to the Russian government. Yet in fairness, it must be acknowledged that even had the West given clear advice and warning, it might not have been heeded,

---

86. Paul Goble, testimony before the U.S. Congressional Commission on Security and Cooperation in Europe hearings, January 19, 1995. Goble was previously Special Assistant on the Soviet Nationalities to the Assistant Secretary of State for European Affairs.

87. Mikhail Gorbachev, interview with *U.S. News and World Report*, Vol. 118, No. 6 (February 13, 1995), p. 65.

88. Testimony by Deputy Secretary of State Strobe Talbott before the Subcommittee on Foreign Operations, February 9, 1995. The OSCE mission, undertaken to provide humanitarian assistance to the civilian population and to "promote human rights and a political settlement," was the only official international organization presence in Chechnya.

given the personalities, Russian domestic political pressures, and the prior record of unwavering U.S. support.

Chechnya represents a serious setback to the U.S. policy objective of continued movement toward political democracy and a market economy in Russia. As Strobe Talbott pointedly put it: "Chechnya has become...a universally recognized synonym for a threat to the survival of reform in Russia."[89] The consequences may be felt on a number of levels. First, Yeltsin's penchant for authoritarian rule seemed to have increased, jeopardizing the development of democratic institutions. Second, without a central figure to encourage reform, the energies of the reformers may be dissipated. As *The Economist* noted, Yeltsin, while never an ideal leader of the reform movement, nevertheless offered a rallying point and the hope that progress toward democracy and a free market economy would continue, albeit in fits and starts.[90] Now, in the aftermath of what many see as Yeltsin's break with democracy, reformers lack a central political figure to implement the total agenda.

Finally, the question remains whether there are likely to be other breakaway republics in Russia and how they might be handled. Some argue that the Russian experience in Chechnya makes repetition unlikely, given the lack of proficiency and relatively large number of casualties on the part of the armed forces, the scourging that the government received at the hands of the press, and lack of support among Russia's population. The cost of the attempt for Chechens has also been enormous, which argues against a repeat performance. Yet other resource-rich regions may have similar intentions. Even if some sort of a deal is struck that keeps the Chechens in the federation, it is no guarantee that other regions will not take the gamble that they might do better. In January 1995, for example, when most had a good idea of the price, seven of the twenty-two non-Russian ethnic regions petitioned Moscow to renegotiate the Russian relationship. In a statement to a U.S. Congressional Commission, Paul Goble pointed out: "Most of the North Caucasians now back Chechnya, something that was not true six months ago. And many of the other autonomous formations within the Russian Federation now believe they should make a move too."[91]

---

89. Ibid.

90. *The Economist*, Vol. 334, No. 7899 (January 28, 1995), p. 21.

91. Paul Goble, testimony before the U.S. Congressional Commission on Security and Cooperation in Europe hearings, January 19, 1995. The report of the hearings contains information on other regions that may attempt to break away despite the experience of the Chechens.

Moreover, the Chechnya experience will have an effect on Moscow's relationships with other states as well. The way Russian troops conducted themselves in Chechnya will make it difficult for Moscow to convince others that it is a viable partner for peace operations in the near abroad or elsewhere. The invasion, coming as it did on the heels of Yeltsin's statement to the Budapest summit, calls his credibility into question.

Although there can be justified criticisms of the course of U.S. policy after December 11, 1994, the real deficiencies of policy occurred earlier, in the failure to be aware of the menacing developments in Chechnya, to anticipate the likely course of events, and to take timely action to promote a negotiated solution.

A Trial Balance

It is far too early for a definitive appraisal of U.S. policy toward the former Soviet republics, and particularly of the handling of ethnic conflict in the region of the old Soviet state. Criticism and praise fluctuate widely in response to immediate developments. After the success of the Zhirinovsky faction in the December 1993 elections, the Clinton administration's Russian policy was widely criticized. When the Baltics, Ukraine, Moldova, Crimea, and Georgia all seemed likely to go the way of Armenia and Azerbaijan, and when Russian troops and influence seemed visibly active throughout the former Soviet territory, there was much handwringing among U.S. analysts. Later, when, apart from Chechnya, the turmoil in the FSU seemed to have quieted somewhat, or at least not erupted further, the administration claimed a foreign policy success. These appraisals reflect the abbreviated time horizons of contemporary policy analysis.

What can probably be said with some confidence is that, with the exception of its almost obsessive commitment to the shock therapy prescription (now widely recognized as a mistake), the United States has had only modest influence on developments in Russia. Its impact has been even smaller on the evolution of ethno-national relations within the successor states of the Soviet Union and within Russia itself. This was the inevitable consequence of the limited character of U.S. commitments and contacts. Except for Ukraine and Kazakhstan, where levels of U.S. economic assistance have been driven by its denuclearization interests, very little in the way of U.S. bilateral financial aid has gone to the NIS, and indeed in relation to the magnitude of the problems, the same is true of Russia itself. This state of affairs sometimes left Washington without much leverage. There has been some shift in the balance, if not the magnitude of U.S. aid. Half of the fiscal year 1995 assistance to the FSU was directed to nations other than Russia, and as indicated, Ukraine is the fourth largest recipient of U.S. Agency for International Development funds. Enterprise funds to promote private investment in small businesses are scheduled for Central Asia, Ukraine, Moldova, and Belarus.[92] But the amounts involved remain almost pitifully small.

As Alexei Arbatov points out in this volume, no responsible Russian government can ignore civil wars and internal clashes on its periphery. Crises are sure to develop in the future. Elementary considerations of security preclude any Russian government from ignoring conditions in which potentially hostile outside powers could gain a foothold in the region. Moreover, stability on the frontiers is closely linked to stability at home. The treatment of Russian minorities in the near abroad is a central issue feeding reactionary nationalist forces. If violence should become widespread in neighboring states, refugee flows would be enormously disruptive and costly. The Russian Federation itself is a fragile political entity, wracked by ongoing struggles against the weak center waged by regional authorities and autonomous republics.

Economic imperatives also point toward further Russian involvement in the affairs of the states of the near abroad. The Soviet Union was a highly interdependent economic system. It was an illusion of the nationalists in the new states that this system could be internally divided into separate economic units, or if not, that the center would pick up the bill. Likewise it was naive of the reformists, both Russian and Western, to think that the Russian economy could be transformed in isolation from the other fragments of the formerly integrated system.[93] In this sense, there is no real alternative to a considerable degree of economic integration in the region. The old republics of the Soviet Union were not created to be independently viable economic entities. Although they have gained political independence, except for Russia, most of them will not be economically

---

92. Testimony of Strobe Talbott, Ambassador-at-Large and Special Adviser to the Secretary of State on the NIS, before the Senate Foreign Relations Committee, March 23, 1994.

93. On the link between economic reform for the region as a whole and continued integration or independence and economic dislocation of all regions, see Jerry F. Hough, "Perilous Ties: Economic Reform and Russian 'Imperialism'," *Brookings Review* (Summer 1994), pp. 5–9.

viable for a long time. These realities have begun to manifest themselves in CIS meetings on economic integration and may ultimately lead to more politically mature and mutually beneficial relationships that could be nourished by European institutions.

U.S. policy has begun to take account of the interdependence, both in economic and security terms. Perhaps its most serious defect has been the hubris of behaving as if U.S. goals could be achieved by unilateral efforts without a far greater concerted effort through the Western alliance and the array of international organizations operating in the area. Given the U.S. domestic political climate, the agenda of the Clinton administration was ambitious. But accomplishing the objectives it identified will require more than a unilateral effort. The territory, both literally and figuratively, is simply too broad and the available resources—money, expertise, and time—are too limited.

At the 1992 Council of Ministers meeting in Stockholm, U.S. Secretary of State Lawrence Eagleburger urged that all international efforts to assist in resolving the conflicts within the CIS should take place within the framework of the CSCE principles and with CSCE political engagement, and stated that under this umbrella the United States should be prepared to support peacekeeping efforts by Russia and other CIS states.[94] A year later, in September 1993, in disclaiming any formal mediative role for the United States in these controversies, Strobe Talbott avowed that "America's role will often be as an active participant in multilateral efforts through international bodies in which all the New Independent States are members—such as the UN, CSCE, or the NATO Coordinating Council."[95] In October 1993, he argued before a congressional committee for U.S. "involvement in the international effort to foster peace and stability in the former Soviet Union."[96]

Yet U.S. commitment has not matched the rhetoric. It is belied in many ways—not least of which is the arrears in payments to the UN. The United States has not supported the OSCE robustly as a vehicle

---

94. Lawrence Eagleburger, "CSCE: A New Role for a New Era," intervention before the CSCE Council of Ministers Meeting, Stockholm, December 14, 1992, in *Dispatch*, Vol. 3, No. 52 (December 28, 1992), p. 914.

95. Statement before the Senate Foreign Relations Committee by Strobe Talbott, Ambassador-at-Large and Special Adviser to the Secretary of State for the NIS, September 7, 1993.

96. Statement before the House Foreign Affairs Committee by Strobe Talbott, October 6, 1993.

for conflict resolution in Europe. Although U.S. representation to the organization has been effective and dedicated over several administrations, most OSCE activities have gone unnoticed at the highest levels of government. The United States has not provided strong leadership in generating support for international organizations other than NATO. It has failed to provide not only the financial wherewithal, but the energy and imagination necessary to convert rhetoric into effective international action. It was the Netherlands that was instrumental in the conception and establishment of the CSCE's High Commissioner on National Minorities, widely viewed as one of the most effective instruments of preventive diplomacy in recent years. Given the low levels of funding, even a small additional infusion of U.S. dollars could have a disproportionate impact. Much of the blame may rest with the U.S. Congress, but executive leadership has not been strong.

Moreover, there is an important educational job that Americans might assist in doing. As the authors of the case studies in this volume point out, international and regional organizations lack visibility and clout among Russian leaders. Although these organizations have some capability to mediate crises, provide reassurance, monitor agreements and compliance with norms of behavior, and perhaps even marginalize nationalist opposition movements, there is little appreciation of these possibilities among Russian policymakers. Russia has much to learn about positive engagement in international organizations, and the United States, in order to help, must deepen its own commitment to them.

The truth is that the United States itself lacks a clear vision of how international organizations can be integrated into these endeavors. Without that clarity of vision, it is difficult to mobilize the organizations and align objectives adequately enough to be of some service. For example, Russia has continually declared its readiness to accept UN peacekeeping in Georgia, although, admittedly, the details were never very clear. The U.S. responses were less than forthcoming.[97]

In Chechnya, the time for intervention was not after violence broke out, but well before then. And the appropriate instrument was not

---

97. It is said that President Clinton told Georgian President Edward Shevardnadze that the United States would support the creation of a UN peacekeeping operation in that country, and would even help fund it if he could work out the appropriate mechanisms. Testimony of Strobe Talbott, Ambassador-at-Large and Special Adviser to the Secretary of State for the NIS, before the Senate Foreign Relations Committee, March 23, 1994.

bilateral diplomacy, which would have been resented by the Russians, but the OSCE with its recognized mandate for dealing with internal ethnic problems, and which was ultimately accepted.

The most intelligent way of addressing the realities and complexities that continue to beset the area of the former Soviet Union would be to engage Russia in a truly cooperative enterprise for dealing with external and domestic controversies through the major international organizations. In some cases, the task is straightforward—for example helping to strengthen the OSCE both financially and politically. In others, the United States must face complex issues and competing objectives—such as NATO expansion. With respect to the European Union, the United States may have limited influence. Most important is the energetic, imaginative, and sensitive joint involvement in the daily activities of these organizations. Hardest of all is that in such a venture the United States may have to accept the unaccustomed role of equal or perhaps junior partner when it is more appropriate for another country or group of countries to take the lead.

Contributors

Alexei Arbatov is Director of the Center for Geopolitical and Military Forecasts, Moscow, and head of the Department of Arms Control Studies of the Institute for World Economics and International Relations (IMEMO) of the Russian Academy of Sciences. A member of Russia's Duma (lower house of parliament), he is currently Deputy Chairman of the Duma's Defense Committee.

Abram Chayes is the Felix Frankfurter Professor of Law Emeritus at Harvard Law School. He has been on the faculty since 1955, except while serving as Legal Adviser to the U.S. Department of State in the Kennedy administration. He later represented Nicaragua in the World Court in its suit against the United States over the Reagan administration's support for the contras. His area of research is international law, especially environmental and trade issues, peacekeeping and conflict prevention.

Antonia Handler Chayes is a senior adviser at Conflict Management Group, a non-profit conflict-resolution organization in Cambridge, Mass. She is director of the Carnegie Conflict Prevention Project, which studies international organizations, conflict, and conflict prevention in East-Central Europe and the former Soviet Union; a lecturer at the John F. Kennedy School of Government at Harvard University; and a consultant at JAMS/Endispute. She has been president of the Consensus Building Institute; a member of the Commission on Roles and Missions of the U.S. Armed Forces; and Undersecretary of the U.S. Air Force during the Carter administration.

Lara Olson is the Deputy Director of the Norwegian Refugee Council office in Tbilisi, Georgia, and was Project Manager of the Carnegie Conflict Prevention Project at the Consensus Building Institute in Cambridge, Mass.

Nadia Alexandrova-Arbatova is Section Head of the Institute for World Economics and International Relations (IMEMO) in Moscow.

Vladimir Barsamov is a consultant to the Analytical Center of the Federation Council in Russia.

Brian J. Boeck completed his master's degree in Russian, Eastern European, and Central Asian Studies at Harvard University's Russian Research Center in 1994, and is working on a doctoral degree in Russian history at Harvard.

Henry Hale is a doctoral candidate in Harvard University's Department of Government. His research examines patterns of national separatism and international integration in the former Soviet Union.

Michael Lysobey has received a master's degree from the Russian Research Center at Harvard University with a concentration on Russian-Ukrainian relations.

Arthur G. Matirosyan is a consultant with the Former Soviet Union Project at Conflict Management Group. He holds a master's degree in International Relations from Yale University. His research interests include nationalism, conflict, and transitions to democracy in East-Central Europe and the former Soviet Union.

David Mendeloff is a doctoral candidate in political science at the Massachusetts Institute of Technology. His research focuses on Russian nationalism and education policy in post-Soviet Russia.

Olga Osipova is an analyst with the Division for Ethnopolitical Analysis at the Analytical Center of the Federation Council in Russia.

Edward Ozhiganov is Head of the Division for Ethnopolitical Research at the Analytical Center of the Federation Council in Russia.

Tonya Putnam received a master's degree from Harvard University's Russian Research Center. She is a doctoral candidate in political science at Stanford University and is pursuing a law degree from Harvard Law School.

George Raach is the Program Manager of the Project on Organizational Strategies for International Conflict Prevention at George Washington University's Elliott School of International Affairs, where he lectures on international organizations and peacekeeping operations. A retired U.S. Army colonel, he served as a professional staffer with the Commission on the Roles and Missions of the U.S. Armed Forces of the United States, and has been a member of the faculty of the National War College.

Brian D. Taylor is a doctoral candidate in political science at the Massachusetts Institute of Technology, and a research fellow in the International Security Program at the Center for Science and International Affairs at Harvard University's John F. Kennedy School of Government.

Alexander Yusupovsky is a consultant to the Analytical Center of the Federation Council in Russia.

INDEX

A

Abkhazia conflict, 371–400

  historical context, 345–351

  international organizations in, 393–398

  Russian Federation in, 390–393

  stabilization, 389-390

  war, 378-388

  See also Georgia Republic conflict; South Ossetia–Georgia conflict

Abkhazia war losses, 342

American perspectives on the former Soviet Union, 1–18

Armenia, 443–444

assessing post-Soviet conflicts, 19–24

Aushev, Ruslan, 61–66, 68, 73, 78–79

Azerbaijan, 448

B

Baikonur (space complex), 314

Balkan economic sanctions, 469–472

Baltic states

  history of, 225–227

  independence from Soviet Union, 229–230, 242–245

  link to Europe, 225

  Russian policy in, 447–448

  treaties with Russia, 242–245

  U.S. policies toward, 513–516

Belarus, 442–443

Belovezh Accords, 120, 172, 230, 292, 413

Black Sea Fleet, 120–128, 137–138, 141, 143

Bolsheviks, 33–34, 36, 37, 39

C

case study themes, 4–11

  citizenship and language laws, 7–8

  international organizations' role, 10–11

  Russian military presence, 8–10

  Russian minorities in the new republics, 5–7

  Yeltsin's support of nationalism, 4–5

Caucasus region nationalities, 31–34

cease-fire in Moldova, 183–186

Central Asian states, 448–450

Chechen people, 33, 41

Chechen crisis, impact on
Ingushetia–South Ossetia,
71–72

Chechen independence, impact
on Ingushetia, 48–49

Chechen oil industry, 49

Chechnya
Ingushetia conflict as a deterrent to, 56–57, 71–72, 75, 77–79

secession, 425–427

war in, 127, 486–487, 525–532

Chechnya-Ingushetia governments, 38–42

CIS; See Commonwealth of
Independent States

citizen vs. noncitizen rights
(Latvia), 235–241, 263

civil rights abuses (Latvia),
253–254, 264–265

claims to power (Crimea), 99–105,
119

Clinton administration
denuclearization issues,
495–502, 510

interests in Ukraine, 516–520

Russian integration into international community, 496

Clinton, Bill, 259, 483, 485, 488

colonizers; See Russian ethnics
(Latvia)

commentary on
Crimea, 137–143

Georgia, 401–407

Kazakhstan, 333–340

Latvia, 267–272

Moldova, 211–218

North Ossetia–Ingushetia,
77–82

Commonwealth of Independent
States (CIS)
establishment of, 292, 421, 493

in Georgia, 388–390

in Kazakhstan, 292, 323, 338

in Moldova, 185–186

communism defeated by
nationalism, 478

Confederation of Mountain
Peoples, 377–378, 381–383

Conference on Security and
Cooperation in Europe (CSCE)
in Moldova, 205–208

in Crimea, 129–133

in Ingushetia–North Ossetia, 70

in Kazakhstan, 300–302, 323–326

in Latvia, 231–232, 252

See also Organization on Security and Cooperation in Europe

Cossacks

in Crimea, 100

in Kazakhstan, 305–306, 309–310

defend Transdniester, 175–177

regional associations, 290

Council of Europe

in Estonia, 246

in Ingushetia–North Ossetia, 70–71

in Kazakhstan, 326–328

in Latvia, 246

in Moldova, 188

Crimean

Constitution, 101–102, 111, 113, 117, 132

demographics, 83–84

ethnic composition, 83, 89, 96

Transfer Act of 1954, 92, 99, 121–122, 518

Crimean Republic conflict, 83–135

commentary on, 137–143

first years of independence, 101–105

history and sociopolitics

B.C. to the nineteenth century, 85–87

nineteenth century, 87–89

Soviet period, 89–100

international organizations in, 129–133

Kravchuk and Meshkov period, 105–114

Kuchma period, 114–119

Russian Federation in, 119–129

Crimean Tatar National Movement (CTNM), 94–97, 109–110, 119

Crimean Tatars, 118, 133–135, 138–139

vs. Crimean Republic, 104–105, 108, 118–119

history, 86–99

nationalism, 101–105

CSCE; *See* Conference on Security and Cooperation in Europe

D

de facto segregation (Latvia), 269–270

defense of ethnic Russians, 245–249

discrimination in Latvia, 235–241

divide and rule dictum, 28, 38

domestic issues in Russia, 420–428

Druk, Mircea, 160–161, 163–166, 171, 203

Dudaev, Dzhokhar, 1–2, 57, 62, 71, 73, 78, 380, 405, 486

Dudaev government, 425–427, 481, 525

E

economic chaos in Moldova, 170

election violations in Kazakhstan, 300–302

Estonia, 240

history of, 226–227

treaties with Russia, 242–245

ethnic composition (Abkhazia), 374

ethnic conflicts (Russia), 1–2

ethnic foundations of the Soviet state, 34–35

ethnic Germans (Kazakhstan), 290–291

ethnic nationalism

in Georgia, 398–400

in Moldova, 204–209

ethnic polarization (Latvia), 225–235

ethnic politics (Kazakhstan), 304–307, 310

ethnic Russians

in Kazakhstan, 275–276

in the near abroad, 436–439

Euro-Atlantic security, 450–458

F

fifth column, 224, 267, 268

G

Gagauz

people, 146, 150, 154, 161, 163, 165, 179, 192–193

region, 146, 154, 160–162

Gagauzia, Republic of, 146, 159, 163, 166–169, 171–172, 179, 192–193, 196–197

See also Moldovan Republic conflict

Gamsakhurdia regime, 375–378, 387

Gamsakhurdia, Zviad, 356–362, 402

Georgia

economy, 342–343

hypernationalism, 351–354

recent developments, 404

refusal to recognize South Ossetia, 354–357, 360–361, 365

Russian policy in, 443–444

secession from Soviet Union, 357

war in Abkhazia, 378–388

Georgia Republic conflict, 341–400

in Abkhazia, 371–400

cease-fires and stabilization, 362–365

Gamsakhurdia's war, 356–362

historical context, 345–354

impact on North Ossetia, 46–48

international organizations in, 368–371, 393–398

Russian Federation in, 365–368, 390–393

Shevardnadze's war, 378–388

in South Ossetia, 354–371

stabilization, 388–390

See also Abkhazia conflict; South Ossetia–Georgia conflict

Gorbachev, Mikhail

in Abkhazian and Georgian conflict, 372–374

on war in Chechnya, 530

and Crimea, 121

government ends, 493–495

and Kazakhstan, 311–312

and Moldova, 158, 164, 167

perestroika in Moldova, 154–155

in Yugoslavia, 461–463

H

historical interpretations by the Latvians and Russians, 225–235

hordes, 277–278

host/guest ideology, 370, 373, 399

I

IMF; *See* International Monetary Fund

indigenization *(korenizatsia)*, 90, 153, 155, 279, 283, 347

Ingush people

history of, 33

post-Stalin era, 41–43

Ingushetia

assistance to Chechnya, 73

economic status, 29–30

industrial base, 48–49

lack of government structure, 46, 50, 52, 53

Ingushetia-Chechnya treaty, 62

Ingushetia–North Ossetia conflict, 27–75

commentary on, 77–83

evolution of conflict, 43–57

factors leading to violence, 28–30

historical origins, 31–43

impact of war in Chechnya, 30–31

international organizations in, 69–71

refugee problems, 28, 70, 71

territorial disputes, 27–29, 36

war, 49–57

warning to Chechnya, 56

See also North Ossetia

integration (Latvia), 265, 270–272

interethnic relations

in Kazakhstan, 277–292

in Latvia, 267–268

interethnic tensions in Kazakhstan, 288–292, 316–319

international human rights norms, 224–225

International Monetary Fund (IMF), 498, 506–508

international organizations

in Crimea, 129–133

in Georgia, 393–398

in Ingushetia–North Ossetia, 69–71

in Kazakhstan, 322–328, 339–340

in Latvia, 251–254

in Moldova, 187–189

in Ukraine, 129–130

international reactions (Latvian citizenship policies), 251–254 irredentism, 333–336, 338–340

Islamic influences (Kazakhstan), 311

K

Kazakhs, 277–278, 304

Kazakhstan conflict, 273–331

commentary on, 333–340

creation of, 277–281

CSCE in, 300–302, 324–326

economy, 292–295

election violations, 300–302

ethnic composition, 275

future scenarios, 328–331

geography, 274–275

interethnic tensions, 316–319

international organizations in, 322–328

Islamic influences, 311

lack of a parliament, 299–303, 327

language laws, 286, 296–299

link between Europe and Asia, 274, 311

mining enterprises, 293

nationality policies

after independence, 295–299

during perestroika, 281–285

of the Soviet period, 279–281

nuclear weapons disposition, 315–316

political organizations, 288–292

presidential power, 299–303

republic, 292–310

Russian policy in, 445–447

United Nations in, 326

Kazakhstani Constitution, 275, 296–299

Kazakhstani regional relations, 319–322

Kazakhstani-Russian relations, 311–316

Khrushchev, Nikita, 29, 41, 92–93, 518

korenizatsia (indigenization), 90, 153, 155, 279, 283, 347

Kozyrev, Andrei, 463, 511–512

Kravchuk, Leonid, 103, 120–123, 131, 134, 141, 200, 518–519

and Meshkov, 105–114

Kuchma, Leonid, 112, 114–119, 125–126, 129, 134, 440

Kunaev, Dinmukhamed, 281–285

Kyrgyzstan, 443–444

L

language laws (Kazakhstan), 296–299

Latvian anti-Russian laws, 220, 230–232

Latvian Department of Citizenship and Immigration, 238–240, 252

Latvian employment by ethnicity, 261

Latvian interethnic relations, 267–268

Latvian Republic conflict, 219–265

    author recommendations, 261–265

    citizenship and language laws, 229–232, 235–241, 251–254, 262

    civil rights abuses in, 253–254, 264–265

    commentary on, 267–272

    ethnic polarization, 225–235

    evolution of Russian policy in, 241–250

    international organizations in, 251–254

    Pytalovo-Abrene district, 259–260

    third-party states, 254–259

Latvian Republic goals, 223

Latvian voting blocs, 233–234

Lebed, Alexander, 148, 182, 195–197, 199–200

legacy of communism, 481–482

Lithuanian zero option, 237–238

M

Majlis, 98, 101–105, 107, 109–110, 118, 131

market economy in Russia, 504–509

Meshkov, Yuri, 100, 110–115, 139

Milly Firka, 88–91

Milošević, Slobodan, 460, 462, 471, 477, 479, 481, 485, 488

mirror effect of the Yugoslov conflict, 485–487

Moldovan Constitution, 175, 206, 209

Moldovan Republic conflict, 145–209

beginnings of, 154–164

cease-fire, 183–187

commentary on, 211–218

Gagauz Republic, 146, 150, 154, 179, 192–193, 196–197

history and background, 148–154

international organizations in, 187–189

peace negotiations, 189–197

stabilization, 183–197

Romania and, 201–204

Russian Federation and, 197–200

Soviet 14th Army involvement in, 147–148, 174–175, 177–183, 194–196

Soviet policy in, 447–448

Transdniester war, 164–183

Ukraine and, 200–201

See also Gagauz; Transdniester

Moldovan ethnic composition, 152–154

Moldovan language laws, 156–158

Moldovan nationalism, 160–161

Moldovan violent clashes, 158–159, 163–164, 168–169

Monrovsky Doctrine, 13, 423–424, 428, 431, 489

Moscow

low foreign policy profile, 483, 490

pressure on Ukraine, 441–442

threatened by NATO expansion, 522–524

N

NATO

expansion, 520–525

mission, 455–456

restructured, 520–524

Nazerbaev, Nursultan, 285–288, 299–303, 336–337, 340

near abroad (definition), 415

negotiation vs. force in post-Soviet government, 74–75

nomadic peoples (in Kazakhstan), 280

North Ossetia

commentary on, 77–82

Prigorodny district, 27–29, 42–43, 54

See also Ingushetia–North Ossetia conflict; Ossetians

North Ossetia–Ingushetia; *See* Ingushetia–North Ossetia conflict

Nuclear Non-Proliferation Treaty (NPT), 500–502

nuclear test site (Semipalatinsk), 287, 289

nuclear weapons disposition (in Kazakhstan), 315–316

O

occupiers; *See* Russian ethnics (Latvia)

Organization of the Crimean Tatar National Movement (OCNM), 94, 101–104, 107

Organization on Security and Cooperation in Europe (OSCE)

in Georgia, 368–371

in Latvia, 516

mission, 456–458

in South Ossetia, 367–371

See also Conference on Security and Cooperation in Europe

Ossetians

history of, 32–33

North and South aid each other, 363, 365–366

See also Abkhazia conflict; Georgia Republic conflict; Ingushetia–North Ossetia; North Ossetia; South Ossetia–Georgia conflict

P

People's Front of Moldova, 157–159, 161, 162, 171

perestroika

failure, 478

in Kazakhstan, 281–285

in Latvia, 227–231

in Moldova, 154–155, 158

plebiscitary presidency, 170–172, 177

political organizations (in Kazakhstan), 288–292

power struggle between Yeltsin and parliament, 508–509

presidential power (in Kazakhstan), 299–303

Prigorodny district (North Ossetia), 27–29, 42–43, 54

pro-Romanian movement, 156–159, 161–162, 164–165, 171

Pytalovo-Abrene district, 259–260 *See* also Latvian Republic conflict

R

regional relations (Kazakhstan), 319–322

Romania in Moldovan war, 178

Romanians in Ukraine, 201

Romania pressures Moldova for reunification, 201–204

Russia

Balkan policy, 464–467, 474–487

and Crimea, 124–129

defends its ethnics, 245–249

and Kazakhstan, 339

near abroad dilemmas, 415–417

place in the international environment, 419–420

posture on Yugoslavia, 461–463

reactions to Western attitudes, 22–24, 254–259

relations with the far abroad, 417–419

resources, 413–444

shift to foreign policy independence, 483–485

treaties with Baltic states, 242–245

and war in Chechnya, 525–532

Russia and the West

partners vs. rivals, 489–491

policies toward Yugoslavia, 459–474

Russian domestic

economic weakness, 422–423, 506–507

issues, 420–428

politics regarding their ethnics, 249–250

Russian ethnics (Latvia)

goals, 223–224

historical interpretations, 225–235

lack of citizenship, 222–228

reasons for, 221

Russian Federation

composition of, 35

in Crimea, 119–129

in Ingushetia-Ossetia, 30

in Georgia, 390–393

and Moldova, 197–200

resources, 413

Russian foreign policy

deficiencies, 423–425

priorities, 432–433

Russian interests in the near abroad, 428–439

Russian military balance, 417–419

Russian nationalities policy, 75

Russian perceptions

    of Yugoslav conflict, 459–491

    of Western prejudice against Serbs, 482–483

Russian perspectives on the former Soviet Union (FSU), 1–18

Russian and U.S. policy implications, 12–18

Russian policy in post-Soviet regions, 439–450

    Azerbaijan, 448

    Central Asian states, 448–450

    Georgia, Armenia, Kazakhstan, Kyrgyzstan, 443–447

    Moldova and the Baltic states, 447–448

    Ukraine and Belarus, 439–443

Russian security interests, 411–458

    domestic factors, 420–428

    with Euro-Atlantic organizations, 450–458

    in the near abroad, 428–439

    policy in post-Soviet regions, 439–450

    situation in Moscow, 413–420

Russian speakers; See Russian ethnics (Latvia)

Russian transition to democracy, 2–3

Russian troops

    in Abkhazia, 384–386

    in Prigorodny, 55

    stations of, 453

Russification policies, 261–262

S

Sebastopol, 121–123, 125–126, 129

Semipalatinsk, 287, 289

Shevardnadze, Edward, 362, 402

shock therapy, 474–475, 503–504, 507, 532

Smirnov, Igor, 172, 173, 187

Snegur, Mircea, 157, 159, 163–164, 203

    post-war negotiations, 189–191, 195–197

    stabilization of Moldovan conflict, 183–185, 187–188

    Transdniester war, 165, 168, 171–173, 177, 181

South Ossetia–Georgia conflict, 341–400

    Gamsakhurdia's war, 356–362

historical context, 345–354

impact on North Ossetia, 46–48

international organizations in, 368–371

pre-conflict situation, 351–354

Russian Federation's role in, 365–368

steps toward a settlement, 362–365

See also Abkhazia conflict; Georgia Republic conflict

South Ossetian war losses, 342, 347, 356, 362

Soviet

14th Army, 147–148, 174–175, 177–183, 194–196

Balkan policy evolution, 463–467

nationality policies in Kazakhstan, 278–281

Soviet empire

colonization, 20–21

dissolution, 21–22

Soviet Union

collapse (effects in Latvia), 231–235

dissolution, 411, 413–414, 493–494, 498–499

expands its influence in Mediterranean, 463–464

stabilizing the Moldovan conflict, 183–197

Stalin, Joseph, 38–39

Stalinist cartographers, 198

START I Treaty, 499–501, 511

stateless Russians; *See* Russian ethnics (Latvia)

state sovereignty vs. right to self-determination, 434

Switzerland scenario, 265

T

Tajikistan, 448–450

Talbott, Strobe, 509–510, 512–513, 527–528, 530–531, 534

Tito, Josip Broz, 476, 479, 481

titular nationalists, 334–335, 338–339

Topal, Sergei, 161, 168, 172

Transcaucasus Military District, 379, 383–384, 391–392

Transdniester

armed conflict in Transdniester, 172–174

conflict beginnings, 154–164

ethnic composition, 155

history, 148–154

seeks independence, 193–194

war, 264–283

See also Moldovan Republic
conflict; Soviet 14th Army

Tskhinvali, 354–361

Turkmenistan, 448–450

U

Ukraine

economic decline, 518, 520

economy, 105–106

ethnic composition, 105

Russian policy in, 439–442

U.S. financial aid to, 520

U.S. policies toward, 516–520

Ukraine and Moldova, 200–201

Ukraine-Crimean struggle,
114–119

Ukraine-Russian relations,
122–129, 133–135

United Nations

in Georgia-Abkhazia conflict,
394–398

in Kazakhstan, 326

U.S. financial aid to former Soviet
Union, 504–506, 520

U.S. policies toward former Soviet
Union, 493–536

democracy and marketization,
503–509

inclusion of Newly
Independent States (NIS),
509–510

reduction of nuclear arsenal,
495–502, 510

successes and failures, 532–536

U.S. policy toward

Baltic states, 513–516

Moscow, 494–496, 499, 504

NATO's expansion, 520–525

Ukraine, 516–520

U.S. reverses neglect of the near
abroad, 16–18

U.S. two-tiered policy, 497

U.S. and war in Chechnya,
523–530

Uzbekistan, 448–450

V

Vance-Owen plan, 470, 473, 482

van der Stoel, Max, 131–132, 192, 251, 252, 254

W

war
losses in Moldova, 146

in Moldova, 176–179, 184

in Transdniester, 164–183

Washington's democracy and marketization objectives for Russia, 503–509

West and Russia (partners or rivals), 489–491

Western and Russian policy toward Yugoslavia, 459–474

Western attitudes toward Russia, 254–259

Western disregard for Russian input, 484–489

Western indifference to Russian minorities, 480

West uninvolved in Yugoslavia problems, 460–461

Y

Yeltsin, Boris
administrative failings, 421–422

and Baltic states, 230–231, 243–244

and Crimea, 120–123, 126–127, 134

defense of ethnic Russians, 246

disorganized administration, 425–427

encourages nationalistic movement, 466, 511

and Kazakhstan, 311, 339

and Moldova, 181, 198–199

return of refugees to Prigorodny, 67

and Russian domestic politics, 209

and the Russian parliament, 184

and the Soviet 14th Army, 127–128

and Ukraine, 106–107, 126

Yeltsin policies
in Georgia, 358, 367

in Ingushetia–North Ossetia, 28, 45–46, 53, 58, 70, 72–74

Yugoslav conflict

  implications for the West and
  Russia, 487–491

  Russian perceptions, 459–491

Yugoslavia, 11–12

  peace operations, 472–474

  and Soviet disintegration parallels, 476–482, 485–486

Z

zero option, 237–238, 248, 265